NEW PERSPECTIVES ON
Microsoft® PowerPoint® 2013

COMPREHENSIVE

NEW PERSPECTIVES ON

Microsoft® PowerPoint® 2013

COMPREHENSIVE

Beverly B. Zimmerman
Brigham Young University

S. Scott Zimmerman
Brigham Young University

Katherine T. Pinard

CENGAGE
Learning®

Australia • Brazil • Mexico • Singapore • United Kingdom • United States

New Perspectives on Microsoft PowerPoint 2013, Comprehensive

Product Director: Kathleen McMahon

Senior Director of Development: Marah Bellegarde

Senior Product Team Manager: Donna Gridley

Associate Product Manager: Amanda Lyons

Product Development Manager: Leigh Hefferon

Senior Content Developer: Kathy Finnegan

Content Developer: Julia Leroux-Lindsey

Developmental Editor: Kim T. M. Crowley

Product Assistant: Melissa Stehler

Senior Market Development Manager: Eric LaScola

Market Development Manager: Kristie Clark

Marketing Manager: Gretchen Swann

Marketing Coordinator: Elizabeth Murphy

Senior Content Project Manager:
    Jennifer Goguen McGrail

Composition: GEX Publishing Services

Art Director: GEX Publishing Services

Text Designer: Althea Chen

Cover Art: © Rick Hanley/Flickr/Getty Images

Copyeditor: Michael Beckett

Proofreader: Lisa Weidenfeld

Indexer: Alexandra Nickerson

For product information and technology assistance, contact us at
Cengage Learning Customer & Sales Support, 1-800-354-9706

For permission to use material from this text or product, submit all requests online at **www.cengage.com/permissions**
Further permissions questions can be emailed to
permissionrequest@cengage.com

Some of the product names and company names used in this book have been used for identification purposes only and may be trademarks or registered trademarks of their respective manufacturers and sellers.

Microsoft and the Office logo are either registered trademarks or trademarks of Microsoft Corporation in the United States and/or other countries. Cengage Learning is an independent entity from the Microsoft Corporation, and not affiliated with Microsoft in any manner.

Disclaimer: Any fictional data related to persons or companies or URLs used throughout this book is intended for instructional purposes only. At the time this book was printed, any such data was fictional and not belonging to any real persons or companies.

Library of Congress Control Number: 2013953095

ISBN-13: 978-1-285-16182-2

ISBN-10: 1-285-16182-3

Cengage Learning
200 First Stamford Place, 4th Floor
Stamford, CT 06902
USA

Cengage Learning is a leading provider of customized learning solutions with office locations around the globe, including Singapore, the United Kingdom, Australia, Mexico, Brazil, and Japan. Locate your local office at:
international.cengage.com/global

Cengage Learning products are represented in Canada by Nelson Education, Ltd.

For your course and learning solutions, visit **www.cengage.com.**

Purchase any of our products at your local college store or at our preferred online store **www.cengagebrain.com**

ProSkills Icons © 2014 Cengage Learning.

Printed in the United States of America
2 3 4 5 6 7 19 18 17 16 15 14

Preface

The New Perspectives Series' critical-thinking, problem-solving approach is the ideal way to prepare students to transcend point-and-click skills and take advantage of all that Microsoft Office 2013 has to offer.

In developing the New Perspectives Series, our goal was to create books that give students the software concepts and practical skills they need to succeed beyond the classroom. We've updated our proven case-based pedagogy with more practical content to make learning skills more meaningful to students.

With the New Perspectives Series, students understand *why* they are learning *what* they are learning, and are fully prepared to apply their skills to real-life situations.

About This Book

This book provides complete coverage of PowerPoint 2013, and includes the following:
- The framework in which students can create well-designed presentations using the fundamental features of PowerPoint 2013, including slide layouts, placeholders, themes, transitions, and animations
- Coverage of the most important PowerPoint skills—planning and creating a presentation; creating bulleted lists; inserting photos, videos, tables, shapes, SmartArt diagrams, and audio; customizing presentations; and running slide shows
- Exploration of the new features in PowerPoint 2013, including theme variants, the easier to use Presenter view, and the updated Backstage view

New for this edition!
- Each tutorial has been updated with new case scenarios throughout, which provide a rich and realistic context for students to apply the concepts and skills presented.
- A new Troubleshoot type of Case Problem, in which certain steps of the exercise require students to identify and correct errors—which are intentionally placed in the files students work with—promotes problem solving and critical thinking.
- The content has been developed so that students and instructors can work seamlessly on either the Windows 7 or Windows 8 operating system.

System Requirements

This book assumes a typical installation of Microsoft PowerPoint 2013 and Microsoft Windows 8. (You can also complete the material in this text using another version of Windows 8 or using Windows 7. You may see only minor differences in how some windows look.) The browser used for any steps that require a browser is Internet Explorer 10.

www.cengage.com/series/newperspectives

The New Perspectives Approach

Context
Each tutorial begins with a problem presented in a "real-world" case that is meaningful to students. The case sets the scene to help students understand what they will do in the tutorial.

Hands-on Approach
Each tutorial is divided into manageable sessions that combine reading and hands-on, step-by-step work. Colorful screenshots help guide students through the steps. **Trouble?** tips anticipate common mistakes or problems to help students stay on track and continue with the tutorial.

VISUAL OVERVIEW

Visual Overviews
Each session begins with a Visual Overview, a two-page spread that includes colorful, enlarged screenshots with numerous callouts and key term definitions, giving students a comprehensive preview of the topics covered in the session, as well as a handy study guide.

PROSKILLS

ProSkills Boxes and Exercises
ProSkills boxes provide guidance for how to use the software in real-world, professional situations, and related ProSkills exercises integrate the technology skills students learn with one or more of the following soft skills: decision making, problem solving, teamwork, verbal communication, and written communication.

KEY STEP

Key Steps
Important steps are highlighted in yellow with attached margin notes to help students pay close attention to completing the steps correctly and avoid time-consuming rework.

INSIGHT

InSight Boxes
InSight boxes offer expert advice and best practices to help students achieve a deeper understanding of the concepts behind the software features and skills.

TIP

Margin Tips
Margin Tips provide helpful hints and shortcuts for more efficient use of the software. The Tips appear in the margin at key points throughout each tutorial, giving students extra information when and where they need it.

REVIEW

APPLY

Assessment
Retention is a key component to learning. At the end of each session, a series of Quick Check questions helps students test their understanding of the material before moving on. Engaging end-of-tutorial Review Assignments and Case Problems have always been a hallmark feature of the New Perspectives Series. Colorful bars and headings identify the type of exercise, making it easy to understand both the goal and level of challenge a particular assignment holds.

REFERENCE

TASK REFERENCE

GLOSSARY/INDEX

Reference
Within each tutorial, Reference boxes appear before a set of steps to provide a succinct summary and preview of how to perform a task. In addition, a complete Task Reference at the back of the book provides quick access to information on how to carry out common tasks. Finally, each book includes a combination Glossary/Index to promote easy reference of material.

Our Complete System of Instruction

BRIEF

INTRODUCTORY

COMPREHENSIVE

Coverage To Meet Your Needs

Whether you're looking for just a small amount of coverage or enough to fill a semester-long class, we can provide you with a textbook that meets your needs.

- Brief books typically cover the essential skills in just 2 to 4 tutorials.
- Introductory books build and expand on those skills and contain an average of 5 to 8 tutorials.
- Comprehensive books are great for a full-semester class, and contain 9 to 12+ tutorials.

So if the book you're holding does not provide the right amount of coverage for you, there's probably another offering available. Go to our Web site or contact your Cengage Learning sales representative to find out what else we offer.

COURSECASTS

CourseCasts – Learning on the Go. Always available…always relevant.

Want to keep up with the latest technology trends relevant to you? Visit http://coursecasts.course.com to find a library of weekly updated podcasts, CourseCasts, and download them to your mp3 player.

Ken Baldauf, host of CourseCasts, is a faculty member of the Florida State University Computer Science Department where he is responsible for teaching technology classes to thousands of FSU students each year. Ken is an expert in the latest technology trends; he gathers and sorts through the most pertinent news and information for CourseCasts so your students can spend their time enjoying technology, rather than trying to figure it out. Open or close your lecture with a discussion based on the latest CourseCast.

Visit us at http://coursecasts.course.com to learn on the go!

Instructor Resources

We offer more than just a book. We have all the tools you need to enhance your lectures, check students' work, and generate exams in a new, easier-to-use and completely revised package. This book's Instructor's Manual, ExamView testbank, PowerPoint presentations, data files, solution files, figure files, and a sample syllabus are all available on a single CD-ROM or for downloading at http://www.cengage.com.

SAM: Skills Assessment Manager

Get your students workplace-ready with SAM, the premier proficiency-based assessment and training solution for Microsoft Office! SAM's active, hands-on environment helps students master computer skills and concepts that are essential to academic and career success.

Skill-based assessments, interactive trainings, business-centric projects, and comprehensive remediation engage students in mastering the latest Microsoft Office programs on their own, allowing instructors to spend class time teaching. SAM's efficient course setup and robust grading features provide faculty with consistency across sections. Fully interactive MindTap Readers integrate market-leading Cengage Learning content with SAM, creating a comprehensive online student learning environment.

Certification Prep Tool

This textbook was developed to instruct on the Microsoft® Office® 2013 certification objectives. Microsoft Corporation has developed a set of standardized, performance-based examinations that you can take to demonstrate your overall expertise with Microsoft Office 2013 programs. Microsoft Office 2013 certification provides a number of benefits for you:

- Differentiate yourself in the employment marketplace from those who are not Microsoft Office Specialist or Expert certified.
- Prove skills and expertise when using Microsoft Office 2013.
- Perform at a higher skill level in your job.
- Work at a higher professional level than those who are not certified.
- Broaden your employment opportunities and advance your career more rapidly.

For more information about Microsoft Office 2013 certification, including a complete list of certification objectives, visit the Microsoft web site, http://www.microsoft.com/learning. To see which Microsoft Office 2013 certification objectives are addressed by the contents of this text and where each is included in the text, visit the Certification resource on the Student Companion Site located on www.cengagebrain.com. For detailed instructions about accessing available resources, visit www.cengage.com/ct/student download or contact your instructor for information about accessing the required files.

Acknowledgments

The authors would like to thank the following reviewers for their valuable feedback on this book: Rollie Cox, Madison Area Technical College; Maryann Gallant, Curry College; Jennifer Gwizdala, Rasmussen College; Bill Hutchinson, Charter College; and Bradley West, Sinclair Community College. We also would like to thank the always hard-working editorial and production teams at Cengage Learning, including Donna Gridley, Executive Editor; Amanda Lyons, Associate Acquisitions Editor; Leigh Hefferon, Product Development Manager; Julia Leroux-Lindsey, Product Manager; Melissa Stehler, Editorial Assistant; Jennifer Goguen McGrail, Senior Content Product Manager; Chris Scriver, Manuscript Quality Assurance (MQA) Project Leader; and MQA Testers John Freitas, Serge Palladino, Susan Pedicini, and Danielle Shaw. Special thanks to Kathy Finnegan, Senior Product Manager, whose leadership on the New Perspectives Series results in such beautiful, high-quality books, and to Kim Crowley, Developmental Editor, whose thoroughness and commitment to quality and accuracy were invaluable. Thank you also to Scott and Beverly Zimmerman for the opportunity to work on this book. And special thanks to my family for putting up with me while I virtually ignored them for the past year as I worked on this project.
–Katherine T. Pinard

We have had the honor and privilege of working with the wonderful people at Course Technology for 24 years, ever since the company's inception in 1989. We thank all of them—the present and past managers, editors, marketers, and others—for their expertise, enthusiasm, and professionalism. We especially thank our colleague, co-author, and dear friend, Katherine Pinard, for her kindness, diligence, and high standard of excellence in all that she does. In this and the previous eight editions of *New Perspectives on Microsoft PowerPoint*, she has played a key role in making this book so successful.
–Scott and Beverly Zimmerman

BRIEF CONTENTS

FILE MANAGEMENT

Managing Your Files . . . . FM 1
Organizing Files and Folders with Windows 8

POWERPOINT

Presentation Concepts: Planning, Developing, and
Giving a Presentation . . . . PRES 1
Preparing a Presentation for an After-School Program

Tutorial 1 Creating a Presentation . . . . PPT 1
Presenting Information About Community Supported Agriculture

Tutorial 2 Adding Media and Special Effects . . . . PPT 69
Using Media in a Presentation for a Norwegian Tourism Company

Tutorial 3 Applying Advanced Formatting to Objects . . . . PPT 137
Formatting Objects in a Presentation for a Seminar Management Company

Tutorial 4 Advanced Animations and Distributing Presentations . . . . . PPT 189
Creating an Advanced Presentation for a Wireless Control Systems Company

Tutorial 5 Integrating PowerPoint with Other Programs . . . . PPT 241
Creating a Presentation for a Challenge Course Company

Tutorial 6 Customizing Presentations and the PowerPoint
Environment . . . . PPT 301
Creating a Presentation for a Conservation Group

Additional Cases . . . . **ADD 1**

Glossary/Index   **REF 1**

Task Reference   **REF 9**

TABLE OF CONTENTS

Preface v

Managing Your Files
Organizing Files and Folders with Windows 8 . . .**FM 1**

Visual Overview: Comparing Windows 7 &
Windows 8 . . . . .FM 2

Exploring the Differences Between Windows 7
and Windows 8 . . . . .FM 4

Organizing Files and Folders . . . . .FM 5

   Understanding How to Organize Files and
   Folders . . . . .FM 6

Exploring Files and Folders . . . . .FM 8

   Navigating to Your Data Files . . . . .FM 10

   Changing the View .FM 12

Managing Files and Folders . . . . .FM 14

   Opening a File . . . . .FM 15

   Saving a File . . . . .FM 16

   Creating Folders . . . . .FM 19

   Moving and Copying Files and Folders . . . . .FM 20

   Deleting Files and Folders . . . . .FM 25

   Renaming Files . . . . .FM 26

Working with Compressed Files . . . . .FM 26

Quick Check . . . . .FM 29

Review Assignments . . . . .FM 30

Case Problems . . . . .FM 31

**Presentation Concepts: Planning, Developing,
and Giving a Presentation**
*Preparing a Presentation for an After-School
Program* . . . .**PRES 1**

Session 1 Visual Overview: Planning
a Presentation . . . . .PRES 2

Understanding Presentations and Presentation
Media . . . . .PRES 4

Planning a Presentation . . . . .PRES 5

Determining the Form of the Presentation . . . .PRES 5

Determining the Presentation's Purposes and
Desired Outcomes . . . . .PRES 6

   Determining the Purposes . . . . .PRES 6

   Identifying Desired Outcomes . . . . .PRES 7

Analyzing Your Audience's Needs and
Expectations . . . . .PRES 9

Session 1 Quick Check . . . . .PRES 11

Session 2 Visual Overview: Creating
a Presentation . . . . .PRES 12

Creating the Presentation . . . . .PRES 14

Focusing Your Presentation . . . . .PRES 14

Identifying Your Key Points . . . . .PRES 15

Developing an Introduction . . . . .PRES 15

   Gaining Your Audience's Attention . . . . . . .PRES 15

   Providing an Overview of Your
   Presentation . . . . .PRES 18

Developing the Body of Your Presentation . . .PRES 18

   Gathering Information . . . . .PRES 18

   Evaluating Information . . . . .PRES 19

   Organizing Your Information . . . . .PRES 19

   Developing Your Conclusion . . . . .PRES 23

Creating Visuals . . . . .PRES 24

   Using Text as Visuals . . . . .PRES 25

   Using Graphics as Visuals . . . . .PRES 26

Creating Handouts . . . . .PRES 30

Session 2 Quick Check . . . . .PRES 31

Session 3 Visual Overview: Delivering a Presentation . . . . PRES 32

Preparing for the Delivery of an Oral Presentation. . . . . PRES 34

Choosing a Delivery Method. . . . . PRES 34

Preparing for Audience Interaction. . . . . PRES 35

Anticipating Audience Questions. . . . . . . PRES 35

Preparing for Audience Participation . . . . . PRES 36

Rehearsing the Presentation . . . . PRES 37

Connecting to Your Audience. . . . . PRES 39

Referring to Visuals During Your Presentation . . . . PRES 42

Evaluating Your Appearance. . . . . PRES 42

Setting Up for Your Presentation . . . . PRES 43

Preparing Copies of Your Content . . . . PRES 44

Assessing the Technology and Staff Available . . . . PRES 44

Becoming Familiar with the Room . . . . PRES 45

Identifying Other Needed Supplies . . . . . . PRES 45

Evaluating Your Performance . . . . PRES 46

Session 3 Quick Check . . . . PRES 47

Review Assignments . . . . PRES 48

Tutorial 1 Creating a Presentation
Presenting Information About Community Supported Agriculture. . . . . **PPT 1**

Session 1.1 Visual Overview: The PowerPoint Window . . . . PPT 2

Planning a Presentation. . . . . PPT 4

Starting PowerPoint and Creating a New Presentation . . . . PPT 5

Working in Touch Mode . . . . PPT 6

Creating a Title Slide. PPT 7

Saving and Editing a Presentation . . . . PPT 8

Adding New Slides . . . . PPT 11

Creating Lists. . . . . PPT 14

Creating a Bulleted List. . . . . PPT 14

Creating a Numbered List . . . . PPT 16

Creating an Unnumbered List. . . . . PPT 17

Formatting Text. . . . . PPT 19

Moving and Copying Text. . . . . PPT 22

Converting a List to a SmartArt Diagram . . . . PPT 24

Manipulating Slides. PPT 27

Closing a Presentation. . . . . PPT 30

Session 1.1 Quick Check . . . . PPT 31

Session 1.2 Visual Overview: Slide Show and Presenter Views. . . . . PPT 32

Opening a Presentation and Saving It with a New Name. . . . . PPT 34

Changing the Theme and the Theme Variant . . . . PPT 35

Working with Photos . . . . PPT 38

Inserting Photos Stored on Your Computer or Network . . . . PPT 39

Cropping Photos. . . . . PPT 40

Modifying Photo Compression Options. . . . PPT 42

Resizing and Moving Objects . . . . PPT 45

    Resizing and Moving Pictures . . . . PPT 45

    Resizing and Moving Text Boxes . . . . PPT 48

Adding Speaker Notes . . . . PPT 49

Checking Spelling . . . . PPT 51

Running a Slide Show . . . . PPT 52

    Using Slide Show View and Presenter
    View . . . . PPT 53

    Using Reading View . . . . PPT 55

Printing a Presentation . . . . PPT 56

Exiting PowerPoint . . . . PPT 60

Session 1.2 Quick Check . . . . PPT 60

Review Assignments . . . . PPT 61

Case Problems . . . . PPT 63

Tutorial 2 Adding Media and Special Effects
*Using Media in a Presentation for a Norwegian
Tourism Company* . . . . **PPT 69**

Session 2.1 Visual Overview: Formatting
Graphics . . . . PPT 70

Applying a Theme Used in Another
Presentation . . . . PPT 72

Inserting Online Pictures . . . . PPT 74

Inserting Shapes . . . . PPT 77

Formatting Objects . . . . PPT 79

    Formatting Shapes . . . . PPT 79

    Formatting Pictures . . . . PPT 81

Rotating and Flipping Objects . . . . PPT 83

Creating and Formatting Tables . . . . PPT 84

    Creating and Adding Data to a Table . . . . . PPT 84

    Inserting and Deleting Rows and
    Columns . . . . PPT 86

    Formatting a Table . . . . PPT 88

Inserting Symbols and Characters . . . . PPT 94

Changing the Proofing Language . . . . PPT 95

Session 2.1 Quick Check . . . . PPT 97

Session 2.2 Visual Overview: Using Transitions
and Animations . . . . PPT 98

Applying Transitions . . . . PPT 100

Applying Animations . . . . PPT 102

    Animating Objects . . . . PPT 103

    Changing How an Animation Starts . . . . . . PPT 107

    Animating Lists . . . . PPT 109

Adding and Modifying Video . . . . PPT 111

    Adding Video to Slides . . . . PPT 111

    Modifying Video Playback Options . . . . . . PPT 114

    Understanding Animation Effects Applied
    to Videos . . . . PPT 115

    Setting a Poster Frame . . . . PPT 117

    Trimming Videos . . . . PPT 118

Compressing Media . . . . PPT 119

Adding Footers and Headers . . . . PPT 121

Session 2.2 Quick Check . . . . PPT 124

Review Assignments . . . . PPT 125

Case Problems . . . . PPT 127

ProSkills Exercise: Verbal Communication . . . PPT 134

Tutorial 3 Applying Advanced Formatting to Objects
Formatting Objects in a Presentation for a Seminar Management Company . . . . **PPT 137**

Session 3.1 Visual Overview: Creating a Chart on a Slide . . . . PPT 138

Creating SmartArt Diagrams . . . . PPT 140

    Modifying a SmartArt Diagram . . . . PPT 142

    Animating a SmartArt Diagram . . . . PPT 144

Adding Audio to Slides . . . . PPT 145

Adding a Chart to a Slide . . . . PPT 147

    Creating a Chart . . . . PPT 147

    Modifying a Chart . . . . PPT 151

Inserting and Formatting Text Boxes . . . . PPT 153

Applying WordArt Styles to Text . . . . PPT 156

Session 3.1 Quick Check . . . . PPT 159

Session 3.2 Visual Overview: Formatting Shapes and Pictures . . . . PPT 160

Editing Photos . . . . PPT 162

Removing the Background from Photos . . . . . PPT 164

Applying Artistic Effects to Photos . . . . PPT 166

Creating a Custom Shape . . . . PPT 168

    Using the Adjustment Handle to Modify Shapes . . . . PPT 169

    Aligning Objects . . . . PPT 170

    Merging Shapes . . . . PPT 171

Applying Advanced Formatting to Shapes . . . PPT 173

Making Presentations Accessible . . . . PPT 177

    Adding Alt Text . . . . PPT 177

Checking the Order Objects Will Be Read by a Screen Reader . . . . PPT 179

Renaming Objects in the Selection Pane . . . PPT 180

Session 3.2 Quick Check . . . . PPT 181

Review Assignments . . . . PPT 182

Case Problems . . . . PPT 184

Tutorial 4 Advanced Animations and Distributing Presentations
Creating an Advanced Presentation for a Wireless Control Systems Company . . . . **PPT 189**

Session 4.1 Visual Overview: Understanding Advanced Animations . . . . PPT 190

Adding More Than One Animation to an Object . . . . PPT 192

Using the Animation Pane . . . . PPT 196

Setting Animation Triggers . . . . PPT 198

Changing the Slide Background . . . . PPT 200

Creating and Editing Hyperlinks . . . . PPT 204

    Creating a Link . . . . PPT 205

    Adding Action Buttons . . . . PPT 207

Customizing Theme Colors . . . . PPT 211

    Deleting Custom Theme Colors . . . . PPT 214

Session 4.1 Quick Check . . . . PPT 215

Session 4.2 Visual Overview: Automatic Slide Timings . . . . PPT 216

Creating a Self-Running Presentation . . . . . . PPT 218

    Setting the Slide Timings . . . . PPT 218

    Rehearsing the Slide Timings . . . . PPT 220

    Recording Slide Timings and Narration . . . PPT 221

Controlling Options for Overriding the
Automatic Timings. . . . . PPT 225

Applying Kiosk Browsing. . . . . PPT 225

Using the Document Inspector . . . . PPT 227

Saving the Presentation for Distribution. . . . . PPT 229

Saving a Presentation as a Video . . . . PPT 229

Saving the Presentation as a Picture
Presentation . . . . PPT 231

Packaging a Presentation for CD . . . . PPT 233

Session 4.2 Quick Check. . . . . PPT 235

Review Assignments . . . . PPT 236

Case Problems. . . . . PPT 237

ProSkills Exercise: Teamwork. . . . . PPT 242

Tutorial 5 Integrating PowerPoint with Other Programs

*Creating a Presentation for a Challenge
Course Company* . . . . **PPT 241**

Session 5.1 Visual Overview: Understanding
Layers. . . . . PPT 242

Creating a Presentation by Importing
a Word Outline . . . . PPT 244

Resetting Slides. . . . . PPT 247

Inserting Slides from Another Presentation . . PPT 249

Working in Outline View . . . . PPT 252

Dividing a Presentation into Sections . . . . . . PPT 254

Working with Layers . . . . PPT 257

Modifying Advanced Animation Effect
Options . . . . PPT 260

Session 5.1 Quick Check . . . . PPT 269

Session 5.2 Visual Overview: Importing,
Embedding, and Linking . . . . PPT 270

Inserting a Word Table . . . . PPT 272

Formatting Cells in Tables. . . . . PPT 273

Inserting Excel Data and Objects . . . . PPT 277

Embedding an Excel Worksheet. . . . . PPT 277

Linking an Excel Chart . . . . PPT 282

Formatting Chart Elements. . . . . PPT 285

Breaking Links . . . . PPT 287

Annotating Slides During a Slide Show. . . . . PPT 288

Creating Handouts by Exporting a
Presentation to Word . . . . PPT 290

Session 5.2 Quick Check . . . . PPT 292

Review Assignments . . . . PPT 293

Case Problems. . . . . PPT 294

Tutorial 6 Customizing Presentations and the PowerPoint Environment

*Creating a Presentation for a Conservation
Group.* . . . . **PPT 301**

Session 6.1 Visual Overview: Slide Master
View. . . . . PPT 302

Sharing and Collaborating with Others . . . . . PPT 304

Comparing Presentations . . . . PPT 304

Working with Comments . . . . PPT 307

Modifying Themes. . . . . PPT 310

Changing Theme Fonts. . . . . PPT 310

Changing Theme Colors. . . . . PPT 312

Working in Slide Master View . . . . PPT 314

Modifying the Slide Master . . . . PPT 315

Modifying Individual Layouts . . . . PPT 315

Modifying the Style of Lists . . . . PPT 316

Creating a Custom Layout. . . . . PPT 319

Session 6.1 Quick Check . . . . PPT 329

Session 6.2 Visual Overview: File Properties . . . PPT 330

Saving a Presentation as a Template. . . . . PPT 332

Creating a Custom Show. . . . . PPT 334

Working with File Properties. . . . . PPT 336

Checking for Accessibility Issues. . . . . PPT 339

Encrypting a Presentation . . . . PPT 341

Marking the Presentation as Final. . . . . PPT 344

Presenting Online . . . . PPT 346

Session 6.2 Quick Check. . . . . PPT 348

Review Assignments . . . . PPT 349

Case Problems. . . . . PPT 350

ProSkills Exercise: Verbal Communication . . . PPT 355

Additional Case 1 Creating a Presentation
About a Town Plan for Open Space . . . . . . ADD 1

Additional Case 2 Geddes Trinkets . . . . . . ADD 3

GLOSSARY/INDEX . . . . REF 1

TASK REFERENCE . . . . REF 9

OBJECTIVES

- Explore the differences between Windows 7 and Windows 8
- Plan the organization of files and folders
- Use File Explorer to view and manage libraries, folders, and files
- Open and save files
- Create folders
- Copy and move files and folders
- Compress and extract files

Managing Your Files

Organizing Files and Folders with Windows 8

Case | Savvy Traveler

After spending a summer traveling in Italy, Matt Marino started Savvy Traveler, a travel company that organizes small tours in Europe. To market his company, Matt created flyers, brochures, webpages, and other materials that describe the tours he offers. Matt uses the Savvy Traveler office computer to locate and store photos, illustrations, and text documents he can include in his marketing materials. He recently hired you to help manage the office. To keep Matt connected to the office while traveling, he just purchased a new laptop computer running Windows 8. He is familiar with Windows 7, so he needs an overview explaining how Windows 8 is different. Matt asks you to train him on using Windows 8 to organize his files and folders. Although he has only a few files, he knows it's a good idea to set up a logical organization now so he can find his work later as he stores more files and folders on the computer.

In this tutorial, you'll explore the differences between Windows 7 and Windows 8, especially those related to file management tools. You'll also work with Matt to devise a plan for managing his files. You'll learn how Windows 8 organizes files and folders, and then create files and folders yourself and organize them on Matt's computer. You'll also use techniques to display the information you need in folder windows, and explore options for working with compressed files.

STARTING DATA FILES

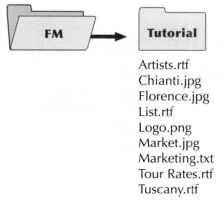

FM →	Tutorial	Review	Case1	Case2
	Artists.rtf	Banner.png	Fall Classes.rtf	Budget1.xlsx
	Chianti.jpg	Colosseum.jpg	Instructors.txt	Budget2.xlsx
	Florence.jpg	Lectures.xlsx	Kings Canyon.jpg	Report1.xlsx
	List.rtf	Rome.jpg	Mojave.jpg	Report2.xlsx
	Logo.png	Rome.rtf	Redwoods.jpg	Report3.xlsx
	Market.jpg	Schedule.rtf	Spring Classes.rtf	Report4.xlsx
	Marketing.txt	Tours.rtf	Summer Classes.rtf	Tips1.rtf
	Tour Rates.rtf		Winter Classes.rtf	Tips1 – Copy.rtf
	Tuscany.rtf		Workshops.rtf	Tips2.rtf
			Yosemite.jpg	Tips2 – Copy.rtf

Visual Overview:

In Windows 7, you use **Windows Explorer** to navigate the contents of your computer.

Use the arrow buttons in the Address bar to navigate to other locations on your computer.

The **file path** is a notation that indicates a file's location on your computer.

You use the Change your view button to change the size of the icons in the window.

Use the Search box to search for files in the current folder.

The Windows Explorer **toolbar** provides buttons for completing tasks.

Windows Explorer includes a **navigation pane**, which displays icons and links to resources and locations on your computer.

By default, Windows Explorer includes the **Details pane** at the bottom of the window, which displays the properties of the selected object.

Windows provides **libraries** so you can organize files by category—documents, music, pictures, and video.

A thumbnail image previews the file contents for certain types of files.

The zipped folder icon indicates a **compressed folder**, which stores files so they take up less disk space.

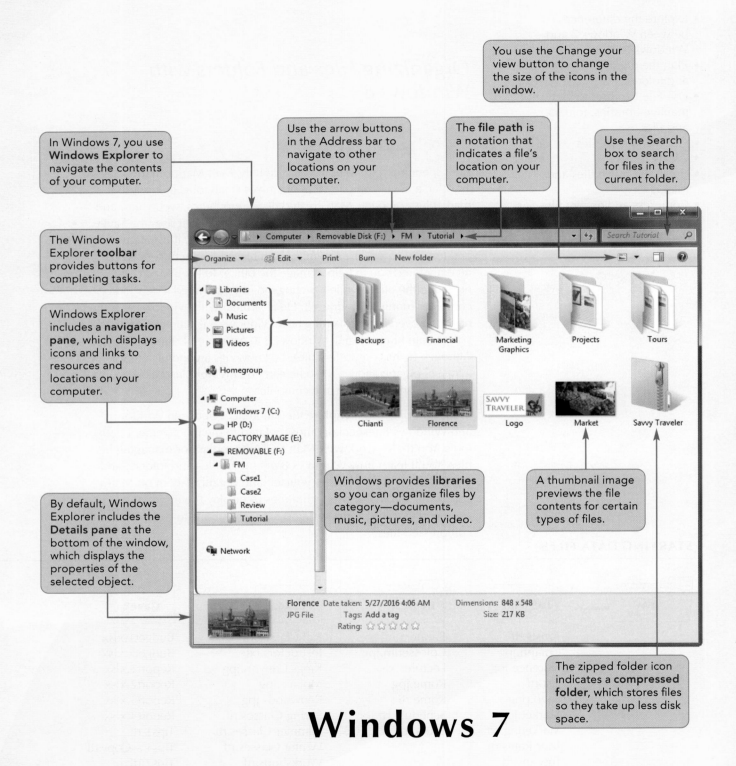

Windows 7

Comparing Windows 7 & Windows 8

The **View tab** on the ribbon contains options for specifying how the information displays in File Explorer.

Windows provides **libraries** so you can organize files by category—documents, music, pictures, and videos.

The **Quick Access toolbar** contains buttons for viewing properties and creating a folder.

Use the arrow buttons in the Address bar to navigate to other locations on your computer.

The **file path** in the Address bar shows a file's location on your computer.

In Windows 8, you use **File Explorer** to navigate the contents of your computer.

File Explorer includes a ribbon with tools organized on tabs for working with files and folders.

A thumbnail image previews the file contents for certain types of files.

A **filename** is the name you give to a file when you save it to identify the file's contents.

A **file icon** indicates the file type.

Clicking the Computer icon in the navigation pane shows the drives on your computer.

Data Files for this tutorial are stored on a removable disk on this computer.

File Explorer includes a **navigation pane**, which displays icons and links to resources and locations on your computer.

You can use the Large icons view button on the status bar or in the Layout group on the View tab to switch to Large icons view.

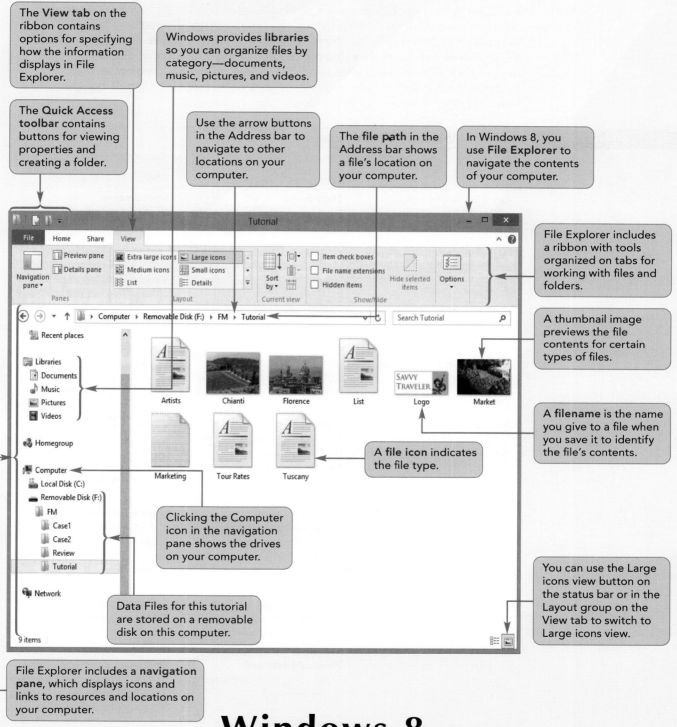

Windows 8

Exploring the Differences Between Windows 7 and Windows 8

Windows 8, the most recent version of the Microsoft operating system, is significantly different from Windows 7, the previous version. The major difference is that Windows 8 is designed for touchscreen computers such as tablets and laptops with touch-activated displays, though it runs on computers with more traditional pointing devices such as a mouse or a trackpad. This design change affects many of the fundamental Windows features you use to work on a computer. Figure 1 compares how to perform typical tasks in Windows 7 and Windows 8.

Figure 1	Comparing Windows 7 and Windows 8

Task	Windows 7 Method	Windows 8 Method
Start applications (sometimes called apps)	**Start menu** Open the Start menu by clicking the Start button.	**Start screen** The Start screen appears when you start Windows.
Access applications, documents, settings, and other resources	**Start menu** Use the Start menu, All Programs list, and Search box.	**Charms bar** The Charms bar appears when you point to the upper-right or lower-right corner of the screen, and displays buttons, called charms, for interacting with Windows 8 and accessing applications.
Select objects and commands	**Icons** Icons are small and detailed, designed for interaction with mechanical pointing devices.	**Icons and tiles** Icons and tiles are large and simplified, designed for interaction with your fingertips.
Open and work in applications	**Desktop** Applications all use a single desktop interface featuring windows and dialog boxes.	**Windows 8 and desktop** Applications use one of two interfaces: the Windows 8 interface (featuring tiles and a full-screen layout) or the desktop.
Display content out of view	**Vertical scrolling** Applications allow more vertical scrolling than horizontal scrolling.	**Horizontal scrolling** The Start screen and applications allow more horizontal scrolling than vertical scrolling to take advantage of wide-screen monitors.
Store files	**Physical storage devices** Windows primarily provides access to disks physically connected to the computer.	**Cloud storage locations** A Microsoft user account provides access to information stored online.
Enter text	**Physical keyboard** Type on the keyboard attached to the computer.	**On-screen keyboard** If your computer does not have a physical keyboard, type using the on-screen keyboard.

© 2014 Cengage Learning

Although Windows 7 introduced a few gestures for touchscreen users, Windows 8 expands the use of gestures and interactions. In Windows 8, you can use touch gestures to do nearly everything you can do with a pointing device. Figure 2 lists common Windows 8 interactions and their touch and mouse equivalents.

| Figure 2 | Windows 8 touch and mouse interactions |

Interaction	Touch Gesture	Mouse Action
Display a ScreenTip, text that identifies the name or purpose of the button	Touch and hold (or press) an object such as a button.	Point to an object such as a button.
Display an Apps bar, which displays options related to the current task and access to the Apps screen	Swipe from the top or bottom of the screen toward the center.	Right-click the bottom edge of the screen.
Display the Charms bar	Swipe from the right edge of the screen toward the center.	Point to the upper-right or lower-right corner of the screen.
Display thumbnails of open apps (the Switch List)	Swipe from the left edge of the screen toward the center.	Point to the upper-left corner of the screen, and then drag the pointer down.
Drag an object	Press and then drag.	Click, hold, and then drag.
Scroll the Start screen	Swipe from the right edge of the screen to the left.	Click the scroll arrows, or drag the scroll bar.
Select an object or perform an action such as starting an app	Tap the object.	Click the object.
Zoom	Pinch two fingers to zoom out or move the fingers apart to zoom in.	Click the Zoom button.

© 2014 Cengage Learning

Despite the substantial differences between how you interact with Windows 7 and Windows 8, the steps you follow to perform work in either operating system are the same. In a typical computer session, you start an application and open a **file**, often referred to as a document, which is a collection of data that has a name and is stored on a computer. You view, add, or change the file contents, and then save and close the file. You can complete all of these steps using Windows 7 or Windows 8. Because most of your work involves files, you need to understand how to save and organize files so you can easily find and open them when necessary.

Organizing Files and Folders

Knowing how to save, locate, and organize computer files makes you more productive when you are working with a computer. After you create a file, you can open it, edit its contents, print the file, and save it again—usually using the same application you used to create the file. You organize files by storing them in folders. A **folder** is a container for files. You need to organize files and folders so that you can find them easily and work efficiently.

A file cabinet is a common metaphor for computer file organization. As shown in Figure 3, a computer is like a file cabinet that has two or more drawers—each drawer is a storage device, or **disk**. Each disk contains folders that hold files. To make it easy to retrieve files, you arrange them logically into folders. For example, one folder might contain financial data, another might contain your creative work, and another could contain information you're gathering for an upcoming vacation.

Figure 3   Computer as a file cabinet

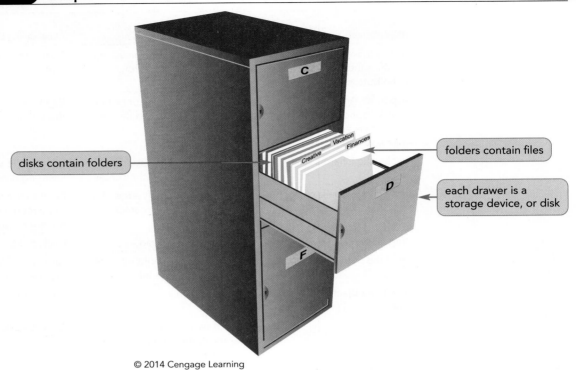

disks contain folders

folders contain files

each drawer is a storage device, or disk

© 2014 Cengage Learning

A computer can store folders and files on different types of disks, ranging from removable media—such as **USB drives** (also called USB flash drives) and digital video discs (DVDs)—to **hard disks**, or fixed disks, which are permanently housed in a computer. Hard disks are the most popular type of computer storage because they provide an economical way to store many gigabytes of data. (A **gigabyte**, or **GB**, is about 1 billion bytes, with each byte roughly equivalent to a character of data.)

To have your computer access a removable disk, you must insert the disk into a **drive**, which is a device that can retrieve and sometimes record data on a disk. A computer's hard disk is already contained in a drive inside the computer, so you don't need to insert it each time you use the computer.

A computer distinguishes one drive from another by assigning each a drive letter. The hard disk is assigned to drive C. The remaining drives can have any other letters, but are usually assigned in the order that the drives were installed on the computer— so your USB drive might be drive D or drive F.

Understanding How to Organize Files and Folders

Windows stores thousands of files in many folders on the hard disk of your computer. These are system files that Windows needs to display the Start screen and desktop, use drives, and perform other operating system tasks. To keep the system stable and to find files quickly, Windows organizes the folders and files in a hierarchy, or **file system**. At the top of the hierarchy, Windows stores folders and important files that it needs when you turn on the computer. This location is called the **root directory** and is usually drive C (the hard disk). As Figure 4 shows, the root directory contains all the other folders and files on the computer. The figure also shows that folders can contain other folders. An effectively organized computer contains a few folders in the root directory, and those folders contain other folders, also called **subfolders**.

Figure 4   **Organizing folders and files on a hard disk**

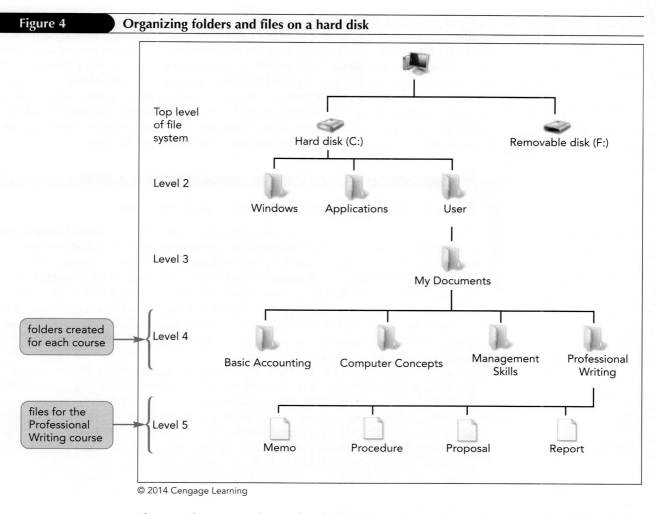

© 2014 Cengage Learning

The root directory is the top level of the hard disk and is for system files and folders only. You should not store your own work in the root directory because your files could interfere with Windows or an application. (If you are working in a computer lab, you might not be allowed to access the root directory.)

Do not delete or move any files or folders from the root directory of the hard disk; doing so could disrupt the system so that you can't start or run the computer. In fact, you should not reorganize or change any folder that contains installed software because Windows 8 expects to find the files for specific applications within certain folders. In Figure 4, folders containing software are stored at Level 2 of the file system. If you reorganize or change these folders, Windows 8 can't locate and start the applications stored in those folders. Likewise, you should not make changes to the folder (usually named Windows) that contains the Windows 8 operating system.

Level 2 of the file system also includes a folder for your user account, such as the User folder. This folder contains all of your system settings, preferences, and other user account information. It also contains subfolders, such as the My Documents folder, for your personal files. The folders in Level 3 of the file system are designed to contain subfolders for your personal files. You can create as many subfolders at Level 4 of the file system as you need to store other folders and files and keep them organized.

Figure 4 shows how you could organize your files on a hard disk if you were taking a full semester of business classes. To duplicate this organization, you would open the main folder for your documents, such as My Documents, create four folders—one each for the Basic Accounting, Computer Concepts, Management Skills, and Professional Writing courses—and then store the writing assignments you complete in the Professional Writing folder.

If you store your files on removable media, such as a USB drive, you can use a simpler organization because you do not have to account for system files. In general, the larger the storage medium, the more levels of folders you should use because large media can store more files and, therefore, need better organization. For example, if you were organizing your files on a 12 GB USB drive, you could create folders in the top level of the USB drive for each general category of documents you store—one each for Courses, Creative, Financials, and Vacation. The Courses folder could then include one folder for each course (Basic Accounting, Computer Concepts, Management Skills, and Professional Writing), and each of those folders could contain the appropriate files.

PROSKILLS

Decision Making: Determining Where to Store Files

When you create and save files on your computer's hard disk, you should store them in subfolders. The top level of the hard disk is off-limits for your files because they could interfere with system files. If you are working on your own computer, store your files within the My Documents folder in the Documents library, which is where many applications save your files by default. When you use a computer on the job, your employer might assign a main folder to you for storing your work. In either case, if you simply store all your files in one folder, you will soon have trouble finding the files you want. Instead, you should create subfolders within a main folder to separate files in a way that makes sense for you.

Even if you store most of your files on removable media, such as USB drives, you still need to organize those files into folders and subfolders. Before you start creating folders, whether on a hard disk or removable disk, you need to plan the organization you will use. Following your plan increases your efficiency because you don't have to pause and decide which folder to use when you save your files. A file organization plan also makes you more productive in your computer work—the next time you need a particular file, you'll know where to find it.

Exploring Files and Folders

As shown in the Visual Overview, you use File Explorer in Windows 8 to explore the files and folders on your computer. File Explorer displays the contents of your computer by using icons to represent drives, folders, and files. When you open File Explorer, it shows the contents of the Windows built-in libraries by default. Windows provides these libraries so you can organize files by category—documents, music, pictures, and video. A library can display these categories of files together, no matter where the files are actually stored. For example, you might keep some music files in a folder named Albums on your hard disk. You might also keep music files in a Songs folder on a USB drive. Although the Albums and Songs folders are physically stored in different locations, you can set up the Music library to display both folders in the same File Explorer window. You can then search and arrange the files as a single collection to quickly find the music you want to open and play. In this way, you use libraries to organize your files into categories so you can easily locate and work with files.

The File Explorer window is divided into two sections, called panes. The left pane is the navigation pane, which contains icons and links to locations on your computer. The right pane displays the contents of the location selected in the navigation pane. If the navigation pane showed all the contents on your computer at once, it could be a very long list. Instead, you open drives and folders only when you want to see what they contain. For example, to display the hierarchy of the folders and other locations on your computer, you select the Computer icon in the navigation pane, and then select the icon for a drive, such as Local Disk (C:) or Removable Disk (F:). You can then open and explore folders on that drive.

If a folder contains undisplayed subfolders, an expand icon appears to the left of the folder icon. (The same is true for drives.) To view the folders contained in an object, you click the expand icon. A collapse icon then appears next to the folder icon; click the collapse icon to hide the folder's subfolders. To view the files contained in a folder, you click the folder icon, and the files appear in the right pane. See Figure 5.

Figure 5	Viewing files in File Explorer

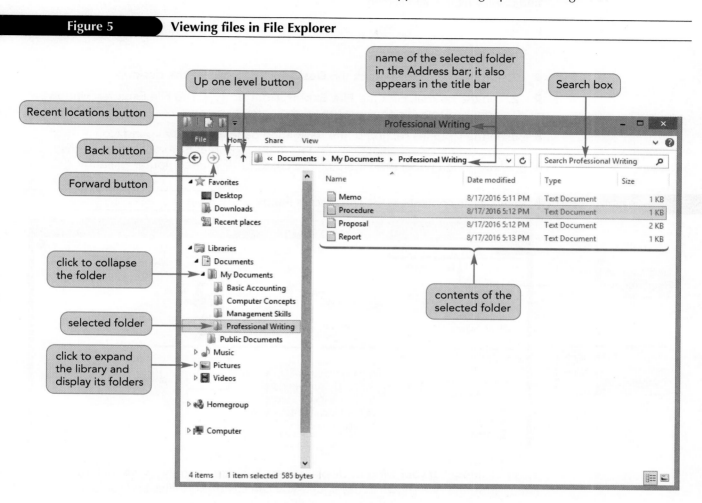

Using the navigation pane helps you explore your computer and orients you to your current location. As you move, copy, delete, and perform other tasks with the files and folders in the right pane of File Explorer, you can refer to the navigation pane to see how your changes affect the overall organization of the selected location.

In addition to using the navigation pane, you can explore your computer in File Explorer using the following navigation techniques:

- Opening drives and folders in the right pane—To view the contents of a drive or folder, double-click the drive or folder icon in the right pane of File Explorer.
- Using the Address bar—You can use the Address bar to navigate to a different folder. The Address bar displays the file path for your current folder. (Recall that a file path shows the location of a folder or file.) Click a folder name such as My Documents in the Address bar to navigate to that folder, or click an arrow button to navigate to a different location in the folder's hierarchy.
- Clicking the Back, Forward, Recent locations, and Up to buttons—Use the Back, Forward, and Recent locations buttons to navigate to other folders you have already opened. Use the Up to button to navigate up to the folder containing the current folder.
- Using the Search box—To find a file or folder stored in the current folder or its subfolders, type a word or phrase in the Search box. The search begins as soon as you

start typing. Windows finds files based on text in the filename, text within the file, and other properties of the file.

You'll practice using some of these navigation techniques later in the tutorial. Right now, you'll show Matt how to open File Explorer. Your computer should be turned on and displaying the Start screen.

To open File Explorer:

▶ **1.** On the Start screen, click the **Desktop** tile to display the desktop.

▶ **2.** On the taskbar, click the **File Explorer** button 📁. The File Explorer window opens, displaying the contents of the default libraries.

▶ **3.** In the Libraries section of the navigation pane, click the **expand** icon ▷ next to the Documents icon. The folders in the Documents library appear in the navigation pane; see Figure 6. The contents of your computer will differ.

Figure 6	Viewing the contents of the Documents library

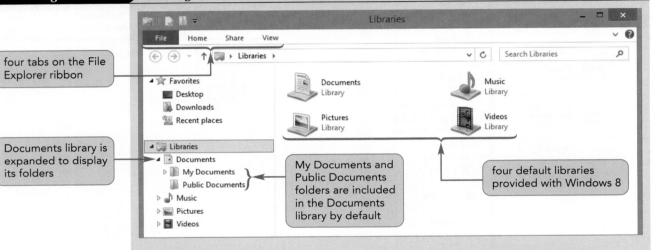

four tabs on the File Explorer ribbon

Documents library is expanded to display its folders

My Documents and Public Documents folders are included in the Documents library by default

four default libraries provided with Windows 8

Trouble? If your window displays icons in a size or arrangement different from the one shown in the figure, you can still explore files and folders. The same is true for all the figures in this tutorial.

▶ **4.** In the navigation pane, click the **My Documents** folder to display its contents in the right pane.

TIP

When you are working in the navigation pane, you only need to click a folder to open it; you do not need to double-click it.

As Figure 6 shows, the File Explorer window includes a ribbon, which is collapsed by default so it displays only tab names, such as File, Home, Share, and View. The Visual Overview shows the expanded ribbon, which displays the options for the selected tab. You'll work with the ribbon and learn how to expand it later in the tutorial.

Navigating to Your Data Files

To navigate to the files you want, it helps to know the file path because the file path tells you exactly where the file is stored in the hierarchy of drives and folders on your computer. For example, Matt has a file named "Logo," which contains an image of the company's logo. If Matt stored the Logo file in a folder named "Marketing" and saved that folder in a folder named "Savvy Traveler" on drive F (a USB drive) on his computer, the Address bar would show the following file path for the Logo file:

Computer ▶ Removable Disk (F:) ▶ Savvy Traveler ▶ Marketing ▶ Logo.png

This path has five parts, with each part separated by an arrow button:

- Computer—The main container for the file, such as "Computer" or "Network"
- Removable Disk (F:)—The drive name, including the drive letter followed by a colon, which indicates a drive rather than a folder
- Savvy Traveler—The top-level folder on drive F
- Marketing—A subfolder in the Savvy Traveler folder
- Logo.png—The name of the file

Although File Explorer uses arrow buttons to separate locations in a file path, printed documents use backslashes (\ ). For example, if you read an instruction to open the Logo file in the Savvy Traveler\Marketing folder on your USB drive, you know you must navigate to the USB drive attached to your computer, open the Savvy Traveler folder, and then open the Marketing folder to find the Logo file.

File Explorer displays the file path in the Address bar so you can keep track of your current location as you navigate between drives and folders. You can use File Explorer to navigate to the Data Files you need for this tutorial. Before you perform the following steps, you should know where you stored your Data Files, such as on a USB drive. The following steps assume that drive is Removable Disk (F:), a USB drive. If necessary, substitute the appropriate drive on your system when you perform the steps.

To navigate to your Data Files:

▶ **1.** Make sure your computer can access your Data Files for this tutorial. For example, if you are using a USB drive, insert the drive into the USB port.

   Trouble? If you don't have the starting Data Files, you need to get them before you can proceed. Your instructor will either give you the Data Files or ask you to obtain them from a specified location (such as a network drive). If you have any questions about the Data Files, see your instructor or technical support person for assistance.

▶ **2.** In the navigation pane of File Explorer, click the **expand** icon ▷ next to the Computer icon to display the drives on your computer, if necessary.

▶ **3.** Click the **expand** icon ▷ next to the drive containing your Data Files, such as Removable Disk (F:). A list of the folders on that drive appears below the drive name.

▶ **4.** If the list of folders does not include the FM folder, continue clicking the **expand** icon ▷ to navigate to the folder that contains the FM folder.

▶ **5.** Click the **expand** icon ▷ next to the FM folder to expand the folder, and then click the **FM** folder so that its contents appear in the navigation pane and in the right pane of the folder window. The FM folder contains the Case1, Case2, Review, and Tutorial folders, as shown in Figure 7. The other folders on your computer might vary.

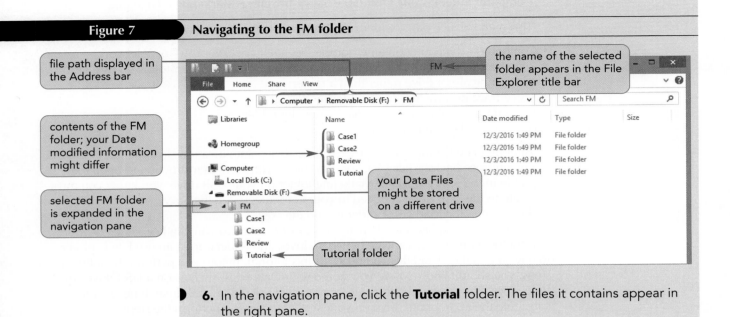

Figure 7   **Navigating to the FM folder**

- file path displayed in the Address bar
- the name of the selected folder appears in the File Explorer title bar
- contents of the FM folder; your Date modified information might differ
- your Data Files might be stored on a different drive
- selected FM folder is expanded in the navigation pane
- Tutorial folder

6. In the navigation pane, click the **Tutorial** folder. The files it contains appear in the right pane.

You can change the appearance of the File Explorer window to suit your preferences. You'll do so next so you can see more details about folders and files.

Changing the View

File Explorer provides eight ways to view the contents of a folder: Extra large icons, Large icons, Medium icons, Small icons, List, Details, Tiles, and Content. For example, the files in the Tutorial folder are currently displayed in Details view, which is the default view for all folders except those stored in the Pictures library. Details view displays a small icon to identify each file's type and lists file details in columns, such as the date the file was last modified, the file type, and the size of the file. Although only Details view lists the file details, you can see these details in any other view by pointing to a file to display a ScreenTip.

To change the view of File Explorer to any of the eight views, you use the View tab on the ribbon. To switch to Details view or Large icons view, you can use the view buttons on the status bar.

REFERENCE

Changing the View in File Explorer

- Click a view button on the status bar.

or

- Click the View tab on the ribbon.
- In the Layout group, click the view option; or click the More button, if necessary, and then click a view option.

You'll show Matt how to change the view of the Tutorial folder in the File Explorer window.

To change the view of the Tutorial folder in File Explorer:

▶ **1.** On the ribbon, click the **View** tab.

▶ **2.** In the Layout group, click **Medium icons**. The files appear in Medium icons view in File Explorer. See Figure 8.

| Figure 8 | Files in the Tutorial folder in Medium icons view |

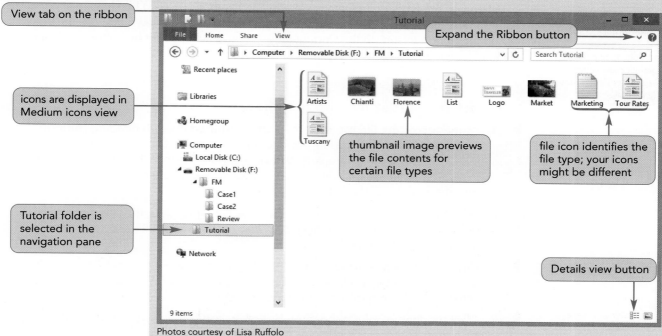

Photos courtesy of Lisa Ruffolo

Because the icons used to identify types of files depend on the applications installed on your computer, the file icons that appear in your window might be different.

TIP

When you change the view, it only changes the view for the currently selected folder.

▶ **3.** On the status bar, click the **Large icons view** button 🖼. The window shows the files with large icons and no file details.

When you clicked the View tab in the previous steps, the ribbon expanded so you could select an option and then collapsed after you clicked the Medium icons option. You can keep the ribbon expanded in the File Explorer window so you can easily access all of its options. You'll show Matt how to expand the ribbon and then use the View tab to switch to Details view.

To expand the ribbon in File Explorer:

▶ **1.** Click the **Expand the Ribbon** button 🔽 to expand the ribbon. The Expand the Ribbon button changes to the Minimize the Ribbon button, which you could click if you wanted to collapse the ribbon.

▶ **2.** On the View tab, in the Layout group, click **Details**. The window shows the files with small icons and lists the file details.

No matter which view you use, you can sort the file list by the name of the files or another detail, such as size, type, or date. When you **sort** files, you list them in ascending order (A to Z, 0 to 9, or earliest to latest date) or descending order (Z to A, 9 to 0, or latest to earliest date) by a file detail. If you're viewing music files, you can sort by details such as contributing artists or album title; and if you're viewing picture files, you can sort by details such as date taken or size. Sorting can help you find a particular file in a long file listing. For example, suppose you want to work on a document that you know you edited on June 4, 2016, but you can't remember the name of the file. You can sort the file list by date modified to find the file you want.

When you are working in Details view in File Explorer, you sort by clicking a column heading that appears at the top of the file list. In other views, you use the View tab on the ribbon to sort. In the Current view group, click the Sort by button, and then click a file detail.

TIP

To sort by a file detail that does not appear as a column heading, right-click any column heading and then select a file detail.

To sort the file list by date modified:

1. At the top of the file list, click the **Date modified** column heading button. The down arrow that appears above the label of the Date modified button indicates that the files are sorted in descending (newest to oldest) order by the date the file was modified. At the top of the list is the List file, which was modified on June 18, 2016.

   Trouble? If your folder window does not contain a Date modified column, right-click any column heading, click Date modified on the shortcut menu, and then repeat Step 1.

2. Click the **Date modified** column heading button again. The up arrow on the Date modified button indicates that the sort order is reversed, with the files listed in ascending (oldest to newest) order.

3. Click the **Name** column heading button to sort the files in alphabetical order by name. The Artists file is now listed first.

Now that Matt is comfortable working in File Explorer, you're ready to show him how to manage his files and folders.

Managing Files and Folders

As discussed earlier, you manage your personal files and folders by storing them according to a logical organization so that they are easy to find later. You can organize files as you create, edit, and save them, or you can do so later by creating folders, if necessary, and then moving and copying files into the folders.

To create a file-organization plan for Matt's files, you can review Figure 8 and look for files that logically belong together. In the Tutorial folder, Chianti, Florence, Logo, and Market are all graphics files that Matt uses for marketing and sales. He created the Artists and Tuscany files to describe Italian tours. The Marketing and Tour Rates files relate to business finances. Matt thinks the List file contains a task list for completing a project, but he isn't sure of its contents. He does recall creating the file using WordPad.

If the List file does contain a project task list, you can organize the files by creating four folders—one for graphics, one for tours, another for the financial files, and a fourth folder for projects. When you create a folder, you give it a name, preferably one that describes its contents. A folder name can have up to 255 characters, and any character is allowed, except / \ : * ? " < > and |. Considering these conventions, you could create four folders to contain Matt's files, as follows:

- Marketing Graphics folder—Chianti, Florence, Logo, and Market files
- Tours folder—Artists and Tuscany files
- Financial folder—Marketing and Tour Rates files
- Projects folder—List file

Before you start creating folders according to this plan, you need to verify the contents of the List file. You can do so by opening the file.

Opening a File

TIP

To select the default application for opening a file, right-click the file in File Explorer, point to Open with, and then click Choose default application. Click an application in the list that opens, and then click OK.

You can open a file from a running application or from File Explorer. To open a file in a running application, you select the application's Open command to access the Open dialog box, which you use to navigate to the file you want, select the file, and then open it. In the Open dialog box, you use the same tools that are available in File Explorer to navigate to the file you want to open. If the application you want to use is not running, you can open a file by double-clicking it in the right pane of File Explorer. The file usually opens in the application that you used to create or edit it.

Occasionally, File Explorer will open the file in an application other than the one you want to use to work with the file. For example, double-clicking a digital picture file usually opens the picture in a picture viewer application. If you want to edit the picture, you must open the file in a graphics editing application. When you need to specify an application to open a file, you can right-click the file, point to Open with on the shortcut menu, and then click the name of the application that you want to use.

Matt says that he might want to edit the List file to add another task. You'll show him how to use File Explorer to open the file in WordPad, which he used to create the file, and then edit it.

To open and edit the List file:

1. In the right pane of File Explorer, right-click the **List** file, and then point to **Open with** on the shortcut menu to display a list of applications that can open the file. See Figure 9.

   Trouble? If a list does not appear when you point to Open with on the shortcut menu, click Open with to display a window asking how you want to open this file.

Figure 9   Shortcut menu for opening a file

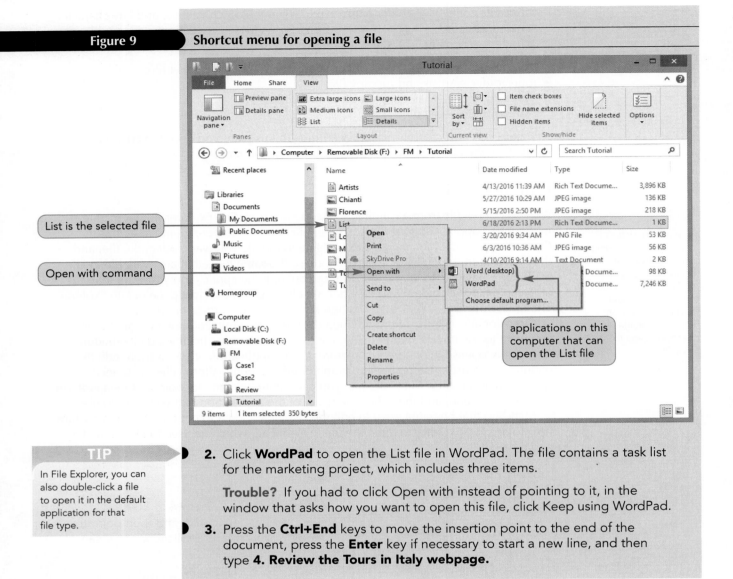

List is the selected file

Open with command

applications on this computer that can open the List file

TIP

In File Explorer, you can also double-click a file to open it in the default application for that file type.

2. Click **WordPad** to open the List file in WordPad. The file contains a task list for the marketing project, which includes three items.

   Trouble? If you had to click Open with instead of pointing to it, in the window that asks how you want to open this file, click Keep using WordPad.

3. Press the **Ctrl+End** keys to move the insertion point to the end of the document, press the **Enter** key if necessary to start a new line, and then type **4. Review the Tours in Italy webpage.**

Now that you've added text to the List file, you need to save it to preserve the changes you made.

Saving a File

As you are creating or editing a file, you should save it frequently so you don't lose your work. When you save a file, you need to decide what name to use for the file and where to store it. Most applications provide a default location for saving a file, which makes it easy to find the file again later. However, you can select a different location depending on where you want to store the file.

Besides a storage location, every file must have a filename, which provides important information about the file, including its contents and purpose. A filename such as Italian Tours.docx has the following three parts:

- Main part of the filename—When you save a file, you need to provide only the main part of the filename, such as "Italian Tours."
- Dot—The dot (.) separates the main part of the filename from the extension.
- Extension—The **extension** includes the three or four characters that follow the dot in the filename and identify the file's type.

Similar to folder names, the main part of a filename can have up to 255 characters. This gives you plenty of room to name your file accurately enough so that you'll recognize the contents of the file just by looking at the filename. You can use spaces and certain punctuation symbols in your filenames. However, filenames cannot contain the symbols / \ : * ? " < > or | because these characters have special meanings in Windows 8.

Windows and other software add the dot and the extension to a filename, though File Explorer does not display them by default. Instead, File Explorer shows the file icon associated with the extension or a thumbnail for some types of files, such as graphics. For example, in a file named Italian Tours.docx, the docx extension identifies the file as one created in Microsoft Word, a word-processing application. File Explorer displays this file using a Microsoft Word icon and the main part of its filename. For a file named Italian Tours.png, the png extension identifies the file as one created in a graphics application such as Paint. In Details view or List view, File Explorer displays this file using a Paint icon and the main part of its filename. In other views, File Explorer does not use an icon, but displays the file contents in a thumbnail. File Explorer treats the Italian Tours.docx and Italian Tours.png files differently because their extensions distinguish them as different types of files, even though the main parts of their filenames are identical.

When you save a new file, you use the Save As dialog box to provide a filename and select a location for the file. You can create a folder for the new file at the same time you save the file. When you edit a file you saved previously, you can use the application's Save command to save your changes to the file, keeping the same name and location. If you want to save the edited file with a different name or in a different location, however, you need to use the Save As dialog box to specify the new name or location.

As with the Open dialog box, you specify the file location in the Save As dialog box using the same navigation techniques and tools that are available in File Explorer. You might need to click the Browse Folders button to expand the Save As dialog box so it displays these tools. In addition, the Save As dialog box always includes a File name box where you specify a filename.

INSIGHT

Saving Files on SkyDrive

Some Windows 8 applications, such as Microsoft Office, include SkyDrive as a location for saving and opening files. **SkyDrive** is a Microsoft service that provides up to 7 GB of online storage space for your files at no charge. You can purchase additional space if you need it. For example, if you create a document in Microsoft Word, your SkyDrive appears as a location for saving the document. (Your SkyDrive appears with your username, such as Matt's SkyDrive.) If you have a Microsoft account, you can select a folder on your SkyDrive to save the document online. (If you don't have a Microsoft account, you can sign up for one by visiting the SkyDrive website.) Because the file is stored online, it takes up no storage space on your computer and is available from any computer with an Internet connection. You access the document by opening it in Word or by visiting the SkyDrive website, and then signing in to your Microsoft account. To share the document with other people, you can send them a link to the document via email. They can use the link to access the document even if they do not have a Microsoft account.

One reason that Matt had trouble remembering the contents of the List file is that "List" is not a descriptive name. A better name for this file is Task List. You will save this document in the Tutorial subfolder of the FM folder provided with your Data Files. You will also use the Save As dialog box to specify a new name for the file as you save it.

To save the List file with a new name:

1. On the ribbon in the WordPad window, click the **File** tab to display commands for working with files.

2. Click **Save as** to open the Save As dialog box, as shown in Figure 10. The Tutorial folder is selected as the storage location for this file because you opened the file from this folder.

Figure 10	Saving a file using the Save As dialog box

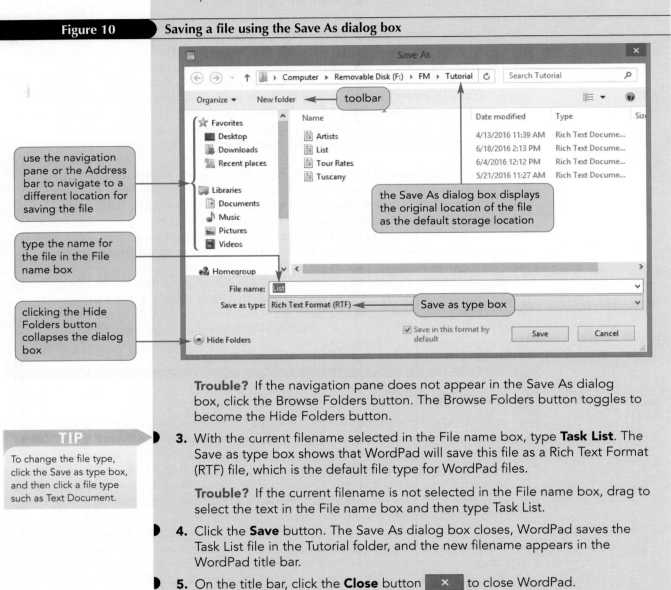

use the navigation pane or the Address bar to navigate to a different location for saving the file

type the name for the file in the File name box

clicking the Hide Folders button collapses the dialog box

the Save As dialog box displays the original location of the file as the default storage location

toolbar

Save as type box

Trouble? If the navigation pane does not appear in the Save As dialog box, click the Browse Folders button. The Browse Folders button toggles to become the Hide Folders button.

3. With the current filename selected in the File name box, type **Task List**. The Save as type box shows that WordPad will save this file as a Rich Text Format (RTF) file, which is the default file type for WordPad files.

   Trouble? If the current filename is not selected in the File name box, drag to select the text in the File name box and then type Task List.

4. Click the **Save** button. The Save As dialog box closes, WordPad saves the Task List file in the Tutorial folder, and the new filename appears in the WordPad title bar.

5. On the title bar, click the **Close** button ❌ to close WordPad.

Now you're ready to start creating the folders you need to organize Matt's files.

Creating Folders

You originally proposed creating four new folders for Matt's files: Marketing Graphics, Tours, Financial, and Projects. Matt asks you to create these folders now. After that, you'll move his files to the appropriate folders. You create folders in File Explorer using one of three methods: using the New folder button in the New group on the Home tab; using the New folder button on the Quick Access Toolbar; or right-clicking to display a shortcut menu that includes the New command.

INSIGHT

Guidelines for Creating Folders

Consider the following guidelines as you create folders:
- Keep folder names short yet descriptive of the folder's contents. Long folder names can be more difficult to display in their entirety in folder windows, so use names that are short but clear. Choose names that will be meaningful later, such as project names or course numbers.
- Create subfolders to organize files. If a file list in File Explorer is so long that you must scroll the window, you should probably organize those files into subfolders.
- Develop standards for naming folders. Use a consistent naming scheme that is clear to you, such as one that uses a project name as the name of the main folder, and includes step numbers in each subfolder name (for example, 1-Outline, 2-First Draft, 3-Final Draft, and so on).

In the following steps, you will create the four folders for Matt in your Tutorial folder. Because it is easier to work with files using large file icons, you'll switch to Large icons view first.

To create the folders:

▶ **1.** On the status bar in the File Explorer window, click the **Large icons view** button 🖼 to switch to Large icons view.

▶ **2.** Click the **Home** tab to display the Home tab on the ribbon.

▶ **3.** In the New group, click the **New folder** button. A folder icon with the label "New folder" appears in the right pane of the File Explorer window. See Figure 11.

Figure 11	Creating a new folder in the Tutorial folder

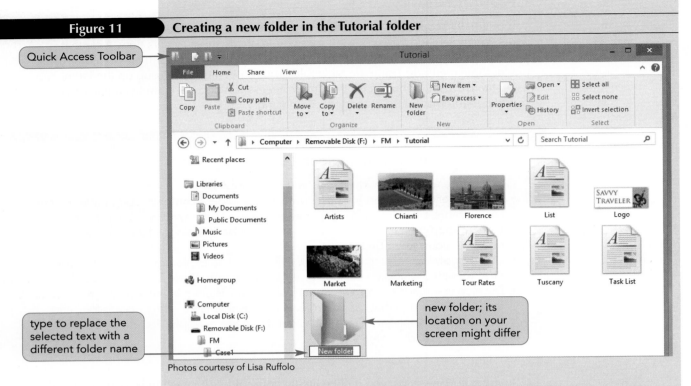

Photos courtesy of Lisa Ruffolo

> **Trouble?** If the "New folder" name is not selected, right-click the new folder, click Rename on the shortcut menu, and then continue with Step 4.
>
> Windows uses "New folder" as a placeholder, and selects the text so that you can replace it immediately by typing a new name. You do not need to press the Backspace or Delete key to delete the text.

4. Type **Marketing Graphics** as the folder name, and then press the **Enter** key. The new folder is named Marketing Graphics and is the selected item in the right pane. To create a second folder, you can use a shortcut menu.

5. In the right pane, right-click a blank area, point to **New** on the shortcut menu, and then click **Folder**. A folder icon appears in the right pane with the "New folder" text selected.

6. Type **Tours** as the name of the new folder, and then press the **Enter** key. To create the third folder, you can use the Quick Access Toolbar.

7. On the Quick Access Toolbar, click the **New folder** button 🔲, type **Financial**, and then press the **Enter** key to create and name the folder.

8. Create a new folder in the Tutorial folder named **Projects**.

After creating four folders, you're ready to organize Matt's files by moving them into the appropriate folders.

Moving and Copying Files and Folders

You can either move or copy a file from its current location to a new location. **Moving** a file removes it from its current location and places it in a new location that you specify. **Copying** a file places a duplicate version of the file in a new location that you specify, while leaving the original file intact in its current location. You can also move and copy folders. When you do, you move or copy all the files contained in the folder. (You'll practice copying folders in a Case Problem at the end of this tutorial.)

In File Explorer, you can move and copy files by using the Move to or Copy to buttons in the Organize group on the Home tab; using the Copy and Cut commands on a file's shortcut menu; or using keyboard shortcuts. When you copy or move files using these methods, you are using the **Clipboard**, a temporary storage area for files and information that you copy or move from one location to place in another.

You can also move files by dragging the files in the File Explorer window. You will now organize Matt's files by moving them to the appropriate folders you have created. You'll start by moving the Marketing file to the Financial folder by dragging the file.

To move the Marketing file by dragging it:

▶ **1.** In File Explorer, point to the **Marketing** file in the right pane, and then press and hold the mouse button.

▶ **2.** While still pressing the mouse button, drag the **Marketing** file to the **Financial** folder. See Figure 12.

Figure 12	Dragging a file to move it to a folder

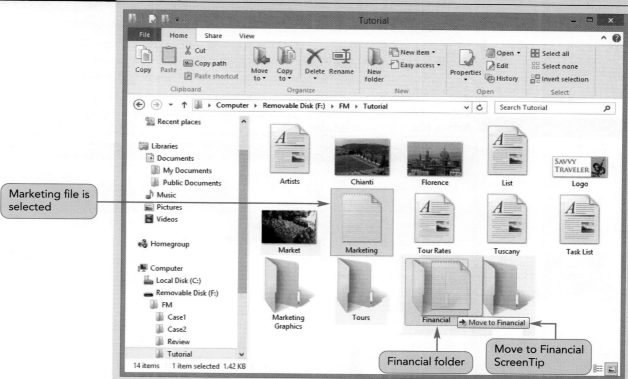

Marketing file is selected

Financial folder

Move to Financial ScreenTip

▶ **3.** When the Move to Financial ScreenTip appears, release the mouse button. The Marketing file is removed from the main Tutorial folder and stored in the Financial subfolder.

Trouble? If you released the mouse button before the Move to Financial ScreenTip appeared, press the Ctrl+Z keys to undo the move, and then repeat Steps 1–3.

Trouble? If you moved the Market file instead of the Marketing file, press the Ctrl+Z keys to undo the move, and then repeat Steps 1–3.

▶ **4.** In the right pane, double-click the **Financial** folder to verify that it contains the Marketing file.

Trouble? If the Marketing file does not appear in the Financial folder, you probably moved it to a different folder. Press the Ctrl+Z keys to undo the move, and then repeat Steps 1–3.

▶ **5.** Click the **Back** button ⊖ on the Address bar to return to the Tutorial folder.

You'll move the remaining files into the folders using the Clipboard.

To move files using the Clipboard:

▶ **1.** Right-click the **Artists** file, and then click **Cut** on the shortcut menu. Although the file icon still appears selected in the right pane of File Explorer, Windows removes the Artists file from the Tutorial folder and stores it on the Clipboard.

▶ **2.** In the right pane, right-click the **Tours** folder, and then click **Paste** on the shortcut menu. Windows pastes the Artists file from the Clipboard to the Tours folder. The Artists file icon no longer appears in the File Explorer window, which is currently displaying the contents of the Tutorial folder.

▶ **3.** In the navigation pane, click the **expand** icon ▷ next to the Tutorial folder, if necessary, to display its contents, and then click the **Tours** folder to view its contents in the right pane. The Tours folder now contains the Artists file. See Figure 13.

| Figure 13 | Artists file in its new location |

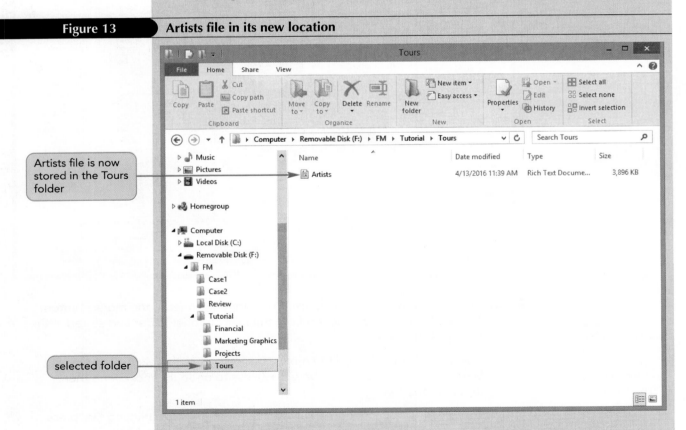

Artists file is now stored in the Tours folder

selected folder

Next, you'll use the Clipboard again to move the Tuscany file from the Tutorial folder to the Tours folder. But this time, you'll access the Clipboard using the ribbon.

4. On the Address bar, point to the **Up to** button ⬆ to display its ScreenTip (Up to "Tutorial"), click the **Up to** button ⬆ to return to the Tutorial folder, and then click the **Tuscany** file to select it.

5. On the Home tab, in the Clipboard group, click the **Cut** button to remove the Tuscany file from the Tutorial folder and temporarily store it on the Clipboard.

6. In the Address bar, click the **arrow** button ▶ to the right of "Tutorial" to display a list of subfolders in the Tutorial folder, and then click **Tours** to display the contents of the Tours folder in File Explorer.

7. In the Clipboard group, click the **Paste** button to paste the Tuscany file in the Tours folder. The Tours folder now contains the Artists and Tuscany files.

Finally, you'll move the Task List file from the Tutorial folder to the Projects folder using the Move to button in the Organize group on the Home tab. This button and the Copy to button are ideal when you want to move or copy files without leaving the current folder. When you select a file and then click the Move to or Copy to button, a list of locations appears, including all of the Windows libraries and one or more folders you open frequently. You can click a location in the list to move the selected file to that library or folder. You can also select the Choose location option to open the Move Items or Copy Items dialog box, and then select a location for the file, which you'll do in the following steps.

To move the Task List file using the Move to button:

1. In the Address bar, click **Tutorial** to return to the Tutorial folder, and then click the **Task List** file to select it.

2. On the Home tab, in the Organize group, click the **Move to** button to display a list of locations to which you can move the selected file. The Projects folder is not included on this list because you haven't opened it yet.

3. Click **Choose location** to open the Move Items dialog box. See Figure 14.

Figure 14	Move Items dialog box

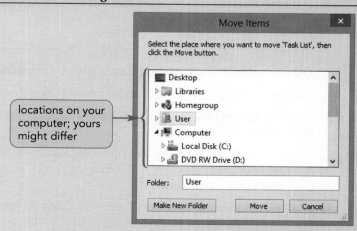

locations on your computer; yours might differ

4. If necessary, scroll the list of locations, and then click the **expand** icon ▷ next to the drive containing your Data Files, such as Removable Disk (F:).

5. Navigate to the FM ▸ Tutorial folder, and then click the **Projects** folder to select it.

6. Click the **Move** button to close the dialog box and move the Task List file to the Projects folder.

7. Open the Projects folder to confirm that it contains the Task List file.

One way to save steps when moving or copying multiple files or folders is to select all the files and folders you want to move or copy, and then work with them as a group. You can use several techniques to select multiple files or folders at the same time, which are described in Figure 15.

Figure 15   Selecting multiple files or folders

Items to Select in the Right Pane of File Explorer	Method
Files or folders listed together	Click the first item, press and hold the Shift key, click the last item, and then release the Shift key.
	or
	Drag the pointer to create a selection box around all the items you want to include.
Files or folders not listed together	Press and hold the Ctrl key, click each item you want to select, and then release the Ctrl key.
All files and folders	On the Home tab, in the Select group, click the Select all button.

Items to Deselect in the Right Pane of File Explorer	Method
Single file or folder in a selected group	Press and hold the Ctrl key, click each item you want to remove from the selection, and then release the Ctrl key.
All selected files and folders	Click a blank area of the File Explorer window.

© 2014 Cengage Learning

Next, you'll copy the four graphics files from the Tutorial folder to the Marketing Graphics folder using the Clipboard. To do this efficiently, you will select multiple files at once.

To copy multiple files at once using the Clipboard:

1. Display the contents of the Tutorial folder in File Explorer.

2. Click the **Chianti** file, press and hold the **Shift** key, click the **Market** file, and then release the **Shift** key.

3. Press and hold the **Ctrl** key, click the **List** file to deselect it, and then release the **Ctrl** key. Four files—Chianti, Florence, Logo, and Market—are selected in the Tutorial folder window.

4. Right-click a selected file, and then click **Copy** on the shortcut menu. Windows copies the selected files to the Clipboard.

5. Right-click the **Marketing Graphics** folder, and then click **Paste** on the shortcut menu.

6. Open the **Marketing Graphics** folder to verify it contains the four files you copied, and then return to the Tutorial folder.

7. Right-click the **Tour Rates** file, and then click **Copy** on the shortcut menu.

8. In the right pane, double-click the **Financial** folder to open it, right-click a blank area of the right pane, and then click **Paste** on the shortcut menu.

INSIGHT

Duplicating Your Folder Organization

If you work on two computers, such as one computer at an office or school and another computer at home, you can duplicate the folders you use on both computers to simplify the process of transferring files from one computer to another. For example, if you have four folders in your My Documents folder on your work computer, create these same four folders on a USB drive and in the My Documents folder of your home computer. If you change a file on the hard disk of your home computer, you can copy the most recent version of the file to the corresponding folder on your USB drive so the file is available when you are at work. You also then have a **backup**, or duplicate copy, of important files. Having a backup of your files is invaluable if your computer has a fatal error.

All the files that originally appeared in the Tutorial folder are now stored in appropriate subfolders. You can streamline the organization of the Tutorial folder by deleting the duplicate files you no longer need.

Deleting Files and Folders

TIP

In most cases, a file deleted from a USB drive does not go into the Recycle Bin. Instead, it is deleted when Windows 8 removes its icon, and the file cannot be recovered.

You should periodically delete files and folders you no longer need so that your main folders and disks don't get cluttered. In File Explorer, you delete a file or folder by deleting its icon. When you delete a file from a hard disk, Windows 8 removes the file from the folder but stores the file contents in the Recycle Bin. The Recycle Bin is an area on your hard disk that holds deleted files until you remove them permanently. When you delete a folder from the hard disk, the folder and all of its files are stored in the Recycle Bin. If you change your mind and want to retrieve a deleted file or folder, you can double-click the Recycle Bin on the desktop, right-click the file or folder you want to retrieve, and then click Restore. However, after you empty the Recycle Bin, you can no longer recover the files it contained.

Because you copied the Chianti, Florence, Logo, Market, and Tour Rates files to the subfolders in the Tutorial folder, you can safely delete the original files. You can also delete the List file because you no longer need it. You can delete a file or folder using various methods, including using a shortcut menu or selecting one or more files and then pressing the Delete key.

To delete files in the Tutorial folder:

1. Display the Tutorial folder in the File Explorer window.

2. In the right pane, click **Chianti**, press and hold the **Shift** key, click **Tour Rates**, and then release the **Shift** key. All files in the Tutorial folder are now selected. None of the subfolders should be selected.

Make sure you have copied the selected files to the Marketing Graphics and Financial folders before completing this step.

3. Right-click the selected files, and then click **Delete** on the shortcut menu. A message box appears, asking if you're sure you want to permanently delete these files.

4. Click the **Yes** button to confirm that you want to delete the files.

Renaming Files

After creating and naming a file or folder, you might realize that a different name would be more meaningful or descriptive. You can easily rename a file or folder by using the Rename command on the file's shortcut menu.

Now that you've organized Matt's files into folders, he reviews your work and notes that the Artists file was originally created to store text specifically about Florentine painters and sculptors. You can rename that file to give it a more descriptive filename.

To rename the Artists file:

▶ **1.** In the right pane of the File Explorer window, double-click the **Tours** folder to display its contents.

▶ **2.** Right-click the **Artists** file, and then click **Rename** on the shortcut menu. The filename is highlighted and a box appears around it.

▶ **3.** Type **Florentine Artists**, and then press the **Enter** key. The file now appears with the new name.

Trouble? If you make a mistake while typing and you haven't pressed the Enter key yet, press the Backspace key until you delete the mistake and then complete Step 3. If you've already pressed the Enter key, repeat Steps 2 and 3 to rename the file again.

Trouble? If your computer is set to display filename extensions, a message might appear asking if you are sure you want to change the filename extension. Click the No button, and then repeat Steps 2 and 3.

TIP

To rename a file, you can also click the file, pause, click it again to select the filename, and then type to enter a new filename.

Working with Compressed Files

You compress a file or a folder of files so it occupies less space on the disk. It can be useful to compress files before transferring them from one location to another, such as from your hard disk to a removable disk or vice versa, or from one computer to another via email. You can then transfer the files more quickly. Also, if you or your email contacts can send and receive files only up to a certain size, compressing large files might make them small enough to send and receive. Compare two folders—a folder named Photos that contains files totaling about 8.6 MB, and a compressed folder containing the same files but requiring only 6.5 MB of disk space. In this case, the compressed files use about 25 percent less disk space than the uncompressed files.

You can compress one or more files in File Explorer using the Zip button, which is located in the Send group on the Share tab of the ribbon. Windows stores the compressed files in a special type of folder called an **archive**, or a compressed folder. File Explorer uses an icon of a folder with a zipper to represent a compressed folder. To compress additional files or folders, you drag them into the compressed folder. You can open a file directly from a compressed folder, although you cannot modify the file. To edit and save a compressed file, you must extract it first. When you **extract** a file, you create an uncompressed copy of the file in a folder you specify. The original file remains in the compressed folder.

Matt suggests that you compress the files and folders in the Tutorial folder so that you can more quickly transfer them to another location.

To compress the folders and files in the Tutorial folder:

TIP

Another way to compress files is to select the files, right-click the selection, point to Send to on the shortcut menu, and then click Compressed (zipped) folder.

1. In File Explorer, navigate to the Tutorial folder, and then select all the folders in the Tutorial folder.

2. Click the **Share** tab on the ribbon.

3. In the Send group, click the **Zip** button. After a few moments, a new compressed folder appears in the Tutorial window with the filename selected. By default, File Explorer uses the name of the first selected item as the name of the compressed folder. You'll replace the name with a more descriptive one.

4. Type **Savvy Traveler**, and then press the **Enter** key to rename the compressed folder. See Figure 16.

Figure 16   Compressing files and folders

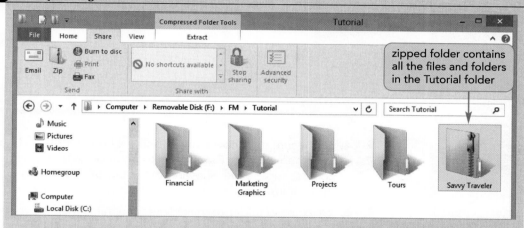

5. Double-click the **Savvy Traveler** compressed folder to open it, open the **Tours** folder, and then note the size of the compressed Tuscany file, which is 1,815 KB.

6. Navigate back to the Tutorial folder.

You can move and copy the files and folders from an opened compressed folder to other locations, although you cannot rename the files. More often, you extract all of the files from the compressed folder to a new location that you specify, preserving the files in their original folders as appropriate.

To extract the compressed files:

1. Click the **Savvy Traveler** compressed folder to select it, and then click the **Compressed Folder Tools Extract** tab on the ribbon.

2. In the Extract all group, click the **Extract all** button. The Extract Compressed (Zipped) Folders Wizard starts and opens the Select a Destination and Extract Files dialog box.

3. Press the **End** key to deselect the path in the box and move the insertion point to the end of the path, press the **Backspace** key as many times as necessary to delete the Savvy Traveler text, and then type **Backups**. The final three parts of the path in the box should be \FM\Tutorial\Backups. See Figure 17.

| Figure 17 | Extracting files from a compressed folder |

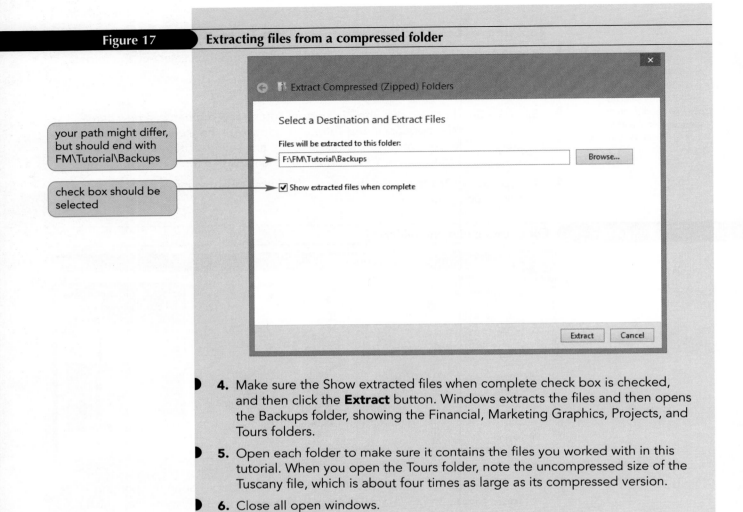

your path might differ, but should end with FM\Tutorial\Backups

check box should be selected

4. Make sure the Show extracted files when complete check box is checked, and then click the **Extract** button. Windows extracts the files and then opens the Backups folder, showing the Financial, Marketing Graphics, Projects, and Tours folders.

5. Open each folder to make sure it contains the files you worked with in this tutorial. When you open the Tours folder, note the uncompressed size of the Tuscany file, which is about four times as large as its compressed version.

6. Close all open windows.

In this tutorial, you examined the purpose of organizing files and folders, and you planned and created an organization for a set of related files and folders. You also explored your computer using File Explorer and learned how to navigate to your Data Files using the navigation pane. You used File Explorer to manage files and folders by opening and saving files; creating folders; and selecting, moving, and copying files. You also renamed and deleted files according to your organization plan. Finally, you compressed and extracted files.

REVIEW

Quick Check

1. You organize files by storing them in _____.
2. What is the purpose of the Address bar in File Explorer?
3. A filename _____ identifies the file's type and indicates the application that created the file.
4. Explain how to use File Explorer to navigate to a file in the following location: E: ▸ Courses ▸ Computer Basics ▸ Operating Systems.txt.
5. One way to move files and folders is to use the _____, a temporary storage area for files and information that you copied or moved from one place and plan to use somewhere else.
6. What happens if you click the first file in a folder window, press the Shift key, click the last file, and then release the Shift key?
7. When you delete a file from a hard disk, Windows removes the file from the folder but stores the file contents in the _____.
8. Describe how to compress a file or folder.
9. What are the benefits of compressing files and folders?

PRACTICE

Review Assignments

Data Files needed for the Review Assignments: Banner.png, Colosseum.jpg, Lectures.xlsx, Rome.jpg, Rome.rtf, Schedule.rtf, Tours.rtf

Matt has saved a few files from his old computer to a removable disk. He gives you these files in a single, unorganized folder, and asks you to organize them logically into subfolders. To do this, you will need to devise a plan for managing the files, and then create the subfolders you need. Next, you will rename, copy, move, and delete files, and then perform other management tasks to make it easy for Matt to work with these files and folders. Complete the following steps:

1. Use File Explorer to navigate to and open the FM ▶ Review folder provided with your Data Files. Examine the seven files in this folder and consider the best way to organize the files.

2. Open the **Rome** text file in WordPad, and then add the following tip to the end of the document: **Dine on the Italian schedule, with the main meal in the middle of the day.**

3. Save the document as **Rome Dining Tips** in the Review folder. Close the WordPad window.

4. In the Review folder, create three folders: **Business**, **Destinations**, and **Supplements**.

5. To organize the files into the correct folders, complete the following steps:
   - Move the Banner and Schedule files from the Review folder to the Business folder.
   - Move the Colosseum and Rome JPEG image files and the Rome Dining Tips and Tours text files to the Destinations folder.
   - Copy the Lectures file to the Supplements folder.

6. Copy the Tours file in the Destinations folder to the Business folder.

7. Rename the Schedule file in the Business folder as **2016 Schedule**. Rename the Lectures file in the Supplements folder as **On-site Lectures**.

8. Delete the Lectures file and the Rome text file from the Review folder.

9. Create a compressed (zipped) folder in the Review folder named **Rome** that contains all the files and folders in the Review folder.

10. Extract the contents of the Rome compressed folder to a new folder named **Rome Backups** in the Review folder. (*Hint:* The file path will end with \FM\Review\Rome Backups.)

11. Close the File Explorer window.

APPLY

Case Problem 1

See the Starting Data Files section at the beginning of this tutorial for the list of Data Files needed for this Case Problem.

Bay Shore Arts Center   Casey Sullivan started the Bay Shore Arts Center in Monterey, California, to provide workshops and courses on art and photography. Attracting students from the San Francisco and San José areas, Casey's business has grown and she now holds classes five days a week. She recently started a course on fine art landscape photography, which has quickly become her most popular offering. Casey hired you to help her design new classes and manage other parts of her growing business, including maintaining electronic business files and communications. Your first task is to organize the files on her new Windows 8 computer. Complete the following steps:

1. Open File Explorer. In the FM ► Case1 folder provided with your Data Files, create three folders: **Classes**, **Landscapes**, and **Management**.
2. Move the Fall Classes, Spring Classes, Summer Classes, and Winter Classes files from the Case1 folder to the Classes folder.
3. Rename the four files in the Classes folder by deleting the word "Classes" from each filename.
4. Move the four JPEG image files from the Case1 folder to the Landscapes folder.
5. Copy the remaining two files to the Management folder.
6. Copy the Workshops file to the Classes folder.
7. Delete the Instructors and Workshops files from the Case1 folder.
8. Make a copy of the Landscapes folder in the Case1 folder. The name of the duplicate folder appears as Landscapes – Copy. Rename the Landscapes – Copy folder as **California Photos**.
9. Copy the Workshops file from the Classes folder to the California Photos folder. Rename this file **California Workshops**.
10. Compress the graphics files in the California Photos folder in a new compressed folder named **Photos**.
11. Move the compressed Photos folder to the Case1 folder.
12. Close File Explorer.

Case Problem 2

See the Starting Data Files section at the beginning of this tutorial for the list of Data Files needed for this Case Problem.

Charlotte Area Business Incubator Antoine Jackson is the director of the Charlotte Area Business Incubator, a service run by the University of North Carolina in Charlotte to consult with new and struggling small businesses. You work as an intern at the business incubator and spend part of your time organizing client files. Since Antoine started using Windows 8, he has been having trouble finding files on his computer. He sometimes creates duplicates of files and then doesn't know which copy is the most current. Complete the following steps:

1. Navigate to the FM ▶ Case2 folder provided with your Data Files, and then examine the files in this folder. Based on the filenames and file types, begin to create an organization plan for the files.

🔧 **Troubleshoot** 2. Open the Tips1 and the Tips1 – Copy files and consider the problem these files could cause. Close the files and then fix the problem, renaming one or more files as necessary to reflect the contents.

🔧 **Troubleshoot** 3. Open the Tips2 and the Tips2 – Copy files and compare their contents. Change the filenames to clarify the purpose and contents of the files.

4. Complete the organization plan for Antoine's files. In the FM ▶ Case2 folder, create the subfolders you need according to your plan.

5. Move the files in the Case2 folder to the subfolders you created. When you finish, the Case2 folder should contain at least two subfolders containing files.

6. Rename the spreadsheet files in each subfolder according to the following descriptions.
   - Budget1: **Website budget**
   - Budget2: **Marketing budget**
   - Report1: **Travel expense report**
   - Report2: **Project expense report**
   - Report3: **Balance sheet**
   - Report4: **Event budget**

🔧 **Troubleshoot** 7. Make sure all files have descriptive names that accurately reflect their contents.

🔧 **Troubleshoot** 8. Based on the work you did in Steps 6 and 7, move files as necessary to improve the file organization.

9. Close File Explorer.

Planning, Developing, and Giving a Presentation

Preparing a Presentation for an After-School Program

Case | *Team Kidz*

Jon Rivera was a physical education teacher in Albany, NY public schools for 15 years, and during that time, he recognized that many of the children he taught would benefit from additional opportunities to stay active. He founded Team Kidz, a network of volunteers and programs that provides free or low-cost physical activities for the city's children. He recently opened the Team Kidz Center and greatly expanded the programs offered. He wants to promote the program to parents, faculty at city schools, and other community leaders. He needs to create a presentation to help him do this.

In this tutorial, you'll learn how to plan presentations by determining their purposes and outcomes and by analyzing the needs and expectations of your audience. You'll also understand the importance of identifying a clear focus for the presentations and outlining your key points, and how to apply this information as you develop an introduction, organized body, and conclusion for presentations. You'll also learn about the types of visuals and handouts you can use to support the content of a presentation and about the criteria for assessing the situation and facilities for giving the presentation. Finally, you will learn the value of rehearsing your delivery and preparing your appearance, and how to evaluate your performance.

STARTING DATA FILES

There are no starting Data Files needed for this tutorial.

Session 1 Visual Overview:

Knowing whether the presentation will be delivered in front of a live audience or over the Internet or if it will be self-running affects how you will use presentation media.

Presentations can be informative, persuasive, or demonstrative.

Understanding what you want your listeners to know, think, feel, or do after listening to your message helps keep you focused on your audience's needs.

Determine the form of the presentation

Determine the purpose of the presentation

Identify the desired outcome

Form, Purpose, and Outcome

What form is the presentation?	☐	Oral delivery	☐	Self-running

What is the primary purpose of your presentation? Check one and add specific details.

☐   Inform:

☐   Persuade:

☐   Demonstrate or train:

What is the primary desired outcome of your presentation? Specifically, what should the audience know, think, feel, or do after listening to your message?

Does your presentation have a secondary purpose? Check one and add specific details.

☐   Inform:

☐   Persuade:

☐   Demonstrate or train:

☐   None

If there is a secondary purpose, what is the secondary desired outcome?

Planning a Presentation

Identifying your audience's relationship to you can help you determine the appropriate style for your presentation.

Learning the characteristics of your audience will help you deliver an effective presentation.

Determine the audience's relationship to you

Determine the demographics of the audience

Audience Analysis, continued

How will your listeners use this information? Check and explain all that apply.

☐ Make decisions:

Audience Analysis

Who is your audience? Check all that apply and add details about each selected group.

☐ Peers:

☐ Superiors:

☐ Subordinates:

☐ Strangers:

What characteristics do you know about your audience? Check all that apply and add details about each selected characteristic.

☐ Age

☐ Education:

☐ Cultural background:

☐ Other:

What level of expertise does your audience have with regards to your topic? Add details to describe the selected level of expertise.

☐ Expert:

☐ Intermediate:

☐ Beginner/Some knowledge:

☐ Complete novice:

Understanding Presentations and Presentation Media

A **presentation** is a talk in which the person speaking—the **presenter**—is communicating with an audience in an effort to explain new concepts or ideas, sell a product or service, entertain, train the audience in a new skill or technique, or achieve a wide variety of other goals. The ability to give an interesting and informative presentation has become an important skill for students and professionals in all types of businesses.

Some talented presenters are able to simply stand in front of an audience and speak. They don't need any **presentation media**—the visual and audio aids that you display to support your points—because they are able to captivate the audience and clearly explain their topics simply by speaking. Most of us, however, want to use presentation media to help hold the audience's interest and enhance their understanding.

Presentation media can include photos, lists, music, video, and objects that the presenter holds or even passes around the room. You can also use the following tools to display presentation media:

- Presentation software, such as Microsoft PowerPoint
- Whiteboard
- Flip chart
- Posters
- Overhead transparencies
- Handouts
- Chalkboard

Presentation software like PowerPoint makes it very easy for presenters to create bulleted lists of information points. This sometimes results in all of the presenter's content listed on a screen behind them, which they then proceed to read to their audience. Since most people can read faster than someone can speak, the audience finishes reading the words before the presenter finishes speaking, and then sits, bored, waiting for the presenter to move on to new information. Even if the presenter has additional information to communicate, the audience, anticipating that they will be able to read the information on the screen, has probably stopped listening. Sometimes visuals contain so many words that to make them all fit, the presenter must use a small font, making it difficult or impossible for the audience to read, leading to frustration as well as boredom.

| Figure 1 | A bored audience member |

Yuri Acurs/Shutterstock.com

Although brief bulleted lists can be very helpful when the presenter is explaining facts, people attend presentations to hear the speaker and perhaps to see diagrams or other illustrations that will help them understand and retain the information. When you give a presentation, you should take advantage of this opportunity to thoroughly engage your audience. For example, if you display a graphic that supports your statements, your presentation will be more interesting, and the audience will pay attention to you and what you are saying, rather than tuning you out while trying to read words on the screen.

| Figure 2 | An interested, engaged audience |

Kzenon/Shutterstock.com

In order to deliver a successful presentation, you need to spend time developing it. There are three stages to developing a presentation: planning, creating, and preparing your delivery. In this session, you will focus on the planning stage.

Planning a Presentation

When you plan a presentation, you need to consider some of the same factors you consider when planning a written document—your purpose, audience, and situation. Planning a presentation in advance will improve the quality of your presentation, make it more effective and enjoyable for your audience, and, in the long run, save you time and effort.

As you plan your presentation, you should ask yourself the following questions:

- Will I deliver the presentation in front of a live audience or over the Internet, or will it be a self-running presentation?
- What are the purposes and desired outcomes of this presentation?
- Who is the audience for my presentation, and what do they need and expect?

The following sections will help you answer these questions so that you can create a more effective presentation, and enable you to feel confident in presenting your ideas.

Determining the Form of the Presentation

Usually when someone refers to a presentation, they mean an oral presentation given by a presenter to a live audience. When giving an oral presentation, a person might present to a small audience in a room the size of a classroom, to an audience in a hall large enough to require using a microphone, or over the Internet in webinar format. A **webinar** is a presentation in which the audience signs in to a shared view of the presenter's computer screen and calls in to a conference call to hear the presenter over the telephone line. If the presenter is using video technology, such as a webcam, the webinar audience will be able to see the presenter as well.

With PowerPoint and other presentation software, you can also create a presentation that is self-running or that is controlled by the person viewing it. Sometimes, this type of presentation includes recorded audio, but often it includes only the presentation content. This type of presentation can be challenging to create because the person who prepares the content needs to avoid making it simply a wordy substitute for a written document.

If you are presenting in front of a live audience, you can rely on facial expressions and body language to help convey your points. You can also see your audience's facial expressions and body language, which can help to indicate how they are feeling about your presentation. For example, if you see confused expressions, you might decide to pause for questions. If you are presenting via a webinar you need to make sure all the visuals that you use to help explain your points are very clear, and you need to figure out how to interact with your audience in a way that won't disrupt the flow of your presentation. If the presentation will be self-running, the content will need to be compelling enough on its own to make the audience want to watch the entire presentation. For this reason, the content of a self-running presentation must be even more visually interesting then if it were appearing on a screen behind a speaker because the presenter will not have the opportunity to directly engage the audience.

Determining the Presentation's Purposes and Desired Outcomes

When you are planning a presentation, you need to know what the purpose of the presentation is. Most presentations have one of three purposes: to inform, to persuade, or to demonstrate.

Determining the Purposes

Informative presentations are designed to inform or educate. This type of presentation provides the audience with background information, knowledge, and specific details about a topic that will enable them to gain understanding, make informed decisions, or increase their expertise on a topic. Examples of informative presentations include:

- Summary of research findings at an academic conference
- Briefings on the status of projects
- Overview, reviews, or evaluations of products and services
- Reports at company meetings

Persuasive presentations are designed to persuade or sell. They have the specific purpose of influencing how an audience feels or acts regarding a particular position or plan, or trying to convince the audience to buy something. Persuasive presentations are usually designed as balanced arguments involving logical as well as emotional reasons for supporting an action or viewpoint. Examples of persuasive presentations include:

- Recommendations of specific steps to take to achieve goals
- Sales presentations to sell a product or service
- Motivational presentations

Demonstrative (or **training**) **presentations** show an audience how something works, educate them on how to perform a task, or help them to understand a process or procedure. Sometimes you will provide listeners with hands-on experience, practice, and feedback so they can correct their mistakes and improve their performances. Examples of demonstrative presentations include:

- Software demonstrations
- Process explanations
- Employee training
- Seminars and workshops
- Educational classes and courses

You should always identify the primary purpose of your presentation. However, presenters often have more than one goal, which means your presentation might have additional, secondary purposes. For example, the primary purpose of a presentation might be to inform an audience about a wildlife preserve and describe it to them. But the secondary purpose might be to raise funds for that preserve. Identifying the primary purpose of a presentation helps you focus the content; however, by acknowledging secondary purposes, you can be prepared to answer or deflect questions until after the presentation so that the primary purpose remains the focus of the presentation.

Figure 3 summarizes the three categories of presentation purposes and their goals.

Figure 3	Purposes for giving presentations

Purpose	Goal	Examples
Informative	Present facts and details	Summary of research findings, status reports, briefings, discussions of products and services
Persuasive	Influence feelings or actions	Recommendation reports, sales presentations, motivational presentations
Demonstrative (Training)	Show how something works and provide practice and feedback	Software demos, process explanations, employee training, seminars and workshops, educational courses

© 2014 Cengage Learning

When Jon gives his presentation about Team Kidz, his primary purpose will be to persuade the parents in his audience to register their children for the programs he offers. His secondary purpose will be to inform them of the benefits of regular physical activity for children.

Identifying Desired Outcomes

In addition to determining the purpose of a presentation, you should also consider what you hope to achieve in giving your presentation. That means you need to determine the desired outcomes of your presentation—what you want your listeners to know, think, feel, or do after listening to the message. Focusing on the desired outcomes of your presentation forces you to make it more audience-oriented. Just as when you determined the purpose of your presentation, you might find that although you have a primary desired outcome, secondary outcomes might be acceptable as well.

You should be able to concisely express the purpose and desired outcomes of your presentation. Writing down the purpose and desired outcomes helps you decide what to include in the presentation, enabling you to create a more effective presentation. A good statement of your purpose and desired outcomes will also help when you write the introduction and conclusion for your presentation. Consider the following examples of specific purpose statements with specific outcomes:

- **Purpose:** To demonstrate to staff members a newly purchased projector that can be used for giving presentations to small groups.
  Outcome: Staff members will understand how to use the new equipment.

- **Purpose:** To inform department heads at a college about the benefits of a new website where students can receive tutoring.
Outcome: Audience will understand the benefits of the program.
Secondary Purpose: To persuade department heads to recruit tutors for the program.
Secondary Outcome: Department heads will ask their faculty to identify potential tutors.

The desired outcome of Jon's presentation is that parents will register their children for his program and that faculty in the city's schools will be enthusiastic about it.

Figure 4 shows a basic worksheet for helping determine the form, purpose, and outcome of a presentation. This worksheet is filled out with Jon's information.

| **Figure 4** | Form, Purpose, and Outcome worksheet for Team Kidz presentation |

Form, Purpose, and Outcome

What form is the presentation?	☒ Oral delivery	☐ Self-running

What is the primary purpose of your presentation? Check one and add specific details.

☐ Inform:

☒ Persuade: Persuade parents to register their children for Team Kidz.

☐ Demonstrate or train:

What is the primary desired outcome of your presentation? Specifically, what should the audience know, think, feel, or do after listening to your message?

The audience will know about the various activities that Team Kidz offers and understand the benefits the program has for children. As a result, they will want to send their children to the program.

Does your presentation have a secondary purpose? Check one and add specific details.

☒ Inform: Describe benefits of regular physical activity for children.

☐ Persuade:

☐ Demonstrate or train:

☐ None

If there is a secondary purpose, what is the secondary desired outcome?

The audience will understand the benefits of regular physical activity for children.

Analyzing Your Audience's Needs and Expectations

The more you know about your listeners, the more you'll be able to adapt your presentation to their needs. By putting yourself in your listeners' shoes, you'll be able to visualize your audience as more than just a group of passive listeners, and you can anticipate what they need and expect from your presentation. Anticipating the needs of your audience also increases the chances that your audience will react favorably to your presentation.

The first step in analyzing your audience is to determine their relationship to you. If you are speaking to your peers, you could adopt a less formal style than if you are speaking to your superiors or people who report to you. Also, if you are speaking to a room full of people who know you and your credentials, you might be able to present in a more informal, familiar manner than if you are speaking to people who have never met you.

The second step in analyzing your audience is to find out about their demographics. **Demographics** are characteristics that describe your audience. Some of the demographics that affect your presentations are:

- **Age**—People of different age groups vary in terms of attention span and the way they absorb information. For example, young children have shorter attention spans and generally can't sit still as long as adults, so presentations to young children should be divided into short sessions interspersed with physical activity.
- **Education**—Audiences with more education expect a higher level of technicality than audiences with less education.
- **Cultural background**—Each culture has its own expectations for how to write, speak, and communicate, including nonverbal conventions such as gestures and body movement. It is important to remember that cultural differences can occur even in the same country.
- **Expertise**—Audiences with specialized training expect examples that use terms and concepts from their field. Audiences who are unfamiliar with a topic will require more definitions and explanation to understand the presentation.

INSIGHT

Understanding the Needs of an International Audience

If you're presenting to an international audience, whether over the Internet or in person, it is important to understand the different cultural expectations that international audiences may have for your presentation, including expectations for nonverbal communication. These cultural expectations are subtle but powerful, and you can immediately create a negative impression if you don't understand them. For example, audiences from cultures outside the United States may expect you to speak and dress more formally than you are used to in the United States. In addition, some cultures are hesitant to debate an issue or present disagreement towards popular views.

There are no universal guidelines that would enable you to characterize the needs of all international audiences; however, there are some commonsense recommendations. You should analyze the hand gestures and symbols you use routinely to see if they have different meaning for other cultures. Be cautious about using humor because it is easy to misinterpret. And take special care to avoid using cultural stereotypes.

Understanding who your audience is and their needs and expectations helps you adapt the content of your presentation to a particular audience. Figure 5 shows a worksheet that Jon used to analyze the needs and expectations of his audience.

Figure 5   **Audience Analysis worksheet for Team Kidz presentation**

Audience Analysis

Who is your audience? Check all that apply and add details about each selected group.

☐ Peers:

☐ Superiors:

☐ Subordinates:

☒ Strangers: Parents and maybe teachers.

What characteristics do you know about your audience? Check all that apply and add details about each selected characteristic.

☒ Age: 20s – 50s

☒ Education: Varied, from no high school diploma through PhD.

☒ Cultural background: Varied, but all currently living in the city.

☒ Other: Socio-economic backgrounds will be varied as well.

What level of expertise does your audience have with regards to your topic? Add details to describe the selected level of expertise.

☐ Expert:

☐ Intermediate:

☒ Beginner/Some knowledge: Everyone will be familiar with children's needs, but not with the specific programs at Team Kidz.

☐ Complete novice:

Audience Analysis, continued

How will your listeners use this information? Check and explain all that apply.

☒ Make decisions: Decide whether to sign their children up for program.

☐ Perform a task:

☒ Form an opinion: Form an opinion about the Team Kidz program.

☒ Increase understanding: Learn more about the Team Kidz program and the benefits of physical activity for children.

☐ Follow a process:

☐ Other:

© 2014 Cengage Learning

Teamwork: Planning Collaborative Presentations

Because much of the work in business and industry is collaborative, it's only natural that presentations in these settings often are created and presented by a team of people. These types of presentations are referred to as collaborative presentations and they provide many benefits, including:

- Sharing a greater range of expertise and ideas
- Provoking more discussion due to different presentation styles and a wider range of information being shared
- Providing more people with exposure and the rewards of a task accomplished
- Allowing more people to gain valuable experience in communicating ideas

In addition to creating compelling content, a successful collaborative presentation depends on your group's ability to plan thoroughly and practice together. To ensure a successful group presentation, consider the following as you plan your presentation:

- Involve the whole team in the planning.
- Show respect for the ideas of all team members, and be sensitive to personality and cultural differences among the team members.
- Convey clear time constraints to each speaker and ensure that all speakers are prepared to limit themselves to the time allotted.
- Plan for the transitions between speakers.

In this session you learned how to plan a presentation and to consider the needs and expectations of your audience. In the next session, you will learn about the steps for creating the content of a presentation.

Session 1 Quick Check

1. Describe the difference between a presentation and presentation media.
2. List the three categories of presentation purposes.
3. Give an example of each category of presentation purpose.
4. Why is it important to focus on the desired outcomes of a presentation?
5. List three examples of audience demographics.
6. Why is it helpful for the presenter to understand the audience's relationship to him or her?

Session 2 Visual Overview:

A presentation's focus can be based on the chronology of events, a geography or region, categories or classifications, a particular component or segment, or a point of view.

An effective introduction should engage the audience and state the purpose for your presentation.

Information gathered from a variety of sources can help support your statements, as long as the information is accurate and up-to-date and the source is reputable.

Establish a focus and identify key points

Write an introduction

Gather and evaluate information

Focus and Organization

How will you focus your presentation? Select one and describe the selected strategy.

☐ Time or chronology   ☐ Geography or region

☐ Category or classification   ☐ Component or element

☐ Segment or portion   ☐ Point of view

Explanation:

What are your key points of your presentation?

How will you gain your audience's attention? Select one and describe the selected strategy.

☐ Anecdote   ☐ Statistic or relevant data

☐ Quotation, familiar phrase, or definition   ☐ Question(s)

☐ Current problem or issue   ☐ Comment about audience or occasion

☐ State purpose

Explanation:

Will you provide an overview of your presentation?   ☐ Yes   ☐ No

If so, how?

Creating a Presentation

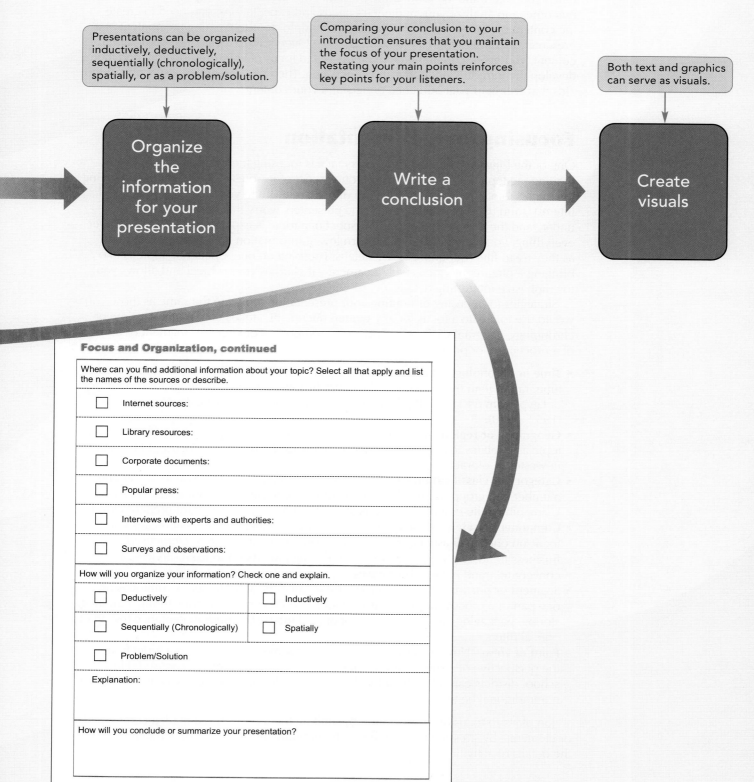

Presentations can be organized inductively, deductively, sequentially (chronologically), spatially, or as a problem/solution.

Comparing your conclusion to your introduction ensures that you maintain the focus of your presentation. Restating your main points reinforces key points for your listeners.

Both text and graphics can serve as visuals.

Organize the information for your presentation

Write a conclusion

Create visuals

Focus and Organization, continued

Where can you find additional information about your topic? Select all that apply and list the names of the sources or describe.

☐ Internet sources:

☐ Library resources:

☐ Corporate documents:

☐ Popular press:

☐ Interviews with experts and authorities:

☐ Surveys and observations:

How will you organize your information? Check one and explain.

☐ Deductively		☐ Inductively	
☐ Sequentially (Chronologically)		☐ Spatially	
☐ Problem/Solution			

Explanation:

How will you conclude or summarize your presentation?

Creating the Presentation

Once you determine the form of the presentation, determine your purpose and outcome, and analyze your audience's needs and expectations, you need to create the content of your presentation. There are multiple steps to creating the content of a presentation. As shown in the Session 2 Visual Overview, to create the presentation's content, you need to identify the main ideas and focus of your presentation, and then develop the introduction, body, and conclusion. Then you can create visual and audio aids that will help your audience understand your content.

Focusing Your Presentation

One of the biggest challenges presenters face is focusing their presentations, that is, limiting the topic by concentrating on one aspect of it. You should begin by identifying the major points or main ideas that are directly relevant to your listeners' needs and interests, and then focus on those. Some presenters worry that audiences will not understand the material unless every aspect of a topic is explained. If you try to cover everything, you'll give your audience irrelevant information and they'll lose interest as they try to filter out unnecessary details. Focusing on one aspect of a topic is like bringing a picture into focus with a camera—it clarifies your subject and allows you to emphasize interesting details.

Strategies for focusing or limiting your presentation topic are the same as those you would use to create a focus for any written document—focus on a particular time or chronology, geography or region, category, component or element, segment or portion of a procedure, or point of view.

- **Time or chronology**—Limiting a topic by time means you focus on a segment of time, rather than trying to cover the entire history of a topic. *Unfocused:* The history of Egypt from 640 to 2000. *Focused:* The history of Egypt during the Nasser years (1952–1970).
- **Geography or region**—Limiting a topic by geography or region means you look at a topic as it relates to a specific location. *Unfocused:* Fly fishing. *Focused:* Fly fishing in western Colorado.
- **Category or classification**—Limiting a topic by category means you focus on one member of a group or on a limited function. *Unfocused:* Thermometers. *Focused:* Using bimetallic-coil thermometers to control bacteria in restaurant-prepared foods.
- **Component or element**—Limiting a topic by component or element means you focus on one small aspect or part of an organization or problem. *Unfocused:* Business trends. *Focused:* Blending accounting practices and legal services, a converging trend in large businesses.
- **Segment or portion**—Limiting a topic by segment or portion means you focus on one part of a process or procedure. *Unfocused:* Designing, manufacturing, handling, storing, packaging, and transporting of optical filters. *Focused:* Acceptance testing of optical filters.
- **Point of view**—Limiting a topic by point of view means you look at a topic from the perspective of a single group. *Unfocused:* Employee benefits. *Focused:* How school districts can retain their teachers by providing child-care assistance and other nontraditional benefits.

Jon plans to focus his presentation by limiting the topic—focusing on a component or element—by stressing the benefits of the program, and not spending much time on the details of activities.

Identifying Your Key Points

Once you have determined your focus, you need to identify the key points of your presentation. To help you continue to design your presentation with the listener in mind, phrase the key points as the conclusions you want your audience to draw from the presentation.

As you identify the key points, order them in a numbered list with the most important idea listed first and the least important point listed last. This will help you maintain the focus and ensure that the most important points receive the most attention. For example, the key points for Jon's presentation about the Team Kidz program are:

1. Children need physical activity to promote good physical, emotional, and mental health.
2. The program provides many opportunities for physical activity.
3. Program activities are fun and engaging.

Once you've established a focus and identified your key points, you need to create the introduction, body, and conclusion of your presentation. Good presentations start with an effective introduction, continue with a well-organized body, and end with a strong conclusion.

Developing an Introduction

The introduction, or opening statement, of a presentation enables you to gain your listeners' attention, establish a relationship with your audience, and preview your key points. The introduction sets the tone for the entire presentation. An inadequate introduction can ruin the rest of your presentation no matter how well you've prepared. Consider these guidelines to avoid common mistakes:

- Don't begin by apologizing about any aspect of your presentation, such as how nervous you are or your lack of preparation. Apologies destroy your credibility and guarantee that your audience will react negatively to what you present.
- Don't use gimmicks to begin your presentation, such as making a funny face, singing a song, or ringing a bell. Members of your audience won't know how to respond and will feel uncomfortable.
- Avoid trite, flattering, or phony statements, such as, "Ladies and gentlemen, it is an unfathomable honor to be in your presence." Gaining respect requires treating your audience as your equal.
- Be cautious when using humor. It's difficult to predict how audiences will respond to jokes and other forms of humor; therefore, you should avoid using humor unless you know your audience well.

Gaining Your Audience's Attention

The purpose of the introduction is to provide the listeners with an organizational overview of your presentation; however, it is also important to remember that the introduction provides the audience with their first impression of you and your presentation. Even if your audience is interested in your topic, they can be easily distracted, so it's important to create an effective introduction that will immediately grab their attention. A truly effective introduction captures the attention of your audience and establishes a rapport with them. Some effective ways to gain your audience's attention are:

- Share anecdotes.
- Discuss statistics or relevant data.
- Mention a quotation, familiar phrase, or definition.
- Ask questions.
- Raise a current problem or issue.
- Comment about the audience or occasion.
- State the purpose of the presentation.

Share Anecdotes

Sharing anecdotes (short stories or personal experiences that demonstrate a specific point) is a very effective method of gaining your audience's attention. Anecdotes allow your audience to relate to you as a person and make your topic more relevant. For example, Jon could begin his presentation relating his story about how he first thought of creating the Team Kidz program:

"Last year, I became frustrated because when I was teaching physical education classes, the time periods were so short that the children were not able to complete any games. Also, children weren't placed in the same physical education classes based on their interest in specific activities, so it was difficult to keep all the children engaged. I thought that a program run outside of regular school hours, with plenty of time to finish games and plenty of choices of activities, would fill this need. And Team Kidz was born."

Discuss Statistics and Quantitative Data

Another way to engage your audience is to discuss interesting statistics and quantitative data relating to the needs of your audience. To be effective, make sure that the statistics and data you use are current, accurate, and easily understood.

In Jon's presentation, he could share statistics and data about how children who get plenty of physical activity demonstrate better behavior and are much healthier.

Mention a Quotation, Familiar Phrase, or Definition

Short quotes, familiar phrases, or definitions are another way to gain your audience's attention. This strategy works because your audience wants to know how the quote, phrase, or definition relates to your topic, and this leads naturally into the rest of your talk. Jon could use a quotation such as the following one by Plato to introduce his presentation:

"Lack of activity destroys the good condition of every human being, while movement and methodical physical exercise save it and preserve it."

Ask Questions

TIP

Be aware that an audience member might call out humorous or otherwise unwanted answers to your questions, which can detract from the effectiveness of your introduction.

Asking questions to introduce your topic can be effective if the questions are thought-provoking and the issues are important. This can be especially effective in small group settings or situations where you're attempting to find new ways to approach ideas. Asking audience members to give tentative answers to an informal quiz or questionnaire allows you to adjust your presentation to accommodate their responses.

Rhetorical questions (questions you don't expect the audience to answer) are especially effective. Rhetorical questions engage the audience right away because the audience members instinctively reply to the question internally.

In his presentation, Jon could ask parents, "How often do your children engage in physical activity?"

Raise a Current Problem or Issue

Another way to grab the attention of your audience is to raise a current problem or unresolved issue. This provides you with an opportunity to suggest a change or a solution to the problem. By defining a problem for your audience, you develop a common ground upon which you can provide insight, examine alternatives, and make recommendations.

In Jon's presentation, he could raise current problems such as the following:

- "Obesity rates in this country are soaring, and lifelong patterns of a sedentary lifestyle begin in childhood."
- "Although we provide physical education classes during school, in reality this means that kids are actively moving for only about 30 minutes each class. With classes occurring only twice a week, this just isn't enough."

Comment About the Audience or Occasion

To show your enthusiasm about the group you're addressing, as well as about your topic, you can make comments about the audience or occasion. If you do this, your comments should be brief and sincere. Referring to the occasion can be as simple as Jon saying:

- "I'm happy that you're giving me this opportunity to tell you about my new Team Kidz program."
- "Thanks for letting me tell you about the Team Kidz program. I think you'll find that we have a wide range of activities with something for everyone."

State the Purpose of the Presentation

Simply announcing your purpose works well as an introduction if your audience is already interested in your topic or if your time is limited. Most audiences, however, will appreciate a more creative approach than simply stating, "I'm going to try to convince you that Team Kidz has a range of activities that are beneficial to children." For example, in Jon's presentation to parents, he might say something like, "My purpose is to discuss a situation that affects your children every day."

Figure 6 summarizes the ways to gain your audience's attention.

Figure 6	Ways to gain your audience's attention

Method	Result
Share anecdotes	Helps audience relate to you as a real person
Discuss statistics and quantitative data	Increases audience interest in topic
Mention a quotation, familiar phrase, or definition	Leads in well to remainder of presentation
Ask questions	Gets audience thinking about topic
Raise a current problem or issue	Prepares audience to consider solutions or recommendations for change
Comment about the audience or occasion	Enables you to show your enthusiasm
State the purpose of the presentation	Works well if audience is already interested

© 2014 Cengage Learning

Providing an Overview of Your Presentation

Once you have gained the attention of your audience, you might choose to provide them with an overview of your presentation. Overviews, sometimes called advance organizers or previews, prepare your audience for the points that will follow. They can be very effective for longer presentations or for presentations that cover complex or technical information. Overviews help your audience remember your presentation by providing a road map of how it is organized. Overviews should be brief and simple, stating what you plan to do and in what order. After you've given your audience an overview of your presentation, it's important that you follow that same order.

Once you've created your introduction, you're ready to develop the body of your presentation.

Developing the Body of Your Presentation

The body of your presentation is where you present pertinent information, supporting evidence, and important details. To develop the body, you need to gather information on your key points, determine the organizational approach, add supporting details and other pertinent information, and provide transitions from one point to the next.

Gathering Information

Most of the time, you'll give presentations on topics about which you're knowledgeable and comfortable. Other times, you might have to give presentations on topics that are new to you. In either case, you'll need to explain the reasoning behind your statements, provide support for claims, present sensible recommendations, and anticipate objections to your statements or conclusions. This means you need to go beyond your personal experience and do in-depth research to provide relevant and up-to-date information, verifiable facts, truthful statistics, and expert testimony.

You can find additional information on your topic by consulting the following:

- Internet sources—The Internet is an excellent place to find information on any topic.
- Library resources—You can access library resources, such as books, encyclopedias, academic journals, government publications, and other reference materials, using the library's computerized catalog, indexes, and professional database services.
- Corporate documents and office correspondence—Since using these materials might violate your company's nondisclosure policy, you might need to obtain your company's permission or get legal clearance to use the information.
- Popular press items from newspapers, radio, TV, the web, and magazines—This information, geared for general audiences, provides large-scale details and personal opinions that may need to be supplemented by additional research.
- Interviews with experts and authorities in the field or other members of your organization—Talking to other people who are knowledgeable about your topic will give you additional insight.
- Surveys and observations—If you do your own interviews, surveys, and observations, be prepared with a list of specific questions, and always be respectful of other people's time.

Figure 7 | **Gathering information from a variety of sources**

Jaimie Duplass/Shutterstock.com

Evaluating Information

Not all of the information you gather will be of equal value. You must evaluate the information you gather by asking whether it is accurate, up-to-date, and reputable. When evaluating Internet sources in particular, it's important that you ascertain whether the websites you use as sources contain a bias or viewpoint that influences the information, such as a sales pitch.

You should also evaluate whether the information is pertinent to your particular topic. The scope of some topics is so broad, you will need to whittle down the information to only that which serves to clarify or enhance the specific key points of your presentation. Consider whether the information supports your purpose and focus.

For his presentation, Jon collected the following additional information: a book from the library titled *A Guide for Parents about Nutrition and Exercise*; the latest data from the USDA (United States Department of Agriculture); an article from the *Albany News* titled "Studies Show 17% of Kids Clinically Obese"; information from interviews with local doctors and physical therapists; and an informal survey of 25 children who are interested in participating in activities but are currently unable to due to cost or accessibility. Although all of the information is accurate, current, and interesting, the information on nutrition is not relevant to Jon's topic.

Organizing Your Information

After you have fully researched your topic and evaluated the information you've gathered, you're ready to organize the information in an understandable and logical manner so that your listeners can easily follow your ideas. You should choose an organizational approach for your information based upon the purpose, audience, and situation of each presentation. Sometimes your company or supervisor might ask you to follow a specific organizational pattern or format in giving your presentations. Other times you might be able to choose your own organizational approach. Some common organizational options include deductive, inductive, chronological, spatial, and problem-solution.

Deductive organization means that you present your conclusions or solutions first, and then explain the information that led you to your conclusions. See Figure 8. Deductive organization is the most common pattern used in business because it presents the most important or bottom-line information first.

Figure 8   **Deductive organization**

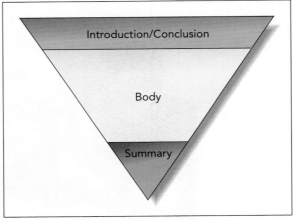

© 2014 Cengage Learning

Organizing Jon's presentation in a deductive manner would mean that Jon would begin by describing his program and then give details about how regular physical activity is vital to children for their health and happiness.

When you begin with the individual facts and save your conclusions until the end of your presentation, you are using **inductive organization**. See Figure 9. Inductive organization is useful when your purpose is to persuade your audience to follow an unusual plan of action, or you feel your audience might resist your conclusions. However, inductively organized presentations can be more difficult to follow because the most important information may come at the end of the presentation.

Figure 9   **Inductive organization**

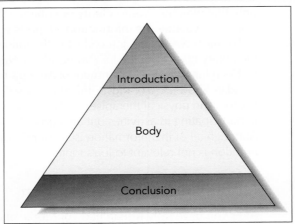

© 2014 Cengage Learning

If Jon is concerned that parents will think his program is completely unnecessary, he could organize his presentation inductively by presenting facts about childhood obesity and the benefits of regular physical activity, and then provide his program as a solution to this problem.

When you use **sequential** or **chronological organization**, you organize information in a step-by-step fashion or according to a time sequence. See Figure 10. Sequential organization works best when you must demonstrate a procedure, train someone to use a piece of equipment, or explain the evolution of a concept. Failing to present sequential information in the proper order can leave your listeners confused and might result in wasting time and resources.

| Figure 10 | Sequential (chronological) organization |

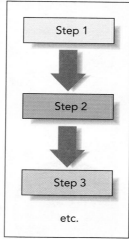

© 2014 Cengage Learning

If Jon was confident that his audience wanted to register for his program, he could organize his presentation sequentially by explaining the details of signing up for specific types of programs—drop-in games, mini-tournaments, or the commitment required for signing up for a seasonal team.

Spatial organization is used to provide a logical and effective order for describing the physical layout of an item or system. See Figure 11.

| Figure 11 | Spatial organization |

© 2014 Cengage Learning

If Jon thought that it was important to describe the physical locations of the program, he might present a city map to show the locations of all the schools for the programs conducted at schools, and then describe the layout of the Team Kidz center by describing all the rooms on the bottom floor, then proceed to the second floor and describe all the rooms on that floor, and then describe the outside layout.

Problem-solution organization consists of presenting a problem, outlining various solutions to the problem, and then explaining the solution you recommend. See Figure 12. Problem-solution presentations work best for recommending a specific action or solution.

Figure 12	Problem-solving organization

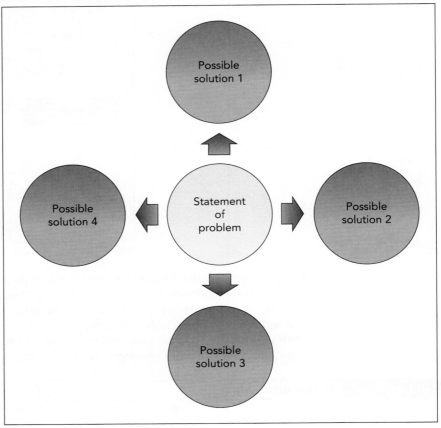

© 2014 Cengage Learning

If Jon uses problem-solving organization in his presentation, he would present the problems—children's lack of physical activity and the need for something fun and interesting to do after school—and then recommend his solution: that children attend Team Kidz.

Figure 13 summarizes the ways you can organize a presentation.

Figure 13	Ways to organize a presentation

Organizational Pattern	Explanation of Pattern
Deductive	Present conclusions or solutions first
Inductive	Present conclusions or solutions last
Sequential (Chronological)	Order by sequence or time
Spatial	Order by space or position
Problem/Solution	Present problem and various solutions, then recommend solution

© 2014 Cengage Learning

Developing Your Conclusion

Conclusions are valuable because they allow you to restate your key points, thus helping your listeners remember important information from your presentation. You can also suggest appropriate actions and recommend further resources. The conclusion is the last thing your audience hears and sees, and will likely stay with them longer than individual points you made—if it's effective. Therefore, you should give the same amount of attention and effort to developing the conclusion as you did to your introduction.

The following suggestions will help you create an effective conclusion:

- Use a clear transition to move into your conclusion. This will signal your audience that you're moving from the body of your presentation to the closing statements. Avoid ending with a trite statement like "I see my time is up, so I'll quit," which sends a general message to your audience that you did not develop a conclusion or prepare adequately to present all the relevant information in the amount of time available.
- Keep your conclusion short and simple. Audiences appreciate speakers who keep their presentations within the allotted time limit.
- Make sure the conclusion reiterates only the central points or essential message of your presentation. Don't introduce new ideas; simply remind your audience why they should care about your topic. Audiences won't appreciate a rehash of your entire presentation.
- Relate your conclusion to your introduction. Consider writing your conclusion at the same time you write your introduction to make sure that they both provide the same focus. Whenever you write your conclusion, compare it to your introduction to make sure they are complementary.
- If your purpose was to persuade your audience to take a specific action, use your conclusion to suggest what the audience should do now.
- If possible, suggest where your audience can find additional resources by providing web addresses, email addresses, phone numbers, or physical addresses.

Jon could conclude his presentation to parents by stating, "Now that you've seen the benefits of my Team Kidz program, I'd like to briefly summarize the main points I've made today. All children need regular physical activity. Team Kidz fills this need for your children by providing fun, low-cost activities at a variety of locations with a wide age-range appeal."

Figure 14 shows a worksheet Jon used to determine the focus and organization for his presentation.

Figure 14   **Focus and Organization worksheet for Team Kidz presentation**

Focus and Organization

How will you focus your presentation? Select one and describe the selected strategy.

☐	Time or chronology	☐	Geography or region
☐	Category or classification	☒	Component or element
☐	Segment or portion	☐	Point of view

Explanation:
Stress the benefits of the program and not spend too much time on the details of each activity.

What are your key points of your presentation?
Explain benefits of physical activity; how program provides this; program is fun

How will you gain your audience's attention? Select one and describe the selected strategy.

☐	Anecdote	☐	Statistic or relevant data
☐	Quotation, familiar phrase, or definition	☐	Question(s)
☒	Current problem or issue	☐	Comment about audience or occasion
☐	State purpose		

Explanation:
State known problem of kids not having healthy choices for after school activity in our city.

Will you provide an overview of your presentation?   ☒ Yes   ☐ No

If so, how?
Orally—explain that program will be described and there will be an opportunity to sign up at end

Focus and Organization, continued

Where can you find additional information about your topic? Select all that apply and list the names of the sources or describe.

☒ Internet sources: government sites, physical education sites

☐ Library resources:

☐ Corporate documents:

☒ Popular press: current news and magazine articles

☐ Interviews with experts and authorities:

☒ Surveys and observations: work as youth phys ed instructor

How will you organize your information? Check one and explain.

☒	Deductively	☐	Inductively
☐	Sequentially (Chronologically)	☐	Spatially
☐	Problem/Solution		

Explanation:
Describe program (the solution) then mention problems

How will you conclude or summarize your presentation?
Reiterate importance of regular physical activity; summarize variety of Team Kidz activities and wide age-range appeal. Distribute brochures and sign up sheets.

© 2014 Cengage Learning

Creating Visuals

Once you have written the content of your presentation, you can create your visuals. As you create your visuals, remember that they are intended to clarify your points, not contain the full content of your presentation. The exception to this is when you are creating a self-running presentation that users can view on their own. Even then, you need to remember that you are creating a presentation, not a document, so the information should be communicated in a creative manner, not just via long bulleted lists.

Using visuals to supplement your presentation does the following:

- Increases the listeners' understanding—Visuals are especially helpful in explaining a difficult concept, displaying data, and illustrating the steps in a process.
- Helps listeners remember information—Audiences will remember information longer when visuals highlight or exemplify the main points, review conclusions, and explain recommendations.
- Adds credibility to the presentation—Speakers who use visuals in their presentation are judged by their audiences as more professional and better prepared.
- Stimulates and maintains the listeners' attention—It's much more interesting to see how something functions, rather than just hear about it.

The primary thing to remember is that the visuals are supposed to enhance the audience's understanding and help keep their attention. Visuals shouldn't draw attention to themselves in such a way as to distract from your main points.

Using Text as Visuals

When you use text as visuals, you allow your audience to absorb the information you are conveying by reading as well as listening. This can help audience members retain the information presented. Text can be formatted as bulleted lists or treated like a graphic.

A common pitfall for presenters is to use too much text. You don't want your presentation to turn into a bedtime story with you reading all the words on your visual as the audience falls asleep. Therefore, if you use bulleted lists, keep the bullet points short. Bullet points should be brief descriptions of your main points, giving your audience a broad overview of what you will be discussing and serving as reminders to help you remember what you want to say.

Instead of creating a bulleted list, one alternative is to display key words in a decorative, large font. You could also use relevant images as the bullets, or use a photo of a person accompanied by dialog balloons, like those in a drawn comic, that contain the text you want to display. Compare the four visuals shown in Figure 15. The text in the first visual is clear enough, but the second is visually more interesting. The third visual uses graphical bullets that relate to the text in each bullet point, and the fourth eliminates text completely and just uses images.

Figure 15   **A simple bulleted list and alternatives**

Hybrid Automobiles

- Better gas mileage
- Reduced emissions
- Possible tax breaks

Hybrid Automobiles

Better gas mileage

Reduced emissions

Possible tax breaks

Hybrid Automobiles

 Better gas mileage

 Reduced emissions

 Possible tax breaks

Hybrid Automobiles

© 2014 Cengage Learning; images used with permission from Microsoft.

When you use text as a visual, keep in mind the following:

- Follow the 7x7 Rule, which says that when you display bulleted lists, use no more than seven bullet points per visual, with no more than seven words per bullet. Some presenters restrict themselves to 4x4—no more than four bullet points per visual or page with no more than four words per bullet.
- Keep phrases parallel. For example, if one bulleted item starts with a verb (such as "Summarize"), the other bulleted items should also start with a verb (such as "Include," "List," or "Review").
- Use simple fonts in a size large enough to be read from the back of the room. Only use decorative fonts for a single word or a few related words for maximum impact.
- Use dark-colored text on a light or white background to make it easy for the audience to quickly read the content. Do not layer text on top of a busy background graphic because the text will be difficult to read and the graphic will compete with the text for the audience's attention.
- Proofread your presentations. One sure way to reduce your credibility as a presenter is to have typographical errors in your presentation. It is especially important to double-check the spelling of proper names.

In his presentation, Jon could list facts about exercise, overall health, and obesity in a bulleted list.

Using Graphics as Visuals

You can help your listeners comprehend and retain the ideas from your presentation by supplementing it with effective graphics. A **graphic** is a picture, shape, design, graph or chart, diagram, or video. The old adage "A picture is worth a thousand words" especially applies to presentations because listeners understand ideas more quickly when they can see and hear what you're talking about.

You can choose from many types of visuals for your presentations: tables (text and numerical), graphs and charts (bar, line, pie, organizational, flow), illustrations (drawings, diagrams, maps, and photographs), and video. Selecting appropriate visuals for your purpose is a matter of knowing the strengths and weaknesses of the types of visuals. For example, if you want your audience to know facts and figures, a table might be sufficient; however, if you want your audience to make a particular judgment about the data, then a bar graph, line graph, or pie chart might be better. If you want to show processes and procedures, diagrams are better than photographs.

In Jon's presentation, he might want to present data showing how childhood obesity rates have risen. He could read a summary of the numbers, as shown in Figure 16.

Figure 16   Childhood obesity rate data as a presenter would read it

"In the 1970s, the percentage of children in the United States who were clinically obese was 4.4. Then for the next several years, through 1980, it rose by between 0.2% and 0.4%. Then from 1980 to 1982, from 1982 to 1984, and again from 1984–1986, it rose by 0.8%. It continued to rise fairly steadily from 1986–1990. Then, from 1990 to 1992, it rose by more than one full percentage point from 9.4% to 10.1%. From 1992 to 1994, it rose only 0.8%, but after that the increases were much larger. From 1994–1996, it rose from 10.9% to 12.2%; it then rose to 13.6% in 1998, to 15.0% in 2000, to 16.5% in 2002, and to 18.1% in 2004. The percentage declined slightly in 2006 to 16.5%, but then it rose again to its highest level in 2008 to 18.9%." *(interpolated from data on cdc.gov)*

© 2014 Cengage Learning

However, this is not the most interesting way of communicating the data, and Jon's audience will find it difficult to understand this long series of numbers if he just speaks them. By using visuals, he can present the same data in a format that's easier to understand, and more interesting. For example, he could present the data in tabular format, as shown in Figure 17.

Figure 17   Childhood obesity rate data in tabular format

Percentage of children ages 6–19 in the U.S. who are obese	
Year	Percentage*
1970	4.4
1972	4.8
1974	5.1
1976	5.3
1978	5.6
1980	5.8
1982	6.6
1984	7.3
1986	8.0
1988	8.7
1990	9.4
1992	10.1
1994	10.9
1996	12.2
1998	13.6
2000	15.0
2002	16.5
2004	18.1
2006	16.5
2008	18.9

interpolated from data on cdc.gov

© 2014 Cengage Learning

Although presenting the data in this manner does allow the audience members to read and absorb the numbers as he is speaking, this is still quite a lot of numerical data and many people can't visualize what this means. So, Jon could create a line graph instead, as shown in Figure 18.

| Figure 18 | Childhood obesity rate data in line chart format |

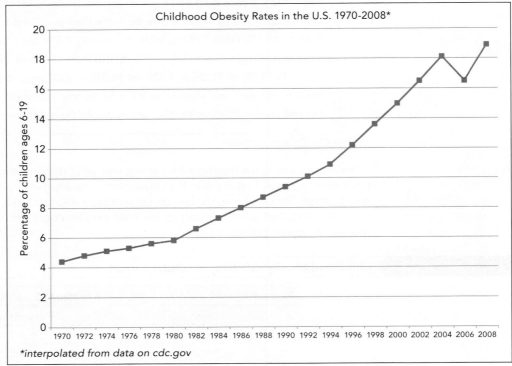

Childhood Obesity Rates in the U.S. 1970-2008*

*interpolated from data on cdc.gov

© 2014 Cengage Learning

The line graph clearly shows how rates have risen. The chart is somewhat visually deceiving because the values on the vertical axis go from 0 to 20, but the numbers shown are percentages. To give a true picture, the vertical axis should go from 0 to 100. This might result in a graph that's hard to read from the back of a room. Jon's alternative is to try two simple pie charts, as shown in Figure 19.

| Figure 19 | Childhood obesity rate data in pie charts |

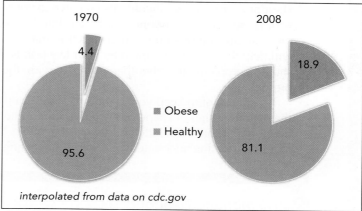

By showing only the data from 1970 and 2008, the two pie charts more clearly illustrate the point that Jon wants to make—that a much higher percentage of children are obese now than years ago. The actual numbers each year don't really matter that much and are distracting from Jon's main point.

Jon plans to use the charts shown in Figure 19 in his presentation. He also plans to include photos showing the Team Kidz center and photos of children playing various games. He is considering showing video of kids at the center as well.

PROSKILLS

Decision Making: Text, Graphics, or Both?

Some people think that presentation visuals should consist exclusively of graphics; that is, they should not contain any bulleted or numbered lists at all. Using graphics without any bulleted lists can help keep your audience's attention on you and your message. The audience sees the graphic and then focuses on you as you explain your point and the relevance of the graphic. However, this is not necessarily the best choice if you are presenting facts, summarizing a process, or presenting in an academic setting. Some business and academic audiences expect to see bullet points in a presentation. In these cases, you should give your audience what they expect. Self-running presentations also usually require more text than visuals compared to an oral presentation.

If you decide to use bulleted lists, re-evaluate the content after you create it to see if the list is necessary or if you can use a graphic or series of graphics instead. Whether you decide to use all bulleted lists, all graphics, or a combination, always review your content to make sure it supplements your oral presentation to make it clearer or that your self-running presentation is interesting enough to make someone want to watch it to the end.

Creating Handouts

Handouts are printed documents you give to your audience before, during, or after your presentation. Handouts can be a printed version of your presentation, but they can also be brochures, an instruction manual, booklets, or anything you think will help the audience remember your key points. The information in handouts should complement, rather than compete with, the information contained in your presentation.

It's important to keep your handouts simple and easy to read. Begin by considering the overall design or shape of the page. Your audience is more apt to read your handout if it looks uncluttered and approachable. You can do this by providing ample margins, creating adequate white space, and using prominent headings.

INSIGHT

Distributing Handouts

The decision of when to distribute handouts depends on how you want the audience to use them. If you are presenting complex information about which the audience will probably need to take notes, you should distribute the handouts at the start of your presentation. If you want the audience's undivided attention while you are speaking and your handouts will serve simply as a reminder of your key points, distribute them after your presentation.

Jon has a brochure for Team Kidz that describes the program, schedule, and cost, and he has a sign-up form. He feels these will be more beneficial handouts than a printed version of his presentation. He will distribute them at the end of his presentation.

After developing the content of a presentation and creating supporting visuals, you can begin to prepare to deliver your presentation. You will learn how to prepare for delivering a presentation in the next session.

REVIEW

Session 2 Quick Check

1. List at least three methods for focusing your topic.
2. Why should you phrase the key points of your presentation as conclusions you want your audience to draw?
3. List at least three ways to gain your audience's attention and the benefit of each.
4. What is the difference between organizing your presentation deductively and inductively, and when would you use each of these organizational formats?
5. Why are conclusions important?
6. If you use bulleted lists as visuals, what is a good rule of thumb for how much text should be shown at one time?
7. What is a graphic?
8. What is a handout?

Session 3 Visual Overview:

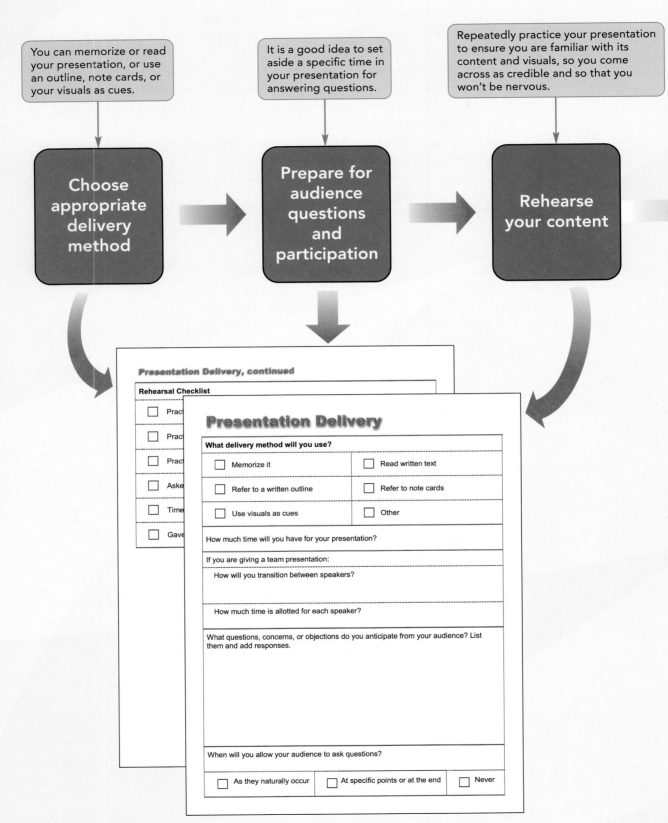

You can memorize or read your presentation, or use an outline, note cards, or your visuals as cues.

It is a good idea to set aside a specific time in your presentation for answering questions.

Repeatedly practice your presentation to ensure you are familiar with its content and visuals, so you come across as credible and so that you won't be nervous.

Choose appropriate delivery method

Prepare for audience questions and participation

Rehearse your content

Presentation Delivery, continued

Rehearsal Checklist

- [ ] Prac
- [ ] Prac
- [ ] Prac
- [ ] Aske
- [ ] Time
- [ ] Gave

Presentation Delivery

What delivery method will you use?

- [ ] Memorize it
- [ ] Read written text
- [ ] Refer to a written outline
- [ ] Refer to note cards
- [ ] Use visuals as cues
- [ ] Other

How much time will you have for your presentation?

If you are giving a team presentation:

How will you transition between speakers?

How much time is allotted for each speaker?

What questions, concerns, or objections do you anticipate from your audience? List them and add responses.

When will you allow your audience to ask questions?

- [ ] As they naturally occur
- [ ] At specific points or at the end
- [ ] Never

Delivering a Presentation

It is important to dress appropriately for your presentation.

Check that all your equipment is working properly, make sure you have all the supplies you need, and make sure the room is arranged so that all audience members can clearly see you.

Obtaining feedback on your presentation and its delivery will help improve your future presentations.

Evaluate your appearance

Set up the location for your presentation

Evaluate your performance

Situation Assessment and Facilities Checklist, continued

Physical Setup

Situation Assessment and Facilities Checklist

How large will your audience be?

What will the room be like and how will it be arranged? Add details.

- [ ] Small room:
- [ ] Large room:
- [ ] Webinar:
- [ ] Other:

Did you test your electronic equipment in the room? Check each after you test it.

- [ ] Computer
- [ ] Connection to projector
- [ ] Wireless remote
- [ ] Microphone
- [ ] Other

Where did you store copies of your PowerPoint file?

- [ ] On your laptop
- [ ] On a flash drive
- [ ] On the Internet
- [ ] Other

Internet Connection

| Do you need an Internet connection? | [ ] Yes | [ ] No |
| If yes, did you check it in the room with your laptop, tablet, or smartphone to make sure you know how to connect and that it is reliable? | [ ] Yes | [ ] No |

Presentation Evaluation

Content (10 points)					
Topic was relevant and focused	5	4	3	2	1
Information was credible and reliable	5	4	3	2	1
Organization (20 points)					
Main points were identified and supported	5	4	3	2	1
Introduction was interesting	5	4	3	2	1
Visuals increased understanding of topic	5	4	3	2	1
Conclusion was concise	5	4	3	2	1
Delivery (35 points)					
Established credibility and built a rapport	5	4	3	2	1
Stood up straight	5	4	3	2	1
Established eye contact	5	4	3	2	1
Spoke fluently and was easy to understand	5	4	3	2	1
Used natural voice and hand movements	5	4	3	2	1
Used proper grammar and pronunciation	5	4	3	2	1
Free of annoying mannerisms and fillers	5	4	3	2	1
Total (65 points)					

Strengths of the presentation:

Weaknesses of the presentation:

Other suggestions:

Preparing for the Delivery of an Oral Presentation

If you need to give an oral presentation, planning and creating the content of your presentation and creating your visuals are only part of the necessary preparation. In order to give a successful presentation, you need to prepare your delivery. The best oral presentations are prepared well in advance. As shown in the Session 3 Visual Overview, the first step in preparing is to choose a delivery method.

Choosing a Delivery Method

After you have created the content of your presentation, you need to decide if you want to memorize it exactly, read it word for word, or review it thoroughly so that glancing at keywords or your visuals is enough of a trigger to indicate which information to present at a given point in your talk.

Some presenters like to write their entire presentation out, word for word, and then memorize it so they can recite the presentation to the audience from memory. If you've never given a presentation before, this might be the best approach. If you are using presentation media, you can also use your visuals as reminders of the points you want to make. This works well for speakers who are comfortable speaking in front of an audience and who know their topic very well.

You can also read your written presentation word for word, if necessary. This is not the most engaging method of presenting, however, because you may tend to keep your head down and your voice low. It is better if you can maintain eye contact with your audience and stand up straight so that your voice is loud and clear.

Written or memorized presentations don't leave a lot to chance, so they work well in formal settings when you must stick to a topic and stay on schedule. They're also helpful if you think you'll forget what you prepared, or become nervous and tongue-tied as a result of your inexperience with the topic or with giving presentations. However, once you've memorized your presentation, it's not easy to alter it in response to changes in time limits or audience questions. Perhaps the biggest drawback to written or memorized presentations is that it's difficult to sound natural while reading your presentation or reciting it from memory, causing your listeners to lose interest.

Another delivery approach is to create an outline on paper or notecards that you can use to deliver your presentation without memorization. This type of delivery allows you to have a more natural-sounding presentation and the ability to adapt it for audience questions or participation. You still need to thoroughly review your notes to avoid leaving out crucial information, lacking precision when explaining your ideas, or stumbling because you are nervous and unfamiliar with the material.

INSIGHT

Giving an Impromptu Presentation

Impromptu presentations involve speaking without notes, an outline, or memorized text. Impromptu presentations work best when you're in the following situations:

- Extremely familiar with your topic and audience
- Speaking to a small, intimate group, or in your office setting
- More interested in getting the views of your audience than in persuading them or giving them specific information

Generally, you should be wary of impromptu presentations because they leave too much to chance. Speaking without notes may result in taking too much time, saying something that offends your audience, or appearing unorganized. If you think you might be asked to give an impromptu presentation, jot down some notes beforehand so you'll be prepared.

Jon will prepare his oral delivery and memorize it. He knows his material well, so he plans to use his visuals as cues rather than written notes.

Preparing for Audience Interaction

Allowing your audience to ask questions or actively participate in your presentation by offering their own ideas makes the presentation more personal for your audience. This also helps to keep them interested.

Anticipating Audience Questions

You need to decide whether you want your audience to have an opportunity to ask questions or actively participate in your presentation. You should welcome the idea of questions from the audience, rather than trying to avoid them. The absence of questions may indicate that your audience had no interest in what you said or that you spoke for too long. Adopting the attitude that interested listeners will have questions enables you to anticipate and prepare for the questions your audience will ask.

Figure 20 | **Interested listeners have questions**

Andrey_Popov/Shutterstock.com

If you plan to invite your audience to ask questions, you need to decide when you want this to happen. The size of your audience and the formality of the presentation might affect this decision. For example, four or five co-workers in a small conference room would probably expect to be able to interrupt your presentation and ask questions or express their own views, whereas a large audience in a lecture hall would not.

Allowing people to ask questions freely during your presentation means that the questions will be relevant and the answers will make sense to all members of the audience. If you allow this, keep an eye on the time and be prepared to halt questions if you need to. To allow you a little more control, you can build time for questions into your presentation as you transition from one section to another.

You can also ask your audience to hold all questions until the end of your presentation. If you do this, you will have more control over the time. However, people might forget their questions by the end of the presentation, and other audience members might not pay any attention at all to a question about something you discussed 30 minutes earlier.

If you decide to open the presentation to questions, you should prepare a few that you can pose in case no one responds when you invite questions. You can start with "I've often been asked…" or "A question that comes up frequently is…" This can be especially helpful if you build in time at the end of your presentation for answering questions, but no one has any.

When preparing for questions, keep in mind the following:

- Announce your plan for handling questions at the beginning of your presentation. If you don't plan to allow questions during your presentation, perhaps let people know they can approach you later.
- Repeat questions to make sure everyone in the audience hears them.
- If you don't understand a question, ask the questioner to rephrase it.
- Be prepared to answer questions about information in your presentation that is new, controversial, or unexpected.
- If you can't answer a question, admit it, indicate you will find out the answer and report back to the group, and then move on.
- If one person is completely confused and asks too many questions, especially questions that most of the audience already knows the answer to, ask this person to talk to you after the presentation so that the focus of your presentation doesn't get derailed.
- Don't be defensive about hostile questions. Treat every person's question as important, and respond courteously.
- Keep your answers brief. If you need additional time to respond to a question, arrange for it after your presentation.
- Be prepared to end a question-and-answer session; for example, state, "We have time for one more question."
- Consider offering to answer questions after the session, or provide your contact information and invite people to send you questions.

Jon anticipates that during his presentation audience members might have questions such as, "How will children get to the center?", "How much does the program cost?", and "How do you help children who are not skilled athletically?"

Preparing for Audience Participation

If you involve your audience in your presentation, they will pay closer attention to what you have to say. For example, an easy way to get the audience to participate is to start with a question and invite responses, or to stop partway through to discuss a particularly important point. You can also allow audience members to answer others' questions, contribute their own ideas, or ask for volunteers to help with a demonstration. Alternatively, you could ask audience members to give answers to an informal quiz or questionnaire, and then adjust your presentation to accommodate their responses. Allowing the audience to actively participate in your presentation can be especially effective in small group settings or situations where you're attempting to find new ways to approach ideas.

If you decide to allow your audience to participate in your presentation, you need to take extra precautions to avoid losing control of your presentation. Here are some tips to help you handle audience participation:

- Be prepared with tactful ways to interrupt a participant who monopolizes the time. If necessary, you can simply state, "I'm sorry. We must move on," and then continue with your presentation.
- State a limit on the length of each response (such as 30 seconds) or the number of responses.
- Be prepared to halt comments that are taking too much time by saying something such as "These are great comments, but I'm afraid I need to move on as we have a limited amount of time."
- If you are inexperienced with handling audience participation, consider allowing it only at the end of your presentation.

During his presentation, Jon wants to ask a few of the parents to relate their experiences searching for fun, inexpensive physical activities for their children.

Now that you've determined how you want to deliver your presentation and you're prepared to interact with your audience, it's time to practice delivering the presentation.

Rehearsing the Presentation

Once the presentation content has been created, enhanced, and perfected, and you have determined your delivery method, it is time to prepare you, the presenter. Even the most knowledgeable speakers rehearse to ensure they know how the topics flow, what the main points are, how much time to spend on each point, and where to place emphasis. Presenters who try to stand up and "wing it" in front of a crowd usually reveal this amateur approach the moment they start speaking—by looking down at their notes, rambling off topic, losing track of what they are saying, or turning their backs on the audience frequently to read information displayed on-screen. To avoid this, you need to rehearse your presentation.

Figure 21	Confidence comes with practice

Stephen Coburn/Shutterstock.com

TIP

Consider rehearsing for job interviews using the same techniques as you use for rehearsing for a presentation.

Begin by simply going over the key points of the presentation in your mind. Then rehearse your presentation in private until you are comfortable with the content. Next, practice in front of a few close friends so that they can offer critiques and you can get a feel for what it will be like speaking to an audience. Pay special attention to what your friends say about key aspects of your presentation, such as your introduction, main points, and conclusion. Then, rehearse your presentation again.

During your rehearsals, practice using your visuals to support your points. Know when to pause for a moment to let your audience absorb a visual, and know when to switch to the next visual. Also, time your presentation to make sure it is the correct length. Pay attention to the timing as you are speaking so that you know approximately how much time you have left by where you are in the presentation.

Finally, if you have a video camera, you can record yourself and then review the video. Watching video evidence of your performance often reveals weaknesses that you don't want your audience to see or that your friends or family may be unwilling or unable to identify.

As you rehearse, you should remember to focus on the following areas:

- Connecting to your audience
- Being aware of your body language
- Establishing eye contact
- Speaking in a pleasant, natural, confident voice
- Using proper grammar and pronunciation
- Avoiding fillers

INSIGHT

Overcoming Nervousness

Just thinking about speaking in front of other people may cause your heart to beat faster and your palms to sweat. You aren't alone. Feeling nervous about giving a presentation is a natural reaction. But you don't need to let nervousness interfere with your giving a successful presentation. Being nervous is not all bad. It means your adrenalin is flowing, and you'll have more energy and vitality for your presentation. In most instances, your nervousness will pass once you begin speaking. Sometimes, however, nervousness arises from feelings of inadequacy or from worrying about problems that could occur during a presentation. The most effective way to overcome your nervousness and deliver a smooth presentation is to carefully plan and prepare your presentation, and then to practice, practice, practice.

Experienced public speakers have learned several means of overcoming nervousness:

- Think positively about your presentation. Be optimistic and enthusiastic about your opportunity to gain experience. Visualize yourself as calm and confident.
- Work with your nervousness. Realize that some nervousness is normal and will help make your presentation better. Remember, your audience isn't nearly as concerned about your nervousness as you are.
- Give yourself plenty of time before your presentation. Arrive early to avoid rushing around before your presentation. Devote a few minutes beforehand to relax and review your presentation notes.
- When you first stand up, look at your audience and smile. Then take a few slow breaths to calm yourself before you begin to speak.
- Don't expect everything to be perfect. Have backup plans in case something goes wrong, and be prepared to handle problems with grace and a sense of humor.
- Think about why your audience is there—to learn something from you. When you focus your mind on meeting the needs of your audience, you begin to forget about yourself and how the audience might respond to you.
- Observe other presenters. Make a list of the things they do that you like, and try to implement them into your own presentations. Likewise, note any annoying mannerisms or speech patterns so that you don't duplicate them in your presentation.

Connecting to Your Audience

How an audience perceives a speaker can sometimes be more important than what the speaker says; therefore, it is important to establish a connection with your audience. Begin by introducing yourself and describing your credentials for speaking on your topic. Being aware of your demeanor—your body language, how often you make eye contact, and how you speak—will help you build a rapport with the audience. You often know if you have made a connection with your audience by their behavior and expressions. If your message is getting across, they will instinctively affirm what you're saying by returning your gaze, nodding their heads, or smiling. In Figure 22, the audience is smiling, nodding, and appears engaged with the presenter. If your message is not getting across and you see confused, puzzled, or frustrated expressions, you can make adjustments accordingly.

Figure 22   **Establish a connection with your audience**

iStockphoto.com/kupicoo

Being Aware of Your Body Language

Nonverbal communication is the way you convey a message without saying a word. Most nonverbal communication deals with how you use your body when interacting with people—how you look, stand, and move—in other words, your body language. In your everyday life, your body language is unconscious. However, by becoming aware of your body language, you can use it consciously to help you communicate more effectively.

Start by becoming aware of your posture. Stand up straight to signal confidence. Refrain from slouching, as your audience may interpret this to mean that you don't care or you're insecure.

Be aware of your hand movements as you speak. The best position for your hands is to place them comfortably by your side, in a relaxed position. As you talk, it's fine to use hand gestures to help make a point, but be careful not to overdo it. Informal presentations lend themselves to more gestures and movement than do formal presentations where you're standing in front of a microphone on a podium. But giving a formal presentation doesn't mean you should hide behind the lectern, or behave like a robot. Even formal presentations allow for gestures that are purposeful, spontaneous, and natural.

It is important to recognize your unique mannerisms (recurring or unnatural movements of your voice or body) that can be annoying, such as raising your voice and eyebrows as if you are talking to children; playing with your car keys, a pen, or equipment; or fidgeting, rocking, and pacing. All of these mannerisms can communicate nervousness. If they are pervasive, they will detract from your presentation because your audience will start paying attention to your mannerisms instead of to your topic. Consider asking a friend whether your gestures are distracting, and then practice speaking without them.

Resist the temptation to glance at your watch or cell phone; you don't want to send a signal that you'd rather be someplace else or that you are anxious to have the presentation completed.

Establishing Eye Contact

One of the most common mistakes presenters make is failing to establish eye contact with their audience. Speakers who keep their eyes on their notes, stare at their visuals, or look out over the heads of their audience create an emotional distance between themselves and their listeners. A better method is to look directly at your listeners, even if you have to pause to look up. Smiling and looking directly at your audience members, making eye contact, sends the message that you want to connect and that you can be trusted.

Figure 23	**Establish eye contact**

iStockphoto.com/kupicoo

To establish eye contact, look at individuals; do not just scan the audience. Focus on a particular member of the audience for just a second or two, then move on to someone else until you eventually get to most of the people in the audience or, if the audience is large, to most parts of the presentation room.

Speaking in a Pleasant, Natural, Confident Voice

The best presentations are those in which the presenter appears confident and speaks naturally in a conversational manner. No one enjoys a presentation when the speaker drones on endlessly in a monotone voice. So when delivering your presentation, speak with enthusiasm, with authority, and with a smile. When you project your voice with energy, passion, and confidence, your audience will automatically pay more attention to you. However, be careful not to overdo it. Speaking too loudly or using an overly confident or arrogant tone will quickly turn off an audience and make them stop listening altogether.

Using Proper Grammar and Pronunciation

One of the best ways to be seen as a credible speaker is to use proper grammar and pronunciation. To assure you're pronouncing a word correctly, check its pronunciation in a dictionary.

Here are some common pronunciation problems:

- Mispronunciations caused by dropping a letter, such as "liberry" instead of "library," or "satistics" instead of "statistics"
- Mispronunciations caused by adding a letter or inserting the wrong letter, such as "acrost" instead of "across," "learnt" instead of "learned," or "stadistics" instead of "statistics"
- Colloquial expressions, such as "crick" instead of "creek," or "ain't" instead of "isn't" or "aren't"
- Lazy pronunciation caused by dropping the final consonant, such as "speakin" rather than "speaking"

Avoiding Fillers

Fillers consist of sounds, words, and phrases such as *um, ah, like, you know?*, and other such breaks in speech that dilute a speaker's message because they are not essential to the meaning of what's being spoken. Fillers don't add any value, yet add length to sentences. At best, they can make you sound unprofessional. At worst, they can distract your audience and make your message incomprehensible.

Jon used the worksheet shown in Figure 24 to help him when practicing the delivery of his presentation. Note that he still needs to practice in front of others to get their feedback.

Figure 24	Presentation Delivery worksheet for the Team Kidz presentation

Presentation Delivery

What delivery method will you use?

☐ Memorize it	☐ Read written text
☐ Refer to a written outline	☐ Refer to note cards
☒ Use visuals as cues	☐ Other

How much time will you have for your presentation? 30 minutes

If you are giving a team presentation: N/A

How will you transition between speakers?

How much time is allotted for each speaker?

What questions, concerns, or objections do you anticipate from your audience? List them and add responses.

How will they get to the center? Shuttle from schools ($1/ride) or they walk

What is the cost? $10/month plus $1/shuttle ride

My child is not very athletic. Will he/she be able to participate? Yes, there will be programs at all levels. We will provide beginner training for kids who need it.

When will you allow your audience to ask questions?

☐ As they naturally occur	☒ At specific points or at the end	☐ Never

Presentation Delivery, continued

Rehearsal Checklist

☒	Practiced presentation in private
☐	Practiced presentation in front of friends or sample audience
☒	Practiced with presentation tools (PowerPoint file, props, etc.)
☐	Asked friends for suggestions and feedback on presentation
☒	Timed your presentation. Time in minutes: _30_____
☒	Gave particular attention to introduction, main points, and conclusion

PROSKILLS

Verbal Communication: Avoiding Business Jargon

Business jargon has crept into our everyday language more and more over the past several years, to the point that many expressions are cliché. As you prepare your delivery, avoid using business jargon. For example, avoid saying things like "maximize our growth potential," "leverage our content," "using all our available bandwidth," "productivity solution," and "we need a hard stop here." Think about what you're trying to say and break it down into its simplest, most direct terms. If your audience is used to hearing business jargon, they'll tune out your message because they've heard it all before. If your audience is not used to hearing business jargon, they'll spend most of their time trying to figure out what exactly you're trying to tell them. And if your audience is spending time figuring out what you just said, they are no longer listening to what you are currently saying. After you prepare your oral delivery, go back through and replace any jargon with simple direct language that anyone could understand.

Referring to Visuals During Your Presentation

As you rehearse your presentation, you'll need to plan how to manage and present your visuals so they effectively support your content. Follow these simple guidelines for effectively using visuals when giving your presentation:

- Introduce and interpret the visual. Explain to your audience what they should be looking at in the visual and point to what is important.
- If the visual is text, don't read it word for word; use it as a cue for what you want to say next.
- Stand to the side, not in front, of the visuals. Avoid turning your back on your audience as you refer to a visual. Talk directly to your audience, rather than turning toward or talking at the visual.
- Display the visual as you discuss it and remove the visual after you're through discussing it. Don't let your visuals get ahead of or behind your verbal presentation.

Evaluating Your Appearance

Before a single word is spoken in a presentation, the audience sizes up the way the presenter looks. Your appearance creates your audience's first impression of you, so make sure your dress and grooming contribute to the total impression you want to convey to your audience. You want to make sure you look professional and competent. Dress appropriately for the situation, and in a manner that doesn't detract from your presentation. For example, for a formal presentation, you should wear business attire, such as a suit and tie for a man and a suit or tailored dress for a woman. Consider your audience and situation, but always make sure your appearance is neat, clean, and well-coordinated, and that you choose appropriate clothing. For example, the presenters shown in Figure 25 are appropriately dressed to speak in a professional setting.

Figure 25   **Dress appropriately**

Serg Zastavkin/Shutterstock.com

Setting Up for Your Presentation

It's important to include the setup, or physical arrangements, for your presentation as a critical element of preparation. Even the best-planned and practiced presentation can fail if your audience can't see or hear your presentation, or if they're uncomfortable. You've probably attended a presentation where the speaker stepped up to the microphone only to find that it wasn't turned on. Or, the speaker tried to start a PowerPoint presentation but nothing appeared on the screen or it was displayed incorrectly.

Much of the embarrassment and lost time can be prevented if you plan ahead. Make sure the equipment works and make sure you know how to use it, especially if it works differently from equipment with which you are familiar. Of course, there are some things over which you have no control. For example, if you're giving your presentation as part of a professional conference, you can't control whether the room you're assigned is the right size for your audience. You often can't control what projection systems are available, the thermostat setting in the room, or the quality of the sound system. But you can control many of the factors that could interfere with or enhance the success of your presentation, if you consider them in advance.

Preparing Copies of Your Content

Usually, the original copy of visuals for a presentation is sufficient and will be available to you when you give your presentation. However, electronic storage can be damaged or files erased, and physical handouts and posters can be accidentally destroyed, for example, by getting wet. Therefore, it's always a good idea to have backups or copies of your visuals.

If you prepared a presentation file, you should make backups of the file on a portable storage device, such as a flash drive. If you are traveling on a plane, consider carrying a copy of your presentation in your carry-on bag and another copy in your checked bags. In addition, send a copy of the presentation via email to yourself on an email service that you can access via the web, or store a copy of the presentation file in the cloud, such as on Microsoft SkyDrive, where you can easily retrieve it if necessary.

If you have handouts or posters, consider making extra copies of them and storing them separately from the original versions. This might not be possible in the case of posters, but you could take photos of the posters and bring your camera or storage card with you so that you could recreate the posters if something happens to the originals.

Assessing the Technology and Staff Available

You need to think about the technology you will be using. Check with your host or the presentation organizer ahead of time to make sure you know the type of equipment that will be available in the presentation room. If you are planning to use presentation software such as PowerPoint, you need a computer, a projector, and a screen. If you need to access the Internet during your presentation, obtain the password, if needed, and make sure you test the connection. If you have posters that need to be displayed, make sure an easel or place to mount the posters is available as well as thumbtacks or adhesive. If you want to take notes that people can see, make sure there is a whiteboard and markers or a chalkboard and chalk.

When you arrive at the location where you will be giving the presentation, verify that the presentation tools you need are physically in the room. If you will be using presentation software, connect the computer with the presentation on it to the projector device, making sure you have adequate space for your equipment and access to electrical outlets. Then open the presentation file and start the presentation to make sure that it will be displayed correctly. Make sure that each visual is displayed as you expect it to be. Do this well in advance of the time you are scheduled to give your presentation.

Figure 26   **Setting up for the presentation**

Goygel-Sokol Dmitry/Shutterstock.com

If the venue is going to be providing you with the computer, rather than you using your own, take the time to familiarize yourself with that computer and make sure you know exactly which folder your presentation is stored in. Consider bringing your own computer as a backup just in in case the one provided to you doesn't display the presentation file correctly.

Even with the most carefully laid plans, unexpected problems can come up. If you are giving a presentation at a large facility, such as in a conference room at a hotel, make sure you know how to contact the appropriate staff in case you have technical or other problems.

Becoming Familiar with the Room

It's helpful to know the size and shape of the room where your presentation will occur and the seating arrangement. The setting for a presentation can affect audience expectations and, therefore, will dictate the appropriate level of formality. A small conference room with a round table and moveable chairs would call for a much more informal presentation than a large lecture hall with fixed seating.

Examine the room in which you'll give your presentation. You'll want to check whether the room is properly ventilated, adequately lighted, and free from distracting noises, such as clanking of dishes in the kitchen, hammering and sawing by work crews, or interference from the speakers in adjacent rooms. You might not be authorized to change things like temperature settings or the arrangement of chairs, so you may need to adjust your presentation somewhat.

In considering the layout of the room, you'll want to make sure the chairs are arranged so that everyone in the audience can see and hear your presentation. You'll also want to make sure a podium or table provides enough room for your notes, or that the equipment, such as the computer, is close enough so that you won't have to walk back and forth to your notes.

Identifying Other Needed Supplies

In addition to your presentation visuals, you should make sure that you have any other supplies that you need. For example, if you are using technology, make sure you have extension cords. If you need them, make sure a whiteboard or flip chart is available. You should also have pen and paper in case you need to take notes.

If you are going to have handouts, make sure you have enough copies for all your audience members. Even if you don't plan to pass out business cards to everyone in the room, make sure you have some with you in case someone asks for one.

Finally, it's also a good idea to have a glass of water or water bottle available in case your throat or lips get dry.

Figure 27 shows a worksheet Jon used to assess the situation and facilities for this and other presentations.

Figure 27   Situation Assessment and Facilities Checklist worksheet for the Team Kidz presentation

Situation Assessment and Facilities Checklist

How large will your audience be? 20-50

What will the room be like and how will it be arranged? Add details.

☒ Small room: Classroom or gym/auditorium but with everyone seated near front

☐ Large room:

☐ Webinar:

☐ Other:

Did you test your electronic equipment in the room? Check each after you test it.

☒ Computer	☒ Connection to projector
☒ Wireless remote	☒ Microphone
☒ Other: Lighting	

Where did you store copies of your PowerPoint file?

| ☒ On your laptop | ☒ On a flash drive |
| ☒ On the Internet | ☐ Other |

Internet Connection

| Do you need an Internet connection? | ☒ Yes | ☐ No |
| If yes, did you check it in the room with your laptop, tablet, or smartphone to make sure you know how to connect and that it is reliable? | ☒ Yes | ☐ No |

Situation Assessment and Facilities Checklist, continued

Physical Setup

☒ Microphone height OK

☒ Extension cords available if you need them

☒ Extension cords and other wires out of the way

In addition to your PowerPoint file, laptop, and projection equipment, do you have other equipment available to use?

☐ Whiteboard	☐ White board markers and eraser
☐ Flip chart	☐ Permanent marker
☐ Chalkboard	☐ Chalk and eraser
☐ Other	

Additional Supplies

| ☒ Drinking water | ☒ Paper and pen |
| ☒ Business cards | ☐ Other |

Who will assist you with the equipment and other situational aspects?

| ☐ Technical support staff | ☒ Friend or colleague |
| ☐ Room monitor | ☐ Other |

What other aspects must you consider for your presentation?
Arrange for coffee and snacks after so people linger and we can answer questions.

© 2014 Cengage Learning

For his presentation, Jon will have a colleague available to help him with technical details, but he will not be able to adjust the temperature or change the arrangement of chairs. He plans to access the room in which he will be speaking a day ahead of time so he can become familiar with its setup. When he visits, he will connect his laptop to the projector provided by the facility to make sure that his PowerPoint presentation file will be displayed correctly. He decides that he doesn't need a whiteboard, chalkboard, or flip chart.

Jon feels confident that he has done everything possible to prepare for his presentation.

Evaluating Your Performance

TIP

If you ask someone to critique your presentation, be prepared to take criticism. Even if you think the criticism is unjustified, ask yourself, "How can I use this criticism to improve my presentation?"

An important step in any presentation (and the step that is most often left out) is to review your performance after it is over to determine how you can improve your next presentation. Evaluating your performance and setting goals for improvement ensures that your next presentation will be even better than your last one. After you give your oral presentation, you can also ask your audience to evaluate your presentation. Having written feedback or a numerical score for each aspect of your presentation can be especially helpful in highlighting where you have room for improvement.

You can evaluate your own performance or ask friends or audience members to evaluate your presentation. Jon plans to ask colleagues and faculty to evaluate his presentation using the Presentation Evaluation sheet shown in Figure 28.

Figure 28   Presentation Evaluation worksheet

Presentation Evaluation

Content (10 points)					
Topic was relevant and focused	5	4	3	2	1
Information was credible and reliable	5	4	3	2	1
Organization (20 points)					
Main points were identified and supported	5	4	3	2	1
Introduction was interesting	5	4	3	2	1
Visuals increased understanding of topic	5	4	3	2	1
Conclusion was concise	5	4	3	2	1
Delivery (35 points)					
Established credibility and built a rapport	5	4	3	2	1
Stood up straight	5	4	3	2	1
Established eye contact	5	4	3	2	1
Spoke fluently and was easy to understand	5	4	3	2	1
Used natural voice and hand movements	5	4	3	2	1
Used proper grammar and pronunciation	5	4	3	2	1
Free of annoying mannerisms and fillers	5	4	3	2	1
Total (65 points)					

Strengths of the presentation:

Weaknesses of the presentation:

Other suggestions:

© 2014 Cengage Learning

Session 3 Quick Check

REVIEW

1. What is a good approach for delivering a presentation if you are not used to giving them?
2. What is one benefit of allowing audience members to ask questions during a presentation at the point when questions occur to them?
3. Name three reasons why you should rehearse your presentation.
4. Why is being aware of your body language helpful when giving presentations?
5. What are fillers and why should you avoid them?
6. Why should you create backups or copies of your visuals?
7. If you will be using a computer and projector to display a presentation file, what should you do when you arrive at the facility where you will be giving your presentation?
8. Why is it useful to evaluate your performance?

Review Assignments

The principals asked Jon to return and give a presentation to the children at the schools. He will have 15 minutes to present, and they will allow up to another 15 minutes for questions. All of these presentations will be presented in the school gymnasiums. Some of the schools have a combination gymnasium and auditorium so there will be a stage. At the smallest school, he will be presenting to approximately 100 children; at the largest, he will present to over 300 children.

Complete the following steps (note that your instructor may provide you with files containing the different worksheets you need to complete):

1. Complete a Purposes and Outcomes worksheet for Jon's presentation.
2. Complete an Audience Analysis worksheet for Jon's presentation.
3. Complete a Focus and Organization worksheet for Jon's presentation, using the following information:
   a. Keep in mind that the audience is composed of children.
   b. Prepare an introduction for the presentation using a fictional story or anecdote describing a current program member who was very tentative at first and is now a strong leader in the program.
   c. Prepare a conclusion for the presentation that includes a fictional quote from a current program member.
4. Complete a Presentation Delivery worksheet for Jon's presentation (skip the Rehearsal Checklist). Include at least three questions (and fictional responses) that you think the audience will have.
5. Describe what Jon should wear for his presentation. (Remember, his audience consists of young children in a school setting.)
6. Complete a Situation and Media Assessment Worksheet for Jon's presentation. Assume the following:
   a. Jon will have access to a projector to which you can connect your laptop.
   b. A microphone will be available.
   c. Jon has a wireless remote to switch from one visual to another.
   d. Jon does not need a connection to the Internet.
   e. A room monitor will be available to assist.
7. Divide into groups of two and deliver a one-minute presentation to your partner. Present a topic that Jon would cover or any topic of your choice. Have your partner fill out a Presentation Evaluation worksheet for you. Then have your partner present, and you fill out a Presentation Evaluation worksheet for him or her.

Creating a Presentation

Presenting Information About Community Supported Agriculture

OBJECTIVES

Session 1.1
- Plan and create a new presentation
- Create a title slide and slides with lists
- Edit and format text
- Move and copy text
- Convert a list to a SmartArt diagram
- Duplicate, rearrange, and delete slides
- Close a presentation

Session 1.2
- Open an existing presentation
- Change the theme and theme variant
- Insert and crop photos
- Modify photo compression options
- Resize and move objects
- Create speaker notes
- Check the spelling
- Run a slide show
- Print slides, handouts, speaker notes, and the outline

Case | *Valley Falls CSA*

Isaac DeSoto graduated from Claflin University in Orangeburg, South Carolina, with a degree in Agriculture Production Technology. He began his career working for the South Carolina Department of Agriculture. Recently, he bought a large farm near Spartanburg, South Carolina, and started a community-supported agriculture program, or CSA. In a CSA, people buy shares each season and, in return, receive weekly portions of produce from the farm. Isaac also created a partnership with other local farmers and founded Valley Falls CSA. Isaac wants to use a PowerPoint presentation to attract new co-op members.

Microsoft PowerPoint 2013 (or simply **PowerPoint**) is a computer program you use to create a collection of slides that can contain text, charts, pictures, sounds, movies, multimedia, and so on. In this tutorial, you'll use PowerPoint to create a presentation that Isaac can use to explain what Valley Falls CSA is and what it has to offer to potential members and the community. After Isaac reviews it, you'll add graphics and speaker notes to the presentation. Finally, you'll check the spelling, run the slide show to evaluate it, and print the file.

STARTING DATA FILES

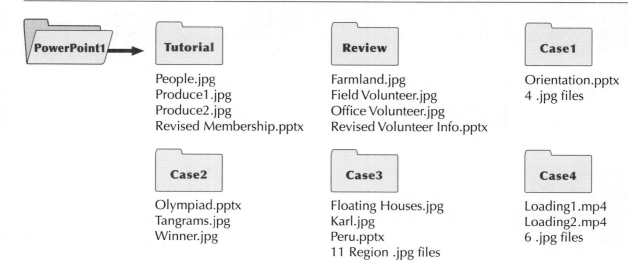

PowerPoint1

Tutorial
People.jpg
Produce1.jpg
Produce2.jpg
Revised Membership.pptx

Review
Farmland.jpg
Field Volunteer.jpg
Office Volunteer.jpg
Revised Volunteer Info.pptx

Case1
Orientation.pptx
4 .jpg files

Case2
Olympiad.pptx
Tangrams.jpg
Winner.jpg

Case3
Floating Houses.jpg
Karl.jpg
Peru.pptx
11 Region .jpg files

Case4
Loading1.mp4
Loading2.mp4
6 .jpg files

Session 1.1 Visual Overview:

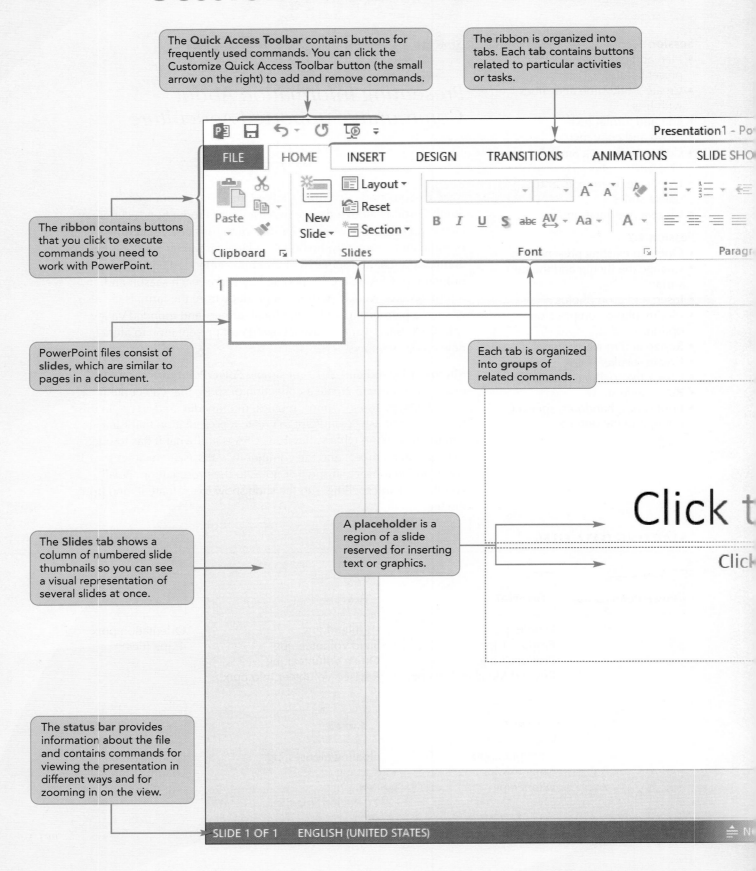

The **Quick Access Toolbar** contains buttons for frequently used commands. You can click the Customize Quick Access Toolbar button (the small arrow on the right) to add and remove commands.

The ribbon is organized into tabs. Each **tab** contains buttons related to particular activities or tasks.

The **ribbon** contains buttons that you click to execute commands you need to work with PowerPoint.

PowerPoint files consist of **slides**, which are similar to pages in a document.

Each tab is organized into **groups** of related commands.

The **Slides tab** shows a column of numbered slide thumbnails so you can see a visual representation of several slides at once.

A **placeholder** is a region of a slide reserved for inserting text or graphics.

The **status bar** provides information about the file and contains commands for viewing the presentation in different ways and for zooming in on the view.

The PowerPoint Window

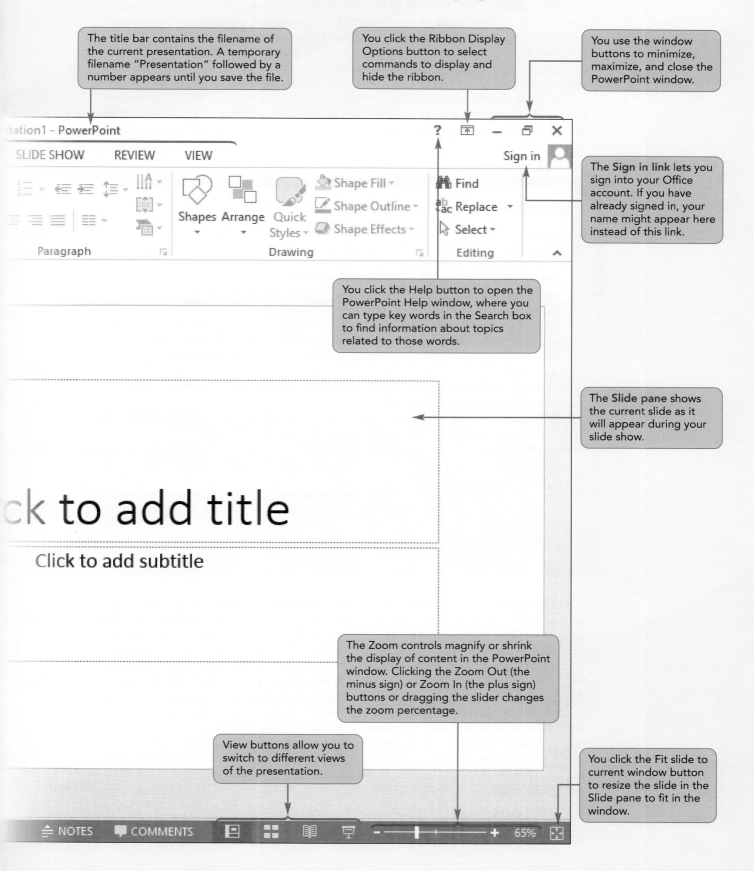

The title bar contains the filename of the current presentation. A temporary filename "Presentation" followed by a number appears until you save the file.

You click the Ribbon Display Options button to select commands to display and hide the ribbon.

You use the window buttons to minimize, maximize, and close the PowerPoint window.

The **Sign in link** lets you sign into your Office account. If you have already signed in, your name might appear here instead of this link.

You click the Help button to open the PowerPoint Help window, where you can type key words in the Search box to find information about topics related to those words.

The **Slide pane** shows the current slide as it will appear during your slide show.

The Zoom controls magnify or shrink the display of content in the PowerPoint window. Clicking the Zoom Out (the minus sign) or Zoom In (the plus sign) buttons or dragging the slider changes the zoom percentage.

View buttons allow you to switch to different views of the presentation.

You click the Fit slide to current window button to resize the slide in the Slide pane to fit in the window.

tation1 - PowerPoint

SLIDE SHOW   REVIEW   VIEW

Sign in

Shapes   Arrange   Quick Styles

Shape Fill
Shape Outline
Shape Effects

Find
Replace
Select

Paragraph   Drawing   Editing

ck to add title

Click to add subtitle

NOTES   COMMENTS   65%

Planning a Presentation

A **presentation** is a talk (lecture) or prepared file in which the person speaking or the person who prepared the file—the presenter—wants to communicate with an audience to explain new concepts or ideas, sell a product or service, entertain, train the audience in a new skill or technique, or any of a wide variety of other topics.

Most people find it helpful to use **presentation media**—visual and audio aids to support key points and engage the audience's attention. Microsoft PowerPoint is one of the most commonly used tools for creating effective presentation media. The features of PowerPoint make it easy to incorporate photos, diagrams, music, and video with key points of a presentation. Before you create a presentation, you should spend some time planning its content.

PROSKILLS

Verbal Communication: Planning a Presentation

Answering a few key questions will help you create a presentation using appropriate presentation media that successfully delivers its message or motivates the audience to take an action.

- **What is the purpose of your presentation?** In other words, what action or response do you want your audience to have? For example, do you want them to buy something, follow instructions, or make a decision?
- **Who is your audience?** Think about the needs and interests of your audience as well as any decisions they'll make as a result of what you have to say. What you choose to say to your audience must be relevant to their needs, interests, and decisions or it will be forgotten.
- **What are the main points of your presentation?** Identify the information that is directly relevant to your audience.
- **What presentation media will help your audience absorb the information and remember it later?** Do you need lists, photos, charts, or tables?
- **What is the format for your presentation?** Will you deliver the presentation orally or will you create a presentation file that your audience members will view on their own, without you present?
- **How much time do you have for the presentation?** Keep that in mind as you prepare the presentation content so that you have enough time to present all of your key points.
- **Will your audience benefit from handouts?** Handouts are printed documents you give to your audience before, during, or after your presentation.

The purpose of Isaac's presentation is to sell shares in the new CSA. His audience will be members of the local community who are interested in the benefits of belonging to a CSA and want to learn more about it. His key points are that being a member of a CSA is good for consumers because they will be eating fresher, more nutritious food, and good for the community because local farms are supported and there is less of an impact on the environment. He also plans to explain pricing and how members get their produce so that audience members have enough information to make a decision about becoming a member. Isaac will use PowerPoint to display lists and graphics to help make his message clear. He plans to deliver his presentation orally to small groups of people in a classroom-sized room, and his presentation will be 15 to 20 minutes long. For handouts, he plans to have membership applications available to distribute to anyone who is interested, but he will not distribute anything before his presentation because he wants the audience's full attention to be on him and the details are not complex enough that the audience will need a sheet to refer to as he is speaking.

Once you know what you want to say or communicate, you can prepare the presentation media to help communicate your ideas.

Starting PowerPoint and Creating a New Presentation

Microsoft PowerPoint 2013 is a tool you can use to create and display visual and audio aids on slides to help clarify the points you want to make in your presentation or to create a presentation that people view on their own without you being present.

When PowerPoint starts, the Recent screen in Backstage view is displayed. **Backstage view** contains commands that allow you to manage your presentation files and PowerPoint options. When you first start PowerPoint, the only actions available to you in Backstage view are to open an existing PowerPoint file or create a new file. You'll start PowerPoint now.

To start PowerPoint:

▶ **1.** Display the Windows Start screen, if necessary.

  Using Windows 7? To complete Step 1, click the Start button on the taskbar.

▶ **2.** Click the **PowerPoint 2013** tile. PowerPoint starts and displays the Recent screen in Backstage view. See Figure 1-1. In the orange bar on the left is a list of recently opened presentations, and on the right are options for creating new presentations.

Figure 1-1   Recent screen in Backstage view

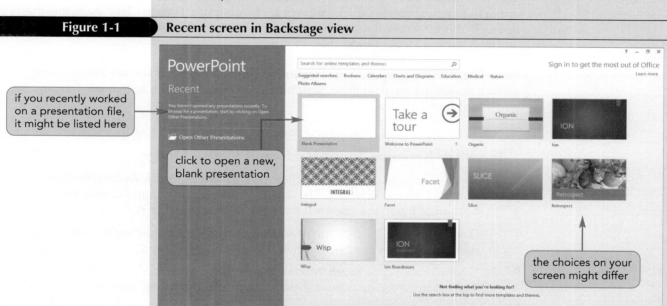

Trouble? If you don't see the PowerPoint 2013 tile, type PowerPoint to display the Apps screen with the PowerPoint 2013 tile highlighted, and then click the tile.

Using Windows 7? To complete Step 2, point to All Programs on the Start menu, click Microsoft Office 2013, and then click PowerPoint 2013.

▶ **3.** Click **Blank Presentation**. Backstage view closes and a new presentation window appears. The temporary filename "Presentation1" appears in the title bar. There is only one slide in the new presentation—Slide 1.

Trouble? If you do not see the area on the ribbon that contains buttons and you see only the ribbon tab names, click the HOME tab to expand the ribbon and display the commands, and then in the bottom-right corner of the ribbon, click the Pin the ribbon button ⊞ that appears.

Trouble? If the window is not maximized, click the Maximize button ▢ in the upper-right corner.

When you create a new presentation, it is displayed in Normal view. **Normal view** displays slides one at a time in the Slide pane, allowing you to see how the text and graphics look on each slide, and displays **thumbnails**—miniature images—of all the slides in the presentation in the Slides tab on the left. The HOME tab on the ribbon is orange to indicate that it is selected when you first open or create a presentation. The Session 1.1 Visual Overview identifies elements of the PowerPoint window.

Working in Touch Mode

In Office 2013, you can work with a mouse or, if you have a touch screen, you can work in Touch Mode. In **Touch Mode** the ribbon increases in height so that there is more space around each button on the ribbon, making it easier to use your finger to tap the specific button you need. Also, in the main part of the PowerPoint window, the instructions telling you to "Click" are replaced with instructions to "Tap." Note that the figures in this text show the screen with Mouse Mode on. You'll switch to Touch Mode and then back to Mouse Mode now.

Note: The following steps assume that you are using a mouse. If you are instead using a touch device, please read these steps but don't complete them, so that you remain working in Touch Mode.

To switch between Touch Mode and Mouse Mode:

1. On the Quick Access Toolbar, click the **Customize Quick Access Toolbar** button ▾. A menu opens. The Touch/Mouse Mode command near the bottom of the menu does not have a checkmark next to it.

   Trouble? If the Touch/Mouse Mode command has a checkmark next to it, press the Esc key to close the menu, and then skip Step 2.

2. On the menu, click **Touch/Mouse Mode**. The menu closes and the Touch/Mouse Mode button appears on the Quick Access Toolbar.

3. On the Quick Access Toolbar, click the **Touch/Mouse Mode** button 👆. A menu opens listing Mouse and Touch, and the icon next to Mouse is shaded orange to indicate it is selected.

   Trouble? If the icon next to Touch is shaded orange, press the Esc key to close the menu and skip Step 4.

4. On the menu, click **Touch**. The menu closes and the ribbon increases in height so that there is more space around each button on the ribbon. Notice that the instructions in the main part of the PowerPoint window changed by replacing the instruction to "Click" with the instruction to "Tap." See Figure 1-2. Now you'll change back to Mouse Mode.

Figure 1-2   **PowerPoint window with Touch mode active**

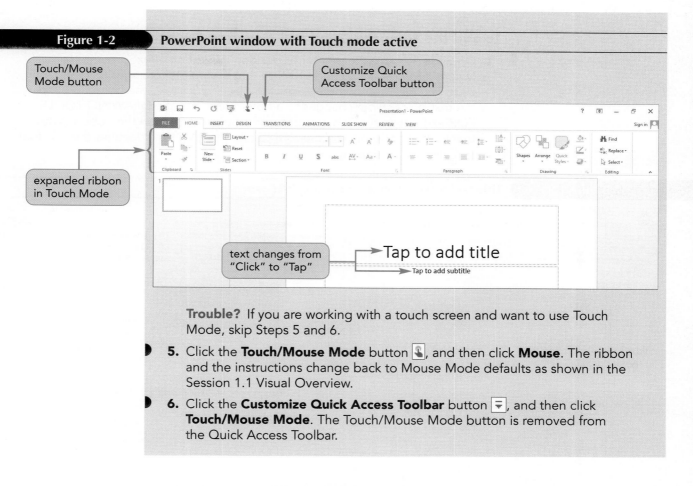

Touch/Mouse Mode button

Customize Quick Access Toolbar button

expanded ribbon in Touch Mode

text changes from "Click" to "Tap"

Tap to add title

Tap to add subtitle

Trouble? If you are working with a touch screen and want to use Touch Mode, skip Steps 5 and 6.

5. Click the **Touch/Mouse Mode** button 👆, and then click **Mouse**. The ribbon and the instructions change back to Mouse Mode defaults as shown in the Session 1.1 Visual Overview.

6. Click the **Customize Quick Access Toolbar** button ⩢, and then click **Touch/Mouse Mode**. The Touch/Mouse Mode button is removed from the Quick Access Toolbar.

Creating a Title Slide

The **title slide** is the first slide in a presentation. It generally contains the title of the presentation plus any other identifying information you want to include, such as a company's slogan, the presenter's name, or a company name. The **font**—a set of characters with the same design—used in the title and subtitle may be the same or may be different fonts that complement each other.

The title slide contains two objects called text placeholders. A placeholder is a region of a slide reserved for inserting text or graphics. A **text placeholder** is a placeholder designed to contain text. Text placeholders usually display text that describes the purpose of the placeholder and instructs you to click so that you can start typing in the placeholder. The larger text placeholder on the title slide is designed to hold the presentation title, and the smaller text placeholder is designed to contain a subtitle. Once you enter text into a text placeholder, it is no longer a placeholder and becomes an object called a **text box**.

When you click in the placeholder, the **insertion point**, which indicates where text will appear when you start typing, appears as a blinking line in the center of the placeholder. In addition, a contextual tab, the DRAWING TOOLS FORMAT tab, appears on the ribbon. A **contextual tab** appears only in context—that is, when a particular type of object is selected or active—and contains commands for modifying that object.

You'll add a title and subtitle for Isaac's presentation now. Isaac wants the title slide to contain the company name and slogan.

To add the company name and slogan to the title slide:

▸ **1.** On **Slide 1**, move the pointer to position it in the title text placeholder (where it says "Click to add title") so that the pointer changes to I, and then click. The insertion point replaces the placeholder text; the border around the text placeholder changes to a dotted line, and the DRAWING TOOLS FORMAT contextual tab appears as the rightmost tab on the ribbon. Note that in the Font group on the HOME tab, the Font box identifies the title font as Calibri Light. See Figure 1-3.

Figure 1-3	Title text placeholder after clicking in it

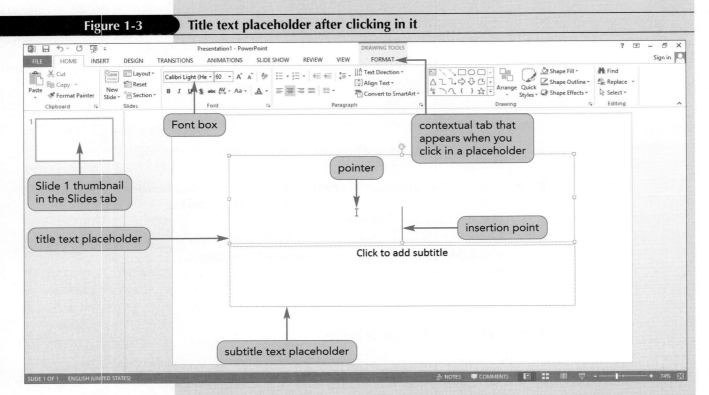

Trouble? The insertion point might appear as a thin, blue rectangle with the Mini toolbar above and to the right of it. Ignore this and continue with Step 2.

▸ **2.** Type **Valley Farms CSA**. The placeholder is now a text box.

▸ **3.** Click a blank area of the slide. The border of the text box disappears, and the DRAWING TOOLS FORMAT tab no longer appears on the ribbon.

▸ **4.** Click in the **subtitle text placeholder** (where it says "Click to add subtitle"), and then type **Freshest, most delicious food!**. Notice in the Font group that the subtitle font is Calibri, a font which works well with the Calibri Light font used in the title text.

▸ **5.** Click a blank area of the slide.

Saving and Editing a Presentation

Once you have created a presentation, you should name and save the presentation file. You can save the file on a hard drive or a network drive, on an external drive such as a USB drive, or to your account on SkyDrive, Microsoft's free online storage area.

To save the presentation for the first time:

1. On the Quick Access Toolbar, point to the **Save** button 🖫. The button becomes shaded and its ScreenTip appears. A **ScreenTip** identifies the names of buttons; sometimes they also display a key combination you can press instead of clicking the button and information about how to use the button. In this case, the ScreenTip displays the word "Save" and the key combination for the Save command, Ctrl+S.

2. Click the **Save** button 🖫. The Save As screen in Backstage view appears. See Figure 1-4. Because a presentation is open, more commands are available in Backstage view than when you started PowerPoint. The **navigation bar** on the left contains commands for working with the file and program options.

Figure 1-4 Save As screen in Backstage view

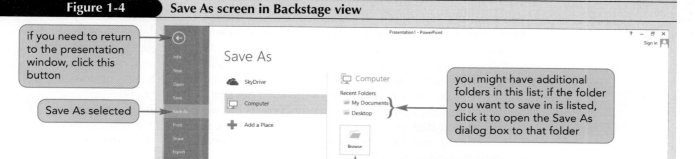

if you need to return to the presentation window, click this button

Save As selected

navigation bar

you might have additional folders in this list; if the folder you want to save in is listed, click it to open the Save As dialog box to that folder

click to open the Save As dialog box

3. Click **Computer**, if necessary, and then click the **Browse** button. The Save As dialog box opens, similar to the one shown in Figure 1-5.

Figure 1-5 Save As dialog box

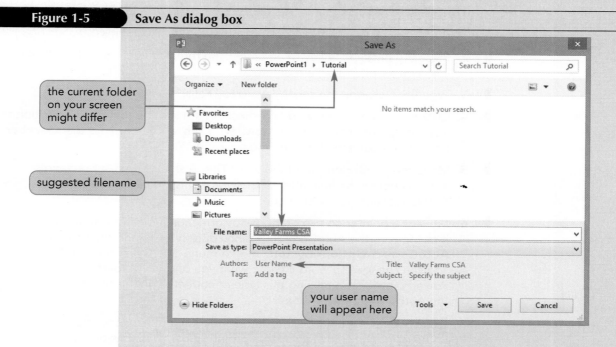

the current folder on your screen might differ

suggested filename

your user name will appear here

> **Trouble?** If you are saving your files to your SkyDrive account, click SkyDrive on the Save As screen, log in to your account if necessary, and then click the Browse button.

> 4. Navigate to the drive and folder where you are storing your Data Files, and then click in the **File name** box. The suggested filename, Valley Falls CSA, is selected.

> 5. Type **Membership Info**. The text you type replaces the selected text in the File name box.

> 6. Click the **Save** button. The file is saved, the dialog box and Backstage view close, and the presentation window appears again with the new filename in the title bar.

Once you have created a presentation, you can make changes to it. For example, if you need to change text in a text box, you can easily edit it. The Backspace key deletes characters to the left of the insertion point, and the Delete key deletes characters to the right of the insertion point.

If you mistype or misspell a word, you might not need to correct it because the **AutoCorrect** feature automatically corrects many commonly mistyped and misspelled words after you press the spacebar or the Enter key. For instance, if you type "cna" and then press the spacebar, PowerPoint corrects the word to "can." If you want AutoCorrect to stop making a particular change, you can display the AutoCorrect Options menu, and then click Stop making the change. (The exact wording will differ depending on the change made.)

After you make changes to a presentation, you will need to save the file again so that the changes are stored. Because you have already saved the presentation with a permanent filename, using the Save command does not open the Save As dialog box; it simply saves the changes you made to the file.

To edit the text on Slide 1 and save your changes:

> 1. On Slide 1, click the **title**, and then use the ← and → keys as needed to position the insertion point to the right of the word "Farms."

> 2. Press the **Backspace** key three times. The three characters to the left of the insertion point, "rms," are deleted.

> 3. Type **lls** to change the second word to "Falls."

> 4. Click to the left of the word "Freshest" in the subtitle text box to position the insertion point in front of that word, type **Teh**, and then press the **spacebar**. PowerPoint corrects the word you typed to "The."

> 5. Move the pointer on top of the word **The**. A small, very faint rectangle appears below the first letter of the word. This indicates that an AutoCorrection has been made.

> 6. Move the pointer on top of the AutoCorrection indicator box so that it changes to the AutoCorrect Options button ⬚ ▾, and then click the **AutoCorrect Options button** ⬚ ▾. A menu opens, as shown in Figure 1-6. You can change the word back to what you originally typed, instruct PowerPoint to stop making this type of correction in this file, or open the AutoCorrect dialog box.

> **Trouble?** If you can't see the AutoCorrection indicator box, point to the letter T, and then slowly move the pointer down until it is on top of the box and changes it to the AutoCorrect Options button.

Figure 1-6   AutoCorrect Options button menu

Figure 1-6   AutoCorrect Options button menu

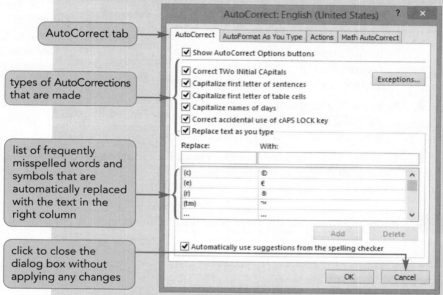

click to undo this AutoCorrection and to stop this type of AutoCorrection from occurring in this file

AutoCorrect Options button

Valley Falls CSA

The Freshest, most delicious food!

Change back to "Teh"
Stop Automatically Correcting "teh"
Control AutoCorrect Options...

click to open the AutoCorrect dialog box

7. Click **Control AutoCorrect Options**. The AutoCorrect dialog box opens with the AutoCorrect tab selected. See Figure 1-7.

Figure 1-7   AutoCorrect tab in the AutoCorrect dialog box

AutoCorrect tab

types of AutoCorrections that are made

list of frequently misspelled words and symbols that are automatically replaced with the text in the right column

click to close the dialog box without applying any changes

AutoCorrect: English (United States)

AutoCorrect | AutoFormat As You Type | Actions | Math AutoCorrect

☑ Show AutoCorrect Options buttons

☑ Correct TWo INitial CApitals
☑ Capitalize first letter of sentences   Exceptions...
☑ Capitalize first letter of table cells
☑ Capitalize names of days
☑ Correct accidental use of cAPS LOCK key
☑ Replace text as you type

Replace: With:

(c)   ©
(e)   €
(r)   ®
(tm)   ™
...   ...

Add   Delete

☑ Automatically use suggestions from the spelling checker

OK   Cancel

8. Examine the types of changes the AutoCorrect feature makes, and then click the **Cancel** button.

9. Click to the left of the "F" in "Freshest, if necessary, press the **Delete** key, and then type **f**. The subtitle now is "The freshest, most delicious food!" Now that you have modified the presentation, you need to save your changes.

10. On the Quick Access Toolbar, click the **Save** button 🖫. The changes you made are saved to the file you named Membership Info.

Adding New Slides

Now that you've created the title slide, you need to add more slides. Every slide has a **layout**, which is the arrangement of placeholders on the slide. The title slide uses the Title Slide layout. A commonly used layout is the Title and Content layout, which contains a title text placeholder for the slide title and a content placeholder.

A **content placeholder** is a placeholder designed to hold several types of slide content including text, a table, a chart, a picture, or a video.

To add a new slide, you use the New Slide button in the Slides group on the HOME tab. When you click the top part of the New Slide button, a new slide is inserted with the same layout as the current slide, unless the current slide is the title slide; in that case the new slide has the Title and Content layout. If you want to create a new slide with a different layout, click the bottom part of the New Slide button to open a gallery of layouts, and then click the layout you want to use.

You can change the layout of a slide at any time. To do this, click the Layout button in the Slides group to display the same gallery of layouts that appears in the Add Slide gallery, and then click the slide layout you want to apply to the selected slide.

As you add slides, you can switch from one slide to another by clicking the slide thumbnails in the Slides tab. You need to add several new slides to the file.

To add new slides and apply different layouts:

1. Make sure the HOME tab is displayed on the ribbon.

2. In the Slides group, click the **New Slide** button (that is, click the top part of the button). A new slide appears in the Slide pane and its thumbnail appears in the Slides tab below Slide 1. The new slide has the Title and Content layout applied. This layout contains a title text placeholder and a content placeholder. In the Slides tab, an orange border appears around the new Slide 2, indicating that it is the current slide.

3. In the Slides group, click the **New Slide** button again. A new Slide 3 is added. Because Slide 2 had the Title and Content layout applied, Slide 3 also has that layout applied.

4. In the Slides group, click the **New Slide button arrow** (that is, click the bottom part of the New Slide button). A gallery of the available layouts appears. See Figure 1-8.

Figure 1-8	Gallery of layouts on the New Slide button menu

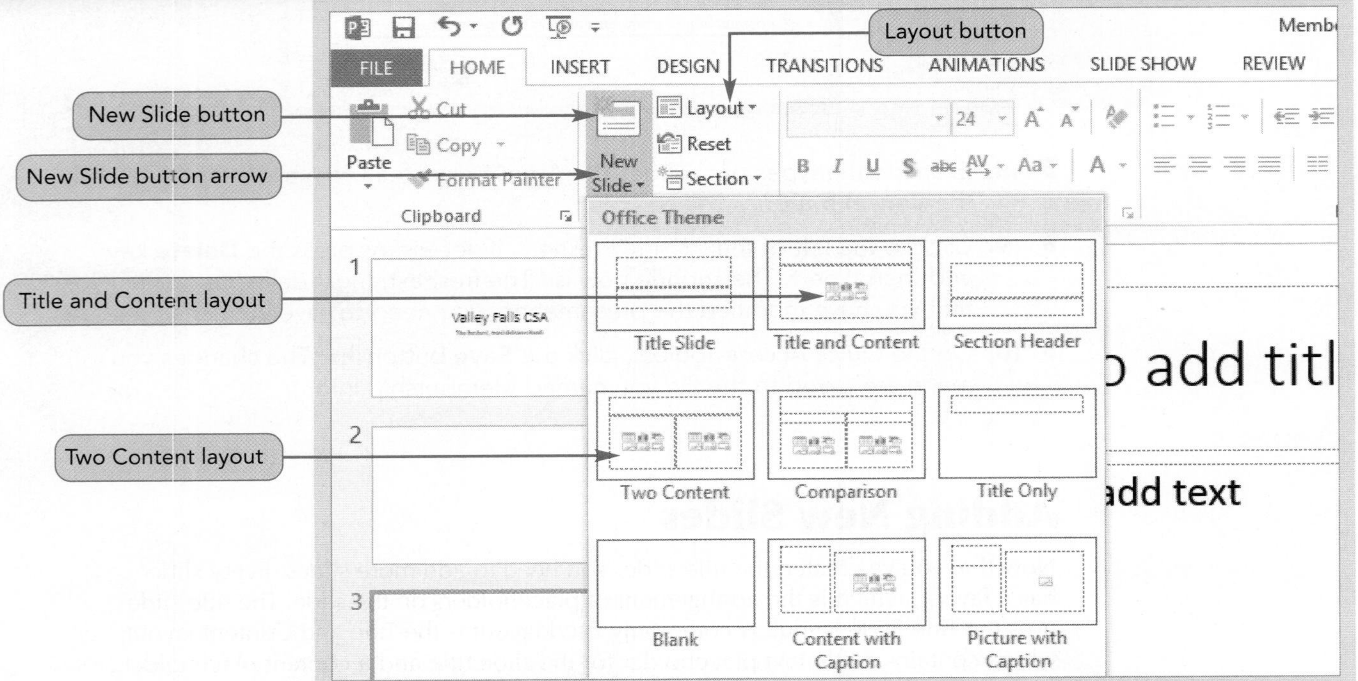

5. In the gallery, click the **Two Content** layout. The gallery closes and a new Slide 4 is inserted with the Two Content layout applied. This layout includes three objects: a title text placeholder and two content placeholders.

6. In the Slides group, click the **New Slide** button. A new Slide 5 is added to the presentation. Because Slide 4 had the Two Content layout applied, that layout is also applied to the new slide. You need to change the layout of Slide 5.

7. In the Slides group, click the **Layout** button. The same gallery of layouts that appeared when you clicked the New Slide button arrow appears. The Two Content layout is selected, as indicated by the orange shading behind it, showing you that this is the layout applied to the current slide, Slide 5.

8. Click the **Title and Content** layout. The layout of Slide 5 is changed to Title and Content.

9. In the Slides group, click the **New Slide** button three more times to add three more slides with the Title and Content layout. There are now eight slides in the presentation. In the Slides tab, Slides 1 through 3 have scrolled up out of view, and vertical scroll bars are now visible in both the Slides tab and in the Slide pane.

10. In the Slides tab, drag the **scroll box** to the top of the vertical scroll bar, and then click the **Slide 2** thumbnail. Slide 2 becomes the current slide—it appears in the Slide pane and is selected in the Slides tab. See Figure 1-9.

Figure 1-9	Slide 2 with the Title and Content layout

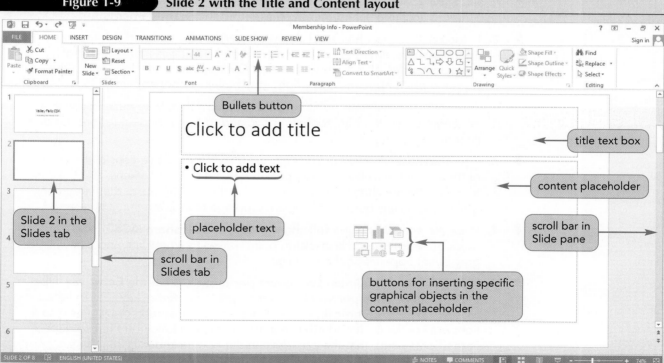

11. On the Quick Access Toolbar, click the **Save** button 🔲. The changes you made are saved in the file.

If you accidentally close a presentation without saving changes and need to recover it, you can do so by clicking the FILE tab, clicking Open in the navigation bar, and then clicking the Recover Unsaved Presentations button.

Creating Lists

One way to help explain the topic or concept you are describing in your presentation is to use lists. For oral presentations, the intent of lists is to enhance the oral presentation, not replace it. In self-running presentations, items in lists might need to be longer and more descriptive. However, keep in mind that PowerPoint is a presentation graphics program intended to help you present information in a visual, graphical manner, not create a written document in an alternate form.

Items in a list can appear at different levels. A **first-level item** is a main item in a list; a **second-level item**—sometimes called a **subitem**—is an item beneath and indented from a first-level item. Usually, the font size—the size of the text—in subitems is smaller than the size used for text in the level above. Text is measured in **points**, which is a unit of measurement. Text in a book is typically printed in 10- or 12-point type; text on a slide needs to be much larger so the audience can easily read it.

Creating a Bulleted List

A **bulleted list** is a list of items with some type of bullet symbol in front of each item or paragraph. When you create a subitem in the list, a different or smaller symbol is often used. You need to create a bulleted list that describes the requirements of a membership in Valley Farms CSA.

To create bulleted lists on Slides 2 and 3:

1. On **Slide 2**, click in the **title text placeholder** (with the placeholder text "Click to add title"), and then type **Membership Requirements**.

2. In the content placeholder, click any area where the pointer is shaped as I; in other words, anywhere except on one of the buttons in the center of the placeholder. The placeholder text "Click to add text" disappears, the insertion point appears, and a light gray bullet symbol appears.

   Trouble? The insertion point might appear as a thin, blue rectangle with a rectangle called the Mini toolbar above and to the right of it. Ignore this and continue with Step 3.

3. Type **Purchase**. As soon as you type the first character, the icons in the center of the content placeholder disappear, the bullet symbol darkens, and the content placeholder changes to a text box. On the HOME tab, in the Paragraph group, the Bullets button is shaded orange to indicate that it is selected.

4. Press the **spacebar**, type **full-share ($425) or half-share ($250)**, and then press the **Enter** key. The insertion point moves to a new line and a new, light gray bullet appears on the new line.

5. Type **Volunteer minimum two hours per month**, press the **Enter** key, type **Pick up share once per week**, and then press the **Enter** key. The bulleted list now consists of three first-level items, and the insertion point is next to a light gray bullet on the fourth line in the text box. Notice on the HOME tab, in the Font group, that the point size in the Font Size box is 28 points.

6. Press the **Tab** key. The bullet symbol and the insertion point indent one-half inch to the right, the bullet symbol changes to a smaller size, and the number in the Font Size box changes to 24. See Figure 1-10.

Figure 1-10   **Subitem created on Slide 2**

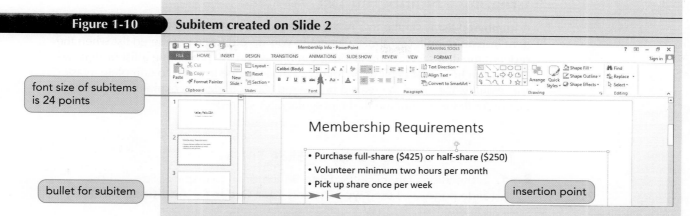

font size of subitems is 24 points

bullet for subitem

insertion point

7. Type **Fridays, 3 p.m. - 5 p.m.** and then press the **Enter** key. When you pressed the spacebar key after typing 5, AutoCorrect changed the dash to an en-dash, a typographical character slightly longer than a hyphen.

8. Type **Saturdays, 7 a.m. - noon**, and then press the **Enter** key. A third subitem is created. You will change it to a first-level item using a key combination. In this book, when you need to press two keys together, the keys will be listed separated by a plus sign. You don't need to press the keys at exactly the same time—press and hold the first key, press and release the second key, and then release the first key.

9. Press the **Shift+Tab** keys. The bullet symbol and the insertion point shift back to the left margin of the text box, the bullet symbol changes back to the larger size, and 28 again appears in the Font Size box because this line is now a first-level bulleted item.

10. Type **Or have it delivered (additional fee)**, press the **Enter** key, and then type **October community celebration**.

11. In the Slides tab, click the **Slide 3** thumbnail to display Slide 3 in the Slide pane, click in the **title text placeholder**, and then type **Members Receive**.

12. In the content placeholder, click the **placeholder text**, type **Share of pre-selected produce**, press the **Enter** key, and then type **Self-selected items**.

TIP

Avoid putting information on the bottom quarter of the slide because people in the back of a large room will not be able to see it.

If you add more text than will fit in the text box with the default font sizes and line spacing, **AutoFit** adjusts these features to make the text fit. When AutoFit is activated, the AutoFit Options button appears below the text box. You can click this button and then select from among several options, including turning off AutoFit for this text box and splitting the text between two slides. Although AutoFit can be helpful, be aware that it also allows you to crowd text on a slide, making the slide less effective.

PROSKILLS

Written Communication: How Much Text Should I Include?

Text can help audiences retain the information you are presenting by allowing them to read the main points while hearing you discuss them. But be wary of adding so much text to your slides that your audience can ignore you and just read the slides. Try to follow the 7x7 rule—no more than seven items per slide, with no more than seven words per item. A variation of this rule is 6x6, and some presenters even prefer 4x4. If you create a self-running presentation (a presentation file others will view on their own) you will usually need to add more text than you would if you were presenting the material in person.

Creating a Numbered List

A **numbered list** is similar to a bulleted list except that numbers appear in front of each item instead of bullet symbols. Generally you should use a numbered list when the order of the items is important—for example, if you are presenting a list of step-by-step instructions that need to be followed in sequence in order to complete a task successfully. You need to create a numbered list on Slide 5 to explain how members can order items in addition to their regular CSA share.

To create a numbered list on Slide 5:

1. In the Slides tab, click the **Slide 5** thumbnail to display Slide 5 in the Slide pane, and then type **Placing Your Order for Additional Items** as the title text.

2. In the content placeholder, click the **placeholder text**.

3. On the HOME tab, in the Paragraph group, click the **Numbering** button ▤. The Numbering button is selected, the Bullets button is deselected, and in the content placeholder, the bullet symbol is replaced with the number 1 followed by a period.

   Trouble? If a menu containing a gallery of numbering styles appears, you clicked the Numbering button arrow on the right side of the button. Click the Numbering button arrow again to close the menu, and then click the left part of the Numbering button.

4. Type **Place online by Wednesday**, and then press the **Enter** key. As soon as you start typing, the number 1 darkens to black. After you press the Enter key, the insertion point moves to the next line, next to the light gray number 2.

5. Type **Verify payment information**, and then press the **Enter** key. The number 3 appears on the next line.

6. In the Paragraph group, click the **Increase List Level** button ▤. The third line is indented to be a subitem under the second item, and the number 3 that had appeared changes to a number 1 in a smaller size than the first-level items. Clicking the Increase List Level button is an alternative to pressing the Tab key to create a subitem.

7. Type **Credit card**, press the **Enter** key, type **Debit from checking account**, press the **Enter** key.

8. In the Paragraph group, click the **Decrease List Level** button ▤. The fifth line is now a first-level item and the number 3 appears next to it. Clicking the Decrease List Level button is an alternative to pressing the Shift+Tab keys to promote a subitem.

9. Type **Submit**. The list now consists of three first-level numbered items and two subitems under number 2.

10. In the second item, click before the word "Verify," and then press the **Enter** key. A blank line is inserted above the second item.

11. Press the ↑ key. A light-gray number 2 appears in the blank line. The item on the third line in the list is still numbered 2.

12. Type **Specify pickup or delivery**. As soon as you start typing, the new number 2 darkens in the second line and the third item in the list is numbered 3. Compare your screen to Figure 1-11.

Figure 1-11   Numbered list on Slide 5

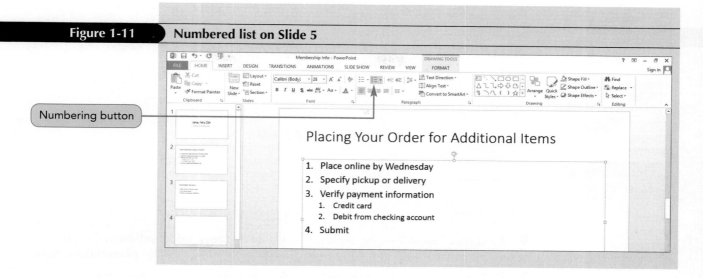

Numbering button

Creating an Unnumbered List

An **unnumbered list** is a list that does not have bullets or numbers preceding each item. Unnumbered lists are useful in slides when you want to present information on multiple lines without actually itemizing the information. For example, contact information for the presenter, including his or her email address, street address, city, and so on would be clearer if it were in an unnumbered list.

As you have seen, items in a list have a little extra space between each item to visually separate bulleted items. Sometimes, you don't want the extra space between lines. If you press the Shift+Enter keys instead of just the Enter key, a new line is created, but it is still considered to be part of the item above it. Therefore, there is no extra space between the lines. Note that this also means that if you do this in a bulleted or numbered list, the new line will not have a bullet or number next to it because it is not a new item.

You need to create a slide that defines CSA. Also, Isaac asks you to create a slide containing contact information.

To create unnumbered lists on Slides 4 and 7:

1. In the Slides tab, click the **Slide 4** thumbnail to display Slide 4 in the Slide pane. Slide 4 has the Two Content layout applied.

2. Type **What Is a CSA?** as the title text, and then in the left content placeholder, click the **placeholder text**.

3. On the HOME tab, in the Paragraph group, click the **Bullets** button. The button is no longer selected, and the bullet symbol disappears from the content placeholder.

4. Type **Community**, press the **Enter** key, type **Supported**, press the **Enter** key, and then type **Agriculture**. Compare your screen to Figure 1-12.

Figure 1-12 | **Unnumbered list on Slide 4**

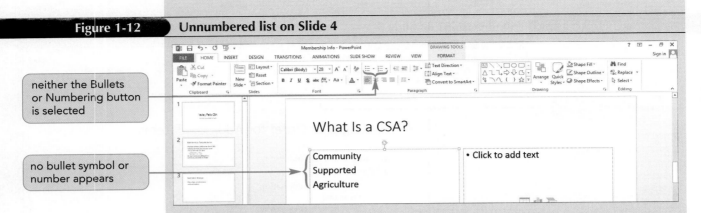

neither the Bullets or Numbering button is selected

no bullet symbol or number appears

5. Display **Slide 7** in the Slide pane, type **For More Information** in the title text placeholder, and then in the content placeholder, click the **placeholder text**.

6. In the Paragraph group, click the **Bullets** button to remove the bullets, type **Valley Falls CSA**, and then press the **Enter** key. A new line is created, but there is extra space above the insertion point. This is not how addresses usually appear.

7. Press the **Backspace** key to delete the new line and move the insertion point back to the end of the first line, and then press the **Shift+Enter** keys. The insertion point moves to the next line and, this time, there is no extra space above it.

8. Type **300 County Fair Road**, press the **Shift+Enter** keys, and then type **Spartanburg, SC 29301**. You need to insert the phone number on the next line, the general email address for the group on the line after that, and the website address on the last line. The extra space above these lines will set this information apart from the address and make it easier to read.

9. Press the **Enter** key to create a new line with extra space above it, type **(864) 555-FOOD**, press the **Enter** key, type **csainfo@valleyfallscsa.example.org**, and then press the **Enter** key. The insertion point moves to a new line with extra space above it, and the email address you typed changes color to blue and is underlined.

   When you type text that PowerPoint recognizes as an email or website address and then press the spacebar or Enter key, it automatically formats it as a link that can be clicked during a slide show, and changes its color and adds the underline to indicate this. You can only click links during a slide show.

10. Type **www.valleyfallscsa.example.org**, and then press the **spacebar**. The text is formatted as a link. Isaac plans to click the link during his presentation to show the audience the website, so he wants it to stay formatted as a link. However, there is no need to have the email address formatted as a link because no one will click it during the presentation.

11. Right-click **csainfo@valleyfallscsa.example.org**. A shortcut menu opens.

12. On the shortcut menu, click **Remove Hyperlink**. The email address is no longer formatted as a hyperlink. Compare your screen to Figure 1-13.

Figure 1-13 List on Slide 7

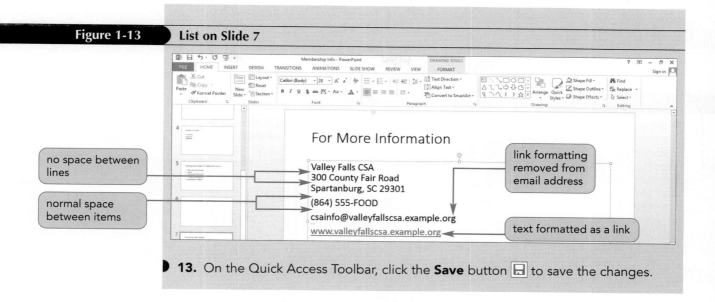

no space between lines

normal space between items

link formatting removed from email address

text formatted as a link

▶ **13.** On the Quick Access Toolbar, click the **Save** button 🖫 to save the changes.

Formatting Text

Slides in a presentation should have a cohesive look and feel. For example, the slide titles and the text in content placeholders should be in complementary fonts. However, there are times when you need to change the format of text. For instance, you might want to make specific words bold to make them stand out more.

To apply a format to text, either the text or the text box must be selected. If you want to apply the same formatting to all the text in a text box, you can click the border of the text box. When you do this, the dotted line border changes to a solid line to indicate that the contents of the entire text box are selected.

The commands in the Font group on the HOME tab are used to apply formatting to text. Some of these commands are also available on the Mini toolbar, which appears when you select text with the mouse. The **Mini toolbar** contains commonly used buttons for formatting text. If the Mini toolbar appears, you can use the buttons on it instead of those in the Font group.

Some of the commands in the Font group use the Microsoft Office **Live Preview** feature, which previews the change on the slide so you can instantly see what the text will look like if you apply that format.

Isaac wants the contact information on Slide 7 to be larger. He also wants the first letter of each item in the unnumbered list on Slide 4 ("What Is a CSA?") formatted so they are more prominent.

To format the text on Slides 4 and 7:

▶ **1.** On **Slide 7** ("For More Information"), position the pointer on the text box border so that it changes to ⬚, and then click the border of the text box containing the contact information. The border changes to a solid line to indicate that the entire text box is selected.

▶ **2.** On the HOME tab, in the Font group, click the **Increase Font Size** button A̅ twice. All the text in the text box increases in size with each click.

▶ **3.** Display **Slide 4** ("What Is a CSA?") in the Slide pane.

▶ **4.** In the unnumbered list, click to the left of "Community," press and hold the **Shift** key, press the → key, and then release the **Shift** key. The letter "C" is selected. See Figure 1-14.

Figure 1-14   **Text selected to be formatted**

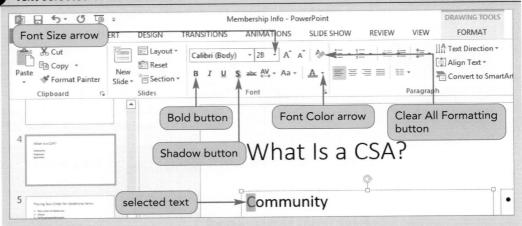

▶ **5.** In the Font group, click the **Bold** button **B**. The Bold button becomes selected and the selected text is formatted as bold.

▶ **6.** Make sure the letter "C" is still selected, and then in the Font group, click the **Shadow** button **S**. The selected text is now bold with a slight drop shadow.

▶ **7.** In the Font group, click the **Font Size arrow** to open the Font Size menu, and then click **48**. The selected text is now 48 points.

▶ **8.** In the Font group, click the **Font Color arrow**. A menu containing colors opens.

▶ **9.** Under Theme Colors, move the pointer over each color, noting the ScreenTips that appear and watching as Live Preview changes the color of the selected text as you point to each color. Figure 1-15 shows the pointer pointing to the Orange, Accent 2, Darker 25% color.

Figure 1-15   **Font Color button menu**

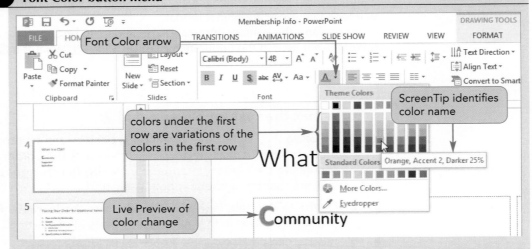

▶ **10.** Using the ScreenTips, locate the **Orange, Accent 2, Darker 25%** color and then click it. The selected text changes to the orange color you clicked.

Now you need to format the first letters in the other words in the list to match the letter "C." You can repeat the steps you did when you formatted the letter "C," or you use the Format Painter to copy all the formatting of the letter "C" to the other letters you need to format.

Also, Isaac wants the text in the unnumbered list to be as large as possible. Because the first letters of each word are larger than the rest of the letters, the easiest way to do this is to select all of the text, and then use the Increase Font Size button. All of the letters will increase in size by four points with each click.

To use the Format Painter to copy and apply formatting on Slide 4:

1. Make sure the letter "C" is still selected.

2. On the HOME tab, in the Clipboard group, click the **Format Painter** button, and then move the pointer back to the Slide pane. The button is selected, and the pointer changes to ▲I.

3. Position the pointer before the letter "S" in "Supported," press and hold the mouse button, drag over the letter **S**, and then release the mouse button. The formatting you applied to the letter "C" is copied to the letter "S" and the Mini toolbar appears. See Figure 1-16. The Mini toolbar appears whenever you drag over text to select it.

Figure 1-16	The Mini toolbar

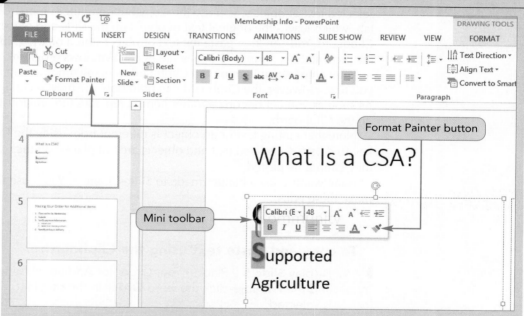

4. On the Mini toolbar, click the **Format Painter** button, and then drag across the letter **A** in Agriculture.

5. Click the border of the text box to select the entire text box, and then in the Font group, click the **Increase Font Size** button five times. In the Font group, the Font Size button indicates that the text is 48+ points. This means that in the selected text box, the text that is the smallest is 48 points and there is some text that is a larger point size.

6. On the Quick Access Toolbar, click the **Save** button to save the changes.

Undoing and Redoing Actions

If you make a mistake or change your mind about an action as you are working, you can reverse the action by clicking the Undo button on the Quick Access Toolbar. You can undo up to the most recent 20 actions by continuing to click the Undo button, or by clicking the Undo button arrow and then selecting as many actions in the list as you want. You can also Redo an action that you undid by clicking the Redo button on the Quick Access Toolbar.

When there are no actions that can be redone, the Redo button changes to the Repeat button. You can use the Repeat button to repeat an action, such as formatting text as bold. If the Repeat button is light gray, this means it is unavailable because there is no action to repeat (or to redo).

Moving and Copying Text

You can move or copy text and objects in a presentation using the Clipboard. The **Clipboard** is a temporary storage area available to all Windows programs on which text or objects are stored when you cut or copy them. To **cut** text or objects—that is, remove the selected text or objects from one location so that you can place it somewhere else— you select the text or object, and then use the Cut button in the Clipboard group on the HOME tab to remove the selected text or object and place it on the Clipboard. To **copy** selected text or objects, you use the Copy button in the Clipboard group on the HOME tab, which leaves the original text or object on the slide and places a copy of it on the Clipboard. You can then **paste** the text or object stored on the Clipboard anywhere in the presentation, or, in fact, in any file in any Windows program.

You can paste an item on the Clipboard as many times and in as many locations as you like. However, the Clipboard can hold only the most recently cut or copied item. As soon as you cut or copy another item, it replaces the previously cut or copied item on the Clipboard.

Note that cutting text or an object is different from using the Delete or Backspace key to delete it. Deleted text and objects are not placed on the Clipboard; this means they cannot be pasted.

Isaac wants a few changes made to Slides 5 and 3. You'll use the Clipboard as you make these edits.

To copy and paste text using the Clipboard:

▶ 1. Display **Slide 5** ("Placing Your Order for Additional Items") in the Slide pane, and then double-click the word **Order** in the title text. The word "Order" is selected.

▶ 2. On the HOME tab, in the Clipboard group, click the **Copy** button. The selected word is copied to the Clipboard.

▶ 3. In the last item in the numbered list, click after the word "Submit," and then press the **spacebar**.

▶ 4. In the Clipboard group, click the **Paste** button. The text is pasted and picks up the formatting of its destination; that is, the pasted text is the 28-point Calibri font, the same font and size as the rest of the first-level items in the list, instead of 44-point Calibri Light as in the title. The Paste Options button 🗐 (Ctrl)▾ appears below the pasted text.

▶ 5. Click the **Paste Options** button 🗐 (Ctrl)▾. A menu opens with four buttons on it. See Figure 1-17.

Figure 1-17   **Buttons on the Paste Options button menu when text is on the Clipboard**

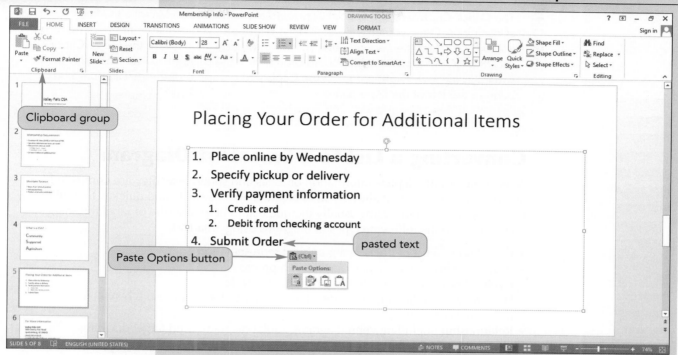

6. Point to each button on the menu, reading the ScreenTips and watching to see how the pasted text changes in appearance. The first button is the Use Destination Theme button ⬛, and this is the default choice when you paste text.

7. Click a blank area of the slide to close the menu without making a selection, click to the left of "Order" in the last item in the numbered list, press the **Delete** key, and then type **o**. The word "order" in in the numbered list is now all lowercase.

8. Display **Slide 2** ("Membership Requirements") in the Slide pane. The last bulleted item ("October community celebration") belongs on Slide 3.

9. In the last bulleted item, position the pointer on top of the bullet symbol so that the pointer changes to ✥, and then click. The entire bulleted item is selected.

10. In the Clipboard group, click the **Cut** button. The last bulleted item is removed from the slide and placed on the Clipboard.

11. Display **Slide 3** ("Members Receive") in the Slide pane, click after the second bulleted item, and then press the **Enter** key to create a third line.

12. In the Clipboard group, click the **Paste** button. The bulleted item you cut is pasted as the third bulleted item on Slide 3 using the default Paste option of Use Destination Theme. The insertion point appears next to a fourth bulleted item.

13. Press the **Backspace** key twice. The extra line is deleted.

Using the Office Clipboard

The **Office Clipboard** is a special Clipboard available only to Microsoft Office applications. Once you activate the Office Clipboard, you can store up to 24 items on it and then select the item or items you want to paste. To activate the Office Clipboard, click the HOME tab. In the Clipboard group, click the Dialog Box Launcher (the small square in the lower-right corner of the Clipboard group) to open the Clipboard task pane to the left of the Slide pane.

Converting a List to a SmartArt Diagram

A **diagram** visually depicts information or ideas and shows how they are connected. **SmartArt** is a feature that allows you to create diagrams easily and quickly. In addition to shapes, SmartArt diagrams usually include text to help describe or label the shapes. You can create the following types of diagrams using SmartArt:

- **List**—Shows a list of items in a graphical representation
- **Process**—Shows a sequence of steps in a process
- **Cycle**—Shows a process that is a continuous cycle
- **Hierarchy** (including organization charts)—Shows the relationship between individuals or units
- **Relationship** (including Venn diagrams, radial diagrams, and target diagrams)— Shows the relationship between two or more elements
- **Matrix**—Shows information in a grid
- **Pyramid**—Shows foundation-based relationships
- **Picture**—Provides a location for a picture or pictures that you insert

There is also an Office.com category of SmartArt, which, if you are connected to the Internet, displays additional SmartArt diagrams available in various categories on Office.com, a Microsoft website that contains tools for use with Office programs.

A quick way to create a SmartArt diagram is to convert an existing list. When you select an existing list and then click the Convert to SmartArt Graphic button in the Paragraph group on the HOME tab, a gallery of SmartArt layouts appears. For SmartArt, a **layout** is the arrangement of the shapes in the diagram. Each first-level item in the list is converted to a shape in the SmartArt diagram. If the list contains subitems, you might need to experiment with different layouts to find one that best suits the information in your list.

Converting a Bulleted List into a SmartArt Diagram

- Click anywhere in the bulleted list.
- In the Paragraph group on the HOME tab, click the Convert to SmartArt Graphic button, and then click More SmartArt Graphics.
- In the Choose a SmartArt Graphic dialog box, select the desired SmartArt type in the list on the left.
- In the center pane, click the SmartArt diagram you want to use.
- Click the OK button.

Isaac wants the numbered list on Slide 5 converted into a SmartArt diagram.

To convert the list on Slide 5 into a SmartArt diagram:

▶ **1.** Display **Slide 5** ("Placing Your Order for Additional Items") in the Slide pane, and then click anywhere on the numbered list to make the text box border appear.

▶ **2.** On the HOME tab, in the Paragraph group, click the **Convert to SmartArt Graphic** button. A gallery of SmartArt layouts appears.

▶ **3.** Point to the first layout. The ScreenTip identifies this layout as the Vertical Bullet List layout, and Live Preview shows you what the numbered list will look like with that layout applied. See Figure 1-18. Notice that the subitems are not included in a shape in this diagram.

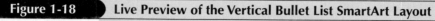

Figure 1-18   **Live Preview of the Vertical Bullet List SmartArt Layout**

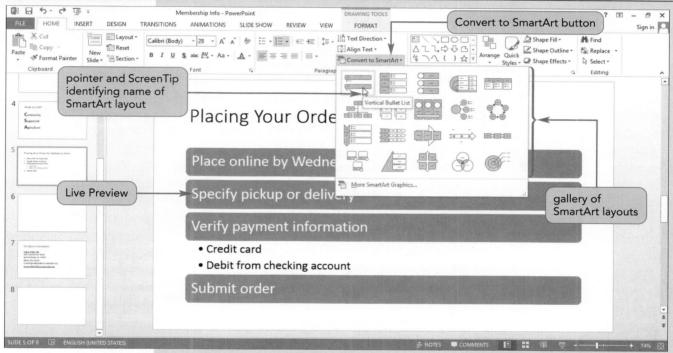

▶ **4.** Point to several other layouts in the gallery, observing the Live Preview of each one. In some of the layouts, the subitems are included in a shape.

▶ **5.** At the bottom of the gallery, click **More SmartArt Graphics**. The Choose a SmartArt Graphic dialog box opens. See Figure 1-19. You can click a type in the left pane to filter the middle pane to show only that type of layout.

| Figure 1-19 | Choose a SmartArt Graphic dialog box |

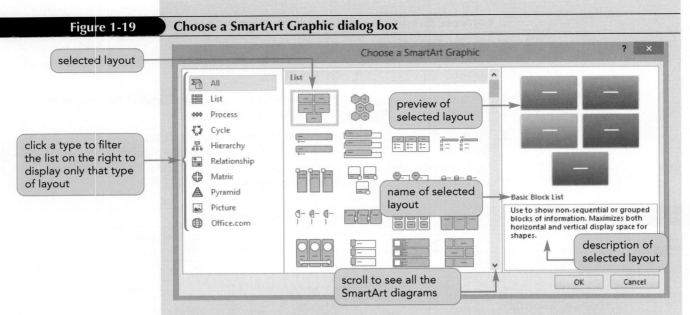

6. In the left pane, click **Process**, and then in the middle pane, click the **Continuous Block Process** layout, using the ScreenTips to identify it (it's the first layout in the third row). The right pane changes to show a description of that layout.

7. Click the **OK** button. The dialog box closes, and each of the first level items in the list appears in the square shapes in the diagram. The items also appear as a bulleted list in the Text pane, which is open to the left of the diagram. The SMARTART TOOLS contextual tabs appear on the ribbon. See Figure 1-20.

In this layout, the subitems below "Verify payment information" are included in the third square; they are not placed in their own shapes in the diagram. Isaac decides the information in the subitems does not need to be on the slide because people will see those options on the website when they log in.

Trouble? If you do not see the Text pane, click the Text pane button ◀ on the left border of the selected SmartArt diagram.

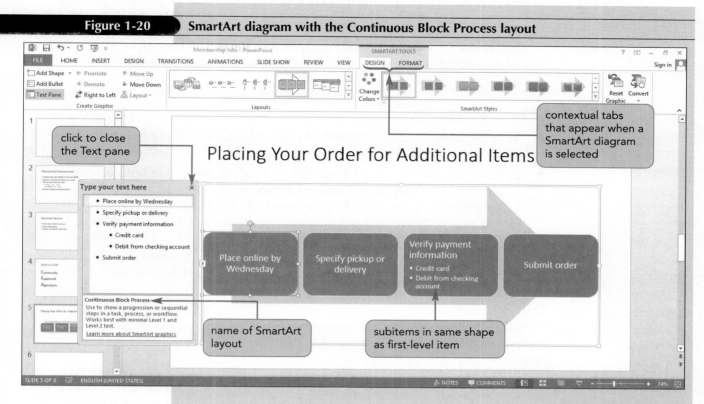

Figure 1-20   **SmartArt diagram with the Continuous Block Process layout**

8. In the "Verify payment information shape," select **Debit from checking account**, and then press the **Delete** key. The text is deleted from the shape and from the Text pane.

9. In the Text pane, click after the word "card," press the **Backspace** key as many times as necessary to delete all of the bullet text, and then press the **Backspace** key once more. The bullet changes to a first-level bullet and a new square shape is inserted in the diagram.

10. Press the **Backspace** key one more time. The empty bullet and the blank line are deleted in the Text pane, and the newly added shape is removed from the diagram. The "Verify payment information" square now contains only the first-level item. Notice that AutoFit increased the size of the text in all the boxes so that the text still fills the boxes and is as large as possible.

11. Click a blank area of the slide to deselect the diagram, and then on the Quick Access Toolbar, click the **Save** button to save your changes.

Manipulating Slides

You can manipulate the slides in a presentation to suit your needs. For instance, if you need to create a slide that is similar to another slide, you can duplicate the existing slide and then modify the copy. If you decide that slides need to be rearranged, you can reorder them. And if you no longer want to include a slide in your presentation, you can delete it.

To duplicate, rearrange, or delete slides, you select the slides in the Slides tab in Normal view or switch to Slide Sorter view. In **Slide Sorter view** all the slides in the presentation are displayed as thumbnails in the window; the Slides tab does not appear. You already know that to select a single slide you click its thumbnail. You can also select more than one slide at a time. To select sequential slides, click the first slide, press and hold the Shift key, and then click the last slide you want to select. To select nonsequential slides, click the first slide, press and hold the Ctrl key, and then click any other slides you want to select.

Isaac wants to show the slide that explains what the letters "CSA" stand for at the end of the presentation. You will duplicate that slide instead of recreating it.

To duplicate Slide 4:

▶ **1.** In the Slides tab, click the **Slide 4** ("What Is a CSA?") thumbnail to display Slide 4 in the Slide pane.

▶ **2.** On the HOME tab, in the Slides group, click the **New Slide button arrow**, and then click **Duplicate Selected Slides**. Slide 4 is duplicated and the copy is inserted as a new Slide 5 in the Slides tab. Slide 5 is now the current slide. If more than one slide were selected, they would all be duplicated. The duplicate slide doesn't need the title; Isaac just wants to reinforce the term.

▶ **3.** Click in the title "What Is a CSA?", click the text box border to select the text box, and then press the **Delete** key. The title and the title text box are deleted and the title text placeholder reappears.

You could delete the title text placeholder, but it is not necessary. When you display the presentation to an audience as a slide show, any unused placeholders will not appear.

Next you need to rearrange the slides. You need to move the duplicate of the "What Is a CSA?" slide so it is the last slide in the presentation because Isaac wants to leave it displayed after the presentation is over. He hopes this visual will reinforce for the audience that CSAs are good for the entire community. Isaac also wants the "Members Receive" slide moved so it appears before the "Membership Requirements" slide, and he wants the original "What Is a CSA?" slide to be the second slide in the presentation.

To move slides in the presentation:

▶ **1.** In the Slides tab, scroll up, if necessary, so that you can see Slides 2 and 3, and then drag the **Slide 3** ("Members Receive") thumbnail above the Slide 2 ("Membership Requirements") thumbnail. As you drag, the Slide 3 thumbnail follows the pointer and Slide 2 moves down. The "Members Receive" slide is now Slide 2 and "Membership Requirements" is now Slide 3. You'll move the other two slides in Slide Sorter view.

TIP

You can also use the buttons in the Presentation Views group on the VIEW tab to switch views.

▶ **2.** On the status bar, click the **Slide Sorter** button ⊞. The view switches to Slide Sorter view. Slide 2 has an orange border, indicating that it is selected.

▶ **3.** On the status bar, click the **Zoom Out** button ▬ as many times as necessary until you can see all nine slides in the presentation. See Figure 1-21.

| Figure 1-21 | Slide Sorter view |

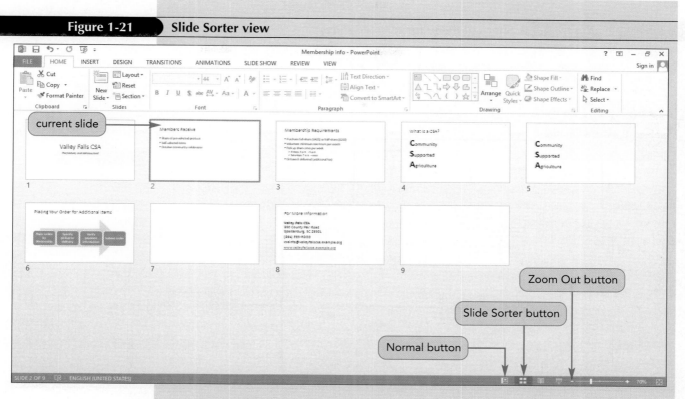

4. Drag the **Slide 4** ("What Is a CSA?") thumbnail between Slides 1 and 2. As you drag, the other slides move out of the way. The slide is repositioned and the slides are renumbered so that the "What Is a CSA?" slide is now Slide 2.

5. Drag the **Slide 5** (the CSA slide without a title) thumbnail so it becomes the last slide in the presentation (Slide 9).

Now you need to delete the two blank slides. To delete a slide, you need to right-click its thumbnail to display a shortcut menu.

To delete slides:

1. Click **Slide 6** (a blank slide), press and hold the **Shift** key, and then click **Slide 8** (the other blank slide), and then release the **Shift** key. The two slides you clicked are selected, as well as the slide between them. You want to delete only the two blank slides.

2. Click a blank area of the window to deselect the slides, click **Slide 6**, press and hold the **Ctrl** key, click **Slide 8**, and then release the **Ctrl** key. Only the two slides you clicked are selected.

3. Right-click either selected slide. A shortcut menu appears. See Figure 1-22.

Figure 1-22   Shortcut menu for selected slides

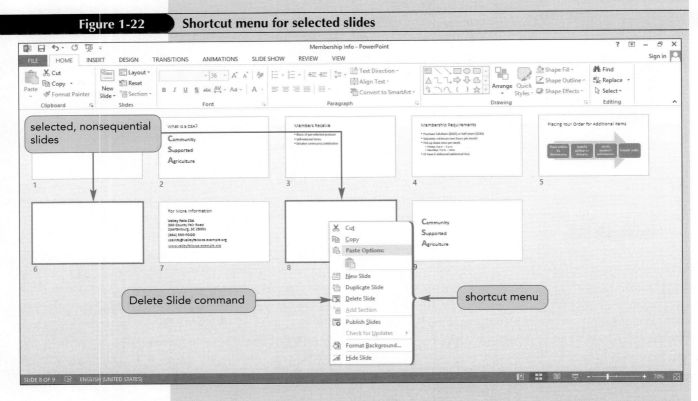

4. On the shortcut menu, click **Delete Slide**. The shortcut menu closes and the two selected slides are deleted. The presentation now contains seven slides.

5. On the status bar, click the **Normal** button ▣. The presentation appears in Normal view.

6. On the Quick Access Toolbar, click the **Save** button ▤ to save the changes to the presentation.

TIP

You can also double-click a slide thumbnail in Slide Sorter view to display that slide in the Slide pane in Normal view.

Closing a Presentation

When you are finished working with a presentation, you can close it and leave PowerPoint open. To do this, you click the FILE tab to open Backstage view, and then click the Close command. If you click the Close button ✕ in the upper-right corner of the PowerPoint window and only one presentation is open, you will not only close the presentation, you will exit PowerPoint as well.

You're finished working with the Membership Info file for now, so you will close it. First you will add your name to the title slide.

To close the Membership Info presentation:

1. Display **Slide 1** (the title slide) in the Slide pane, click the **subtitle**, position the insertion point after "food!," press the **Enter** key, and then type your full name.

2. On the ribbon, click the **FILE** tab. Backstage view appears with the Info screen displayed. See Figure 1-23. The Info screen contains information about the current presentation, including the name, drive, and folder of the current presentation.

Figure 1-23   **Info screen in Backstage view**

Info selected in the navigation bar

drive and folder in which current file is stored

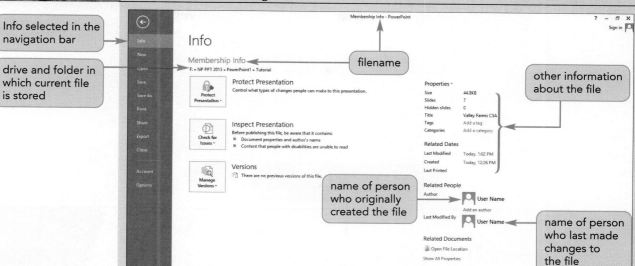

filename

other information about the file

name of person who originally created the file

name of person who last made changes to the file

3. In the navigation bar, click **Close**. Backstage view closes and a dialog box opens asking if you want to save your changes.

4. In the dialog box, click the **Save** button. The dialog box and the presentation close, and the empty presentation window appears.

   Trouble? If you want to take a break, you can exit PowerPoint by clicking the Close button in the upper-right corner of the PowerPoint window.

You've created a presentation that includes slides to which you added bulleted, numbered, and unnumbered lists. You also edited and formatted text, converted a list to a SmartArt diagram, and duplicated, rearranged, and deleted slides. You are ready to give the presentation draft to Isaac to review.

REVIEW

Session 1.1 Quick Check

1. Define "presentation."

2. How do you display Backstage view?

3. What is the main area of the PowerPoint window called?

4. What is a layout?

5. In addition to a title text placeholder, what other placeholder do most layouts contain?

6. What is the term for an object that contains text?

7. What is the difference between the Clipboard and the Office Clipboard?

8. How do you convert a list to a SmartArt diagram?

Session 1.2 Visual Overview:

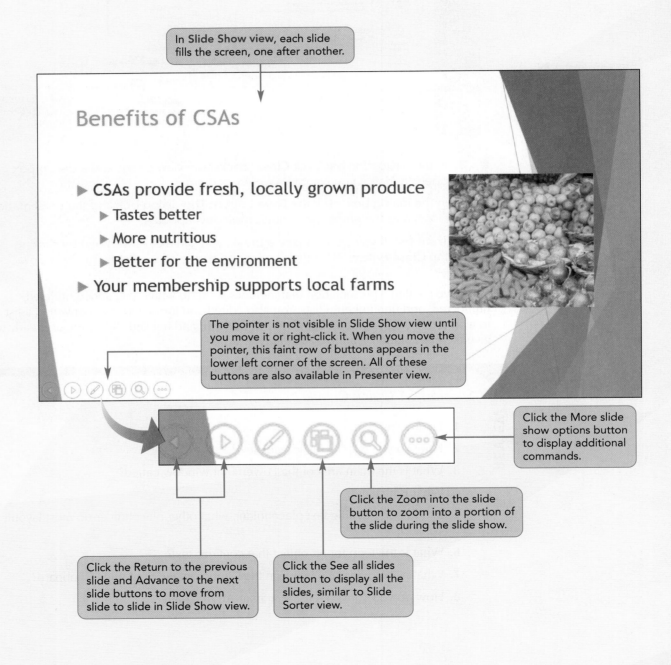

In **Slide Show view**, each slide fills the screen, one after another.

Benefits of CSAs

▶ CSAs provide fresh, locally grown produce
  ▶ Tastes better
  ▶ More nutritious
  ▶ Better for the environment
▶ Your membership supports local farms

The pointer is not visible in Slide Show view until you move it or right-click it. When you move the pointer, this faint row of buttons appears in the lower left corner of the screen. All of these buttons are also available in Presenter view.

Click the More slide show options button to display additional commands.

Click the Zoom into the slide button to zoom into a portion of the slide during the slide show.

Click the Return to the previous slide and Advance to the next slide buttons to move from slide to slide in Slide Show view.

Click the See all slides button to display all the slides, similar to Slide Sorter view.

Slide Show and Presenter Views

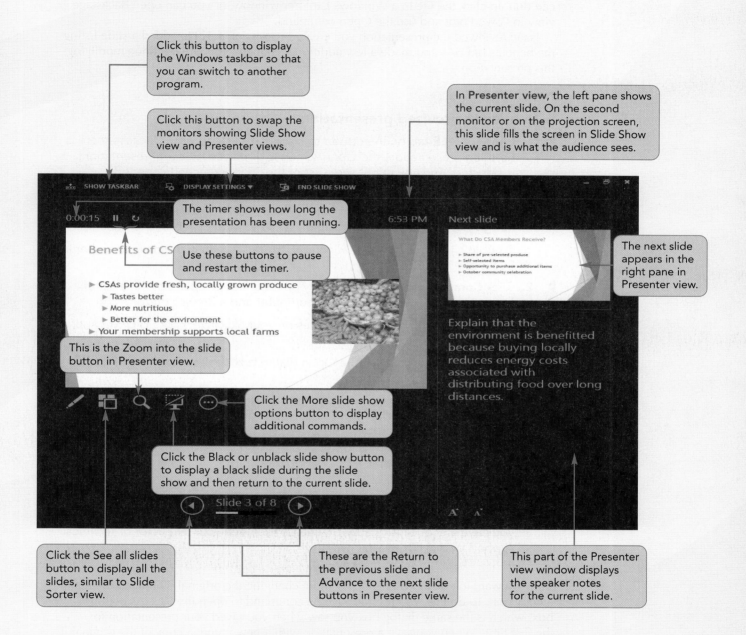

Click this button to display the Windows taskbar so that you can switch to another program.

Click this button to swap the monitors showing Slide Show view and Presenter views.

In **Presenter view**, the left pane shows the current slide. On the second monitor or on the projection screen, this slide fills the screen in Slide Show view and is what the audience sees.

The timer shows how long the presentation has been running.

Use these buttons to pause and restart the timer.

This is the Zoom into the slide button in Presenter view.

The next slide appears in the right pane in Presenter view.

Click the More slide show options button to display additional commands.

Click the Black or unblack slide show button to display a black slide during the slide show and then return to the current slide.

Click the See all slides button to display all the slides, similar to Slide Sorter view.

These are the Return to the previous slide and Advance to the next slide buttons in Presenter view.

This part of the Presenter view window displays the speaker notes for the current slide.

Opening a Presentation and Saving It with a New Name

If you have closed a presentation, you can always reopen it to modify it. To do this, you can double-click the file in a Windows Explorer window, or you can open Backstage view in PowerPoint and use the Open command.

Isaac reviewed the presentation you created in Session 1.1. He added a slide listing the benefits of CSAs and made a few additional changes. You will continue modifying this presentation.

To open the revised presentation:

1. Click the **FILE** tab on the ribbon to display Backstage view. Because there is no open presentation, the Open screen is displayed. Recent Presentations is selected, and you might see a list of the 25 most recently opened presentations on the right.

   Trouble? If PowerPoint is not running, start PowerPoint, and then in the navigation bar on the Recent screen, click the Open Other Presentations link.

   Trouble? If another presentation is open, click Open in the navigation bar in Backstage view.

2. Click **Computer**. The list of recently opened files is replaced with a list of recently accessed folders on your computer and a Browse button.

   Trouble? If you are storing your files on your SkyDrive, click SkyDrive, and then log in if necessary.

3. Click the **Browse** button. The Open dialog box appears. It is similar to the Save As dialog box.

4. Navigate to the drive that contains your Data Files, navigate to the **PowerPoint1 ▸ Tutorial** folder, click **Revised Membership** to select it, and then click the **Open** button. The Open dialog box closes and the Revised Membership presentation opens in the PowerPoint window, with Slide 1 displayed in the Slide pane.

   Trouble? If you don't have the starting Data Files, you need to get them before you can proceed. Your instructor will either give you the Data Files or ask you to obtain them from a specified location (such as a network drive). If you have any questions about the Data Files, see your instructor or technical support person for assistance.

If you want to edit a presentation without changing the original, you need to create a copy of it. To do this, you use the Save As command to open the Save As dialog box, which is the same dialog box you saw when you saved your presentation for the first time. When you save a presentation with a new name, a copy of the original presentation is created, the original presentation is closed, and the newly named copy remains open in the PowerPoint window.

To save the Revised Membership presentation with a new name:

1. Click the **FILE** tab, and then in the navigation bar, click **Save As**. The Save As screen in Backstage view appears.

2. Click **Computer**, if necessary. On the right under Computer is a list of recently accessed folders with the folder containing the current file at the top.

3. If the folder in which you are saving your Data Files is listed on the right, click it; if the folder in which you are saving your files is not listed, click the **Browse** button. The Save As dialog box opens.

4. If necessary, navigate to the drive and folder where you are storing your Data Files.

5. In the File name box, change the filename to **CSA New Member**, and then click the **Save** button. The Save As dialog box closes, a copy of the file is saved with the new name CSA New Member, and the CSA New Member presentation appears in the PowerPoint window.

Changing the Theme and the Theme Variant

A **theme** is a coordinated set of colors, fonts, backgrounds, and effects. All presentations have a theme. If you don't choose one, the default Office theme is applied; that is the theme currently applied to the CSA New Member presentation.

You saw the Office theme set of colors when you changed the color of the text on the "What Is a CSA?" slide. You have also seen the Office theme fonts in use on the slides. In the Office theme, the font of the slide titles is Calibri Light and the font of the text in content text boxes is Calibri. In themes, the font used for slide titles is the Headings font, and the font used for the content text boxes is the Body font.

In PowerPoint, each theme has several variants with different coordinating colors and sometimes slightly different backgrounds. A theme and its variants are called a **theme family**. PowerPoint comes with several installed themes, and many more themes are available online at Office.com. In addition, you can use a custom theme stored on your computer or network.

You can select a different installed theme when you create a new presentation by clicking one of the themes on the New or Recent screen in Backstage view instead of clicking Blank Presentation, and then clicking one of the variants. If you want to change the theme of an open presentation, you can choose an installed theme on the DESIGN tab or you can apply a custom theme stored on your computer or network. When you change the theme, the colors, fonts, and slide backgrounds change to those used in the new theme.

Isaac wants the theme of the CSA New Member presentation changed to one that has more color in the background. First you'll display Slide 2 in the Slide pane so you can see the effect a different theme has on the text formatted with a theme color.

To examine the current theme and then change the theme and theme variant:

1. Display **Slide 2** ("What Is a CSA?") in the Slide pane, and then, in the unnumbered list select the orange letter **C**.

2. On the HOME tab, in the Font group, click the **Font Color arrow**. Look at the colors under Theme Colors and note the second to last color is selected in the column containing shades of orange. Notice also the row of Standard Colors below the theme colors.

3. In the Font group, click the **Font arrow**. A menu of fonts installed on the computer opens. At the top under Theme Fonts, Calibri (Body) is selected because the letter C that you selected is in a content text box. See Figure 1-24.

Figure 1-24 Theme fonts on the Font box menu

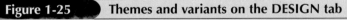

4. On the ribbon, click the **DESIGN** tab. The Font menu closes and the installed themes appear in the Themes gallery on the DESIGN tab. See Figure 1-25. The current theme is the first theme listed in the Themes group on the DESIGN tab. The next theme is the Office theme, which, in this case, is also the current theme.

Figure 1-25 Themes and variants on the DESIGN tab

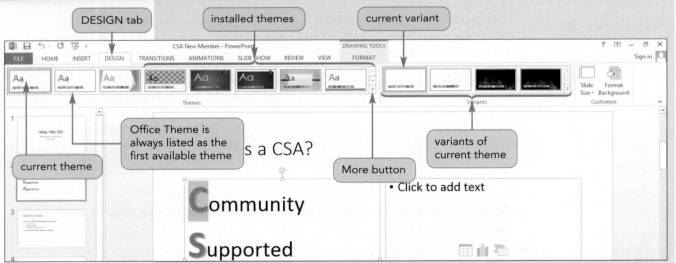

TIP

To apply a theme from a presentation stored on your computer or network, click the Themes More button, and then click Browse for Themes.

To see all of the installed themes, you need to scroll through the gallery by clicking the up and down scroll buttons on the right end of the gallery or clicking the More button to expand the gallery to see all of the themes at once. The **More button** appears on all galleries that contain additional items or commands that don't fit in the group on the ribbon.

5. In the Themes group, click the **More** button ⊽. The gallery of themes opens. See Figure 1-26. When the gallery is open, the theme applied to the current presentation appears in the first row. In the next row, the first theme is the Office theme, and then the rest of the installed themes appear. Some of these themes appear on the Recent and New screens in Backstage view.

Figure 1-26   **Theme gallery expanded**

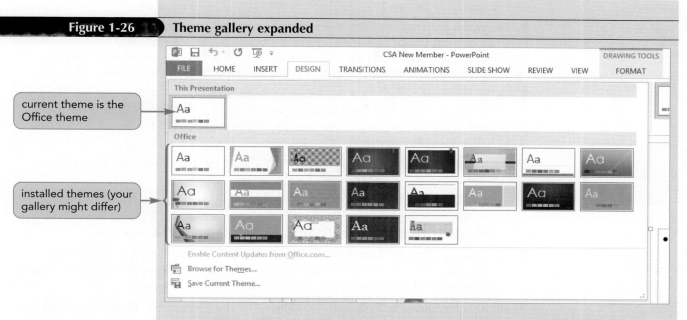

current theme is the Office theme

installed themes (your gallery might differ)

6. Point to several of the themes in the gallery to display their ScreenTips and to see a Live Preview of the theme applied to the current slide, and then click the **Facet** theme. The gallery closes and the Facet theme is applied to all the slides with the default variant (the first variant in the Variants group).

   The title text on each slide changes from black to green, the letters that you had colored orange on Slide 2 are dark green, the bullet symbols change from black circles to green triangles, and in the Slides tab, you can see on the Slide 6 thumbnail that the SmartArt shapes are now green as well.

7. In the Variants group, point to the other three variants to see a Live Preview of each of them. Isaac likes the default green variant best, so you will not change it.

8. Click the **HOME** tab, and then in the Font group, click the **Font Color arrow**. The selected color—the color of the selected letter "C"—is now a shade of green in the Theme Colors of the Facet theme. Notice also that the row of Standard Colors is the same as it was when the Office theme was applied.

9. In the Font group, click the **Font arrow**. You can see that the Theme Fonts are now Trebuchet MS for both Headings (slide titles) and the Body (content text boxes).

10. Press the **Esc** key. The Font menu closes.

After you apply a new theme, you should examine your slides to make sure that they look the way you expect them to. The font sizes used in the Facet theme are considerably smaller than those used in the Office theme. You know that Isaac wants the slides to be legible and clearly visible from a distance, so you will increase the font sizes on some of the slides. The title slide and Slide 2 are fine, but you need to examine the rest of the slides.

To examine the slides with the new theme and adjust font sizes:

1. Display **Slide 3** ("Benefits of CSAs") in the Slide pane, and then in the bulleted list, click the first bulleted item. (This is the new slide that Isaac added.) In the Font group, the font size is 18 points, quite a bit smaller than the font size of first-level bulleted items in the Office theme, which is 28 points. You can see that the font size of the subitems is also fairly small.

▶ **2.** In the bulleted list, click the text box border to select the entire text box. In the Font group, 16+ appears in the Font Size box. The smallest font size used in the selected text box—the font size of the subitems—is 16, and the plus sign indicates that there is text in the selected text box larger than 16 points.

▶ **3.** In the Font group, click the **Increase Font Size** button $\boxed{A}$ three times. The font size of the first-level bullets changes to 28 points, and the font size of the second-level bullets changes to 24 points. This is the same as the font sizes used in lists in the Office theme.

   Trouble? If the DRAWING TOOLS FORMAT tab becomes selected on the ribbon, click the HOME tab.

▶ **4.** Display **Slide 4** ("What Do CSA Members Receive?") in the Slide pane, and then increase the size of the text in the bulleted list to 28 points. There are misspelled words on this slide and on Slide 5; ignore them for now.

▶ **5.** Display **Slide 5** ("Membership Requirements") in the Slide pane, and then increase the font size of the text in the bulleted list so that the font size of the first-level items is 28 points and of the subitems is 24 points.

▶ **6.** Display **Slides 6, 7, 8,** and then **Slide 1** in the Slide pane. These remaining slides look fine.

▶ **7.** On the Quick Access Toolbar, click the **Save** button $\boxed{}$. The changes to the presentation are saved.

INSIGHT

Understanding the Difference Between Themes and Templates

As explained earlier, a theme is a coordinated set of colors, fonts, backgrounds, and effects. A **template**, like any presentation, has a theme applied, but it also contains text, graphics, and placeholders to help direct you in creating content for a presentation. You can create and save your own custom templates or find everything from calendars to marketing templates among the thousands of templates available on Office.com. To find a template on Office.com, display the Recent or New screen in Backstage view, type key words in the Search box or click one of the category links below the Search box to display templates related to the search terms or category. If you create a new presentation based on a template, you can make any changes you want to the slides.

   If a template is stored on your computer, you can apply the theme used in the template to an existing presentation. However, if you want to apply the theme used in a template on Office.com to an existing presentation, you need to download and save the template to your computer first, and then you can apply it to an existing presentation.

Working with Photos

Most people are exposed to multimedia daily and expect to have information conveyed visually as well as verbally. In many cases, graphics are more effective than words for communicating an important point. For example, if a sales force has reached its sales goals for the year, including a photo in your presentation of a person reaching the top of a mountain can convey a sense of exhilaration to your audience.

Inserting Photos Stored on Your Computer or Network

Content placeholders contain buttons that you can use to insert things other than a list, including photos stored on your hard drive, a network drive, a USB drive, an SD card from a digital camera, or any other medium to which you have access. You can also use the Picture button in the Images group on the INSERT tab to add photos to slides.

Isaac has photos showing produce from his farm that he wants inserted on two of the slides in the presentation. He also wants a photo of people volunteering on the farm to appear on the last slide in the presentation.

To insert photos stored on your computer or network on slides:

1. Display **Slide 2** ("What Is a CSA?") in the Slide pane, and then in the content placeholder on the right, click the **Pictures** button. The Insert Picture dialog box appears. This dialog box is similar to the Open dialog box.

2. Navigate to the **PowerPoint1 ▸ Tutorial** folder included with your Data Files, click **Produce1**, and then click the **Insert** button. The dialog box closes, and a picture of produce in bins appears in the placeholder and is selected. The contextual PICTURE TOOLS FORMAT tab appears on the ribbon to the right of the VIEW tab and is the active tab. See Figure 1-27.

| Figure 1-27 | Picture inserted on Slide 2 |

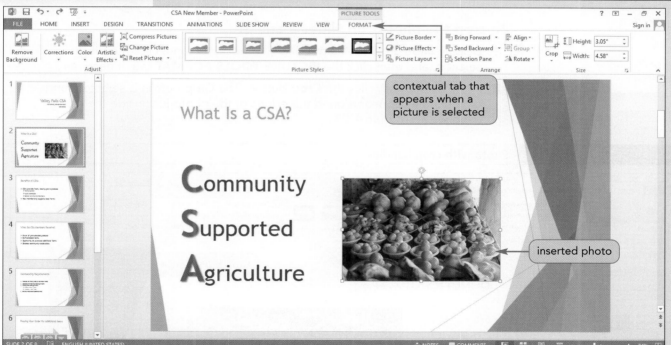

Photo courtesy of S. Scott Zimmerman

3. Display **Slide 3** ("Benefits of CSAs") in the Slide pane. This slide uses the Title and Content layout and does not have a second content placeholder. You can change the layout to include a second content placeholder or you can use a command on the ribbon to insert a photo.

4. Click the **INSERT** tab, and then in the Images group, click the **Pictures** button. The Insert Picture dialog box opens.

5. In the PowerPoint1 ► Tutorial folder, click **Produce2**, and then click the **Insert** button. The dialog box closes and the picture is added to the center of the slide, covering much of the bulleted list. You will fix this later.

6. Display **Slide 8** (the copy of the "What Is a CSA?" slide), and then click the **INSERT** tab on the ribbon.

7. In the Images group, click the **Pictures** button, click **People** in the PowerPoint1 ► Tutorial folder, and then click the **Insert** button. The picture replaces the content placeholder on the slide.

Cropping Photos

Sometimes you want to display only part of a photo. For example, if you insert a photo of a party scene that includes a bouquet of colorful balloons, you might want to show only the balloons. To do this, you can **crop** the photo—cut out the parts you don't want to include. In PowerPoint, you can crop it manually to any size you want, crop it to a preset ratio, or crop it to a shape.

On Slide 2, Isaac wants you to crop the photo to a diamond shape to make it more interesting, and to crop the photo on Slide 3 to make the dimensions of the final photo smaller without making the images in the photo smaller.

To crop the photos on Slides 2 and 3:

1. Display **Slide 3** ("Benefits of CSAs") in the Slide pane, click the photo to select it, and then click the **PICTURE TOOLS FORMAT** tab, if necessary.

2. In the Size group, click the **Crop** button. The Crop button is selected, and crop handles appear around the edges of the photo just inside the sizing handles. See Figure 1-28.

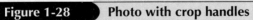

Figure 1-28   Photo with crop handles

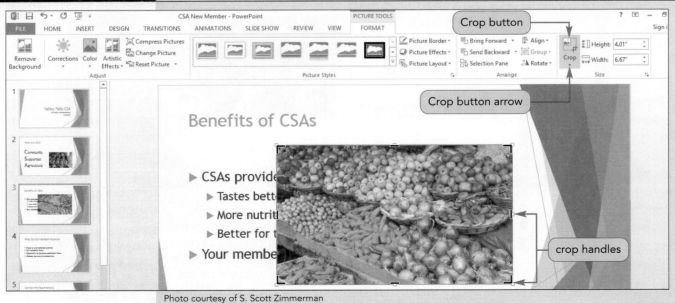

Photo courtesy of S. Scott Zimmerman

3. Position the pointer directly on top of the **left-middle crop handle** so that it changes to ⊣, press and hold the mouse button, and then drag the crop handle to the right approximately two inches.

4. Drag the crop handles on the bottom and right of the photo to match the cropped photo shown in Figure 1-29.

Figure 1-29 Cropped photo

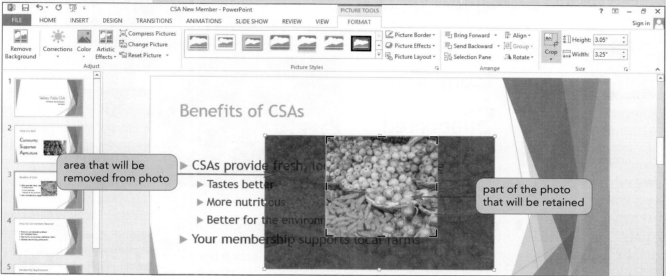

Photo courtesy of S. Scott Zimmerman

5. Click the **Crop** button again. The Crop feature is turned off, but the photo is still selected and the FORMAT tab is still the active tab. The photo is still on top of the bulleted list, but you'll fix this later.

6. Display **Slide 2** ("What Is a CSA?") in the Slide pane, click the photo to select it, and then click the **FORMAT** tab, if necessary.

7. In the Size group, click the **Crop button arrow**. The Crop button menu opens. See Figure 1-30.

| Figure 1-30 | Crop button menu |

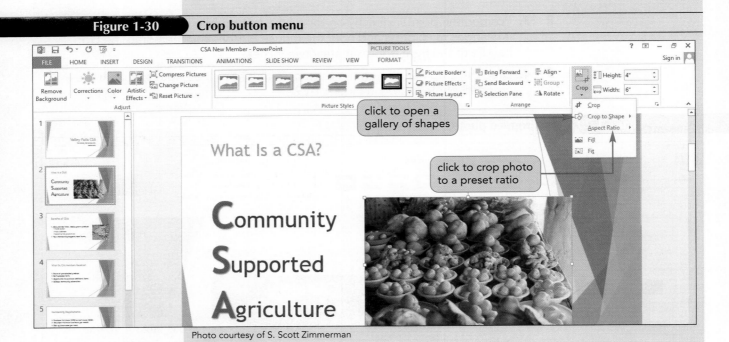

Photo courtesy of S. Scott Zimmerman

▶ **8.** Point to **Crop to Shape** to open a gallery of shapes, and then under Basic Shapes, click the **Diamond** shape. The photo is cropped to a diamond shape. Notice that the rectangular selection border of the original photo is still showing.

▶ **9.** In the Size group, click the **Crop** button. You can now see the cropped portions of the original, rectangle photo that are shaded gray.

▶ **10.** Click a blank area of the slide. The picture is no longer selected and the HOME tab is the active tab on the ribbon.

Modifying Photo Compression Options

When you save a presentation that contains photos, PowerPoint automatically compresses the photos to a resolution of 220 pixels per inch (ppi). (For comparison, photos printed in magazines are typically 300 ppi.) Compressing photos reduces the size of the presentation file, but it also reduces the quality of the photos. See Figure 1-31 for a description of the compression options available. If an option in the dialog box is gray, the photo is a lower resolution than that setting. Note that many monitors and projectors are capable of displaying resolutions only a little higher (98 ppi) than the resolution designated for email (96 ppi).

Figure 1-31	Photo compression settings

Compression Setting	Description
220 ppi	Photos are compressed to 220 pixels per inch; use when you need to maintain the quality of the photograph when the slides are printed. This is the default setting for PowerPoint presentations. (Note that although this setting compresses the photos minimally, they are still compressed, and if photograph quality is the most important concern, do not compress photos at all.)
150 ppi	Photos are compressed to 150 pixels per inch; use when the presentation will be viewed on a monitor or screen projector.
96 ppi	Photos are compressed to 96 pixels per inch; use for presentations that need to be emailed or uploaded to a Web page or when it is important to keep the overall file size small.
Document resolution	Photos are compressed to the resolution specified on the Advanced tab in the PowerPoint Options dialog box. The default setting is 220 ppi.
No compression	Photos are not compressed at all; used when it is critical that photos remain at their original resolution.

© 2014 Cengage Learning

You can change the compression setting for each photo that you insert or you can change the settings for all the photos in the presentation. If you cropped photos, you also can discard the cropped areas of the photo to make the presentation file size smaller. (Note that when you crop to a shape, the cropped portions are not discarded.) If you insert additional photos or crop a photo after you apply the new compression settings to all the slides, you will need to apply the new settings to the new photos.

REFERENCE

Modifying Photo Compression Settings and Removing Cropped Areas

- After all photos have been added to the presentation file, click any photo in the presentation to select it.
- Click the PICTURE TOOLS FORMAT tab. In the Adjust group, click the Compress Pictures button.
- Click the option button next to the resolution you want to use.
- To apply the new compression settings to all the photos in the presentation, click the Apply only to this picture check box to deselect it.
- To keep cropped areas of photos, click the Delete cropped area of pictures check box to deselect it.
- Click the OK button.

You will adjust the compression settings to make the file size of the presentation as small as possible so that Isaac can easily send it or post it for others without worrying about file size limitations on the receiving server.

To modify photo compression settings and remove cropped areas from photos:

1. On **Slide 2** ("What Is a CSA?"), click the photo, and then click the **PICTURE TOOLS FORMAT** tab, if necessary.

2. In the Adjust group, click the **Compress Pictures** button. The Compress Pictures dialog box opens. See Figure 1-32. Under Target output, the Use document resolution option button is selected.

Figure 1-32   Compress Pictures dialog box

deselect to apply new settings to all photos currently in slides

keep selected to remove cropped areas of photos

default resolution

3. Click the **E-mail (96 ppi)** option button. This setting compresses the photos to the smallest possible size. At the top of the dialog box under Compression options, the Delete cropped area of pictures check box is already selected. This option is not applied to cropped photos until you open this dialog box and then click the OK button to apply it. Because you want the presentation file size to be as small as possible, you do want cropped portions of photos to be deleted, so you'll leave this selected. The Apply only to this picture check box is also selected; however, you want the settings applied to all the photos in the file.

4. Click the **Apply only to this picture** check box to deselect it.

5. Click the **OK** button.

    The dialog box closes and the compression settings are applied to all the photos in the presentation. You can confirm that the cropped areas of photos were removed by examining the photo on Slide 3. (The photo on Slide 2 was cropped to a shape, so the cropped areas on it were not removed.)

6. Display **Slide 3** ("Benefits of CSAs") in the Slide pane, click the photo to select it, click the **FORMAT** tab, if necessary, and then in the Size group, click the **Crop** button. The Crop handles appear around the photo, but the portions of the photo that you cropped out no longer appear.

7. Click the **Crop** button again to deselect it, and then save the changes to the presentation.

Be sure you are satisfied with the way you cropped the photo on Slide 3 before you delete the cropped areas.

INSIGHT

Keeping Photos Uncompressed

Suppose you are a photographer and want to create a presentation to show your photos. In that case, you would want to display them at their original, uncompressed resolution. To do this, you need to change a setting in the PowerPoint Options dialog box before you add photos to slides. Click the FILE tab to open Backstage view, click Options in the navigation bar to open the PowerPoint Options dialog box, click Advanced in the navigation bar, and then locate the Image Size and Quality section. To keep images at their original resolution, click the Do not compress images in file check box to select it. Note that you can also change the default compression setting for photos in this dialog box; you can increase the compression or choose to automatically discard cropped portions of photos. Note that these changes affect only the current presentation.

Resizing and Moving Objects

You can resize and move any object to best fit the space available on a slide. One way to resize an object is to drag a sizing handle. **Sizing handles** are the small squares that appear in the corners and in the middle of the sides of the border of a selected object. When you use this method, you can adjust the size of the object so it best fits the space visually. If you need to size an object to exact dimensions, you can modify the measurements in the Size group on the FORMAT tab that appears when you select the object.

You can also drag an object to reposition it anywhere on the slide. If more than one object is on a slide, **smart guides**, dashed red lines, appear as you drag to indicate the center and the top and bottom borders of the objects. Smart guides can help you position objects so they are aligned and spaced evenly.

In addition to using the smart guides, it can be helpful to display rulers and gridlines in the window. The rulers appear along the top and left sides of the Slide pane. Gridlines are one-inch squares made up of dots one-sixth of an inch apart. As you drag an object, it snaps to the grid, even if it is not visible.

Resizing and Moving Pictures

Pictures and other objects that cause the PICTURE TOOLS FORMAT tab to appear when selected have their aspect ratios locked by default. The **aspect ratio** is the ratio of the object's height to its width. When the aspect ratio is locked, if you resize the photo by dragging a corner sizing handle or if you change one dimension in the Size group on the PICTURE TOOLS FORMAT tab, the other dimension will change by the same percentage. However, if you drag one of the sizing handles in the middle of an object's border, you will override the locked aspect ratio setting and resize the object only in the direction you drag. Generally you do not want to do this with photos because the images will become distorted.

You need to resize and move the cropped photo on Slide 3 so it is not obscuring the text. You also want to resize and move the photos you inserted on Slides 2 and 8 so the slides are more attractive. You'll display the rulers and gridlines to help you as you do this.

To move and resize the photos:

1. Click the **VIEW** tab, and then in the Show group, click the **Ruler** and the **Gridlines** check boxes. Rulers appear along the top and left sides of the Slide pane, and the gridlines appear in the Slide pane.

2. On **Slide 3** ("Benefits of CSAs"), select the photo, if necessary, and then position the pointer on the photo anywhere except on a sizing handle so that the pointer changes to ⊹.

3. Press and hold the mouse button, drag the photo down and to the right so that the right edge of the photo is approximately one inch from the right side of the slide and a smart guide appears indicating that the top of the photo and the top of the bulleted list text box are aligned, as shown in Figure 1-33.

TIP

If you don't want objects you are moving to snap to the grid, press and hold the Alt key while you are dragging.

| Figure 1-33 | Repositioning photo on Slide 3 using smart guides and gridlines |

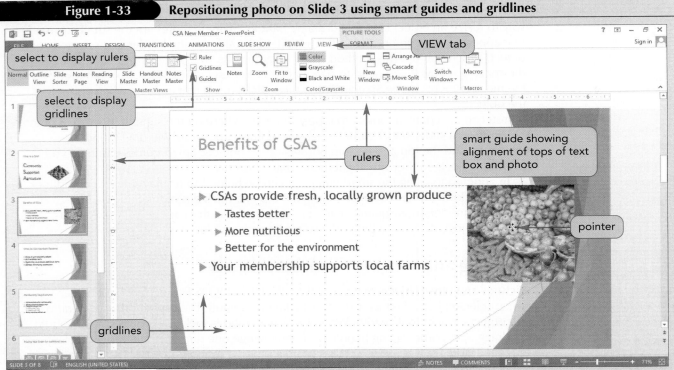

Photo courtesy of S. Scott Zimmerman

4. Release the mouse button. The photo is repositioned to the right of the bulleted list.

5. Display **Slide 2** ("What Is a CSA?") in the Slide pane, click the photo to select it, and then click the **PICTURE TOOLS FORMAT** tab if necessary. Instead of the border and sizing handles being on the diamond border, a rectangular border appears representing the original, uncropped photo's borders. (Remember that cropped portions of photos that are cropped to a shape are not removed.)

6. In the Size group, click in the **Height** box to select the current measurement, type **4**, and then press the **Enter** key. The measurement in the Width box in the Size group changes proportionately, and the new measurements are applied to the photo.

7. Drag the photo up and to the left until a horizontal smart guide appears indicating the alignment of the middle of the text box and the middle of the photo, and a vertical smart guide appears on the left side of the photo indicating the alignment of the left edge of the photo and the right edge of the bulleted list text box, as shown in Figure 1-34.

Figure 1-34 Moving resized photo on Slide 2

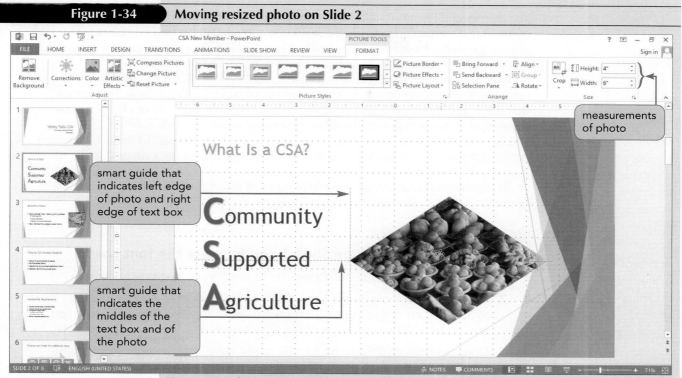

Photo courtesy of S. Scott Zimmerman

▶ **8.** Display **Slide 8** (the last slide in the presentation) in the Slide pane, click the photo to select it, position the pointer on the top-middle sizing handle to that it changes to ↕, press and hold the mouse button, and then drag the sizing handle approximately two inches up. The photo is two inches taller, but the image is distorted.

▶ **9.** On the Quick Access Toolbar, click the **Undo** button ↶. You need to resize the photo by dragging a corner sizing handle to maintain the aspect ratio.

▶ **10.** Click the **FORMAT** tab, and note the measurements in the Size group. The photo is 3.05 inches high and 4.58 inches wide.

▶ **11.** Position the pointer on the bottom-right corner sizing handle so that it changes to ⬂, press and hold the mouse button, and then drag the sizing handle down. Even though you are dragging in only one direction, because you are dragging a corner sizing handle, both the width and height are changing proportionately.

▶ **12.** When the photo is approximately four inches high and six inches wide, release the mouse button. Note that the measurements in the Height and Width boxes changed to reflect the picture's new size.

▶ **13.** Drag the photo up until the top of the photo aligns with the 2-inch mark on the ruler on the left and the right edge of the photo is aligned with the 6-inch mark on the ruler at the top of the Slide pane. You are done using the ruler and gridlines so you can turn these features off.

▶ **14.** Click the **VIEW** tab, and then click the **Ruler** and **Gridlines** check boxes to deselect them.

Resizing and Moving Text Boxes

The themes and layouts installed with PowerPoint are designed by professionals, so much of the time it's a good idea to use the layouts as provided to be assured of a cohesive look among the slides. However, occasionally there will be a compelling reason to adjust the layout of objects on a slide, by either resizing or repositioning them.

Text boxes and other objects that cause the DRAWING TOOLS FORMAT tab to appear when selected do not have their aspect ratios locked by default. This means that when you resize an object by dragging a corner sizing handle or changing one dimension in the Size group, the other dimension is not affected.

Like any other object on a slide, you can reposition text boxes. To do this, you must position the pointer on the text box border, anywhere except on a sizing handle, to drag it to its new location.

To improve the appearance of Slide 8, you will resize the text box containing the unnumbered list so it vertically fills the slide.

To resize the text box on Slide 8 and increase the font size:

▶ **1.** On Slide 8, click the unnumbered list to display the text box border.

▶ **2.** Position the pointer on the top-middle sizing handle so that it changes to $\updownarrow$, and then drag the sizing handle up until the top edge of the text box is aligned with the top edge of the title text placeholder.

▶ **3.** Drag the right-middle sizing handle to the right until the right edge of the text box is touching the left edge of the photo.

▶ **4.** Click the **HOME** tab, and then in the Font group, click the **Increase Font Size** button $\boxed{A^{\hat{}}}$ three times. Even though the title text placeholder will not appear during a slide show, you will delete it so that it is easier to see how the final slide will look.

▶ **5.** Click the title text placeholder border, and then press the **Delete** key. See Figure 1-35 and adjust the position of the photo if necessary.

Figure 1-35   Slide 8 with resized text box

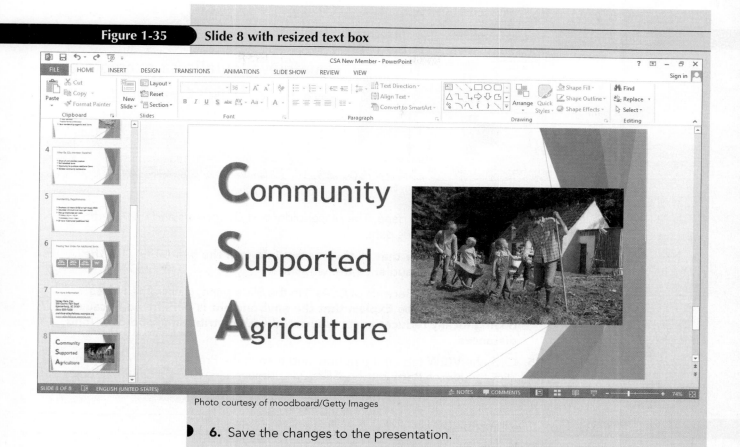

Photo courtesy of moodboard/Getty Images

▶ **6.** Save the changes to the presentation.

Adding Speaker Notes

Speaker notes, or simply **notes**, are information you add about slide content to help you remember to bring up specific points during the presentation. Speaker notes should not contain all the information you plan to say during your presentation, but they can be a useful tool for reminding you about facts and details related to the content on specific slides. You add notes in the **Notes pane**, which you can display below the Slide pane in Normal view, or you can switch to **Notes Page view**, in which an image of the slide appears in the top half of the presentation window and the notes for that slide appear in the bottom half.

To add notes to Slides 3 and 7:

▶ **1.** Display **Slide 7** ("For More Information") in the Slide pane, and then, on the status bar, click the **NOTES** button. The Notes pane appears below the Slide pane with "Click to add notes" as placeholder text. See Figure 1-36.

Figure 1-36 Notes pane below the Slide pane

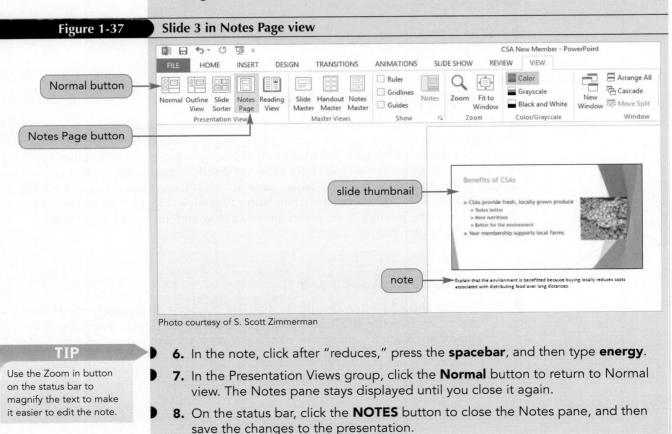

Notes pane

csainfo@valleyfallscsa.example.org

www.valleyfallscsa.example.org

NOTES button

Click to add notes

SLIDE 7 OF 8   ENGLISH (UNITED STATES)   ≜ NOTES

Photo courtesy of moodboard/Getty Images

2. Click in the **Notes** pane. The placeholder text disappears and the insertion point is in the Notes pane.

3. Type **Tell audience that all the contact info is in the handouts. Use the link to show the audience the website**.

4. Display **Slide 3** ("Benefits of CSAs") in the Slide pane, click in the **Notes** pane, and then type **Explain that the environment is benefitted because buying locally reduces costs associated with distributing food over long distances**.

5. Click the **VIEW** tab on the ribbon, and then in the Presentation Views group, click the **Notes Page** button. Slide 3 is displayed in Notes Page view. See Figure 1-37.

Figure 1-37 Slide 3 in Notes Page view

Normal button

Notes Page button

slide thumbnail

note

Photo courtesy of S. Scott Zimmerman

TIP

Use the Zoom in button on the status bar to magnify the text to make it easier to edit the note.

6. In the note, click after "reduces," press the **spacebar**, and then type **energy**.

7. In the Presentation Views group, click the **Normal** button to return to Normal view. The Notes pane stays displayed until you close it again.

8. On the status bar, click the **NOTES** button to close the Notes pane, and then save the changes to the presentation.

Checking Spelling

You should always check the spelling and grammar in your presentation before you finalize it. To make this task easier, you can use PowerPoint's spelling checker. You can quickly tell if there are words on slides that are not in the built-in dictionary by looking at the Spelling button at the left end of the status bar. If there are no words flagged as possibly misspelled, the button is [ ]; if there are flagged words, the button changes to [ ]. To indicate that a word might be misspelled, a wavy red line appears under it.

To correct misspelled words, you can right-click a flagged word to see a list of suggested spellings on the shortcut menu, or you can check the spelling of all the words in the presentation. To check the spelling of all the words in the presentation, you click the Spelling button in the Proofing group on the REVIEW tab. This opens the Spelling task pane to the right of the Slide pane and starts the spell check from the current slide. A **task pane** is a pane that opens to the right or left of the Slide pane and contains commands and options related to the task you are doing. When a possible misspelled word is found, suggestions are displayed for the correct spelling. Synonyms for the selected correct spelling are also listed.

To check the spelling of words in the presentation:

1. Display **Slide 4** ("What Do CSA Members Receive?") in the Slide pane, and then right-click the misspelled word **Oportunity**. A shortcut menu opens listing spelling options. See Figure 1-38.

| Figure 1-38 | Shortcut menu for a misspelled word |

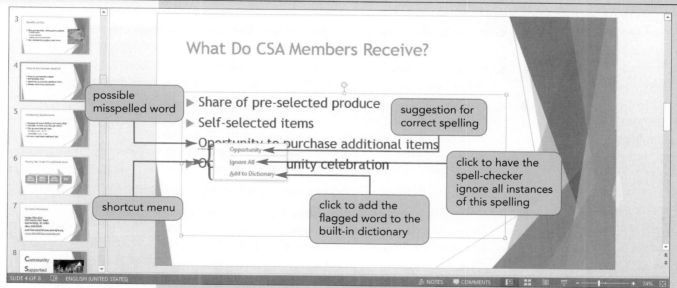

Photos courtesy of S. Scott Zimmerman and moodboard/Getty Images

2. On the shortcut menu, click **Opportunity**. The menu closes and the spelling is corrected.

TIP

You can also click the Spelling button on the status bar to start the spell check.

3. Click the **REVIEW** tab, and then in the Proofing group, click the **Spelling** button. The Spelling task pane opens to the right of the Slide pane, and the next slide that contains a possible misspelled word, Slide 5 ("Membership Requirements"), appears in the Slide pane with the flagged word, "minmum," highlighted. See Figure 1-39. In the Spelling task pane, the first suggested correct spelling is selected. The selected correct spelling also appears at the bottom of the task pane with synonyms for the word listed below it and a speaker icon next to it.

Figure 1-39   Spelling task pane displaying a misspelled word

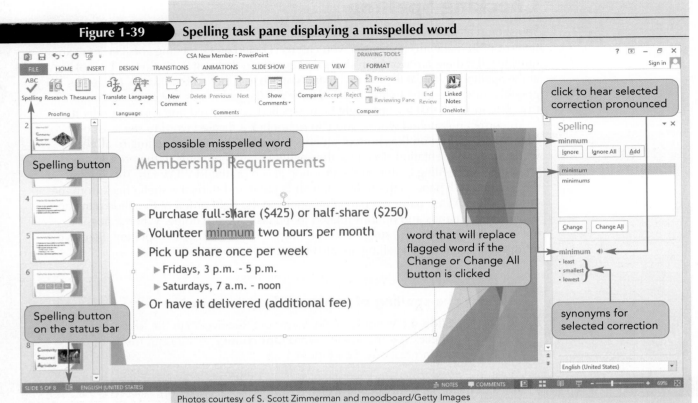

Photos courtesy of S. Scott Zimmerman and moodboard/Getty Images

4. In the Spelling task pane, click the **speaker** icon. A male voice says the word "minimum."

5. In the list of suggested corrections, click **minimums**. The word at the bottom of the task pane changes to "minimums," and the synonyms change also.

6. In the list of suggested corrections, click **minimum**, and then click the **Change** button. The word is corrected and the next slide containing a possible misspelled word, Slide 1, appears in the Slide pane with the flagged word, "DeSoto," highlighted and listed in the Spelling task pane. This is Isaac's last name so you want the spell checker to ignore this.

   Trouble? If the spell checker finds any other misspelled words, correct them.

7. In the task pane, click the **Ignore All** button. Because that was the last flagged word in the presentation, the Spelling task pane closes and a dialog box opens telling you that the spell check is complete.

8. Click the **OK** button. The dialog box closes. The last flagged word, DeSoto, is still selected on Slide 1.

9. Click a blank area of the slide to deselect the text, and then save the changes to your presentation.

Running a Slide Show

After you have created and proofed your presentation, you should view it as a slide show to see how it will appear to your audience. There are several ways to do this—Slide Show view, Presenter view, and Reading view.

Using Slide Show View and Presenter View

You can use Slide Show view if your computer has only one monitor and you don't have access to a screen projector. If your computer is connected to a second monitor or a screen projector, Slide Show view is the way an audience will see your slides. Refer to the Session 1.2 Visual Overview for more information about Slide Show view.

Isaac asks you to review the slide show in Slide Show view to make sure the slides look good.

To use Slide Show view:

TIP
To start the slide show from the current slide, click the Slide Show button on the status bar.

1. On the Quick Access Toolbar, click the **Start From Beginning** button. Slide 1 appears on the screen in Slide Show view. Now you need to advance the slide show.

2. Press the **spacebar**. Slide 2 ("What Is a CSA?") appears on the screen.

3. Click the mouse button. The next slide, Slide 3 ("Benefits of CSAs"), appears on the screen.

4. Press the **Backspace** key. The previous slide, Slide 2, appears again.

5. Type **7**, and then press the **Enter** key. Slide 7 ("For More Information") appears on the screen.

6. Move the mouse to display the pointer, and then position the pointer on the website address **www.valleyfoodscsa.example.org**. The pointer changes to indicate that this is a link, and the ScreenTip that appears shows the full website address including "http://". If this were a real website, you could click the link to open your Web browser and display the website to your audience. Because you moved the pointer, a very faint row of buttons appears in the lower-left corner. See Figure 1-40.

Figure 1-40   Link and buttons in Slide Show view

(864) 555-FOOD
csainfo@valleyfallscsa.example.org
www.valleyfallscsa.example.org

pointer on a link in Slide Show view

row of buttons that appears when you move the pointer

ScreenTip identifying the link

7. Move the pointer again, if necessary, to display the row of buttons that appears in the lower left corner of the screen, and then click the **Return to the previous slide** button four times to return to Slide 3 ("Benefits of CSAs").

   Trouble? If you can't see the buttons on the toolbar, move the pointer to the lower left corner so it is on top of the first button to darken that button, and then move the pointer to the right to see the rest of the buttons.

8. Display the faint row of buttons again, and then click the **Zoom into the slide** button. The pointer changes to and three-quarters of the slide is darkened. See Figure 1-41.

Figure 1-41 **Zoom feature activated in Slide Show view**

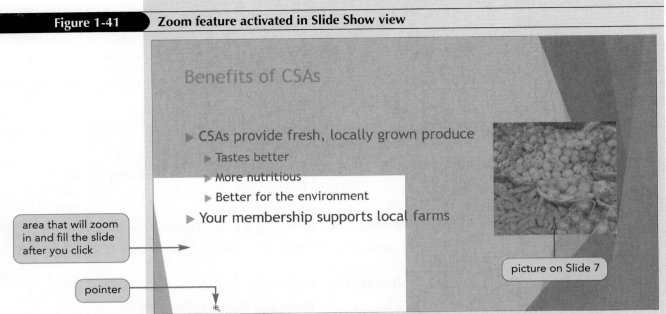

area that will zoom in and fill the slide after you click

picture on Slide 7

pointer

Photo courtesy of S. Scott Zimmerman

9. Move the pointer to the picture, watching as the bright rectangle follows it, and then click the picture. The view zooms so that the part of the slide inside the bright rectangle fills the screen, and the pointer changes to 🖑.

10. Press and hold the mouse button to change the pointer to 🖑, and then drag down and to the right to pull another part of the zoomed in slide into view.

11. Press the **Esc** key to zoom back out to see the whole slide.

Presenter view provides additional tools for running a slide show. In addition to seeing the current slide, you can also see the next slide, speaker notes, and a timer showing you how long the slide show has been running. Refer to the Session 1.2 Visual Overview for more information about Presenter view. Because of the additional tools available in Presenter view, you should consider using it if your computer is connected to a second monitor or projector. If, for some reason, you don't want to use Presenter view in that circumstance, you can switch to Slide Show view.

If your computer is connected to a projector or second monitor, and you start a slide show in Slide Show view, Presenter view starts on the computer and Slide Show view appears on the second monitor or projection screen. If you want to practice using Presenter view when your computer is not connected to a second monitor or projector, you can switch to Presenter view from Slide Show view.

Isaac wants you to switch to Presenter view and familiarize yourself with the tools available there.

To use Presenter view to review the slide show:

1. Move the pointer to display the row of buttons in the lower left corner of the screen, click the **More slide show options** button ⦿ to open a menu of commands, and then click **Show Presenter View**. The screen changes to show the presentation in Presenter view.

2. Below the current slide, click the **See all slides** button ▦. The screen changes to show thumbnails of all the slides in the presentation, similar to Slide Sorter view.

3. Click the **Slide 4** thumbnail. Presenter view reappears, displaying Slide 4 ("What Do CSA Members Receive?") as the current slide.

4. Click anywhere on the current slide, Slide 4. The slide show advances to display Slide 5.

5. At the bottom of the screen, click the **Advance to the next slide** button ▶. Slide 6 ("Placing Your Order for Additional Items") appears.

6. Press the **spacebar** twice. The slide show advances again to display Slides 7 and then 8.

7. Press the **spacebar** again. A black slide appears. As noted on the slide, the black screen indicates the end of the slide show.

8. Press the **spacebar** once more. Presentation view closes and you return to Normal view.

PROSKILLS

Decision Making: Displaying a Blank Slide During a Presentation

Sometimes during a presentation, the audience has questions about the material and you want to pause the slide show to respond to their questions. Or you might want to refocus the audience's attention on you instead of on the visuals on the screen. In these cases, you can display a blank slide (either black or white). When you do this, the audience, with nothing else to look at, will shift all of their attention to you. Some presenters plan to use blank slides and insert them at specific points during their slide shows. Planning to use a blank slide can help you keep your presentation focused and remind you that the purpose of the PowerPoint slides is to provide visual aids to enhance your presentation; the slides themselves are not the presentation.

If you did not create blank slides in your presentation file, but during your presentation you feel you need to display a blank slide, you can easily do this in Slide Show or Presenter view by pressing the B key to display a blank black slide or the W key to display a blank white slide. You can also click the Menu button in the row of buttons or right-click the screen to open a menu, point to Screen on the menu, and then click Black or White. To remove the black or white slide and redisplay the slide that had been on the screen before you displayed the blank slide, press any key on the keyboard or click anywhere on the screen. In Presenter view, you can also use the Black or unblack slide show button ▨ to toggle a black slide on or off.

An alternative to redisplaying the slide that had been displayed prior to the blank slide is to click the Advance to the next slide button ▶. This can be more effective than redisplaying the slide that was onscreen before the blank slide because, after you have grabbed the audience's attention and prepared them to move on, you won't lose their focus by displaying a slide they have already seen.

Using Reading View

Reading view displays the slides so that they almost fill the screen, similar to Slide Show view; however, in Reading view, a status bar appears identifying the number of the current slide and providing buttons to advance the slide show. You can also resize the window in Reading view to allow you to work in another window on the desktop.

To use Reading view to review the presentation:

1. Display **Slide 2** ("What Is a CSA?"), in the Slide pane, and then on the status bar, click the **Reading View** button. The presentation changes to Reading view with Slide 2 displayed. See Figure 1-42.

Figure 1-42 | **Slide 2 in Reading view**

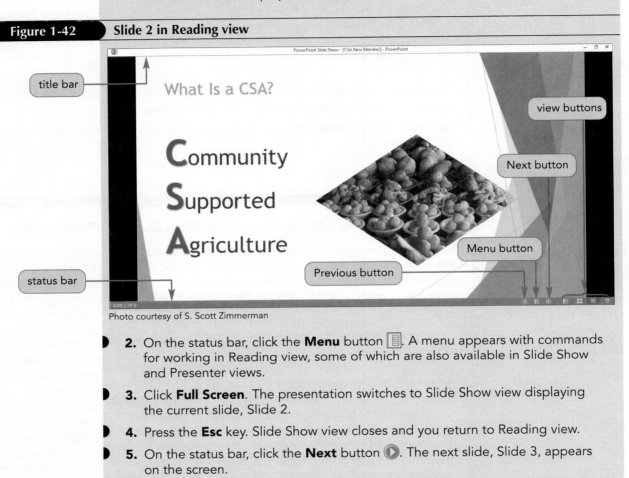

Photo courtesy of S. Scott Zimmerman

2. On the status bar, click the **Menu** button. A menu appears with commands for working in Reading view, some of which are also available in Slide Show and Presenter views.

3. Click **Full Screen**. The presentation switches to Slide Show view displaying the current slide, Slide 2.

4. Press the **Esc** key. Slide Show view closes and you return to Reading view.

5. On the status bar, click the **Next** button. The next slide, Slide 3, appears on the screen.

6. On the status bar, click the **Normal** button to return to Normal view with Slide 1 displayed in the Slide pane.

Printing a Presentation

Before you deliver your presentation, you might want to print it. PowerPoint provides several printing options. For example, you can print the slides in color, grayscale (white and shades of gray), or pure black and white, and you can print one, some, or all of the slides in several formats.

You use the Print screen in Backstage view to set print options such as specifying a printer and color options.

First, you will replace Isaac's name on Slide 1 with your name.

To choose a printer and color options:

1. Display **Slide 1** in the Slide pane, and then replace Isaac's name in the subtitle with your name.

2. Click the **FILE** tab to display Backstage view, and then click **Print** in the navigation bar. Backstage view changes to display the Print screen. The Print screen contains options for printing your presentation, and a preview of the first slide as it will print with the current options. See Figure 1-43.

Figure 1-43	Print screen in Backstage view

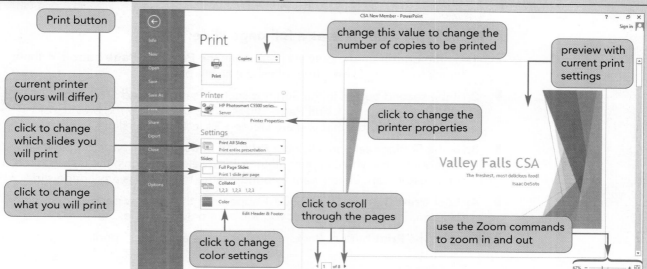

3. If you are connected to a network or to more than one printer, make sure the printer listed in the Printer box is the one you want to use; if it is not, click the **Printer** button, and then click the correct printer in the list.

4. Click the **Printer Properties** link to open the Properties dialog box for your printer. Usually, the default options are correct, but you can change any printer settings, such as print quality or the paper source, in this dialog box.

5. Click the **Cancel** button to close the Properties dialog box. Now you can choose whether to print the presentation in color, black and white, or grayscale. If you plan to print in black and white or grayscale, you should change this setting so you can see what your slides will look like without color and to make sure they are legible.

6. Click the **Color** button, and then click **Grayscale**. The preview changes to grayscale.

7. At the bottom of the preview pane, click the **Next Page** button ▶ twice to display Slide 3 ("Benefits of CSAs"). The slides are legible in grayscale.

8. If you will be printing in color, click the **Grayscale** button, and then click **Color**.

In the Settings section on the Print screen, you can click the Full Page Slides button to choose from among several choices for printing the presentation, as described below:

- **Full Page Slides**—Prints each slide full size on a separate piece of paper.
- **Notes Pages**—Prints each slide as a notes page.
- **Outline**—Prints the text of the presentation as an outline.
- **Handouts**—Prints the presentation with one or more slides on each piece of paper. When printing four, six, or nine slides, you can choose whether to order the slides from left to right in rows (horizontally) or from top to bottom in columns (vertically).

Isaac wants you to print the title slide as a full page slide so that he can use it as a cover page for his handouts.

To print the title slide as a full page slide:

1. At the bottom of the preview pane, click the **Previous Page** button ◀ three times to display Slide 1 (the title slide) as the preview.

2. If the second button in the Settings section is not labeled "Full Page Slides," click it, and then click **Full Page Slides**. Note that below the preview of Slide 1, it indicates that you are viewing Slide 1 of eight slides to print.

3. In the Settings section, click the **Print All Slides** button. Note on the menu that opens that you can print all the slides, selected slides, the current slide, or a custom range. You want to print just the title slide as a full page slide.

4. Click **Print Current Slide**. Slide 1 appears in the preview pane, and at the bottom, it now indicates that you will print only one slide.

5. Click the **Print** button. Backstage view closes and Slide 1 prints.

Next, Isaac wants you to print the slides as a handout, with all eight slides on a single sheet of paper.

To print the slides as a handout:

1. Click the **FILE** tab, and then click **Print** in the navigation bar.

2. In the Settings section, click the **Full Page Slides** button. A menu opens listing the various ways you can print the slides. See Figure 1-44.

Figure 1-44   Print screen in Backstage view with print options menu open

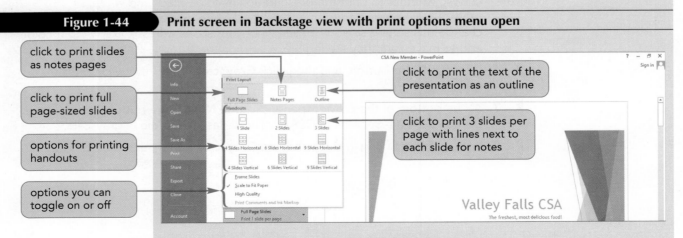

click to print slides as notes pages

click to print full page-sized slides

options for printing handouts

options you can toggle on or off

click to print the text of the presentation as an outline

click to print 3 slides per page with lines next to each slide for notes

3. In the Handouts section, click **9 Slides Horizontal**. The preview changes to show Slide 1 in the upper-left corner. You need to specify that all eight slides will print.

4. Click the **Print Current Slide** button, and then click **Print All Slides**. All eight slides appear in the preview pane, arranged in order horizontally, that is, in three rows from left to right. Notice that the current date appears in the top-right corner and a page number appears in the bottom-right corner.

5. At the top of the Print section, click the **Print** button. Backstage view closes and the handout prints.

Recall that you created speaker notes on Slides 3 and 7. Isaac would like you to print these slides as notes pages.

To print the nonsequential slides containing speaker notes:

1. Open the Print screen in Backstage view again, and then click the **9 Slides Horizontal** button. The menu opens. "9 Slides Horizontal" appeared on the button because that was the last printing option you chose.

2. In the Print Layout section of the menu, click **Notes Pages**. The menu closes and the preview displays Slide 1 as a Notes Page.

3. In the Settings section, click in the **Slides** box, type **3,7** and then click a blank area of the Print screen.

4. Scroll through the preview to confirm that Slides 3 and 7 will print, and then click the **Print** button. Backstage view closes and Slides 3 and 7 print as notes pages.

Finally, Isaac would like you to print the outline of the presentation. Recall that Slide 8 is designed to be a visual Isaac can leave displayed at the end of the presentation, so you don't need to include it in the outline.

To print Slides 1 through 7 as an outline on a single page:

1. Open the Print tab in Backstage view, click the **Notes Pages** button, and then in the Print Layout section, click **Outline**. The text on Slides 3 and 7 appears as an outline in the preview pane.

2. Click in the **Slides** box, type **1-7**, and then click a blank area of the Print screen. See Figure 1-45.

Figure 1-45	Print screen in Backstage view with Slides 1-7 previewed as an outline

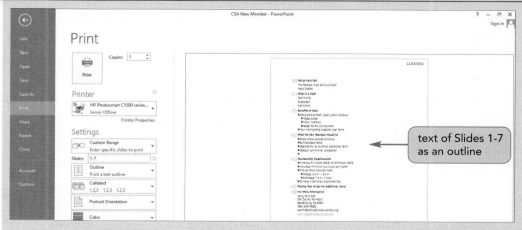

3. At the top of the Print section, click the **Print** button. Backstage view closes and the text of Slides 1-7 prints on one sheet of paper.

Exiting PowerPoint

When you are finished working with your presentation, you can exit PowerPoint. If there is only one presentation open, you click the Close button ✕ in the upper-right corner of the program window to exit the program. If more than one presentation is open, clicking this button will only close the current presentation; to exit PowerPoint, you would need to click the Close button in each of the open presentation's windows.

To exit PowerPoint:

1. In the upper-right corner of the program window, click the **Close** button ✕. A dialog box opens asking if you want to save your changes. This is because you did not save the file after you replaced Isaac's name with your own.

2. In the dialog box, click the **Save** button. The dialog box closes, the changes are saved, and PowerPoint exits.

In this session, you opened an existing presentation and saved it with a new name, changed the theme, added and cropped photos and adjusted the photo compression, and resized and moved objects. You have also added speaker notes and checked the spelling. Finally, you printed the presentation in several forms and exited PowerPoint. Your work will help Isaac give an effective presentation to potential customers of Valley Farms CSA.

Session 1.2 Quick Check

REVIEW

1. Explain what a theme is and what changes with each variant.
2. Describe what happens when you crop photos.
3. Describe sizing handles.
4. Describe smart guides.
5. Why is it important to maintain the aspect ratio of photos?
6. What is the difference between Slide Show view and Presenter view?
7. List the four formats for printing a presentation.

ASSESS

SAM Projects

Put your skills into practice with SAM Projects! SAM Projects for this tutorial can be found online. If you have a SAM account, go to www.cengage.com/sam2013 to download the most recent Project Instructions and Start Files.

PRACTICE

Review Assignments

Data Files needed for the Review Assignments: Farmland.jpg, Field Volunteer.jpg, Office Volunteer.jpg, Revised Volunteer Info.pptx

Chris Kopache is the Volunteer Coordinator for Valley Falls CSA. He needs to create a presentation for CSA members to explain the various ways they can volunteer. He will give the presentation to small groups. He doesn't want to overwhelm people, but he wants them to have enough information about each type of job so that they can choose one that best suits their abilities. He asks you to begin creating the presentation.

1. Start PowerPoint and create a new, blank presentation. On the title slide, type **Information for Volunteers** as the title, and then type your name as the subtitle. Save the presentation as **Volunteer Info** to the drive and folder where you are storing your files.
2. Edit the title by adding **Valley Falls CSA** before the word "Volunteers."
3. Add a new Slide 2 with the Title and Content layout, type **Jobs for Volunteers** as the slide title, and then in the content placeholder type the following:
   - **Field work**
   - **Work in store**
   - **Deliver shares**
   - **Office work**
     - **Must be familiar with Excel and Word**
     - **Only 3 positions available**
4. Create a new Slide 3 with the Title and Content layout. Add **Expectations** as the slide title, and then type the following as a numbered list on the slide:
   1. **Submit job preferences with membership application**
   2. **Volunteer minimum two hours per month**
   3. **Submit shift changes one week in advance**
   4. **Contact Chris Kopache**
5. Create a new Slide 4 using the Two Content layout. Add **Questions?** as the slide title.
6. Use the Cut and Paste commands to move the last bulleted item on Slide 3 ("Contact Chris Kopache") to the left content placeholder on Slide 4.
7. On Slide 4, remove the bullet symbol from the text you pasted, and then add the following as the next two items in the unnumbered list:
   Email: c_kopache@example.org
   Cell: 803-555-8723
8. Click after "Kopache" in the first item in the list, and then create a new line below it without creating a new item in the list and so that there is no extra space above the new line. On the new line, type **Volunteer Coordinator**.
9. Remove the hyperlink formatting from the email address.

10. Create a new Slide 5 using the Title and Content layout. Delete the title text placeholder. In the content placeholder, type **Thank You!** as a single item in an unnumbered list. Increase the size of the text "Thank You!" to 96 points, and then change the color of this text to Blue, Accent 1.

11. On Slide 3 ("Expectations"), change the numbered list to a SmartArt graphic. Use the Vertical Curved List layout, which is a List type of diagram.

12. Save your changes, and then close the presentation.

13. Open the file **Revised Volunteer Info**, located in the PowerPoint1 ▸ Review folder included with your Data Files, add your name as the subtitle on the title slide, and then save it as **New CSA Volunteers** to the drive and location where you are storing your files.

14. Change the theme to Wisp and keep the default variant. On Slide 2, change the size of the text in the bulleted list so that the size of the text of the first-level items is 28 points.

15. On Slide 1 (the title slide), insert the photo **Farmland**, located in the PowerPoint1 ▸ Review folder included with your Data Files. Resize the photo, maintaining the aspect ratio, so that it is the same width as the slide, and then reposition the photo so that the top of the photo aligns with the top of the slide. Crop the photo from the bottom, up to the base of the trees on the right, leaving approximately one-quarter inch between the bottom of the photo and the slide title.

16. Change the layout of Slide 4 ("Volunteer in the Fields") to Title and Content, and then duplicate Slide 4. In the title of Slide 5 (the duplicate slide), replace "Fields" with **Office**.

17. On Slide 4, insert the photo **Field Volunteer**, located in the PowerPoint1 ▸ Review folder. Resize the photo so it is 4.9 inches high, maintaining the aspect ratio, and reposition it so it is approximately centered in the space below the slide title.

18. On Slide 5, insert the photo **Office Volunteer**. Crop the top portion of the photo so that there is approximately one-half inch of wall above the top of the paintings in the photo. Resize the cropped photo so it is 5.1 inches high, maintaining the aspect ratio, and then reposition the photo as you did for the photo on Slide 4.

19. Move Slide 5 ("Volunteer in the Office") so it becomes Slide 7.

20. On Slide 9 ("Questions?"), crop the photo to the Oval shape. Increase the size of the text in the unnumbered list to 24 points, and then resize the text box to make it wide enough so that the line containing the email address fits on one line.

21. Compress all the photos in the slides to 96 ppi and delete cropped areas of pictures.

22. Display Slide 3 ("Description of Volunteer Jobs") in the Slide pane and review the information on this slide. Chris wants to include this information as notes on Slides 4 through 7 instead of displaying it as a bulleted list. He has already added the notes to Slides 5 and 6. Display Slide 4 ("Volunteer in the Fields") in the Slide pane, display the Notes pane, and then add **Field workers pull weeds and participate in harvesting produce.** in the Notes pane. Then display Slide 7 ("Volunteer in the Office") in the Slide pane, and add **Office workers use Excel to maintain volunteer schedules and use Word to publish the newsletter.** as a note on this slide.

23. Delete Slide 3 ("Description of Volunteer Jobs") and the last slide (the blank slide).

24. Correct the two spelling errors on Slide 2 and the error on Slide 7, and ignore all instances of Chris's last name. If you made any additional spelling errors, correct them as well. Save the changes to the presentation.

25. Review the slide show in Slide Show, Presenter, and Reading views.

26. View the slides in grayscale, and then print the following: the title slide as a full page-sized slide in color or in grayscale depending on your printer; Slides 1–9 as a handout on a single piece of paper with the slides in order horizontally; Slides 3 and 6 as notes pages, and Slides 1–8 as an outline. Close the presentation when you are finished.

Case Problem 1

APPLY

Data Files needed for this Case Problem: Apartment.jpg, Center.jpg, Couple.jpg, Orientation.pptx, Room.jpg

Wind Lake Assisted Living Center Sylvia Prater is director of human resources at Wind Lake Assisted Living Center in Muskego, Wisconsin. She is in charge of hiring employees and training them. She decided to create a presentation that she will give to new employees as part of their orientation. She asks you to help her create PowerPoint slides that she will use while she gives her presentation. Complete the following steps:

1. Open the presentation named **Orientation**, located in the PowerPoint1 ▶ Case1 folder included with your Data Files, and then save it as **Employee Orientation** to the drive and folder where you are storing your files.

2. Insert a new slide using the Title Slide layout. Move this new slide so it is Slide 1. Type **Employee Orientation** as the presentation title on the title slide. In the subtitle text placeholder, type your name.

3. Create a new Slide 2 with the Title and Content layout. Type **What Is Assisted Living?** as the slide title, and **Residence for people who need some assistance with daily living activities**. as the only item in the content placeholder. Change this to an unnumbered list.

4. Apply the View theme, and then apply its third variant. (If the View theme is not listed in the Themes gallery, choose any other theme and variant that uses a white or mostly white background, places the slide titles at the top of the slides, uses bullet symbols for first-level bulleted items, and positions the content in the bulleted lists starting at the top of the content text box, not the middle.)

5. On Slide 2 ("What Is Assisted Living?"), increase the size of the text of the in the text box below the slide titles to 28 points. On Slide 3 ("What Do We Provide?") increase the size of the text in the bulleted list so it is 24 points. On Slide 4 ("Our Employees") and Slide 7 ("Our Residents"), increase the size of the text in the bulleted list so that the first-level items are 28 points.

6. On Slide 2, insert the photo **Center**, located in the PowerPoint1 ▶ Case1 folder. Crop the top part of the photo off so that there is about one inch of sky above the building. Position the photo so the bottom of the photo aligns with the bottom of the slide and the left edge of the photo aligns with the right edge of the gray bar on the left. Resize the photo, maintaining the aspect ratio, so that it stretches from the gray bar on the left to the orange bar on the right. (If you used a different theme, center the photo horizontally in the space at the bottom of the slide.)

7. On Slide 3 ("What Do We Provide?"), add the speaker note **Personal care, such as bathing, grooming, and dressing, is provided by certified personal care attendants**.

8. On Slide 6 ("Living Quarters"), change the layout to the Comparison layout, which includes two content placeholders and a small text placeholder above each content placeholder. In the large content placeholder on the left, insert the photo **Room**, and in the large content placeholder on the right, insert the photo **Apartment**. Resize the Room photo so it is approximately the same height as the Apartment photo, maintaining the aspect ratio, and then reposition it, if needed, so that it is center-aligned with the caption placeholder above it and top-aligned with the Room photo on the left.

9. On Slide 5 ("Our Facility"), cut the first bulleted item, and then paste it in on Slide 6 in the small text placeholder on the left. If a blank line is added below the pasted text, delete it. On Slide 5, cut the remaining bulleted item, and then paste it on Slide 6 in the small text placeholder on the right, deleting the blank line if necessary.

10. On Slide 7 ("Our Residents"), add **Age** as the third bulleted item in the list, and then add **Minimum 60 years** and **Average 78 years** as subitems under the "Age" first-level item. Change the layout to Two Content.

11. On Slide 7, in the content placeholder, insert the photo **Couple**, located in the PowerPoint1 ▶ Case1 folder. Crop off the part of the photo to the right of the man, resize the photo so it is 5 inches high, maintaining the aspect ratio, and then reposition it as needed so that the top of the photo and the top of the content text box are aligned.

12. Compress all the photos in the presentation to 96 ppi and delete cropped portions of photos.

13. On Slide 8 ("New Employee To Do List"), change the list to a numbered list, and then add the following as a new item 2:

 2. Attend certification seminars
 1. First aid
 2. CPR

14. On Slide 8, convert the numbered list to a SmartArt diagram using the Vertical Block List layout, which is a List type of diagram. In the Text pane, click before "Confidentiality agreement," and then press the Tab key to make it a subitem under "Fill out paperwork." Change "W-4 and other personnel forms" to a second subitem under "Fill out paperwork."

15. Delete Slide 5 ("Our Facility"). Move Slide 4 ("Our Employees") so it becomes Slide 6.

16. Check the spelling in the presentation, and then read the text in the presentation carefully. On Slide 3 ("What Do We Provide?"), change the incorrect word "sight" to **site**.

17. Save the changes to the presentation, view the slide show in Presenter view, and then print the title slide as a full page slide, print Slides 2–7 as a handout using the 6 Slides Horizontal arrangement, and print Slide 3 as a notes page.

Case Problem 2

TROUBLESHOOT

Data Files needed for this Case Problem: Olympiad.pptx, Tangrams.jpg, Winner.jpg

Chandler, AZ School District Manuel Resendez is the Director of Science Curriculum Development for the Chandler, Arizona school district. One of his responsibilities is to organize an annual district-wide Math and Science Olympiad, during which school children in grades 4 through 6 can demonstrate their skills in math and science. To make sure that the teachers, coaches, parents, and volunteers at the Olympiad understand the purpose of the event and the activities the students will be doing, he plans to visit each school and give a presentation to those involved. He created a PowerPoint presentation with text describing the event, and he asks you to finish it by inserting photos from the previous year's event. Complete the following steps:

1. Open the file named **Olympiad**, located in the PowerPoint1 ▶ Case2 folder included with your Data Files, and then save it as **Math-Science Olympiad** to the drive and folder where you are storing your files. Add your name as the subtitle on Slide 1.

2. Apply the Frame theme. Change the variant to the third variant.

⚙ **Troubleshoot** 3. Evaluate the problem that the theme change caused on the title slide and fix it.

4. On Slide 3, in the first item in the bulleted list, move "9:00 a.m. to 8:00 p.m." to a new line below the first line starting with "When" without creating a new bulleted item. Do the same with "180 S. Arizona Ave." in the second item.

5. Move Slide 4 ("Rules") so it becomes Slide 10.

6. On Slide 10 ("Rules"), change the bulleted list to a numbered list. Add as a new item 4 **Only event administrators allowed on the contest floor**. Change the size of the text in the numbered list to 28 points.

7. Change the layout of Slide 9 ("Tangrams") to Two Content, and then insert the photo **Tangrams**, located in the PowerPoint1 ▸ Case2 folder, in the content placeholder. Increase the size of the picture, maintaining the aspect ratio, and reposition it so it better fills the space on the right.

8. Change the layout of Slide 11 ("Awards") to Two Content, and then insert the photo **Winner**, located in the PowerPoint1 ▸ Case2 folder, in the content placeholder.

☼ **Troubleshoot** 9. One of the slides contains information that should be explained orally rather than presented as a list. Review the presentation to identify this slide and change that information to a speaker note on that slide. Make any other adjustments necessary to make this an effective slide.

☼ **Troubleshoot** 10. Review the presentation to identify the slide that contains information that is repeated in the presentation and delete that slide.

☼ **Troubleshoot** 11. Consider how changing the theme in Step 2 affected the readability of the lists on the slides. Make the appropriate changes to the slides.

12. Compress all the photos in the presentation to 96 ppi, check the spelling in the presentation, and then save the changes. (*Hint*: If the E-mail (96 ppi) option in the Compress Pictures dialog box is gray and not available, close the dialog box, select a different picture, and try again.)

13. View the slide show in Presenter view, zooming in on the pictures of the different events.

14. Print the title slide as a full page slide in grayscale. Print Slides 1–3 and Slides 5–10 as an outline by typing **1-3, 5-10** in the Slides box.

Case Problem 3

CREATE

Data Files needed for this Case Problem: Floating Houses.jpg, Karl.jpg, Peru.pptx, Region1.jpg – Region8 Right.jpg

Karl Benson Photography Karl Benson is a photographer who specializes in scenic photos. He also teaches a course for beginner photographers. Karl recently returned from a trip to Peru. On his trip, he was very interested to learn that Peru has eight distinct regions with different geography and climates. Karl asks you to create a presentation that contains some of the photos he took on his trip. He will not be giving an oral presentation using this file. Instead, he wants his students to view the slides on their own, so he prepared a file with text describing the photos and the regions in Peru. Slides 2 through 10 of the final presentation are shown in Figure 1-46. Refer to Figure 1-46 as you complete the following steps:

Figure 1-46   Slides 2-11 of Peruvian Regions presentation

Maps used with permission of Microsoft Corporation; Photos courtesy of S. Scott Zimmerman

1. Open the file named **Peru**, located in the PowerPoint1 ▸ Case3 folder included with your Data Files, and then save it as **Peruvian Regions** to the drive and folder where you are storing your files.

2. Add a new slide with the Title Slide layout, and move it so it is Slide 1. Type **The Eight Regions of Peru** as the title and your name as the subtitle.

3. Change the variant of the Office theme to the third variant.

4. On Slide 2, drag the map of Peru on top of the map of South America as in Figure 1-46. (Use the left edges of the maps as a guide.) Resize the title text box to 4" x 5", change the font size of the text in the title text box to 32 points, and then position it on the left side of the slide, approximately centered vertically.

5. Change the layout of Slides 3 through 7 to Picture with Caption. On all five slides, change the font size of the captions in the text boxes below the titles from 16 points to 18 points.

6. Use the Region numbers on the slides to reorder Slides 3 through 10 in order by Region, starting with Region 1 on Slide 3 and ending with Region 8 on Slide 10.

7. On Slides 3 through 10, insert the photos provided in the PowerPoint1 ▸ Case3 folder that correspond to the region numbers described on each slide. Refer to Figure 1-46 as needed.

8. On Slide 11 ("Want More?"), insert the **Floating Houses** photo, located in the PowerPoint1 ▸ Case3 folder, in the content placeholder on the left and the **Karl** photo, located in the PowerPoint1 ▸ Case3 folder, in the content placeholder on the right.

9. Karl needs to post this presentation to a website that has file size limitations, so he needs the presentation file size to be as small as possible, even though he realizes that compressing the photos will reduce their quality. Compress all the photos in the presentation to 96 ppi.

10. Save the changes to the presentation, and then view the presentation in Reading view.

Case Problem 4

CHALLENGE

Data Files needed for this Case Problem: Cargo.jpg, Corpus Christi.jpg, Freight.jpg, Loading1.mp4, Loading2.mp4, Submit.jpg, URL.jpg, Woman.jpg

Corpus Christi Freight Transport, Inc. Quentin Hershey is a customer relations representative for Corpus Christi Freight Transport, Inc., a large shipping company headquartered in Corpus Christi, Texas, and with offices in Argentina and Sydney. He wants you to help him create a PowerPoint presentation to explain features of the company and the services it offers. Quentin wants to give the presentation to organizations that require shipping services to U.S. waterways and to foreign ports. Complete the following steps:

⊕ **Explore** 1. Create a new presentation using the Striped black border presentation template from Office.com. (*Hint*: Use **striped black border** as the search term. If you get no results, type **white** as the search term, and then choose a template with a simple theme.)

2. Replace the title text on the title slide with **Corpus Christi Freight Transport, Inc**. and replace the subtitle text with your name. Save the presentation as **Freight Transport** to the drive and folder where you are storing your files.

3. Delete all the slides except the title slide.

4. Add a new Slide 2 with the Two Content layout. Type **Who We Are** as the title, and then type the following as a bulleted list in the left content placeholder:
   - **International shipping company**
   - **Licensed by Federal Maritime Commission**
   - **Bonded as international freight transporter**
   - **Registered as cosmetic freight forwarder**

5. On Slide 2, in the right content placeholder, insert the photo **Freight**, located in the PowerPoint1 ▸ Case4 folder included with your Data Files. Resize it, maintaining the aspect ratio, so it is 4.8 inches high, and then reposition it as needed so that the middle of the photo and the middle of the bulleted list text box are aligned.

6. Add a new Slide 3 with the Title and Content layout. Type **Online Scheduling** as the title, and then type the following as a bulleted list in the content placeholder:

- **Register at www.freight.example.com**
- **Enter type and amount**
- **Submit information**
- **Receive confirmation within 24 hours**

7. On Slide 3, remove the link formatting from the website address in the first bulleted item.

8. On Slide 3, convert the bulleted list to a SmartArt diagram with the Vertical Picture List layout, which is a List type of diagram.

⊕ **Explore** 9. Change the colors of the diagram to Colored Fill – Accent 3 by using the Change Colors button in the SmartArt Styles group on the SMARTART TOOLS DESIGN tab.

⊕ **Explore** 10. Insert the following pictures, located in the PowerPoint1 ▸ Case4 folder, in the picture placeholders in the SmartArt diagram, in order from top to bottom: **URL, Cargo, Submit,** and **Woman**.

11. Add a new Slide 4 with the Two Content layout. Type **U.S. Office** as the title. In the content placeholder on the left, type the following as an unnumbered list without extra space between the lines:

Corpus Christi Freight

2405 Shoreline Road

Corpus Christi, TX 78401

12. On Slide 4, add the phone number **(361) 555-1254** and the website address **www.freight.example.com** as new items in the unnumbered list. Press the spacebar after typing the website address to format it as a link.

13. On Slide 4, add the photo **Corpus Christi**, located in the PowerPoint1 ▸ Case4 folder, to the content placeholder on the right. Resize it so it is 3.9 inches high, maintaining the aspect ratio, and then position it so the top edge aligns with the top edge of the text box on the left and there is approximately one inch of space between the right side of the photo and the right edge of the slide.

14. Compress all the photos in the presentation to 96 ppi, and then save the changes.

15. Add a new Slide 5 with the Comparison layout. Type **How Are Containers Loaded?** as the title, type **First a container is selected** in the small text placeholder on the left, and then type **Then it is transported to the ship and loaded** in the small text placeholder on the right. Move this slide so it becomes Slide 4.

⊕ **Explore** 16. On Slide 4 ("How Are Containers Loaded?"), insert the video **Loading1**, located in the PowerPoint1 ▸ Case4 folder, in the left content placeholder, and insert the video **Loading2**, located in the same folder, in the right content placeholder. (The video objects might be filled with black when they are inserted.)

⊕ **Explore** 17. Open the Info tab in Backstage view. Use the Compress Media command to compress the videos to the lowest quality possible. Use the Back button at the top of the navigation bar in Backstage view to return to Normal view.

18. Run the slide show in Slide Show view. When Slide 4 ("How Are Containers Loaded?") appears, point to each video to make a Play button appear, and then click the Play button to play each video. Note that there is no sound in the videos. (*Hint*: Point to the video as it plays to display the play bar again.)

POWERPOINT

OBJECTIVES

Session 2.1
- Apply a theme used in another presentation
- Insert online pictures
- Insert shapes
- Format shapes and pictures
- Rotate and flip objects
- Create a table
- Modify and format a table
- Insert symbols
- Change the proofing language

Session 2.2
- Apply and modify transitions
- Animate objects and bulleted lists
- Change how an animation starts
- Add video and modify playback options
- Understand animation effects applied to videos
- Trim video and set a poster frame
- Compress media
- Add footers and headers

Adding Media and Special Effects

Using Media in a Presentation for a Norwegian Tourism Company

Case | *Essential Norway Tours*

Inger Halvorsen was born and raised in Myrdal, Norway, not far from the Flåm Railway that travels through the beautiful mountains of central Norway. She attended college in the United States and graduated with a degree in geography. She then returned to her home country and started a travel agency, Essential Norway Tours, in Oslo. She hired a photographer to take photos and video of scenes from one of her tours from Hønefoss to Myrdal on the Bergen Train, from Myrdal to Flåm on the Flåm Train, and by boat through Aurlandsfjord and Nærøfjords, two of the most beautiful fjords in Norway. She wants to include the photos and video in a presentation that she wants you to give to U.S. travel agents and others who might be interested in booking trips through her agency.

In this tutorial, you will modify a presentation to highlight the beautiful scenery visitors will enjoy when they go on an Essential Norway tour. You will add formatting and special effects to photos and shapes, add transitions and animations to slides, and add and modify video.

STARTING DATA FILES

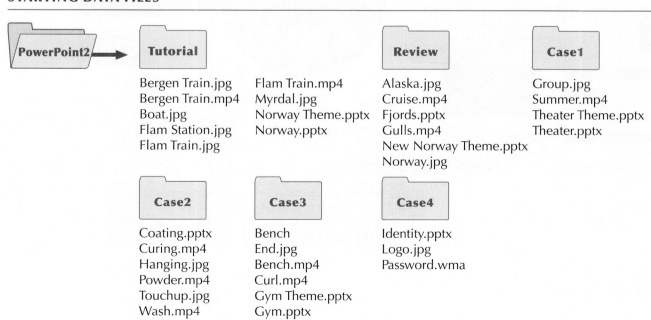

PowerPoint2 → Tutorial		Review	Case1
Bergen Train.jpg	Flam Train.mp4	Alaska.jpg	Group.jpg
Bergen Train.mp4	Myrdal.jpg	Cruise.mp4	Summer.mp4
Boat.jpg	Norway Theme.pptx	Fjords.pptx	Theater Theme.pptx
Flam Station.jpg	Norway.pptx	Gulls.mp4	Theater.pptx
Flam Train.jpg		New Norway Theme.pptx	
		Norway.jpg	

Case2	Case3	Case4
Coating.pptx	Bench	Identity.pptx
Curing.mp4	End.jpg	Logo.jpg
Hanging.jpg	Bench.mp4	Password.wma
Powder.mp4	Curl.mp4	
Touchup.jpg	Gym Theme.pptx	
Wash.mp4	Gym.pptx	
Welding.jpg	Military.mp4	

Session 2.1 Visual Overview:

Use the Shape Fill button to change the **fill**, the formatting of the area inside the shape.

To change the color, weight (thickness), or style (solid line, dashed line, and so on) of a shape's border, use the Shape Outline button.

The DRAWING TOOLS FORMAT tab appears when a drawing or a text box—including the slide's title and content placeholders—is selected.

The Shape Height box contains the height measurement of the selected shape, and the Shape Width box contains the width measurement.

To insert a shape, click a shape in the Shapes gallery.

Click the Shape Effects button to add special effects, such as a shadow, reflection, glow, soft edges, beveled edges, or a 3D rotation, to a shape.

You can drag a **rotate handle** to rotate an object, or you can click the Rotate button to open a menu of Rotate and Flip commands.

Use the Shape Styles gallery to apply a **style**, which is a combination of several formats, to a shape.

Draw the yellow **adjustment handle** on a shape to change its proportions without changing the size of the shape.

Like text boxes and pictures, you can drag a sizing handle to resize shapes.

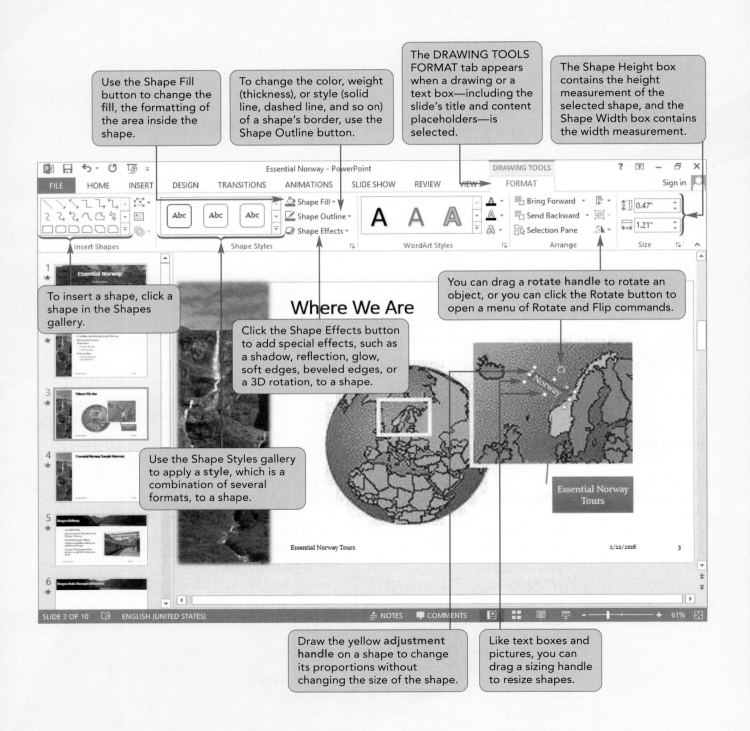

Formatting Graphics

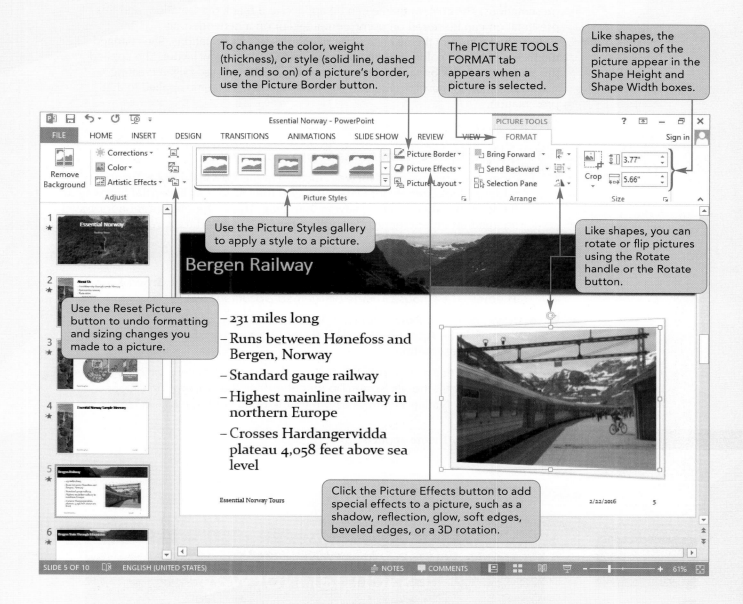

To change the color, weight (thickness), or style (solid line, dashed line, and so on) of a picture's border, use the Picture Border button.

The PICTURE TOOLS FORMAT tab appears when a picture is selected.

Like shapes, the dimensions of the picture appear in the Shape Height and Shape Width boxes.

Use the Picture Styles gallery to apply a style to a picture.

Like shapes, you can rotate or flip pictures using the Rotate handle or the Rotate button.

Use the Reset Picture button to undo formatting and sizing changes you made to a picture.

Click the Picture Effects button to add special effects to a picture, such as a shadow, reflection, glow, soft edges, beveled edges, or a 3D rotation.

Applying a Theme Used in Another Presentation

As you learned earlier, an installed theme can be applied by clicking one in the Themes group on the DESIGN tab. An installed theme is actually a special type of file that is stored with PowerPoint program files. You can also apply themes that are applied to any other presentation stored on your computer. For example, many companies want to promote their brand through their presentations, so they hire presentation design professionals to create custom themes that can be applied to all company presentations. The custom theme can be applied to a blank presentation, and this presentation can be stored on users' computers or on a network drive.

Inger had a custom theme created for her company's presentations. She changed the theme fonts and colors, modified layouts, and created a new layout. She applied this theme to a blank presentation that she sent to you. Inger also began creating her presentation for travel agents, and she wants the custom theme applied to that presentation.

To apply a theme from another presentation:

1. Open the presentation **Norway**, located in the **PowerPoint2 ▸ Tutorial** folder included with your Data Files, and then save it as **Essential Norway** in the location where you are saving your files. This is the presentation for travel agents that Inger created. The Office theme is applied to it. You need to apply Inger's custom theme to it.

2. On the ribbon, click the **DESIGN** tab.

3. In the Themes group, click the **More** button, and then click **Browse for Themes**. The Choose Theme or Themed Document dialog box opens.

4. Navigate to the **PowerPoint2 ▸ Tutorial** folder, click **Norway Theme**, and then click the **Apply** button. The custom theme is applied to the Essential Norway presentation.

5. In the Themes group, point to the first theme in the gallery, which is the current theme. Its ScreenTip identifies it as the Norway Theme. See Figure 2-1. Notice that this custom theme does not have any variants.

| Figure 2-1 | Custom Norway Theme applied |

Photos courtesy of S. Scott Zimmerman

6. Click the **HOME** tab, and then on Slide 1 (the title slide), click the title text.

7. In the Font group, click the **Font** arrow. Notice that the theme fonts for the Norway theme are Calibri Light and Constantia. This is different from the Office theme, which uses Calibri for the body text.

8. In the Slides group, click the **Layout** button. The Layout gallery appears. The custom layouts that Inger created are listed in the gallery, as shown in Figure 2-2.

Figure 2-2 **Custom layouts in the Norway Theme**

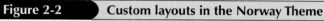

Photos courtesy of S. Scott Zimmerman

Notice the customized Title Slide layout has a photo as a slide background, the Title and Content customized layout has a photo along the left edge of the slide of water running down a cliff, and the customized Two Content layout includes a photo under the slide title. Inger also provided an additional custom layout called Photo Title & Content, which is for a slide with a title and one content placeholder.

9. Press the **Esc** key to close the Layout gallery.

When you applied the custom theme from the Norway Theme presentation, the title slide and the slides with the Title and Content layout and Two Content layout were changed to use the customized versions of these layouts. Slides 4 and 6 have the Two Content layout applied and contain information about the Bergen and Flåm railways. Slides 5 and 7 have the Title and Content layout applied. Currently they only contain a title, but later you will add videos related to the Bergen and Flåm trains to these slides. Inger wants you to change the layout of these two slides to the new Photo Title & Content layout so they better match the slides with the Two Content layouts.

To apply a custom layout to Slides 5 and 7:

1. Display **Slide 5** ("Bergen Train Through Mountains") in the Slide pane.

2. In the Slides group, click the **Layout** button. The Layout gallery appears.

3. Click the **Photo Title & Content** layout. The custom layout is applied to Slide 5.

4. Apply the **Photo Title & Content** layout to Slide 7 ("Flåm Train in Station").

5. Save your changes.

INSIGHT

Saving a Presentation as a Theme

If you need to use a custom theme frequently, you can save a presentation file as an Office Theme file. A theme file is a different file type than a presentation file. You can then store this file so that it appears in the Themes gallery on the DESIGN tab. To save a custom theme, click the FILE tab, click Save As in the navigation bar, and then click the Browse button to open the Save As dialog box. To change the file type to Office Theme, click the Save as type arrow, and then click Office Theme. This changes the current folder in the Save As dialog box to the Document Themes folder, which is a folder created on the hard drive when Office is installed and where the installed themes are stored. If you save a custom theme to the Document Themes folder, that theme will be listed in its own row above the installed themes in the Themes gallery. (You need to click the More button in the Themes gallery to see this row.) You can also change the folder location and save the custom theme to any location on your computer or network or to a folder on your SkyDrive. If you do this, the theme will not appear in the Themes gallery, but you can still access it using the Browse for Themes command on the Themes gallery menu.

Inserting Online Pictures

In addition to adding pictures stored on your computer or network to slides, you can also add pictures stored on websites. To do this, you click the Online Pictures button in a content placeholder or in the Images group on the INSERT tab. When you do this, the Insert Pictures window opens, in which you can choose to search for an image on Office.com or use the Bing search engine to search for images across the Internet. The images stored on Office.com are often called clip art, which are images stored in collections so that you can easily locate and use them.

After selecting where you want to search (Office.com or the Internet using the Bing search engine), click in the Search box next to your choice, and then type keywords. **Keywords** are words or phrases that describe an image. When you use the Bing search engine, you get the same results that you would get if you were to type keywords in the Search box on the Bing home page in your browser.

Images stored on Office.com have keywords directly associated with them. For example, a photo of a train might have the keywords "train" and "engine" associated with it. If the photo is a train going over a bridge, additional keywords might be "bridge" and "trestle." The more keywords you use, the narrower (more specific) your search results will be; conversely, to broaden your search, use fewer keywords.

Inger wants you to add a new Slide 3 to the presentation and then insert a map of Norway. You'll search for an image of this on <u>Office.com</u>.

To insert a picture of a map from Office.com:

1. Display **Slide 2** ("About Us") in the Slide pane, and then in the Slides group, click the **New Slide** button. A new Slide 3 is inserted with the same layout as Slide 2, Title and Content.

2. Type **Where We Are** as the slide title.

3. In the content placeholder, click the **Online Pictures** button. The Insert Pictures window opens with the insertion point in the Office.com Clip Art search box. See Figure 2-3.

Figure 2-3   Insert Pictures window

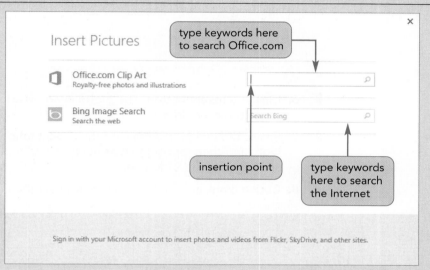

4. In the **Office.com Clip Art** search box, type **Norway map**, and then click the **Search** button. After a moment, images that match your keywords appear in the window.

5. Click the drawing of a globe with Scandinavia pulled out in a detail map. The keywords associated with the selected image and the image's measurements in pixels are in the bottom-left corner of the window, as shown in Figure 2-4.

Figure 2-4   **Images found on Office.com in Insert Pictures window**

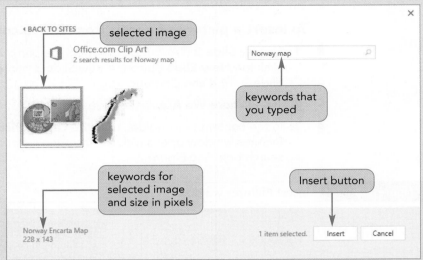

Images used with permission of Microsoft Corporation

6. Click the **Insert** button. The globe image is added to the slide in place of the content placeholder.

7. Resize the image, maintaining the aspect ratio, so that it is about five inches high, and then reposition it as necessary to roughly center it in the white space below the slide title.

8. Click a blank area of the slide to deselect the image, and then save your changes.

PROSKILLS

Written Communication: Respecting Intellectual Property

Make sure you understand and abide by copyright laws. If you use someone else's photograph, illustration, video, music, diagram, or chart, or if you use someone else's data to create your own visuals, give proper credit. Students can, for educational purposes only, use copyrighted material on a one-time basis without getting permission from the copyright holder. On the other hand, if you work for a business or nonprofit organization, much stricter copyright laws apply. You must obtain explicit permission from the copyright owner, and in some cases pay a fee to that person or company. You may use all the images on Office.com in your presentations as long as you are not creating the presentation for commercial purposes. If you need to use an image for a commercial purpose, you need to check to see who owns the image. To do this, go to Office.com, search for the image there, point to the image you want to use, and then click View Details. The image appears on a new webpage with information about the image listed on the right. At the top of this list of information, the name of the copyright holder appears, such as Fotalia or iStockphoto. Contact the copyright holder directly for permission to use the image. If there is no copyright holder listed, the image is owned by Microsoft and you cannot use it for commercial purposes. If you use the Bing search engine when you insert an online picture, you should go to the website from which you are copying the photo and determine if you need to get permission to use the image.

Inserting Shapes

You can add many shapes to a slide, including lines, rectangles, stars, and more. To draw a shape, click the Shapes button in the Illustrations group on the INSERT tab, click a shape in the gallery, and then click and drag to draw the shape in the size you want. Like any object, a shape can be resized after you insert it.

You've already had a little experience with one shape—a text box, which is a shape specifically designed to contain text. You can add additional text boxes to slides using the Text Box shape. You can also add text to any shape you place on a slide.

Inger wants you to add a few labels to the map image. First, she wants you to add a label to identify Norway in the detail map of Scandinavia.

To insert and position an arrow shape with text on Slide 3:

1. With **Slide 3** ("Where We Are") in the Slide pane, click the **INSERT** tab, and then in the Illustrations group, click the **Shapes** button. The Shapes gallery opens. See Figure 2-5. The gallery is organized into nine categories of shapes, plus the Recently Used Shapes group at the top.

Figure 2-5   Shapes gallery

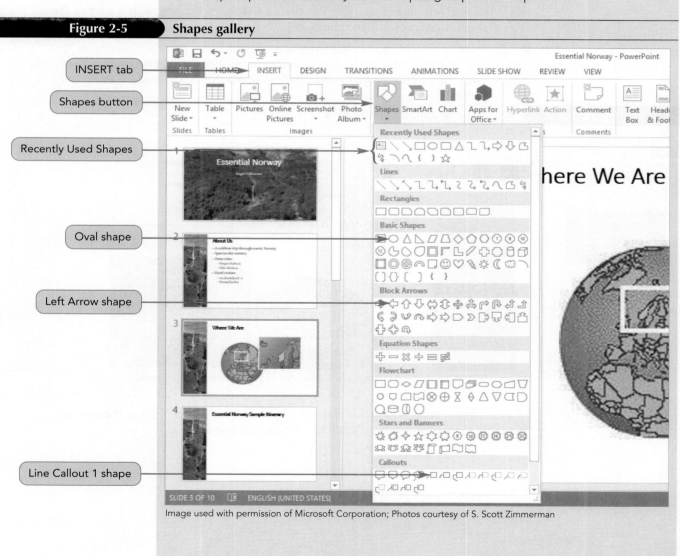

Image used with permission of Microsoft Corporation; Photos courtesy of S. Scott Zimmerman

2. Under Block Arrows, click the **Left Arrow** shape ⇦. The gallery closes and the pointer changes to ┼.

3. On the slide, click above the top-left corner of the pop-out, detail map, and then drag to the right to create an arrow approximately 1¼-inches long and ½-inch high.

   A blue, left-pointing arrow appears. (Don't worry about the exact placement or size of the arrow; you will move it later.) Note that the DRAWING TOOLS FORMAT tab is the active tab on the ribbon.

4. With the shape selected, type **Norway**. The text you type appears in the arrow. It might not all fit on one line and it may be too tall to fit inside the arrow.

5. If necessary, drag the right-middle sizing handle on the end of the arrow to the right to lengthen the arrow until the word "Norway" fits on one line.

6. If necessary, drag the bottom-middle sizing handle down until the arrow is tall enough to display all of the text. Now you need to position the arrow shape on the map. When you drag a shape with text, it is similar to dragging a text box, which means you need to drag a border of the shape or a part of the shape that does not contain text.

7. Position the pointer on the arrow shape so that the pointer changes to ⬩, and then drag the arrow shape on top of the map so that it points to the right-lower side of the yellow area in the detail map of Scandinavia. See Figure 2-6.

> Make sure you drag the pointer, not just click it. Otherwise the inserted shape will be tiny.

| Figure 2-6 | Arrow shape with text on Slide 3 |

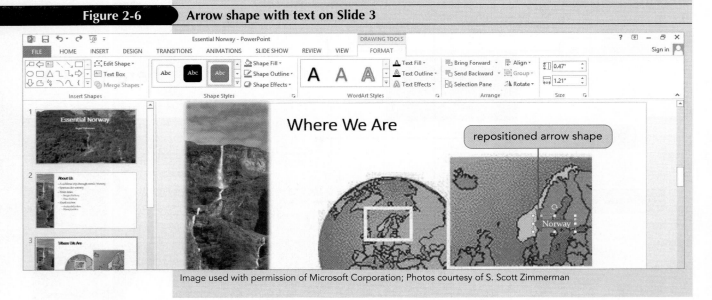

Image used with permission of Microsoft Corporation; Photos courtesy of S. Scott Zimmerman

Next, Inger wants you to add a shape to point to the part of Norway that she is featuring in the presentation. You'll use a callout shape for this.

To insert and position a callout shape with text on Slide 3:

TIP

You can also insert a shape using the Shapes gallery in the Drawing group on the HOME tab.

▶ **1.** On the ribbon, click the **INSERT** tab.

▶ **2.** In the Illustrations group, click the **Shapes** button. The Shapes gallery opens.

▶ **3.** Under Callouts, click the **Line Callout 1** shape.

▶ **4.** Below the detail map, drag to create a box approximately two inches wide and one inch high, and then type **Essential Norway Tours**.

▶ **5.** Resize the square part of the callout shape, if necessary, so that the text "Essential Norway" fits on one line.

▶ **6.** Save your changes.

Formatting Objects

Recall that both shapes and pictures, such as photos and clip art, are treated as objects in PowerPoint. The PICTURE TOOLS and DRAWING TOOLS FORMAT tabs contain tools for formatting these objects. For both shapes and pictures, you can use these tools to apply borders or outlines, special effects such as drop shadows and reflections, and styles. You can also resize and rotate or flip these objects. Some formatting tools are available only to one or the other type of object. For example, the Remove Background tool is available only to pictures, and the Fill command is available only to shapes. Refer to the Session 2.1 Visual Overview for more information about the commands on the FORMAT tabs.

Formatting Shapes

You can modify the fill of a shape by filling it with a color, a gradient (shading in which one color blends into another or varies from one shade to another), a textured pattern, or a picture. When you add a shape to a slide, the default fill is the Accent 1 color from the set of theme colors, and the default outline is a darker shade of that color.

The default blue of the arrow shape blends into the blue color of the image, so you'll change it.

To change the fill of the arrow and the style of the callout:

▶ **1.** Click the **Norway** arrow, and then click the **DRAWING TOOLS FORMAT** tab, if necessary.

▶ **2.** In the Shape Styles group, click the **Shape Fill button arrow**. The Shape Fill menu opens. See Figure 2-7. You can fill a shape with a color, a picture, a gradient, or a texture, or you can remove the fill by clicking No Fill.

Figure 2-7   **Shape Fill button menu**

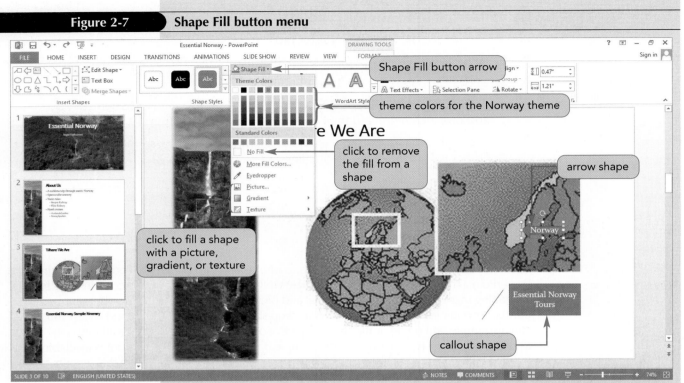

Image used with permission of Microsoft Corporation; Photos courtesy of S. Scott Zimmerman

> **3.** Under Theme Colors, click **Red, Accent 2**. The shape fill of the selected arrow changes to the red color. Next, you'll apply a style to the callout shape.

> **4.** Click the callout shape, and then in the Shape Styles group, click the **More** button. The Shape Styles gallery opens.

> **5.** Click the **Moderate Effect – Red, Accent 2** style. The style, which fills the shape with gradient shades of red and changes the shape outline to the Red, Accent 2 color, is applied to the callout shape.

On some shapes, you can drag the yellow adjustment handle to change the shape's proportions. For instance, if you dragged the adjustment handle on the arrow shape, you would change the size of the arrow head relative to the size of the arrow. The callout shape has two adjustment handles, one on either end of the line that extends out from the part of the shape that contains text. You can drag these adjustment handles to more clearly identify what the callout is pointing to.

You need to position the callout shape and adjust the line so that the line is pointing to the area of Norway highlighted in the presentation.

To move and adjust the callout shape and change its outline weight:

▶ **1.** Drag the callout shape so that the right edge is aligned with the right side of the map image and there is approximately one-quarter inch space between the callout and the bottom of the detail portion of the map.

▶ **2.** Drag the yellow adjustment handle on the left end of the callout line so that it points to the lower-left portion of Norway on the map. The callout line is hard to see on top of the map, so you will make the shape's outline thicker by changing its weight.

▶ **3.** In the Shape Styles group, click the **Shape Outline button arrow**, point to **Weight**, and then click **3 pt**. Compare your screen to Figure 2-8 and make any adjustments necessary to match the figure.

Figure 2-8   **Formatted and positioned callout shape**

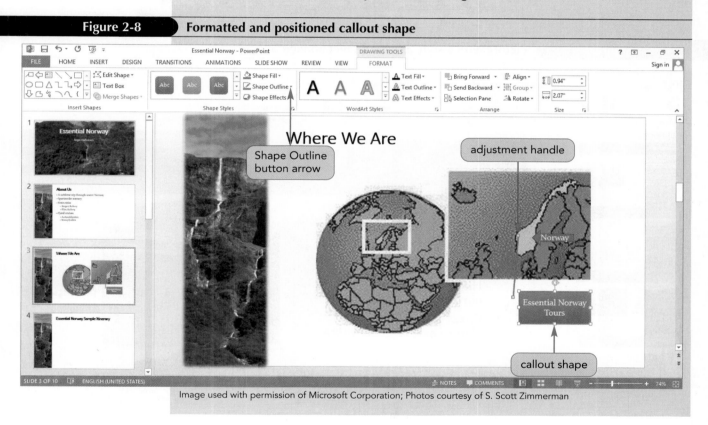

Image used with permission of Microsoft Corporation; Photos courtesy of S. Scott Zimmerman

Formatting Pictures

You can format photos as well as shapes. To format photos, you use the tools on the PICTURE TOOLS FORMAT tab.

Inger wants you to format the pictures on Slides 5 and 7 by adding a frame and a 3-D effect. To create the frame, you could apply a thick outline, or you can apply one of the styles that includes a frame.

To format the photos on Slides 5 and 7:

TIP

Click the Reset Picture button in the Adjust group on the PICTURE TOOLS FORMAT tab to remove formatting from a picture or resize the picture to its original size.

1. Display **Slide 5** ("Bergen Railway") in the Slide pane, click the photo of the train, and then click the **PICTURE TOOLS FORMAT** tab.

2. In the Picture Styles group, click the **Beveled Matte, White** style. This style applies a 15-point white border with a slight beveled edge and a slight shadow to the photo. Now you need to add a 3-D rotation to the picture.

3. In the Picture Styles group, click the **Picture Effects** button, and then point to **3-D Rotation**. A gallery of 3-D rotation options opens.

4. Under Perspective, click the **Perspective Left** option. The picture rotates slightly to the left. See Figure 2-9. You need to apply the same formatting to the photo on Slide 7. You can repeat the same formatting steps or you can copy the formatting.

Figure 2-9	Picture with a style and 3-D effect applied

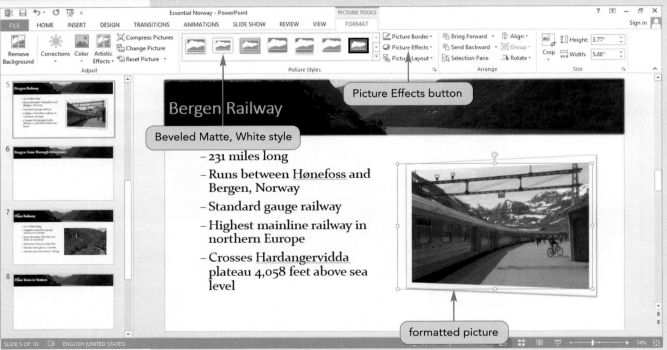

Photos courtesy of S. Scott Zimmerman

5. With the photo on Slide 5 still selected, click the **HOME** tab.

6. In the Clipboard group, click the **Format Painter** button, and then move the pointer to the Slide pane. The pointer changes to ⬚.

7. In the Slides tab, click the **Slide 7** thumbnail, and then in the Slide pane, click the photo next to the bulleted list. The style and 3-D rotation formatting is copied from the photo on Slide 5 and applied to the photo on Slide 7.

8. Save your changes.

Rotating and Flipping Objects

You can rotate and flip any object on a slide. To flip an object, you use the Flip commands on the Rotate button menu in the Arrange group on the DRAWING TOOLS FORMAT tab. To rotate an object, you can use the Rotate commands on the Rotate button menu to rotate objects in 90-degree increments. You can also drag the Rotate handle that appears above the top-middle sizing handle when the object is selected to rotate it to any position that you want, using the center of the object as a pivot point.

The Norway arrow would look better if it were pointing to the west coast of the country on the map. To correctly position the Norway arrow, you first need to flip it.

To flip the arrow shape on Slide 3:

1. Display **Slide 3** ("Where We Are") in the Slide pane, and then click the **Norway** arrow.

TIP

You can also click the Arrange button in the Drawing group on the HOME tab to access the Rotate and Flip commands.

2. Position the pointer on the Rotate handle ⟳ so that the pointer changes to ⟳, and then drag the Rotate handle ⟳ until the Norway arrow is pointing to the right. The arrow is pointing in the correct direction, but the text is upside-down.

3. Undo the rotation, and then click the **DRAWING TOOLS FORMAT** tab.

4. In the Arrange group, click the **Rotate** button. The Rotate menu opens. See Figure 2-10.

Figure 2-10	Rotate button menu

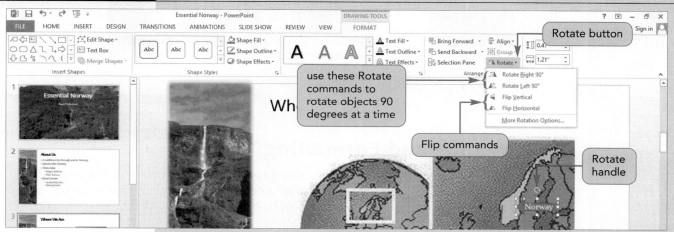

Image used with permission of Microsoft Corporation; Photos courtesy of S. Scott Zimmerman

5. Click **Flip Horizontal**. The arrow flips horizontally and is now pointing right. Unlike when you rotated the arrow so that it pointed right, the text is still right-side up.

Now you need to rotate and reposition the Norway arrow so that it is pointing to the west coast of Norway on the map.

To rotate the arrow shape and reposition it:

▶ **1.** Position the pointer on the Rotate handle so that the pointer changes to ↻.

▶ **2.** Drag the Rotate handle to the right to rotate the arrow so that it points down and to the right at approximately a 45-degree angle.

▶ **3.** Drag the Norway arrow so it is pointing down to approximately the center of Norway's west coast.

▶ **4.** Click a blank area of the slide to deselect the shape, compare your screen to Figure 2-11, and then make any adjustments needed to match the figure.

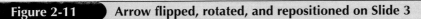

| Figure 2-11 | Arrow flipped, rotated, and repositioned on Slide 3 |

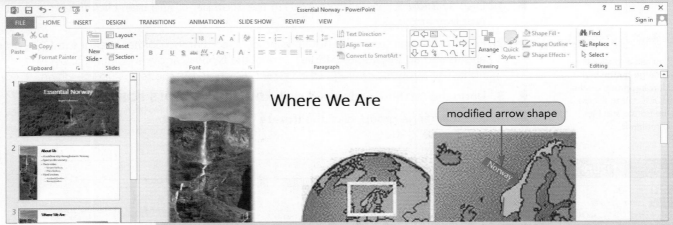

Image used with permission of Microsoft Corporation; Photos courtesy of S. Scott Zimmerman

▶ **5.** Save your changes.

Creating and Formatting Tables

A **table** is information arranged in horizontal rows and vertical columns. The area where a row and column intersect is called a **cell**. Each cell contains one piece of information. A table's structure is indicated by borders, which are lines that outline the rows and columns.

Creating and Adding Data to a Table

Inger wants you to add a table to Slide 4 to list a typical tour itinerary. This table will have three columns—one to describe the activity, one to list the time that the activity starts, and one to list notes.

Inserting a Table

- In a content placeholder, click the Insert Table button; or, click the INSERT tab on the ribbon, click the Table button in the Tables group, and then click Insert Table.
- Specify the numbers of columns and rows.
- Click the OK button.

or

- On the ribbon, click the INSERT tab, and then in the Tables group, click the Table button to open a grid.
- Click a box in the grid to create a table of that size.

Inger hasn't decided how much data to include in the table, so she asks you to start by creating a table with four rows.

To add a table to Slide 4:

1. Display **Slide 4** ("Essential Norway Sample Itinerary") in the Slide pane.

2. Click the **INSERT** tab, and then in the Tables group, click the **Table** button. A menu opens with a grid of squares above three commands.

3. Point to the squares on the grid, and without clicking the mouse button, move the pointer down and to the right. As you move the pointer, the label above the grid indicates how large the table will be, and a preview of the table appears on the slide. See Figure 2-12.

Figure 2-12	Inserting a 3x4 table on Slide 3

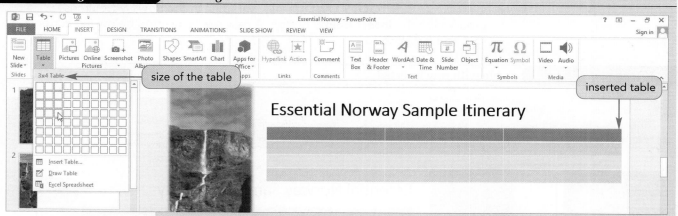

Photos courtesy of S. Scott Zimmerman

4. When the label above the grid indicates 3x4 Table, click to insert a table with three columns and four rows. A selection border appears around the table, and the insertion point is in the first cell in the first row.

Now you're ready to fill the blank cells with the information about the tour. To enter data in a table, you click in the cells in which you want to enter data, and then start typing. You can also use the Tab and arrow keys to move from one cell to another.

To add data to the table:

▶ 1. In the first cell in the first row, type **Activity**. The text you typed appears in the first cell.

▶ 2. Press the **Tab** key. The insertion point moves to the second cell in the first row.

▶ 3. Type **Time**, press the **Tab** key, type **Notes**, and then press the **Tab** key. The insertion point is in the first cell in the second row.

▶ 4. In the first cell in the second row, type **Bergen train from Honefoss**, press the **Tab** key, and then type **8:13 a.m.**

▶ 5. Click in the first cell in the third row, type **Arrive Myrdal for lunch, shopping**, press the **Tab** key, and then type **11:41 a.m.**

▶ 6. Click in the first cell in the last row, type **Flam train from Myrdal**, press the **Tab** key, and then type **1:11 p.m.**

Inserting and Deleting Rows and Columns

You can modify the table by adding or deleting rows and columns. You need to add more rows to the table for additional itinerary items. Inger also wants to make the table a little more interesting by adding a new first column in which you will insert pictures related to that part of the itinerary.

To insert rows in the table:

▶ 1. Make sure the insertion point is in the last row in the table.

▶ 2. Click the **TABLE TOOLS LAYOUT** tab, and then in the Rows & Columns group, click the **Insert Below** button. A new row is inserted below the current row. See Figure 2-13.

Figure 2-13 | **Table with row inserted**

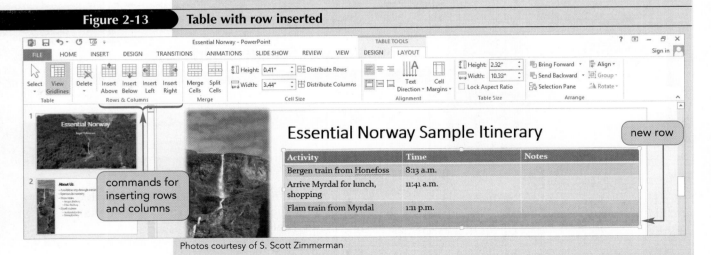

Photos courtesy of S. Scott Zimmerman

   3. Click in the first cell in the new last row, type **Arrive Flam**, and then press the **Tab** key.

   4. Type **2:05 p.m.**, and then press the **Tab** key. The insertion point is in the last cell in the last row.

   5. Press the **Tab** key. A new row is created and the insertion point is in the first cell in the new row.

   6. Type **Check in at hotel**, press the **Tab** key, and then type **4:30 p.m.** You need to insert a row above the last row.

   7. In the Rows & Columns group, click the **Insert Above** button. A new row is inserted above the current row.

   8. Click in the first cell in the new row, type **Fjord cruises from Flam**, press the **Tab** key, and then type **2:20 p.m.**

Inger decided she doesn't want to add notes to the table, so you'll delete the last column. She also decides that the information in the last row in the table about checking into the hotel isn't needed, so you'll delete that row.

To delete a column and a row in the table:

   1. Click in any cell in the last column. This is the column you will delete.

   2. On the TABLE TOOLS LAYOUT tab, in the Rows & Columns group, click the **Delete** button. The Delete button menu opens.

   3. Click **Delete Columns**. The current column is deleted, and the entire table is selected.

   4. Click in any cell in the last row. This is the row you want to delete.

   5. In the Rows & Columns group, click the **Delete** button, and then click **Delete Rows.**

   6. Click a blank area of the slide to deselect the table. See Figure 2-14.

Figure 2-14   **Table after adding and deleting rows and deleting the third column**

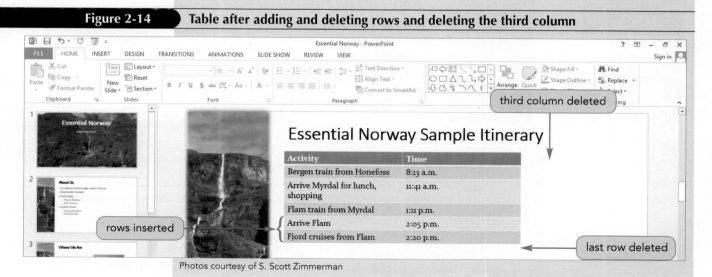

Photos courtesy of S. Scott Zimmerman

Formatting a Table

After you insert data into a table, you need to think about how the table looks and whether the table will be readable for the audience. As with any text, you can change the font, size, or color, and as with shapes and pictures, you can apply a style to a table. You can also change how the text fits in the table cells by changing the height of rows and the width of columns. You can also customize the formatting of the table by changing the border and fill of table cells.

You need to make the table text larger so that an audience will be able to read it. You will also increase the width of the Activity column so that it is as wide as the widest entry.

To change the font size and adjust the column size in the table:

1. Click any cell in the table. You want to change the size of all the text in the table, so you will select the entire table. Notice that a selection border appears around the table. This border appears any time the table is active.

2. Click the **TABLE TOOLS LAYOUT** tab, and then in the Table group, click the **Select** button. The Select button menu appears with options to select the entire table, the current column, or the current row.

3. Click **Select Table**. The entire table is selected. Because the selection border appears any time the table is active, the only visual cues you have that it is now selected are that the insertion point is no longer blinking in the cell that you clicked in Step 1 and the Select button is gray and unavailable. See Figure 2-15.

| Figure 2-15 | Table selected on Slide 4 |

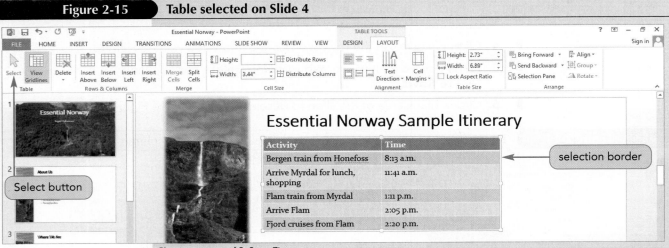

Photos courtesy of S. Scott Zimmerman

4. On the ribbon, click the **HOME** tab.

5. In the Font group, click the **Font Size** arrow, and then click **28**. Because the entire table is selected, the size of all the text in the table changes to 28 points.

6. Position the pointer on the column line between the two columns in the table so that the pointer changes to ⁺‖⁺, and then double-click. The width of the first column expands so that all the text in each cell in the first column fits on one line.

Inger wants you to change the format of the table so it looks more attractive and so that its colors complement the photo in the slide's layout. You will do this by applying a style to the table. When you apply a style to a table, you can specify whether the header and total rows and the first and last columns are formatted differently from the other rows and columns in the table. You can also specify whether to use banded rows or columns; that is, whether to fill alternating rows or columns with different shading.

To apply a style to the table:

1. Click the **TABLE TOOLS DESIGN** tab on the ribbon, if necessary. In the Table Styles group, the second style, Medium Style 2 – Accent 1, is selected. In the Table Style Options group, the Header Row and Banded Rows check boxes are selected, which means that the header row will be formatted differently than the rest of the rows and that every other row will be filled with shading. See Figure 2-16.

Figure 2-16	Default formatting applied to the table

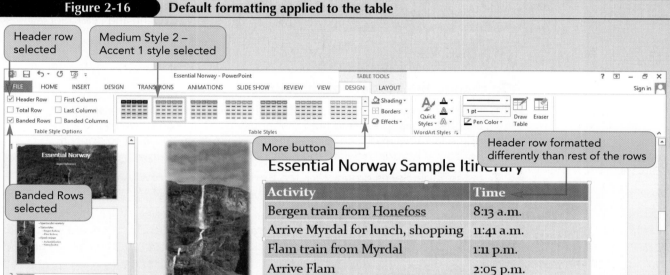

Photos courtesy of S. Scott Zimmerman

2. In the Table Styles group, click the **More** button. The Table Styles gallery opens.

3. Click the **Medium Style 3 – Accent 3** style, and then click a blank area of the slide to deselect the table.

The color in the first row is a little too bright. You can change the fill of table cells in the same manner that you change the fill of shapes.

To change the fill of cells in the table:

▶ 1. In the table, click in the first row, and then click the **LAYOUT** tab.

▶ 2. In the Table group, click the **Select** button, and then click **Select Row**. The first row in the table is selected.

▶ 3. Click the **TABLE TOOLS DESIGN** tab.

▶ 4. In the Table Styles group, click the **Shading button arrow**. The Shading menu is similar to the Shape Fill menu you worked with earlier.

▶ 5. Click **Olive Green, Accent 3, Darker 50%**. The menu closes and the cells in the first row are shaded with olive green.

In addition, the table might be easier to read if the horizontal borders between the rows were visible. You can add these by using the Borders button arrow and the buttons in the Draw Borders group on the TABLE TOOLS DESIGN tab. When you use the Borders button arrow, you can apply borders to all the selected cells at once. The borders will be the style, weight, and color specified by the Pen Style, Pen Weight, and Pen Color buttons in the Draw Borders group.

To change the borders of the table:

▶ 1. Position the pointer to the left of the first cell in the second row so that it changes to ➡, press and hold the mouse button, drag down to the left of the last row, and then release the mouse button. You want to apply a horizontal border between the rows below the header row.

▶ 2. In the Table Styles group, click the **Borders button arrow**. A menu opens listing borders that you can apply to the selected cells.

▶ 3. Click **Inside Horizontal Border**. A border appears between each row below the header row. As indicated in the Draw Table group, the borders are solid line borders, one point wide, and black. See Figure 2-17. You can change any of these attributes.

Figure 2-17   **Table with inside horizontal borders added**

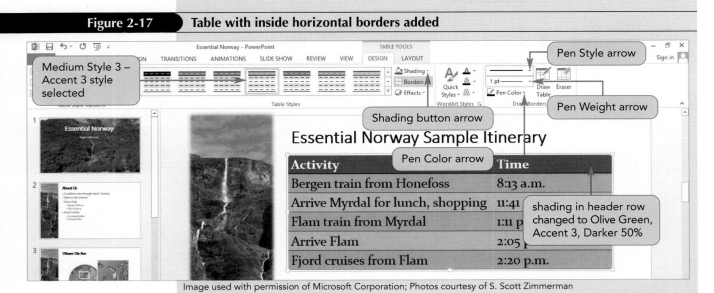

Image used with permission of Microsoft Corporation; Photos courtesy of S. Scott Zimmerman

▶ **4.** In the Draw Borders group, click the **Pen Weight** arrow, and then click **½ pt**. The pointer changes to 𝒾. You could drag this pointer along each border to draw them individually. Instead, you will use the Borders button again to apply the new settings to all of the selected cells. Because Inside Horizontal Borders was the last option chosen on the Borders button menu, it is the default option for the Borders button.

▶ **5.** In the Table Styles group, click the **Borders** button. The weight of the borders between each selected row is changed to one-half point.

Inger decides that she wants you to add a picture to each row that is related to that part of the itinerary. Recall that one of the things you can fill a shape with is a picture. You can do the same with cells. First, you'll need to insert a new first column.

To insert a new column and fill the cells with pictures:

▶ **1.** Click in any cell in the first column, and then click the **LAYOUT** tab.

▶ **2.** In the Rows & Columns group, click the **Insert Left** button. A new column is inserted to the left of the current column.

▶ **3.** Position the pointer on the column line between the new first column and the second column, and then drag left until the column line is approximately below the middle of the "n" in "Essential" in the slide title. The text in each cell in the second column again fits on one line. In the Cell Size group, the measurement in the Width box should be approximately 1.2". See Figure 2-18.

Figure 2-18 | **New column added to table**

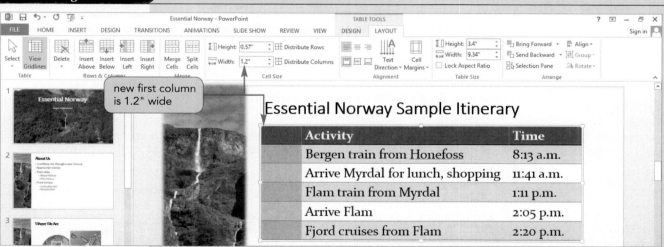

Image used with permission of Microsoft Corporation; Photos courtesy of S. Scott Zimmerman

▶ **4.** Click in the first cell in the second row, and then click the **TABLE TOOLS DESIGN** tab.

▶ **5.** In the Table Styles group, click the **Shading button arrow**, and then click **Picture**. The Insert Pictures window opens. See Figure 2-19.

Figure 2-19   Insert Pictures window with option for locating a file on your computer

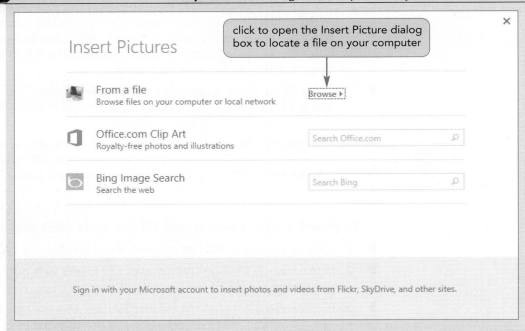

6. Next to From a file, click the **Browse** button. The Insert Picture dialog box opens.

7. Navigate to the **PowerPoint2 ▸ Tutorial** folder, click **Bergen Train**, and then click the **Insert** button. The photo fills the cell.

8. Insert the following photos, all located in the **PowerPoint2 ▸ Tutorial** folder, in the first cells in the next four rows: **Myrdal**, **Flam Train**, **Flam Station**, **Boat**.

The text in the table is large enough, but the photos are too small, and some of them are fairly distorted because they were stretched horizontally to fill the cells. You'll increase the height of the rows below the heading row in the table.

To increase the row height in the table and adjust cell alignment:

1. Select all the rows except the heading row.

2. On the ribbon, click the **LAYOUT** tab.

3. In the Cell Size group, click in the **Height** box, delete the selected value, type **1**, and then press the **Enter** key. The height of each selected rows changes to one inch.

Finally, the text in all cells in the table is horizontally left-aligned and vertically aligned at the top of the cells. The headings would look better centered horizontally in the cells, and the text in the other rows would look better vertically aligned in the center of the cells.

You also need to reposition the table on the slide to better fill the space. You move a table the same way you move any other object. The pointer must be positioned on the table border in order to change it to ⊹⥅.

To adjust the alignment of text in cells and reposition the table:

▶ **1.** Make sure all the rows except the heading row are still selected.

▶ **2.** In the Alignment group, click the **Center Vertically** button ▤. The text in the selected rows is now centered vertically in the cells.

▶ **3.** In the first row, drag across the second and third cells to select them.

▶ **4.** In the Alignment group, click the **Center** button ▤. The headings are now centered horizontally in the cells. Now you will adjust the table's placement on the slide.

▶ **5.** Position the pointer on the table border so that it changes to ⊹⥅, and then drag the table so that its left edge is approximately aligned with the left of the letter "E" in "Essential" in the slide title and vertically centered in the white space below the title. Compare your screen to Figure 2-20.

Figure 2-20   **Final formatted table**

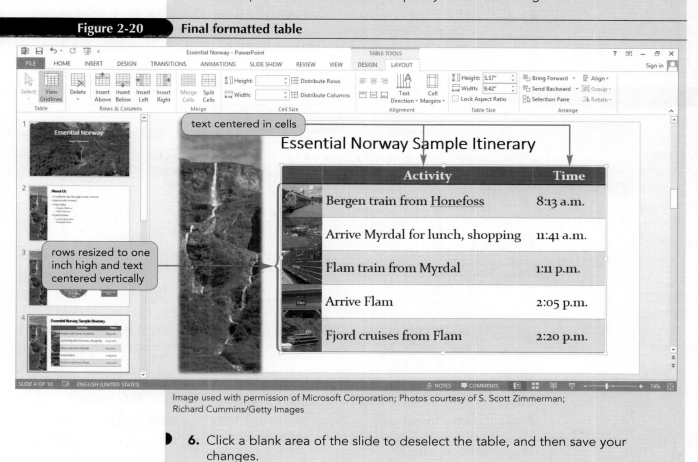

Image used with permission of Microsoft Corporation; Photos courtesy of S. Scott Zimmerman; Richard Cummins/Getty Images

▶ **6.** Click a blank area of the slide to deselect the table, and then save your changes.

Inserting Symbols and Characters

The Norwegian alphabet contains three letters that are not in the English alphabet: æ (pronounced like the "a" in "cat"), ø (pronounced like the "u" in "hurt"), and å (pronounced like the "o" in "more"). The city names Flåm and Hønefoss use two of these letters. To insert these letters using a keyboard with only English letters, you can use the Symbol button in the Symbols group on the INSERT tab.

You need to correct the spelling of Flåm and Hønefoss in the table you inserted on Slide 4.

To insert the special characters:

1. Display **Slide 4** ("Essential Norway Sample Itinerary") in the Slide pane, if necessary.

2. In the row below the table header, click after the "H" in "Honefoss," and then press the **Delete** key to delete the "o."

3. Click the **INSERT** tab, and then in the Symbols group, click the **Symbol** button. The Symbol dialog box opens.

4. Drag the scroll box to the top of the vertical scroll bar, click the **Subset** arrow, click **Latin-1 Supplement**, and then click the **down scroll arrow** four times. The bottom row contains the letter ø, and the row above it contains the letter å. See Figure 2-21.

Figure 2-21	Symbol dialog box

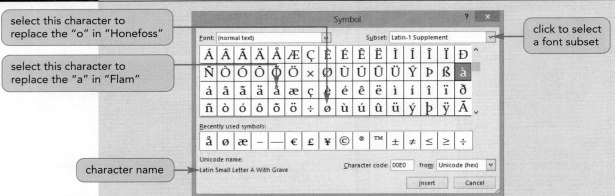

select this character to replace the "o" in "Honefoss"

select this character to replace the "a" in "Flam"

character name

click to select a font subset

Trouble? If the letters do not appear in the rows mentioned in Step 4, someone might have resized the Symbol dialog box. Refer to Figure 2-21 for help locating the symbols.

5. In the bottom row, click **ø**. In the bottom-left corner of the Symbol dialog box, the name of the selected character is "Latin Small Letter O With Stroke."

6. Click the **Insert** button. The letter ø is inserted in the table, and the Cancel button in the dialog box changes to the Close button.

▶ **7.** Click the **Close** button. The cell below the header "Activity" now contains the text "Bergen train from Hønefoss."

▶ **8.** In the third row below the header row, click after the "a" in "Flam," and then press the **Backspace** key to delete the "a."

▶ **9.** In the Symbols group, click the **Symbol** button to open the Symbols dialog box, scroll up one row, and then click **å**, which has the name "Latin Small Letter A With Ring Above."

▶ **10.** Click the **Insert** button, and then click the **Close** button. The cell now contains the text "Flåm train from Myrdal."

▶ **11.** Double-click **Flåm**, click the **HOME** tab, and then, in the Clipboard group, click the **Copy** button.

▶ **12.** In the next row in the table, double-click **Flam**, and then in the Clipboard group, click the **Paste** button.

▶ **13.** In the last row in the table, replace **Flam** with the text **Flåm** on the Clipboard.

▶ **14.** Save your changes.

Changing the Proofing Language

The spell checker can be very helpful, but when it flags words that are spelled correctly, the wavy red lines can be distracting as you work with the presentation. In the Essential Norway presentation, some of the Norwegian city and fjord names have been flagged as misspelled. This is because the proofing language for the presentation is set to English.

You can change the proofing language for the entire presentation or only for specific words to any language supported by Microsoft Office. If the proofing language you specify is not installed on your computer, PowerPoint will stop flagging the words in that language as misspelled, but it will not be able to determine if the foreign language words are spelled correctly. However, if you open the file on a computer that has the other language installed, you can use the spell checker to check the words in that language.

You will set the proofing language of the Norwegian words to Norwegian to help Inger as she reviews the final presentation.

To set the proofing language for specific words to Norwegian:

▶ **1.** Display **Slide 4** ("Essential Norway Sample Itinerary") in the Slide pane, if necessary.

▶ **2.** In the second row of the table, double-click **Hønefoss**. The word is selected.

▶ **3.** On the status bar, click **ENGLISH (UNITED STATES)**. The Language dialog box opens. See Figure 2-22. The default is for the selected text to be marked as English. The spell check icon next to English indicates that this language is installed.

Figure 2-22	Language dialog box

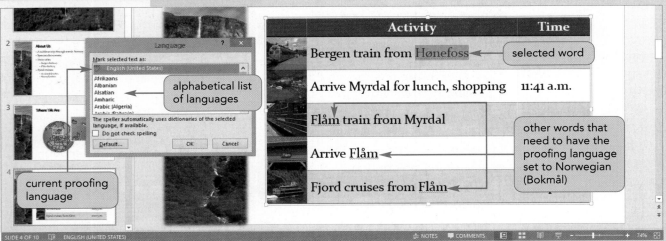

Image used with permission of Microsoft Corporation; Photos courtesy of S. Scott Zimmerman; Richard Cummins/Getty Images

Trouble? If ENGLISH (UNITED STATES) does not appear on the status bar, click the REVIEW tab, click the Language button in the Language group, and then click Set Proofing Language.

4. Scroll down the alphabetical list until you see **Norwegian (Bokmål)**. There is no spell check icon next to this language because Microsoft Office sold in English-speaking countries comes only with English, French, and Spanish languages installed.

Trouble? If there is a spell check icon next to Norwegian (Bokmål), then that language is installed on your computer.

5. Click **Norwegian (Bokmål)**, and then click the **OK** button. The wavy red line under the selected word disappears, and next to the Spelling icon on the status bar, the language is now Norwegian (Bokmål).

6. In the fourth row in the table, double-click **Flåm**. Because specifying the Norwegian language as the proofing language was the most recent action, a quicker way to specify it for additional words you select is to use the Repeat button to repeat that action.

7. On the Quick Access Toolbar, click the **Repeat** button . As indicated on the status bar, the language for the selected word is changed to Norwegian.

8. In the fifth and sixth rows of the table, select **Flåm**, and then set the proofing language for both instances to **Norwegian (Bokmål)**.

9. Save your changes.

You have modified a presentation by applying a theme used in another presentation, inserting and formatting online pictures and shapes, and inserting a table and characters that are not on your keyboard. You also changed the proofing language for Norwegian words. In the next session, you will continue modifying the presentation by applying and modifying transitions and animations, adding and modifying videos, and adding footer and header information.

REVIEW

Session 2.1 Quick Check

1. What are keywords?
2. Which contextual tab appears on the ribbon when a shape is selected?
3. What is a style?
4. What is a shape's fill?
5. In a table, what is the intersection of a row and column called?
6. How do you know if an entire table is selected and not just active?
7. How do you insert characters that are not on your keyboard?

Session 2.2 Visual Overview:

Use commands on the TRANSITIONS tab to apply **transitions**, the manner in which a new slide appears on the screen in place of the previous slide during a slide show.

Click the Preview button on the TRANSITIONS tab to preview transitions.

Click the More button to open the gallery of transitions.

If a transition has an effect that you can modify, click the Effect Options button to select one.

Click the Sound box arrow to select a sound to add to a transition.

The Transition gallery contains transitions that you can apply.

Click the Apply To All button to apply a selected transition to all the slides in the presentation.

Change the duration to change the speed of a transition.

The "About Us" slide is transitioning onto the screen with the Cube transition.

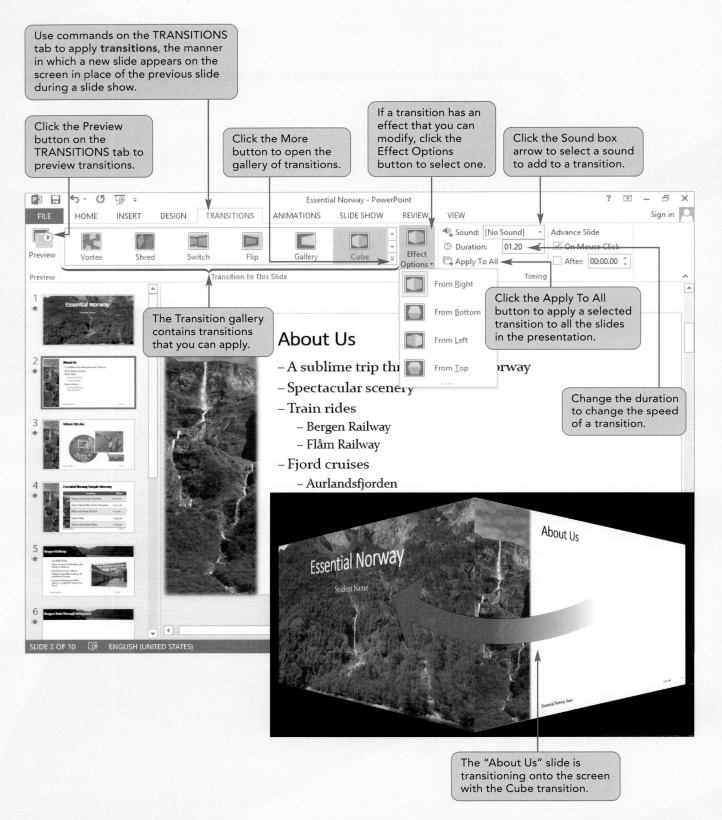

Using Transitions and Animations

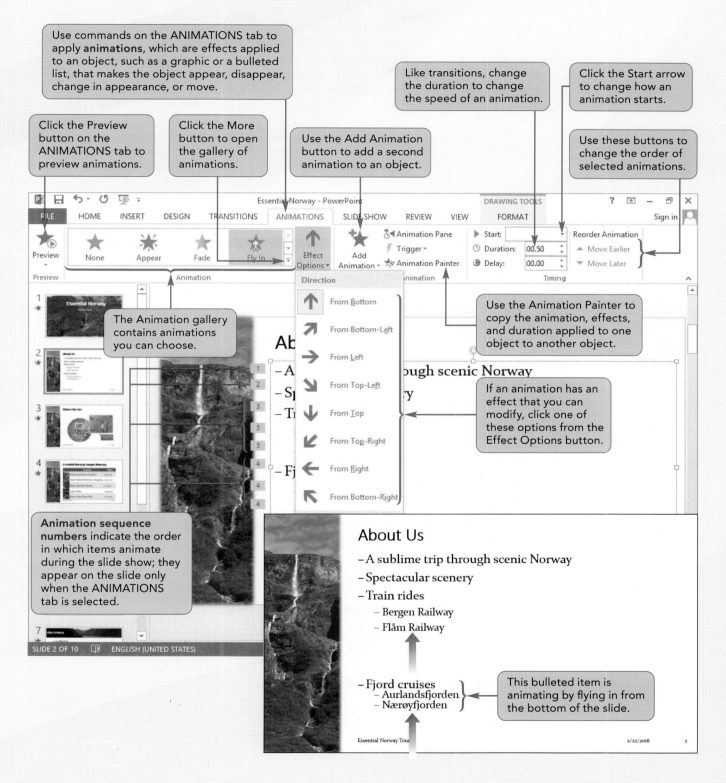

Use commands on the ANIMATIONS tab to apply **animations**, which are effects applied to an object, such as a graphic or a bulleted list, that makes the object appear, disappear, change in appearance, or move.

Like transitions, change the duration to change the speed of an animation.

Click the Start arrow to change how an animation starts.

Click the Preview button on the ANIMATIONS tab to preview animations.

Click the More button to open the gallery of animations.

Use the Add Animation button to add a second animation to an object.

Use these buttons to change the order of selected animations.

The Animation gallery contains animations you can choose.

Use the Animation Painter to copy the animation, effects, and duration applied to one object to another object.

If an animation has an effect that you can modify, click one of these options from the Effect Options button.

Animation sequence numbers indicate the order in which items animate during the slide show; they appear on the slide only when the ANIMATIONS tab is selected.

This bulleted item is animating by flying in from the bottom of the slide.

About Us

– A sublime trip through scenic Norway
– Spectacular scenery
– Train rides
  – Bergen Railway
  – Flåm Railway

– Fjord cruises
  – Aurlandsfjorden
  – Nærøyfjorden

Essential Norway Tour   2/22/2016   2

Applying Transitions

The TRANSITIONS tab contains commands for changing slide transitions. Refer to the Session 2.2 Visual Overview for more information about transitions. Unless you change it, the default is for one slide to disappear and the next slide to immediately appear on the screen. You can modify transitions in Normal or Slide Sorter view.

Transitions are organized into three categories: Subtle, Exciting, and Dynamic Content. Dynamic Content transitions are a combination of the Fade transition for the slide background and a different transition for the slide content. If slides have the same background, it looks like the slide background stays in place and only the slide content moves.

Inconsistent transitions can be distracting and detract from your message, so generally it's a good idea to apply the same transition to all of the slides in the presentation. Depending on the audience and topic, you might choose different effects of the same transition for different slides, such as changing the direction of a Wipe or Push transition. If there is one slide you want to highlight, for instance, the last slide, you can use a different transition for that slide.

REFERENCE

Adding Transitions

- In the Slides tab in Normal view or in Slide Sorter view, select the slide(s) to which you want to add a transition, or, if applying to all the slides, select any slide.
- On the ribbon, click the TRANSITIONS tab.
- In the Transition to This Slide group, click the More button to display the gallery of transitions, and then click a transition in the gallery.
- If desired, in the Transition to This Slide group, click the Effect Options button, and then click an effect.
- If desired, in the Timing group, click the Transition Sound arrow to insert a sound effect to accompany each transition.
- If desired, in the Timing group, modify the time in the Duration box to modify the speed of the transition.
- To apply the transition to all the slides in the presentation, in the Timing group, click the Apply to All button.

The Essential Norway presentation contains photos of beautiful vistas. Inger wants a transition between the slides that gives the audience a feel for moving through the open spaces in the photos.

To apply transitions to the slides:

1. If you took a break after the previous session, make sure the Essential Norway presentation is open, and then display **Slide 2** ("About Us") in the Slide pane.

2. On the ribbon, click the **TRANSITIONS** tab. See Figure 2-23.

Figure 2-23   Commands on the TRANSITIONS tab

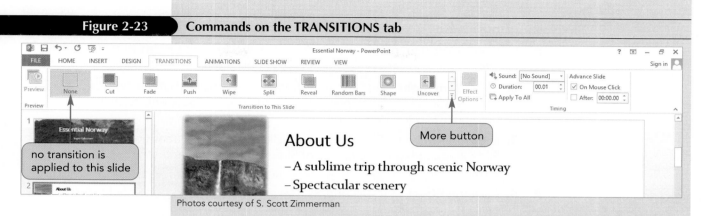

Photos courtesy of S. Scott Zimmerman

> **3.** In the Transition to This Slide group, click **Reveal**. The transition previews in the Slide pane as Slide 1 (the title slide) appears, fades away, and then Slide 2 fades in. The Reveal transition is now highlighted in orange in the gallery. In the Slides tab, a star appears next to the Slide 2 thumbnail. If you missed the preview, you can see it again.

> **4.** In the Preview group, click the **Preview** button. The transition previews in the Slide pane again.

> **5.** In the Transition to This Slide group, click the **More** button. The gallery opens listing all the transitions. See Figure 2-24.

Figure 2-24   Transitions gallery

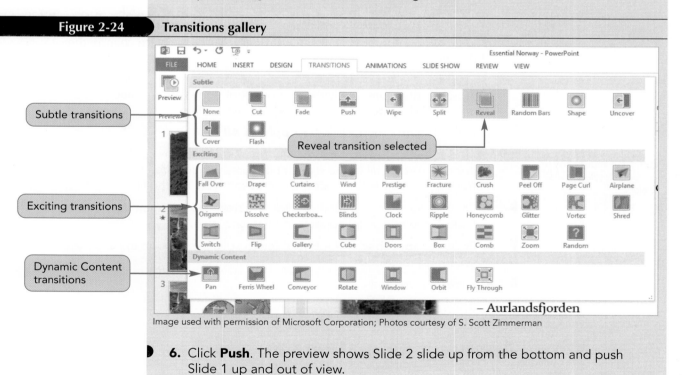

Image used with permission of Microsoft Corporation; Photos courtesy of S. Scott Zimmerman

> **6.** Click **Push**. The preview shows Slide 2 slide up from the bottom and push Slide 1 up and out of view.

Most transitions have effects that you can modify. For example, the Peel Off transition can peel from the bottom left or the bottom right corner, and the Wipe transition can wipe from any direction. You'll modify the transition applied to Slide 2.

To modify the transition effect for Slide 2:

▶ 1. In the Transition to This Slide group, click the **Effect Options** button. The effects that you can modify for the Push transition are listed on the menu.

▶ 2. Click **From Right**. The Push transition previews again, but this time Slide 2 slides from the right to push Slide 1 left. The available effects change depending on the transition selected.

▶ 3. In the Transition to This Slide group, click **Shape**. The transition previews with Slide 2 appearing in the center of Slide 1 inside a circle that grows to fill the slide.

▶ 4. Click the **Effect Options** button. The effects that you can modify for the Shape transition are listed.

▶ 5. Click **Out**. The preview of the transition with this effect displays Slide 2 in the center of Slide 1 inside a rectangle that grows to fill the slide.

Finally, you can also change the duration of a transition. The duration is how long it takes the transition to finish; in other words, the speed of the transition. To make the transition faster, decrease the duration; to slow the transition down, increase the duration. Inger likes the Shape transition, but she thinks it is a little fast, so you will increase the duration. Then you can apply the modified transition to all the slides.

To change the duration of the transition and apply it to all the slides:

▶ 1. In the Timing group, click the **Duration up** arrow twice to change the duration to 1.5".

▶ 2. In the Preview group, click the **Preview** button. The transition previews once more, a little more slowly than before. Right now, the transition is applied only to Slide 2. You want to apply it to all the slides.

▶ 3. In the Timing group, click the **Apply To All** button.

In the Slides tab, the star indicating that a transition is applied to the slide appears next to all of the slides in the presentation. You should view the transitions in Slide Show view to make sure you like the final effect.

Make sure you click the Apply To All button or the transition is applied only to the currently selected slide or slides.

▶ 4. On the Quick Access Toolbar, click the **Start From Beginning** 🔲 button. Slide 1 (the title slide) appears in Slide Show view.

▶ 5. Press the **spacebar** or the **Enter** key to advance through the slide show. The transitions look fine.

▶ 6. Save your changes.

Applying Animations

Animations add interest to a slide show and draw attention to the text or object being animated. For example, you can animate a slide title to fly in from the side or spin around like a pinwheel to draw the audience's attention to that title. Refer to the Session 2.2 Visual Overview for more information about animations.

Animation effects are grouped into four types:

• **Entrance**—Text and objects are not shown on the slide until the animation occurs; one of the most commonly used animation types.

- **Emphasis**—Text and objects on the slide change in appearance or move.
- **Exit**—Text and objects leave the screen before the slide show advances to the next slide.
- **Motion Paths**—Text and objects follow a path on a slide.

Animating Objects

You can animate any object on a slide, including pictures, shapes, and text boxes. To animate an object you click it, and then select an animation in the Animation group on the ANIMATIONS tab.

REFERENCE

Applying Animations

- In the Slide pane in Normal view, select the object you want to animate.
- On the ribbon, click the ANIMATIONS tab.
- In the Animation group, click the More button to display the gallery of animations, and then click an animation in the gallery.
- If desired, in the Animation group, click the Effect Options button, and then click a direction effect; if the object is a text box, click a sequence effect.
- If desired, in the Timing group, modify the time in the Duration box to modify the speed of the animation.
- If desired, in the Timing group, click the Start arrow, and then click a different start timing.

Slide 9 contains two pictures of fjords, one of Aurlandsfjord and one of Nærøyfjord. Inger wants you to add an animation to the title text on this slide.

To animate the title on Slide 9:

1. Display **Slide 9** ("Views of the Fjords") in the Slide pane, and then click the **ANIMATIONS** tab on the ribbon. The animations in the Animation group are grayed out, indicating they are not available. This is because nothing is selected on the slide.

2. Click the **Views of the Fjords** title text. The animations in the Animation group darken to indicate that they are now available. See Figure 2-25. All of the animations currently visible in the Animation group are entrance animations.

Figure 2-25   **Animations available on the ANIMATIONS tab after an object is selected**

Photos courtesy of S. Scott Zimmerman

3. In the Animation group, click **Fly In**. This entrance animation previews in the Slide pane—the title text disappears and then flies in from the bottom. In the Timing group, the Start box displays On Click, which indicates that this animation will occur when you advance the slide show by clicking the mouse or pressing the spacebar or the Enter key.

Notice the animation sequence number 1 in the box to the left of the title text box, which indicates that this is the first animation that will occur on the slide. You can preview the animation again if you missed it.

4. In the Preview group, click the **Preview** button. The animation previews again.

5. In the Animation group, click the **More** button. The Animation gallery opens. The animation commands are listed by category, and each category appears in a different color. At the bottom are four commands, each of which opens a dialog box listing all the effects in that category. See Figure 2-26. You will try an emphasis animation.

Figure 2-26	Animations gallery

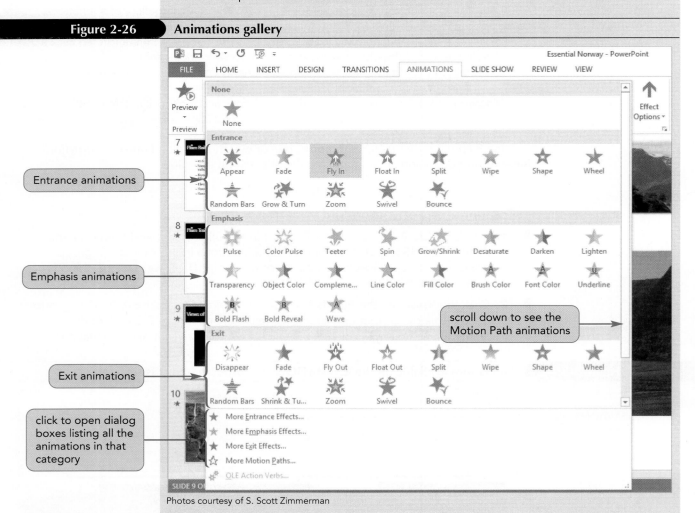

Photos courtesy of S. Scott Zimmerman

6. Under Emphasis, click **Underline**. The Underline animation replaces the Fly In animation, and the slide title is underlined in the preview in the Slide pane. The text did not disappear before the animation started because an emphasis animation causes something to happen to an object already on the slide.

The Underline animation you applied to the slide title is an example of an emphasis animation that is available only to text. You cannot apply that animation to objects such as pictures.

Slide 9 contains photos showing scenic views that customers will see if they book a tour. To focus the audience's attention on one photo at time, you will apply an entrance animation to the photos so that they appear one at a time during the slide show.

To apply entrance animations to the photos on Slide 9:

▶ **1.** With **Slide 9** ("Views of the Fjords") in the Slide pane, click the picture on the right.

▶ **2.** In the Animation group, click the **More** button. Notice that in the Emphasis section, six of the animations, including the Underline animation you just applied to the slide title, are gray, which means they are not available for this object. These six animations are available only for text.

▶ **3.** In the Entrance section, click **Split**. The picture fades in starting from the left and right edges and fading into the center. In the Timing group, On Click appears in the Start box, indicating that this animation will occur when you advance the slide show. The animation sequence number to the left of the selected picture is 2, which indicates that this is the second animation that will occur on the slide when you advance the slide show.

Like transitions, animations can be modified by changing the effect or the duration (the speed). You need to change the direction from which this animation appears, and you want to slow it down.

To change the effect and duration of the animation applied to the photo:

▶ **1.** In the Animation group, click the **Effect Options** button. See Figure 2-27. This menu contains Direction options.

Figure 2-27   **Effect options for the Fly In entrance animation**

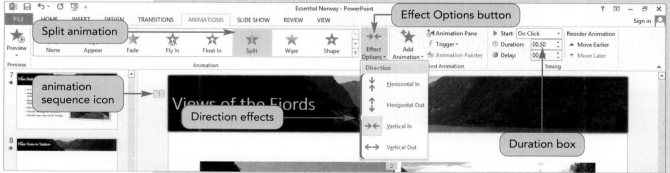

Photos courtesy of S. Scott Zimmerman

▶ **2.** Click **Vertical Out**. The preview fades the picture in starting from the center and building out to the left and right edges.

▶ **3.** In the Timing group, click the **Duration up** arrow once. The duration changes from .50 seconds to .75 seconds.

After you have applied and customized the animation for one object, you can use the Animation Painter to copy that animation to other objects. You will copy the Split entrance animation with the Vertical Out effect and a duration of .75 seconds to the other photo on Slide 9.

To use the Animation Painter to copy the animation on Slide 9:

▶ **1.** Click the photo on the right to select it.

▶ **2.** In the Advanced Animation group, click the **Animation Painter** button, and then move the pointer onto the Slide pane. The pointer changes to ⬚.

▶ **3.** Click the photo on the left. The Split animation with the Vertical Out effect and a duration of .75 seconds is copied to the photo on the left.

After you apply animations, you should watch them in Slide Show, Presenter, or Reading view to see what they will look like during a slide show. Remember that On Click appeared in the Start box for each animation that you applied, which means that to see the animation during the slide show, you need to advance the slide show.

To view the animations on Slide 9 in Slide Show view:

▶ **1.** Make sure **Slide 9** ("Views of the Fjords") is displayed in the Slide pane.

▶ **2.** On the status bar, click the **Slide Show** button 🖵. Slide 9 appears in Slide Show view. Only the photo that is part of the layout and the title appear on the slide.

▶ **3.** Press the **spacebar** to advance the slide show. The first animation, the emphasis animation that underlines the title, occurs.

▶ **4.** Press the **spacebar** again. The photo on the right fades in starting at the center of the photo and building out to the left and right edges.

▶ **5.** Click anywhere on the screen. The photo on the left fades in with the same animation as the photo on the right.

▶ **6.** Press the **Esc** key. Slide 9 appears in Normal view.

Inger doesn't like the emphasis animation on the slide title. It's distracting because the title is not the focus of this slide, the photos are. Also, it would be better if the photo on the left appeared before the photo on the right. To fix this, you can remove the animation applied to the title and change the order of the animations applied to the photos.

To remove the title animation and change the order of the photo animations:

▶ **1.** Click the title. In the Animation group, the yellow emphasis animation Underline is selected.

▶ **2.** In the Animation group, click the **More** button, and then at the top of the gallery, click **None**. The animation applied to the title is removed, the animation sequence icon no longer appears next to the title text box, and the other two animation sequence icons on the slide are renumbered 1 and 2.

TIP

You can also click the animation sequence icon, and then press the Delete key to remove an animation.

Now you need to select the animation applied to the photo on the left and change it so that it occurs first. You can select the object or the animation sequence icon to modify an animation.

3. Next to the left photo, click the animation sequence icon **2**. In the Animation group, the green Split entrance animation is selected. See Figure 2-28.

Figure 2-28   **Animation selected to change its order**

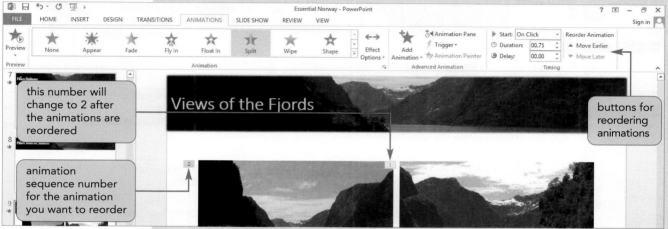

Photos courtesy of S. Scott Zimmerman

4. In the Timing group, click the **Move Earlier** button. The animation sequence icon next to the photo on the left changes from 2 to 1, and the animation sequence icon next to the photo on the right changes from 1 to 2.

5. In the Preview group, click the **Preview** button. The photo on the left fades in, and then the photo on the right fades in.

Changing How an Animation Starts

Remember that when you apply an animation, the default is for the object to animate On Click, which means when you advance through the slide show. You can change this so that an animation happens automatically, either at the same time as another animation or when the slide transitions, or after another animation.

Inger wants the photo on the right to appear automatically, without the presenter needing to advance the slide show.

To change how the animation for the photo on the right starts:

1. With **Slide 9** ("Views of the Fjords") displayed in the Slide pane, click the photo on the right. The entrance animation Split is selected in the Animation group, and in the Timing group, On Click appears in the Start box.

2. In the Timing group, click the **Start** arrow. The three choices for starting an animation appear. See Figure 2-29.

Figure 2-29   Options on the Start menu for animations

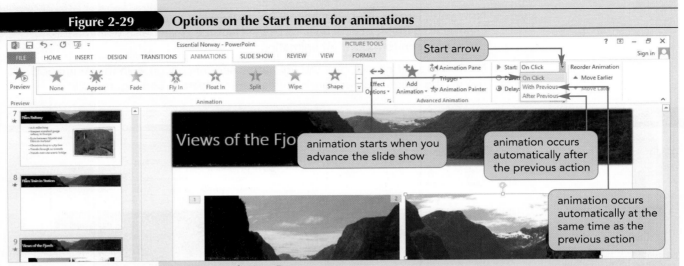

Photos courtesy of S. Scott Zimmerman

3. Click **After Previous**. Now this photo will appear automatically after the photo on the left fades in. Notice that the animation sequence number next to this photo changed to 1, the same number as the animation sequence number next to the photo on the left. This is because you will not need to advance the slide show to make this animation happen.

When you preview an animation, it plays automatically on the slide in the Slide pane, even if the timing setting for the animation is On Click. To make sure the timing settings are correct, you need to watch the animation in a slide show.

To preview and test the animations:

1. On the status bar, click the **Slide Show** button 🖵. Slide 9 appears in Slide Show view.

2. Press the **spacebar**. The photo on the left fades in, and then the photo on the right fades in.

3. Press the **Esc** key to end the slide show.

When you set an animation to occur automatically during the slide show, it happens immediately after the previous action. If that is too soon, you can add a pause before the animation. To do this, you increase the time in the Delay box in the Timing group.

To give the audience time to look at the first photo before the second photo appears on Slide 9, you will add a delay to the animation that is applied to the photo on the right.

To add a delay to the After Previous animation:

1. Click the photo on the right, if necessary. In the Timing group, 00.00 appears in the Delay box.

2. In the Timing group, click the **Delay up** arrow four times to change the time to one second. This means that after the photo on the left appears (the previous animation), the photo on the right will appear after a delay of one second. You'll view the slide in Slide Show view again to see the change.

3. On the status bar, click the **Slide Show** button 🖵. Slide 9 appears in Slide Show view.

4. Press the **spacebar**. The photo on the left fades in, and then after a one-second delay, the photo on the right fades in.

5. Press the **Esc** key to end the slide show.

Animating Lists

If you animate a list, the default is for the first-level items to appear one at a time. In other words, each first-level bulleted item is set to animate On Click. This type of animation focuses your audience's attention on each item, without the distraction of items that you haven't discussed yet.

Inger wants you to add an Entrance animation to the bulleted list on the "About Us" slide. She wants each first-level bulleted item to appear on the slide one at a time so that the audience won't be able to read ahead while you are discussing each point.

To animate the bulleted lists:

1. Display **Slide 2** ("About Us") in the Slide pane, and then click anywhere in the bulleted list to make the text box active.

2. On the ANIMATIONS tab, in the Animation group, click **Fly In**. The animation previews in the Slide pane as the bulleted items fly in from the bottom. When the "Train rides" and "Fjord cruises" items fly in, their subitems fly in with them. After the preview is finished, the numbers 1 through 4 appear next to the bulleted items. Notice that the subitems have the same animation sequence number as their first-level items. This means that the start timing for the subitems is set to With Previous or After Previous. See Figure 2-30.

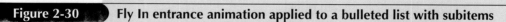

Figure 2-30   **Fly In entrance animation applied to a bulleted list with subitems**

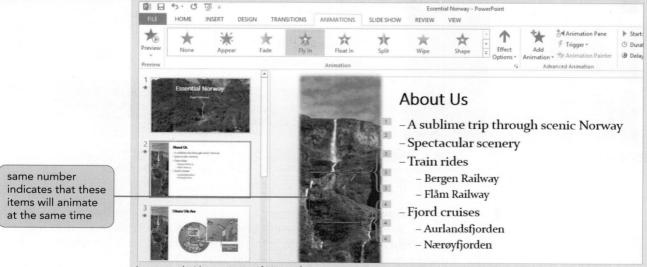

same number indicates that these items will animate at the same time

Image used with permission of Microsoft Corporation; Photos courtesy of S. Scott Zimmerman

3. Next to the Train rides bullet item, click the animation sequence icon **3** to select it. In the Timing group, On Click appears in the Start box.

▶ **4.** Next to the subitem "Bergen Railway," click the animation sequence icon **3**. In the Timing group, With Previous appears in the Start box.

If you wanted to change how the items in the list animate during the slide show, you could change the start timing of each item, or you could change the sequence effect. Sequence options appear on the Effect Options menu in addition to the Direction options when an animation is applied to a text box. The default is for the items to appear By Paragraph. This mean each first-level item animates one at a time, with its subitems if there are any, when you advance the slide show. You can change this so that the entire list animates at once as one object, or so that each first-level item animates at the same time but as separate objects.

To examine the Sequence options for the animated list:

▶ **1.** Click in the bulleted list, and then in the Animation group, click the **Effect Options** button. The Sequence options appear at the bottom of the menu, below the Direction options, and By Paragraph is selected. See Figure 2-31.

Figure 2-31   **Animation effect options for a bulleted list**

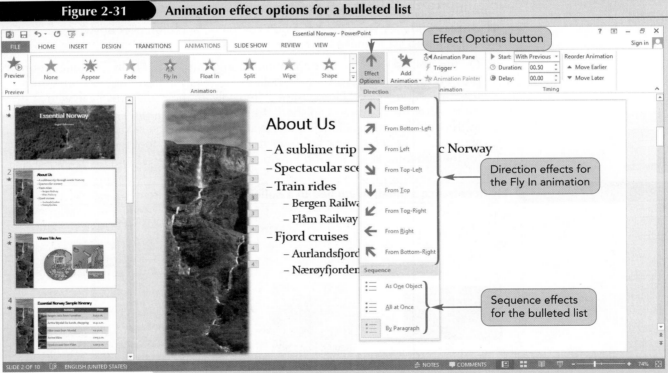

Image used with permission of Microsoft Corporation; Photos courtesy of S. Scott Zimmerman; Richard Cummins/Getty Images

▶ **2.** Click **As One Object**. The animation preview shows the entire text box fly in. After the preview, only one animation sequence icon appears next to the text box, indicating that the entire text box will animate as a single object. In the Timing group, On Click appears in the Start box.

▶ **3.** In the Animation group, click the **Effect Options** button, and then under Sequence, click **All At Once**. The animation previews again, but this time each of the first-level items fly in as separate objects, although they all fly in at the same time. After the preview, animation sequence icons, all numbered 1, appear next to each bulleted item, indicating that each item will animate separately but you only need to advance the slide show once.

▶ **4.** Next to the first bulleted item, click the animation sequence icon. In the Timing group, On Click appears in the Start box.

▶ **5.** Next to the second bulleted item, click the animation sequence icon. In the Timing group, With Previous appears in the Start box.

▶ **6.** In the Animation group, click the **Effect Options** button, and then click **By Paragraph**. The sequence effect is changed back to its original setting.

▶ **7.** Save your changes.

PROSKILLS

Decision Making: Just Because You Can Doesn't Mean You Should

PowerPoint provides you with many tools that enable you to create interesting and creative slide shows. However, you need to give careful thought before deciding to use a tool to enhance the content of your presentation. Just because a tool is available doesn't mean you should use it. For example, the Add or Remove Columns button in the Paragraph group on the HOME tab allows you to create multiple columns in a text box. If you need to include two columns of bullet items on a slide, it is almost always a better choice to use a layout that has two content placeholders. Another example of a tool to use sparingly is a sound effect with transitions. Most of the time you do not need to use sound to highlight the fact that one slide is leaving the screen while another appears.

You will also want to avoid using too many or frivolous animations. It is easy to go overboard with animations, and they can quickly become distracting and make your presentation seem less professional. Before you apply an animation, you should know what you want to emphasize and why you want to use an animation. Remember that animations should always enhance your message. When you are finished giving your presentation, you want your audience to remember your message, not your animations.

Adding and Modifying Video

You can add video to slides to play during your presentation. PowerPoint supports various file formats, but the most commonly used are the MPEG-4 format, the Windows Media Audio/Video format, and the Audio Visual Interleave format, which appears in Explorer windows as the Video Clip file type. After you insert a video, you can modify it by changing playback options, changing the length of time the video plays, and applying formats and styles to the video.

Adding Video to Slides

To insert video stored on your computer or network, click the Insert Video button in a content placeholder, and then in the Insert Video window next to "From a file," click Browse to open the Insert Video dialog box. You can also click the Video button in the Media group on the INSERT tab, and then click Video on My PC to open the same Insert Video dialog box.

REFERENCE

Adding Videos Stored on Your Computer or Network

- In a content placeholder, click the Insert Video button to open the Insert Video window, and then next to "From a file," click Browse to open the Insert Video dialog box; or click the INSERT tab on the ribbon, and then in the Media group, click the Video button, and then click Video on My PC to open the Insert Video dialog box.
- Click the video you want to use, and then click the Insert button.
- If desired, click the VIDEO TOOLS PLAYBACK tab, and then in the Video Options group:
  - Click the Start arrow, and then click Automatically to change how the video starts from On Click.
  - Click the Play Full Screen check box to select it to have the video fill the screen.
  - Click the Rewind after Playing check box to select it to have the poster frame display after the video plays.
  - Click the Volume button, and then click a volume level or click Mute.

Inger has several videos she wants you to add to Slides 6 and 8.

To add a video to Slide 6 and play it:

1. Display **Slide 6** ("Bergen Train Through Mountains") in the Slide pane, and then in the content placeholder, click the **Insert Video** button . The Insert Video window opens.

2. Next to "From a file," click **Browse**. The Insert Video dialog box opens.

3. In the **PowerPoint2 ▸ Tutorial** folder, click **Bergen Train**, and then click the **Insert** button. The video is inserted on the slide. The first frame of the video is displayed, and a play bar with controls for playing the video appears below it. See Figure 2-32.

Figure 2-32   **Video added to Slide 6**

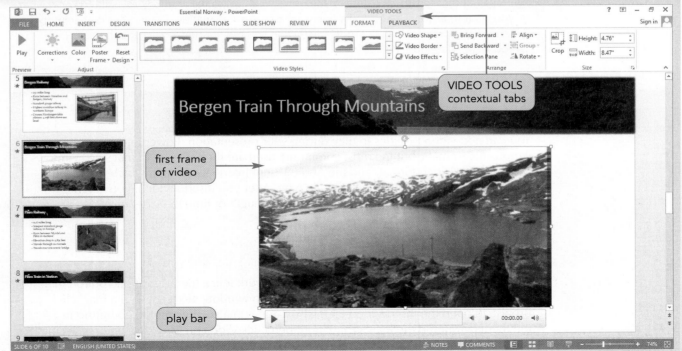

Photos courtesy of S. Scott Zimmerman

Trouble? Depending on your computer, the video might appear as a black box on the slide. It should still play.

Trouble? This video includes sound, so you might want to adjust your speakers if needed to avoid disturbing others when you complete the next step.

▶ **4.** On the play bar, click the **Play** button ▶. The Play button changes to the Pause button ‖ and the video plays. Watch the 14-second video. Next, you'll watch the video in Slide Show view.

▶ **5.** On the status bar, click the **Slide Show** button 🖳. Slide 6 appears in Slide Show view.

▶ **6.** Point to the video. The play bar appears, and the pointer changes to 🖑. You don't need to click the Play button to play the video in Slide Show view; you can click anywhere on the video to play it as long as the pointer is visible. While the video is playing, you can click it again to pause it.

▶ **7.** Click anywhere on the video. The video plays.

Trouble? If Slide 7 appeared instead of the video playing, the pointer wasn't visible or you didn't click the video object, so clicking the slide advanced the slide show. Press the Backspace key to return to Slide 6, move the mouse over the video to make the pointer visible, and then click the video.

▶ **8.** Before the video finishes playing, move the pointer to make it visible, and then click the video again. The video pauses.

▶ **9.** Move the pointer to make it visible, if necessary, click the video to finish playing it, and then press the **Esc** key to end the slide show.

As you just saw, you clicked the video to play it during the slide show. When you insert a video, its start timing is set to On Click. This start timing means something different for videos than for animations. For animations, On Click means you can do anything to advance the slide show to cause the animation to start. For videos, On Click means you need to click the video object or the Play button on the play bar. If you click somewhere else on the screen or do anything else to advance the slide show, the video will not play. The start timing setting is on the VIDEO TOOLS PLAYBACK tab.

You'll add the video to Slide 8 and then examine the start timing setting.

To add a video to Slide 8 and examine the start timing:

▶ **1.** Display **Slide 8** ("Flåm Train in Station") in the Slide pane, and then click the **INSERT** tab on the ribbon.

▶ **2.** In the Media group, click the **Video** button, and then click **Video on My PC**. The Insert Video dialog box opens.

▶ **3.** Click **Flam Train**, and then click the **Insert** button. The video is inserted in the content placeholder.

▶ **4.** On the play bar, click the **Play** button ▶. Watch the 10-second video.

▶ **5.** On the ribbon, click the **VIDEO TOOLS PLAYBACK** tab. In the Video Options group, On Click appears in the Start box. See Figure 2-33.

Figure 2-33   Options on the VIDEO TOOLS PLAYBACK tab

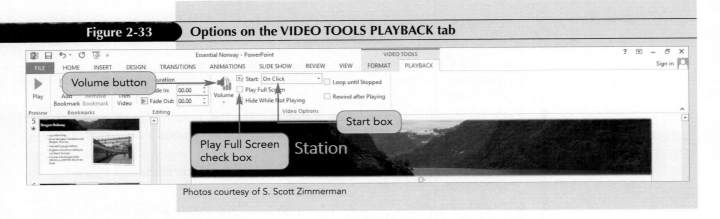

Photos courtesy of S. Scott Zimmerman

Modifying Video Playback Options

You can change several options for how a video plays. For instance, you can change the start timing so that the video plays automatically when the slide appears during the slide show. The video playback options are listed in Figure 2-34.

Figure 2-34   Video playback options

Video Option	Function
Volume	Change the volume of the video from high to medium or low or mute it.
Start	Change how the video starts, either when the presenter clicks it or the Play button on the play bar or automatically when the slide appears during the slide show.
Play Full Screen	The video fills the screen during the slide show.
Hide While Not Playing	The video does not appear on the slide when it is not playing; make sure the video is set to play automatically if this option is selected.
Loop until Stopped	The video plays until the next slide appears during the slide show.
Rewind after Playing	The video rewinds after it plays so that the first frame or the poster frame appears again.

© 2014 Cengage Learning

Both videos that you inserted have sound. Inger doesn't want you to mute them, but she would like you to lower the volume. You could adjust this while the videos are playing by using the volume control on the play bar, but she wants you to set the default volume lower so that you don't have to worry about it during the presentation. Inger also wants the video on Slide 8 to fill the screen when it plays, and for it to start automatically when the slide appears during the slide show.

To modify the playback options of the videos:

1. On **Slide 8** ("Flåm Train in Station"), click the video to select it, if necessary, and make sure the PLAYBACK tab is active on the ribbon. First you'll set the volume to low.

2. In the Video Options group, click the **Volume** button, and then click **Low**. Now you will set the video to play full screen.

3. In the Video Options group, click the **Play Full Screen** check box to select it. Finally, you will set this video to play automatically.

4. Click the **Start** arrow, and then click **Automatically**. Now you need to lower the volume of the video on Slide 6.
5. Display **Slide 6** ("Bergen Train Through Mountains") in the Slide pane, click the video, and then click the **PLAYBACK** tab, if necessary. In the Video Options group, On Click appears in the Start box.
6. Set the volume of the video to **Low**. You'll view the videos again in Slide Show view.
7. On the status bar, click the **Slide Show** button. Slide 6 appears in Slide Show view.
8. Move the mouse to make the pointer visible, and then click the video. The video plays.
9. After the video finishes playing, press the **spacebar** to advance to Slide 7, and then press the **spacebar** again. Slide 8 ("Flåm Train in Station") briefly appears, and then the Flam Train video fills the screen and plays automatically. When the video is finished playing, Slide 8 appears again.
10. Press the **Esc** key to end the slide show.

Understanding Animation Effects Applied to Videos

TIP

The Media animation category appears only when a media object—either video or audio—is selected on a slide.

When you insert a video (or audio) object, an animation is automatically applied to the video so that you can click anywhere on the video to start and pause it when the slide show is run. This animation is the Pause animation in the Media animation category and it is set to On Click. The Pause animation is what makes it possible to start or pause a video during a slide show by clicking anywhere on the video object. (When you click the video to play it, you are actually "unpausing" it.)

When you change the Start setting of a video on the PLAYBACK tab to Automatically, a second animation, the Play animation in the Media animation category, is applied to the video as well as the Pause animation, and the start timing of the Play animation is set to After Previous. If there are no other objects on the slide set to animate before the video, the Play animation has an animation sequence number of zero, which means that it will play immediately after the slide transition.

To see these animations, click the ANIMATIONS tab on the ribbon, and then select a video object on a slide. The Pause and Play animations appear in the Animation gallery in the Media category.

You'll examine the video animations now.

To examine the Media animation effects for the videos:

1. Display **Slide 6** ("Bergen Train Through Mountains") in the Slide pane. Remember that the video on this slide is set to play On Click.
2. On the ribbon, click the **ANIMATIONS** tab, and then click the video. See Figure 2-35. The animation sequence icon next to the video contains a lightning bolt instead of a number. In the Animation group, Pause is selected, and in the Timing group, On Click appears in the Start box. This animation is applied automatically to all videos when you add them to slides.

Figure 2-35 Pause animation applied to video

Photos courtesy of S. Scott Zimmerman

3. In the Animation group, click the **More** button. The Media category appears at the top of the Animation gallery because a media object is selected.

4. Press the **Esc** key to close the gallery, display **Slide 8** ("Flåm Train in Station") in the Slide pane, and then click the video. Because you set this video to start automatically, two animation sequence icons appear next to it, one containing a zero and one containing a lightning bolt. In the Animation group, Multiple is selected because two animations are applied to this video.

   When more than one animation is applied to any object, you need to click each animation sequence icon to see which animation is associated with each icon.

5. Click the **lightning bolt** animation sequence icon. In the Animation group, Pause is selected, and in the Timing group, On Click appears in the Start box. This allows you to click the video during a slide show to play or pause it.

6. Click the animation sequence icon **0**. In the Animation group, Play is selected, and in the Timing group, After Previous appears in the Start box. This Play animation was added to this video when you selected Automatically on the PLAYBACK tab. See Figure 2-36.

Figure 2-36 Play animation settings for video set to play automatically

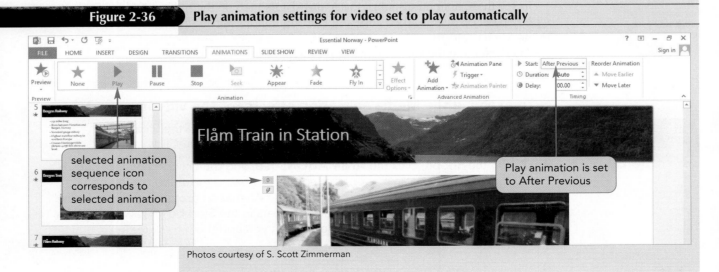

Photos courtesy of S. Scott Zimmerman

Setting a Poster Frame

The frame that appears when the video is not playing is called the **poster frame**. You can set the poster frame to be any frame in the video or you can set the poster frame to any image stored in a file. The default poster frame for a video is the first frame of the video. You can change this so that any frame from the video or any image stored in a file is the poster frame. The video on Slide 8 is of the Flåm train. To make it clear that this is the Flåm train, you want the poster frame to be the frame in the video in which you can see the train name on the side of the train.

To set a poster frame for the video on Slide 8:

1. With **Slide 8** ("Flåm Train in Station") displayed in the Slide pane, click the video, and then click the **FORMAT** tab.

2. Point to the **play bar** below the video. A ScreenTip appears identifying the time of the video at that point. See Figure 2-37.

Figure 2-37   Setting a poster frame

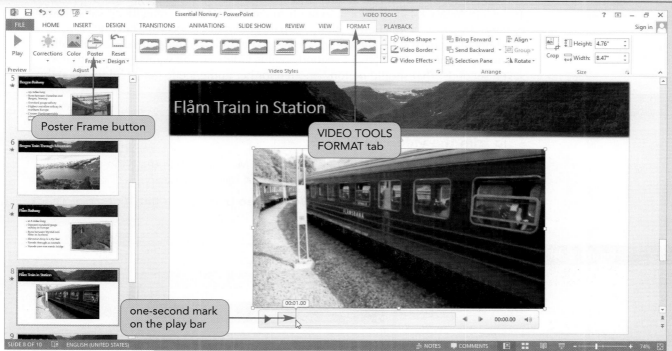

Photos courtesy of S. Scott Zimmerman

TIP

If you see a black square when you insert a video, you can override this by setting a poster frame.

3. On the play bar, click at approximately the **one-second mark**. The video advances to the one-second mark, and the frame showing the car with the name of the train, FLÅMSBANA, appears in the video object.

4. In the Adjust group, click the **Poster Frame** button. The Poster Frame menu opens.

5. Click **Current Frame**. The message "Poster Frame Set" appears in the video's play bar, and the frame currently visible in the video object is set as the poster frame.

After you play a video during a slide show, the last frame of the video appears in the video object. You can make the poster frame appear if you set the video to rewind after playing. Inger wants you to do this for the Flåm Train video.

To set the video on Slide 8 to rewind:

1. On **Slide 8** ("Flåm Train in Station"), click the video, if necessary, and then click the **PLAYBACK** tab.

2. In the Video Options group, click the **Rewind after Playing** check box to select it.

3. On the play bar, click the **Play** button ▶. The video plays, and then the poster frame appears again.

Trimming Videos

If a video is too long, or if there are parts you don't want to show during the slide show, you can trim it. To do this, click the Trim Video button in the Editing group on the VIDEO TOOLS PLAYBACK tab, and then, in the Trim Video dialog box, drag the green start slider or the red stop slider to a new position to mark where the video will start and stop.

Although in person the view from the Bergen train is stunning, Inger doesn't think the audience needs to watch 13 seconds of this video, so she wants you to trim it to seven seconds. That should be long enough for her audience to get a feel for what the train ride through the mountains is like.

To trim the video on Slide 6:

1. Display **Slide 6** ("Bergen Train Through Mountains") in the Slide pane, click the video, and then click the **PLAYBACK** tab, if necessary.

2. In the Editing group, click the **Trim Video** button. The Trim Video dialog box opens. See Figure 2-38.

Figure 2-38   **Trim Video dialog box**

Photo courtesy of S. Scott Zimmerman

3. Drag the red **Stop** tab to the left until the time in the End Time box is approximately seven seconds, and then click the **OK** button.

4. On the play bar under the video on the right, click the **Play** button ▶. The video plays, but stops after playing for seven seconds.

5. Save your changes.

Compressing Media

As with pictures, you can compress media files. If you need to send a file via email or you need to upload it, you should compress media files to make the final PowerPoint file smaller. The more you compress files, the smaller the final presentation file will be, but also the lower the quality. For videos, you can compress using the following settings:

• **Presentation Quality**—compresses the videos slightly and maintains the quality of the videos
• **Internet Quality**—compresses the videos to a quality suitable for streaming over the Internet
• **Low Quality**—compresses the videos as small as possible

With all of the settings, any parts of videos that you trimmed off will be deleted, similar to deleting the cropped portions of photos.

After you compress media, you should watch the slides containing the videos using the equipment you will be using when giving your presentation to make sure the reduced quality is acceptable. Usually, if the videos were high quality to start with, the compressed quality will be fine. However, if the original video quality was grainy, the compressed quality might be too low, even for evaluation purposes. If you decide that you don't like the compressed quality, you can undo the compression.

You will compress the media files you inserted. You need to send the presentation to Inger via email, so you will compress the media as much as possible.

To compress the videos in the presentation:

1. Click the **FILE** tab. Backstage view appears displaying the Info screen. See Figure 2-39.

Figure 2-39 **Info screen in Backstage view**

click to display compression options

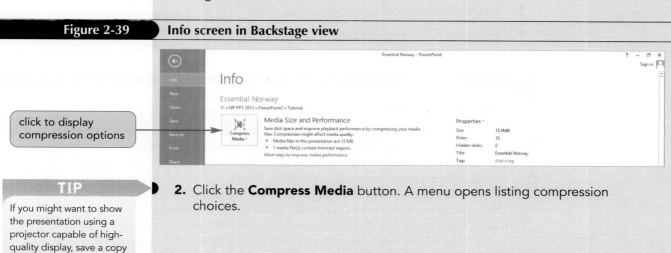

TIP

If you might want to show the presentation using a projector capable of high-quality display, save a copy of the presentation before you compress the media.

2. Click the **Compress Media** button. A menu opens listing compression choices.

3. Click **Low Quality**. The Compress Media dialog box opens listing the two video files in the presentation with a progress bar appearing next to each one in the Status column to show you the progress of the compression. After each file is compressed, the progress bar is replaced by a message indicating that compression for the file is complete and stating how much the video file size was reduced. See Figure 2-40.

Figure 2-40 **Compress Media dialog box**

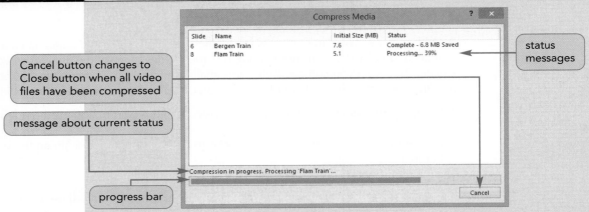

After all the videos have been compressed, a message appears at the bottom of the dialog box stating that the compression is complete and indicating how much the file size of the presentation was reduced.

4. Click the **Close** button. Next to the Compress Media button on the Info screen, the bulleted list states that the presentation's media was compressed to Low Quality and that you can undo the compression if the results are unsatisfactory. Now you need to view the compressed videos.

5. At the top of the navigation bar, click the **Back** button ⬅ to display Slide 6 ("Bergen Train Through Mountains") in the Slide pane.

6. On the status bar, click the **Slide Show** button 🖵 to display the slide in Slide Show view, and then click the video to play it. The quality is lower, but sufficient for Inger to get the general idea after you send it to her via email.

7. Press the **Esc** key to end the slide show.

8. Save your changes.

INSIGHT

Optimizing Media

If you insert videos saved in older video formats, such as the Audio Visual Interleave format (whose file type is listed in File Explorer windows as Video Clip and which uses the filename extension ".avi") and the Windows Media Video format (whose file type is listed in File Explorer windows as Windows Media Audio/Video file and which uses the filename extension ".wmv"), the Info screen in Backstage view contains an Optimize Media button as well as the Compress Media button. If you click the Optimize Media button first, any potential problems with the video on the slides, such as problems that might make it difficult to play the video on another computer or would cause the video to stutter during playback, are repaired.

Adding Footers and Headers

Sometimes it can be helpful to have information on each slide such as the title of the presentation or the company name. This is called a **footer**. It can also be helpful to have the slide number displayed. For example, you might need to distribute handouts that reference slide numbers. And some presentations need the date to appear on each slide, especially if the presentation contains time-sensitive information. You can easily add this information to all the slides. Usually this information is not needed on the title slide, so you can also specify that it not appear on there.

To add a footer, slide numbers, and the date to slides:

TIP

Clicking the Date & Time button and the Slide Number button also opens the Header & Footer dialog box.

1. Click the **INSERT** tab on the ribbon, and then in the Text group, click the **Header & Footer** button. The Header and Footer dialog box opens with the Slide tab selected.

2. Click the **Footer** check box to select it, and then click in the **Footer** box. In the Preview box on the right, the left placeholder on the bottom is filled with black to indicate where the footer will appear on slides. See Figure 2-41. Note that the position of the footer, slide number, and date changes in different themes.

Figure 2-41 Slide tab in the Header and Footer dialog box

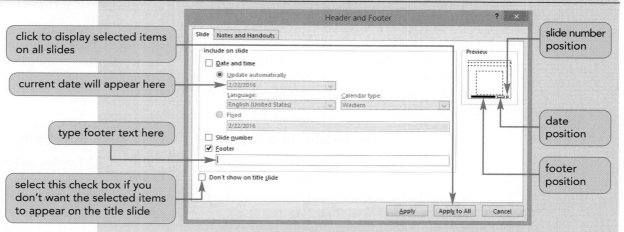

- click to display selected items on all slides
- current date will appear here
- type footer text here
- select this check box if you don't want the selected items to appear on the title slide
- slide number position
- date position
- footer position

3. Type **Essential Norway Tours**.

4. Click the **Slide number** check box to select it. In the Preview box, the box in the bottom-right is filled with black.

5. Click the **Date and time** check box to select it. The options under this check box darken to indicate that you can use them, and in the Preview box, the box in the middle on the bottom is filled with black.

   You don't want the date in the presentation to update automatically each time the presentation is opened. You want it to show today's date so people will know that the information is current as of that date.

 6. Click the **Fixed** option button. Now you want to prevent the footer, slide
number, and date from appearing on the title slide.

 7. Click the **Don't show on title slide** check box to select it, and then click the
Apply to All button. On Slide 6, the footer, date, and slide number display.
See Figure 2-42.

Figure 2-42 **Footer, date, and slide number on Slide 6**

Photos courtesy of S. Scott Zimmerman

In common usage, a footer is any text that appears at the bottom of every page in a
document or every slide in a presentation. However, as you saw when you added the
footer in the Header and Footer dialog box, in PowerPoint a footer is specifically the text
that appears in the Footer box on the Slide tab in that dialog box and in the footer text
box on the slides. This text box can appear anywhere on the slide; in some themes the
footer appears at the top of slides. This information does not appear on notes pages and
handouts. You need to add footers to notes pages and handouts separately.

A **header** is information displayed at the top of every page. Slides do not have
headers, but you can add a header to handouts and notes pages. Like a footer, in
PowerPoint a header refers only to the text that appears in the Header text box on
handouts and notes pages. In addition to headers and footers, you can also display a
date and the page number on handouts and notes pages.

To modify the header and footer on handouts and notes pages:

 1. On the INSERT tab, in the Text group, click the **Header & Footer** button.
The Header and Footer dialog box opens with the Slide tab selected.

 2. Click the **Notes and Handouts** tab. This tab includes a Page number check
box and a header box. The Page number check box is selected, and in the
Preview, the lower-right rectangle is bold to indicate that this is where the
page number will appear.

 3. Click the **Header** check box to select it, click in the **Header** box, and then
type **Essential Norway Tours**.

 4. Click the **Footer** check box to select it, click in the **Footer** box, and then
type your name.

 5. Click the **Apply to All** button. To see the effect of modifying the handouts
and notes pages, you need to look at the print preview.

 6. Click the **FILE** tab, and then in the navigation bar, click **Print**.

7. Under Settings, click the **Full Page Slides** button, and then click **Notes Pages**. The preview shows Slide 6 as a notes page. The header and footer you typed appear, along with the page number. See Figure 2-43.

Figure 2-43   Header and footer on the Slide 6 notes page

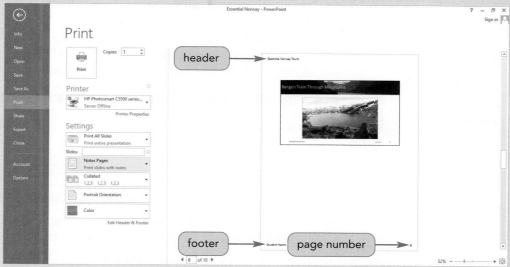

Photos courtesy of S. Scott Zimmerman

8. At the top of the navigation bar, click the **Back** button to return to Normal view.

9. Display **Slide 1** (the title slide) in the Slide pane, replace Inger's name in the subtitle text box with your name, and then save the changes to the presentation.

Now that you have finished working on the presentation, you should view the completed presentation as a slide show.

To view the completed presentation in Slide Show view:

1. On the Quick Access Toolbar, click the **Start From Beginning** button. Slide 1 appears in Slide Show view.

2. Press the **spacebar**. Slide 2 ("About Us") appears in Slide Show view displaying the photo on the slide layout, the slide background, the slide title, and the footer, date, and slide number.

3. Press the **spacebar** four times to display all the bulleted items, and then press the **spacebar** again to display Slide 3 ("Where We Are").

4. Press the **spacebar** three times to display Slide 4 ("Essential Norway Sample Itinerary"), Slide 5 ("Bergen Railway"), and finally Slide 6 ("Bergen Train Through Mountains").

5. Click the video object. The video plays on the slide.

6. After the video has finished playing, press the **spacebar** to display Slide 7 ("Flåm Railway"), and then press the **spacebar** to display Slide 8 ("Flåm Train in Station"). Slide 8 briefly appears, and then the video of the train fills the screen and plays automatically. After the video finishes playing, Slide 8 appears again in Slide Show view displaying the poster frame you set.

> **7.** Press the **spacebar** to display Slide 9 ("Views of the Fjords"), and then press the **spacebar** again. The photo on the left fades in with the Split animation, and then after a one-second delay, the photo on the right fades in.

> **8.** Press the **spacebar** to display Slide 10 ("Contact Us"), press the **spacebar** again to display the black slide that appears at the end of a slide show, and then press the **spacebar** once more to return to Normal view.

The final presentation file with transitions, animations, and video is interesting and should enhance the presentation you will give to travel agents in the United States. You can confidently send it to Inger in Norway for a final review.

REVIEW

Session 2.2 Quick Check

1. What is a transition?
2. What are animations?
3. How do you change the speed of a transition or an animation?
4. When you apply an animation to a bulleted list with subitems, how do the first-level items animate? How do the second-level items animate?
5. What does "On Click" mean for a video?
6. What animation is applied to every video that you add to a slide?
7. What is a poster frame?
8. In PowerPoint, what is a footer?

ASSESS

SAM Projects

Put your skills into practice with SAM Projects! SAM Projects for this tutorial can be found online. If you have a SAM account, go to www.cengage.com/sam2013 to download the most recent Project Instructions and Start Files.

PRACTICE

Review Assignments

Data Files needed for the Review Assignments: Alaska.jpg, Cruise.mp4, Fjords.pptx, Gulls.mp4, New Norway Theme.pptx, Norway.jpg

Travel agents often ask Inger Halvorsen questions about fjords. Inger decided to create a PowerPoint presentation that describes fjords. She also revised the custom theme she created for her company so that it uses a different photo in the background on the title slide, and she created two new custom layouts to show three items on a slide. Complete the following:

1. Open the presentation **Fjords.pptx**, located in the PowerPoint2 ► Review folder included with your Data Files, add your name as the subtitle, and then save it as **Information about Fjords** to the drive and folder where you are storing your files.

2. Apply the theme from the presentation **New Norway Theme**, located in the PowerPoint2 ► Review folder.

3. Change the layout of Slide 5 ("Fjords in Other Countries") to Three Comparison. Type **Chile** in the text placeholder above the picture on the right. Delete "Chile" in the text box above the content placeholder in the middle, and then type **Alaska**. In the empty content placeholder, insert the photo **Alaska**, located in the PowerPoint2 ► Review folder. Apply the Compound Frame, Black style and the Reflection effect "Half Reflection, touching" to the three pictures.

4. Change the layout of Slide 6 ("Norwegian Fjords") to Three Content, insert the photo **Norway**, located in the PowerPoint2 ► Review folder in the empty content placeholder, and then apply the Compound Frame, Black style to the three photos.

5. On Slide 2 ("What Is a Fjord?"), insert an online picture from Office.com in the content placeholder using **Norway fjord cliff** as the keywords. Apply the Compound Frame, Black style to the picture, and then apply the Perspective Left 3-D Rotation effect.

6. Click the photo you just inserted, and then compress all the photos in the presentation to 96 ppi.

7. On Slide 3 ("Where Are Fjords Located?"), copy the "North America northwest coast" callout, paste it on the same slide, and then flip the pasted copy horizontally. Position the flipped callout so it points to the red circle on the map, and then delete the red circle. Edit the text of the flipped callout by changing "northwest" to **"northeast."**

8. On Slide 3, add a Left Arrow shape. Type **Norway** in the arrow, and then resize the shape so it just fits the text on one line. Rotate the arrow approximately 45 degrees to the right so that it points up to the left, and then position it so that it points to the area of the map indicated by the top of the red triangle. Change the fill color of the arrow to Orange, Accent 6, and then delete the red triangle.

9. On Slide 4 ("Facts About Countries with Fjords"), insert a 3x6 table. In the first row in the table, type **Location, Famous examples, Flag**.

10. In the first cell in the second row, type **Canada--British Columbia**. (When you press the spacebar after typing "British," AutoCorrect changes the two dashes to an em dash, which is a long dash.)

11. Refer to Figure 2-44 to add the rest of the data to the table. Add a row if needed. (*Hint*: To activate AutoCorrect to change the two dashes after "United States" to an em dash, press the Tab key to move the insertion point to the next cell instead of clicking in the next cell.)

Figure 2-44   **Data for table on Slide 4 in the Information about Fjords presentation**

Location	Famous examples	Flag
Canada—British Columbia	Howe Sound	
Chile	Aisen Fjord	
Greenland	Ilulissat Icefjord	
Iceland	East Fjords	
New Zealand	Milford Sound, Doubtful Sound	
United States--Alaska	Kenai Fjords	

© 2014 Cengage Learning

12. In the table, delete the Flag column. Add a new row above the row containing "United States—Alaska." Type **Norway** in the new cell in the Location column, and then type **Geirangerfjord, Naeroyfjord** in the Famous examples column.

13. In the table, in the "Chile" row, replace the "e" in "Aisen" with **é**. Then in the Norway row, in the word "Naeroyfjord," replace the "ae" with **æ** and replace the first "o" with **ø** so the word is spelled "Nærøyfjord." (All three letters are in the Latin-1 Supplement subset.)

14. In the table, set the proofing language for the two words in the Famous examples column in the Norway row to Norwegian (Bokmål), and then set the proofing language for the two words in the Famous examples column in the Greenland row to Greenlandic.

15. Apply the Light Style 3 - Accent 1 table style, and then change the font size of all of the text in the table to 24 points.

16. Insert a new column to the left of the Location column. Use online pictures on Office.com to fill each cell with a picture of the flag of the country listed in the Location column. To locate each flag, type the keywords listed below in the box next to Office.com in the Insert Pictures dialog box. When more than one result appears, click each result and look at the keywords and measurements in the lower-left corner of the dialog box, and then use the result that has a width measurement of 600 pixels.
    - Canada: type **Canada flag country**
    - Chile: type **Chile flag country**
    - Greenland: type **Greenland flag**
    - Iceland: type **Iceland flag country**
    - New Zealand: type **New Zealand flag**
    - Norway: type **Norway flag country**
    - United States: type **United States flag country**

17. In the table, change the width of the first column so it is 0.8 inches wide, and then make the second and third columns just wide enough to hold the widest entry on one line. Reposition the table so the left edge is approximately aligned with the left edge of the title text and so the table is approximately centered vertically in the space below the title.

18. Apply the Uncover transition. Change the Effect Options to From Top, and then change the duration to .50 seconds. Apply this transition to all of the slides.

19. On Slide 2 ("What Is a Fjord?"), animate the bulleted list using the Fade animation. Change the duration of the animation to .75 seconds.

20. On Slide 5 ("Fjords in Other Countries"), apply the Wipe animation using the From Left effect to the "New Zealand" caption. Apply the same animation to the other two text captions.

21. Apply the Wipe animation with the From Left effect to the photo under "New Zealand," and then change the start timing of that animation to After previous. Move the animation applied to the photo earlier so it has the same animation sequence number as the caption above it (it should be a 1). Apply the same animation using the After previous start timing to the photos under "Alaska" and "Chile," and adjust the animation order so that each photo has the same animation sequence number as the caption above it.

22. On Slide 7, add the video **Cruise**, located in the PowerPoint2 ▸ Review folder, in the content placeholder on the left, and set it to play Automatically and Full Screen and to rewind after playing. (This video has no sound.) Set the poster frame to the frame at approximately the 2.30-second mark.

23. Add the video **Gulls**, located in the PowerPoint2 ▸ Review folder, in the content placeholder on the right. This video should play On Click and Full Screen. Set the volume to Low. Leave the poster frame as the first frame of the video.

24. Trim the Gulls video by adjusting the end time so the video is approximately 10 seconds long.

25. Compress the media to Low Quality.

26. Add **Fjords presented by Essential Norway Tours** as the footer on all the slides except the title slide, and display the slide number on all the slides except the title slide. On the Notes and Handouts, add **Essential Norway Tours** as the header and your name as the footer.

27. Save your changes, and then watch the final presentation in Slide Show view.

Case Problem 1

APPLY

Data Files needed for this Case Problem: Group.jpg, Summer.mp4, Theater Theme.pptx, Theater.pptx

Ottawa Children's Theatre Workshop   Adrielle Schlosser is the director of the Ottawa Children's Theatre Workshop in Ontario, Canada. One of her responsibilities is to inform parents, teachers, and volunteers about the organization. She asked you to help her prepare the PowerPoint presentation, which will include photos, a video, and a table to provide details her audience might be interested in knowing. Complete the following steps:

1. Open the file named **Theater**, located in the PowerPoint2 ▸ Case1 folder included with your Data Files, add your name as the subtitle on Slide 1, and then save it as **Children's Theater** to the drive and folder where you are storing your files.

2. Apply the theme from the presentation **Theater Theme**, located in the PowerPoint2 ▸ Case1 folder.

3. Apply the picture style Moderate Frame, White to the pictures on Slides 2, 3, 4, and 5.

4. On Slide 3 ("Eligibility"), animate the bulleted list using the Float In animation with the Float Down effect, and change the duration to .50 seconds. Animate the bulleted list on Slide 5 ("Performances") using the same animation.

5. On Slide 6 ("Recent Summer Performance"), insert the video **Summer**, located in the PowerPoint2 ▸ Case1 folder. Set the movie to play Automatically and to rewind after playing, and set the volume to Low. Trim the video by changing the end time to approximately the 18.5-second mark. Set the poster frame to the frame at approximately the 13-second mark.

6. Compress the media to Low Quality.

7. On Slide 7 ("Classes"), add a new row above the last row with the following data: **Junior Jazzers**, **7th – 9th**, **Rarford Koskosky**, **Tues & Thurs, 4 p.m.** (*Hint*: To activate AutoCorrect to change the "th" after 9 to a superscript, press the Tab key to move to the next cell instead of clicking in the cell.)

8. Change the table style to Medium Style 1 – Accent 1. Select all of the text in the table in the rows below the header row, and then change the font color to Pink, Background 1, Darker 50%. Reposition the table so it is approximately centered vertically in the blank area below the title.

9. On Slide 8, which has the Blank layout applied, draw a rectangle shape so it almost fills the slide but fits inside the purple and pink borders on the slide. (*Hint*: Change the fill color of the rectangle to one of the blue colors in the Theme Colors so that you can more easily see where the rectangle and the purple border lines meet.) After the rectangle is sized to the correct size, fill the shape with the picture **Group**, located in the PowerPoint2 ▶ Case1 folder.

10. On Slide 8, draw another rectangle shape that is one inch high and stretches from the inside of the pink borders on the left and right. Position this rectangle directly below the purple line at the top of the slide. Remove the fill from the shape and remove the outline (that is, change the fill to No Fill and change the outline to No Outline).

11. In the second rectangle, type **See You at the Theater!**. Change the font to Broadway (Headings), and change the font size to 44 points. (If the font color is not White, or if you can't see the text, click the border of the rectangle to select the entire shape, and then change the font color to White.)

12. On Slide 8, animate the text box using the entrance animation Grow & Turn. Set its duration to .50 seconds, set its start timing to After previous, and set a delay of one second.

13. Apply the Drape transition to all the slides using the default Left effect. Then apply the Curtains transition to only Slides 1 and 8. On Slide 8, change the duration of the transition to two seconds.

14. Save your changes, and then watch the slide show in Slide Show view. Remember to wait for the video on Slide 6 ("Recent Summer Performance") to start automatically, and, after the transition to Slide 8, wait for the text box to animate automatically.

Case Problem 2

CREATE

Data Files needed for this Case Problem: Coating.pptx, Curing.mp4, Hanging.jpg, Powder.mp4, Touchup.jpg, Wash.mp4, Welding.jpg

Powder Coating Power Plus   Yung Hoang owns Powder Coating Power Plus, a company that uses a process called powder coating to paint metal surfaces. Powder coating results in a high-quality painted metal surface because it bonds with the metal instead of sitting on top of it. His company paints items such as exhaust fans, intake vents, pipes, and bike frames. Potential clients want to know the advantages and the process of powder coating, so Yung decided to create a PowerPoint presentation to provide this information and approximate costs. He started with the Project planning overview presentation template from Office.com and added a custom layout. Complete the following steps:

1. Open the presentation **Coating**, located in the PowerPoint2 ▸ Case2 folder included with your Data Files, add your name as the subtitle, and then save the presentation as **Powder Coating** to the drive and folder where you are storing your files.

2. Change the layout of Slides 3 through 8 to the custom layout Two Content Modified.

3. Refer to Figure 2-45 and insert the pictures and video as shown on Slides 3 through 8. All the files are located in the PowerPoint2 ▸ Case2 folder. Note that none of the videos in the presentation have sound.

Figure 2-45   **Slides 3 – 8 in the Powder Coating presentation**

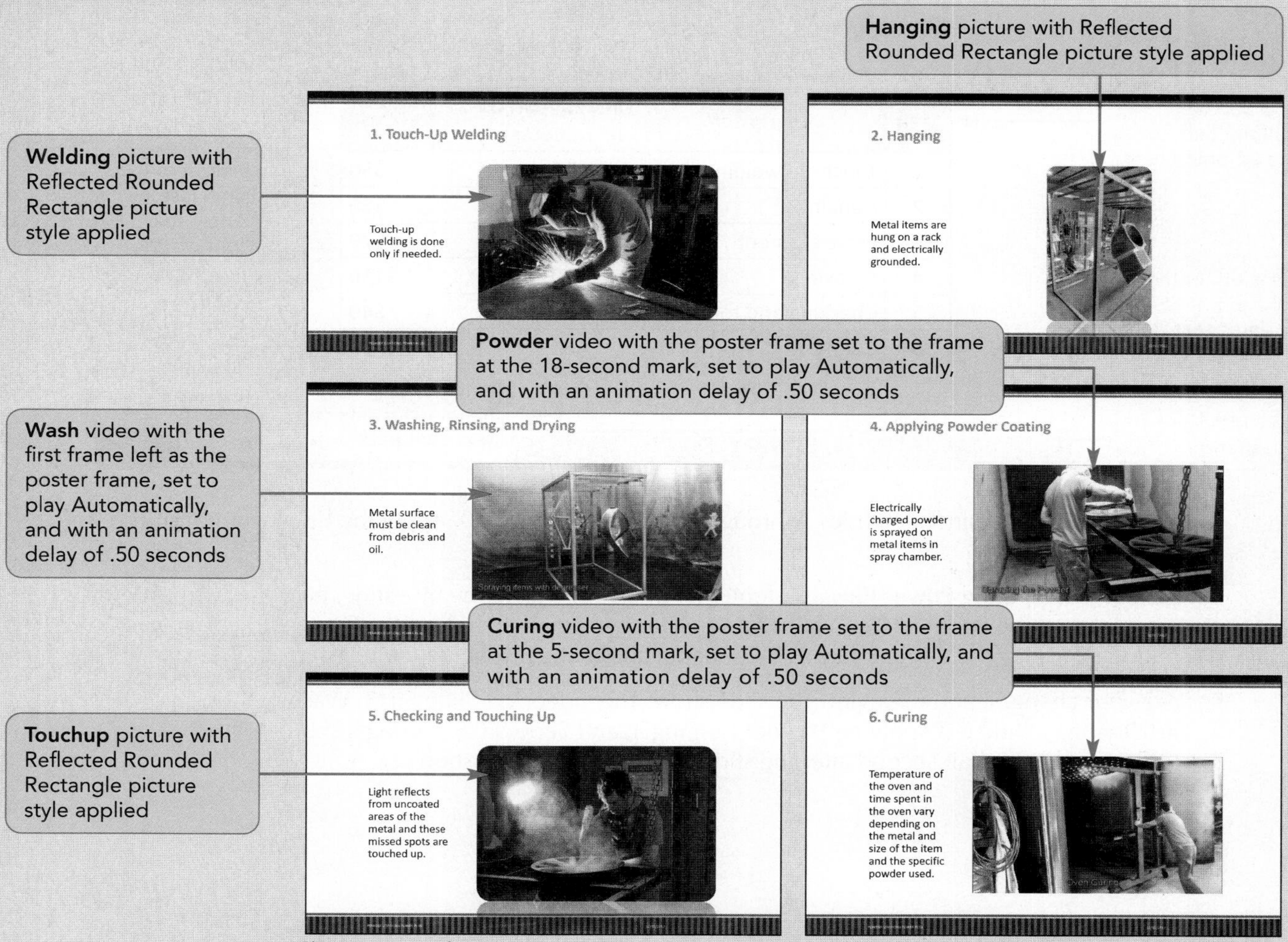

Photos courtesy of S. Scott Zimmerman

4. Compress all the photos to 96 ppi, and compress the media to Low Quality.

5. On Slide 2 ("Why Is Powder Coating Better Than Paint?"), animate the bulleted list to Wipe with the From Top effect.

6. On Slide 9 ("Procedures and Costs"), create the table shown in Figure 2-46, and apply the formatting as described in the figure.

Figure 2-46   **Table on Slide 9 in the Power Coating presentation**

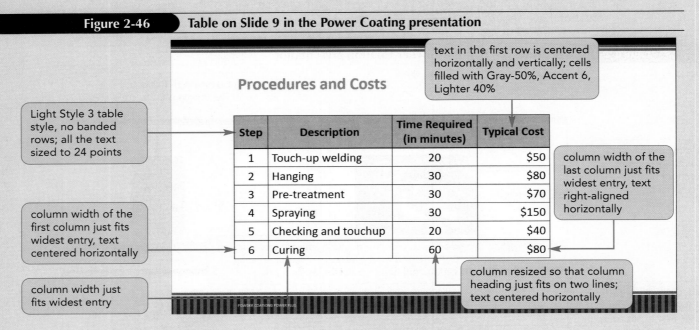

7. Apply the Fade transition to Slides 1 through 3 and Slides 9 and 10. Apply the Conveyor transition to Slides 4 through 8.

8. Add **Powder Coating Power Plus** as a footer on all slides except the title slide, and display the current date to be updated automatically on all slides except the title slide. On the notes and handouts, display the current date to be updated automatically, and add your name as a header.

9. Save your changes, and then view the slide show. The videos on Slide 5 ("3. Washing, Rinsing, and Drying"), Slide 6 ("Applying Powder Coating"), and Slide 8 ("6. Curing") should play automatically one-half second after the slide appears in the slide show.

Case Problem 3

Data Files needed for this Case Problem: Bench End.jpg, Bench.mp4, Curl.mp4, Gym Theme.pptx, Gym.pptx, Military.mp4

St. Louis Fitness Consultants   St. Louis Fitness Consultants provides consulting and training services to gyms, municipal fitness centers, and large companies. Bianca Kocherhans, a personal trainer and sales consultant who works at St. Louis Fitness, realized that many people want the convenience of having a home gym. She approached the company's owners and was given approval to offer consulting to retail stores that sell fitness equipment and to large companies with employees interested in setting up their own home gym. She prepared a PowerPoint presentation with some information on setting up a home gym and doing a few basic weight-lifting exercises. Complete the following steps:

1. Open the presentation named **Gym**, located in the PowerPoint2 ▸ Case3 folder included with your Data Files, add your name as the subtitle, and then save it as **Home Gym** to the drive and folder where you are storing your files.

2. Apply the theme from the presentation **Gym Theme**, located in the PowerPoint2 ▸ Case3 folder.

3. On Slide 10 ("Bench Press Technique"), change the layout to Comparison Three, insert the picture **Bench End** in the content placeholder, and then type **Ending position** in the text placeholder below this photo. Compress this photo to 96 ppi.

4. Apply the Drop Shadow Rectangle picture style to the three photos on Slide 10.

5. On Slide 3 ("Why a Power Cage?"), add the Line Callout 1 shape to the left of the bottom part of the picture. Type **Safety bar to catch barbell** in the shape. Apply the Moderate Effect – Black, Dark 1 shape style, and then change the outline weight to 3 points. Resize the box part of the callout containing the text so that all the text fits on two lines with "Safety bar to" on the first line.

6. Flip the callout shape horizontally, and then drag the end of the callout line to point to the part of the horizontal safety bar in the photo indicated by the red circle shape. Delete the red circle shape.

7. On Slide 4 ("Typical Costs"), insert a 3x6 table. Keep the default style Medium Style 2 – Accent 1 applied to the table. Enter the data shown in Figure 2-47.

Figure 2-47   Data for table on Slide 4 in the Home Gym presentation

Item	Cost per Item	Total Cost
Power cage (1)	$650	$650
Bench (1)	$200	$200
Barbell (2)	$50	$100
Barbell plates (12 pairs)	$30	$360
Dumbbells (9 pairs)	$20	$180

© 2014 Cengage Learning

8. Add a new bottom row to the table. Type **TOTAL** in the first cell in the new row, and then type **$1,490** in the last cell in the new row.

9. Increase the size of all the text in the table to 24 points. Resize the first column so it is just wide enough to fit the widest entry, and then resize the second and third columns so they are 2.5 inches wide.

10. Horizontally center the text in the first row. Horizontally right-align the dollar values in the second and third columns, and then right-align "TOTAL" in its cell in the last row.

11. Add a Gray-50%, Accent 6, Darker 50%, 3-point horizontal border between the last row and the row above it, and then add a 1-point border using the same color to the top and bottom of the table.

12. On Slide 7 ("Executing the Arm Curl"), insert the video **Curl**, on Slide 9 ("Executing the Military Press"), insert the video **Military**, and on Slide 11 ("Executing the Bench Press"), insert the video **Bench**. All three videos are located in the PowerPoint2 ▶ Case3 folder. (None of the videos in this presentation have sound.) For all three videos, keep the first frame as the poster frame.

13. Trim each video as necessary so that only two repetitions of the exercise are shown.

14. Copy the callout you added on Slide 3 ("Why a Power Cage?") to Slide 11 ("Executing the Bench Press"). Reposition the callout to point to the same location on the safety bar that you pointed to on Slide 3.

15. Animate the bulleted list on Slide 3 ("Why a Power Cage?") with the Appear entrance animation, and then animate the callout on Slide 3 with the same animation.

16. Change the start timing of the animation applied to the callout so that it appears at the same time as the "Safe" bulleted item.

17. Compress the media in the presentation.

18. Add **St. Louis Fitness Consultants** as the footer on all of the slides, including the title slide, and display the slide number on all of the slides. Add your name as a header on the notes and handouts.

19. Apply the Gallery transition to all of the slides except the first one using the default effect options From Right.

20. Save your changes, and then view the slide show.

Case Problem 4

Data Files needed for this Case Problem: Identity.pptx, Logo.jpg, Password.wma

CHALLENGE

KeepMeMine ID Dudley Zaunbrecher is a regional sales representative for KeepMeMine ID, an insurance and security company headquartered in Fort Smith, Arkansas that protects, monitors, insures, and recovers personal identity. Dudley travels throughout his region meeting with new customers. He wants to use PowerPoint to give a presentation to explain the seriousness of identity theft and how to create strong passwords, and then wrap up by trying to sign up new clients. He has asked you to help him prepare the presentation. Complete the following steps:

1. Open the presentation **Identity**, located in the PowerPoint2 ▶ Case4 folder included with your Data Files, add your name as the subtitle, and then save the presentation as **Identity Theft** to the drive and folder where you are storing your files.

2. Apply the installed Organic theme, and then change the variant to the fourth variant.

3. On Slide 4 ("What Is a Strong Password?"), insert a picture from Office.com. Use the keyword **password**, and insert the picture of asterisks in a password box.

4. On Slide 4, animate the bulleted list using the Wipe animation with the From Left effect.

5. Slide 5 ("Creating a Strong Password") contains four individual text boxes, not the usual bulleted list in one text box. Click the first bulleted item, press and hold the Shift key, click each of the other three items, and then release the Shift key. Apply the entrance animation Appear to the selected text boxes.

⊕ **Explore** 6. On Slide 5, select the four animated text boxes, and then modify the Appear animation so that the letters appear one by one. (*Hint*: Use the Animation group Dialog Box Launcher, and then change the setting in the Animate text box on the Effect tab.) Speed up the effect by changing the delay between letters to 0.1 seconds.

⊕ **Explore** 7. On Slide 5, insert the audio clip **Password**, located in the PowerPoint2 ▶ Case4 folder included with your Data Files. Position the sound icon to the right of the slide title so that the centers and right edges of the icon object and the title text object are aligned. Point to the sound icon, and then click the Play button. Listen to the recording and notice how it relates to the bulleted items on the slide.

⊕ **Explore** 8. Add bookmarks to the play bar for the sound icon to mark four distinct points in the recording at approximately 9, 15, 19, and 32 seconds to correspond to the four text boxes on the slide. (*Hint*: Click the sound icon, and then click the AUDIO TOOLS PLAYBACK tab. Point to the sound icon, click the Play button, and then click the Add Bookmark button in the Bookmarks group on the PLAYBACK tab at the appropriate times, or click the play bar at the point where you want to add the bookmark.)

⊕ **Explore** 9. Set the animation of the bulleted list to play automatically as the recording hits each bookmark. (*Hint*: Select each text box, and then use the Trigger button in the Advanced Animation group on the ANIMATIONS tab.)

10. Display Slide 5 in Slide Show view, point to the sound icon, and then click the Play button. Watch as the text in the text boxes animates automatically, one letter at a time, as each bookmark is reached. End the slide show.

11. On Slide 6 ("We Can Help"), insert the picture **Logo**, located in the PowerPoint2 ▶ Case4 folder.

12. Compress all the pictures to 96 ppi, and then compress the media to the lowest quality.

13. Apply the Switch transition to all the slides in the presentation.

14. Save your changes, and then run the slide show.

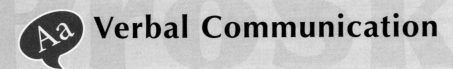

Verbal Communication

Rehearsing Your Presentation

The best presentations are planned well in advance of their delivery. Once the content has been created, enhanced, and perfected, it is time to prepare you, the presenter. Presenters who try to stand up and "wing it" in front of a crowd usually reveal this amateur approach the moment they start speaking—by looking down at their notes, rambling off topic, or turning their back on the audience frequently to read from the slides displayed on-screen.

To avoid being seen as an amateur, you need to rehearse your presentation. Even the most knowledgeable speakers rehearse to ensure they know how the topic flows, what the main points are, how much time to spend on each slide, and where to place emphasis. Experienced presenters understand that while practice may not make them perfect, it will certainly make them better.

Where you practice isn't that important. You can talk to a mirror, your family, or a group of friends. If you have a video camera, you can record yourself and then review the video. Watching video evidence of your performance often reveals the weaknesses you don't want your audience to see and that your friends or family may be unwilling or unable to identify. Whatever you choose to do, the bottom line is this: If you practice, you will improve.

As you rehearse, you should remember to focus on the following steps:

- Practice speaking fluently.
- Work on your tone of voice.
- Decide how to involve your audience.
- Become aware of your body language.
- Check your appearance.

Speaking Fluently

Be sure to speak in an easy, smooth manner, and avoid using nonwords and fillers. Nonwords consist of ums, ahs, hms, and other such breaks in speech. Fillers are phrases that don't add any value yet add length to sentences. Both can dilute a speaker's message because they are not essential to the meaning of what's being spoken. At best, they can make you sound unprofessional. At worst, they can distract your audience and make your message incomprehensible.

Considering Your Tone of Voice

When delivering your presentation, you usually want to speak passionately, with authority, and with a smile. If you aren't excited about your presentation, how will your audience feel? By projecting your voice with energy, passion, and confidence, your audience will automatically pay more attention to you. Smile and look directly at your audience members and make eye contact. If your message is getting across, they will instinctively affirm what you're saying by returning your gaze, nodding their heads, or smiling. There's something compelling about a confident speaker whose presence commands attention. However, be careful not to overdo it. Speaking too loudly or using an overly confident or arrogant tone will turn off an audience and make them stop listening altogether.

Involving Your Audience

If you involve your audience in your presentation, they will pay closer attention to what you have to say. When an audience member asks a question, be sure to affirm them before answering. For example, you could respond with "That's a great question. What do the rest of you think?" or "Thanks for asking. Here's what my research revealed." An easy way to get the audience to participate is to start with a question and invite responses, or to stop partway through to discuss a particularly important point.

Being Aware of Your Body Language

Although the content of your presentation plays a role in your message delivery, it's your voice and body language during the presentation that make or break it. Maintain eye contact to send the message that you want to connect and that you can be trusted. Stand up straight to signal confidence. Conversely, avoid slouching, which can convey laziness, lack of energy, or disinterest, and fidgeting or touching your hair, which can signal nervousness. Resist the temptation to glance at your watch; you don't want to send a signal that you'd rather be someplace else. Finally, be aware of your hand movements. The best position for your hands is to place them comfortably by your side, in a relaxed position. As you talk, it's fine to use hand gestures to help make a point, but be careful not to overdo it.

Evaluating Your Appearance

Just as a professional appearance makes a good impression during a job interview, an audience's first impression of a speaker is also based on appearance. Before a single word is spoken, the audience sizes up the way the presenter looks. You want to make sure you look professional and competent. Make sure your appearance is neat, clean, and well-coordinated, and dress in appropriate clothing.

As you spend time practicing your presentation, you will naturally develop appropriate body language, tone of voice, and a fluent delivery, ensuring a clear connection with your audience and a professional delivery of your presentation's message.

PROSKILLS

Create and Deliver a Training Presentation

If you hold a job for any length of time, as part of your employment, you might have to train new employees in their work tasks. For example, if you work in a library, you might have to explain how to process returned books, or if you work in a chemistry stockroom at a college, you might have to describe how to make up solutions for the school's chemistry laboratories. A PowerPoint presentation can be an effective way to start the training process. With a presentation, you can give an overview of the job without needing to repeat yourself to explain detailed aspects. Then you can customize the rest of the training to fit the needs of the specific employee.

In this exercise, you'll create a presentation containing information of your choice, using the PowerPoint skills and features presented in Tutorials 1 and 2, and then you will practice techniques for delivering the presentation.

Note: Please be sure not to include any personal information of a sensitive nature in the documents you create to be submitted to your instructor for this exercise. Later on, you can update the documents with such information for your own personal use.

1. Create a new PowerPoint presentation and apply an appropriate theme. Make sure you choose a theme that is relevant to the job you are describing and to your audience. Consider using a template from Office.com.
2. On Slide 1, make the presentation title the same as the title of your job or the job for which you are giving the training. Add your name as a subtitle.
3. Create a new slide for each major category of tasks. For example, task categories for a library job might be "Punching In," "Checking in with Your Supervisor," "Gathering Books from Drop-Off Stations," "Scanning Returned Books into the Computer," "Checking Books for Damage or Marks," "Processing Abused Books," "Processing Late Books," "Sorting Books," "Shelving Books," and "Punching Out."
4. On each slide, create a bulleted list to explain the particular task category or to provide the steps required to perform the task, or consider if a graphic, such as a SmartArt diagram or a table, would better illustrate your point.
5. Where applicable, include clip art, photographs, or a video. For example, you might include a photograph of the punch clock (time clock) used by hourly workers in the library, or a photograph of a book with serious damage relative to one with normal wear.

6. On one or more slides, insert a shape, such as a rectangle, triangle, circle, arrow, or star. For example, you might want to place a small colored star next to a particularly important step in carrying out a task.

7. Apply appropriate formatting to the graphics on the slides.

8. Examine your slides. Are you using too many words? Can any of your bulleted lists be replaced with a graphic?

9. Reevaluate the theme you chose. Do you think it is still appropriate? Does it fit the content of your presentation? If not, apply a different theme.

10. Add appropriate transitions and animations. Remember that the goal is to keep your audience engaged without distracting them.

11. Check the spelling of your presentation, and then proofread it to check for errors that would not be caught by the spell check. Save the final presentation.

12. Rehearse the presentation. Consider your appearance, and decide on the appropriate clothing to wear. Practice in front of a mirror and friends or family, and if you can, create a video of yourself. Notice and fine tune your body language, tone of voice, and fluency to fully engage your audience.

OBJECTIVES

Session 3.1
- Create a SmartArt diagram
- Modify a SmartArt diagram
- Add an audio clip to a slide
- Create a chart
- Modify a chart
- Insert and format text boxes
- Apply a WordArt style to text

Session 3.2
- Correct photos using photo editing tools
- Remove the background from a photo
- Apply an artistic effect to a photo
- Create a custom shape
- Adjust and align shapes
- Fill a shape with a texture and a custom gradient
- Add alt text to graphics

Applying Advanced Formatting to Objects

Formatting Objects in a Presentation for a Seminar Management Company

Case | *Spring Lake Seminar Management, Inc.*

Rashad Menche is a senior coordinator for Spring Lake Seminar Management, an international seminar management company with headquarters in Champaign, Illinois. The company provides assistance in planning and implementing seminars for companies and facilitating follow-up activities. As a senior coordinator, Rashad is responsible for everything from identifying and inviting appropriate speakers, to organizing the activities for the event, and finally sending out thank you letters and surveys to obtain feedback. He is preparing a presentation to potential clients about the services offered by the company, and he asks for your help in enhancing the presentation with some more advanced formatting of the presentation's content.

In this tutorial, you will add interest to the presentation by creating a SmartArt graphic and a chart and by inserting an audio clip. You will also create a text box and use WordArt styles. You will improve the photos in the presentation using PowerPoint's photo editing tools. In addition, you will create a custom shape, and apply advanced formatting to the shape. Finally, you will add text to describe some of the graphics to make the presentation more accessible for people who use screen readers.

STARTING DATA FILES

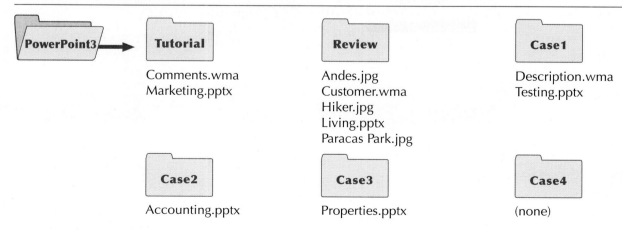

PowerPoint3 →

Tutorial
Comments.wma
Marketing.pptx

Review
Andes.jpg
Customer.wma
Hiker.jpg
Living.pptx
Paracas Park.jpg

Case1
Description.wma
Testing.pptx

Case2
Accounting.pptx

Case3
Properties.pptx

Case4
(none)

Session 3.1 Visual Overview:

When you insert a chart, a spreadsheet appears in which you enter the data to create the chart. A **spreadsheet** (called a worksheet in Microsoft Excel) is a grid of cells that contain numbers and text.

If you need additional tools and Excel is installed on your computer, click the Edit Data in Microsoft Excel button to open the spreadsheet in an Excel workbook.

As in a table, the intersection of a row and a column is a **cell**, and you add data and labels in cells. Cells in a datasheet are referenced by their column letter and row number. This cell is cell B1.

Colored borders and shading of cells indicate that they are included in the chart.

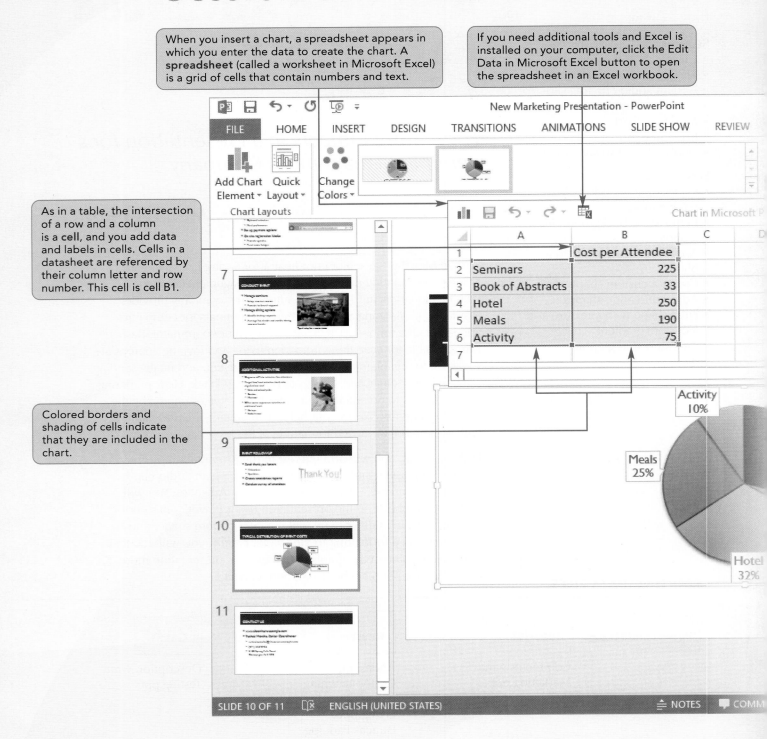

Creating a Chart on a Slide

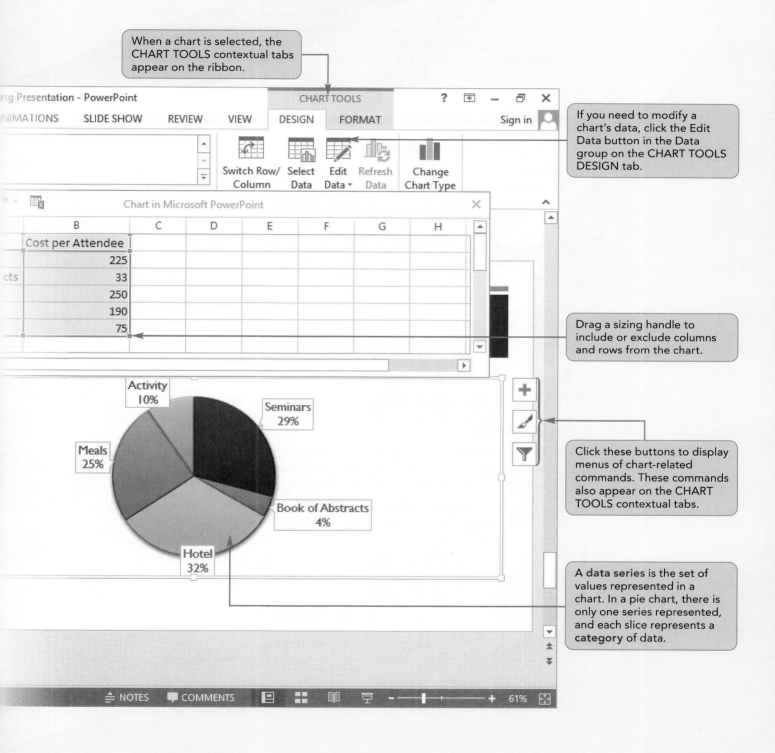

When a chart is selected, the CHART TOOLS contextual tabs appear on the ribbon.

If you need to modify a chart's data, click the Edit Data button in the Data group on the CHART TOOLS DESIGN tab.

Drag a sizing handle to include or exclude columns and rows from the chart.

Click these buttons to display menus of chart-related commands. These commands also appear on the CHART TOOLS contextual tabs.

A **data series** is the set of values represented in a chart. In a pie chart, there is only one series represented, and each slice represents a **category** of data.

Creating SmartArt Diagrams

In addition to creating a SmartArt diagram from a bulleted list, you can create one from scratch and then add text or pictures to it. Once you create a SmartArt diagram, you can change its layout, add or remove shapes from it, reorder, promote, or demote the shapes, and change the style, color, and shapes used to create the SmartArt. To create a SmartArt diagram, you can click the Insert a SmartArt Graphic button in a content placeholder, or in the Illustrations group on the INSERT tab, click the SmartArt button to open the Choose a SmartArt Graphic dialog box.

REFERENCE

Creating a SmartArt Diagram

- Switch to a layout that includes a content placeholder, and then in the content placeholder, click the Insert a SmartArt Graphic button; or click the INSERT tab on the ribbon, and then in the Illustrations group, click the SmartArt button.
- In the Choose a SmartArt Graphic dialog box, select the desired SmartArt category in the list on the left.
- In the center pane, click the SmartArt diagram you want to use.
- Click the OK button.

Rashad wants you to create a SmartArt diagram on Slide 3 of his marketing presentation. The diagram will list a general overview of the presentation.

To create a SmartArt diagram:

1. Open the presentation **Marketing**, located in the PowerPoint3 ▸ Tutorial folder included with your Data Files, and then save it as **New Marketing Presentation**.

2. Display **Slide 3** ("Let Us Plan Your Seminar or Conference") in the slide pane, and then in the content placeholder, click the **Insert a SmartArt graphic** button. The Choose a SmartArt Graphic dialog box opens.

3. In the List category, click the **Lined List** layout, and then click the **OK** button. A SmartArt diagram containing placeholder text is inserted on the slide, and the SMARTART TOOLS DESIGN tab is selected on the ribbon.

4. In the Create Graphic group, click the **Text Pane** button. The text pane appears to the left of the diagram. See Figure 3-1. The insertion point is in the first bullet in the text pane.

    Trouble? If the text pane is already displayed, skip Step 4.

Figure 3-1   SmartArt inserted on Slide 3

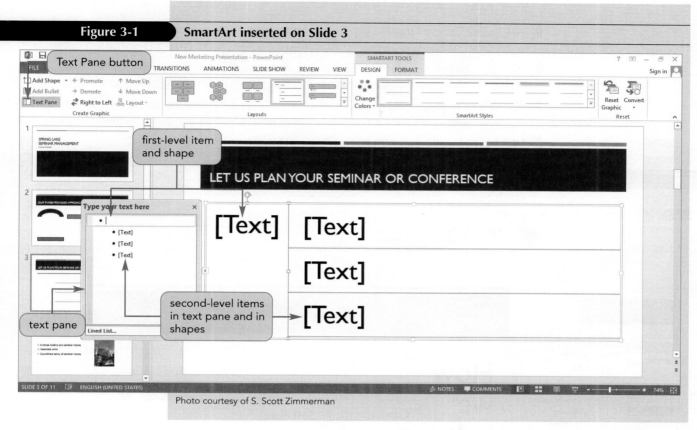

Photo courtesy of S. Scott Zimmerman

Now that you've added the diagram to the slide, you can add content to it. You need to add a first-level item and subitems to the diagram.

To add text to the SmartArt diagram and reorder it:

1. With the insertion point in the first bulleted item in the text pane, type **How we help**. The text appears in the bulleted list in the text pane and in the leftmost rectangle in the diagram.

2. In the first subbullet in the bulleted list, click **[Text]**. The placeholder text disappears and the insertion point appears.

3. Type **Choose site**, and then in the text pane, click the **Close** button ✖.

4. In the diagram, click the placeholder text in the box under the "Choose site" shape, and then type **Coordinate registration**.

5. Click the last empty box in the diagram, and then type **Invite speakers**. The "Invite speakers" shape needs to be moved so it is the second shape in the diagram.

6. Make sure the insertion point is in the Invite speakers shape, and then in the Create Graphic group, click the **Move Up** button. The current shape moves up into the second position in the diagram. You need to add two more shapes to the diagram.

7. Click in the **Coordinate registration shape**, and then in the Create Graphic group, click the **Add Shape** button. A new shape is added to the bottom of the diagram at the same level as the "Coordinate registration" shape. This shape does not have placeholder text, so you need to reopen the text pane to add the text.

TIP

To switch the order of the shapes, click the Right to Left button in the Create Graphic group on the SMARTART TOOLS DESIGN tab.

▶ **8.** In the Create Graphic group, click the **Text Pane** button. The text pane opens with an additional subbullet below the "Coordinate registration" item.

▶ **9.** Click to the right of the subbullet below the "Coordinate registration" item, and then type **Conduct event**. You need to add one more item to the list.

▶ **10.** With the insertion point after the word "event," press the **Enter** key. A fifth subbullet is created and an additional shape appears in the SmartArt diagram.

▶ **11.** Type **Handle follow-up**. See Figure 3-2.

Figure 3-2	SmartArt with text added

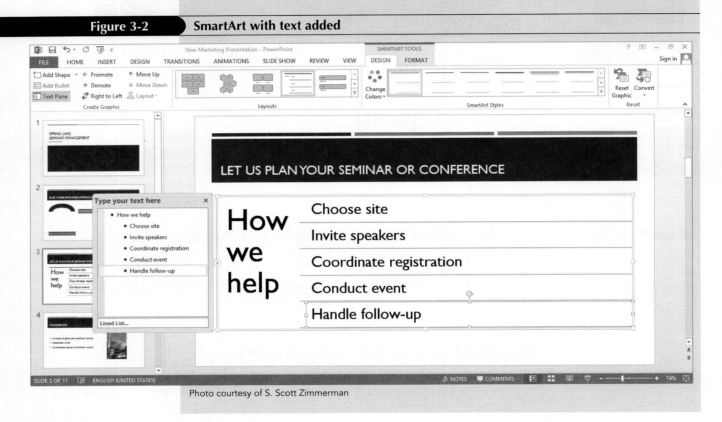

Photo courtesy of S. Scott Zimmerman

Modifying a SmartArt Diagram

There are many ways to modify a SmartArt diagram. For example, you can change the layout of the diagram so the information is presented differently. You can also change the level of items in the diagram. You will change this next.

To change the layout of the SmartArt diagram:

▶ **1.** On the SMARTART TOOLS DESIGN tab, in the Layouts group, click the **More** button. The gallery of layouts in the List category opens.

2. Click the **Vertical Block List** layout. The layout of the diagram changes to the new layout. Now you need to change the five subbullets to first-level bullets and delete the "How we help" shape.

3. In the text pane, click in the **Choose site** bulleted item.

4. On the SMARTART TOOLS DESIGN tab, in the Create Graphic group, click the **Promote** button. The item is promoted to a first-level item in both the text pane and in the diagram. See Figure 3-3.

Figure 3-3 | **SmartArt after changing the layout and promoting a shape**

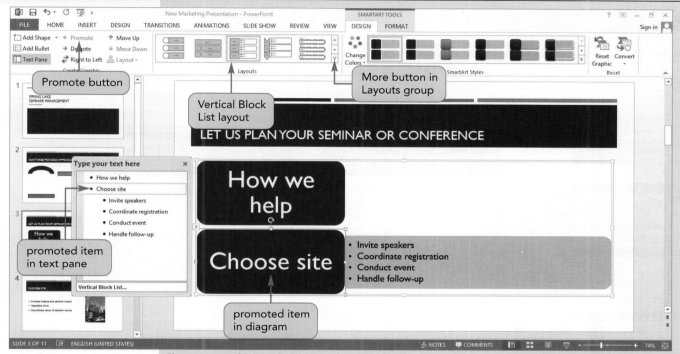

Photo courtesy of S. Scott Zimmerman

5. Promote the other four subbulleted items. All the text in the diagram is now in first-level shapes, and because there are no longer any subbullets, the first-level items are centered in the SmartArt diagram.

6. In the text pane, select **How we help** (the first bulleted item), and then press the **Delete** key. The text and the bullet item are deleted. In the diagram, the first shape is deleted as well.

Trouble? If there is still a bullet at the top of the text pane and an empty shape above the "Choose site" shape in the diagram, click in the empty line in the text pane, and then press the Delete key.

7. In the text pane, click the **Close** button ☒.

SmartArt diagrams contain multiple objects that are grouped as one object which is then treated as a whole. So when you apply a style or other effect to the diagram, the effect is applied to the entire object. You can also apply formatting to individual shapes within the diagram if you want. You just need to select the specific shape first.

To apply a style to the SmartArt diagram and change its colors:

1. On the SMARTART TOOLS DESIGN tab, in the SmartArt Styles group, click the **More** button to open the gallery of styles available for the graphic.

2. In the gallery, click the **Inset** style. The style of the graphic changes to the Inset style.

3. In the SmartArt Styles group, click the **Change Colors** button. A gallery of color styles opens.

4. Under Accent 1, click the **Colored Outline – Accent 1** style. See Figure 3-4.

| Figure 3-4 | SmartArt with color and style changed |

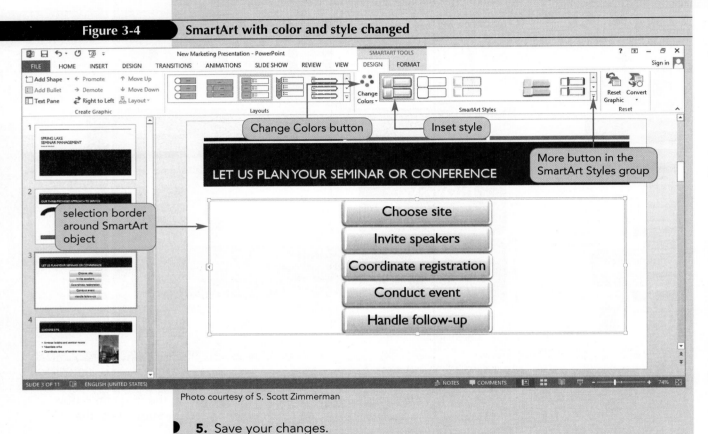

Photo courtesy of S. Scott Zimmerman

5. Save your changes.

Animating a SmartArt Diagram

You animate a SmartArt diagram in the same way you animate any object. The default is for the entire object to animate as a single object. But similar to a bulleted list, after you apply an animation, you can use the Effect Options button and choose a different sequence effect. For example, you can choose to have each object animate one at a time.

Rashad wants the shapes in the SmartArt diagram to appear on the slide one at a time during his presentation.

To animate the SmartArt diagram:

▶ **1.** On the ribbon, click the **ANIMATIONS** tab.

▶ **2.** In the Animation group, click the **Appear** animation. The animation previews and the object quickly appears on the slide. One animation sequence icon appears to the left of the diagram object in the Slide pane.

▶ **3.** In the Animation group, click the **Effect Options** button. The selected effect is As One Object.

▶ **4.** Click **One by One**. The animation previews and each shape in the diagram appears one at a time.

▶ **5.** On the status bar, click the **Slide Show** button 🖵. Slide 3 appears in Slide Show view.

▶ **6.** Advance the slide show five times to display each of the shapes on the screen, one at a time.

▶ **7.** Press the **Esc** key to end the slide show.

▶ **8.** Save your changes.

INSIGHT

Converting a SmartArt Diagram to Text or Shapes

You can convert a SmartArt diagram to a bulleted list or to its individual shapes. To convert a diagram to a bulleted list, select the diagram, and then on the SMARTART TOOLS DESIGN tab, in the Reset group, click the Convert button, and then click Convert to Text. To convert a group to its individual shapes, click Convert to Shapes on the Convert menu or use the Ungroup command. In both cases, the shapes are converted from a SmartArt diagram into a set of grouped shapes. To completely ungroup them, you would need to use the Ungroup command a second time. Keep in mind that if you convert the diagram to shapes, you change it from a SmartArt object into ordinary drawn shapes, and you will no longer have access to the commands on the SmartArt Tools contextual tabs.

Adding Audio to Slides

Audio in a presentation can be used for a wide variety of purposes. For example, you might want to add a sound clip of music to a particular portion of the presentation to evoke emotion, or perhaps include a sound clip that is a recording of a customer expressing their satisfaction with a product or service. To add a sound clip to a slide, you use the Audio button in the Media group on the INSERT tab. When a sound clip is added to a slide, a sound icon and a play bar appear on the slide. Similar to videos, the options for changing how the sound plays during the slide show appear on the AUDIO TOOLS PLAYBACK tab. For the most part, they are the same options that appear on the VIDEO TOOLS PLAYBACK tab. For example, you can trim an audio clip or set it to rewind after playing. You can also compress audio in the same way that you compress video.

REFERENCE

Inserting an Audio Clip into a Presentation

- Display the slide in which you want to insert the sound in the Slide pane.
- On the ribbon, click the INSERT tab, click the Audio button in the Media group, and then click Audio on My PC.
- In the Insert Audio dialog box, navigate to the folder containing the sound clip, click the audio file, and then click the Insert button.
- If desired, click the AUDIO TOOLS PLAYBACK tab, and then in the Audio Options group:
  - Click the Start arrow, and then click Automatically.
  - Click the Hide During Show check box to select it to hide the icon during a slide show.
  - Click the Volume button, and then click a volume level or click Mute.

Rashad wants you to add a sound clip to the presentation—a recording of a recent customer praising the company. The recorded message is a Windows Media Audio file, which is the most common file format for short sound clips.

To add a sound clip to Slide 3:

1. With **Slide 3** ("Let Us Plan Your Seminar or Conference") displayed in the Slide pane, click the **INSERT** tab on the ribbon.

2. In the Media group, click the **Audio** button, and then click **Audio on My PC**. The Insert Audio dialog box opens.

3. Navigate to the PowerPoint3 ► Tutorial folder, click the **Comments** file, and then click the **Insert** button. A sound icon appears in the middle of the slide with a play bar below it, and the AUDIO TOOLS PLAYBACK tab is selected on the ribbon. See Figure 3-5. As with videos, the default start setting is On Click.

TIP

To record an audio clip, click the Audio button, and then click Record Audio.

Figure 3-5　Sound icon on Slide 2

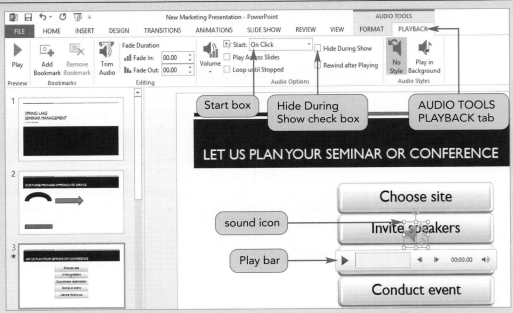

> To make it easier to see the sound icon, you can reposition it on the slide.
>
> ▶ **4.** Drag the sound icon to the lower-right corner of the slide.
>
> ▶ **5.** On the play bar, click the **Play** button ▶. The sound clip plays, which is a comment from a customer complimenting the company on their service. Rashad wants the clip to play automatically after the slide appears on the screen.
>
> ▶ **6.** On the PLAYBACK tab, in the Audio Options group, click the **Start box arrow**, and then click **Automatically**. Because the clip will play automatically, there is no need to have the sound icon be visible on the screen during a slide show.
>
> ▶ **7.** In the Audio Options group, click the **Hide During Show** check box to select it.
>
> ▶ **8.** Save the presentation.

INSIGHT

Playing Music Across Slides

You can add an audio clip to a slide and have it play throughout the slide show. On the AUDIO TOOLS PLAYBACK tab, in the Audio Styles group, click the Play in Background button. When you select this option, the Start timing in the Audio Options group is changed to Automatically, and the Play Across Slides, Loop until Stopped, and Hide During Show check boxes become selected. Also, the Play in Background command changes the trigger animation automatically applied to media to a With Previous animation set to zero so that the sound will automatically start playing after the slide transitions. These setting changes ensure the audio clip will start playing when the slide appears on the screen during a slide show and will continue playing, starting over if necessary, until the end of the slide show.

Adding a Chart to a Slide

The terms "chart" and "graph" often are used interchangeably; however, they do, in fact, have distinct meanings. **Charts** are visuals that use lines, arrows, and boxes or other shapes to show parts, steps, or processes. **Graphs** show the relationship between variables along two axes or reference lines: the independent variable on the horizontal axis and the dependent variable on the vertical axis.

Despite these differences in the definitions, in PowerPoint a chart is any visual depiction of data in a spreadsheet, even if the result is more properly referred to as a graph (such as a line graph). Refer to the Session 3.1 Visual Overview for more information about creating charts in PowerPoint.

Creating a Chart

To create a chart, you click the Insert Chart button in a content placeholder or use the Chart button in the Illustrations group on the INSERT tab. Doing so will open a window containing a spreadsheet with sample data, and a sample chart will appear on the slide. You can then edit the sample data in the window to reflect your own data to be represented in the chart on the slide.

Creating a Chart

- Switch to a layout that includes a content placeholder, and then click the Insert Chart button in the content placeholder to open the Insert Chart dialog box; or click the INSERT tab, and then, in the Illustrations group, click the Chart button to open the Insert Chart dialog box.
- In the list on the left, click the desired chart type.
- In the row of styles, click the desired chart style, and then click the OK button.
- In the spreadsheet that opens, enter the data that you want to plot.
- In the spreadsheet window, click the Close button.

Rashad wants you to create a chart on Slide 10 to illustrate the percentage of each of the costs associated with a typical event that his company organizes. To do this, you'll create a pie chart.

To create a chart on Slide 10:

1. Display **Slide 10** ("Typical Distribution of Event Costs") in the Slide pane.

2. In the content placeholder, click the **Insert Chart** button. The Insert Chart dialog box opens. Column is selected in the list of chart types on the left, and the Clustered Column style is selected in the row of styles at the top and shown in the preview area. See Figure 3-6.

Figure 3-6 **Insert Chart dialog box**

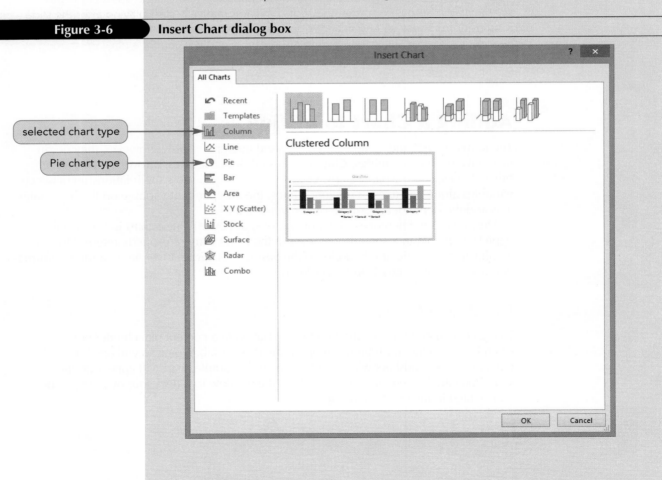

selected chart type

Pie chart type

3. In the list of chart types, click **Pie**. The row of chart styles changes to pie chart styles. The Pie style is selected.

4. Click the **OK** button. A sample chart is inserted on Slide 10, and a small spreadsheet (sometimes called a datasheet) opens above the chart, with colored borders around the cells in the spreadsheet indicating which cells of data are included in the chart. See Figure 3-7.

Figure 3-7   **Spreadsheet and chart with sample data**

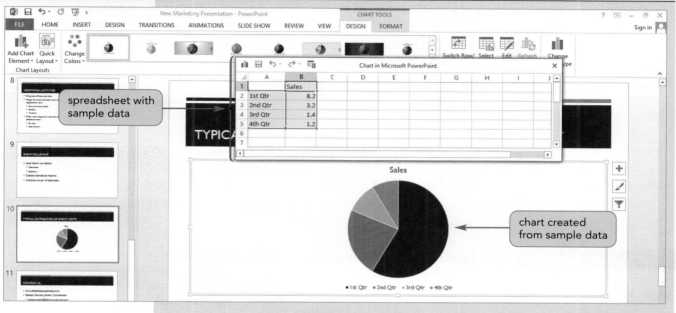

To create the chart for Rashad's presentation, you need to edit the sample data in the spreadsheet. When you work with a worksheet, the cell in which you are entering data is the **active cell**. The active cell has a green border around it.

To enter the data for the chart:

1. In the spreadsheet, click cell **A2**. A green border surrounds cell A2, indicating it is selected.

2. Type **Seminars**, and then press the **Enter** key. Cell A3 becomes the active cell. In the chart, the name in the legend for the blue data series changes to "Seminars".

3. Enter the following in cells **A3** through **A5**:

Book of Abstracts

Hotel

Meals

Trouble? The text you type in cell A3 will be cut off, but this is not a problem.

4. In cell A6, type **Activity**, and then press the **Enter** key. The active cell is cell A7 and the colored borders around the cells included in the chart expands to include row 6. In the chart, a new series (slice) is added to the pie chart.

5. Click in cell **B1** to make it the active cell, type **Cost per Attendee**, and then press the **Enter** key. The active cell is now cell B2.

6. In cell **B2**, type **250**, and then press the **Enter** key. The slice in the pie chart that represents the percentage showing the cost of the Seminars increases to almost fill the chart. This is because the value 250 is so much larger than the sample data values in the rest of the rows in column B. As you continue to enter the data, the slices in the pie chart will adjust as you add each value.

7. In cells **B3** through **B6**, enter the following values:

   33

   250

   180

   75

8. Position the pointer on the column divider between the column A and column B headings so that it changes to ↔, and then double-click. Column A widens to fit the widest entry—the text in cell A3.

9. Double-click the column divider between the column B and column C headings to widen column B. See Figure 3-8.

Figure 3-8 **Spreadsheet and chart after entering formulas in column B**

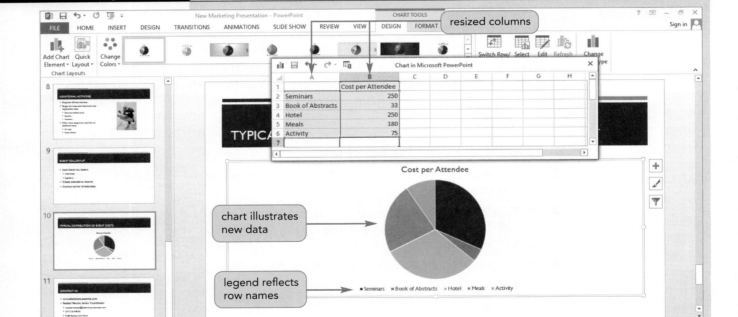

Photo courtesy of Beverly B. Zimmerman

10. In the spreadsheet, click the **Close** button ☒.

Modifying a Chart

Once the chart is on the slide, you can modify it by changing or formatting its various elements. For example, you can edit the data; apply a style; add, remove, or reposition chart elements; add labels to the data series; and modify the formatting of text in the chart.

You need to make several changes to the chart you created on Slide 10. First, Rashad informs you that some of the data he provided was incorrect, so you need to edit the data.

To change the data used to create the chart:

1. On the CHART TOOLS DESIGN tab, in the Data group, click the **Edit Data** button. The spreadsheet reappears.

2. Click cell **B2**, type **225**, and then press the **Enter** key. The slices in the pie chart adjust to accommodate the new value.

3. Click cell **B5**, type **190**, and then press the **Enter** key. The slices in the pie chart adjust again.

4. Close the spreadsheet.

Rashad also wants you to make several formatting changes to the chart. He wants you to change the chart style. Also, there is no need for a title on the chart because the slide title describes the chart. Finally, Rashad wants you to remove the legend and, instead, label the pie slices with the series name and the percentage value.

To format and modify the chart:

1. On the CHART TOOLS DESIGN tab, in the Chart Styles group, click the **More** button, and then click **Style 12**. The chart is formatted with the selected style.

2. To the right of the chart, click the **Chart Elements** button ⊞. The CHART ELEMENTS menu opens to the left of the chart. See Figure 3-9.

| Figure 3-9 | CHART ELEMENTS menu on Slide 9 |

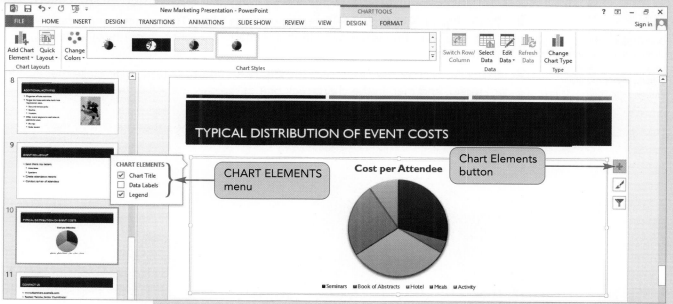

Photo courtesy of Beverly B. Zimmerman

Trouble? If labels appear on the pie slices on your screen, this is not a problem. You will adjust this shortly.

▸ **3.** On the CHART ELEMENTS menu, point to **Data Labels**. A small arrow appears.

▸ **4.** Click the **arrow** ▸ to open the Data Labels submenu. See Figure 3-10.

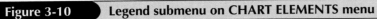

Figure 3-10   **Legend submenu on CHART ELEMENTS menu**

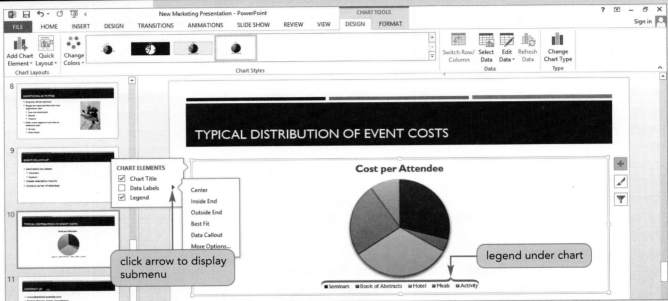

Photo courtesy of Beverly B. Zimmerman

▸ **5.** On the submenu, click **Data Callout**. Callouts containing the series names and percentages appear on the slices in the chart. With the slices labeled, there is no need for the legend.

▸ **6.** On the CHART ELEMENTS menu, click the **Legend** check box to deselect it. The legend is removed from the chart. Now you can remove the chart title.

▸ **7.** On the CHART ELEMENTS menu, click the **Chart Title** check box to deselect it. The chart title is removed from the chart. The font size of the callouts is a little small.

▸ **8.** To the right of the chart, click the **Chart Elements** button ⊞ to close the menu, and then in the chart, click one of the callouts. All of the callouts are selected.

▸ **9.** On the ribbon, click the **HOME** tab, and then change the font size of the selected callouts to **18 points**. See Figure 3-11.

Figure 3-11   Final chart on Slide 9

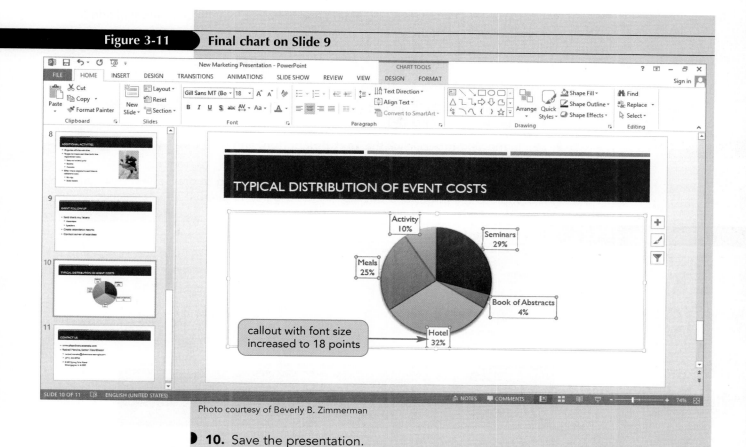

Photo courtesy of Beverly B. Zimmerman

> **10.** Save the presentation.

Decision Making: Selecting the Correct Chart Type

To use charts effectively, you need to consider what you want to illustrate with your data. Column charts use vertical columns and bar charts use horizontal bars to represent values. These types of charts are useful for comparing the values of items over a period of time or a range of dates or costs. Line charts use a line to connect points that represent values. They are effective for showing changes over time, and they are particularly useful for illustrating trends. Area charts are similar to line charts, but show shading from the line down to the x-axis. Line and area charts are a better choice than column or bar charts when you need to display large amounts of information and exact quantities that don't require emphasis. Pie charts are used to show percentages or proportions of the parts that make up a whole.

Inserting and Formatting Text Boxes

Sometimes you need to add text to a slide in a location other than in one of the text box placeholders included in the slide layout. You could draw any shape and add text to it, or you can add a text box shape. Unlike shapes that are filled with the Accent 1 color by default, text boxes by default do not have a fill. Another difference between the format of text boxes and shapes with text in them is that the text in a text box is left-aligned and text in shapes is center-aligned. Regardless of the differences, after you create a text box, you can format the text and the text box in a variety of ways, including adding a fill, adjusting the internal margins, and rotating and repositioning it.

Rashad wants you to add a description under the photo on Slide 7. You will add a text box to accomplish this.

To add a text box to Slide 7:

1. Display **Slide 7** ("Conduct Event") in the Slide pane, and then click the **INSERT** tab on the ribbon.

2. In the Text group, click the **Text Box** button, and then move the pointer to the slide. The pointer changes to ↓.

3. Position ↓ below the photo, and then click and drag to draw a text box half as wide as the photo and one-half inch high. See Figure 3-12.

Figure 3-12	Text box inserted on Slide 7

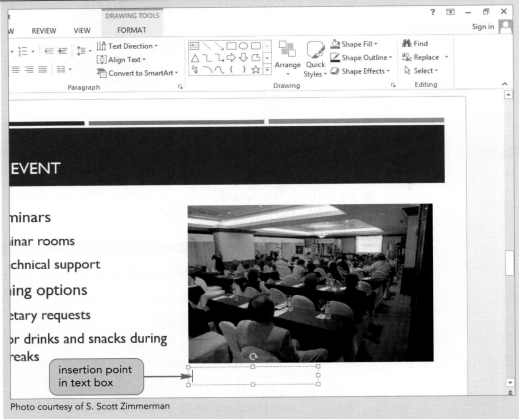

Photo courtesy of S. Scott Zimmerman

Trouble? If your text box is not positioned exactly as shown in Figure 3-12, don't worry. You'll reposition it later.

4. Type **Typical setup for a seminar room**. As you type the text in the text box, the height of the text box changes and the additional text wraps to the next line.

Trouble? If all the text fits on one line, drag the right middle sizing handle to the left until the word "room" appears on the next line so that you can complete the next sets of steps.

The default setting for text boxes you insert is for text to wrap and for the height of the box to resize to accommodate the text you type. This differs from text boxes created from title and content placeholders and shapes with text in them. Recall that text boxes created from placeholders have AutoFit behavior that reduces the font size of the text if you add more text than can fit. If you add more text than can fit to a shape, the text extends outside of the text box.

The caption under the photo would be easier to read if it were all on one line. You can widen the text box, or if you do not want text to wrap to the next line regardless of how much text is in the text box, you can change the text wrapping option.

To modify and reposition the text box:

1. Right-click the text box, and then on the shortcut menu, click **Format Shape**. The Format Shape task pane opens to the right of the Slide pane. At the top, the SHAPE OPTIONS tab is selected. This tab contains categories of commands for formatting the shape, such as changing the fill. See Figure 3-13.

Figure 3-13   Format Shape task pane and formatted text box

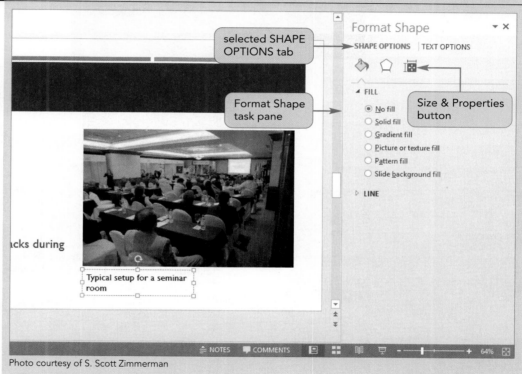

Photo courtesy of S. Scott Zimmerman

2. Click the **TEXT OPTIONS** tab. This tab contains commands for formatting the text and how it is positioned.

3. Click the **Textbox** button [A≡]. The task pane changes to show the TEXT BOX section.

4. Click **TEXT BOX**, if necessary, to display commands for formatting the text box. First you want to change the wrap option so the text does not wrap in the text box.

▶ 5. Click the **Wrap text in shape** check box to deselect it. The text in the text box appears all on one line. Next, you want to decrease the space between the first word in the text box and the left border of the box. In other words, you want to change the left margin in the text box.

▶ 6. Click the **Left margin down arrow**. The value in the box changes to 0" and the text shifts left in the text box.

▶ 7. If necessary, drag the text box so its left edge is aligned with the left edge of the photo and its top edge is aligned with the bottom edge of the photo. See Figure 3-14.

| Figure 3-14 | Format Shape task pane and formatted text box |

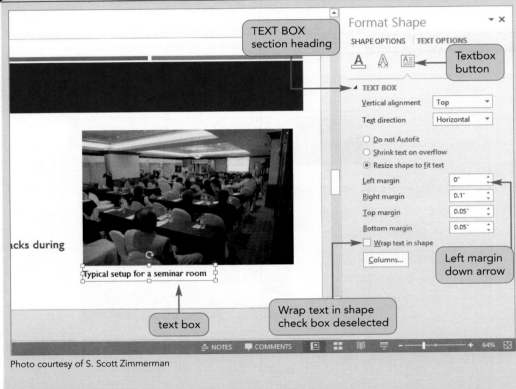

Photo courtesy of S. Scott Zimmerman

▶ 8. In the task pane, click the **Close** button ✖ to close the task pane.

▶ 9. Save the presentation.

Applying WordArt Styles to Text

WordArt is a term used to describe formatted, decorative text in a text box. WordArt text has a fill color, which is the same as the font color, and an outline color. To create WordArt, you can insert a new text box or format an existing one. You can apply one of the built-in WordArt styles or you can use the Text Fill, Text Outline, and Text Effects buttons in the WordArt Styles group on the DRAWING TOOLS FORMAT tab.

Slide 9 describes services the Spring Lake Seminar Management company provides at the conclusion of an event. Rashad would like you to add a text box that contains WordArt to Slide 9 to reinforce the content on this slide.

To create a text box containing WordArt on Slide 9:

1. Display **Slide 9** ("Event Follow-up") in the Slide pane, and then click the **INSERT** tab on the ribbon.

2. In the Text group, click the **WordArt** button to open the WordArt gallery. See Figure 3-15.

Figure 3-15 | WordArt gallery

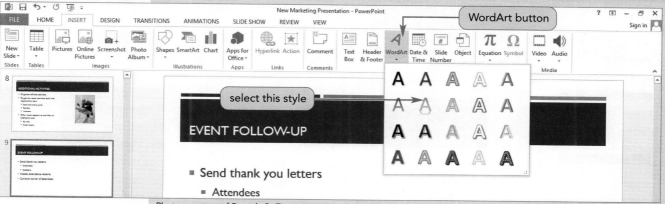

Photo courtesy of Beverly B. Zimmerman

3. Click the **Gradient Fill – Green, Accent 1, Reflection** style. A text box containing the placeholder text "Your text here" appears on the slide, and the DRAWING TOOLS FORMAT tab is selected on the ribbon. The placeholder text is formatted with the style you selected in the WordArt gallery.

4. Type **Thank You!**. The text you typed replaces the placeholder text. You want to change the color used in the gradient fill from green to blue.

5. Click the border of the text box to select the entire object.

6. On the FORMAT tab, in the WordArt Styles group, click the **Text Fill button arrow**, and then click the **Dark Blue, Accent 1** color. Now you need to change this solid fill color to a gradient.

7. Click the **Text Fill button arrow** again, and then point to **Gradient**. The Gradient submenu opens. The gradients on the submenu use shades of the Blue, Accent 1 color.

8. Under Light Variations, click the **Linear Diagonal – Top Left to Bottom Right** gradient.

9. Change the font size of the text in the WordArt text box to **72** points.

10. Drag the text box to position it roughly centered in the white space to the right of the bulleted list.

The shape of text in a text box can be transformed into waves, circles, and other shapes. To do this, use the Transform submenu on the Text Effects menu on the DRAWING TOOLS FORMAT tab. Rashad wants you to change the shape of the WordArt on Slide 9.

To change the shape of the WordArt by applying a transform effect:

▶ **1.** Click the **FORMAT** tab, if necessary.

▶ **2.** In the WordArt styles group, click the **Text Effects** button, and then point to **Transform**. The Transform submenu appears. See Figure 3-16.

Figure 3-16   **Transform submenu**

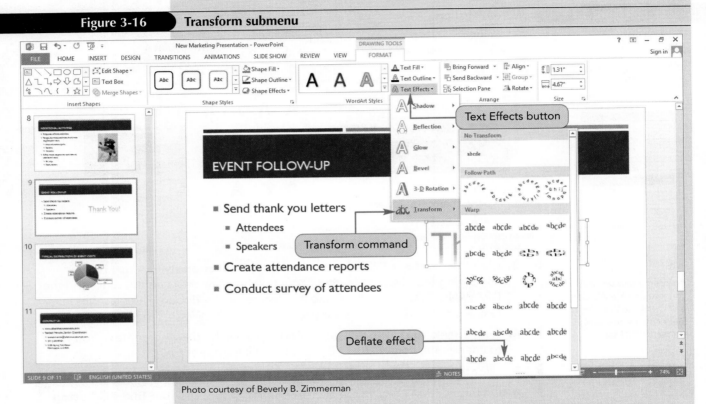

Photo courtesy of Beverly B. Zimmerman

▶ **3.** In the sixth row under Warp, click the **Deflate** effect, and then click a blank area of the slide. See Figure 3-17.

Figure 3-17 **WordArt after applying Deflate transform effect**

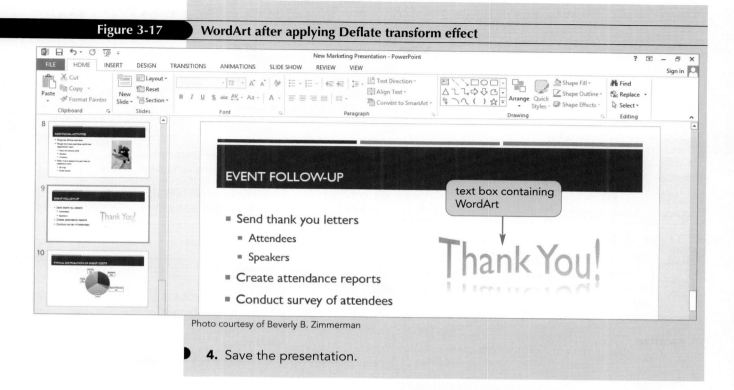

Photo courtesy of Beverly B. Zimmerman

4. Save the presentation.

Decision Making: Selecting Appropriate Font Colors

When you select font colors, make sure your text is easy to read during your slide show. Font colors that work well are dark colors on a light background, or light colors on a dark background. Avoid red text on a blue background or blue text on a green background (and vice versa) unless the shades of those colors are in strong contrast. These combinations might look fine on your computer monitor, but they are almost totally illegible to an audience viewing your presentation on a screen in a darkened room. Also avoid using red/green combinations, which color-blind people find illegible.

PROSKILLS

Session 3.1 Quick Check

REVIEW

1. How do you change the animation applied to a SmartArt diagram so that each shape animates one at a time?
2. What happens when you click the Play in Background button in the Audio Styles group on the AUDIO TOOLS PLAYBACK tab?
3. What is the difference between a chart and a graph?
4. What is a spreadsheet?
5. How do you identify a specific cell in a spreadsheet?
6. What is WordArt?

Session 3.2 Visual Overview:

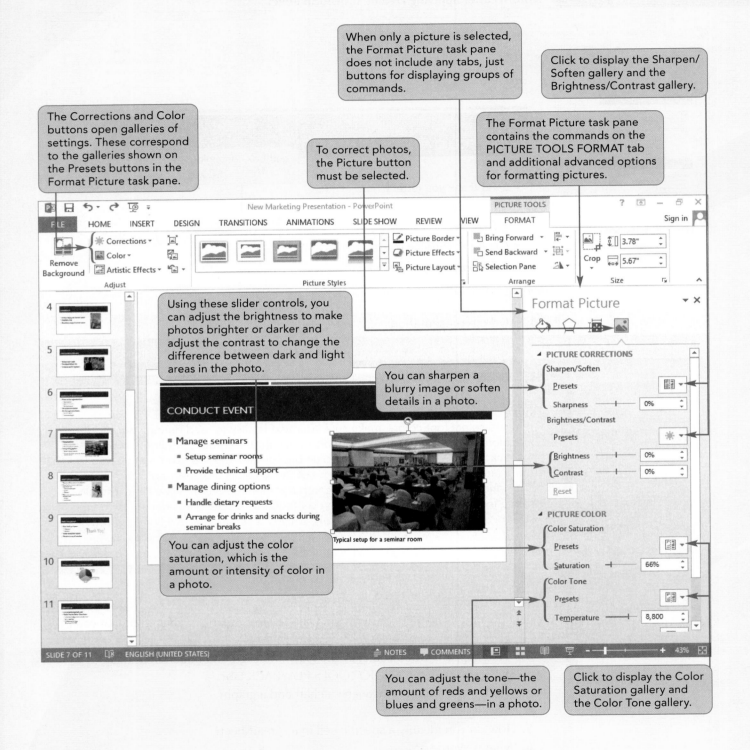

When only a picture is selected, the Format Picture task pane does not include any tabs, just buttons for displaying groups of commands.

Click to display the Sharpen/Soften gallery and the Brightness/Contrast gallery.

The Corrections and Color buttons open galleries of settings. These correspond to the galleries shown on the Presets buttons in the Format Picture task pane.

To correct photos, the Picture button must be selected.

The Format Picture task pane contains the commands on the PICTURE TOOLS FORMAT tab and additional advanced options for formatting pictures.

Using these slider controls, you can adjust the brightness to make photos brighter or darker and adjust the contrast to change the difference between dark and light areas in the photo.

You can sharpen a blurry image or soften details in a photo.

You can adjust the color saturation, which is the amount or intensity of color in a photo.

You can adjust the tone—the amount of reds and yellows or blues and greens—in a photo.

Click to display the Color Saturation gallery and the Color Tone gallery.

Formatting Shapes and Pictures

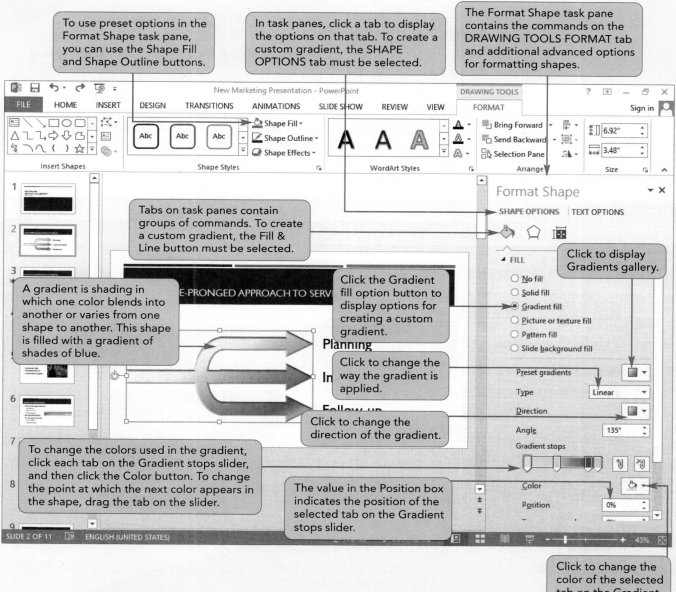

To use preset options in the Format Shape task pane, you can use the Shape Fill and Shape Outline buttons.

In task panes, click a tab to display the options on that tab. To create a custom gradient, the SHAPE OPTIONS tab must be selected.

The Format Shape task pane contains the commands on the DRAWING TOOLS FORMAT tab and additional advanced options for formatting shapes.

Tabs on task panes contain groups of commands. To create a custom gradient, the Fill & Line button must be selected.

A gradient is shading in which one color blends into another or varies from one shape to another. This shape is filled with a gradient of shades of blue.

Click the Gradient fill option button to display options for creating a custom gradient.

Click to display Gradients gallery.

Click to change the way the gradient is applied.

Click to change the direction of the gradient.

To change the colors used in the gradient, click each tab on the Gradient stops slider, and then click the Color button. To change the point at which the next color appears in the shape, drag the tab on the slider.

The value in the Position box indicates the position of the selected tab on the Gradient stops slider.

Click to change the color of the selected tab on the Gradient stops slider.

Editing Photos

TIP

If you make changes to photos and then change your mind, you can click the Reset Picture button in the Adjust group on the PICTURE TOOLS FORMAT tab.

If photos you want to use in a presentation are too dark or require other fine-tuning, you can use PowerPoint's photo correction tools to correct the photos. These photo correction tools appear on the ribbon and in the Format Picture task pane. Refer to the Session 3.2 Visual Overview for more information about correcting photos and the Format Picture task pane.

Rashad thinks there is too much contrast between the dark and light areas in the photo on Slide 5. You will correct this aspect of the photo.

To change the contrast of a photo:

1. If you took a break after the previous session, make sure the **New Marketing Presentation** file is open.

2. Display **Slide 5** ("Arrange for Speakers") in the Slide pane, and then click the photo to select it.

3. On the ribbon, click the **PICTURE TOOLS FORMAT** tab, and then in the Adjust group, click the **Corrections** button. A menu opens showing options for sharpening and softening the photo and adjusting the brightness and the contrast. See Figure 3-18.

Figure 3-18   Corrections menu

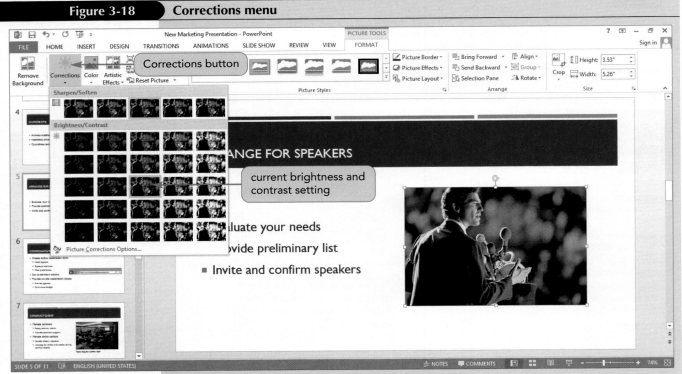

Photos courtesy of S. Scott Zimmerman and Chabruken/Getty Images

TIP

You can also right-click the photo, and then click Format Picture on the shortcut menu to open the Format Picture task pane.

4. In the Brightness/Contrast section, click the **Brightness 0% (Normal) Contrast -20%** style (the third style in the second row). The contrast of the image changes. Because you chose a style with a Brightness percentage of 0%, the brightness of the photo is unchanged.

You want to decrease the contrast just a little more. However, the gallery provides options that change the contrast in increments of 20%, which will be more of an adjustment than you are looking for. For selecting a more precise contrast setting, you need to open the Format Picture task pane.

5. Click the **Corrections** button again, and then click **Picture Corrections Options**. The Format Picture task pane opens with the Picture button selected and the PICTURE CORRECTIONS section expanded.

6. Drag the **Contrast** slider to the left until the box next to the slider indicates -30%. The contrast increases slightly.

   Trouble? If you can't position the slider exactly, click the up or down arrow in the box containing the percentage as needed, or select the current percentage and then type -30.

7. Close the task pane.

Next, Rashad wants you to adjust the saturation and tone of the photo on Slide 7. He wants you to reduce the saturation and increase the tone so the overall photo is a little brighter.

To change the saturation and tone of the photo on Slide 7:

1. Display **Slide 7** ("Conduct Event") in the Slide pane, click the photo to select it, and then click the **PICTURE TOOLS FORMAT** tab on the ribbon, if necessary.

2. In the Adjust group, click the **Color** button. A menu opens with options for adjusting the saturation and tone of the photo's color. See Figure 3-19.

| Figure 3-19 | Color menu |

Photos courtesy of S. Scott Zimmerman and Chabruken/Getty Images

TIP

To recolor a photo so it is all one color, click the Color button in the Adjust group on the PICTURE TOOLS FORMAT tab, and then click a Recolor option.

3. Under Color Saturation, click the **Saturation: 66%** option. The colors in the photo are less intense.

4. Click the **Color** button again.

5. Under Color Tone, click the **Temperature: 8800K** option. More reds and yellows are added to the photo.

Finally, Rashad wants you to sharpen the photo on Slide 8 so that the scuba diver and fish are more in focus.

To sharpen the photo on Slide 8:

1. Display **Slide 8** ("Additional Activities") in the Slide pane, click the photo to select it, and then click the **PICTURE TOOLS FORMAT** tab on the ribbon.

2. In the Adjust group, click the **Corrections** button. The options for sharpening and softening photos appear at the top of the menu.

3. Under Sharpen/Soften, click the **Sharpen: 50%** option.

4. Save the presentation.

Removing the Background from Photos

Sometimes a photo is more striking if you remove its background. You can also layer a photo with the background removed on top of another photo to create an interesting effect. To remove the background of a photo, you can use the Remove Background tool. When you click the Remove Background button in the Adjust group on the PICTURE TOOLS FORMAT tab, the photograph is analyzed; part of it is marked to be removed and part of it is marked to be retained. If the analysis removes too little or too much of the photo, you can adjust it.

REFERENCE

Removing the Background of a Photograph

- Click the photo, and then click the PICTURE TOOLS FORMAT tab on the ribbon.
- In the Adjust group, click the Remove Background button.
- Drag the sizing handles on the remove background border to make broad adjustments to the area marked for removal.
- In the Refine group on the BACKGROUND REMOVAL tab, click the Mark Areas to Keep or the Mark Areas to Remove button, and then click or drag through an area of the photo that you want marked to keep or remove.
- Click a blank area of the slide or click the Keep Changes button in the Close group to accept the changes.

Rashad wants you to modify the photo of the scuba diver on Slide 8 so that the background looks like a drawing, but the scuba diver and the fish stay the same. To create this effect, you will need to work with two versions of the photo. You will use the Duplicate command to make a copy of the photo, and then remove the background from the duplicate photo.

To duplicate the photo on Slide 8 and then remove the background from the copy:

1. Make sure the photo is selected on **Slide 8** ("Additional Activities"), and then, on the ribbon, click the **HOME** tab.

2. In the Clipboard group, click the **Copy button arrow**. Because the selected item is an object and not text, there are two available commands on the menu—Copy and Duplicate.

3. Click **Duplicate**. The photo is duplicated on the slide and the duplicate is selected.

4. Point to the selected duplicate photo so that the pointer changes to ⇱, and then drag it left to position it to the left of the original photo.

5. With the duplicate photo selected, click the **PICTURE TOOLS FORMAT** tab on the ribbon.

6. In the Adjust group, click the **Remove Background** button. The areas of the photograph marked for removal are colored purple. A sizing box appears around the general area of the photograph that will be retained, and a new tab, the BACKGROUND REMOVAL tab, appears on the ribbon and is the active tab. See Figure 3-20. You can adjust the area of the photograph that is retained by dragging the sizing handles on the sizing box.

Figure 3-20   **Photograph after clicking the Remove Background button**

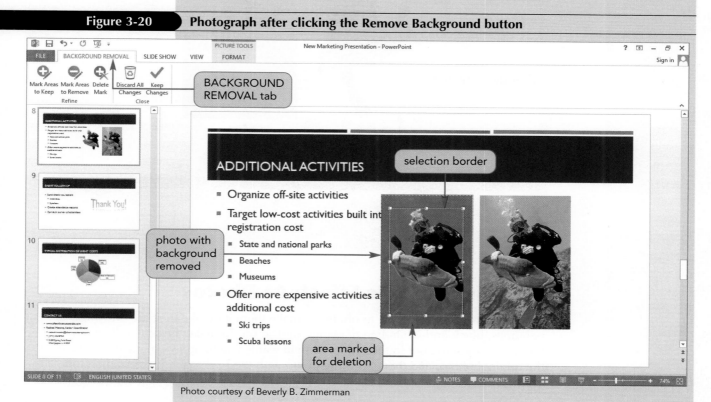

Photo courtesy of Beverly B. Zimmerman

7. Drag the left middle sizing handle to the left edge of the photo. The tail of the fish is colored normally.

TIP

If the background of a photo is all one color, you can click the Color button in the Adjust group on the PICTURE TOOLS FORMAT tab, click Set Transparent Color, and then click the color you want to make transparent.

8. Drag the bottom middle sizing handle down to the bottom border of the photo. The diver's flipper is colored normally.

Trouble? If any of the background of the photo is colored normally, click the Mark Areas to Remove button in the Refine group on the BACKGROUND REMOVAL tab, and then drag through the area that should be removed.

9. On the BACKGROUND REMOVAL tab, in the Close group, click the **Keep Changes** button. The changes you made are applied to the photograph, and the BACKGROUND REMOVAL tab is removed from the ribbon. See Figure 3-21.

Figure 3-21	Duplicate photo with background removed

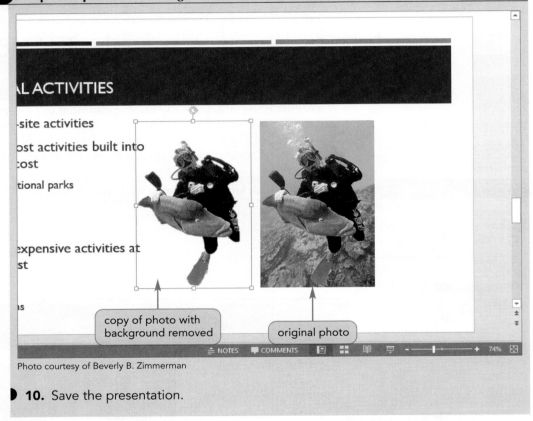

Photo courtesy of Beverly B. Zimmerman

10. Save the presentation.

Applying Artistic Effects to Photos

You can apply artistic effects to photos to make them look like they are drawings, paintings, black-and-white line drawings, and so on. To make the scuba diver and the fish really stand out in the photo, Rashad wants you to apply an artistic effect to the original photo, and then place the photo with the background removed on top of the photo with the artistic effect. You'll do this now.

To apply an artistic effect to the original photo on Slide 8:

1. On **Slide 8** ("Additional Activities"), click the original photo with the background still visible, and then click the **PICTURE TOOLS FORMAT** tab to select it, if necessary.

2. In the Adjust group, click the **Artistic Effects** button. See Figure 3-22.

Figure 3-22   **Artistic Effects menu**

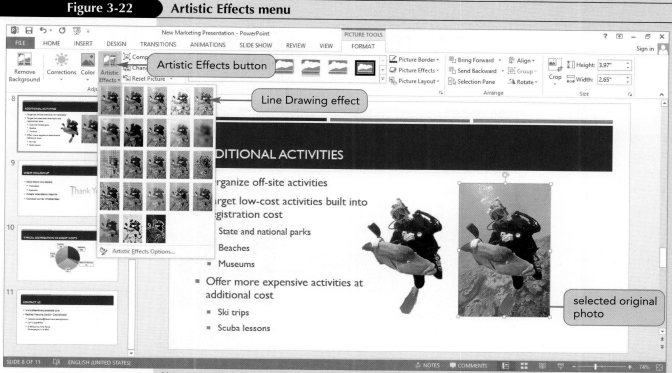

Photo courtesy of Beverly B. Zimmerman

3. Click the **Line Drawing** effect. The photo changes so it looks more like a drawing. Now you will place the photo with the background removed on top of the photo with the artistic effect.

4. Drag the photo with the background removed on top of the photos with the artistic effect applied and position it directly on top of the diver in the photo with the artistic effect applied. See Figure 3-23.

Figure 3-23 Final photo on Slide 7

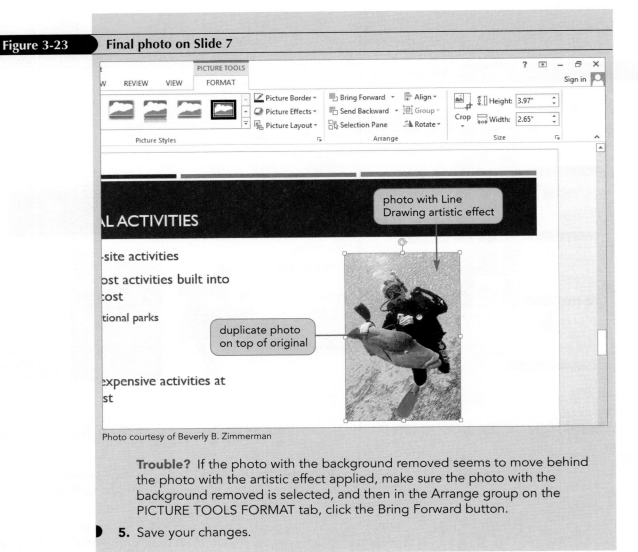

Photo courtesy of Beverly B. Zimmerman

> **Trouble?** If the photo with the background removed seems to move behind the photo with the artistic effect applied, make sure the photo with the background removed is selected, and then in the Arrange group on the PICTURE TOOLS FORMAT tab, click the Bring Forward button.

5. Save your changes.

Creating a Custom Shape

You have learned how to insert and format shapes on slides. In PowerPoint you can also create a custom shape by merging two or more shapes. Then you can position and format the custom shape as you would any other shape.

Rashad wants to illustrate the company's three-pronged approach to service of planning, implementation, and follow-up with a graphic, but none of the SmartArt diagrams matches the idea he has in mind. He asks you to create a custom shape similar to the one shown in Figure 3-24 that illustrates this concept.

Figure 3-24   **Rashad's sketch of the logo**

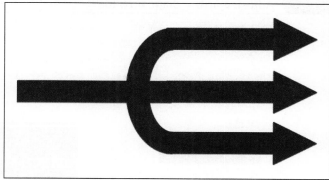

© 2014 Cengage Learning

Using the Adjustment Handle to Modify Shapes

To create the custom shape for Rashad, you will merge several shapes. One of the shapes is an arrow shape. First, you will adjust the arrow so that the arrowhead is longer. You can adjust many shapes using the yellow adjustment handles that appear on a selected shape.

To adjust the arrow shape and duplicate it on Slide 2:

1. Display **Slide 2** ("Our Three-Pronged Approach to Service") in the Slide pane.

2. Click the **arrow** shape to select it, and then drag the adjustment handle on the top corner of the arrowhead one-half inch to the left so that the arrowhead lengthens and the bottom of the arrowhead is aligned between the "T" and "O" in "TO" in the slide title. See Figure 3-25. You need two more arrow shapes exactly the same size as this one.

Figure 3-25 | Adjusted arrow shape on Slide 2

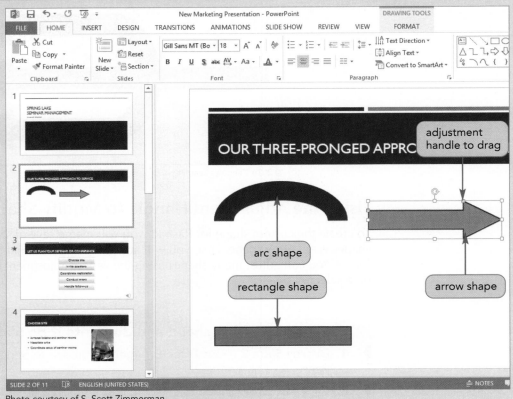

Photo courtesy of S. Scott Zimmerman

▶ **3.** Duplicate the arrow shape twice.

Aligning Objects

You now have all the shapes on the slide that you need to create the custom shape. First you need to arrange and align the three arrow shapes.

To align the three arrow shapes:

▶ **1.** Drag the selected arrow down about two inches so it is positioned just above and to the right of the rectangle shape, and then drag the other duplicated arrow down to position it so it is evenly spaced between the top and bottom arrows. There should be approximately one inch between the left ends of each arrow.

▶ **2.** Click the top arrow, press and hold the **Shift** key, and then click the other two arrows. The three arrows are selected.

▶ **3.** On the HOME tab, in the Drawing group, click the **Arrange** button, and then point to **Align**. The Align submenu opens. See Figure 3-26.

Figure 3-26   Align menu

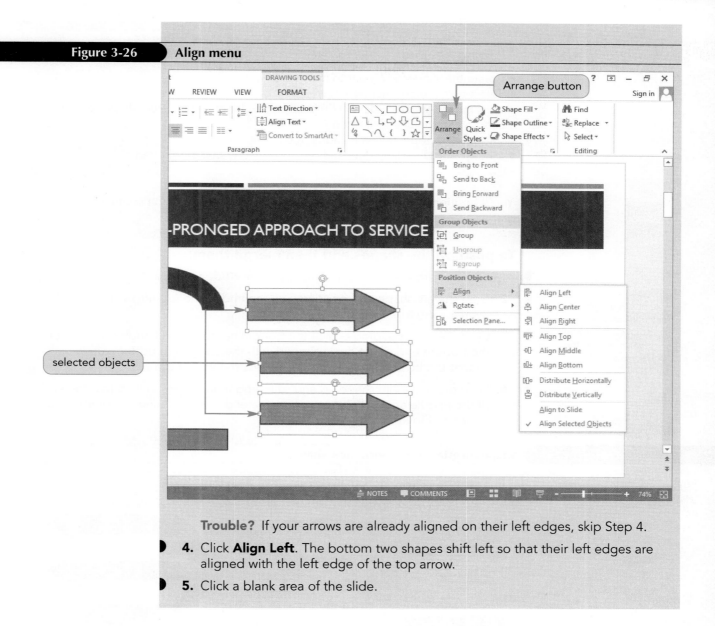

Trouble? If your arrows are already aligned on their left edges, skip Step 4.

4. Click **Align Left**. The bottom two shapes shift left so that their left edges are aligned with the left edge of the top arrow.

5. Click a blank area of the slide.

Merging Shapes

To merge shapes, you need to use the commands on the Merge Shapes menu in the Insert Shapes group on the DRAWING TOOLS FORMAT tab. Each command has a different effect on selected shapes:

- **Union**—Combines selected shapes without removing any portions
- **Combine**—Combines selected shapes and removes the sections of the shapes that overlap
- **Fragment**—Separates overlapping portions of shapes into separate shapes
- **Intersect**—Combines selected shapes and removes everything except the sections that overlap
- **Subtract**—Removes the second shape selected, including any part of the first shape that is overlapped by the second shape

REFERENCE

Merging Shapes

- Create the shapes you want to merge.
- Select two or more shapes.
- Click the DRAWING TOOLS FORMAT tab, and then in the Insert Shapes group, click the Merge Shapes button.
- Click the appropriate command on the menu.
- Modify the style, fill, and outline color of the new shape if desired.

You'll position the shapes and then merge them using the Union command.

To position the shapes and then merge them:

1. Click the arc shape, and then rotate it left **90 degrees**.

2. Drag the arc shape and position it so the end of the top arrow shape slightly overlaps the top end of the arc.

Make sure you slightly overlap the arc and arrow shape or the shapes won't merge when you use the Union command.

3. On the arc shape, drag one of the bottom corner sizing handles up so that the bottom end of the arc is aligned with the end of the bottom arrow and so that the bottom arrow slightly overlaps the end of the arc.

4. Drag the rectangle shape up and to the right and position it so that the end of the middle arrow slightly overlaps the end of the rectangle. Compare your screen to Figure 3-27.

Figure 3-27 | **Shapes overlapping to form new shape**

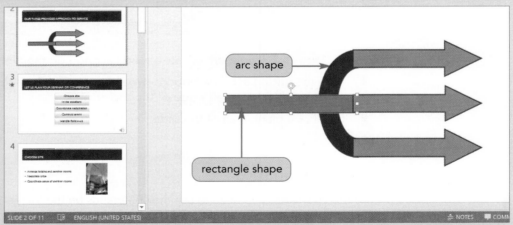

Photo courtesy of S. Scott Zimmerman

5. Click the **DRAWING TOOLS FORMAT** tab. In the Insert Shapes group, the Merge Shapes button is gray and unavailable. At least two shapes need to be selected to use the commands on the Merge Shapes menu.

6. Press and hold the **Shift** key, and then click the middle arrow. The rectangle and the middle arrow shape are now selected, and the Merge Shapes button is now available.

7. In the Insert Shapes group, click the **Merge Shapes** button, and then click **Union**. The two shapes are merged into a new shape formatted the same as the rectangle shape. When you merge shapes that have different formatting, the format of the first shape selected is applied to the merged shape.

8. Click the **arc** shape, press and hold the **Shift** key, click each of the arrow shapes, including the merged shape, and then release the **Shift** key.

9. In the Insert Shapes group, click the **Merge Shapes** button, and then click **Union**. The four shapes are merged into a blue shape, matching the formatting of the first shape selected.

10. Save the presentation.

Applying Advanced Formatting to Shapes

You know that you can fill a shape with a solid color or with a picture. You can also fill a shape with a texture—a pattern that gives a tactile quality to the shape, such as crumpled paper or marble—or with a gradient. You'll change the fill of the custom shape to a texture.

To change the shape fill to a texture:

1. Make sure the custom shape is selected, and then click the DRAWING TOOLS FORMAT tab on the ribbon, if necessary.

2. In the Shape Styles group, click the **Shape Fill button arrow**, and then point to **Texture**. The Texture submenu opens. See Figure 3-28.

Figure 3-28 Texture submenu

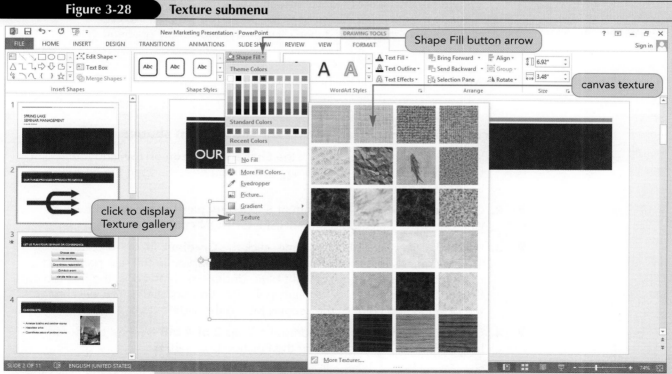

Photo courtesy of S. Scott Zimmerman

3. Click the **Canvas** texture, which is the second texture in the first row. The custom shape is filled with a texture resembling canvas. Rashad doesn't like any of the textures as a fill for the shape. He asks you to remove the texture.

▶ **4.** In the Shapes Styles group, click the **Shape Fill button arrow**, and then click **No Fill**. The texture is removed from the custom shape and only the outline of the custom shape remains.

The texture did not achieve the effect Rashad wanted for the shape. He now asks you to use a gradient to simulate the look of metal or silver. As you have learned, you can apply gradients on the Shape Fill menu that use shades of the Accent 1 color in the theme color palette. You can also create a custom gradient using the options in the Format Shape task pane. To create a custom gradient, you select the colors to use, specify the position in the shape where the color will change, and specify the direction of the gradient in the shape. Refer to the Session 3.2 Visual Overview for more information about using the Format Shape task pane to create a custom gradient.

REFERENCE

Creating a Custom Gradient in a Shape

- Select the shape.
- Click the DRAWING TOOLS FORMAT tab.
- In the Shape Styles group, click the Shape Fill button arrow, point to Gradient, and then click More Gradients to open the Format Shape task pane.
- In the Format Shape task pane, on the SHAPE OPTIONS tab with the Fill & Line button selected, click the Gradient fill option button.
- On the Gradient stops slider, click each tab, click the Color button, and then select a color.
- Drag each tab on the slider to the desired position.
- Click the Type arrow, and then click a type of gradient you want to use.
- Click the Direction button, and then click the direction of the gradient.

You will apply a custom gradient to the custom shape now.

To create a custom gradient fill for the custom shape:

▶ **1.** In the Shape Styles group, click the **Shape Fill button arrow**, and then point to **Gradient**. To create a custom gradient, you need to open the Format Shape task pane.

▶ **2.** Click **More Gradients**. The Format Shape task pane opens with the Fill & Line button [icon] selected on the SHAPE OPTIONS tab.

▶ **3.** In the FILL section of the task pane, click the **Gradient fill** option button. The commands for modifying the gradient fill appear in the task pane, and the shape fills with shades of light blue. Under Gradient stops, the first tab on the slider is selected, and its value in the Position box is 0%. You will change the position and color of the second tab on the slider.

▶ **4.** On the Gradient stops slider, drag the **Stop 2 of 4 tab** (second tab from the left) to the left until the value in the Position box is **40%**.

   Trouble? If you accidentally add a tab to the slider, click it, and then click the Remove gradient stop button [icon] to the right of the slider.

TIP

Click the Preset gradients button to select from gradients of all six of the accent colors in the theme color palette.

5. With the Stop 2 of 4 tab selected, click the **Color** button. The color palette opens.

6. Click the **Blue-Gray, Accent 4, Lighter 80%** color. Next you need to change the color of the third tab.

7. Click the **Stop 3 of 4 tab**, click the **Color** button, and then click the **Gray-25%, Background 2, Darker 50%** color.

8. Drag the **Stop 4 of 4 tab** to the left until the value in the Position box is **95%**, and then change its color to **Gray-25%, Background 2**. Next you will change the direction of the gradient. Above the Gradient stops slider, in the Type box, Linear is selected. This means that the shading will vary linearly—that is, top to bottom, side to side, or diagonally. You will change the direction to a diagonal.

9. Click the **Direction** button. A gallery of gradient options opens.

10. Click the **Linear Diagonal – Top Left to Bottom Right** direction. The shading in the shape changes so it varies diagonally. See Figure 3-29.

Figure 3-29	Final custom gradient in shape

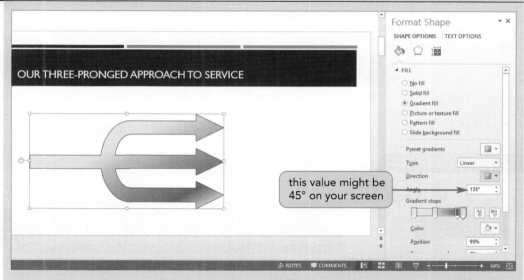

Trouble? If the darker part of the shape isn't in the lower-right as in Figure 3-29, click the Direction button again, and then click the Linear Diagonal–Top Right to Bottom Left direction.

11. In the Format Shape task pane, click the **Close** button ✖.

Now you can finish formatting the shape by changing the outline color and applying a bevel effect.

To finish formatting the custom shape:

1. On the ribbon, click the **DRAWING TOOLS FORMAT** tab, if necessary.

2. In the Shape Styles group, click the **Shape Outline button arrow**, and then click the **Gray-25%, Background 2** color.

TIP

To save a custom shape as a picture file so that you can use it in other files, right-click it, and then click Save as Picture on the shortcut menu.

3. In the Shape Styles group, click the **Shape Effects** button, point to **Bevel**, and then click the **Circle** bevel.

4. Drag the shape to the left so its left edge aligns with the left edge of the title text box.

Now you need to complete the slide by adding text boxes that list the three elements of the company's service.

To add text boxes to the slide:

1. To the right of the shape's top arrow, draw a text box approximately two inches wide, and then type **Planning**.

2. Duplicate the text box twice, and then position the duplicates to the right of the shape's other two arrows.

3. In the text box to the right of the middle arrow, replace "Planning" with **Implementation**.

4. In the text box to the right of the bottom arrow, replace "Planning" with **Follow-up**.

5. Select all three text boxes, and then change the font size to **40** points.

6. With all three text boxes selected, drag one of the right middle sizing handles to the right until "Implementation" fits on one line.

7. With all three boxes still selected, position them so the Implementation text box is about one-quarter inch to the right of the middle arrow. Compare your screen to Figure 3-30, and make any adjustments if necessary.

| Figure 3-30 | Custom shape with final gradient fill |

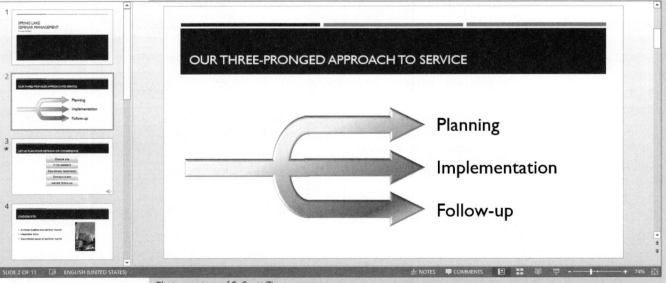

Photo courtesy of S. Scott Zimmerman

8. Save the presentation.

Using the Format Shape and Format Picture Task Panes

Many options are available to you in the Format Shape and Format Picture task panes. Most of the commands are available on the DRAWING TOOLS and PICTURE TOOLS FORMAT tabs on the ribbon, but you can refine their effects in the task panes. For example, you can fill a shape with a color and then use a command in the Format Shape task pane to make the fill color partially transparent so you can see objects behind the shape. Because these task panes are so useful, you can access them in a variety of ways. Once a picture or shape is selected, you can do one of the following to open the corresponding task pane:

- Click any of the Dialog Box Launchers on the DRAWING TOOLS or PICTURE TOOLS FORMAT tab.
- Right-click a shape or picture, and then click Format Shape or Format Picture on the shortcut menu.
- Click a command at the bottom of a menu, such as the More Gradients command at the bottom of the Gradients submenu on the Fill Color menu or the Picture Corrections Options command at the bottom of the Corrections menu.

Making Presentations Accessible

People with physical impairments or disabilities can use computers because of technology that makes them accessible. For example, people who cannot use their arms or hands instead can use foot, head, or eye movements to control the pointer. One of the most common assistive technologies is the screen reader. The screen reader identifies objects on the screen and produces an audio of the text.

Graphics and tables cause problems for users of screen readers unless they have **alternative text**, often shortened to **alt text**. Alt text is text added to an object that describes the object. For example, the alt text for a SmartArt graphic might describe the intent of the graphic.

Adding Alt Text

You can add alt text for any object on a PowerPoint slide. Many screen readers can read the text in title text boxes and bulleted lists, so you usually do not need to add alt text for those objects. For now, you will add alt text for the chart on Slide 10 and the SmartArt diagram on Slide 3 because these graphics contain critical information for understanding the contents of those slides and the presentation overall.

Make sure you select the entire SmartArt object and not just one shape. If you select a shape, the alt text will be available only for that individual shape.

To add alt text for the chart and SmartArt graphic:

1. Display **Slide 3** ("Let Us Plan Your Seminar or Conference") in the Slide pane.

2. Right-click to the right or left of the shapes in the SmartArt graphic to select the entire graphic.

3. On the shortcut menu, click **Format Object**. The Format Shape task pane opens with the SHAPE OPTIONS tab selected.

▶ **4.** In the task pane, click the **Size & Properties** button 🔲, and then at the bottom of the task pane, click **ALT TEXT** to display the boxes below it. See Figure 3-31.

Figure 3-31   **Options for adding alt text in the Format Chart Area task pane**

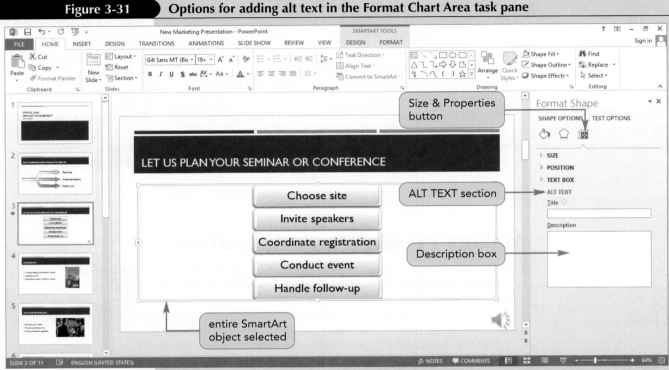

Photos courtesy of S. Scott Zimmerman and Chabruken/Getty Images

▶ **5.** Under ALT TEXT, click in the **Description** box, and then type **Graphic listing services offered by Spring Lake Seminar Management.** (including the period).

▶ **6.** Display **Slide 10** ("Typical Distribution of Event Costs") in the Slide pane, and then click the chart.

▶ **7.** On the ribbon, click the **CHART TOOLS FORMAT** tab.

▶ **8.** In the Current Selection group, click the **Chart Elements arrow** (the arrow on the top box in the group), and then click **Chart Area.**

▶ **9.** If necessary, click the **CHART OPTIONS** tab, click the **Size & Properties** button 🔲, and then click **ALT TEXT** to expand the section.

▶ **10.** Click in the **Description** box, and then type **Pie chart illustrating the distribution of event costs.** (including the period).

▶ **11.** Close the Format Chart Area task pane.

You could add alt text to each shape in the SmartArt graphic. However, because you identified the entire SmartArt object for a screen reader by adding alt text, someone using a screen reader will know to open the text pane, and many screen readers can read the text in the text pane.

Rashad will add alt text for the rest of the graphics in the presentation later. Next, you need to make sure that the objects on slides will be identified in the correct order for screen readers.

Checking the Order Objects Will Be Read by a Screen Reader

In PowerPoint, most screen readers first explain that a slide is displayed. After the user signals to the screen reader that he is ready for the next piece of information (for example, by pressing the Tab key), the reader identifies the first object on the slide. In PowerPoint, objects are identified in the order that they were added to the slide. For most slides, this means that the first object is the title text box. The second object is usually the content placeholder on the slide. To check the order of objects on the slide, you can use the Tab key or open the Selection task pane. You'll check the order of objects on Slide 8.

To identify the order of objects on Slide 8:

1. Display **Slide 8** ("Additional Activities") in the Slide pane, and then click above the bars at the top of the slide. The Slide pane is active, but nothing on the slide is selected.

2. Press the **Tab** key. The title text box is selected.

3. Press the **Tab** key again. The bulleted list text box is selected next. A screen reader will read the title text first, then the text in the bulleted list.

4. Press the **Tab** key once more. The photo is selected. However, remember that there are two photos here, one placed on top of the other. To see which one is selected, you can use the Selection pane.

5. On the HOME tab, in the Editing group, click the **Select** button, and then click **Selection Pane**. The Selection task pane opens. See Figure 3-32.

Figure 3-32	Selection task pane

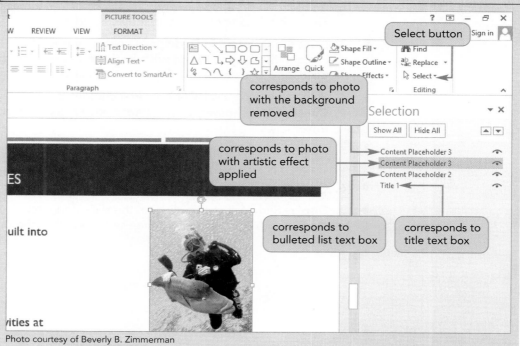

Photo courtesy of Beverly B. Zimmerman

The items are listed in the reverse order they were added to the slide, so the title text box—the first thing selected—appears at the bottom of the list. (The blue box at the bottom of the slide and the three blue bars at the top of the slide aren't listed in the Selection task pane because they are part of the slide background.)

Rashad will examine the order of the objects on the rest of the slides later.

Reordering Objects in the Selection Pane

If an object was in the wrong order in the Selection pane—for example, if the content placeholder was identified first and the title second—you could change this in the Selection pane. To do this, click the object you want move, and then at the top of the task pane, click the Bring Forward ▲ or Send Backward ▼ buttons at the top of the task pane to move the selected object up or down in the list.

Renaming Objects in the Selection Pane

In the Selection task pane for Slide 8, there are two objects with the same name. This is because Slide 8 has the Two Content layout applied, and Rashad added the photo of the scuba diver to the content placeholder on the right. Then you duplicated that photo, so the name in the Selection pane was duplicated as well. To make it clearer which items on slides are listed in the Selection task pane, you can rename each object in the list.

To rename objects in the Selection task pane:

1. In the Slide pane, click the photo, and then drag left. The version of the photo with the background removed moves to the left. The top Content Placeholder 3 is selected in the Selection task pane.

2. In the Selection task pane, click the selected Content Placeholder 3. An orange border appears around the selected item in the task pane. The insertion point appears in the selected text.

3. Press the **Delete** and **Backspace** keys as needed to delete Content Placeholder 3, type **Photo with background removed**, and then press the **Enter** key. The name is changed in the task pane.

4. In the task pane, click **Content Placeholder 3**, click it again, delete the text **Content Placeholder 3**, type **Photo with artistic effect**, and then press the **Enter** key.

5. Drag the photo with the background removed back on top of the photo with the artistic effect applied.

6. Close the Selection task pane.

7. Display **Slide 1** (the title slide) in the slide pane, replace Rashad's name in the subtitle with your name, and then save and close the presentation.

Decision Making: Selecting the Right Tool for the Job

Many programs with advanced capabilities for editing and correcting photos and other programs for drawing complex shapes are available. Although the tools provided in PowerPoint for accomplishing these tasks are useful, if you need to do more than make simple photo corrections or create a simple shape, consider using a program with more advanced features or choose to hire someone with skills in graphic design to help you.

You have created and saved a custom shape and used advanced formatting techniques for shapes and photos in the presentation. Rashad is pleased with the presentation. With the alt text you've added, he is also confident that users of screen readers will be able to understand the slides containing the SmartArt and the chart.

Session 3.2 Quick Check

1. What are the five corrections you can make to photos in PowerPoint?
2. What happens when you use the Remove Background command?
3. What are artistic effects?
4. What happens when you merge shapes?
5. How do you create a custom gradient?
6. What is alt text?

ASSESS

SAM Projects

Put your skills into practice with SAM Projects! SAM Projects for this tutorial can be found online. If you have a SAM account, go to www.cengage.com/sam2013 to download the most recent Project Instructions and Start Files.

PRACTICE

Review Assignments

Data Files needed for the Review Assignments: Andes.jpg, Customer.wma, Hiker.jpg, Living.pptx, Paracas Park.jpg

Rashad Menche of Spring Lake Seminar Management was hired by Chasqui International Living in Lima, Peru to manage their annual sales conference. Chasqui International Living builds and manages condominium homes in Lima and Urubamba, Peru. (During the Inca period in Peru, a *chasqui* was a runner who carried news from one city to another.) These homes are specifically targeted to North Americans who are interested in retiring to Peru because of its low cost of living, low taxes, and cultural diversity. One of the jobs they want Rashad to do is to create their presentation for the conference. They also asked him to design a logo for their company. Complete the following:

1. Open the presentation **Living**, located in the PowerPoint3 ▸ Review folder included with your Data Files, add your name as the Slide 1 subtitle, and then save it as **International Living** to the location where you are storing your files.
2. On Slide 9 ("Interested?"), create a SmartArt diagram using the Vertical Picture Accent List layout, which is a List type diagram. Replace the text in the rectangular shapes with **Complete contact sheet**, **Tour model condo**, and **Meet with onsite loan officer**.
3. In the circles in the SmartArt diagram, click the Insert Picture buttons, and then insert the picture **Hiker** in the top circle, insert the picture **Andes** in the second circle, and insert the picture **Paracas Park** in the third circle. All three photos are located in the PowerPoint3 ▸ Review folder.
4. Change the color of the SmartArt diagram to the Colored Outline – Accent 1 style, and then change the style to the Inset style.
5. On Slide 9 ("Interested?"), add the audio clip **Customer**, located in PowerPoint3 ▸ Review folder. Set it to play automatically and hide the icon during the slide show. Position it in the upper-right corner of the slide.
6. On Slide 8 ("Monthly Cost of Living Comparison"), add a clustered bar chart. Use the data shown in Figure 3-33 to create the chart. Expand columns A and B in the data sheet to fit their widest entries.

Figure 3-33 Data for Slide 8

	United States	Lima	Urubamba
Mortgage	2000	1200	700
Condo Fees	185	50	20
Utilities	300	130	60
Groceries	350	175	100
Medical/Dental	200	100	80

7. Remove the chart title, and then move the legend so it appears to the right of the chart.

8. Change the font size of the labels on the x- and y-axes and in the legend to 16 points.

9. Double-click any value on the x-axis to open the Format Axis task pane. At the bottom of the task pane, expand the NUMBER section. Change the Category to Currency, and then change the number of Decimal places to zero.

10. On Slide 6 ("Urubamba Condos, continued"), add a text box approximately two inches wide and one-half inch high. Type **Inca ruins at Machu Picchu**.

11. Change the format of the text box so the text doesn't wrap and so that the left margin is zero.

12. Change the font size of the text in the text box to 24 points, and then align its left edge with the left edge of the photo and its top edge with the bottom edge of the photo.

13. On Slide 6 ("Urubamba Condos, continued"), change the saturation of the photo to 66%, and change the brightness of the photo to 10% and the contrast to -30%.

14. On Slide 7 ("Features of Both Properties"), change the color tone of the photo on the right to Temperature: 4700K.

15. On Slide 10, remove the background of the photo so that the sky is removed.

16. On Slide 10, sharpen the photo by 25%.

17. On Slide 10, insert a WordArt text box using the Fill - Tan, Background 2, Inner Shadow style. Replace the placeholder text with **Enjoy the beauty of Peru!** and change the font size of the text to 48 points. Position the text box so it is aligned with the left and top edges of the slide. Apply the Linear Down gradient style.

18. On Slide 2, on the donut shape, drag the yellow adjustment handle on the left side of the inside circle to the left to change the width of the donut so it is about half as wide.

19. Drag the adjusted donut shape on top of the large circle. Position the donut shape near the top right of the large circle so that smart guides appear indicating that the top and right of the two shapes are aligned. Subtract the donut shape from the larger circle by selecting the shape you want to keep—the large circle—first, and then selecting the shape you want to subtract—the donut shape—before using the Subtract command.

20. Drag the smaller circle on top of the solid circle that was created in the merged shape. Position the smaller circle near the top right of the solid circle in the merged shape without overlapping the edges of the circles, and then subtract this smaller circle from the merged shape.

21. Create a text box approximately two inches wide and one inch high. Type **CIL** in the text box. Change the font to Bernard MT Condensed, and the font size to 48 points. Deselect the Wrap text in shape option, if necessary.

22. Drag the text box to the center of the white circle created when you subtracted the small circle in the merged shape. Select the merged shape first, and then select the text box. Use the Union command to combine the shapes.

23. Fill the merged shape with the From Bottom Left Corner gradient under Dark Variations on the Gradient submenu on the Shape Fill menu, and then customize the gradient by changing the position of the Stop 2 of 3 tab to 40% and changing the color of the Stop 3 of 3 tab to Lime, Accent 1, Lighter 40%. (*Hint:* Make sure you apply the From Bottom Left Corner gradient using the Shape Fill button arrow first or your colors of the tab stops will be different.)

24. Resize the merged shape so it is 2 inches wide and 2.5 inches high.

25. Copy the custom shape, and then paste it on Slide 1 (the title slide). Position the shape to the left of the title. Position it so its left edge is about one-quarter inch from the right edge of the curve graphic on the left edge of the slide, and then use the Align Middle command to vertically center the shape on the slide. Delete Slide 2.

26. On Slide 7 ("Monthly Cost of Living Comparison"), add the following as alt text to the chart: **Chart showing the difference between the cost of living in the U.S. and in Lima and Urubamba, Peru**.

27. On Slide 8 ("Interested?"), add the following as alt text to the SmartArt shape: **SmartArt diagram listing three steps for buying property.**

28. On Slide 8, edit the Content Placeholder 3 name in the Selection Pane to **SmartArt**.

29. Save and close the presentation.

Case Problem 1

APPLY

Data Files needed for this Case Problem: Description.wma, Testing.pptx

Blue Blazes Testing Centers　Sanjiv Jindia is a senior consultant with Blue Blazes Testing Center Services, headquartered in Chattanooga, Tennessee. The company sets up testing centers at colleges and universities throughout the United States and Canada. Sanjiv visits schools to give presentations on the advantages of a testing center and the services offered by Blue Blazes. He asks you to help him create a PowerPoint presentation for his next visit to a local school. Complete the following steps:

1. Open the presentation **Testing**, located in the PowerPoint3 ▶ Case1 folder included with your Data Files, add your name as the subtitle, and then save the presentation as **Testing Centers** to the location where you are storing your files.
2. On Slide 2 ("What Is a Testing Center?"), apply the Film Grain artistic effect to the photo.
3. On Slide 3 ("A Testing Center Saves Time"), change the brightness of the photo to -20% and the contrast to -40%.
4. On Slide 4 ("A Testing Center Saves Money"), change the saturation of the photo to 200% and the tone to a temperature of 5900 K.
5. On Slide 5 ("A Testing Center Provides More Secure Testing"), remove the background of the photo so it shows only the safe and not the green background or the shadow. Rotate the image slightly to the left so it is straighter.
6. On Slide 5, change the saturation of the photo to 33%, change the tone to a temperature of 4700 K, sharpen it by 50%, and then change the brightness to +20% and the contrast to -40%.
7. On Slide 6 ("Are Testing Centers Effective?"), add a pie chart in the content placeholder. Enter the date shown in Figure 3-34 in the spreadsheet to create the chart.

Figure 3-34　　**Data for chart on Slide 6**

	Responses
Highly Effective	385
Effective	292
Moderately Effective	58
Not Effective	19

8. Adjust the width of column A so that you can see all the text in the cells.
9. Change the style of the chart to Style 8, change the colors of the chart to the Color 2 palette, change the font size of the text in the legend to 18 points, and then change the font size of the data labels—the numbers indicating the percentages on the pie slices—to 18 points.
10. Remove the chart title.
11. On Slide 6, insert the audio clip **Description**, located in the PowerPoint3 ▶ Case1 folder. Hide the icon during a slide show and set it to play automatically.
12. Add the following alt text for the chart: **Chart showing that 51% of instructors think that testing centers are effective and only 2% think they are not effective.**
13. On Slide 7 ("About Blue Blazes Testing Centers"), change the sharpness of the photo so it is 50% sharper.
14. Save and close the presentation.

CHALLENGE

Case Problem 2

Data Files needed for this Case Problem: Accounting.pptx

Medical Dental Accounting Services, Inc.   Shaundra Telanicas is an accountant but her mother was a dentist, so Shaundra knew quite a bit about the healthcare industry when she graduated from college with a double major in accounting and business management. After working as a tax accountant for three years, specializing in the medical and dental industries, she realized that healthcare practices often struggle, not because the healthcare service is poor but because the physicians and dentists themselves were not following sound business and financial practices. She founded Medical-Dental Accounting Services, Inc., located in Boise, Idaho. Her company specializes in financial and consulting services for healthcare practices. She needs to give a sales presentation at an upcoming healthcare convention and asked you to help her prepare it. Complete the following steps:

1. Open the file named **Accounting**, located in the PowerPoint3 ▶ Case2 folder included with your Data Files, add your name as the subtitle on Slide 1, and then save it as **Medical Accounting** to the location where you are storing your files.

2. On Slide 2, duplicate the red filled square shape three times. These are the four squares behind the center square in Figure 3-35. Arrange them as shown in Figure 3-35 so that there is about one-quarter inch of space between each square. Merge the four squares using the Union command.

Figure 3-35	Custom shape for MDAS

3. Apply the From Center Gradient style (a Light Variations gradient style). Customize this gradient by changing the Stop 1 of 3 tab to the Red, Accent 1 color, changing the Stop 2 of 3 tab to the Red, Accent 1, Darker 50% color, and changing the Stop 3 of 3 tab to Red, Accent 1, Lighter 40% color and changing its position to 80%. Then change the gradient Type to Linear and the direction to Linear Down.

4. Create a text box, type **MD**, press the Enter key, type **AS**. Turn off the Wrap text option if necessary, change the font to Castellar, change the font size to 40 points, and then use the Center button in the Paragraph group on the HOME tab to center the text in the box. Fill the text box shape with White. Apply the Preset 5 shape effect to this square (located on the Presets submenu on the Shape Effects menu).

5. Position the text box so it is centered over the custom shape, using the smart guides to assist you.

✪ **Explore** 6. Group the custom shape and the text box. (*Hint:* Use the appropriate command on the DRAWING TOOLS FORMAT tab.)

✪ **Explore** 7. Save the final grouped shape as a picture named **MDAS Logo** to the location where you are storing your files. (*Hint*: Right-click the shape.)

8. Delete Slide 2, and then insert the picture **MDAS Logo** on Slide 1 (the title slide). Resize it, maintaining the aspect ratio, so that it is 2.6 inches square. Position it about one-half inch above the title and so that it is left-aligned with the title text box.

9. Add the following as alt text for the logo: **Company logo**.

10. On Slide 4 ("How We Help You"), change the saturation of the photo to 66%, and sharpen it by 50%.

11. Add the following as alt text for the picture: **Photo of smiling woman at a keyboard**.

12. On Slide 5 ("Financial Concerns of Medical Practices"), insert a SmartArt diagram using the Basic Block List layout (in the List category). Type the following as first-level bullets in the text pane:

   - **Planning for tax purposes**
   - **Keeping overhead down**
   - **Setting up health insurance for employees**
   - **Setting up proper billing**
   - **Containing office setup costs**

✪ **Explore** 13. Reverse the order of the boxes in the diagram. (*Hint:* Use a command in the Create Graphic group on the SMARTART TOOLS DESIGN tab.)

14. Change the style of the SmartArt diagram to the Inset style.

15. Animate the SmartArt diagram with the Wipe entrance animation and the From Left effect. Modify this so that each shape appears one at a time.

16. Add the following as alt text for the SmartArt diagram: **SmartArt diagram listing five financial concerns of medical practice owners**.

17. On Slide 8 ("We Are Here for You"), insert the MDAS Logo in the content placeholder on the left, and add the following as alt text for the logo on Slide 8: **Company logo**.

18. Save and close the presentation.

Case Problem 3

CHALLENGE

Data Files needed for this Case Problem: Properties.pptx

Valley Pike Properties Davion Fusilier is co-owner of Valley Pike Properties in Winchester, Virginia. His company acquired two new properties near the end of last year—a luxury apartment building in the city that he is renovating and condos on Silver Creek. He started preselling the properties in January. Both properties are about 80 percent occupied. Davion regularly holds small sales presentations for people interested in purchasing property. He asks you to help him create his final presentation. Complete the following steps:

1. Open the presentation named **Properties**, located in the PowerPoint3 ▸ Case3 folder included with your Data Files, add your name as the subtitle, and then save it as **Valley Pike Properties** to the location where you are storing your files.

2. On Slide 2 ("Two Luxurious Properties"), sharpen the photo on the right by 25%, and then change its tone to a temperature of 7200 K.

3. On Slide 4 ("Living Room"), change the color tone of both photos to a temperature of 5900 K, and change the color saturation of the photo on the right to 66%.

4. On Slide 7 ("Two Styles of Living Rooms"), sharpen the photo on the left by 50%.

5. On Slide 9 ("Available Properties Going Fast!"), insert a clustered column chart using the data shown in Figure 3-36.

Figure 3-36 **Data for chart on Slide 9**

	Briar Hill	Silver Creek
January	0.37	0.31
March	0.46	0.42
June	0.61	0.56
September	0.7	0.82

⊕ **Explore** 6. In the spreadsheet, drag the small blue selection handle in the lower-right corner of cell D5 to the left to cell C5 so that column D is not included in the chart.

7. Change the style of the chart to Style 5.

⊕ **Explore** 8. In the chart, change the chart title to **Percent Occupancy**.

9. Double-click a value on the y-axis to open the Format Axis task pane. At the bottom of the task pane, expand the NUMBER section. Change the Category to Percentage and then change the number of Decimal places to zero.

⊕ **Explore** 10. In the Format Axis task pane, change the maximum value on the y-axis to 100%. (*Hint*: In the AXIS OPTIONS sections at the top of the Format Axis task pane, change the value in the Maximum box under Bounds to 1.)

⊕ **Explore** 11. Change the color of the columns that represent the Briar Hill occupancy percentages to a light green or teal color, and then change the color of the columns that represent the Silver Creek occupancy percentages to a darker green or teal color. (*Hint*: Click one of the columns, use the Shape Fill button in the Shape Styles group on the CHART TOOLS FORMAT tab.)

12. Change the font size of the labels on the y- and x-axis and the legend to 16 points. Change the font size of the title to 20 points.

⊕ **Explore** 13. Animate the chart with the entrance animation Wipe. Modify the animation so that the chart grid animates first and then each category animates one at a time (in other words, so that the two columns showing occupancy rates in January animate together, then the two columns showing occupancy rates in March animate, and so on). Finally, modify the start timing of the chart grid animation so it animates with the previous action.

14. On Slide 10, insert a WordArt text box using the Gradient Fill – Gray-80%, Accent 1, Reflection style. Enter the text, **Thank you for coming!**. Increase the font size of the text in the text box to 66 points.

15. Save and close the presentation.

Case Problem 4

There are no Data Files needed for this Case Problem.

RESEARCH

Bay Area Speech Makers   Bay Area Speech Makers is a club for people who want to become better public speakers. Their goal is to help people gain confidence in speaking in public. They require members to prepare short presentations for the other club members. As a member of the club, you need to prepare a five minute informative presentation consisting of five or six slides about one aspect of a hobby or special interest. For example, you could prepare a presentation about one aspect of hiking, geology, cooking, race cars, or gardening. Keep the presentation focused so that the short amount of time you have is enough to present your information clearly. Your presentation must contain at least one photo, one SmartArt graphic, and one chart created from factual data. Use the Internet or other sources to find an appropriate photo and research the data. Complete the following steps:

1. Research your topic to find data you can present in a chart. For example, for a presentation about hiking, you could present data showing the number of hikes over 4000 feet in the United States.

2. Decide which information would be clearer or more interesting if it were presented in a SmartArt graphic, and choose the layout you want to use.

3. Plan your presentation slides by writing an outline. Include a title slide and a slide that introduces your topic.

4. Create a new presentation. You can start with a blank presentation and then choose an appropriate theme, or you can create a presentation based on a template from Office.com.

5. Add your name as the subtitle, and then save the presentation with an appropriate name to the location where you are storing your files.

6. Create the slides of your presentation based on your research. Remember to include at least one photo, one SmartArt graphic, and one chart created from factual data. If it would enhance your presentation, consider including a video or audio clip.

7. If you will not be presenting orally, add speaker notes to clarify the information on the slides for your instructor.

8. Add appropriate transitions and animations if they enhance your message.

9. Check the spelling in your presentation and proof it carefully.

10. Save and close the presentation.

Advanced Animations and Distributing Presentations

POWERPOINT

OBJECTIVES

Session 4.1
- Add more than one animation to an object
- Set animation triggers
- Use a picture as the slide background
- Create and edit hyperlinks
- Add action buttons
- Create a custom color palette

Session 4.2
- Create a self-running presentation
- Rehearse slide timings
- Record slide timings and narration
- Set options to allow viewers to override timings
- Inspect a presentation for private information
- Identify features not supported by previous versions of PowerPoint
- Save a presentation in other formats

Creating an Advanced Presentation for a Wireless Control Systems Company

Case | *Duplantis Control Systems*

Duplantis Control Systems manufactures and installs computer-controlled wireless switches and other devices for monitoring and controlling aspects of electrical systems in buildings. For example, Duplantis has designed a system that can allow remote access and control of thermostats, lights, security systems, and other electrical equipment in commercial buildings such as hotels or office buildings. The company also provides smaller systems to be used in residential homes. Ryder Duplantis, owner of Duplantis Control Systems, has created a PowerPoint presentation about his company's products and services appropriate for his commercial customers. He wants your help in finishing the presentation, which he intends to use at trade shows and conventions. Because he hopes to secure some accounts outside of the United States, he wants to be able to distribute the presentation electronically.

In this tutorial, you will enhance Ryder's presentation by adding multiple animations to objects and setting triggers for animations. You'll also add a picture as the slide background, create links to other slides and customize the color of text links, and create a self-running presentation including narration. Finally, you'll save the presentation in other formats for distribution.

STARTING DATA FILES

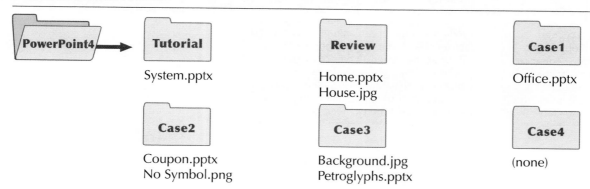

PowerPoint4 → Tutorial

System.pptx

Review

Home.pptx
House.jpg

Case1

Office.pptx

Case2

Coupon.pptx
No Symbol.png

Case3

Background.jpg
Petroglyphs.pptx

Case4

(none)

Session 4.1 Visual Overview:

To add a second animation to an object, click the Add Animation button in the Advanced Animation group on the ANIMATIONS tab.

When multiple animations are applied to an object, select one of the animation sequence icons to display its associated animation in the Animation gallery.

The motion path is indicated by a dotted line. You can drag the green circle or arrow that indicates the starting point or the red circle or arrow that indicates the ending point to modify the path.

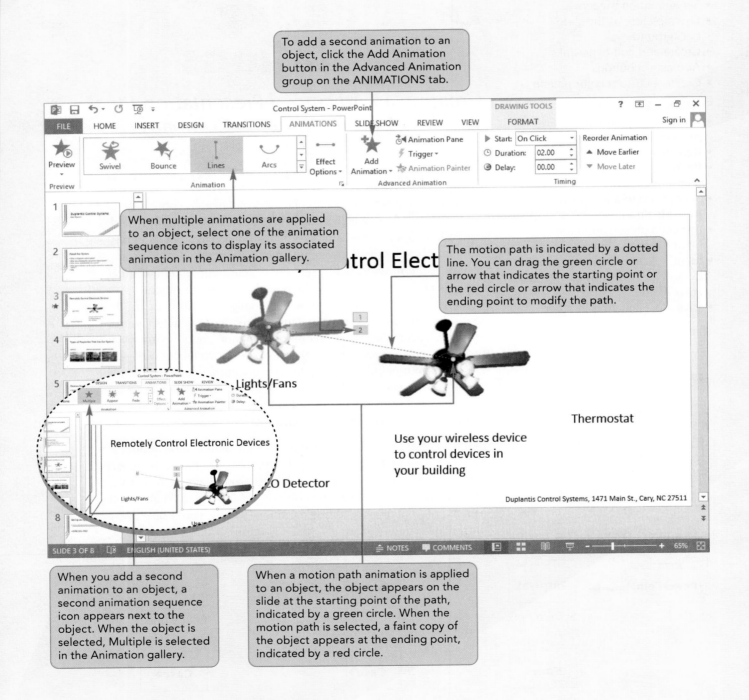

When you add a second animation to an object, a second animation sequence icon appears next to the object. When the object is selected, Multiple is selected in the Animation gallery.

When a motion path animation is applied to an object, the object appears on the slide at the starting point of the path, indicated by a green circle. When the motion path is selected, a faint copy of the object appears at the ending point, indicated by a red circle.

Photos courtesy of S. Scott Zimmerman; Doug Plummer/Getty Images

Understanding Advanced Animations

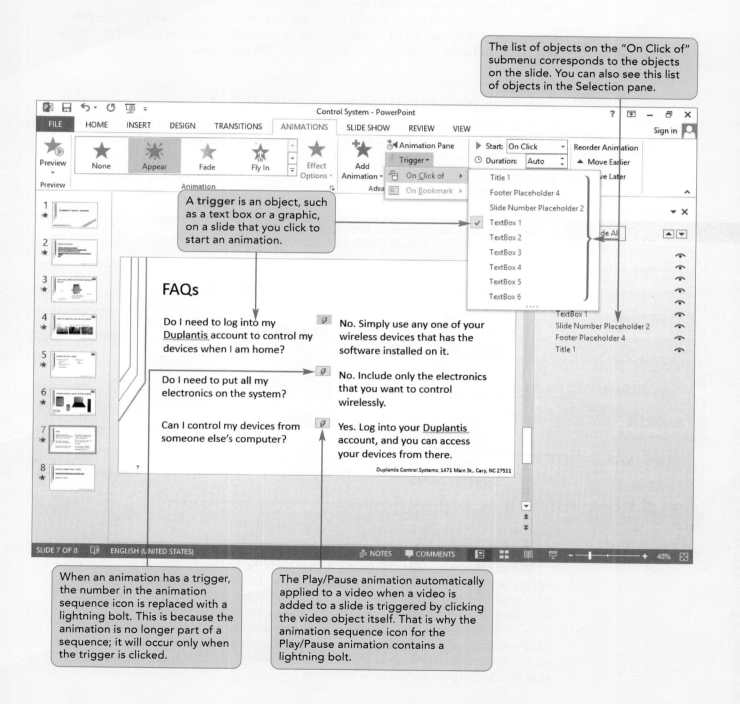

The list of objects on the "On Click of" submenu corresponds to the objects on the slide. You can also see this list of objects in the Selection pane.

A **trigger** is an object, such as a text box or a graphic, on a slide that you click to start an animation.

When an animation has a trigger, the number in the animation sequence icon is replaced with a lightning bolt. This is because the animation is no longer part of a sequence; it will occur only when the trigger is clicked.

The Play/Pause animation automatically applied to a video when a video is added to a slide is triggered by clicking the video object itself. That is why the animation sequence icon for the Play/Pause animation contains a lightning bolt.

Adding More Than One Animation to an Object

You know how to apply an animation to an object and you can determine how the animation starts, its duration, and its speed. An object can have more than one animation applied to it. For example, you might apply an entrance animation to an object by having it fly into a slide, and then once the object is on the slide, you might want to animate it a second time to further emphasize a bullet point on the slide, or to show a relationship between the object and another object on the slide.

Ryder wants Slide 3 to illustrate the concept of a wireless device, such as a mobile phone, controlling various electronic devices in a building. The slide currently contains text boxes and graphic objects. You will examine this slide now.

To open the presentation and examine Slide 3:

1. Open the presentation **System**, located in the **PowerPoint4 ▸ Tutorial** folder included with your Data Files, add your name as the subtitle, and then save it as **Control System**.

2. Display **Slide 3** ("Remotely Control Electronic Devices") in the Slide pane. See Figure 4-1.

| Figure 4-1 | Slide 3 in the Control System presentation |

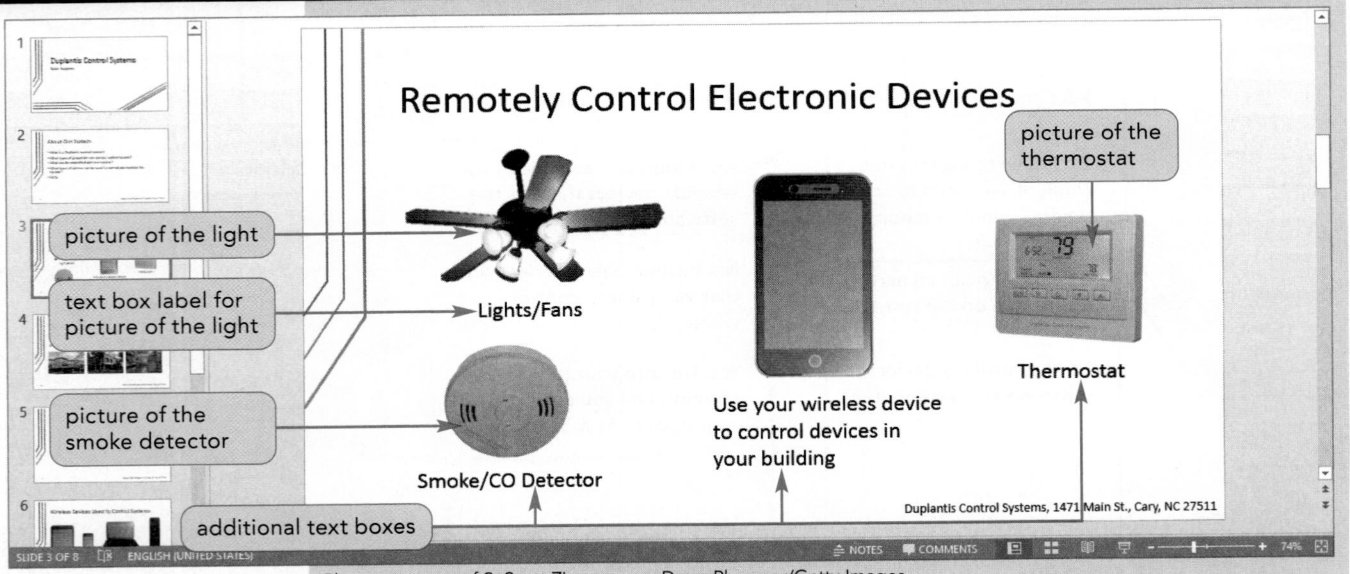

Photos courtesy of S. Scott Zimmerman; Doug Plummer/Getty Images

To make the slide more interesting, Ryder wants the images he has on the slides to appear one at a time in the center of the slide and then move so that they are above their respective text boxes. Then he wants the picture's text box to appear. To create this effect, you will position each picture in the center of the slide and then add two animations to each picture—an entrance animation and then a motion path animation. After you apply and modify the motion path animation to the pictures, you will animate each text box with an entrance animation and modify it so that it appears automatically after the motion path animation is complete.

To add multiple animations to the objects on Slide 3:

1. On **Slide 3** ("Remotely Control Electronic Devices"), drag the picture of the ceiling lights/fan to the center of the slide, on top of the picture of the smartphone. First you need to apply an entrance animation to this image.

2. On the ribbon, click the **ANIMATIONS** tab, and then in the Animation group, click the **Appear** animation. Now you need to add the second animation to the light—the motion path animation. To do this you must use the Add Animation button in the Advanced Animation group; otherwise you will replace the currently applied animation.

3. In the Advanced Animation group, click the **Add Animation** button.

4. Scroll down to locate the Motion Paths section, and then click the **Lines** animation. The animation previews and the light moves down the slide. After the preview, the path appears below the light, and a faint image of the light appears at the end of the path. At the beginning of the path, the green circle indicates the path's starting point, and at the end of the path, the red circle indicates the path's ending point. The second animation sequence icon is selected, and Lines is selected in the Animation group.

5. Click the light to select it. In the Animation gallery, Multiple is selected. This indicates that more than one animation is applied to the selected object.

> Make sure you do not click another animation in the Animation group.

The light needs to move to the left instead of down. You can change the basic direction in which an object moves and then fine-tune the path so it ends up in the correct position. Because two animations are applied to the object, you need to make sure that the correct animation sequence icon is selected and the correct animation is selected in the Animation group on the ANIMATIONS tab.

To modify the motion path animation for the light:

1. Click the **2** animation sequence icon to select it. In the Animation gallery, Lines is selected. This is the animation that corresponds to the selected animation sequence icon.

2. In the Animation group, click the **Effect Options** button, and then click **Left**. The motion path changes to a horizontal line, the light moves left across the slide, and the circles at the beginning and end of the motion path change to arrows. You need to reposition the ending of the motion path so that the light ends up above the Lights/Fans text box. First you need to select the motion path.

3. Point to the **motion path** so that the pointer changes to ⁺↖, and then click. The arrows on the ends of the motion path change to circles and a faint copy of the image appears at the end of the motion path. Now you can drag the start and end points to new locations.

4. Position the pointer on top of the red circle so that it changes to ↙⤢, and then drag the red circle to position it above the Lights/Fans text box. See Figure 4-2.

Figure 4-2 **Repositioned motion path animation**

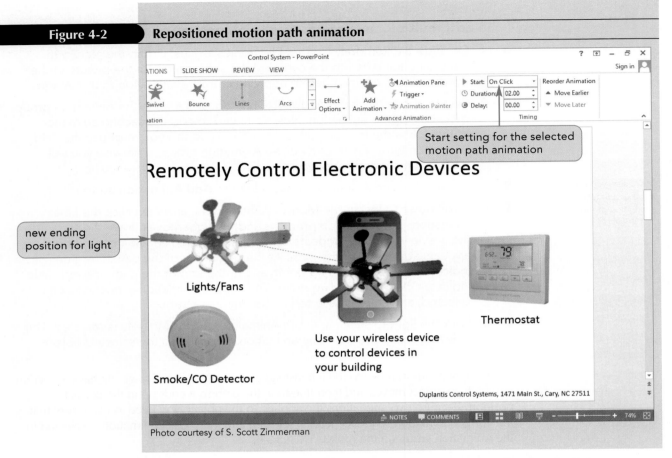

Photo courtesy of S. Scott Zimmerman

Ryder wants the motion path animation to occur automatically after the light appears. The 2 animation sequence icon and the Lines animation in the Animation group are still selected.

To change the start timing of the light's second animation and animate the text box:

1. Make sure the **2** animation sequence icon is selected.

2. In the Timing group, click the **Start** arrow, and then click **After Previous**. Now you need to animate the Lights/Fans text box so it appears automatically after the light finishes moving on the motion path.

3. Click the **Lights/Fans** text box, and then in the Animation group, click the **Appear** animation.

4. In the Timing group, click the **Start** arrow, and then click **After Previous**.

5. In the Preview group, click the **Preview** button. The picture of the light and the Lights/Fans text box disappear from the slide, the picture of the light appears, and then the picture of the light moves from the center of the slide diagonally left. The Lights/Fans text box then appears below the picture of the light.

Now you need to animate the photos of the smoke/CO detector and thermostat and their text boxes in the same manner.

To animate two more photos and their text boxes:

1. Drag the photo of the smoke detector on top of the picture of the lights.

2. Apply the entrance animation **Appear**, and then add the **Lines** motion path animation.

3. Drag the red circle of the motion path so that the picture of the smoke detector ends up above the Smoke/CO Detector text box.

4. If necessary, click the animation sequence icon **3** to select it. In the Animation group on the ANIMATIONS tab, the Lines animation is selected.

5. In the Timing group, click the **Start** arrow, and then click **After Previous**.

6. Click the **Smoke/CO Detector** text box, apply the **Appear** entrance animation to it, and then modify its start timing so that it animates automatically after the previous animation.

7. Drag the picture of the thermostat on top of the picture of the smoke detector, apply the **Appear** entrance animation, and then add the **Lines** animation.

8. Change the Lines animation direction effect so that the picture of the thermostat moves right, and then adjust the end of the motion path as needed so that the picture of the thermostat ends up above the Thermostat text box.

9. Modify the start timing of the Lines animation applied to the thermostat so it starts automatically after the previous animation.

10. Animate the Thermostat text box with the entrance animation Appear, and then modify its start timing so that it animates automatically after the previous animation.

Finally, Ryder wants the photo of a smartphone to appear in the center of the slide, and then for the text box that describes the basic function of the system to appear below the smartphone. The smartphone is below the other three pictures, but you can see the top and bottom of the photo.

To animate the smartphone photo and its text box and view the slide in Slide Show view:

1. Click the picture of the smartphone, and then apply the entrance animation **Appear**.

2. Click the **Use your wireless device…** text box, apply the entrance animation **Appear**, and then change its start timing so that the text box appears automatically after the previous animation. Compare your screen to Figure 4-3.

Figure 4-3   **Slide 3 with animated objects**

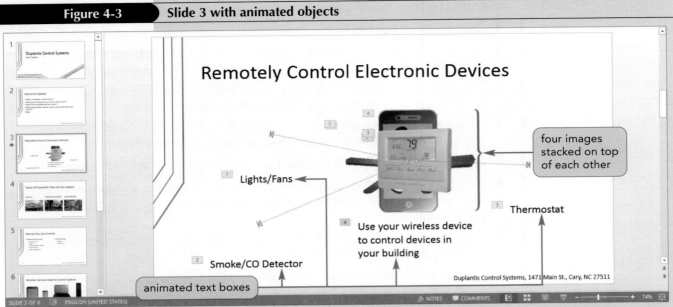

Photos courtesy of S. Scott Zimmerman; Doug Plummer/Getty Images

3. On the status bar, click the **Slide Show** button 🖥 to start the slide show from Slide 3. The slide title, the graphic on the left, and the slide number and footer are the only things visible on the slide.

4. Press the **spacebar** to advance the slide show. The light appears in the center of the slide, moves up and to the left, and then the Lights/Fans text box appears.

5. Press the **spacebar** again, watch the animation of the smoke detector and its text box, and then press the **spacebar** once more to display the thermostat and its text box.

6. Press the **spacebar** again. The smartphone appears followed immediately by its text box.

7. End the slide show, and then save the changes to the presentation.

Using the Animation Pane

When you apply multiple animations to objects and change the start timings, it can be difficult to locate the animation sequence icon associated with a specific animation. To see a list of all the animations on a slide, you can open the Animation Pane. You'll examine the animations on Slide 3 in the Animation Pane.

To examine the animations in the Animation Pane:

1. In the Advanced Animation group, click the **Animation Pane** button. The Animation Pane opens. See Figure 4-4.

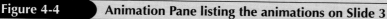

Figure 4-4 — Animation Pane listing the animations on Slide 3

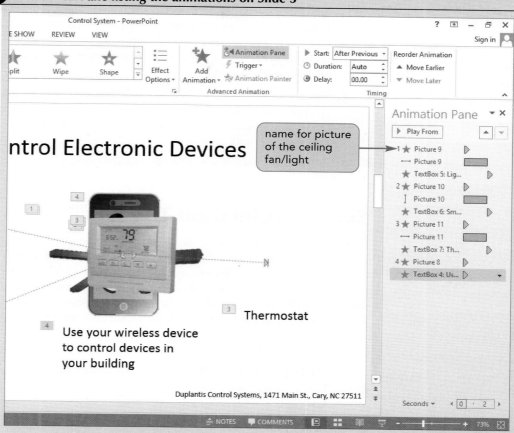

2. In the Animation Pane, point to the first animation in the list, **Picture 9**. The ScreenTip that appears identifies the start timing (On Click), the animation (Appear), and the full name of the object (Picture 9). The picture of the ceiling fan and lights is the first object that is animated on this slide, so you know that Picture 9 identifies that object. The number 1 to the left of the object name is the same number that appears in the animation sequence icon for this animation.

3. In the Animation Pane, point to the second animation in the list, the second **Picture 9**. This is the motion path animation applied to the picture of the ceiling fan and light. There is no number to the left because this animation occurs automatically, not On Click.

4. In the Animation Pane, point to the third animation in the list, **TextBox 5**. The ScreenTip includes the text in the text box, and identifies this object as the Lights/Fans text box. Again, there is no number to the left of the animated item in the list because this animation also occurs automatically.

5. To the right of the first animation in the list, Picture 9, point to the green arrow. The green arrow indicates that the applied animation has no length. This is because the animation is the Appear animation, and this animation does not have a duration that can be adjusted. The ScreenTip also identifies the start time as 0s (zero seconds), which means it starts immediately after the action that causes the animation, in this case, advancing the slide show.

▶ **6.** To the right of the second animation in the list, Picture 9, point to the blue rectangle. Even though this animation is set to start after the previous animation, because the previous animation—Appear—has no length, the ScreenTip indicates that this animation also starts at zero seconds. This animation, however, takes two seconds to complete, so there is an ending time for this animation as well—2s, meaning two seconds.

▶ **7.** To the right of TextBox 5, point to the green arrow. This animation—the Appear animation applied to the Lights/Fans text box—has a start time of 2s because it is set to animate after the previous animation, which ends at the two second mark.

▶ **8.** In the Animation Pane, click the **Close** button ☒.

Setting Animation Triggers

Ryder created a slide listing FAQs—frequently asked questions—and their answers. Ryder created the content on this slide using separate text boxes for each question and answer, instead of using two text boxes created from content placeholders. He wants to be able to click the question to display its answer. To do this, you need to apply an entrance animation to each text box object containing an answer and then set a trigger for that animation. Refer to the Session 4.1 Visual Overview for more information about triggers.

To set triggers for animations on Slide 7:

▶ **1.** Display **Slide 7** ("FAQs") in the Slide pane, and then on the ribbon, click the **HOME** tab.

▶ **2.** In the Editing group, click the **Select** button, and then click **Selection Pane**. Examine the slide contents. Notice that the slide does not contain a list in a single text box. As you can see in the Selection pane, it contains six text boxes in addition to the slide title and footer text box. You can click each object in the slide to identify its name in the Selection pane. See Figure 4-5.

Figure 4-5	Objects on Slide 7 listed in Selection pane

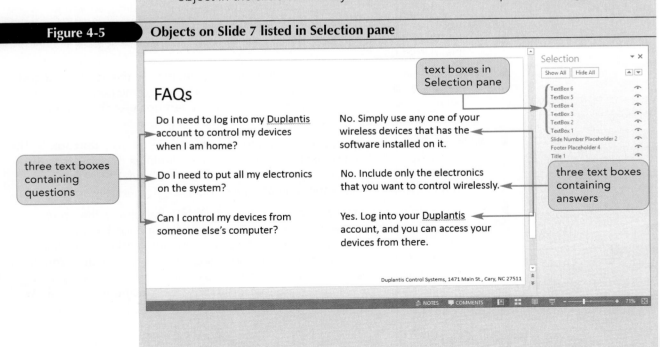

3. On the slide, click the top text box on the left to see that TextBox 1 is selected in the Selection pane, and then click each of the other two text boxes on the left to see their names—TextBox 2 and TextBox 3—selected in the Selection pane.

4. Click the top text box on the right, press and hold the **Shift** key, and then click the two other text boxes on the right. In the Selection pane, TextBox 4, 5, and 6 are selected. You want each of the three text boxes on the right to appear when you click the corresponding text box on the left. First, you need to apply an entrance animation to the text boxes on the right.

5. On the ribbon, click the **ANIMATIONS** tab, and then in the Animation group, click the **Appear** animation. The Appear animation is applied to all three text boxes. Now you need to make the text boxes on the left the triggers for each text box on the right.

6. Next to the top text box on the right, click the **1** animation sequence icon.

7. In the Advanced Animation group, click the **Trigger** button, and then point to **On Click of**. The same list of objects that appears in the Selection pane appears on the submenu.

8. Click **TextBox 1**. The animation sequence icon next to the top right text box changes to a lightning bolt.

9. Next to the middle right text box, click the **0** animation sequence icon, and then set its animation to trigger when you click **TextBox 2**.

10. Next to the bottom right text box, click the **0** animation sequence icon, and then set its animation to trigger when you click **TextBox 3**.

Now you see why Ryder created the slide using six text boxes rather than two lists in two text boxes. If the slide contained only two text boxes, when you clicked any one of the questions on the left, all of the answers in the text box on the right would have appeared at once.

Next you need to test the triggers. You'll view Slide 7 in Slide Show view and click each question to make sure the correct answer appears.

To test the animation triggers in Slide Show view:

1. On the status bar, click the **Slide Show** button 🖵. Slide 7 appears in Slide Show view displaying the slide title and the three text boxes on the left.

2. Click the first question. The text box containing its answer appears on the slide.

3. Click each of the other two questions to display their answers, and then end the slide show.

4. Close the Selection pane, and then save the changes to the presentation.

Changing the Slide Background

The background of a slide can be as important as the foreground when you are creating a presentation with a strong visual impact. To change the background, you use the Format Background task pane. When you change the background, you are essentially changing the fill of the background. The commands are the same as the commands you use when you change the fill of a shape. For example, you can change the color, add a gradient or a pattern, or fill it with a texture or a picture. When you use a picture as the slide background, you can use a picture stored on your computer or network or you can search for one online.

REFERENCE

Adding a Picture to the Slide Background

- On the ribbon, click the DESIGN tab.
- In the Customize group, click the Format Background button to open the Format Background task pane.
- With the Fill button selected, click FILL to expand the section, if necessary.
- Click the Picture or texture fill option button.
- To use an image stored on your computer or network, click the File button to open the Insert Picture dialog box, click the image you want to use, and then click the Insert button; or to use an image on Office.com or another location on the Internet, click the Online button, type keywords in the appropriate box, click the Search button, click the image you want to use, and then click the Insert button.
- If the image is too dark, drag the Transparency slider in the Format Background task pane to the right until the image is the desired transparency.
- Click the Apply to All button if you want to apply the background to all the slides in the presentation.

Ryder wants you to use a photo of circuitry as the slide background. You'll search for a photo of circuits on Office.com and use that as the slide background.

TIP

To add a preset gradient as the background fill, click the More button in the Variants group on the DESIGN tab, point to Background Styles, and then click one of the gradient styles.

To fill the slide background with an online picture:

1. On the ribbon, click the **DESIGN** tab, and then in the Customize group, click the **Format Background** button. The Format Background task pane opens. See Figure 4-6. This task pane has only one button—the Fill button—and one section of commands—the FILL section. It contains the same commands as the FILL section in the Format Shape pane. The Solid fill option button is selected, indicating that the current background has a solid fill.

Figure 4-6   **Format Background task pane**

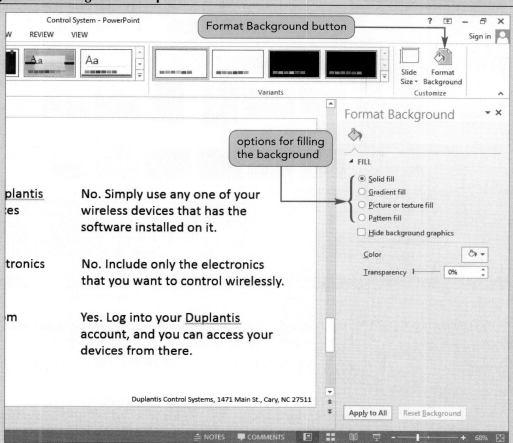

2. Click the **Picture or texture fill** option button. The default texture is applied to the current slide background and the task pane changes to include more commands, including commands for inserting pictures.

3. In the Insert picture from section, click the **Online** button. The Insert Pictures dialog box opens with the insertion point in the Office.com Clip Art box.

4. Type **circuit board chips**, and then click the **Search** button.

5. In the list of results, click the purple picture of a circuit board, as indicated in Figure 4-7.

Figure 4-7 Insert Pictures dialog box displaying search results from Office.com

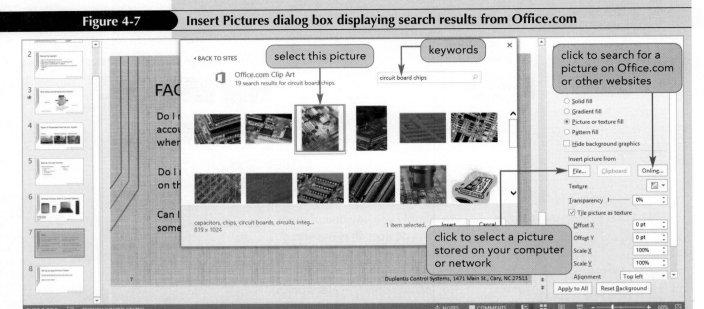

Photos courtesy of S. Scott Zimmerman; Doug Plummer/Getty Images

Trouble? If the picture shown in Figure 4-7 is not available, click any photo of a circuit board with blue or purple colors.

6. Click the **Insert** button. The picture fills the slide background.

You can adjust the position of the photo using the offset options in the task pane. Instead of displaying one image of the picture as the slide background, you can tile it, which means you can make it appear as repeating squares. If you set an image to tile as a background, the four offset options change to offset and scale (size) options. You can adjust the scale of the tiles horizontally (using the Scale X setting) and vertically (using the Scale Y setting). You'll change the picture to tiles.

To change the background picture of the slide to tiles:

1. In the Format Background task pane, click the **Tile picture as texture** check box to select it. The picture changes to a series of tiles on the slide.

2. In the **Scale Y** box, change the value to **75%**, and then press the **Enter** key.

The new background makes it difficult to read the text on the slide. You could adjust the brightness and the contrast of the photo, or you could make the photo more transparent. You'll adjust the transparency of the picture now.

To change the transparency of the background picture:

1. In the Format Background task pane, drag the **Transparency** slider to the right until the value in the Transparency box is **90%**. Now you need to apply this picture background to all the slides.

Trouble? If you can't position the slider so that 90% appears in the Transparency box, click the up or down arrows in the Transparency box as needed to change the value.

2. At the bottom of the task pane, click the **Apply to All** button. Compare your screen to Figure 4-8.

Figure 4-8   **Picture with transparency adjusted tile as slide background**

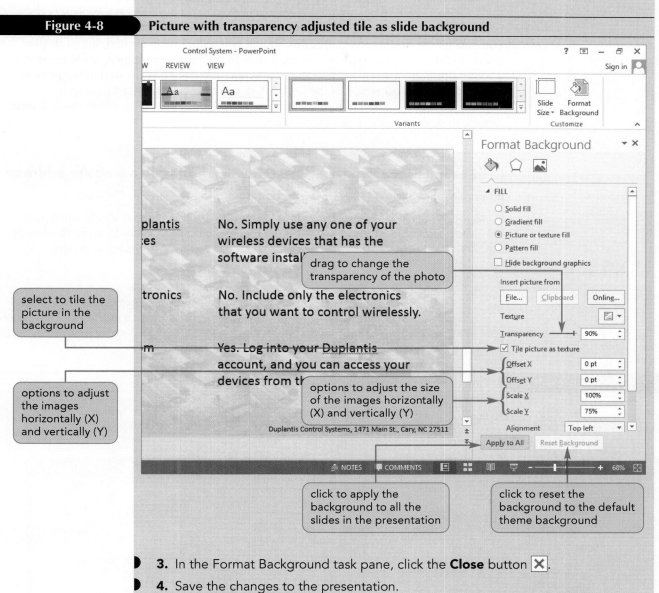

3. In the Format Background task pane, click the **Close** button ⊠.

4. Save the changes to the presentation.

INSIGHT

Hiding Background Graphics

If the theme you are using includes graphics in the background and you need to print the slides in black and white or grayscale, you might want to remove those graphics before printing the slides because the graphic could make the text difficult to read. To hide graphics in the background, select the Hide background graphics check box in the Format Background pane. Note that this will not hide anything you use as a fill for the background, such as the picture you added as the background in this tutorial.

Creating and Editing Hyperlinks

As you know, when you type a web or an email address on a slide, it is formatted as a hyperlink automatically. If you've visited webpages, you've clicked hyperlinks (or links) to "jump to"—or display—other webpages. In PowerPoint, a link on a slide accomplishes the same thing. You can convert any text or object on slide to be a link, and you can set the destination of this link so that when the link is clicked, it will display another slide in the same presentation, a slide in another presentation, a file created in another program, a webpage, or open a new email message addressed to the person whose email address is part of the link. A link can also be set to start a program.

Slide 8 contains a link to Ryder's company's website. You can examine the link more closely to determine the link's destination.

To examine the hyperlink created when you type a website address:

▶ **1.** Display **Slide 8** ("Set Up an Appointment Today!") in the Slide pane.

▶ **2.** Right-click the webpage address hyperlink on the slide. A shortcut menu opens. In addition to the Remove Hyperlink command that you have already used, there are three other commands related to the hyperlink on the shortcut menu.

▶ **3.** Click **Edit Hyperlink**. The Edit Hyperlink dialog box opens. See Figure 4-9. In the Link to list on the left, the Existing File or Web Page option is selected. The web address that is formatted as a hyperlink appears in the Address box at the bottom of the dialog box and also in the Text to display box at the top of the dialog box.

Figure 4-9	Edit Hyperlink dialog box for a link to a webpage

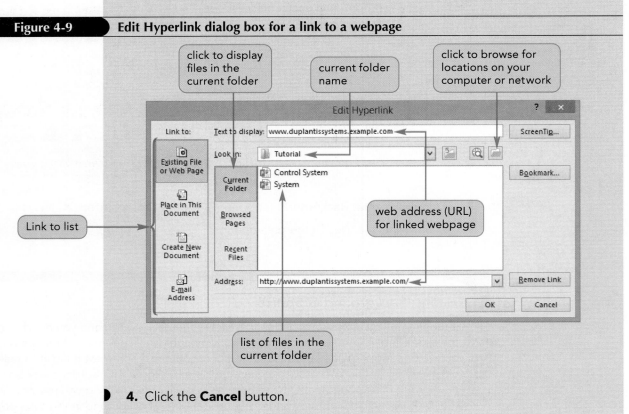

▶ **4.** Click the **Cancel** button.

Creating a Link

You can select any text or object, including graphics or text boxes, and convert them to links. Graphic hyperlinks are visually indistinguishable from graphics that are not hyperlinks, except that when you move the mouse pointer over the object, the pointer changes to 🖑. Text links are usually underlined and a different color than the rest of the text on a slide. After you click a text link during a slide show, the link changes to another color to reflect the fact that it has been clicked, or followed.

Slide 2 in Ryder's presentation is an overview slide. Each bulleted item on this slide describes another slide in the presentation. Ryder wants you to convert each bulleted item to a hyperlink that links to the related slide.

To create a hyperlink to Slide 3 from text on Slide 2:

1. Display **Slide 2** ("About Our System") in the Slide pane.

2. Click the first bullet symbol. The text of the first bulleted item is selected.

3. On the ribbon, click the **INSERT** tab, and then in the Links group, click the **Hyperlink** button. The Insert Hyperlink dialog box opens. In the Link to list on the left, the Existing File or Web Page option is selected. You need to identify the file or location to which you want to link. In this case, you're going to link to a place in the presentation.

4. In the Link to list on the left, click **Place in This Document**. The dialog box changes to show a Select a place in this document box, listing all the slides in the presentation.

5. In the Select a place in this document list, click **3. Remotely Control Electron** The Slide preview area on the right side of the dialog box displays Slide 3. This is the slide to which the text will be linked. See Figure 4-10.

Figure 4-10 | **Insert Hyperlink dialog box displaying slides in this presentation**

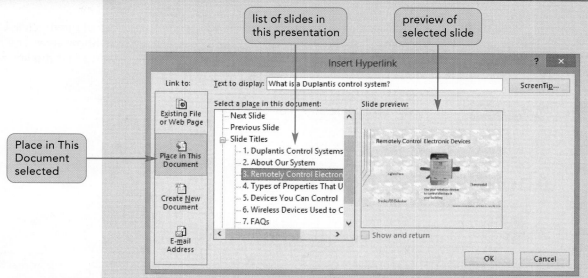

6. Click the **OK** button, and then click a blank area of the slide to deselect the text. The text of the first bullet is now a hyperlink, and it is now formatted in a teal color and underlined. See Figure 4-11.

Figure 4-11	Slide 2 with a hyperlink to Slide 3

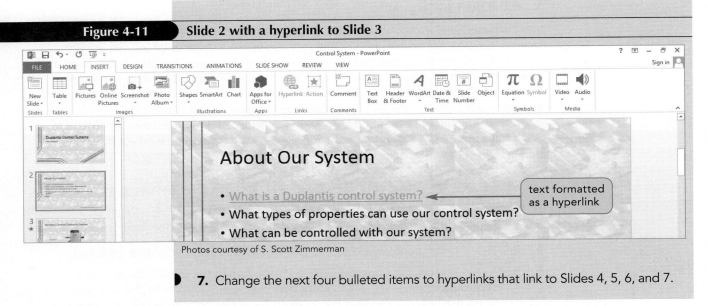

Photos courtesy of S. Scott Zimmerman

▶ **7.** Change the next four bulleted items to hyperlinks that link to Slides 4, 5, 6, and 7.

Now you need to test the links you created. Links are not active in Normal view, so you will switch to Slide Show view.

To test the hyperlinks:

▶ **1.** With Slide 2 ("About Our System") in the Slide pane, on the status bar, click the **Slide Show** button 🖵.

▶ **2.** Click the **What is a Duplantis control system?** hyperlink. Slide 3 ("Remotely Control Electronic Devices") appears in slide show view. (The content of the slide does not appear because you need to advance the slide show to animate the content.)

▶ **3.** Right-click anywhere on the slide, and then on the shortcut menu, click **Last Viewed**. Slide 2 ("About Our System") appears in Slide Show view. The link text in the first bulleted item is now light purple, indicating that the link had been clicked, or was followed. See Figure 4-12.

Figure 4-12	Followed link on Slide 2 in Slide Show view

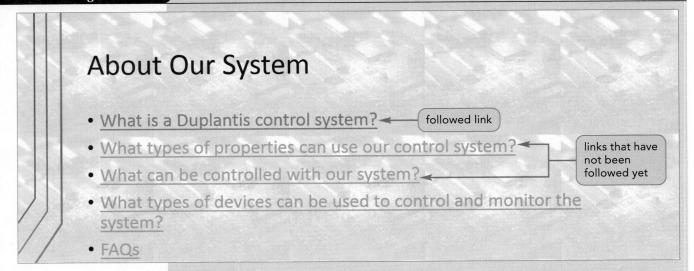

4. Click each of the other links to verify that they display the correct slides, using the Last Viewed command on the shortcut menu to return to Slide 2 each time.

5. End the slide show.

Adding Action Buttons

An action button is a shape intended to be a link. In the Action Button section in the Shapes gallery, 12 action button shapes are available, such as Action Button: Home or Action Button: Sound. Each action button can link to any slide, presentation file, and so on; the various shapes simply offer variety in the way the buttons look. The default format for each button is to link to the slide or file described by the button name.

REFERENCE

Adding an Action Button

- On the ribbon, click the INSERT tab, and then in the Illustrations group, click the Shapes button.
- In the Action Button section, click an action button shape.
- Drag the pointer on the slide to draw the action button the size you want.
- In the Action Settings dialog box, on the Mouse Click tab, click the desired option button.
- Click the arrow below the selected option button and then click the location to which you want to link, or click the Browse button, click the program you want to run, and then click the OK button.
- Click the OK button in the Action Settings dialog box.
- Resize and reposition the action button icon as desired.

Although Ryder can use the commands on the shortcut menu to return to Slide 2 after clicking a link to another slide, it would be easier for him to navigate during the slide show if you added a link back to Slide 2 on each slide. You'll do this now by adding action buttons on Slides 3 through 7.

To add action buttons to link to Slide 2:

1. Display **Slide 3** ("Remotely Control Electronic Devices") in the Slide pane.

2. On the INSERT tab, in the Illustrations group, click the **Shapes** button. The gallery of shapes appears. The action buttons are at the bottom of the gallery.

3. Scroll down to the bottom of the gallery, and then click the **Action Button: Back or Previous** shape in the Action Button section. The pointer changes to ┼.

4. In the upper-right corner of the slide, drag the pointer to draw an action button about one-half inch high and one inch wide. After you release the mouse button, a blue button containing a left-pointing triangle appears on the slide, and the Action Settings dialog box opens with the Mouse Click tab selected. See Figure 4-13. Because you inserted the Back or Previous action button, "Previous Slide" appears in the Hyperlink to box. This is fine because Slide 2 is the slide before Slide 3.

| Figure 4-13 | Action button on Slide 3 and Action Settings dialog box |

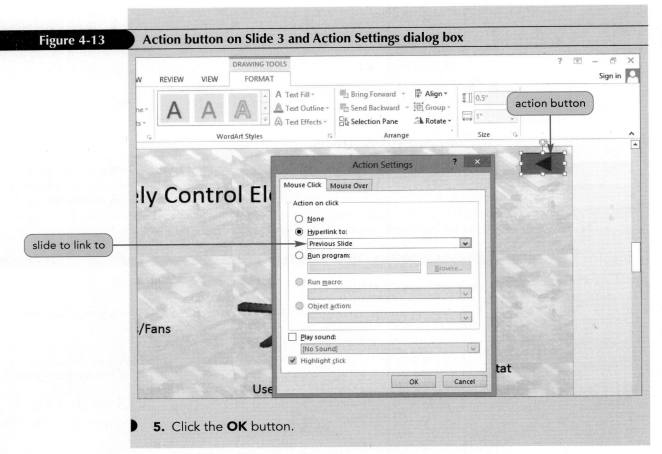

5. Click the **OK** button.

You want the same action button on Slides 4 through 7. You can insert a button on each slide or you can copy the button on Slide 3 and paste it on each slide. You will need to edit the link, however, so that it links to Slide 2 and not the previous slide.

To copy an action button and edit the link:

1. On Slide 3 ("Remotely Control Electronic Systems"), copy the action button to the Clipboard.

2. Display **Slide 4** ("Types of Properties That Use Our System") in the Slide pane, and then paste the contents of the Clipboard to the slide. A copy of the Back or Previous action button appears in the upper-right corner of the slide.

3. Right-click the action button, and then on the shortcut menu, click **Edit Hyperlink**. The Action Settings dialog box opens with the Mouse Click tab selected and Previous Slide selected in the Hyperlink to box.

4. Click the **Hyperlink to** arrow, and then click **Slide**. The Hyperlink to Slide dialog box opens listing the slides in the presentation. See Figure 4-14.

Figure 4-14   **Hyperlink to Slide dialog box**

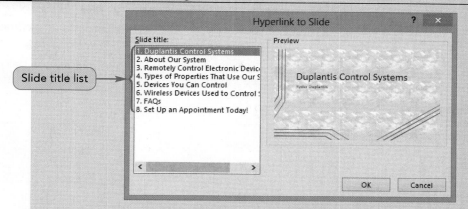

Slide title list →

5. In the Slide title list, click **2. About Our System**, and then click the **OK** button. The title of Slide 2 now appears in the Hyperlink to box in the Action Settings dialog box.

6. Click the **OK** button.

7. Copy the action button on Slide 4 to **Slide 5** ("Devices You Can Control"), **Slide 6** (Wireless Devices Used to Control Systems"), and **Slide 7** ("FAQs").

You need to test the action buttons. Again, you must switch to Slide Show view to do this.

To test the action buttons:

1. Display **Slide 2** ("About Our System") in the Slide pane, and then on the status bar, click the **Slide Show** button 🖥.

2. Click the **What is a Duplantis control system?** hyperlink. Slide 3 ("Remotely Control Electronic Systems") appears in Slide Show view.

3. In the upper-right corner of the slide, click the **action button**. Slide 2 ("About Our System") appears on the screen.

4. Click each of the other links to display those slides, and then click the action buttons on each of those slides to return to Slide 2.

5. End the slide show to return to Slide 2 in Normal view.

Finally, you want to add a link on Slide 2 that links to the last slide in the presentation, Slide 8 ("Set Up an Appointment Today!"). Ryder did not add a bulleted item in the overview on Slide 2 for Slide 8 because as the final slide it is meant to display only as the presentation is concluding. You could add another action button, but instead, you will add a shape and convert it as a link.

To create a link from a shape on Slide 2:

1. With Slide 2 ("About Our System") displayed in the Slide pane, on the ribbon, click the **INSERT** tab.

2. In the Illustrations group, click the **Shapes** button, and then in the Rectangles section, click the **Rounded Rectangle** shape.

▶ **3.** At the bottom of the slide, drag the pointer to draw a rounded rectangle about one-half inch high and four and one-half inches wide.

▶ **4.** With the shape selected, type **Click to set up an appointment**, and then change the font size of the text in the shape to **24** points.

▶ **5.** Drag the shape to position it so it is centered in the area below the bulleted list on the slide. See Figure 4-15. Now you need to convert the shape to a link.

Figure 4-15	Shape added to Slide 2

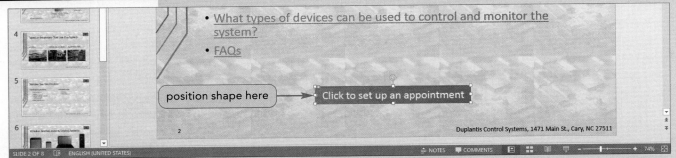

Photos courtesy of S. Scott Zimmerman; Doug Plummer/Getty Images

▶ **6.** On the ribbon, click the **INSERT** tab, and then in the Links group, click the **Hyperlink** button. The Insert Hyperlink dialog box opens with Place in This Document selected in the Link to list.

▶ **7.** Scroll the list of slides, click **8. Set Up an Appointment To**, and then click the **OK** button.

Trouble? If the text in the shape changes so it is formatted as a link, the text was selected before you opened the Insert Hyperlink dialog box instead of the entire shape. On the Quick Access Toolbar, click the Undo button, select the entire shape by clicking the shape border, and then repeat Steps 6 and 7.

Now you need to test the new link. Once again, you will switch to Slide Show view.

To test the shape link in Slide Show view:

▶ **1.** On the status bar, click the **Slide Show** button 🖥. Slide 2 ("About Our System") appears in Slide Show view.

▶ **2.** Click the **Click to set up an appointment** shape. Slide 8 ("Set Up an Appointment Today!") appears.

▶ **3.** End the slide show.

INSIGHT

Linking to Another File

You can create a link to another file so that when you click the link during a slide show, the other file opens. The other file can be any file type; it doesn't need to be a PowerPoint file. To create a link to another file, open the Insert Hyperlink dialog box, click Existing File or Web Page in the Link to list, and then click the Browse for File button. To change the link destination of an action button to another file, open the Action Settings dialog box, click the Hyperlink to option button, click the Hyperlink to arrow, and then click Other PowerPoint Presentation or Other File. For either type of link, a dialog box opens in which you can navigate to the location of the file.

When you create a link to another file, the linked file is not included within the PowerPoint file; only the original path and filename to the files on the computer where you created the links are stored in the presentation. Therefore, if you need to show the presentation on another computer, you must copy the linked files to the other computer as well as the PowerPoint presentation file, and then you need to edit the path to the linked file so that PowerPoint can find the file in its new location. To update the path for a text or graphic link, right-click it, and then click Edit Hyperlink on the shortcut menu to open the Edit Hyperlink dialog box. To edit the path of a file linked to an action button, right-click the action button, and then click Hyperlink to open the Action Settings dialog box.

Customizing Theme Colors

As you know, each theme has its own color palette. In addition, you can switch to one of several built-in color palettes. However, sometimes, you might want to customize a palette. You can change one or all of the theme colors.

REFERENCE

Customizing Theme Colors

- On the ribbon, click the DESIGN tab.
- In the Variants group, click the More button, point to Colors, and then click Customize Colors to open the Create New Theme Colors dialog box.
- Click the button next to the theme color you want to customize.
- Click a color in the Theme Colors section or in the Standard Colors section of the palette, or click More Colors, click a color in the Colors dialog box, and then click the OK button.
- Replace the name in the Name box with a meaningful name for the custom palette.
- Click the Save button.

In the Control Systems presentation, the color of both the light blue unfollowed text links and the light purple followed text links makes them a little hard to see on the slide background. To fix that, you will customize the link colors in the color palette.

To create custom theme colors:

1. On the ribbon, click the **DESIGN** tab.
2. In the Variants group, click the **More** button, and then point to **Colors**. A menu of color palettes opens. See Figure 4-16. If you wanted to change the entire color palette, you could select one of these options. You want to change only the color of hyperlinks.

Figure 4-16   Color palettes on Colors submenu

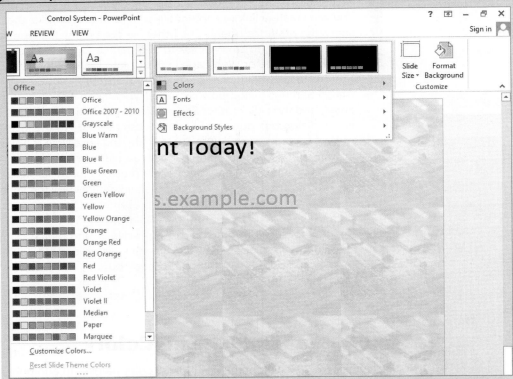

3. At the bottom of the menu, click **Customize Colors**. The Create New Theme Colors dialog box opens. See Figure 4-17. You want to change the color of hyperlinks from light blue to dark blue.

Figure 4-17   Create New Theme Colors dialog box

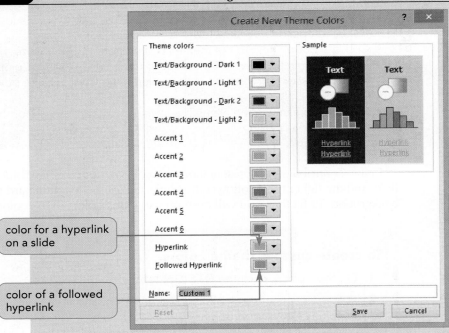

4. Click the **Hyperlink** button to display the complete Theme Colors and Standard Colors palettes.

5. Under Theme Colors, point to the second to last color in the first row. The ScreenTip identifies this as Green, Hyperlink. This is the current color for text hyperlinks.

TIP

Never place dark text on dark background or light text on light background.

6. Under Standard Colors, click the **Dark Blue** color. The Hyperlink color is now the dark blue color you selected, and the top Hyperlink text in the Sample panel in the dialog box is now also dark blue. Next, you'll change the color of the Followed Hyperlinks.

7. Click the **Followed Hyperlink** button to display the color palette. You can choose from additional colors if you open the Colors dialog box.

8. At the bottom of the palette, click **More Colors** to display the Colors dialog box, and then click the **Standard** tab, if necessary.

9. Click the dark purple tile on the right point of the hexagon as shown in Figure 4-18.

| Figure 4-18 | Standard tab in the Colors dialog box |

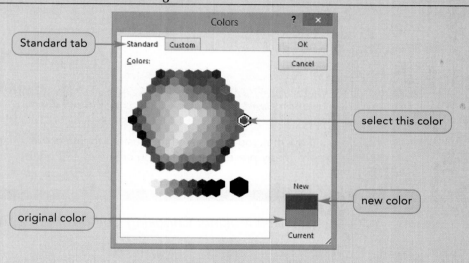

10. Click the **OK** button. The Colors dialog box closes. The Followed Hyperlink color is the dark purple you selected and the bottom Hyperlink text in the Sample panel is dark purple as well. In order to apply the new colors to the presentation, you need to save the new color palette.

11. In the Name box, delete the text Custom 1, and then type **Custom Link Colors**.

12. Click the **Save** button. The dialog box closes and the custom theme colors are applied to the presentation. As you can see in Slide 8 ("Set Up an Appointment Today!"), the link is now dark blue, the color you chose for unfollowed links.

13. Display **Slide 2** ("About Our System") in the Slide pane. The color of the followed links is now dark purple. The followed links will reset to the dark blue of links you haven't followed yet when you close and reopen the presentation. You can also reset the links manually by reapplying the link formatting.

14. Right-click the **What is a Duplantis control system?** link, and then on the shortcut menu, click **Edit Hyperlink**. The Edit Hyperlink dialog box opens. Slide 3 is selected in the list. You don't need to make any changes, so you will simply click the OK button.

Trouble? If a menu of spelling suggestions appears, you right-clicked the word "Duplantis." Right-click any other word in the link.

▶ **15.** Click the **OK** button. The text in the first bullet is reformatted as a link and is colored dark blue. Compare your screen to Figure 4-19.

Figure 4-19	**New link colors**

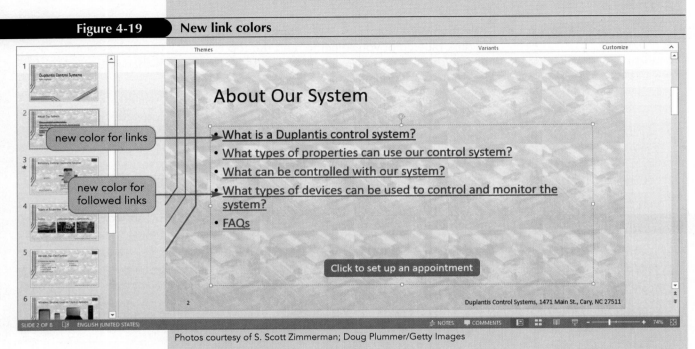

Photos courtesy of S. Scott Zimmerman; Doug Plummer/Getty Images

Now that you have saved the custom theme colors, that color palette is available to apply to any presentation that you create or edit on this computer.

PROSKILLS

Decision Making: Choosing Custom Theme Colors

When creating custom theme colors, you need to be wary of selecting colors that don't match or make text illegible; for example, red text on a blue background might seem like a good combination, but it's actually difficult to read for an audience at a distance from the screen. It's usually safer, therefore, to select one of the built-in theme color sets and stick with it, or make only minor modifications. If you do create a new set of theme colors, select colors that go well together and that maximize the legibility of your slides.

Deleting Custom Theme Colors

When you save a custom theme color palette, the palette is saved to the computer. If you've applied the custom palette to a presentation, and then saved that presentation, that color palette will still be applied to that presentation even if you delete the custom palette from the hard drive. You'll delete the custom theme color palette you created from the computer you are using.

To delete the custom color palette:

▶ **1.** On the DESIGN tab, in the Variants group, click the **More** button, and then point to **Colors**. The Custom Link Colors color palette you created appears at the top of the Colors submenu.

▶ **2.** Right-click the **Custom Link Colors** color palette, and then click **Delete**. A dialog box opens asking if you want to delete these theme colors.

▶ **3.** Click the **Yes** button to delete the custom theme colors. You can confirm that the color palette was deleted from the hard drive.

▶ **4.** In the Variants group, click the **More** button, and then point to **Colors**. The Custom Link Colors palette no longer appears on the Colors submenu.

▶ **5.** Click a blank area of the window to close the menu without making a selection.

▶ **6.** Save your changes.

Ryder is happy with the modifications you've made to the presentation so far. You applied two animations to pictures and modified motion path animations. You changed the slide background by filling the background with a picture, and then making it somewhat transparent so that you can easily see the text of the slides on top of the picture. You created links using text and a graphic and added action buttons. Finally, you changed the color of linked text so that it can be more easily distinguished on the slides. In the next session, you will create a self-running presentation by setting slide timings. You will then record a narration to accompany the self-running presentation. You also will save the presentation in other formats so it can be more easily distributed.

REVIEW

Session 4.1 Quick Check

1. What happens if you try to add a second animation by using the Animation gallery instead of the Add Animation button?
2. What is a trigger?
3. Describe the five types of fill you can add to a slide background.
4. What items on a slide can be a link?
5. What is an action button?
6. What view do you need to be in to test links?

Session 4.2 Visual Overview:

To set automatic timings manually, select the After check box. During a slide show, the slides will advance automatically after the time displayed in the After box.

When the On Mouse Click check box is selected, the slide show can be advanced manually, even if there are saved slide timings. If the On Mouse Click check box is deselected, the slide show may not be advanced manually, although users can still click links.

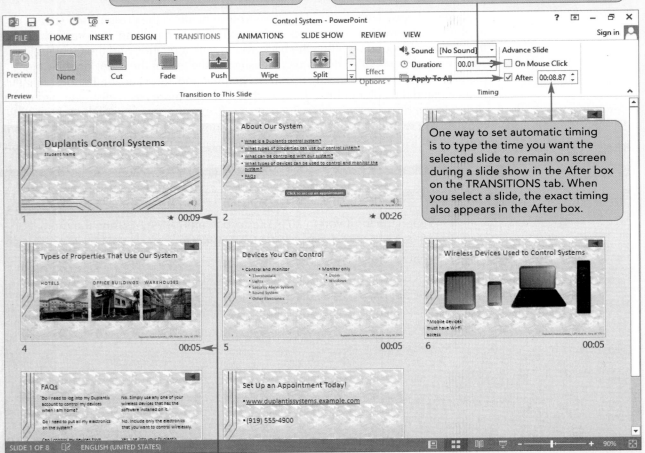

One way to set automatic timing is to type the time you want the selected slide to remain on screen during a slide show in the After box on the TRANSITIONS tab. When you select a slide, the exact timing also appears in the After box.

Automatic timings indicate how many seconds a slide will stay on the screen before transitioning to the next screen during a slide show.

Automatic Slide Timings

A second way to set automatic timings is to click the Rehearse Timings button, and then leave each slide on screen for the desired length of time.

A third way to set automatic timings is to record the slide show, which is similar to rehearsing timings except you have the option to record narrations. When you finish, you can save the narrations only or you can save the narrations and the recorded timings.

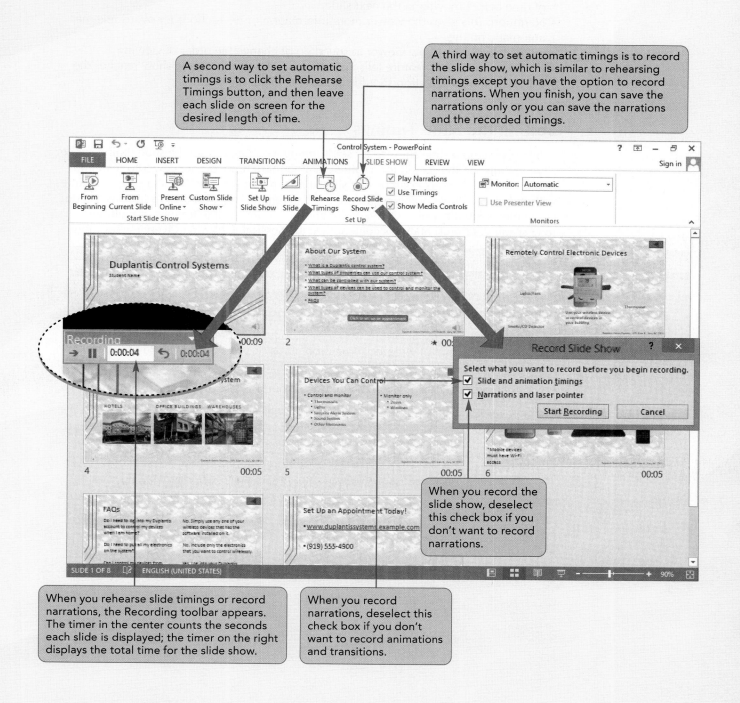

When you record the slide show, deselect this check box if you don't want to record narrations.

When you rehearse slide timings or record narrations, the Recording toolbar appears. The timer in the center counts the seconds each slide is displayed; the timer on the right displays the total time for the slide show.

When you record narrations, deselect this check box if you don't want to record animations and transitions.

Creating a Self-Running Presentation

Ryder intends to use the Control System presentation not only for oral presentations, but also as a self-running presentation on a computer at conventions and exhibitions for contractors. A self-running presentation runs on its own, but it can be set to accept viewer intervention to advance to another slide or return to a previous one. A self-running presentation includes one or more of the following:

- Automatic timing: This feature tells PowerPoint to display slides for a certain amount of time before moving to the next slide.
- Narration: This gives the viewer more information or instructions for overriding the automatic timing.
- Hyperlinks: These allow viewer to speed up or change the order of viewing.
- Kiosk browsing: This feature tells PowerPoint that, when the slide show reaches the last slide, the presentation should start over again at the beginning.

Setting the Slide Timings

When setting up a slide show to be self-running, you need to set the slide timing so the slide remains on the screen for a sufficient amount of time for the viewer to read and comprehend the slide's content. The slide timing might vary for different slides—a slide with only three bullet points might not need to remain on the screen as long as a slide containing six bullet points. PowerPoint allows you to set slide timings in multiple ways to best suit your presentation's content. See the Session 4.2 Visual Overview for more information about setting slide timings.

Ryder asks you to set the timings to five seconds per slide. You'll do this now.

To set the slide timings to five seconds per slide:

1. If you took a break after the last session, make sure the **Control System** presentation you created in Session 4.1 is open in the PowerPoint window in Normal view.

2. On the status bar, click the **Slide Sorter** button ▦ to switch to Slide Sorter view.

3. Click the **Slide 1** (the title slide) thumbnail, press and hold the **Shift** key, scroll down if necessary, and then click the **Slide 8** ("Set Up an Appointment Today!") thumbnail. All the slides are selected.

4. On the ribbon, click the **TRANSITIONS** tab. In the Timing group, the On Mouse Click check box is selected in the Advance Slide section. This means that the slide show will advance when the viewer does something to advance the slide show.

5. In the Timing group, click the **After** check box. The check box is selected, and 00:00 appears below each slide thumbnail. See Figure 4-20.

Figure 4-20   **TRANSITIONS tab with After box selected**

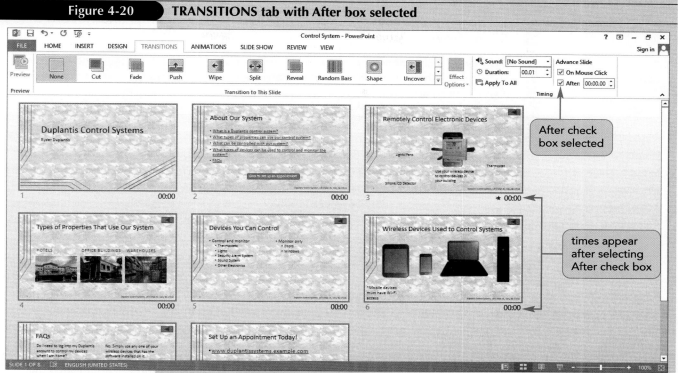

Photos courtesy of S. Scott Zimmerman; Doug Plummer/Getty Images

TIP

If you want to remove slide timings, select all the slides in Slide Sorter view, click the TRANSITIONS tab, and then click the After check box in the Timing group to deselect it.

6. In the Timing group, click the **After** up arrow five times to change the time to five seconds per slide. Under each slide thumbnail, the time changes to 00:05.

7. On the status bar, click the **Slide Show** button 🖵. Watch as the slide show advances through the first three slides.

When Slide 3 ("Remotely Control Electronic Devices") appears on the screen, the animations occur automatically, even though some of them were set to start On Click. This is because the automatic timing overrides the On Click start setting for the animation. Slide 3 remains on the screen for as long as it takes to complete all the animations—a little more than six seconds, even though the automatic timing is set to five seconds. Immediately after the last animation occurs, Slide 4 appears.

8. After Slide 4 ("Types of Properties That Use Our System") appears on the screen, press the **spacebar**. Slide 5 ("Devices You Can Control") appears. You are able to advance the slide show manually because you left the On Mouse Click check box selected.

9. Press the **Esc** key to end the slide show, and then save the presentation.

Aa *Verbal Communication: Preparing to Rehearse Timings and Record a Slide Show*

Before rehearsing timings or recording a slide show, you should first read and look over each slide in the presentation, watching animations and reading the text. For example, if you want to add narration to a slide on which a bulleted list is animated and you want to comment on each bullet as it appears, plan to time your narration to coincide with the animations. Make sure you take the amount of time that you think a viewer would take to view each slide or bulleted item, and then advance from one slide to the next, according to your desired timing of each item. You should move along at a speed for moderately slow readers. Keep in mind that if you move too slowly, your viewers will become bored or wonder if the slide show is working properly; if you move too quickly, viewers will not have enough time to read and absorb the information on each slide.

Rehearsing the Slide Timings

The timing you set does not give the viewer enough time to read and absorb all the information on the slides. To ensure you have the right slide timing for each slide, you'll rehearse the slide show, and then save the slide timings. When you rehearse a slide show, PowerPoint keeps track of the amount of time each slide is displayed during the slide show. You can then save those times for the self-running slide show. See the Session 4.2 Visual Overview for more information about rehearsing presentations.

You'll set new slide timings by using the Rehearse Timings feature. Read through the next set of steps before completing them so that you are prepared to advance the slide show as needed.

To rehearse the slide timings:

1. On the ribbon, click the **SLIDE SHOW** tab, and then in the Set Up group, click the **Rehearse Timings** button. The slide show starts from Slide 1, and the Recording toolbar appears on the screen in the upper-left corner. The toolbar includes a timer on the left that indicates the number of seconds the slide is displayed, and a timer on the right that tracks the total time for the slide show.

2. Leave Slide 1 on the screen for about five seconds, and then advance the slide show. Slide 2 appears on the screen.

3. Leave Slide 2 on the screen for about five seconds, advance to Slide 3, and then press the **spacebar** to make the first animation occur.

4. After the Lights/Fans text box appears, press the **spacebar** three more times to animate the rest of the objects on the slide.

5. Wait about five seconds after displaying the smartphone and its text box, press the **spacebar** again to display Slide 4. You'll leave Slides 4, 5, and 6 on the screen for about five seconds each.

6. Wait five seconds, press the **spacebar** to display Slide 5, wait five seconds, press the **spacebar** to display Slide 6, wait five seconds, and then press the **spacebar** again. Slide 7 appears on the screen.

7. On Slide 7, click each question to display its answer, waiting a few seconds after each answer appears before clicking the next question, and then press the **spacebar** to display Slide 8.

> **TIP**
>
> Click the Pause Recording button on the Recording toolbar to pause the timer; click the Repeat button to restart the timer for the current slide.

▶ **8.** Wait five seconds, and then press the **spacebar**. A dialog box opens asking if you want to save the timings.

▶ **9.** Click the **Yes** button. The timings you rehearsed are saved and the presentation appears in Slide Sorter view. The rehearsed time appears below each slide thumbnail. You can also see the timing assigned to the slides on the TRANSITIONS tab.

▶ **10.** Click the **TRANSITIONS** tab, and then click the **Slide 1** thumbnail. In the Timing group, the recorded timing to the hundredth of a second for the selected slide appears in the After box. The rehearsed timing replaced the five-second slide timing you set previously.

After you rehearse a slide show, you should run the slide show to check the timings.

To play the slide show using the rehearsed slide timings:

▶ **1.** On the Quick Access Toolbar, click the **Start from Beginning** button ⬚. The slide show starts and Slide 1 appears on the screen. The slide show advances to Slide 2 automatically after the saved rehearsal timing elapses. When Slide 3 ("Wirelessly Control") appears, the animations occur automatically at the pace you rehearsed them.

▶ **2.** Continue watching the slide show and evaluate the slide timings. If you feel that a slide stays on the screen for too much or too little time, stop the slide show, click the slide to select it, click the TRANSITIONS tab, and then change the time in the After box in the Timing group.

Trouble? In PowerPoint 2013, sometimes objects that have triggers do not animate correctly when watching a slide show with rehearsed or recorded timings. If that happens with Slide 7 ("FAQs") in this presentation, continue with the steps and this potential issue will be addressed in the next section. If you create your own presentation and this happens, remove the triggers and then rehearse the slide show again.

▶ **3.** When the final black slide appears on the screen, advance the slide show to end it, and then save your changes.

Recording Narration

You can record narration to give viewers more information about presentation content. When you add narration, you should prepare a script for each slide so you won't stumble or hesitate while recording.

If you add narration to a slide, you should not read the text on the slide—the viewers can read that for themselves. Your narration should provide additional information about the slides or instructions for the viewers as they watch the self-running presentation so that they know, for instance, that they can click action buttons to manually advance the presentation. Refer to the Session 4.2 Visual Overview for more information about recording narration.

REFERENCE

Recording Narration

- Confirm that your computer has a microphone.
- On the ribbon, click the SLIDE SHOW tab, and then in the Set Up group, click the Record Slide Show button.
- Click the Start Recording button.
- Speak into the microphone to record the narration for the current slide.
- Press the spacebar to go to the next slide (if desired), record the narration for that slide, and then continue, as desired, to other slides.
- End the slide show after recording the last narration; or continue displaying all the slides in the presentation for the appropriate amount of time, even if you do not add narration to each slide, and then end the slide show as you normally would.

When Ryder sets this presentation to be self-running at a convention or exhibition, he wants viewers to have some guidance in navigating through the presentation. You will record narration for Slides 1, 2, and 7 that tells the viewer how to use the hyperlinks, action buttons, and triggers to navigate the presentation. You will also adjust the timing for these three slides to accommodate their accompanying narrations.

First, you'll record narration for Slides 1 and 2.

To record narration for Slides 1 and 2:

1. Make sure your computer is equipped with a microphone.

    Trouble? If your system doesn't have a microphone, find a computer that does, connect a microphone to your computer, or check with your instructor or technical support person. If you cannot connect a microphone to your computer, read the following steps but do not complete them.

2. On the ribbon, click the **SLIDE SHOW** tab, and then in the Set Up group, click the **Record Slide Show** button. The Record Slide Show dialog box opens. You want to record narration and slide timings, so you will not change the default settings.

    When you click the Start Recording button in the next step, the slide show will start and you can begin recording your narration. Be prepared to start talking as soon as each slide appears, without waiting for the animation to finish. When you are finished recording narration for a slide, wait a couple of seconds before advancing the slide show to avoid the end of your sentence being cut off during the slide show.

3. Click the **Start Recording** button. The dialog box closes and the slide show starts from Slide 1. The Recording dialog box appears on the screen in the upper-left corner as it did when you rehearsed the slide timings.

4. Speak the following into the microphone, using a clear and steady voice: **"Thank you for your interest in Duplantis Control Systems. This presentation will advance automatically from one slide to the next."**

5. Press the **spacebar** to advance to Slide 2, and then say into the microphone, **"If you would rather control your progression through the slide show, click the text links on this slide to jump to the slide containing the related information. On other slides, click the blue button in the upper-right corner to return to this slide. To jump to the last slide, click the 'Click to set up an appointment' button at the bottom of this slide."**

6. Wait for a few seconds (to give the viewer time to examine the slide after the narration is finished), and then press the **Esc** key to end the slide show. The timer in the Recording toolbar stops, and then after a moment, Slide Show view closes and you see the newly recorded timings under the thumbnails for Slides 1 and 2 in Slide Sorter view. If you look closely at the thumbnails for these two slides, you will also see a sound icon in the lower-right corner; this is the narration you recorded on each slide.

Trouble? If you advanced the slide show to Slide 3 instead of pressing the Esc key to end it, when Slide Sorter view appears again, first double-click the Slide 3 thumbnail to display it in the Slide pane in Normal view, click the TRANSITIONS tab, and then change the time in the After box to five seconds. Next, click the sound icon in the lower-right corner of Slide 3, and then press the Delete key to delete it. Return to Slide Sorter view.

After recording the narration for Slide 2, you could have continued the recording and simply not said anything to re-record timings for Slides 3 through 6, and then recorded the narration for Slide 7, but if you did, a sound icon would have appeared on each of those slides and the presentation file size would be larger. Instead, you'll record a narration for just Slide 7.

To record narration for Slide 7:

1. Double-click the **Slide 7** ("FAQs") thumbnail to display it in the Slide pane in Normal view.

2. On the SLIDE SHOW tab, in the Set Up group, click the **Record Slide Show button arrow**, and then click **Start Recording from Current Slide**. The Record Slide Show dialog box appears.

3. Click the **Start Recording** button. Slide 7 appears in Slide Show view.

4. Say into the microphone, "**Click a question to display its answer.**", and then press the **Esc** key to end the slide show. The few seconds it took for you to record the sentence on Slide 7 is not enough time for a viewer to click the questions, so you need to adjust the timing on the TRANSITIONS tab.

5. On the ribbon, click the **TRANSITIONS** tab.

6. In the Timing group, click in the **After** box, type **20**, and then press the **Enter** key. The timing for Slide 7 is now 20 seconds.

You'll run the slide show to test the recorded narration and new slide timings for Slides 1, 2 and 7. The slide timings for Slides 3 through 6 and Slide 8 when you rehearsed the presentation previously remain unchanged.

To play the slide show and use the recorded slide timings:

1. On the Quick Access Toolbar, click the **Start from Beginning** button. The slide show starts, you hear the recording that you made for Slide 1, and then the slide show advances to Slide 2 automatically after the recorded time elapses. Notice that you don't see the sound icon on the slide. Several seconds after the recording on Slide 2 finishes playing, the slide show advances automatically to display Slide 3.

TIP
To remove narration on a slide, delete the sound icon, or click the Record Slide Show button arrow in the Set Up group on the SLIDE SHOW tab, point to Clear, and then click Clear Narration on Current Slide.

Trouble? If Slide 1 transitions to Slide 2 before your recorded voice finishes the sentence, display Slide 1 in the Slide pane in Normal view, click the TRANSITIONS tab, in the Timing group, click the up arrow once or twice to add one or two seconds to the slide timing, and then run the presentation again.

2. Click the blue action button in the upper-right corner of the Slide 3. Slide 2 appears again; however the recording does not play again.

3. Click the **FAQs** link. Slide 7 ("FAQs") appears.

4. Click each of the questions on Slide 7, and then wait until the saved time elapses and Slide 8 ("Set Up an Appointment Today!") appears on the screen.

5. Wait approximately five seconds until the black slide that indicates the end of a slide show appears on the screen, and then press the **spacebar**. The presentation appears in Normal view.

6. Display **Slide 1** (the title slide) in the Slide pane.

7. In the lower-right corner of the slide, click the sound icon, and then on the ribbon, click the **AUDIO TOOLS PLAYBACK** tab. Note that the sound is set to play automatically and the icon will be hidden during the slide show. See Figure 4-21.

Figure 4-21	Settings for the recorded sound

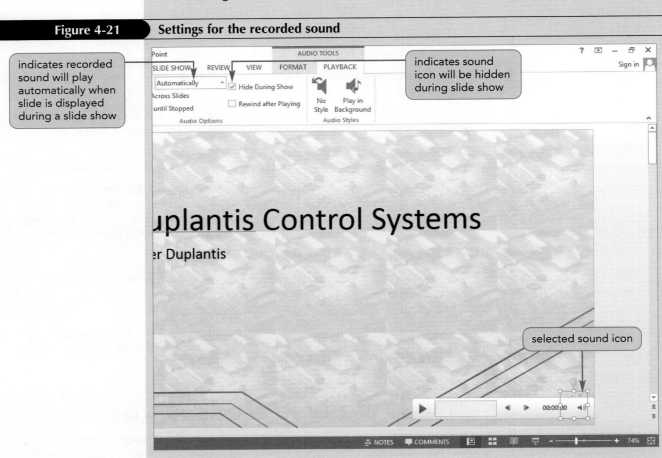

Now that you added sound recordings to the slides, you should optimize the recordings to ensure they will play on any computer.

To optimize the recordings in the presentation:

▶ **1.** On the ribbon, click the **FILE** tab to display the Info screen in Backstage view.

▶ **2.** Click the **Optimize Compatibility** button. The Optimize Media Compatibility dialog box opens and a progress bar shows the progress of the optimization.

▶ **3.** Click the **Close** button in the dialog box. The Optimize Compatibility button no longer appears on the Info screen.

▶ **4.** At the top of the navigation bar, click the **Back** button ⊙ to exit Backstage view.

▶ **5.** Save the changes to the presentation.

Next, you'll continue setting up the self-running slide show by setting options to control the slide show manually.

Setting Options for Overriding the Automatic Timings

As you have seen, when a presentation is set to be self-running, you can allow the viewer to override the timings you set. If the On Mouse Click check box is selected in the Timing group on the TRANSITIONS tab, the viewer can advance the slide show using the normal methods of clicking the left mouse button, pressing the spacebar or the Enter key, and so on. To prevent this, you can deselect the On Mouse Click check box. The links in the presentation will continue to function normally, but the viewer will not be able to manually advance the slide show.

To avoid someone accidentally advancing the slide show by clicking the mouse button or pressing a key, Ryder wants you to deselect the On Mouse Click check box. You'll make this adjustment now.

To change the setting so the viewer cannot advance the slide manually:

▶ **1.** Switch to Slide Sorter view, and then select all the slides.

▶ **2.** On the ribbon, click the **TRANSITIONS** tab.

▶ **3.** In the Timing group, click the **On Mouse Click** check box to deselect it. Now viewers will not accidentally override the timings you set by using the ordinary methods of advancing the slide show.

Applying Kiosk Browsing

Now, Ryder wants you to set up the presentation so that in addition to automatically advancing from one slide to another using the saved slide timings, after the last slide it will loop back to the first slide and run again. To do this, you change the settings in the Set Up Show dialog box. In the Set Up Show dialog box, you can set the presentation to loop continuously or you can set the presentation to be browsed at a kiosk, which automatically applies the loop continuously setting. When you set a presentation to be browsed at a kiosk, the normal methods for advancing a slide show are automatically disabled, so even if the On Mouse Click check box is selected in the Timing group on the TRANSITIONS tab, clicking the mouse button or pressing the spacebar or the Enter key will have no effect. However, a viewer can still click hyperlinks on the screen, including action buttons, and can still press the Esc key to end the slide show.

Now, you'll set up the Control System presentation for kiosk browsing.

To set up the presentation for browsing at a kiosk:

1. On the ribbon, click the **SLIDE SHOW** tab, and then in the Set Up group, click the **Set Up Slide Show** button. The Set Up Show dialog box opens. See Figure 4-22.

Figure 4-22 Set Up Show dialog box set for kiosk browsing

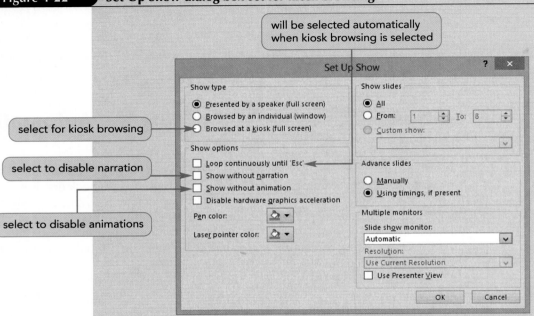

When you run the slide show set for kiosk browsing, it will continue to run until someone presses the Esc key. You'll test that setting.

2. In the Show type section, click the **Browsed at a kiosk (full screen)** option button. Under Show options, the Loop continuously until 'Esc' check box becomes selected. That option has also changed to light gray, indicating that you cannot deselect it.

3. Click the **OK** button. The dialog box closes, and the presentation is set up for kiosk browsing.

TIP

To change the resolution of the slide show, click the Slide show monitor arrow, click the monitor you are showing the slide show on, click the Resolution arrow, and then click the resolution you want to use.

To test the self-running slide show:

1. Click the **Slide 8** ("Set Up an Appointment Today!") thumbnail, and then on the status bar, click the **Slide Show** button ⬚. This is the final slide in the presentation. After the saved timing for Slide 8 elapses, watch as the slide show automatically starts over with Slide 1.

2. After Slide 1 (the title slide) appears on the screen, press the **Esc** key to end the slide show.

3. Save the changes to the presentation.

Using the Document Inspector

The Document Inspector is a tool you can use to check a presentation for hidden data, such as the author's name and other personal information, objects that are in the presentation but are hidden or placed in the area next to a slide instead of on the slide, and speaker notes. Ryder wants you to check the presentation for hidden data.

To check the presentation using the Document Inspector:

1. Double-click the **Slide 1** (the title slide) thumbnail to display Slide 1 in the Slide pane in Normal view, and then on the status bar, click the **NOTES** button. Notice that there is a speaker note on this slide that Ryder added before he gave you the presentation to work with.

2. On the ribbon, click the **FILE** tab. The Info screen in Backstage view appears. On the right, file properties are listed, including the number of slides in the presentation and the author name. On the left, next to the Check for Issues button, a bulleted list informs you that the presentation contains document properties that you might want to delete, speaker notes, and potential problems for people with vision disabilities. See Figure 4-23.

| Figure 4-23 | Info screen in Backstage view |

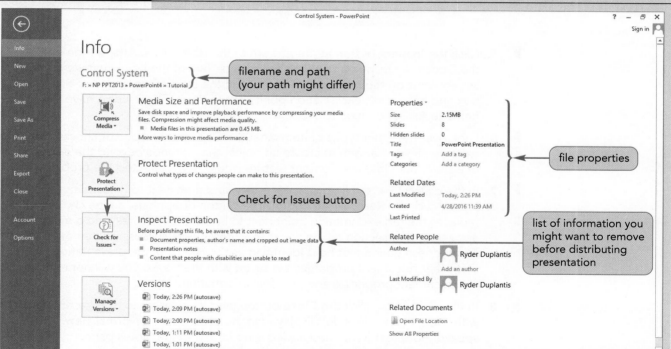

3. Click the **Check for Issues** button, and then click **Inspect Document**. The Document Inspector dialog box opens.

   Trouble? If a dialog box opens telling you that you need to save the presentation first, click the Yes button to save the presentation.

4. Click any of the check boxes in this dialog box that are not checked. See Figure 4-24.

Figure 4-24   **Document Inspector dialog box**

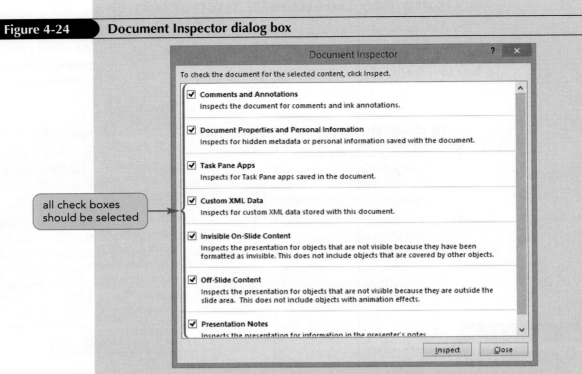

all check boxes should be selected

5.   Click the **Inspect** button at the bottom of the dialog box. After a moment, the Document Inspector displays the results. Two of the items that were listed as problems on the Info screen are listed in the Document Inspector dialog box and have a red exclamation point next to them. These items have a Remove All button next to them.

6.   Look over the other types of items that the Document Inspector checks. For example, if you happen to create an object that extends beyond the edges of a slide, the Off-Slide Content feature would have detected the problem.

7.   In the dialog box, scroll down if necessary, and then next to Presentation Notes, click the **Remove All** button. The button disappears, a blue checkmark replaces the red exclamation point next to Presentation Notes, and a message appears in that section telling you that all items were successfully removed. Ryder doesn't mind that he is identified as the author of the presentation or that other document properties are saved with the file, so you will not remove the document properties and personal information.

8.   In the dialog box, click the **Close** button, and then return to the presentation with Slide 1 (the title slide) displayed in the Slide pane in Normal view. The speaker note that Ryder had added is no longer in the Notes pane.

9.   On the status bar, click the **NOTES** button to close the Notes pane.

10.   Save the changes to the presentation.

Save the changes now because you will be saving the presentation in a different format.

Packaging a Presentation for CD

Ryder will present the slide show at various conventions and exhibitions across the country. He plans to bring his own laptop, but he knows it's a good idea to have backups. One way to back up a presentation is to use the Package a Presentation for CD feature. This puts all the fonts and linked files and anything else needed on a CD or in a folder that you can copy to a USB drive or burn to a DVD using a DVD burner program.

To package the presentation for CD:

▶ **1.** Display the Export screen in Backstage view, and then click **Package Presentation for CD**. The right side of the screen changes to display a description of this command.

▶ **2.** Click the **Package for CD** button. The Package for CD dialog box opens. See Figure 4-25.

Figure 4-25	Package for CD dialog box

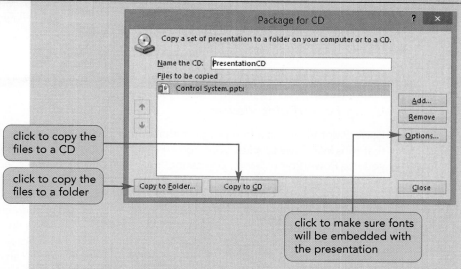

click to copy the files to a CD

click to copy the files to a folder

click to make sure fonts will be embedded with the presentation

▶ **3.** Click the **Options** button. The Options dialog box opens. See Figure 4-26.

Figure 4-26	Options dialog box when packaging a presentation for CD

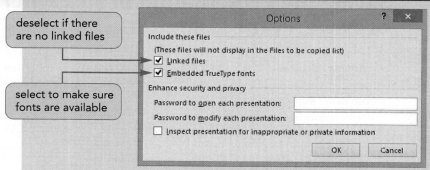

deselect if there are no linked files

select to make sure fonts are available

You will keep the Embed TrueType fonts check box selected to ensure that you will have the fonts used in the presentation available if you run the packaged presentation on another computer. If your presentation contained links to any other files, you would keep the Linked files check box selected to include those files in the package. However, the presentation file does not contain any linked files, so you will deselect that check box.

▶ **4.** Click the **Linked files** check box to deselect it.

▶ **5.** Click the **OK** button. The Package for CD dialog box is visible again.

▶ **6.** Click the **Copy to Folder** button. The Copy to Folder dialog box opens. The default name for the folder you will create to hold the files of the packaged presentation—PresentationCD—appears in the Folder name box.

   Trouble? If you are copying your presentation to a CD, click the Cancel button to close this dialog box, insert a blank CD in the CD drive, click the Copy to CD button, click the No button when the dialog box opens asking if you want to copy the same files to another CD, and then skip to Step 9.

▶ **7.** Click the **Browse** button to open the Choose Location dialog box, navigate to the folder where you are storing your files, and then click the **Select** button.

▶ **8.** Click the **Open folder when complete** check box to deselect it, if necessary, and then click the **OK** button. A dialog box opens briefly as PowerPoint copies all the necessary files to the PresentationCD folder or disc.

▶ **9.** Click the **Close** button in the Package for CD dialog box.

INSIGHT

Using PowerPoint Viewer

PowerPoint Viewer is a free program that you can install and use on any computer that runs Windows to show your PowerPoint presentation in Slide Show view. When you use PowerPoint Viewer, you cannot modify slides and some special effects might not work. To download PowerPoint Viewer, go to www.microsoft.com and use the Search box on the website to search for **PowerPoint Viewer**. In the list of results, click the option to filter the list to show only Downloads, and then click the link for the file with the most recent release date. The file that downloads is an executable file, which means that you double-click it to start the installation process. To be absolutely sure you can show your presentation on another computer, you can download the PowerPoint Viewer executable file and store it on a flash drive to bring with you.

Saving the Presentation in an Earlier Version of PowerPoint

TIP

You can save a presentation in different file types using the options on the Export screen in Backstage view.

You can save a presentation so it is compatible with earlier versions of PowerPoint. Before you do this, it's a good idea to identify features in the presentation that are incompatible with earlier versions of PowerPoint so that you know how the presentation will look for people using the file saved in the earlier format.

Ryder wants to save the presentation as an earlier version of PowerPoint so he can distribute the presentation to potential customers who have not upgraded to PowerPoint 2013. He asks you to check the Control System presentation for features not supported by previous PowerPoint versions.

To check for features not supported by previous versions of PowerPoint:

1. On the ribbon, click the **FILE** tab. The Info screen in Backstage view appears.

2. Click the **Check for Issues** button, and then click **Check Compatibility**. Backstage view closes, and after a moment, the Microsoft PowerPoint Compatibility Checker dialog box opens listing features that aren't supported by earlier versions of PowerPoint.

3. If the Check compatibility when saving in PowerPoint 97-2003 formats check box is not selected, click the **Check compatibility when saving in PowerPoint 97-2003 formats** check box to select it. See Figure 4-27. This ensures that if you save the presentation in the format compatible with PowerPoint versions 97 through 2003, the Compatibility Checker will run automatically.

 Figure 4-27 | Microsoft PowerPoint Compatibility Checker dialog box

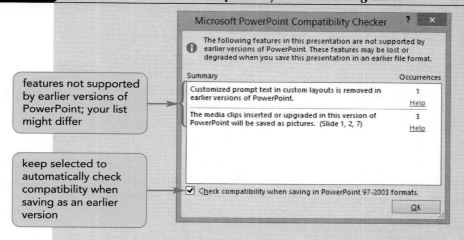

features not supported by earlier versions of PowerPoint; your list might differ

keep selected to automatically check compatibility when saving as an earlier version

4. Click the **OK** button.

Now that Ryder understands which features in the Control System presentation are not supported by earlier versions of PowerPoint, he wants you to save the presentation using an earlier version file type. After you do that, he plans to locate a computer that has an earlier version of PowerPoint installed and review the file to see what adjustments he needs to make to ensure that people he sends the file to will be able to see and understand all the content.

To save a presentation in a file format compatible with earlier versions of PowerPoint:

1. On the ribbon, click the **FILE** tab. The Info screen in Backstage view appears.

2. In the navigation bar, click **Export**. The Export screen appears.

3. Click **Change File Type**. Options for changing the file type appear. See Figure 4-28.

| Figure 4-28 | Change File Type options on the Export screen |

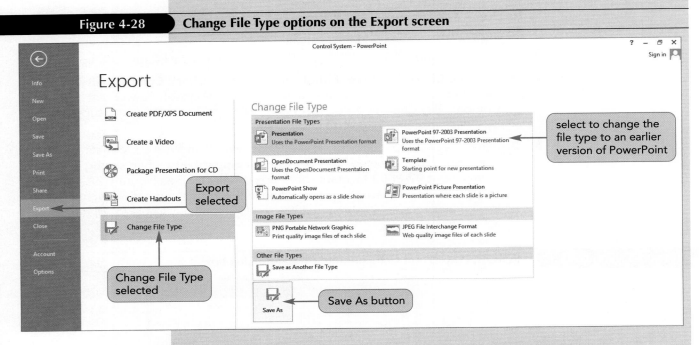

4. Under Change File Type, click **PowerPoint 97-2003 Presentation**, and then click the **Save As** button. The Save As dialog box opens with PowerPoint 97-2003 Presentation in the Save As type box.

5. If necessary, navigate to the location where you are saving your files.

6. Change the name in the File name box to **Control System Earlier Version**, and then click the **Save** button. The Save As dialog box closes and the Microsoft PowerPoint Compatibility Checker dialog box opens. This is because the Check compatibility when saving in PowerPoint 97-2003 formats check box is selected in this dialog box.

7. Click the **Continue** button. In the title bar, "[Compatibility Mode]" appears next to the presentation title, indicating that this file format is an earlier version of PowerPoint.

You have finished the Control System presentation, and ensured that Ryder has the presentation in the formats he needs.

Session 4.2 Quick Check

REVIEW

1. How do you change the amount of time a slide stays on the screen during Slide Show view in a self-running presentation?
2. Do links work in a self-running presentation?
3. How do you prevent viewers from using normal methods of advancing the slide show in a self-running presentation?
4. What does the Document Inspector reveal?
5. Why would you package a presentation to a CD?
6. What does the Compatibility Checker reveal?

ASSESS

SAM Projects

Put your skills into practice with SAM Projects! SAM Projects for this tutorial can be found online. If you have a SAM account, go to www.cengage.com/sam2013 to download the most recent Project Instructions and Start Files.

PRACTICE

Review Assignments

Data Files needed for the Review Assignments: Home.pptx; House.jpg

Ryder Duplantis, owner of Duplantis Control Systems, is expanding his business to include residential homes. He will be attending a home exhibition show, and he wants to bring a self-running presentation that people can watch when they visit his exhibition booth. Complete the following steps:

1. Open the file **Home**, located in the PowerPoint4 ▸ Review folder included with your Data Files, add your name as the subtitle, and then save the presentation as **Home Control Systems**.

2. On Slide 4 ("How Does It Work?"), animate the image of the pointing finger with a motion path animation that ends when it appears as if the finger is on top of the red square.

3. On Slide 4, add the Disappear exit animation to the image of the pointing finger.

4. On Slide 4, click the motion sensors object on the right side of the slide, press and hold the Shift key, and then select the other four objects on the right side of the slide. (Note that each of the five objects on the right side of the slide is a picture and a text box grouped together to form one object.) Apply the Appear entrance animation to the selected objects.

5. Deselect the objects, select the Motion Sensors object, and then change its start timing to With Previous. One at a time, in the following order, change the start timing of the animations applied to the rest of the objects on the right side of the slide to On Click: Wall Speakers, Security Alarms, Porch Light, MP3 Player Docking Station.

6. On Slide 5 ("Typical Device Plan"), select all of the triangles, circles, and the gray rounded rectangle on the floor plan, and then apply the Appear entrance animation.

7. On Slide 5, select only the nine yellow rectangles on the floor plan, and then make the Lights button object the trigger for the animation applied to the triangles. Set the Speakers button object to be the trigger for the animation applied to the three green circles on the floor plan. Set the Thermostat button object to be the trigger for the animation applied to the gray rounded rectangle on the floor plan. Finally, set the Security Alarm button object to be the trigger for the animation applied to the red circle on the floor plan.

8. Add the picture **House**, located in the PowerPoint4 ▸ Review folder, as the slide background. Change the transparency to 85%, and then apply this background to all of the slides. On Slide 1 (the title slide) open the Format Background task pane, and then click the Solid fill option button, to change the background of the title slide back to solid white. Do not apply this change to all the slides.

9. On Slide 2 ("Duplantis Smart Home Features"), convert the "Click to see a typical setup" shape to a link to Slide 5 ("Typical Device Plan"). (*Hint*: Make sure the entire shape is selected before you add the link.)

10. On Slide 2, convert the first bulleted item to a link to Slide 4 ("How Does It Work?").

11. On Slide 4 ("How Does It Work?"), add a Return action button about one-half inch high and three-quarters of an inch wide in the lower left corner and link it to Slide 2 ("Duplantis Smart Home Features"). Copy this action button to Slide 5.

12. On Slide 3 ("What Do I Need?"), convert the "Get a quote" shape to a link to Slide 6 ("Get a Free Quote Today!").

13. Customize the color palette so that the color of hyperlinks is the Indigo, Accent 1 theme color and the color of followed links is the light brown color on the Standard tab of the Colors dialog box (the second color in the second to last row of colors in the color hexagon). Save the custom palette as **Link Colors** to apply the new colors, and then delete the custom palette.

14. Rehearse the slide timings as follows: Leave Slide 1 on the screen for about five seconds and Slides 2 and 3 on the screen for about 10 seconds. On Slide 4, remember to advance the slide show to animate the pointing finger, and then advance the slide show five times to display the rest of the objects on the slide. Wait a few seconds after the last object appears, and then advance to Slide 5. Click each button to trigger the animations, waiting a few seconds between each click. Display Slide 6 for about 5 seconds.

15. Record the following narration for Slide 1: **"This is a self-running presentation. If you want, you can click buttons on each slide to control the presentation."** Press the Esc key to end the slide show after recording this.

16. Optimize the media.

17. Use a command on the TRANSITIONS tab to prevent viewers from advancing the slide show using the ordinary methods (pressing the spacebar or the Enter key and so on).

18. Set up the presentation for kiosk browsing.

19. Save the changes to the presentation, inspect the presentation for hidden information, and then have the Document Inspector remove speaker notes.

20. Save the changes to the presentation.

21. Save the presentation in a format compatible with PowerPoint 97-2003. Name the file **Home Control Systems Earlier Version**.

22. Use the Package Presentation for CD command to package the presentation to a folder named **Duplantis Home**. Do not include linked files (there aren't any) and make sure to embed fonts.

23. Close the file, saving changes if prompted.

Case Problem 1

APPLY

Data Files needed for this Case Problem: Office.pptx

Virtual Office   Dessa Sobieski writes a column titled "The Entrepreneur" in the Park City, Utah newspaper the *Wasatch Mountain Times*. Recently she wrote a column about the "virtual office" a new type of service that provides many benefits to home businesses and smaller companies such as phone answering service, accounting, re-ordering supplies, and other clerical services. Some virtual office companies also offer physical office space on an as-needed basis. Because of her article, Dessa was invited by the Salt Lake City Area Home Business Association to give a presentation at one of their monthly meetings about virtual office services. She has asked you to help her prepare the presentation. Complete the following steps:

1. Open the presentation **Office**, located in the PowerPoint4 ▶ Case1 folder included with your Data Files, and then save the presentation with the filename **Virtual Office**. Add your name as a footer on all the slides. (Do not add your name as the subtitle.)

2. On Slide 1 (the title slide), drag the picture to the center of the slide. Apply the entrance animation Shape to the picture, and change its effect to Out. Add the motion path animation Lines and adjust the path as needed so that the picture ends up on the right side of the slide. Change the start timing of the motion path animation to After Previous.

3. On Slide 1, apply the Split entrance animation to the title, and then change its start timing to After Previous.

4. On Slide 1, set the photo as the trigger for the title animation.

5. On Slide 2 ("Types of Services Provided"), convert the items in the bulleted list to links to Slides 3 through 7.

6. Customize the color palette so that the color of hyperlinks is the White, Text 1 theme color and the color of followed links is the Tan, Accent 1 theme color. Save the custom palette as Office Links, and then delete the Office Links color palette.

7. On Slide 2, in the lower-left corner of the slide, draw an Action Button: End shape about one-half inch high and three-quarters of an inch wide. Keep the default link to the last slide in the presentation.

8. On Slide 3 ("Phone Answering Service"), in the lower-left corner of the slide, draw an Action Button: Back or Previous shape about one-half inch high and three-quarters of an inch wide. Keep the default link to the previous slide.

9. Copy the action button on Slide 3, and then paste it on Slide 4 ("Accounting"). Edit the link destination so it links to Slide 2.

10. Copy the action button on Slide 4 and paste it on Slide 5 ("Website Management"), Slide 6 ("Meeting Spaces"), and Slide 7 ("Professional Address").

11. Use the Document Inspector to remove speaker notes. Save the changes to the presentation.

12. Save the presentation in a format compatible with PowerPoint 97-2003. Name the file **Virtual Office Earlier Version**.

13. Use the Package Presentation for CD command to package the presentation to a folder named **Virtual Office Package**, making sure to embed fonts and without including linked files.

14. Close the presentation, saving changes if prompted.

Case Problem 2

TROUBLESHOOT

Data Files needed for this Case Problem: Coupons.pptx, No Symbol.png

Kritikos Koupons App   Peter Kritikos works full time for a large computer company, but on the side, he creates apps for smartphones and tablets. His most recent app is a coupon app that allows users to find and download coupons for products they want to buy and provides barcodes so that the coupon can be scanned directly from the smartphone or table by the cashier. Peter markets his product online and in person at various consumer events, such as trade shows. He asked you to help him create a self-running PowerPoint presentation. Complete the following steps:

1. Open the presentation **Coupon**, located in the PowerPoint4 ▶ Case2 folder included with your Data Files, add your name as the subtitle, and then save the presentation with the filename **Coupon App**.

2. On Slide 1 (the title slide), change the slide background to a gradient fill. Apply the Medium Gradient – Accent 1 style from the Preset gradients gallery. Change the type to Linear, if necessary, and the direction to Linear Down. Do not apply the background to all the slides (in other words, only Side 1 has the gradient fill background).

⚙ **Troubleshoot** 3. On Slide 1, make any adjustments needed so the text is readable.

4. On Slide 2 ("Save Time and Money"), move the images of the scissors and the finger with a string tied around it so they are out of the way, and then position the stack of newspapers in the center of the space to the right of the text boxes. Apply the Appear entrance animation to the top text box ("No more stacks of newspapers!"). Apply the Appear entrance animation to the picture of the newspaper stacks, and change its start timing to With Previous so that it appears at the same time as the text box.

5. On Slide 2, insert the picture No Symbol, located in the PowerPoint4 ▶ Case2 folder, and position it on top of the newspapers. Apply the entrance animation Appear to the No Symbol picture, change its start timing to After Previous so that it appears after the picture of the newspapers appears, and set a delay of one second.

6. On Slide 2, apply the entrance animation Appear to the middle text box ("No more clipping coupons!").

7. Select the picture of the newspapers (make sure the newspapers picture is selected and not the No Symbol image), and then add the exit animation Disappear as a second animation to the picture of the newspapers. Change the start timing of this animation to With Previous so that it disappears when the middle text box appears.

8. Add the exit animation Disappear as a second animation to the No Symbol picture, and then change the start timing of this animation to With Previous so that it disappears with the newspapers picture.

9. Apply the entrance animation Appear to the picture of the scissors and change its start timing to With Previous so that it appears at the same time as the other two pictures disappear.

10. Select the No Symbol picture and add the Appear animation as a third animation. Change the start timing of this animation to After Previous so it appears after the picture of the scissors appears, and set a delay of one second.

11. Apply the Appear animation to the bottom text box ("No more forgetting coupons at home!"). Add the Disappear animation to the scissors as a second animation, changing its start timing to With Previous. Apply the Appear animation to the picture of the finger with the string tied around it, changing its start timing to With Previous. And add the Disappear animation to the No Symbol picture, changing its start timing to With Previous.

12. Drag the picture of the scissors to the No Symbol picture. It will slide behind the No Symbol picture. Drag the picture of the finger with string tied around it to the No Symbol picture.

🔧 **Troubleshoot** 13. View Slide 2 in Slide Show view, and then add the additional animation needed to the No Symbol picture so it appears one second after the picture of the finger with the string tied around it.

14. On Slide 4 ("Using the Kritikos Koupon App"), apply the Appear animation to the top left text box ("Touch to return to Home screen"), and then add the Disappear animation to that text box.

15. Apply the Appear animation to the second text box on the left, and then add the Disappear animation to that text box.

🔧 **Troubleshoot** 16. Each time you advance the slide show, you want a new callout to appear and the one that was already visible on the slide to disappear at the same time. View Slide 4 in Slide Show view, and then adjust the animations to the second callout as needed to achieve this.

17. Apply the animations and timing that you applied to the second text box to the third and then the fourth text box on the left, and then to the top two text boxes on the right, starting from the top. Apply the Appear animation to the bottom text box on the right, and change its start timing to With Previous. (You don't need the last callout to disappear before the slide show transitions to the next slide.)

18. On Slide 5 ("Start Saving Today!"), apply the Lines motion path animation to the logo so that it moves to the right and ends up to the right of the bulleted list. Change its start timing to After Previous and set a delay of one-half second.

19. On Slide 5, apply the Fly In animation to the bulleted list, change its sequence effect so it animates as one object, and then change its start timing to After Previous.

20. Rehearse and save the timings for the presentation, leaving each slide on the screen a reasonable amount of time and pausing after each animation.

21. Save the changes to the presentation, and then use the Document Inspector to remove document properties and the author's name.

22. Save the changes, and then close the file.

CHALLENGE

Case Problem 3

Data Files needed for this Case Problem: Background.jpg, Petroglyphs.pptx

Kennedy Elementary School   David Stark is a travel writer for a television studio in Tulsa, Oklahoma. He recently reported on his travels to national parks in the Southwest. In his report, he described petroglyphs, which are carvings in rock found in many parts of the world. They first appeared about 12,000 years ago and continued among some cultures up to the 20th century. The principal of Kennedy Elementary School saw his report and asked him to give a presentation to the students at the school. He asked you to help him complete his presentation. Complete the following steps:

1. Open the presentation **Petroglyphs**, located in the PowerPoint4 ▸ Case3 folder included with your Data Files, add your name as the subtitle, and then save the presentation with the filename **Native American Petroglyphs**.
2. Add the picture **Background**, located in the PowerPoint4 ▸ Case3 folder, as the slide background on all slides. Tile the picture as texture, change the vertical offset (Y) to **-100** points, and change the scale in both directions to **60%**.
3. On Slide 1 (the title slide), change the color of the title and subtitle text to White, Background 1.
4. On Slide 3 ("Petroglyph Locations in the Southwest"), draw a rectangle large enough to cover Utah on the map on the slide.
5. Apply the Lines motion path animation to the Canyonlands text box (on top of the top left picture), and adjust it so that the text box ends up below the top-left picture.
6. Animate the rectangle shape you drew so that it disappears at the same time as the text box moves.
7. Animate the top-left picture with the Wheel entrance animation so that it appears after the text box has finished moving.
8. Draw a rectangle on top of Arizona on the slide, and then animate the Chaco Culture text box (on top of the bottom-left picture), the second rectangle you drew, and the picture in the same manner as you did for the first three objects.
9. Draw a rectangle on top of New Mexico on the slide, and then animate the Petrified Forest text box (on top of the picture on the right), the third rectangle you drew, and the picture in the same manner.
⊕ **Explore** 10. Fill the rectangle shapes with the orange color of the wide band behind the images, and remove their outlines. (*Hint*: Use the Eyedropper tool on the Shape Fill menu to match the color.)
11. On Slide 5 ("Examples of Images"), apply the Appear entrance animation to all of the text boxes under the images, and then set the pictures above each text box as a trigger for that text box's animation.
⊕ **Explore** 12. On Slide 4 ("Newspaper Rock, Utah"), start recording from the current slide. In Slide Show view, before you start speaking, right-click to display the shortcut menu, and then change the pointer to a laser pointer. Keep the laser pointer off to the side while saying the first sentence, and then use it to circle the bulleted item "Tse' Hane" while you say the second sentence. Because you need to turn on the laser pointer, there will be silence at the beginning of the recording.

   "There are other newspaper rocks in many other locations around the world. The Navajo word for this rock translates to 'Rock that tells a story.'"
⊕ **Explore** 13. On Slide 4, trim off the silence at the beginning of the audio clip. If there is any at the end of the clip, trim that as well.
14. Optimize the media in the presentation.
15. Save the changes to the presentation, and then close the presentation.

CREATE

Case Problem 4

There are no Data Files needed for this Case Problem.

Bucket List   A "bucket list" is a list of goals that you want to achieve before you die. The term comes from the idiom "kick the bucket." You need to create a self-running PowerPoint presentation that illustrates your real or imaginary bucket list. Your presentation should include at least one slide with recorded narration, one object with multiple animations applied to it, and at least one object with a motion path animation applied to it. Make your presentation attractive and interesting so that viewers want to watch the whole thing. Complete the following steps:

Note: Please be sure not to include any personal information of a sensitive nature in the documents you create to be submitted to your instructor for this exercise. Later on, you can update the documents with such information for your own personal use.

1. Decide what you are going to include as your goals. If you need inspiration to come up with life goals, use a search engine and the search expression "popular life goals bucket lists."

2. Find graphics that illustrate each of your goals. Use your own pictures or search for pictures on Office.com or other site on the Internet.

3. Create a new presentation. Apply an appropriate theme. If you don't want to use one of the installed themes, look at the templates on Office.com.

4. Title the presentation Bucket List, add your name as the subtitle, and then save the presentation as **Bucket List** to the location where you are saving your files.

5. Create at least eight slides in addition to the title slide. Add photos and other illustrations as needed. Remember to keep the presentation content interesting so that viewers will want to watch the entire slide show.

6. Remember to include at least one slide with recorded narration, one object with multiple animations applied to it, and at least one object with a motion path animation applied to it. Any slide that does not have recorded narration must contain enough information to help a viewer understand the slide content. Do not include any links or triggers for animations.

7. Add any other animations you think will add interest. Add transitions if appropriate.

8. Check the spelling in your presentation and proof it.

9. Add timings to the slides using any method so that the presentation is self-running. Prevent viewers from using the mouse or keyboard to advance the slide.

10. Save and close the presentation.

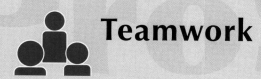

Teamwork

What Is a Team?

The American Heritage Dictionary describes a team as a "group organized to work together." More than just people thrown together, teams consist of individuals who have skills, talents, and abilities that complement each other and, when joined, produce synergy—results greater than those a single individual could achieve. It is this sense of shared mission and responsibility for results that makes a team successful in its efforts to reach organizational goals.

Characteristics of Teams

Have you ever heard someone described as a "team player"? Members on a team get to know how the others work, so they can make contributions where they'll count most. On a football team, not everyone plays the role of quarterback; the team needs other positions working with the quarterback if touchdowns are to be scored. However, before the first play is ever made, the members bring their skills to the team and spend time learning each others' moves so they can catch the pass, block, or run toward the goal line together. Similarly, in a professional environment, the best teams have members whose background, skills, and abilities complement each other.

Managing Workflow on a Team

When team members collaborate on a project, someone needs to manage the workflow. This is especially important if team members are all contributing to a shared file stored on a server or a shared folder on the Internet. Some businesses have the capability to allow team members to co-author a presentation stored on a server. If this capability is not available, however, the team will need to create a strategy for managing the file to make sure that one person's changes do not get overwritten.

One way to manage workflow is to create an ordered list of team members assigned to work on a presentation file, and have team members access and edit the file only after the person preceding them on the list is finished with it. Another way is to allow anyone to access the presentation, but to have each team member save their version of the presentation with a different name—for example, they can add their initials to the end of the filename—and then each person can make their version available for the team member who has been designated to compare all the presentations to create one final version.

PROSKILLS

Create a Collaborative Presentation

Many people volunteer for a program that requires them to work collaboratively. For example, you might be a coach of a youth sports program, a Boy Scout leader, or a member of a local historical society. Often, volunteer groups require their members to meet occasionally to share ideas and information. PowerPoint is a useful tool for collecting notes, data, and images that you can then show everyone all at once. One way to do this could be to create a presentation for the group, post it to a shared folder on the World Wide Web, such as on your SkyDrive, and each person in the group can add slides containing the information they want to share. In this exercise, you'll use PowerPoint to create a presentation for an upcoming meeting for a group of which you are a member, using the skills and features presented in Tutorials 3 and 4.

Note: Please be sure not to include any personal information of a sensitive nature in the documents you create to be submitted to your instructor for this exercise. Later on, you can update the documents with such information for your own personal use.

1. Start a new, blank PowerPoint presentation, and save it with an appropriate name.
2. On Slide 1, type an informative title for your presentation, and add the name of the group as a subtitle.
3. Apply a theme appropriate for the group and the presentation content.
4. Modify the slide background and theme colors to match the colors used by your group or association.
5. Add the group's logo or a photo appropriate to the group to the title slide. Consider creating a logo by creating a custom shape.
6. Create a slide that lists the group members who will contribute to the presentation.
7. Create at least six slides for the presentation. Consider the purpose of the group as well as the purpose of the upcoming meeting. If you know others have information to share, add slides with titles to help guide them.
8. Add SmartArt and charts to the slides to help clarify the content. Add text boxes if needed to help describe the content.
9. Add photos to add interest to your slides. Edit the photos if needed using PowerPoint's photo editing tools.
10. Create an overview slide with a bulleted list corresponding to the other slides in the presentation. Convert the text of each bullet to be a link to the appropriate slide. Add any other links the group thinks are necessary.
11. Add alt text as needed to make the presentation more accessible.
12. Decide whether the presentation should be self-running or given orally. If it will be self-running, decide the best way to set the timings.
13. Save the presentation in at least one other format.
14. Save and close the file.

OBJECTIVES

Session 5.1
- Import a Word outline
- Reset slides
- Reuse slides from another presentation
- Work in Outline view
- Create sections in a presentation
- Move objects through layers on a slide
- Use the Effect Options dialog box to modify animations

Session 5.2
- Embed an Excel worksheet
- Link an Excel chart
- Format a chart with advanced options
- Embed a Word table
- Format a table with advanced options
- Annotate slides during a slide show
- Create handouts in Microsoft Word

Integrating PowerPoint with Other Programs

Creating a Presentation for a Challenge Course Company

Case | *Lakewood Adventure Camp*

Lakewood Adventure Camp in Lakewood, Colorado, offers individuals and groups a variety of physical challenges and tasks. For individuals, the challenges provide an opportunity for developing new strengths and self-awareness. Group challenges provide team building opportunities that promote using the group dynamic to accomplish a task. Laura wants to add two new challenges, and she is collaborating with her team to create a presentation for Laura to present to investors.

In this tutorial, you will import a Word outline to create slides and insert slides from another presentation. You will also divide a presentation into sections, layer objects on a slide, apply advanced animation effects, and embed and link objects created in other programs. Finally, you will annotate slides during a slide show, and create handouts in Microsoft Word.

STARTING DATA FILES

PowerPoint5 →

Tutorial

Adventure.pptx
Challenge Outline.docx
Climber.png
Customer Letter.docx
New Challenges.pptx
Sales.xlsx
Zip Line.jpg

Review

Equipment Memo.docx
Map.jpg
Safety.pptx
Training Log.xlsx
Training Outline.docx
Training.pptx

Case1

Map.jpg
Photos.pptx
Rose Outline.docx
Rose.pptx
Varieties.xlsx

Case2

Coaching Outline.docx
Coaching.pptx
PRRC Photos.pptx
Sample.xlsx

Case3

Calendar.jpg
Layouts and Steps.pptx
Marketing Outline.docx
Marketing.pptx

Case4

Painting List.docx
Paintings.pptx

Session 5.1 Visual Overview:

Each object you place on a slide is placed in a new layer. The first object placed on the slide is in Layer 1—the bottom layer, the next in Layer 2, and so on.

The text box is in the bottom layer—Layer 1. Because it is in the bottom layer, it is covered by both of the other objects.

The image of the climber is in the middle layer—Layer 2. Because it is the layer on top of Layer 1, it covers the text box; because it is in the layer underneath Layer 3, it is covered by the object in Layer 3.

The image of the equipment is in the top layer—Layer 3. Because it is in the top layer, it covers both of the other objects.

If there is anything on the slide background, such as when you use a picture to fill the background, that object is in the Background layer, which is below the bottom layer on the slide. Items on the Background layer do not appear in the Selection pane and cannot be moved to another layer.

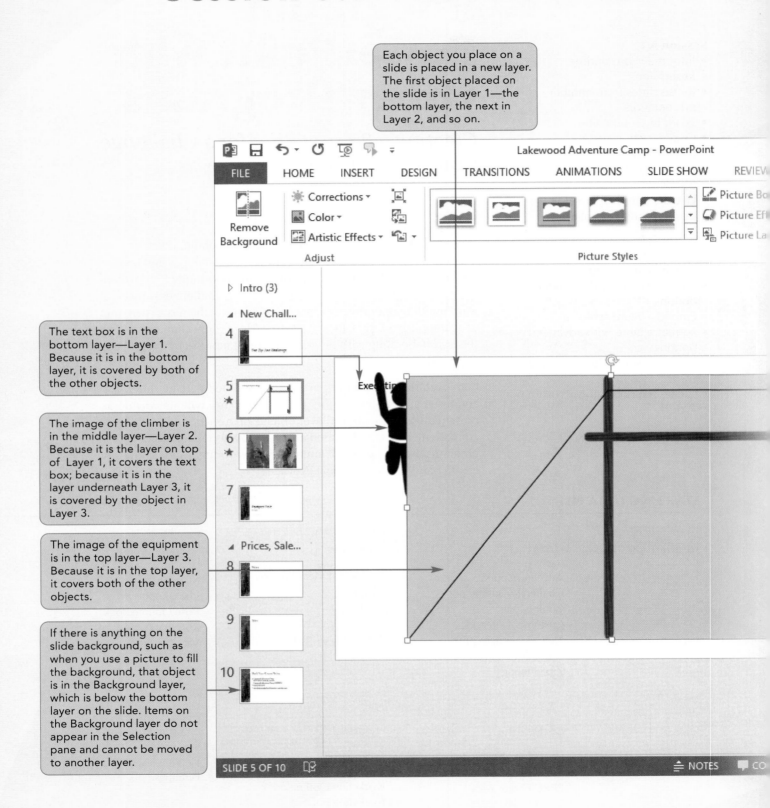

Understanding Layers

Click the Bring Forward button to move an object up in the list in the Selection pane and towards the top layer; to jump an object to the first layer, click the Bring Forward button arrow, and then click Bring to Front.

Click the Send Backward button to move an object down through the layers; to jump an object to the bottom layer, click the Send Backward button arrow, and then click Send to Back.

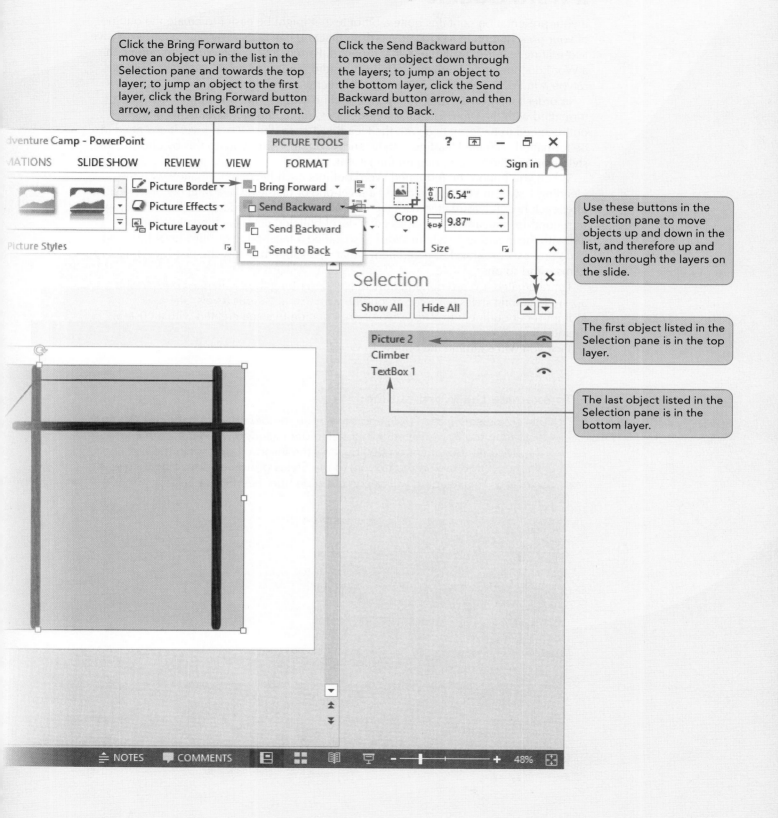

Use these buttons in the Selection pane to move objects up and down in the list, and therefore up and down through the layers on the slide.

The first object listed in the Selection pane is in the top layer.

The last object listed in the Selection pane is in the bottom layer.

Creating a Presentation by Importing a Word Outline

If your presentation contains quite a bit of text, it might be easier to create the outline of your presentation in Microsoft Word, so that you can take advantage of the extensive text-editing features available in that program. Fortunately, if you create an outline in a Word document and utilize the built-in heading styles in Word, you don't need to retype it in PowerPoint; you can import it directly into your presentation.

In order to import a Word outline, the outline levels in the document need to be formatted with the Word Heading styles. For example, the first-level items in the outline need to be formatted with the Heading 1 style, the second-level items need to be formatted with the Heading 2 style, and so on. In Word, you do this by clicking the style name in the Styles group on the HOME tab.

When you import the formatted Word outline, each heading formatted with the Heading 1 style in Word (also called a level-one or first-level heading) becomes a slide title; each heading formatted with the Heading 2 style in Word (also called a level-two or second-level heading) becomes a first-level bulleted item; each heading formatted with the Heading 3 style in Word (also called a level-three or third-level heading) becomes a second-level bulleted item—that is, a subitem below the first-level bulleted items—and so on.

Laura created a Word document with text describing the challenge courses. She applied heading styles to create an outline with text at various levels. She asks you to import her outline into a PowerPoint presentation that she created with a custom theme.

First you will examine the outline in Word.

To examine the Word outline:

1. Start Microsoft Word 2013, and then open the document **Challenge Outline**, located in the PowerPoint5 ▸ Tutorial folder included with your Data Files. The document contains an outline, and the insertion point is in the first line. On the HOME tab on the ribbon, in the Styles group, the Heading 1 style is selected. This heading will become a slide title. See Figure 5-1.

Figure 5-1   **Outline in Word document**

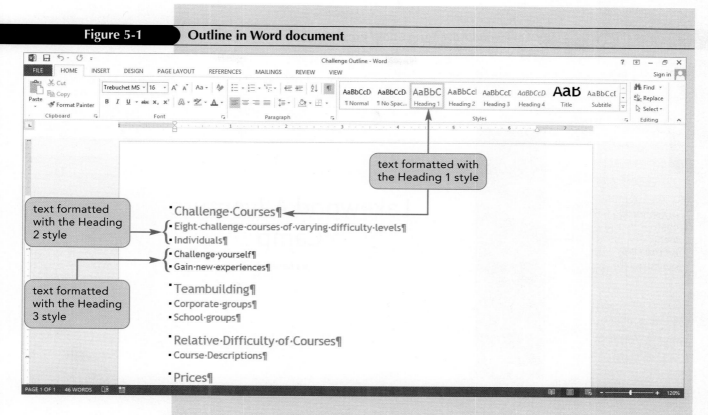

2. Press the ↓ key. The insertion point moves down one line, and in the Styles group, the Heading 2 style is selected. This heading will become a first-level bullet on a slide.

3. Press the ↓ key twice. The insertion point moves down two lines, and in the Styles group, the Heading 3 style is selected. This heading will become a second-level bullet on a slide.

4. Close the document.

Now you will import the outline into PowerPoint. You do this using a command on the New Slide button menu.

To import the Word outline into a presentation:

1. Open the presentation **Adventure** from the PowerPoint5 ▸ Tutorial folder included with your Data Files, change the name in the subtitle to your name, and then save the file with the filename **Lakewood Adventure Camp** to the location where you are saving your files. The presentation consists of only a title slide. See Figure 5-2.

Figure 5-2   **Lakewood Adventure Camp presentation**

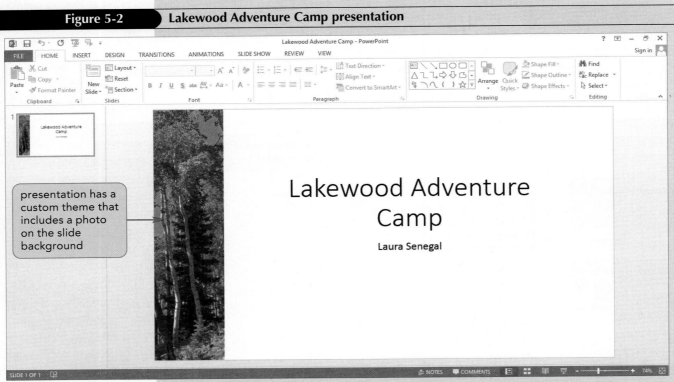

presentation has a custom theme that includes a photo on the slide background

Photo courtesy of S. Scott Zimmerman

2. On the HOME tab, in the Slides group, click the **New Slide button arrow**, and then click **Slides from Outline**. The Insert Outline dialog box opens.

3. Navigate to the PowerPoint5 ▸ Tutorial folder, click **Challenge Outline**, and then click the **Insert** button. The Word outline is inserted as new slides after the current slide in the PowerPoint presentation, with all the Heading 1 text becoming new slide titles. Slide 2 appears in the Slide pane and is currently selected in the Slides tab. See Figure 5-3.

Figure 5-3   Presentation with slides created from imported Word outline

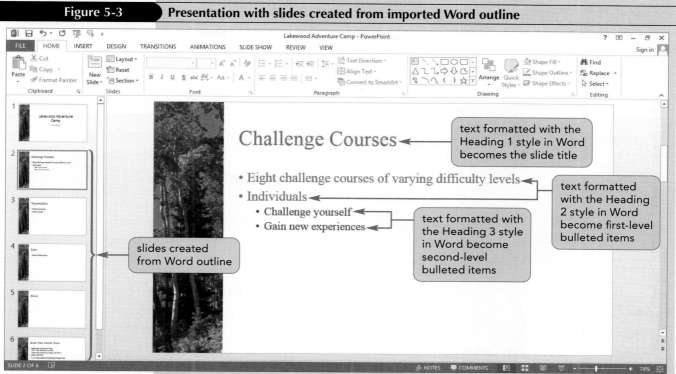

Photo courtesy of S. Scott Zimmerman

Trouble? If Slide 2 is not the current slide, click the Slide 2 thumbnail in the Slides tab.

4. In the Slides group, click the **Layout** button. Notice that a new layout, Title and Text, was created and applied. This layout was applied to all of the slides created by importing the outline.

5. Press the **Esc** key to close the Layout menu.

Resetting Slides

Notice that the text of the slides created by importing the outline retained the fonts and text colors of the outline document rather than picking up those of the presentation theme. You can fix this by resetting the slides. To do this, you use the Reset button in the Slides group on the HOME tab. You can reset a slide any time that formatting is changed unexpectedly or isn't applied as you intended, or if placeholders are modified. When you reset slides, you reset every object on the slides, so if you reset slides that contain objects, you might need to reposition the objects or reapply styles. You'll reset the slides created when you imported the Word outline.

To reset the slides:

1. In the Slides tab, select the **Slide 2** through **Slide 6** thumbnails.

2. On the HOME tab, in the Slides group, click the **Reset** button. The slides are reset to match the presentation theme so the font changes to black Calibri. See Figure 5-4.

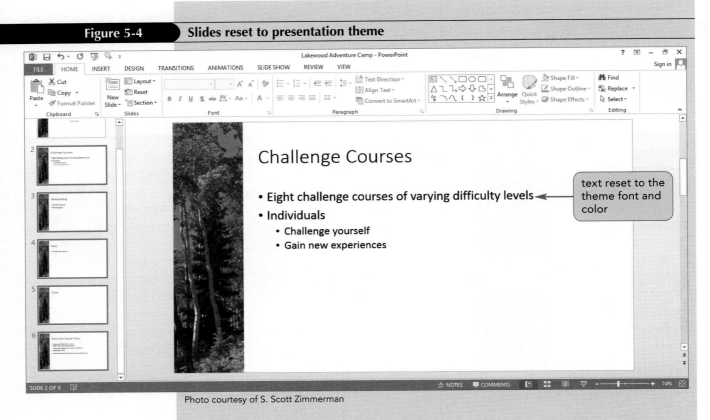

Figure 5-4 **Slides reset to presentation theme**

Photo courtesy of S. Scott Zimmerman

▶ **3.** Save the changes to your presentation.

The imported Word outline is now in the PowerPoint presentation with the Lakewood Adventure Camp theme applied. Because you imported the outline, the text is now part of PowerPoint and has no relationship with the Challenge Outline Word file. Any changes you make to the PowerPoint presentation will have no effect on the Challenge Outline file.

INSIGHT

Changing Slide Size and Orientation

The default for PowerPoint presentations is to be formatted for wide screen displays at a ratio of 16 to 9. You can change this if you need to. To do this, click the Slide Size button in the Customize group on the DESIGN tab. To change the slide size to a 4:3 ratio, click Standard (4:3) on the menu. To select other sizes or to create a custom size, click Custom Slide Size to open the Slide Size dialog box, and then select the size from the Slides sized for list. Slides in a presentation can be in landscape (wider than tall) or portrait (taller than wide) orientation. The default is landscape. Handouts can also be formatted in either orientation; the default for handouts is portrait. To change the orientation of slides or handouts, open the Slide Size dialog box. In the Orientation section of the dialog box, click the Portrait or Landscape options buttons in the Slides or Notes, Handouts, & Outline sections.

Inserting Slides from Another Presentation

TIP

To display two open presentations side by side, click the VIEW tab, and then in the Window group, click the Arrange All button.

In addition to importing a Word outline, you can insert slides from another presentation. To do this, you can open the second presentation in Slide Sorter view, and then use the familiar Copy command to copy a slide. In the presentation in which you want to paste the copied slide, switch to Slide Sorter view, and then click the location where you want to paste the copied slide, and then use the Paste command. You can paste the slide using the destination theme or the source formatting.

You can also use the Reuse Slides command. When you do this, you open the Reuse Slides task pane, in which you can access the slides from another presentation or a slide library. Then you click the slides you want to insert. If the inserted slides have a different theme than the current presentation, the design of the current presentation will override the design of the inserted slides as long as the Keep source formatting check box at the bottom of the Reuse Slides pane is selected.

Like an imported outline, once you insert slides from another presentation, any changes you make to those slides appear only in the current presentation; they do not appear in the original (source) file.

REFERENCE

Reusing Slides from Another Presentation

- Display the slide after which you want to insert slides from another presentation.
- On the HOME tab, in the Slides group, click the New Slide button arrow, and then click Reuse Slides to display the Reuse Slides task pane.
- In the task pane, click the Open a PowerPoint File link, or click the Browse button, and then click Browse File to open the Browse dialog box.
- Navigate to the location of the presentation that contains the slides you want to insert, click the file, and then click the Open button.
- In the task pane, make sure the Keep source formatting check box is not selected to force the inserted slides to use the theme in the current presentation, or click the Keep source formatting check box to retain the theme of the slides you want to import.
- In the task pane, click each slide that you want to insert into the current presentation.

Laura wants her presentation to describe the new challenges she wants to add to the course. She asked the Course Manager, Brian Cooper, to create slides that describe them. Brian started but has not completed the slides yet, so he asked if you could help him. You will insert the slides that he created into the Lakewood Adventure Camp presentation.

To insert slides from another presentation:

1. In the Slides tab, click the **Slide 4** ("Sales") thumbnail. You want to insert the slides from Brian's presentation after Slide 4.

2. On the HOME tab, in the Slides group, click the **New Slide button arrow**, and then click **Reuse Slides**. The Reuse Slides task pane opens. See Figure 5-5.

Figure 5-5   Reuse Slides task pane

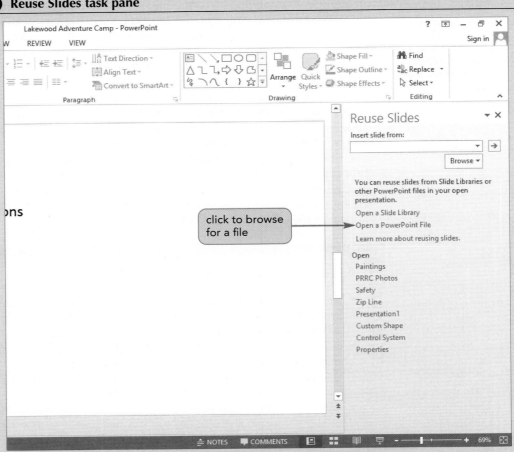

3. In the Reuse Slides task pane, click the **Open a PowerPoint File** link. The Browse dialog box opens.

4. Navigate to the PowerPoint5 ► Tutorial folder, click **New Challenges**, and then click the **Open** button. Thumbnails of the five slides in the New Challenges presentation appear in the Reuse Slides task pane. The Ion theme is applied to these slides. At the bottom of the task pane, the Keep source formatting check box is unchecked. See Figure 5-6.

Figure 5-6 **Reuse Slides task pane with slides from a presentation**

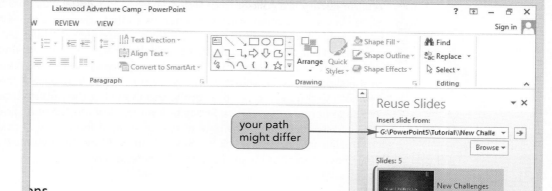

Photos courtesy of S. Scott Zimmerman

5. In the Reuse Slides task pane, click the second slide, "The Zip Line Chal…". The slide is inserted into the Lakewood Adventure Camp presentation after the current slide (Slide 4). Because the Keep source formatting check box is unchecked, the theme used in the Lakewood Adventure Camp presentation is applied to the slide instead of the Ion theme used in the New Challenges presentation.

6. In the Reuse Slides task pane, click **Slide 3**, and then click **Slide 4**. These slides also have the theme of the Lakewood Adventure Camp presentation applied, but they use the Blank layout, and that layout does not include the photo on the left.

7. In the Reuse Slides task pane, click the **Pamper Pole** slide to insert it as a new Slide 8, and then in the Reuse Slides task pane title bar, click the **Close** button ✖.

8. Save the changes to the presentation.

The four slides you inserted from the New Challenges presentation are now Slides 5 through 8 in the Lakewood Adventure Camp presentation.

Using Slides from a Slide Library

A **slide library** is a collection of slides saved as individual files on a SharePoint server. Slide libraries are often used in businesses so that coworkers can share slides that are commonly needed. To add slides to a slide library, click the FILE tab, click Share in the navigation pane, click Publish Slides, and then click the Publish Slides button. This opens the Publish Slides dialog box. Click the check boxes next to the slides you want to add to the slide library. To select the location of the slide library, click the Browse button, navigate to the location of the library, and then click the Publish button. To display slides in a slide library in the Reuse Slides task pane, click the Open a Slide Library link in the Reuse Slides task pane, navigate to the location of the library, click the folder containing the library, and then click the Select button. Note that you must have access to a SharePoint server to reuse slides from a slide library.

Working in Outline View

Outline view displays the outline of the presentation in the Outline tab to the left of the Slide pane. In Outline view, the Slides tab, containing the slide thumbnails, is not visible. In the Outline tab, text is arranged as in an ordinary outline. Slide titles are the top levels in the outline, and the slide content—that is, the bulleted lists—are indented below the slide titles.

You can use the Outline tab to see the outline of the entire presentation and easily move text around, and even change the order of slides. For example, you can move a bulleted item from one slide to another, change a subitem into a first-level item, or change a bulleted item into a slide title, creating a new slide.

Moving an item higher in the outline by, for example, changing a second-level bullet into a first-level bullet or changing a first-level bulleted item into a slide title, is called **promoting** the item. Moving an item lower in the outline by, for example, changing a slide title into a bulleted item on the previous slide or changing a first-level bullet into a second-level bullet, is called **demoting** the item.

The Lakewood Adventure Camp presentation has material from two sources, Laura's outline and Brian's presentation. The presentation needs some organizing. You will do this in the Outline tab in Outline view.

To modify the presentation outline in Outline view:

▶ 1. On the ribbon, click the **VIEW** tab, and then in the Presentation Views group, click the **Outline View** button. The Outline tab, listing the outline of the presentation, replaces the Slides tab, and the Notes pane becomes visible as well. See Figure 5-7.

Figure 5-7   **Outline tab in Outline view**

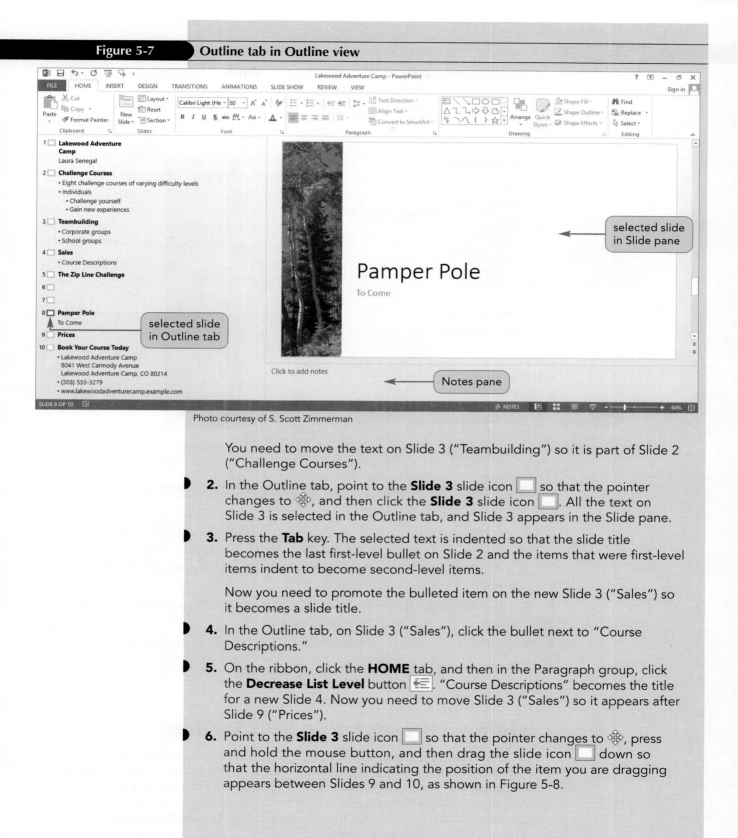

Photo courtesy of S. Scott Zimmerman

You need to move the text on Slide 3 ("Teambuilding") so it is part of Slide 2 ("Challenge Courses").

2. In the Outline tab, point to the **Slide 3** slide icon ☐ so that the pointer changes to ✜, and then click the **Slide 3** slide icon ☐. All the text on Slide 3 is selected in the Outline tab, and Slide 3 appears in the Slide pane.

3. Press the **Tab** key. The selected text is indented so that the slide title becomes the last first-level bullet on Slide 2 and the items that were first-level items indent to become second-level items.

Now you need to promote the bulleted item on the new Slide 3 ("Sales") so it becomes a slide title.

4. In the Outline tab, on Slide 3 ("Sales"), click the bullet next to "Course Descriptions."

5. On the ribbon, click the **HOME** tab, and then in the Paragraph group, click the **Decrease List Level** button ◀≣. "Course Descriptions" becomes the title for a new Slide 4. Now you need to move Slide 3 ("Sales") so it appears after Slide 9 ("Prices").

6. Point to the **Slide 3** slide icon ☐ so that the pointer changes to ✜, press and hold the mouse button, and then drag the slide icon ☐ down so that the horizontal line indicating the position of the item you are dragging appears between Slides 9 and 10, as shown in Figure 5-8.

Figure 5-8	Dragging an item in the Outline tab

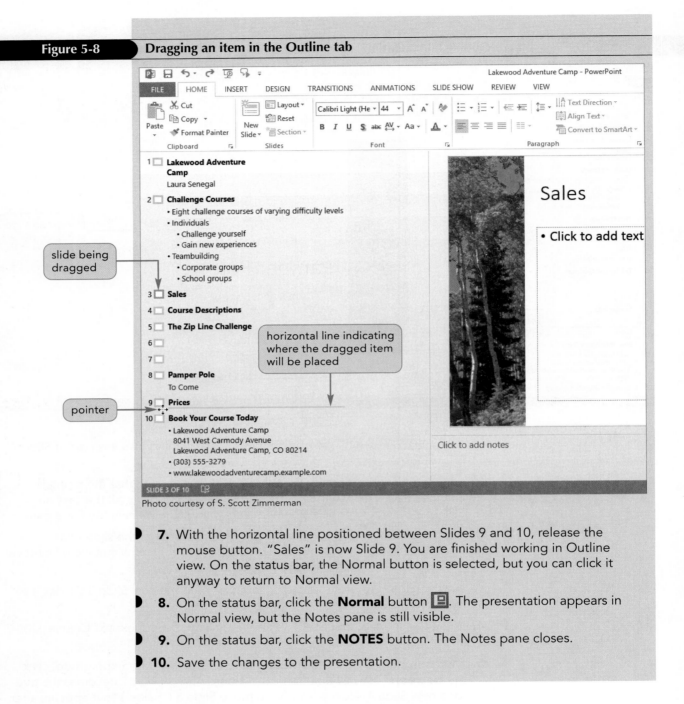

Photo courtesy of S. Scott Zimmerman

▶ **7.** With the horizontal line positioned between Slides 9 and 10, release the mouse button. "Sales" is now Slide 9. You are finished working in Outline view. On the status bar, the Normal button is selected, but you can click it anyway to return to Normal view.

▶ **8.** On the status bar, click the **Normal** button 🔲. The presentation appears in Normal view, but the Notes pane is still visible.

▶ **9.** On the status bar, click the **NOTES** button. The Notes pane closes.

▶ **10.** Save the changes to the presentation.

Dividing a Presentation into Sections

If you are working with a long presentation, it can be helpful to divide it into sections. Presentation sections are different than using a Section Header layout. A Section Header layout is a layout designed to cue the audience that the presentation is shifting to a new topic; sections are designed to help the presentation creator work with and manage a presentation with many slides. Sections can be collapsed, allowing you to focus on one section of slides at a time.

Laura wants you to create a section that consists of the four slides from Brian's presentation so that she knows which slides Brian is responsible for. To do this, you need to first select the slide that will mark the beginning of the section.

To create a section in the presentation:

1. In the Slides tab, click the **Slide 4** ("The Zip Line Challenge") thumbnail. This will be the first slide in the section you will create.

2. On the HOME tab, in the Slides group, click the **Section** button, and then click **Add Section**. The new section is created and is named "Untitled Section" in the Slides tab. Slide 4 and all the slides after it are selected. See Figure 5-9.

Figure 5-9 New section

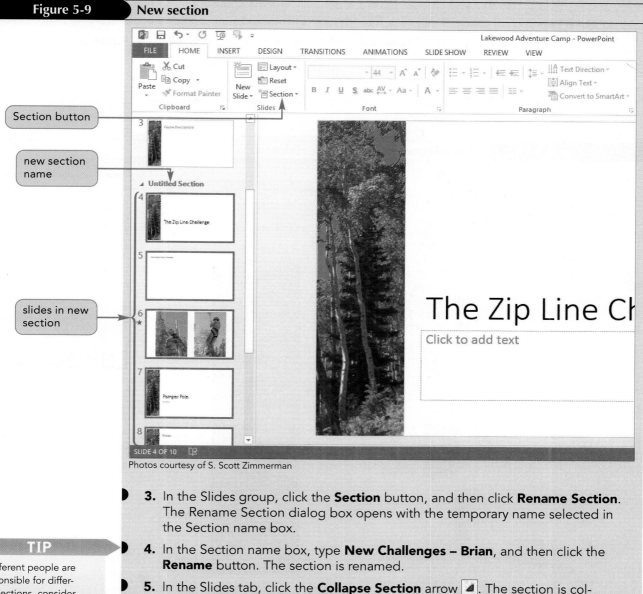

Photos courtesy of S. Scott Zimmerman

3. In the Slides group, click the **Section** button, and then click **Rename Section**. The Rename Section dialog box opens with the temporary name selected in the Section name box.

4. In the Section name box, type **New Challenges – Brian**, and then click the **Rename** button. The section is renamed.

5. In the Slides tab, click the **Collapse Section** arrow ◢. The section is collapsed and the number 7 appears after the section name; this is the number of slides in the section.

TIP

If different people are responsible for different sections, consider naming each section with the name of the person responsible for that section.

The new section should include only the four slides that Brian created. To fix this, you need to create another section that includes the last three slides in the presentation. Also, at the top of the Slides tab, the section name "Default Section" appears. That section includes Slides 1 through 3. You will rename this section.

To create another section in the presentation:

▶ **1.** In the Slides tab, next to New Challenges – Brian (7), click the **Expand Section** arrow ▷. The section expands so that you can see all the slides in it.

▶ **2.** Click a blank area of the Slides tab to deselect the slide thumbnails, and then scroll down to the bottom of the Slides tab.

▶ **3.** Right-click the **Slide 8** ("Prices") thumbnail, and then on the shortcut menu, click **Add Section**.

▶ **4.** In the Slides tab, right-click **Untitled Section**, and then on the shortcut menu, click **Rename Section** to open the Rename Section dialog box.

▶ **5.** Type **Prices, Sales, & Contact Info**, and then click the **Rename** button.

▶ **6.** Scroll to the top of the Slides tab, and then rename the Default Section as **Intro**.

▶ **7.** Collapse the **Intro** and **Prices, Sales, & Contact Info** sections. See Figure 5-10.

TIP

You can also work with sections in Slide Sorter view.

Figure 5-10 Two collapsed sections in the Slides tab

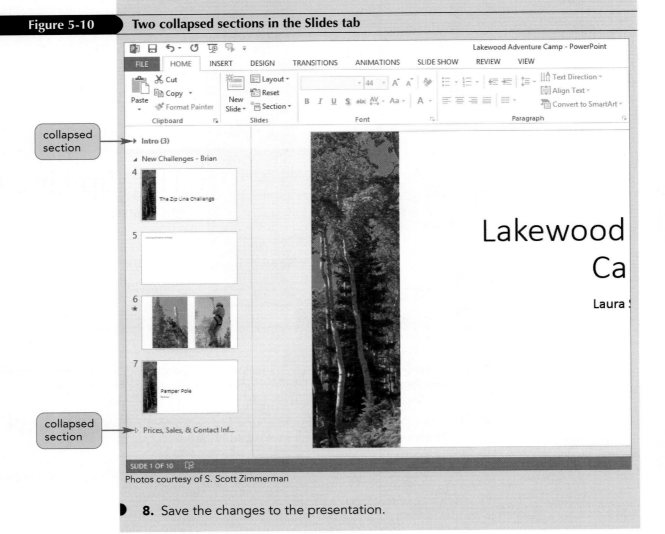

Photos courtesy of S. Scott Zimmerman

▶ **8.** Save the changes to the presentation.

Problem Solving: Creating a Slide Show with Two Orientations

There may be times that the content of your presentation requires you to use a combination of portrait and landscape slide orientations. For example, suppose you are creating a presentation that contains some photos in portrait orientation and some in landscape orientation. In PowerPoint, you cannot create a single presentation file with slides in both orientations. To solve this problem, you need to create two presentations and create links between them. To do this, create one presentation using the default landscape orientation, create a second presentation and change the orientation to portrait, and then add the appropriate photos to each file. Decide which presentation will be the primary file; it should be the presentation that you want to use at the start of your presentation. Then, decide the order in which you want the photos to appear. When you want to display a slide using the orientation used in the other presentation, insert an action button on the slide that will appear prior to displaying the slide with the other orientation. In the Action Settings dialog box, click the Hyperlink to option button, click Other PowerPoint Presentation in the Hyperlink to list, and then select the other presentation. This opens the Hyperlink to Slide dialog box listing the slides in the other presentation. Select the slide you want to display next. If you need to, add an action button in the second presentation linked back to the appropriate slide in the first presentation. It's a good idea to store the two presentations in the same folder so that they will always be together.

Working with Layers

Every time you add an object to a slide, you add it in a new layer. As illustrated in the Session 5.1 Visual Overview, you can send objects to the back (bottom) of the layers on a slide, or you can bring an object to the front (top) of the layers. To change an object's layer, you use commands in the Arrange group on the DRAWING TOOLS FORMAT tab or on the Arrange button menu in the Drawing group on the HOME tab, or you can move objects through layers using the Selection pane.

Brian asks you to add two images to Slide 5 to demonstrate the Zip Line challenge.

To add objects to Slide 5 in layers:

1. Display **Slide 5** (untitled) in the Slide pane. Currently, the only thing on this slide is a text box containing "Executing the Zip Line Challenge." First you will insert an illustration of a climber.

2. Insert the picture **Climber**, located in the PowerPoint5 ▸ Tutorial folder. This picture is in the layer on top of the layer that contains the text box. To see this, you will temporarily position the image on top of the text box.

3. Drag the climber illustration so its head is on top of the word "Challenge." See Figure 5-11. Next you will insert the illustration of the Zip Line equipment.

Figure 5-11   Climber illustration in layer on top of text box

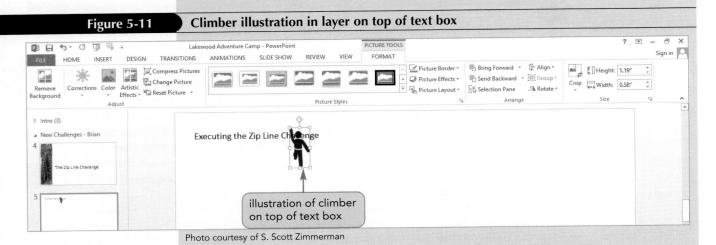

Photo courtesy of S. Scott Zimmerman

4. Insert the picture **Zip Line**, located in the PowerPoint5 ▸ Tutorial folder. This illustration is inserted on top of the illustration of the climber.

The white background of the equipment illustration covers the illustration of the climber and partially covers the text box. The illustration of the equipment is in the top layer on the slide, and the illustration of the climber is in the bottom layer on the slide. To select objects that are not visible because they are in a layer covered by another layer, you need to open the Selection pane and then select the object there. First, to make it easier to see the objects move through the layers, you will temporarily change the background color of the equipment illustration.

To use the Selection pane:

1. With the equipment illustration selected, click the **PICTURE TOOLS FORMAT** tab, if necessary.

2. In the Adjust group, click the **Color** button, and then in the Recolor section, click the **Green, Accent color 6 Dark** option. The picture is recolored, including its background. Now you will open the Selection pane.

TIP

You can also click the Select button in the Editing group on the HOME tab, and then click Selection Pane.

3. In the Arrange group, click the **Selection Pane** button. The Selection pane opens. Every object on the slide is listed in the pane. The object at the top of the list is in the top layer on the slide, and the object at the bottom of the list is in the bottom layer. The selected image of the equipment is listed in the Selection pane as Picture 2.

4. In the Selection pane, click **Picture 1**. The corresponding image of the climber is selected on the slide, even though all you can see is the selection border and sizing handles because the climber is in a layer behind the Zip Line image. See Figure 5-12.

Figure 5-12   **Climber illustration hidden in layer underneath equipment illustration**

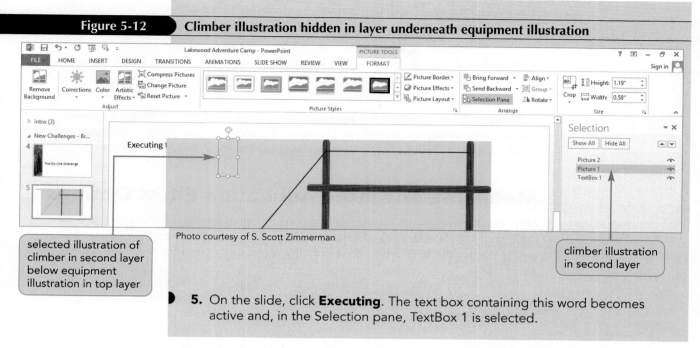

Photo courtesy of S. Scott Zimmerman

selected illustration of climber in second layer below equipment illustration in top layer

climber illustration in second layer

5. On the slide, click **Executing**. The text box containing this word becomes active and, in the Selection pane, TextBox 1 is selected.

To make the climber illustration visible, it needs to be moved up to a layer on top of the layer containing the illustration of the equipment. The text box also needs to be in a layer on top of the layer containing the illustration of the equipment. You will move these objects through the layers now.

To move the text box and the climber illustration through layers on the slide:

1. Make sure the text box is selected, and then on the HOME tab, in the Drawing group, click the **Arrange** button. The Arrange menu contains commands for moving objects up and down through the layers; these same commands can be found in the Arrange group on the DRAWING TOOLS FORMAT tab shown in the Session 5.1 Visual Overview.

2. Click **Bring Forward**. On the slide, nothing appears to change, but in the Selection pane, the selected object, TextBox 1, moved up one place in the list—the text box has moved up one layer so it is now in the second layer on the slide. If you could see the climber illustration, it would be partially covered by the text box. You need to move the text box up one more layer so it is on top of the illustration of the equipment. It might be easier to use the Bring Forward and Send Backward buttons in the Selection pane.

3. In the Selection pane, click the **Bring Forward** button [▲]. The text box moves up one more layer and is now in the top layer on the slide and at the top of the list in the Selection pane. Now you will move the illustration of the climber to the top layer.

4. In the Selection pane, click the **Picture1** object. The selection border and sizing handles appear around the illustration of the climber.

5. On the HOME tab, in the Drawing group, click the **Arrange** button, and then click **Bring to Front**. The illustration of the climber moves to the top of the list and you can now see it on the slide, on top of the text box. Now you will reset the equipment illustration to its original white background.

6. Click the equipment illustration, and then on the ribbon, click the **PICTURE TOOLS FORMAT** tab.

7. In the Adjust group, click the **Reset Picture** button. The picture is reset to its original colors.

You do not need to open the Selection pane to use the Send Backward and Send Forward commands on the ribbon. However, if a slide contains many objects, it can be easier to work with them if you can see the complete list in the Selection pane.

Modifying Advanced Animation Effect Options

Now that the objects are layered so that you can see everything, Brian wants you to apply animations so it looks like the climber climbs up the pole on the right, walks across the horizontal beam holding onto the rope, and then slides down the slanted zip line.

You could try to do this by drawing a custom motion path, but it can be difficult to draw smooth paths. Instead, you will duplicate the image of the climber twice, and then draw three motion paths, one for each climber.

To duplicate the illustration of the climber:

1. On Slide 5 ("Executing the Zip Line Challenge"), drag the climber illustration so it is positioned on the left side of the base of the right vertical pole. See Figure 5-13.

| Figure 5-13 | Climber illustration repositioned on Slide 5 |

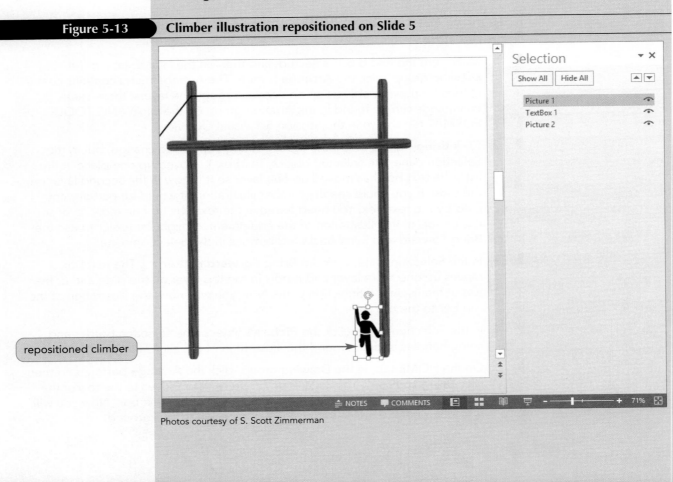

repositioned climber

Photos courtesy of S. Scott Zimmerman

2. With the climber selected, click the **HOME** tab.

3. In the Clipboard group, click the **Copy button arrow**, and then click **Duplicate**. The climber illustration is duplicated on the slide.

4. Drag the duplicate of the climber so it is positioned with the climber's left foot on the horizontal beam just to the left of the right vertical pole and with the climber's right hand touching the horizontal rope.

5. Duplicate the climber illustration again.

   Trouble? If the duplicate appears above the Slide pane, drag it down onto the Slide pane.

6. Drag the duplicate of the climber on top of the left vertical pole, with the climber's left foot on the horizontal pole and the climber's right hand touching the rope slanting down to the left.

7. Click a blank area of the slide, and then compare your screen to Figure 5-14 and make any adjustments necessary.

Figure 5-14	Duplicates of climber illustration repositioned on Slide 5

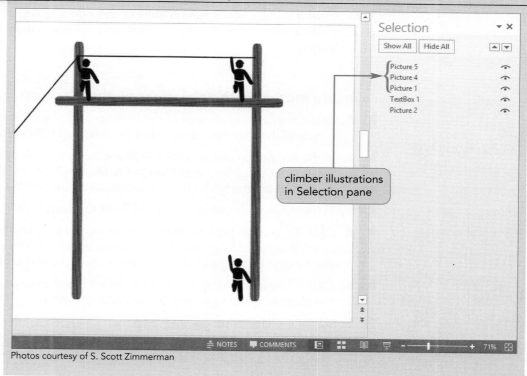

Photos courtesy of S. Scott Zimmerman

You will use the Animation Pane to add animations to the objects. When animated objects are listed in the Animation Pane, they are listed with the same names that are used in the Selection pane. To make it easier to work with the named objects on the slide, you will rename the climber objects in the Selection pane.

To rename slide objects:

▶ **1.** In the Selection pane, click the **Picture 5** object, and then click **Picture 5** again. An orange box appears around the object name and the insertion point appears before the "P" in the box.

   Trouble? If the insertion point does not appear in the box, click in the box.

▶ **2.** Press the **Delete** key as many times as needed to delete all the text, and then type **Left Climber**.

▶ **3.** Click the **Picture 4** object in the list. The climber on the right end of the horizontal pole is selected.

▶ **4.** Click the selected **Picture 4** object, delete all the text, and then type **Right Climber**.

▶ **5.** Click the **Picture 1** object, click it again, delete all the text, type **Bottom Climber**, and then press the **Enter** key.

▶ **6.** In the Selection pane, click the **Close** button ☒, and then save the changes to the presentation.

Now that it is clear which named object corresponds to which object on the slide, you can add animations to the objects. First, you will add a motion path animation to each climber.

To add motion path animations to the climbers:

▶ **1.** Select the bottom climber at the bottom of the right vertical pole, if necessary, and then on the ribbon, click the **ANIMATIONS** tab.

▶ **2.** In the Animation group, click the **More** button, scroll down to the bottom of the Animation gallery, and then in the Motion Paths section, click **Lines**. The animation previews and the climber moves down off the Slide pane.

▶ **3.** In the Animation group, click the **Effect Options** button, and then click **Up**.

▶ **4.** Click the motion path to change the start and stop triangles to the start and stop circles, and then drag the red circle up so that the ending position of the climber is on top of the climber on the right end of the horizontal pole.

▶ **5.** Click a blank area of the slide to deselect the motion path, and then select the climber at the right end of the horizontal pole.

▶ **6.** Apply the **Lines** motion path, and then change the Effect Options to **Left**.

▶ **7.** Drag the end of the motion path you just applied so that the ending position of the climber is on top of the climber on the left end of the horizontal pole, and then deselect the motion path.

▶ **8.** Select the climber at the left end of the horizontal pole, apply the **Lines** motion path, and then drag the end of the motion path so that motion path follows the slanted rope and the ending position of the climber is near the bottom of the slanted rope. See Figure 5-15.

Figure 5-15   **Motion path animations applied to climber illustrations**

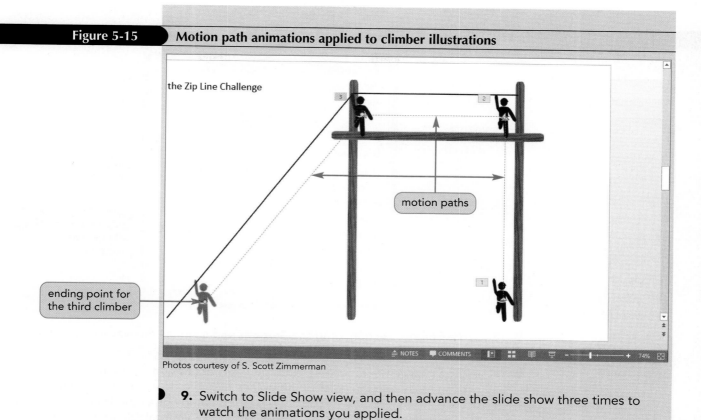

Photos courtesy of S. Scott Zimmerman

> **9.** Switch to Slide Show view, and then advance the slide show three times to watch the animations you applied.

> **10.** Press the **Esc** key to end the slide show.

To make motion paths look smoother, the default is for them to accelerate and decelerate. However, the climber should look like it is moving in one motion. Therefore the first motion path should keep the smooth start setting, and the last motion path down the zip line should keep the smooth end setting, but the rest of the "smooth" settings should be removed.

Also, after the first climber climbs to the top of the pole, it should disappear so it is not still standing there when the second climber moves across the horizontal pole. You could add an exit animation, or you can set the animated object to hide after the animation is finished.

To make these two customizations for the animations, you'll use the Effect Options dialog box. The name and exact contents of this dialog box vary depending on the selected animation, but it always contains an Effect tab and a Timing tab, and it is generically referred to as the Effect Options dialog box even though the title of the dialog box matches the animation name or effect: For entrance, exit, and emphasis animations, the title of the dialog box matches the name of the animation; for most motion path animations, the title of the dialog box matches the selected direction effect.

You will modify the animations now.

To modify the motion path animations:

> **1.** Click the animation sequence icon **1** to select that animation.

> **2.** On the ANIMATIONS tab, in the Animation group, click the **Dialog Box Launcher**. The Effect Options dialog box that opens is titled "Up." This corresponds to the selected direction effect for the motion path. Because this is a motion path animation, the Effect tab contains settings for modifying the path, including how the animation starts and stops. See Figure 5-16.

Figure 5-16   Effect Options dialog box for the Up motion path animation

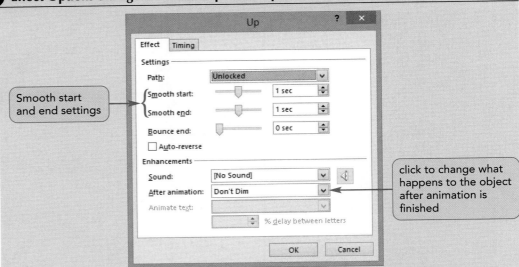

Smooth start and end settings

click to change what happens to the object after animation is finished

  3. In the Settings section, drag the **Smooth end** slider all the way to the left so that the value in the box is 0 sec.

  4. In the Enhancements section, click the **After animation** arrow. You can choose to change the color of the object, hide the object after the animation, or hide the object after the next mouse click (or any other method of advancing the slide show). These options on this menu are available to all entrance, emphasis, and motion path animations.

  5. Click **Hide After Animation**, and then click the **OK** button. You need to change the options for the second animation. This time, you'll access the Effect Options dialog box from the Animation Pane.

  6. On the ANIMATIONS tab, in the Advanced Animation group, click the **Animation Pane** button. The Animation Pane opens listing the three motion path animations applied to the climber objects using the names you typed in the Selection pane. The icon next to each object listed indicates that a motion path is applied.

  7. In the Animation Pane, click the **Right Climber** animation, and then click the arrow □ that appears. A menu opens as shown in Figure 5-17.

Figure 5-17   **Menu for animated object in Animation Pane**

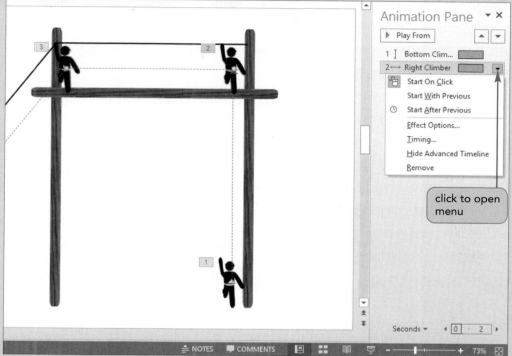

click to open menu

Photos courtesy of S. Scott Zimmerman

8. Click **Effect Options**. The Effect Options dialog box that opens is titled "Left." Because this animation will occur between the other two animations, you want to remove both the smooth start and smooth end settings.

9. In the Settings section, drag the **Smooth start** slider all the way to the left, and then drag the **Smooth end** slider all the way to the left so that the value in both boxes is 0 sec. This object needs to be hidden after it animates as well.

10. In the Enhancements section, click the **After animation** arrow, and then click **Hide After Animation**. You also want this animation to start automatically after the previous animation. You already know how to change this setting on the ANIMATIONS tab on the ribbon, but you can change this setting in the Effect Options dialog box as well.

11. Click the **Timing** tab, click the **Start** arrow, click **After Previous**, and then click the **OK** button. In the Animation Pane, the number 2 no longer appears in front of the Right Climber item, and in the Slide pane, the animation sequence icon next to the climber at the right end of the horizontal pole changes to a 1 because you changed the start timing to After Previous. Now you need to modify the settings for the third motion path.

12. In the Animation Pane, click the **Left Climber** animation (the third item in the list), and then click the arrow ▼ that appears. You can also change the start timing of the animation on this menu.

13. Click **Start After Previous**. The menu closes and the number before the third animation no longer appears.

14. Click ⏷ for the selected item in the Animation Pane, and then click **Effect Options**. You need to change only the Smooth start setting because this is the last animation and you want this climber to remain on the screen after the animation.

15. Drag the **Smooth start** slider all the way to the left, and then click the **OK** button.

Now you will see how the animations look in Slide Show view. After you switch to Slide Show view, you only need to advance the slide show once to see all three animations.

To view the animations on Slide 5 in Slide Show view:

1. Switch to Slide Show view. Slide 5 appears in Slide Show view displaying the text box, the illustration of the zip line, and the three climbers.

2. Advance the slide show. The first climber moves up the vertical pole on the right, and then is hidden. Immediately after, the second climber moves to the left, and is then hidden. Finally, the last climber moves down the slanted rope, and then remains on the screen.

3. Press the **Esc** key to end the slide show.

You need to solve one last problem. The slide is supposed to look like one climber climbs up the pole, walks across the beam, and then slides down the zip line. In order to do this, you need to add the Appear entrance animations to the two climbers "standing" on the horizontal beam. The animations should occur automatically after the previous motion path finishes.

To add the entrance animation Appear to the two climbers on the horizontal beam:

1. In the Slide pane, click the climber at the right end of the horizontal beam.

2. On the ANIMATIONS tab, in the Advanced Animation group, click the **Add Animation** button, and then in the Entrance section, click the **Appear** animation. A second animation sequence icon appears next to the climber, and the animation appears at the bottom of the list in the Animation Pane with the green star next to it indicating that it is an entrance animation. See Figure 5-18.

Figure 5-18   Entrance animation applied to Right Climber object

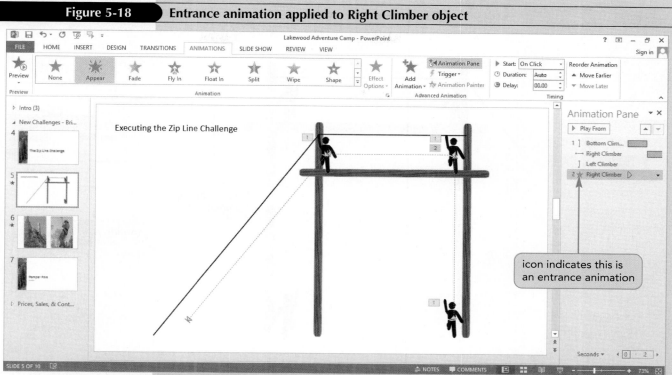

Executing the Zip Line Challenge

icon indicates this is an entrance animation

Photos courtesy of S. Scott Zimmerman

While this animation is still selected, you will change the order of the animation. This animation needs to occur after the first climber moves up the pole, so you need to move this entrance animation earlier in the list in the Animation Pane. Just like the Selection pane, there are buttons in the Animation Pane that you can click to move an animation up or down in the list.

3. In the Animation Pane, point to the **Right Climber entrance animation** so that the pointer changes to ↕, press and hold the mouse button, drag up until the horizontal indicator line is above the Right Climber motion path animation, and then release the mouse button. The Right Climber entrance animation is now second in the list. Now you need to modify the start timing of the entrance animation so that it starts automatically after the previous animation finishes.

4. In the Animation Pane, click the arrow ▾ of the selected animation, and then click **Start After Previous**. Now you need to do the same thing to the climber on the left end of the horizontal beam.

5. Add the entrance animation Appear to the climber on the left end of the horizontal beam, reorder the Appear animation so it occurs before the line motion path animation for the Left Climber, and then change its start timing to **After Previous**. Compare your screen to Figure 5-19.

Figure 5-19 Modified order of entrance animations

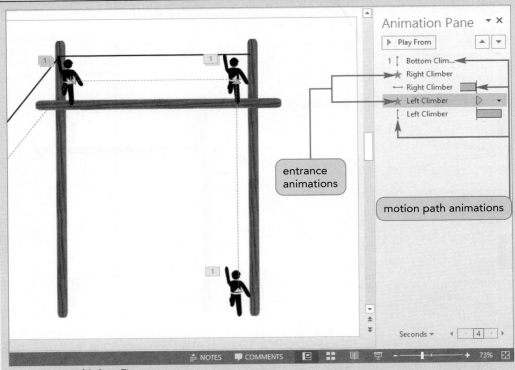

Photos courtesy of S. Scott Zimmerman

6. Switch to Slide Show view, and then advance the slide show. It now looks like a single image of the climber climbs up the pole on the right, moves across the horizontal beam, and then slides down the slanted line (the zip line).

7. Press the **Esc** key to end the slide show.

8. In the Animation Pane, click the **Close** button [X].

9. In the Slides tab, next to the New Challenges - Brian section name, click the **Collapse Section** button [◢], and then save the changes to the presentation.

You have created a presentation by importing an outline and inserting slides from another presentation. You modified the presentation outline in Outline view and divided the presentation into sections. You moved objects through layers and modified animation effects using the Effect Options dialog box. In the next session, you will insert and modify objects created in Excel and Word, and format them using advanced options. You will also annotate slides during a slide show and create handouts in Microsoft Word.

REVIEW

Session 5.1 Quick Check

1. Describe how you use a Word outline to create slides in PowerPoint.
2. Describe how you insert slides from one presentation into another.
3. What happens when you promote a first-level bulleted item in the Outline tab in Outline view?
4. What is the difference between using a Section Header layout and creating a new section in a presentation?
5. How are layers created on a slide?
6. What is another way to cause an animated object to disappear after it animates without adding an Exit animation?

Session 5.2 Visual Overview:

source file (Word table)

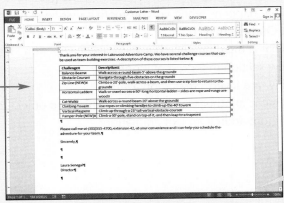

The program used to create the object is called the source program; the file that initially contains the object is called the source file.

When you paste an object, a copy of an object created in a source program becomes part of the destination file; you can edit the object with the tools available in the destination program. There is no connection between the inserted object and its source file or source program.

source file (Excel table)

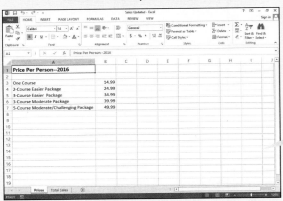

When you embed an object, a copy of the object along with a one-way connection to the source program become part of the destination file, and you can edit the object using the source program's commands. Changes made do not appear in the source file.

source program

You must have access to the source program to edit an embedded object; however, you do not need access to the source file.

source file (Excel chart)

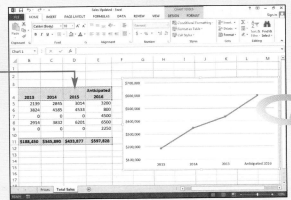

When linking an object, you must have access to the source file if you want to make changes to the source object.

Importing, Embedding, and Linking

destination file
(PowerPoint presentation)

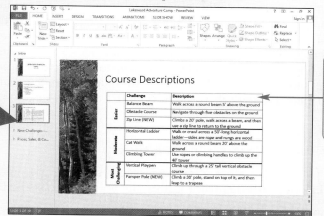

The program used to create the file where you want to insert the object is called the **destination program**; the file where you want to insert the object is called the **destination file**.

destination file
(PowerPoint presentation)

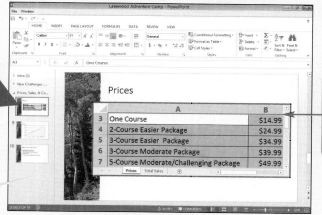

There is no connection between an embedded object and its source file; therefore, changes made to the object in the source file do not appear in the destination file.

When you **link** an object, a direct connection is created between the source and destination programs so that the object exists in only one place—the source file—but the link displays the object in the destination file as well.

destination file
(PowerPoint presentation)

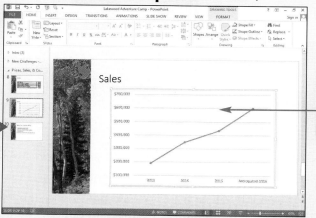

If you edit a linked object in the source file, the link ensures that the changes appear in the destination file.

Photos courtesy of S. Scott Zimmerman

Inserting a Word Table

You know how to use PowerPoint commands to create a table in a slide, but what if you've already created a table using Word? You don't need to re-create it in PowerPoint; instead, you can copy the table from the Word document, and then paste it on a slide. Similar to importing a Word outline or inserting slides from another presentation, once you paste the table, the table becomes part of the PowerPoint file and any changes you make to it will not affect the original table in the source file.

Laura wrote a letter that she sends to companies who have requested information about the challenge courses, and in it, she includes a table listing a description of the courses. She has already modified that table to include descriptions of the two new challenges to be offered at Lakewood Adventure Camp. She wants you to include that table on Slide 3 in the Lakewood Adventure Camp presentation.

To insert a Word table on a slide:

▶ 1. If you took a break after the previous session, open the presentation **Lakewood Adventure Camp** that you created in the first session.

▶ 2. In the Slides tab, expand the Intro section, if necessary, and then collapse the New Challenges - Brian and Prices, Sales, & Contact Info sections, if necessary.

▶ 3. Display **Slide 3** ("Course Descriptions") in the Slide pane, and then change the layout to **Title Only**.

▶ 4. Start Microsoft Word 2013, and then open the document **Customer Letter**, located in the PowerPoint5 ▶ Tutorial folder.

▶ 5. Point to the table so that the Table Select Handle ⊞ appears, and then click the **Table Select Handle** ⊞ to select the entire table. See Figure 5-20.

| Figure 5-20 | Selected table in Word document |

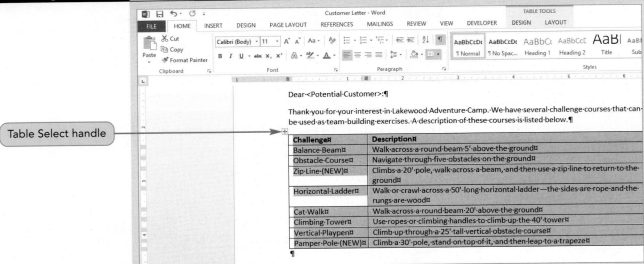

Table Select handle

▶ 6. On the HOME tab, in the Clipboard group, click the **Copy** button.

▶ 7. Switch back to the PowerPoint presentation.

▶ 8. On the HOME tab, in the Clipboard group, click the **Paste button arrow**, and then click the **Keep Source Formatting** button. The table is pasted on the slide as a PowerPoint table with the formatting from the source file (the Word file).

TIP

To insert a Word file on a slide, click the Object button in the Text group on the INSERT tab, click the Create from file option button, browse to the Word file, and then click the OK button.

▶ **9.** Resize the table by dragging the corner sizing handles so that the table is 5 inches high and 9.5 inches wide, and then center it in the blank area on the slide. The text in the table is too small.

▶ **10.** Point just above the first column so that the pointer changes to ↓, and then click and drag to the right to select both columns.

▶ **11.** On the HOME tab, in the Font group, click the **Font Size arrow**, and then click **18**. The font size of the text in the table increases to 18 points.

▶ **12.** Switch back to the Customer Letter Word document, and then close the document and exit Word. You return to the Lakewood Adventure Camp presentation.

Formatting Cells in Tables

Your previous work with tables focused on formatting and modifying the table's appearance and structure. You can also make formatting changes to individual cells. For example, you can merge cells, rotate text in cells, and change the width of borders.

When you merge cells, you combine two or more cells into one. You can merge cells in the same row, the same column, or the same rectangular block of rows and columns. Merging cells is especially useful when you need to enter large amounts of information into a single cell, or when you want to add a heading that spans more than one column. To merge cells, you use the Merge Cells button, which is located in the Merge group on the TABLE TOOLS LAYOUT tab.

At Lakewood Adventure Camp, each course is rated as Easier, Moderate, or Most Challenging. Laura wants you to format the table in the presentation to identify the three categories of courses. To do this, you will add labels in a new first column. Instead of adding a label in each row, you will merge cells to create one larger cell so that each label appears only once.

To create a new first column and merge cells:

▶ **1.** Click in the first column in the table, and then on the ribbon, click the **TABLE TOOLS LAYOUT** tab.

▶ **2.** In the Rows & Columns group, click the **Insert Left** button. A new first column is added to the table.

▶ **3.** Click in the second cell in the new column, press and hold the mouse button, and then drag down to select the second, third, and fourth cells in the column.

▶ **4.** In the Merge group, click the **Merge Cells** button. The three selected cells are merged into one cell. See Figure 5-21.

Figure 5-21 Merged cell in imported table

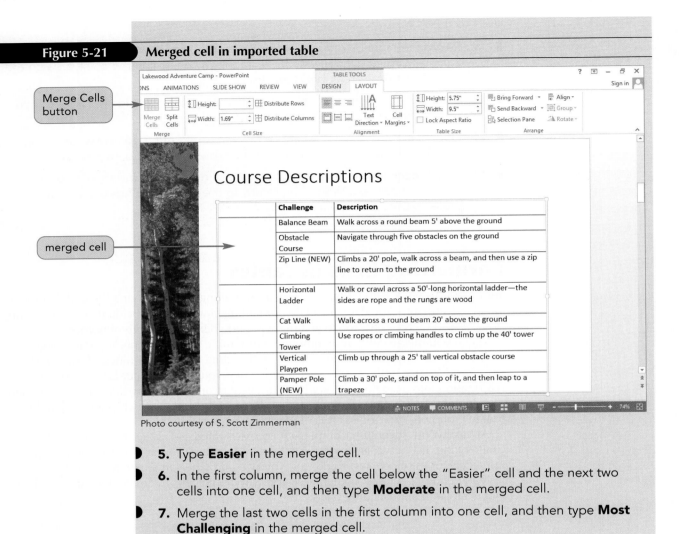

Photo courtesy of S. Scott Zimmerman

▶ **5.** Type **Easier** in the merged cell.

▶ **6.** In the first column, merge the cell below the "Easier" cell and the next two cells into one cell, and then type **Moderate** in the merged cell.

▶ **7.** Merge the last two cells in the first column into one cell, and then type **Most Challenging** in the merged cell.

You can rotate text in a cell to read from the top to the bottom or from the bottom to the top. You will rotate the labels in the merged cells so that they read from bottom to top.

To rotate the text in cells:

▶ **1.** Drag to select the three merged cells in the first column.

▶ **2.** In the Alignment group, click the **Text Direction** button, and then click **Rotate all text 270°**. See Figure 5-22.

Figure 5-22 **Rotated text in merged cells**

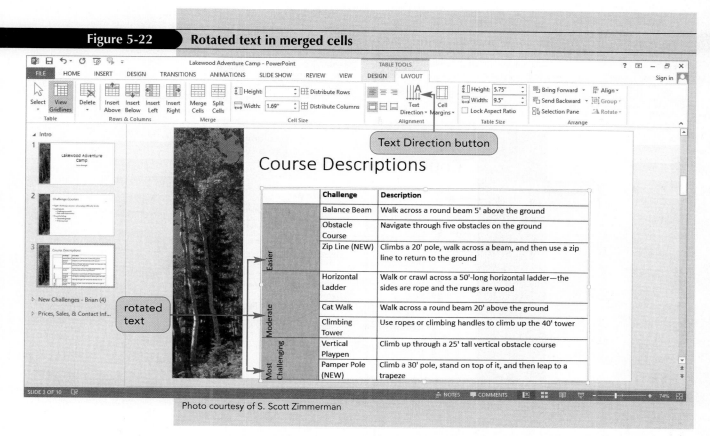

Photo courtesy of S. Scott Zimmerman

To finish formatting the table, you will format the text in the first column so it is bold, and then you'll center-align it. Then you'll adjust the width of the columns and the heights of the rows so the table elements are properly proportioned.

To format and align the text in the merged cells and resize columns and rows:

1. Make sure the three merged cells are still selected, click the **HOME** tab, and then in the Font group, click the **Bold** button **B**.

2. Click the **TABLE TOOLS LAYOUT** tab.

3. In the Alignment group, click the **Center** button ☰, and then click the **Center Vertically** button ☰. The text in the first column is now bold and centered.

4. Resize the first column so it is 1 inch wide, and then resize the third column so it is 5 inches wide. Some of the rows are too tall for their contents.

5. Click in the cell to the right of the Horizontal Ladder cell.

6. On the TABLE TOOLS LAYOUT tab, in the Cell Size group, click in the **Height** box, change the measurement to **0.64"**, and then press the **Enter** key.

7. Click in each cell in the Description column that contains two lines of text, and then, if necessary, change the height of that row to **0.64"**.

8. Drag the table by its border to position it so its left edge is aligned with the left edge of the title text box, and so it is vertically centered in the space below the title. See Figure 5-23.

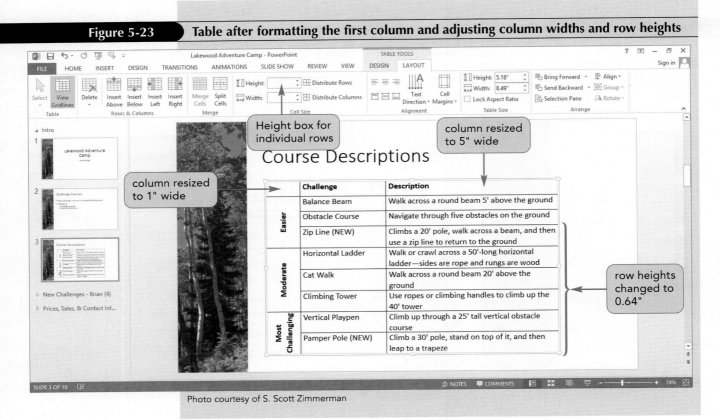

Figure 5-23   **Table after formatting the first column and adjusting column widths and row heights**

Photo courtesy of S. Scott Zimmerman

You can change the borders for individual cells or a group of cells. To further distinguish the courses that meet the different challenge levels, you will make the borders between the sections thicker.

To change the weight of cell borders:

▶ 1. Click the **TABLE TOOLS DESIGN** tab.

▶ 2. In the Draw Borders group, click the **Pen Weight** button [1 pt ———— ▾], and then click **3 pt**. The pointer changes to ⫽ and the Draw Table button in the Draw Borders group becomes selected.

▶ 3. In the table, drag ⫽ all the way across the table along the border below the row containing the Easier cell while holding down the mouse button, and then drag all the way across the table along the border below the row containing the Moderate cell. See Figure 5-24.

Figure 5-24   **Final formatted table on Slide 3**

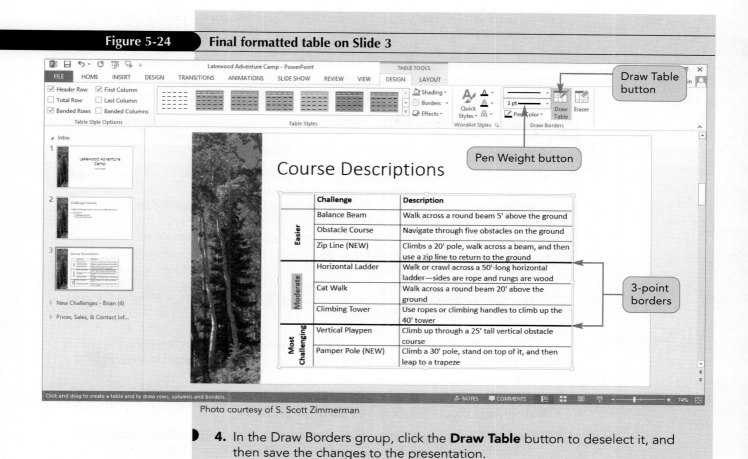

Photo courtesy of S. Scott Zimmerman

▶ **4.** In the Draw Borders group, click the **Draw Table** button to deselect it, and then save the changes to the presentation.

Inserting Excel Data and Objects

You can also insert objects from Excel workbooks and add them to slides. In addition to pasting an object from the Clipboard, you can embed or link it. Pasting, embedding, and linking all involve inserting an object from a source file into a destination file. The difference between them lies in where their respective objects are stored and which program's commands are used to modify the object. Refer to the Session 5.2 Visual Overview for more information about the differences between pasting, embedding, and linking.

If you do not need to access the source program commands from within the destination file, pasting an object is probably a better choice than embedding it. This is because when you embed an object, you insert a link to the source program as well as the object itself, and this increases the file size.

Embedding an Excel Worksheet

TIP

To create an embedded Excel worksheet from within PowerPoint, click the INSERT tab, in the Tables group, click the Table button, and then click Excel Spreadsheet.

You can insert a worksheet created in Excel in a slide. When you do, you can choose to paste it as a table or a picture, embed it, or link it. To paste a worksheet as a table or a picture or to embed it, you use one of the buttons on the Paste menu. If you want to link the data in the worksheet, you need to click the Paste Special command on the Paste menu, and then click the Paste link option button in the Paste Special dialog box that opens.

Laura wants to include pricing information in the Lakewood Adventure Camp presentation. She has an Excel workbook she created that contains pricing and sales data for the company. The workbook contains a worksheet named Total Sales, which lists the number of tickets sold during the past three years and the number of tickets she expects to sell this year. This worksheet also contains the total sales for those years. She calculated her estimate of the total sales for the coming year by multiplying her ticket sale estimates by the prices she plans to charge this year. She also included the new challenges that she wants to add to her course in her estimates. Laura has asked you to embed the pricing information from the workbook into Slide 8 of the presentation.

REFERENCE

Embedding an Excel Worksheet in a Slide

- Start Excel (the source program), open the file containing the worksheet you want to embed, and then select that worksheet's sheet tab.
- In the Excel worksheet, click and drag to select the cells you want to copy, and then on the HOME tab, in the Clipboard group, click the Copy button.
- Switch to the PowerPoint presentation, and then display the slide in which you want to embed the copied cells in the Slide pane.
- On the HOME tab, in the Clipboard group, click the Paste button arrow, and then click the Embed button, or click the Paste button arrow, click Paste Special, make sure Microsoft Excel Worksheet Object is selected in the As list, and then click the OK button.

First, you will open the Excel workbook, and then copy the cells containing the pricing information to be embedded on Slide 8 of Lakewood Adventure Camp presentation.

To embed Excel worksheet data in Slide 8:

1. In the Slides tab, collapse the Intro and New Challenges - Brian sections, if necessary, and then expand the Prices, Sales, & Contact Info section.

2. Display **Slide 8** ("Prices") in the Slide pane, if necessary, and then change the layout to **Title Only**.

3. Start Microsoft Excel 2013, open the file **Sales**, located in the PowerPoint5 ▸ Tutorial folder included with your Data Files, and then save the workbook as **Sales Updated** to the location where you are storing your files. The workbook opens with the Prices worksheet selected. See Figure 5-25.

Figure 5-25   **Prices worksheet in Sales Updated workbook**

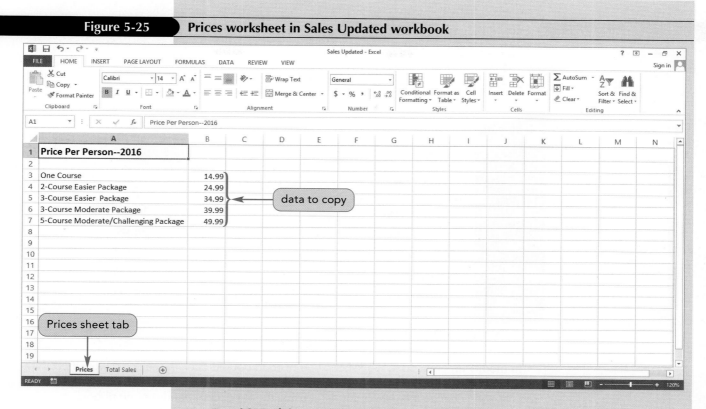

Trouble? If the worksheet is not at 120% zoom, use the Zoom slider on the right end of the status bar to change the zoom to 120%.

4. Click cell **A3**, and then drag to select cells **A3** through **B7**.

5. On the HOME tab, in the Clipboard group, click the **Copy** button.

6. On the taskbar, click the **PowerPoint** button 📭 to display the Lakewood Adventure Camp presentation with Slide 8 in the Slide pane.

7. On the HOME tab, in the Clipboard group, click the **Paste button arrow**, and then click the **Embed** button 🗐. The worksheet is embedded in the slide.

8. Drag the corner sizing handles to resize the worksheet object so it is approximately 3.2 inches high and 10 inches wide, and then drag the table by its outside border to position it in the center of the slide. See Figure 5-26.

Figure 5-26   **Excel data embedded on Slide 8**

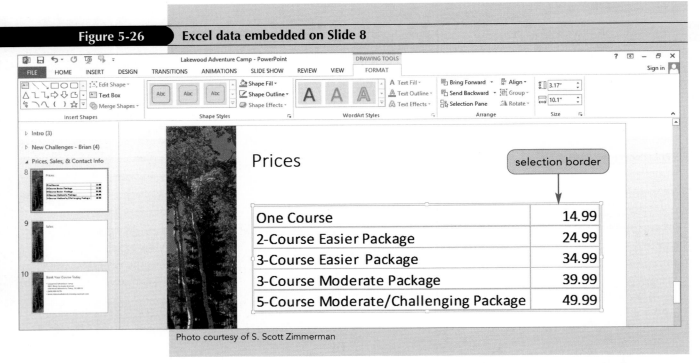

Photo courtesy of S. Scott Zimmerman

To modify an embedded worksheet, you need to double-click the selected worksheet object to display the Excel tabs and commands on the ribbon in the PowerPoint window. You can then change the data or format it using the Excel commands on the ribbon.

Laura wants the prices in the second column formatted with dollar signs. She also thinks the worksheet would be easier to read if the cells had borders.

To modify the embedded worksheet:

1. On **Slide 8** ("Prices"), double-click the selected worksheet object. The ribbon changes to contain the Excel tabs and commands. See Figure 5-27.

| Figure 5-27 | Embedded Excel object with Excel active |

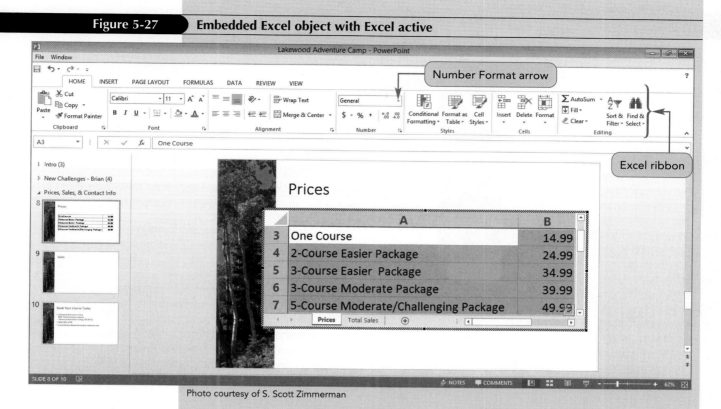

Photo courtesy of S. Scott Zimmerman

2. Click cell **B3**, and then drag down to select cells **B3** through **B7**.

3. On the HOME tab, in the Number group, click the **Number Format** arrow General ▾ , and then click **Currency**. The selected numbers are formatted as currency.

4. Select cells **A3** through **B7**.

5. In the Font group, click the **Border button arrow** ⊞ ▾ , and then click **All Borders**.

6. Click a blank area of the slide. The ribbon changes back to the PowerPoint ribbon, but the embedded object is still selected.

   Trouble? If the presentation window minimized and the Excel window is the active window, click the PowerPoint button on the taskbar. You might need to click it twice.

7. Click a blank area of the slide again to deselect the object. See Figure 5-28.

Figure 5-28   **Formatted data in embedded Excel workbook**

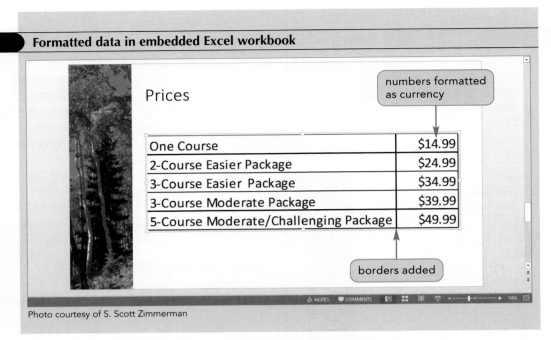

Photo courtesy of S. Scott Zimmerman

Keep in mind that the changes you made to the embedded object did not change the original worksheet in the Excel workbook because embedding maintains a connection only with the program that was used to create the object, not with the original object itself.

Linking an Excel Chart

If you need to include an Excel object in your presentation that is based on data that might change, you can link the object instead of embed it. For example, you might need to include data from an Excel worksheet on a slide, but you know that the final data won't be available for a while or that the data will change over time. In this case, you should link the object so that when the source file is updated, the linked object in the destination file is updated and reflects the changes made to the source file.

INSIGHT

Understanding Linking Options

There are several ways to link Excel data and charts to a slide. The options for linking change depending on whether the Excel data in the worksheet is selected or an Excel chart is selected. The options for formatting the linked data or chart change depending on exactly what was linked and how it was linked.

- If you copy an Excel chart, you can link only the data that was used to create the chart by clicking the Paste button arrow, and then clicking one of the Paste Link buttons. If you link only the data, you can change the data in the source Excel worksheet, and the linked chart in the destination presentation will change to reflect the data changes. However, any formatting changes you make to the chart, including changing the chart type, occurs only in the file in which you make the change. If you break the link to the source file, the chart remains a chart object on the slide that you can format, but you cannot modify the data used to create it.
- If you copy an Excel chart, you can also link the chart object itself by clicking the Paste button arrow, clicking Paste Special to open the Paste Special dialog box, clicking the Paste link option button, and then clicking the OK button. If you use this method, you can change not only the data but also the formatting of the chart in the Excel worksheet source file, and those changes will be reflected in the chart on the slide in the destination file. However, if you break the link, the chart will become a picture object on the slide, and you will not have access to the CHART TOOLS contextual tabs in PowerPoint.
- If you copy data from an Excel worksheet, you must use the Paste Special dialog box to link the data; there are no buttons on the Paste menu that allow you to link worksheet data. As with a chart that you linked using the Paste Special dialog box, if you break the link, the copied data becomes a picture on the slide.

REFERENCE

Linking an Excel Chart to a Slide

- Start Excel (the source program), open the file containing the chart to be linked, and then select the sheet tab of the worksheet that contains the chart.
- Point to the chart to display the ScreenTip "Chart Area," and then click the chart to select it.
- On the HOME tab, in the Clipboard group, click the Copy button.
- Switch to the PowerPoint presentation, and then display the slide to which you want to link the chart in the Slide pane.
- On the HOME tab, in the Clipboard group, click the Paste button, and then click the Use Destination Theme & Link Data button or click the Keep Source Formatting & Link Data button; or click the Paste button arrow, click Paste Special, click the Paste link option button, and then click the OK button.

On the Total Sales worksheet in the Excel workbook, Laura listed the total ticket sales for the past three years as well as the total sales dollars brought in. She then added a column listing the number of tickets she anticipates selling this coming year assuming she adds the two new challenges. She then created a column chart showing the sales growth over the past three years and the anticipated growth this year. Laura wants you to include the chart in the presentation. However, she wants to send the data to her staff to see if they agree with her estimates for the coming year's ticket sales. Therefore, she wants you to link the chart so that it will be updated in the presentation if she changes the data in the worksheet.

To insert a chart linked to the Excel worksheet:

▶ **1.** Display **Slide 9** ("Sales") in the Slide pane, and then change the layout to **Title Only**.

▶ **2.** On the taskbar, click the **Excel** button ⬛, and then at the bottom of the Excel window, click the **Total Sales** sheet tab. See Figure 5-29.

Figure 5-29 Total Sales worksheet in Sales Updated workbook

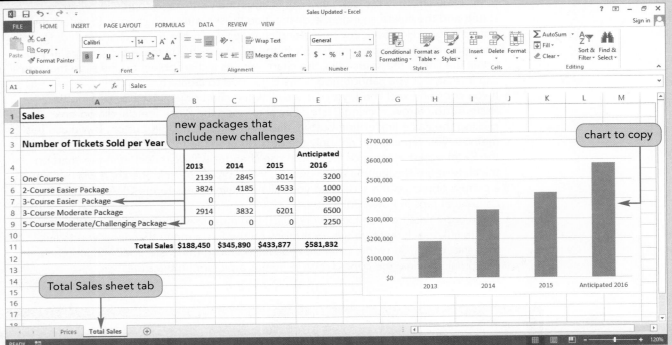

▶ **3.** Point to the chart so that the ScreenTip "Chart Area" appears, and then click to select the chart.

Trouble? If the ScreenTip displays something other than "Chart Area," move the pointer closer to the top or bottom edge of the chart.

▶ **4.** On the HOME tab, in the Clipboard group, click the **Copy** button.

▶ **5.** On the taskbar, click the **PowerPoint** button ⬛. The Lakewood Adventure Camp presentation appears with Slide 9 displayed in the Slide pane.

▶ **6.** In the Clipboard group, click the **Paste button arrow**, and then click the **Use Destination Theme & Link Data** button ⬛. The chart is linked to Slide 9.

▶ **7.** Resize the chart so it is 5.5 inches high and 9 inches wide, and then drag the entire chart to approximately center it in the blank area of the slide.

Laura's staff believes that, based on comments from customers over the past few years, she over-estimated the number of tickets that will be sold for the 2-Course Easier Package and under-estimated the number of tickets that will be sold for the 3-Course Easier Package. Laura has new estimates and asks you to make the changes in the Excel work-sheet, and then make sure the changes are reflected in the PowerPoint presentation.

To modify the data for the linked chart:

▶ **1.** On the ribbon, click the **CHART TOOLS DESIGN** tab.

▶ **2.** In the Data group, click the **Edit Data** button. The Total Sales worksheet in the Sales Updated workbook becomes active.

▶ **3.** Click cell **E6**, type **800**, and then press the **Enter** key.

▶ **4.** Click cell **E7**, type **4500**, and then press the **Enter** key. The chart changes to reflect the new total anticipated sales in 2016 of $597,828.

▶ **5.** On the Quick Access Toolbar, click the **Save** button 🖫.

▶ **6.** Switch to the Lakewood Adventure Camp presentation and notice that the chart has been updated on the slide as well.

Trouble? If the title still appears on the chart, right-click the chart, and then on the shortcut menu, click Update Link.

▶ **7.** Save the changes to the presentation.

TIP

You can also switch to the linked source file by clicking its program button on the taskbar or by opening it if it is closed.

You have now linked and edited an Excel chart in a PowerPoint presentation. Any additional changes made to the workbook will be reflected in the linked object in the PowerPoint slide.

PROSKILLS

Decision Making: Comparing Paste, Embed, and Linking Options

Each method of including objects from another file has advantages and disadvantages. The advantage of pasting or embedding an object instead of linking it is that the source file and the destination file can be stored separately. You can make changes to the object in the destination file, and the source file will be unaffected. The disadvantage of pasting or embedding an object is that you do not have access to the source program from within the destination file to modify the object. The disadvantage of embedding an object is that the destination file size is somewhat larger than it would be if the object were simply imported as a picture or text or linked.

The advantage of linking an object instead of embedding it is that the object remains identical in the source and destination files, and the destination file size does not increase as much as if the object were embedded. The disadvantage is that the source and destination files must be stored together. When you need to copy information from one program to another, consider which option is the best choice for your needs.

Formatting Chart Elements

As you know from your earlier work with creating PowerPoint charts, you can add or remove chart elements, reposition them, and change from one chart style to another, and even change chart type. You can also modify and format the individual elements of a chart. For example, you can change the scale of an axis or change the color of a data series or data points.

Laura thinks that a line chart would better illustrate the increase in sales each year, so she asks you to change the chart type to a line chart. She also wants the vertical axis scale to start at $100,000 instead of starting at $0. You will modify the chart in the source file. First you need to change the chart to a line chart.

To change the chart type:

▶ **1.** On **Slide 9** ("Sales"), click the chart to select it, if necessary.

▶ **2.** On the ribbon, click the **CHART TOOLS DESIGN** tab, and then in the Type group, click the **Change Chart Type** button. The Change Chart Type dialog box opens.

▶ **3.** In the navigation pane on the left, click **Line**.

▶ **4.** In the horizontal list of chart styles at the top of the dialog box, click the **Line with Markers** style, and then click the **OK** button. The chart is changed to a line chart with dots indicating each data point.

Now you need to change the vertical axis scale. The bottom number on the scale is the minimum bound of the axis and the top number is the maximum bound. You need to adjust the minimum bound to $100,000.

To change the vertical axis scale:

▶ **1.** In the chart, right-click any value on the vertical axis, and then on the shortcut menu, click **Format Axis**. The Format Axis task pane opens with the AXIS OPTIONS tab selected and the Axis Options button selected on the tab. The AXIS OPTIONS section is expanded. See Figure 5-30.

Figure 5-30	Format Axis pane for the vertical axis of a chart

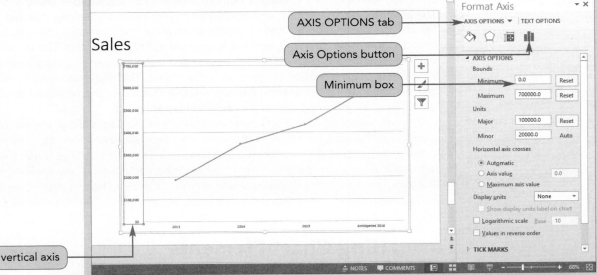

Trouble? If the AXIS OPTIONS section is not expanded, click AXIS OPTIONS.

First you need to change the maximum value on the vertical axis.

▶ **2.** In the Format Axis task pane, in the Bounds section, click in the **Minimum** box, edit the value in the box so it is **100000.0**, and then press the **Enter** key. The line chart changes to reflect this change.

▶ **3.** In the Format Axis task pane, click the **Close** button ⊠.

Finally, you will increase the font size of the labels on both the vertical axis and the horizontal.

To change the font size of the axis labels:

▶ **1.** With the vertical axis selected, click the **HOME** tab.

▶ **2.** In the Font group, click the **Font Size button arrow**, and then click **14**.

▶ **3.** On the horizontal axis, click any value, and then change the font size of the selected axis to **14** points. See Figure 5-31.

| Figure 5-31 | Updated linked chart on Slide 9 |

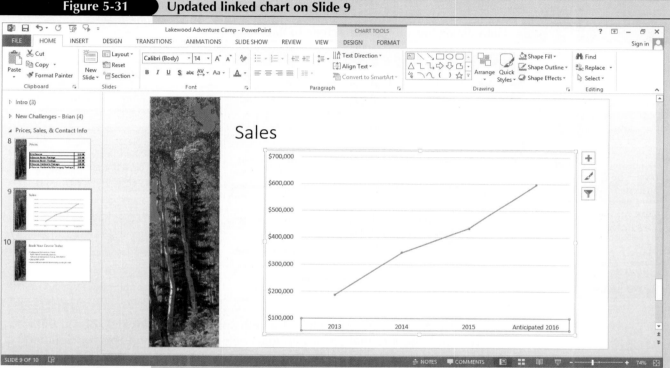

Photo courtesy of S. Scott Zimmerman

Trouble? If the changes were not applied to the chart on the slide, right-click the chart, and then on the shortcut menu, click Update Link.

▶ **4.** Save the changes to the presentation. Because only the data was linked from the source Excel workbook, the formatting changes you made—both changing the chart type and modifying the vertical axis—were not applied to the original chart in the source file. You'll verify this now.

▶ **5.** Switch to the Excel workbook. Notice that the chart is still a column chart and the vertical axis did not change.

▶ **6.** Save the changes to the workbook, and then close the workbook and exit Excel. The Lakewood Adventure Camp presentation is active.

Breaking Links

When you link an object to a slide, you need to keep the source file in its original location so that the link can be maintained. If you move the source file, you need to identify the new location from within the PowerPoint file. You do this by using the Links dialog box, which you can open from the Info screen in Backstage view. You can also change how the object is updated—manually or automatically—from the Links dialog box.

If you plan to send the presentation to others, you should break all links so that when they open the file, they don't see a message asking them if they want to update the links. You will break the link to the Excel data that was used to create the chart on Slide 9.

To examine the Links dialog box:

▶ **1.** On the ribbon, click the **FILE** tab. The Info screen appears in Backstage view.

▶ **2.** In the Related Documents section, click **Edit Links to Files**. The Links dialog box opens. See Figure 5-32.

| Figure 5-32 | Links dialog box on the Info screen in Backstage view |

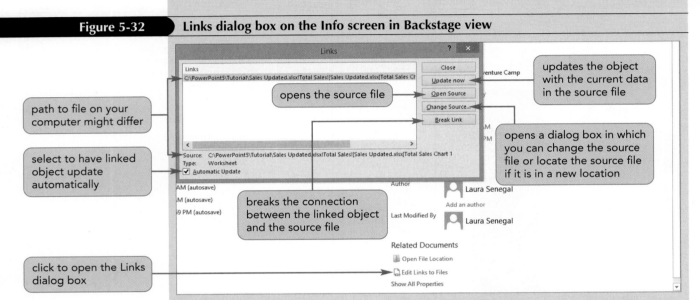

The file name of the object and the path appear in the Links list. Because it is selected, this information also appears below the Links box next to "Source."

▶ **3.** In the Links list, make sure the linked object is selected, and then click the **Break Link** button. The selected item in the list changes and is listed as NULL. Now, if you change the data on which the chart is based in the Excel worksheet, the chart on Slide 9 will not reflect that change.

▶ **4.** In the Links dialog box, click the **Close** button.

▶ **5.** At the top of the navigation bar, click the **Back** button ⬅ to close Backstage view.

Annotating Slides During a Slide Show

During a slide show, you can annotate—mark—the slides to emphasize a point. To do this, you change the pointer to a pen, which allows you to draw lines on a slide during a slide show, or to a highlighter, which allows you to highlight something on a slide during a slide show. For example, you might use the Pen to underline a word or phrase that you want to emphasize or to circle a graphic that you want to point out. You can change the ink color of the Pen or Highlighter you select. You can also select the Eraser tool to remove Pen or Highlighter lines that you draw.

After you go through a presentation and mark it, you have the choice of keeping the markings as graphic objects in the presentation or discarding them.

To use the Pen to mark slides during the slide show:

1. With **Slide 9** ("Sales") displayed in the Slide pane, on the status bar, click the **Slide Show** button 🖵. Slide 9 appears in Slide Show view.

2. Right-click anywhere on the screen, point to **Pointer Options** on the shortcut menu, and then click **Pen**. The mouse pointer becomes a small, red dot.

3. Click and drag to draw a circle around the data point that indicates the antici-pated sales in 2016. Next, you want to highlight the label on the horizontal axis for this data point.

4. Right-click anywhere on the screen, point to **Pointer Options**, and then click **Highlighter**. The pointer changes to a small, yellow rectangle.

5. Click and drag across the label **Anticipated 2016** to highlight it in yellow. When the Pen or the Highlighter is active, you cannot advance the slide show by clicking the mouse button.

6. Press the **spacebar** to move to Slide 10. There is nothing on this slide that you want to annotate, so you'll change the pointer back to its normal shape.

7. Right-click anywhere on the slide, point to **Pointer Options**, and then click the **Highlighter** command. The pointer changes to its normal shape.

8. Advance the slide show to display the black slide that indicates the end of the slide show, and then advance once more. A dialog box opens asking if you want to keep your ink annotations.

9. Click the **Keep** button. Slide 9 ("Sales") appears in Normal view displaying the annotations you made during the slide show. See Figure 5-33.

TIP

If you do not want a slide to be displayed during a slide show, in Normal or Slide Sorter view, select the slide thumbnail, and then on the SLIDE SHOW tab, in the Set Up group, click the Hide Slide button.

Figure 5-33	Annotated slide in Normal view

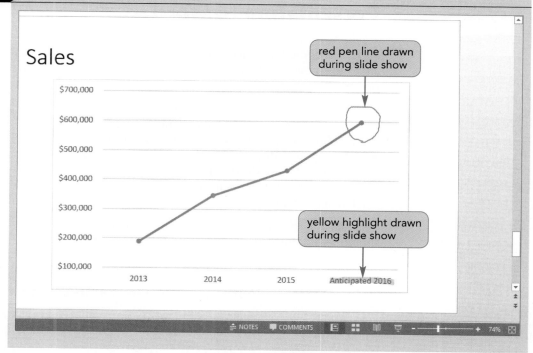

The marks you drew in Slide Show view can be manipulated or deleted just like any object on a slide. When you select an annotation in the Slide pane, the DRAWING TOOLS FORMAT and INK TOOLS PENS tabs appear on the ribbon. You can change the color and width of annotations, as well as move them through layers, align and rotate them, and change their overall size. The tools on the INK TOOLS PEN tab are available only for touchscreens and screens that allow the use of a stylus to write.

You need to delete the highlight mark on Slide 9.

To delete the annotation mark on Slide 9:

1. On **Slide 9** ("Sales"), click the yellow highlight line you drew during the slide show. The highlight line is selected. On the ribbon, in addition to the DRAWING TOOLS FORMAT tab, the INK TOOLS PENS tab appears as well.

2. Press the **Delete** key. The highlight line is deleted.

3. Save the changes to the presentation.

TIP

To erase an annotation in Slide Show view, right-click anywhere on the slide, point to Pointer Options, click Eraser, and then click the annotation.

INSIGHT

Using the Laser Pointer During a Slide Show

You can change the pointer into a red dot that looks like a laser pointer during a slide show so that you can point to objects or text on a slide during your presentation. To do this, right-click a slide during the slide show, point to Pointer Options on the shortcut menu, and then click Laser Pointer. As when you change the pointer to a Pen or Highlighter, you cannot click the mouse button to advance the slide show while the pointer is the Laser Pointer.

Creating Handouts by Exporting a Presentation to Word

You know how to print a presentation using the Handouts setting so that one or more slides are printed per page. You can also use Word to create handouts by exporting the slides to a new Word document. When you do this, you can choose from the following options:

• **Notes next to slides**—lists the speaker notes next to each slide; the number of slides per page depends on how many lines of speaker notes are on each slide
• **Blank lines next to slides**—adds blank lines next to each slide, three slides per page
• **Notes below slides**—lists the speaker notes below each slide; one slide per page
• **Blank lines below slides**—adds blank lines below each slide, one slide per page
• **Outline only**—lists the outline of the presentation as a bulleted list with first-level bulleted items at the same level as slide titles and second-level bulleted items indented

Laura wants you to export the presentation to Word to create handouts displaying thumbnails of the slides with lines for notes to the right of each thumbnail.

To create handouts by exporting the presentation to Word:

1. On the ribbon, click the **FILE** tab to open Backstage view, and then in the navigation bar, click **Export**. The Export screen appears.

2. Click **Create Handouts**. The screen changes to display a description of creating handouts in Microsoft Word and a button for doing this. See Figure 5-34.

Figure 5-34   Export screen in Backstage view with Create Handouts selected

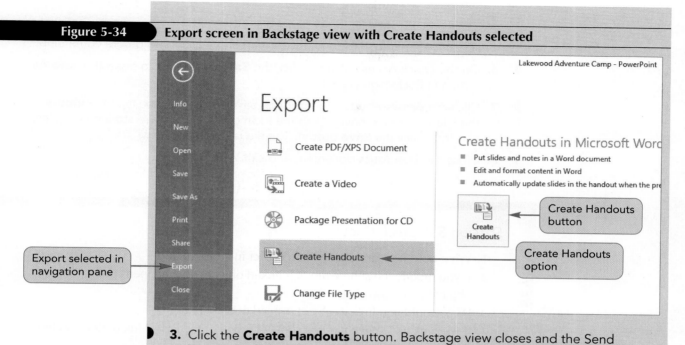

3. Click the **Create Handouts** button. Backstage view closes and the Send To Microsoft Word dialog box opens. You can choose from five options for creating handouts, and you can choose to link the slides instead of simply exporting them. If you choose to link the handouts, when you modify the presentation, the change will be reflected in the handouts. See Figure 5-35.

Figure 5-35   Send to Microsoft Word dialog box

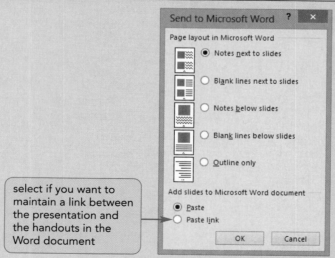

select if you want to maintain a link between the presentation and the handouts in the Word document

TIP

To export only the presentation outline to a document, click the Outline only option button in the Send to Microsoft Word dialog box.

4. Click the **Blank lines next to slides** option button, and then click the **OK** button. The dialog box closes and a new Microsoft Word document is created. On the taskbar, a Microsoft Word button appears and starts blinking, indicating the document is being created. After the document is created, the button stops blinking. The time it takes for this to happen depends on the speed of your computer.

5. On the taskbar, click the **Document1 - Word** program button. The handouts appear in a Word document with thumbnails of three slides on each page and blank lines next to each slide thumbnail.

Trouble? If the pointer blinks and changes to a blue circle, the document is still being created. Wait until the pointer stops changing before continuing.

6. On the Quick Access Toolbar, click the **Save** button 🔲 to open the Save As screen in Backstage view.

7. Click the **Browse** button to open the Save As dialog box, type **Handouts** in the File name box, navigate to the location where you are storing your files, and then click the **Save** button. The file is saved.

8. Close the **Handouts** document and exit Word.

REVIEW

Session 5.2 Quick Check

1. What does it mean to embed an object in a presentation?
2. If you modify the source file of a linked object, what happens to the linked object in the PowerPoint slide?
3. Why would you link an object instead of embed it?
4. If you link an Excel chart to a slide with one of the Paste Link buttons on the Paste menu, is the chart formatting linked as well?
5. How is an annotation that you created during a slide treated in Normal view?
6. Describe how to create handouts in Word.

ASSESS

SAM Projects

Put your skills into practice with SAM Projects! SAM Projects for this tutorial can be found online. If you have a SAM account, go to www.cengage.com/sam2013 to download the most recent Project Instructions and Start Files.

PRACTICE

Review Assignments

Data Files needed for the Review Assignments: Equipment Memo.docx, Map.jpg, Safety.pptx, Training Log.xlsx, Training Outline.docx, Training.pptx

All new staff members of Lakewood Adventure Camp need to be trained on each of the challenges and undergo general safety training. Several staff members have already completed some of the training. Laura scheduled an orientation meeting for the new staff members and asked you to help her create a presentation for this meeting. She created an outline of the presentation in a Word document, and Mike Garcia, a senior staff member in charge of training, created a few slides that he thinks should be included in the presentation. Complete the following steps:

1. Open the presentation **Training**, located in the PowerPoint5 ▸ Review folder, change the name in the subtitle to your name, and then save it as **Staff Training** in the location where you are storing your files.
2. After Slide 2, create slides from the outline in the Word file **Training Outline**, located in the PowerPoint5 ▸ Review folder. Reset the slides you create.
3. Insert Slide 2 ("Safety—Most Impor…"), Slide 3 ("Staff Course Comp…"), and Slide 4 ("Percentage of Cou…") from the **Safety** presentation, located in the PowerPoint5 ▸ Review folder. Insert these slides after Slide 5 so they become Slides 6, 7, and 8 in the Staff Training presentation.
4. In Outline view, reorder the presentation by moving Slide 4 ("Uniform and Supplies") so it becomes Slide 2, and then demote Slide 5 ("During Activity") and its bulleted items so that "During Activity" becomes a second first-level bullet on Slide 4 ("Running a Course").
5. Create four sections in the presentation. The first should include Slides 1 and 2 and be named **Intro**; the second should include Slides 3 and 4 and be named **Courses**; the third should include Slides 5 through 7 and be named **Safety**; and the fourth should include Slide 8 and be named **Conclusion**.
6. On Slide 3 (the slide with the bus illustration and the text boxes), insert the picture **Map**, located in the PowerPoint5 ▸ Review folder, and then move it behind all of the other objects on the slide.
7. In the Selection pane, change the name of the map object to **Map**, and change the name of the other picture object to **Bus**.
8. On Slide 3, animate the text boxes with the entrance animation Wipe and the From Left effect option.
9. Apply the Custom Path motion path animation to the bus illustration, click just below the bus to indicate the start point, and without releasing the mouse button, drag counter-clockwise around the circular road; when you complete the circle, double-click to indicate the ending point.
10. Change the Smooth end setting of the motion path applied to the bus to 0, and hide the bus after the animation finishes. Change the duration of the animation to five seconds.
11. Reorder the animations so the bus animation occurs first.
12. Change the order of the text box animations so the Catwalk text box animates after the bus animation, and then the rest of the text boxes animate in a counter-clockwise direction.
13. Change the start timing of the text box animations to After Previous.

14. Open the Excel workbook **Training Log**, located in the PowerPoint5 ▸ Review folder, and then save it as **Training Log Updated** in the location specified by your instructor.

15. On Slide 6 ("Staff Course Completion") in the Staff Training presentation, embed cells A3 through J14 from the Training worksheet in the Training Log workbook. Resize the embedded object so it is approximately 4 inches high and 10 inches wide.

16. On Slide 6, add borders to cells A3 through J14.

17. On Slide 7 ("Percentage of Courses Completed"), link the chart on the Training worksheet in the Training Log workbook using the destination theme. Resize the linked chart so it is approximately 5 inches high and 8.5 inches wide, and then center the chart in the blank area of the slide.

18. Update the data on which the chart is based by typing **X** in cells B14, C14, F14, and G14 (indicating that Anthony Turner has completed the Safety, Balance Beam, Horizontal Ladder, and Catwalk training). Note that there are formulas in cells B17 and B18 that count the total number of cells in the table that contain Xs (the total number of courses completed) and the number of cells in the table that are empty (the total number of courses remaining). The chart is based on these numbers. Save the changes to the workbook, and then close the workbook and exit Excel.

19. On Slide 7, change the chart type to a pie chart. On the CHART TOOLS DESIGN tab, in the Chart Layouts group, click the Add Chart Element button, point to Legend, and then click Right. Click the legend, and then on the HOME tab, change the font size to 14 points.

20. On Slide 2 ("Uniform and Supplies"), change the layout to Title Only. Copy the table in the Word file **Equipment Memo**, located in the PowerPoint5 ▸ Review folder, to Slide 2 using the destination styles. Close the Equipment Memo document and exit Word.

21. Change the font size of the text in the table to 20 points, and then change the table style to the No Style, Table Grid style. Drag the table back onto the slide.

22. Insert a new first column. Resize the new first column so it is 0.8 inches wide, and then resize the third column so that it is 7 inches wide.

23. In the new first column, merge the second, third, and fourth cells, and then merge the last three cells. In the top merged cell, type **Must Have**, and in the bottom merged cell type **Nice to Have**.

24. Change the font of the text in the first column to Calibri (Body), and then rotate the text in the first column so that it reads from bottom to top.

25. Center the text in the first column so it is centered both horizontally and vertically.

26. Change the border between the "Must Have" and "Nice to Have" rows to a 3-point border.

27. Display Slide 5 ("Safety—Most Important Responsibility") in Slide Show view, circle the word "Safety" in the slide title using the Pen, and then end the slide show, keeping the annotation.

28. Create handouts in a Word document showing the slide thumbnails with blank lines next to them. Save the document as **Training Handouts** in the location where you are storing your files. Close the Training Handouts file and exit Word.

29. Save the changes to the Staff Training presentation.

Case Problem 1

Data Files needed for this Case Problem: Map.jpg, Photos.pptx, Rose Outline.docx, Rose.pptx, Varieties.xlsx

International Rose Importers   Karam Mowad is the Director of Public Relations for International Rose Importers, which is a brokerage house working with rose growers in Fiji and rose sellers in the United States. He wants to create a presentation to help him promote roses and explain his company's business to wholesalers, retailers, and other groups. He has asked you to help him. Complete the following steps:

1. Open the presentation **Rose**, located in the PowerPoint5 ▸ Case1 folder included with your data files, replace the name in the subtitle with your name, and then save the file as **Rose Importers** in the location where you are storing your files.

2. Create additional slides after Slide 2 from the outline contained in Word file **Rose Outline**, located in the PowerPoint5 ▸ Case1 folder. Reset the newly created slides.

3. Insert the four slides from the presentation **Photos**, located in the PowerPoint5 ▸ Case1 folder, in order after Slide 2 ("We Import Roses from Fiji to Boston") so they become the new Slides 3, 4, 5, and 6.

4. On Slide 2 ("We Import Roses from Fiji to Boston"), insert the picture **Map**, located in the PowerPoint5 ▸ Case1 folder.

5. Reorder the objects on Slide 2 in the layers so that the plane is on top of the map. Position the plane below the label "Fiji" on the map.

6. Apply the Lines motion path animation to the plane, and change the effect option to Right. Drag the ending point of the animation to the black dot indicating Boston on the map. Set it to hide after the animation finishes, and change its duration to 3 seconds.

7. Apply the entrance animation Appear to the plane, and then reorder the animations so the Appear animation occurs first.

8. Display Slide 6. Karam wants the photos on Slide 6 to appear in an attractive, interesting way on the slide as he discusses some of the varieties of roses available. There are four objects on the slide. Picture 1, Picture 2, and Picture 3 already have the entrance animation Fade and the exit animation Fade applied to them, and Picture 4 has the entrance animation Split applied to it. Add the following animations to Picture 1, Picture 2, and Picture 3 as follows:

   • Add the Lines motion path animation to Picture 1, and then modify it so that the picture automatically moves in a straight line up to the upper-left corner after the previous animation (After Previous).

   • Add the Lines motion path animation to Picture 2, and then modify it so that the picture automatically moves in a straight line down to the lower-left corner after the previous animation (After Previous).

   • Add the Lines motion path animation to Picture 3 so that the picture automatically moves in a straight line to the right side of the slide after the previous animation (After Previous).

9. Reorder the animations so that the motion path animations applied to each picture occur immediately after the entrance animation for that picture.

10. Open the Excel file **Varieties**, located in the PowerPoint5 ▸ Case1 folder, and then save it as **Varieties Updated** in the location where you are saving your files. Copy cells A3 through B19. Switch to the Rose Imports presentation, and then change the layout of Slide 7 ("Current Varieties of Hybrid Tea Roses") to Title Only. Paste the copied data using the destination styles. (Do not embed the worksheet.)

11. On Slide 7, apply the Themed Style 1 – Accent 2 table style to the table with special formatting for the header row and first column, and use banded rows. Change the font size of the text in the table to 18 points, and then widen the columns as needed to fit the widest entry in each column. Position the table in the blank area of the slide below the title.

12. On Slide 8 ("Color Distribution Among Current Varieties"), change the slide layout to Title Only. Copy the pie chart from the Excel workbook **Varieties Updated**, and then link it to Slide 8 using the source file formatting. Edit the source file by typing **Apricot** in cell C18 and in cell C19 (remember to press the Enter key after typing in each cell). Save the changes to the workbook, and then close the workbook and exit Excel.

13. Resize the chart object so it is 5 inches high and approximately 8.3 inches wide. Save the changes to the presentation.

14. Create handouts in Word showing blank lines next to the slide thumbnails. Save this file as **Roses Handouts** in the location specified by your instructor. Close the Roses Handouts file and exit Word.

APPLY

Case Problem 2

Data Files needed for this Case Problem: Coaching Outline.docx, Coaching.pptx, PRRC Photos. pptx, Sample.xlsx

Personal Remote Running Coach   Sybil Burton was a cross-country runner in college and then, after graduation, took up marathoning. She won several local marathons and finished 47th in the women's division of the Boston Marathon. Recently, she teamed up with two other runners to create Personal Remote Running Coach (PRRC), a company that creates training programs to help runners achieve their race goals. The trainers coach English-speaking runners from all over the world using email, phone, Skype video calls, and FaceTime on iPads and iPhones. Sybil frequently visits running clubs, fitness centers, and marathon race exhibitions to sell PRRC services. She has asked you to help her create a PowerPoint presentation for her sales presentations. Complete the following steps:

1. Open the presentation **Coaching**, located in the PowerPoint5 ▸ Case2 folder included with your Data Files, replace the name in the subtitle with your name, and then save it as **Coaching Presentation** in the location where you are storing your files.

2. Create additional slides for the presentation from the outline contained in the Word document **Coaching Outline**, located in the PowerPoint5 ▸ Case2 folder, and then reset the newly created slides.

3. On Slide 2 ("Who We Are") resize the text box containing the unnumbered list so it is half its width.

4. Insert Slides 2, 3, and 4 from the presentation **PRRC Photos**, located in the PowerPoint5 ▸ Case2 folder, after Slide 5.

5. On Slide 6 ("Sybil, Michaela, and Andrew"), copy the photos and paste them on Slide 2 ("Who We Are"). Resize all three photos so they are 3.5 inches high. Position the middle photo about one-half inch below the top of the slide (overlapping the line under the title) and center it horizontally in the area to the right of the title and the list. Position the other two photos one on either side of the middle photo, about one-half inch above the colored bar at the bottom of the slide.

6. On Slide 8 ("GPS Watch Monitor"), copy the photo of the monitor, and then paste it on Slide 3 ("What We Do"). Position it so that its top and right edges are aligned with the top and right edges of the text box containing the list.

7. On Slide 7 ("Andrew's Boston Marathon Medal"), copy the photo of the medal, and then paste it on Slide 5 ("Contact Us"), centering it in the blank area to the right of the title and the list (it will overlap the line under the title).

8. Delete Slides 6, 7, and 8.

9. Create a new Slide 4 using the Title Only layout. Type **Sample Training Log** as the slide title.

10. Open the Excel workbook **Sample**, located in the PowerPoint5 ▸ Case2 folder, and then save it as **Sample Log** in the location specified by your instructor.

11. On the Training worksheet, copy cells A3 through G10, and then embed it on Slide 4.

12. Modify the embedded worksheet so that borders appear between each row. Resize the embedded object as large as possible, leaving about one-half inch of space on either side of the object.

13. Create a new Slide 5 using the Title Only layout. Type **Sample Distance Log** as the slide title.

14. On the Distance worksheet in the Sample Log workbook, copy cells A3 through E11, and then switch to Slide 5 in the presentation. Link the copied cells to the slide using the Paste Special dialog box. Resize the object so it is 3 inches high, and position it on the left side of the slide.

15. On the Distance worksheet in the Sample Log workbook, copy the chart, and then link it to Slide 5 in the presentation. Resize it so it is about 3.2inches high and 5.5 inches wide, and then position it on the right side of the slide.

16. Edit the worksheet so that the number of miles run on Saturday of Week 1 is **5**. Save the changes to the workbook, and then close the workbook and exit Excel.

17. Save the changes to the presentation.

TROUBLESHOOT

Case Problem 3

Data Files need for this Case Problem: Calendar.jpg, Layouts and Steps.pptx, Marketing Outline. docx, Marketing.pptx

Corners of Your Mind   Alek Latauska is Director of Marketing for Corners of Your Mind, a digital photo printing company. One of the products they sell is photo books. Alek will be attending several Home Expos over the next few months and he wants to create a presentation to showcase the photo books. He also wants to include slides that describe ideas for themes customers can use to build a photo book. He created an outline in Word listing some content for the presentation. He also has slides that he created for another presentation that show some of the page layouts the company offers. He wants you to use these items to create an interesting presentation that he will add more information to later. Complete the following steps:

1. Open the presentation **Marketing**, located in the PowerPoint5 ▸ Case3 folder included with your Data Files, replace the name in the subtitle with your name, and then save it as **Marketing Presentation** in the location where you are storing your files.

2. Create additional slides for the presentation using the outline contained in the Word document **Marketing Outline**, located in the PowerPoint5 ▸ Case3 folder.

⚙ **Troubleshoot** 3. Evaluate the problem with Slides 2 through 5 and fix it. Then increase the font size of the text in the lists on those slides so that the font size of the first-level items is 24 points. On Slide 2, change the layout to Two Content, move the "More sizes" bullet to the content placeholder on the right, and then increase the font size of the text on the slide so that the font size of the first-level items is 24 points.

4. Insert Slides 2 and 3 from the presentation **Layouts and Steps**, located in the PowerPoint5 ▸ Case3 folder, as Slides 2 and 3 in the Marketing Presentation. Then insert Slide 4 from the Layouts and Steps presentation as Slide 6 in the Marketing Presentation.

⚙ **Troubleshoot** 5. Examine the six layers containing objects and animations on Slide 2, and watch the slides in Slide Show view. On Slide 2, one layer of images is never visible. Fix this problem.

⚙ **Troubleshoot** 6. On Slide 3, adjust the animation applied to Layout 6 so that you do not need to advance the slide show twice to have this image disappear.

7. On Slide 6 ("Steps to Create an Interesting Personal History"), modify the Lines motion path animation that is applied to the two photos by turning off the Smooth end effect and hiding the photos after the animation finishes.

8. Reorder the animations so that the exit animation Disappear that is applied to the illustration of the boy occurs after the entrance animation applied to Keep Files.

⚙ **Troubleshoot** 9. The photos should look like they are moving into the folder, not on top of the folder. Fix this problem.

10. On Slide 6, insert the picture **Calendar**, located in the PowerPoint5 ▸ Case3 folder. Position the calendar on top of the illustration of the boy and on top of the folder and photos of the man and woman.

11. Position the pencil so it is above the left edge of the calendar, and then reorder it so it is in the layer above the calendar.

12. Apply the Custom Path motion path animation to the pencil illustration, click on the cursive letter "I," and without releasing the mouse button, trace the cursive writing on the calendar. Double-click when you are finished. Don't worry if you can't trace the writing exactly. Remove the Smooth start and end effects, and hide the pencil after the animation finishes. Change the duration of the animation to four seconds, and change its start timing to With Previous. View the slide in Slide Show view.

13. Draw a Parallelogram shape, 1.5 inches high and 2.4 inches wide, on top of the writing on the calendar. Rotate it so the gray center covers the writing, and then change the shape fill and outline to White, Background 1.

14. Apply the entrance animation Appear to the shape, and then change its start timing to With Previous. Add the exit animation Wipe to the shape, change the effect to From Top, change its duration to four seconds, and then change its start timing to With Previous.

15. Add the entrance animation Appear to the calendar, and then change the start timing to With Previous. Reorder this animation so it occurs before the exit animation Wipe that is applied to the parallelogram.

16. Create a section named **Layouts** that includes Slides 2 through 4. Create a section named **Themes** that includes Slides 5 and 6. Create a section named **Conclusion** that includes Slide 7. Leave the first section named "Default Section."

17. View Slide 7 ("Try It Now!") in Slide Show view, and then use the Pen to circle the title. End the slide show and keep the annotations.

18. Save the changes to the presentation.

Case Problem 4

Data Files needed for this Case Problem: Painting List.docx, Paintings.pptx

Cape Coral Art Club   Jim McLaughlin is a member of the Cape Coral Art Club in Cape Coral, Florida. In addition to organizing trips to museums and holding classes, members meet once a month and take turns giving presentations. Jim recently returned from a trip to Paris, France and he took photos of several paintings in the Louvre. He asked you to help him create a presentation for the art club. Complete the following steps:

1. Create a new presentation. Type **Musée du Louvre** as the presentation title, and type your name as the subtitle. Save the presentation as **Louvre Presentation** in the location where you are storing your files.

2. Apply the Retrospect theme, and then apply the fourth variant.

3. Insert all of the slides from the presentation **Paintings**, located in the PowerPoint5 ▸ Case4 folder included with your Data Files, into the presentation.

4. On Slide 2, reorder the animations so that the exit animation occurs first followed by the entrance animation. Modify the start timing of the entrance animation so it occurs automatically after the exit animation.

5. On Slide 3, preview the animation. Then modify the order of the animations on the bottom row only so that the right-most picture flies in first, followed by the picture that is second to the right, and so on.

6. On Slide 3, change the Smooth end setting for the Fly In animation on all the objects to 0.5 seconds.

7. Create a new Slide 4, apply the Title Only layout, and type **List of Paintings** as the title.

8. Copy the table from the Word file **Painting List**, located in the PowerPoint5 ▸ Case4 folder, and then paste it on Slide 4 using destination styles. Change the font size of all the text in the table to 24 points, and then widen each column to fit its widest entry. Close the Painting List file.

9. In the Artist column, three artists are listed in two cells each. Merge the cells that contain the same name, and then delete the second name in each merged cell. Make sure you delete the blank line below each name as well.

10. In the merged cells, center the text vertically.

⊕ **Explore** 11. Add a Circle bevel to each cell in the table. (*Hint*: Use the Effects button in the Table Styles group on the TABLE TOOLS DESIGN tab.)

12. On Slide 5, apply the Appear animation to both text boxes. Modify the start timing of both animations so they start after the previous action. If necessary, modify the order of the animations so that the title of the painting appears first, followed by the artist's name.

⊕ **Explore** 13. Modify the Appear animation applied to the title text box (which contains "Mona Lisa") so that the text appears one character at a time with 0.2 seconds delay between each character. (*Hint*: Use the appropriate command on the Effect tab in the Effect Options dialog box for the Appear animation.)

14. Apply the same animations and effects to the text boxes on Slides 6 through 12 by repeating Steps 12 and 13 for each of these slides. Make sure the start timing for all of these animations is After Previous.

15. On Slides 5 through 12, resize the pictures so they are as tall as possible on the slides.

⊕ **Explore** 16. Create a custom show named **Favorite Paintings** that includes Slides 5 through 12. (*Hint*: Use the Custom Slide Show button in the Start Slide Show group on the SLIDE SHOW tab.)

⊕ **Explore** 17. Change the color of the laser pointer to green. (*Hint*: Use the Set Up Slide Show button in the Set Up group on the SLIDE SHOW tab.) Switch to Slide Show view and use the pointer.

⊕ **Explore** 18. While in Slide Show view, display Slide 4 ("List of Paintings"). Change the Pen color to green, and then in the table, circle "Rembrandt." Keep the annotation.

19. Save the changes to the presentation.

TUTORIAL 6

POWERPOINT

OBJECTIVES

Session 6.1
- Compare presentations and accept or reject changes
- Add, reply to, and delete comments
- Change theme fonts
- Change theme colors
- Modify elements on the Slide Master
- Modify the style of lists
- Create a custom layout

Session 6.2
- Save a presentation as a template
- Create a custom show
- Modify file properties
- Encrypt a presentation
- Mark a presentation as final
- Present a presentation online

Customizing Presentations and the PowerPoint Environment

Creating a Presentation for a Conservation Group

Case | *International Conservation Group*

Leon Knight founded the International Conservation Group (ICG) in Sheboygan, Wisconsin. ICG is a nonprofit organization dedicated to researching the impact of humans in formerly pristine areas around the world, such as the Antarctic, the Galapagos Islands, and the Amazon. He frequently gives presentations asking for donations to help fund ICG's expenses. Next June, ICG will travel to the Galapagos Islands. Leon started creating a presentation to ask for donations to fund this project. He asks you to help him complete it.

In this tutorial, you will compare two presentations and work with comments. You will modify a theme and the slide master, and you will create a custom layout. Then you will save the presentation as a template. You will also create a custom show and modify file properties. Finally, you will encrypt a presentation, mark it as final, and then learn how to present the presentation online.

STARTING DATA FILES

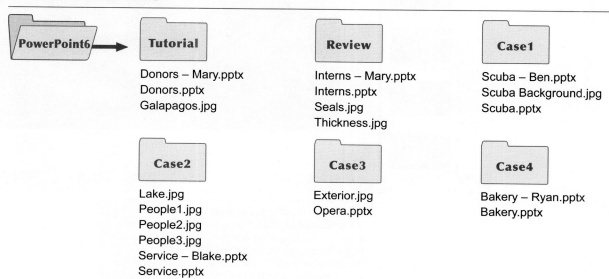

PowerPoint6 →

Tutorial
Donors – Mary.pptx
Donors.pptx
Galapagos.jpg

Review
Interns – Mary.pptx
Interns.pptx
Seals.jpg
Thickness.jpg

Case1
Scuba – Ben.pptx
Scuba Background.jpg
Scuba.pptx

Case2
Lake.jpg
People1.jpg
People2.jpg
People3.jpg
Service – Blake.pptx
Service.pptx

Case3
Exterior.jpg
Opera.pptx

Case4
Bakery – Ryan.pptx
Bakery.pptx

Session 6.1 Visual Overview:

The SLIDE MASTER tab appears in Slide Master view.

The **slide master** contains theme elements and styles, as well as text, formatting, the slide background, and other objects that appear on all the slides in the presentation. Every theme has at least one slide master.

The Title Slide Layout is used by slides with the Title Slide layout applied. This graphic inserted on the Title Slide Layout appears only on slides with the Title Slide layout applied.

The Title and Content Layout is used by slides with the Title and Content layout applied.

The Two Content Layout is used by slides with Two Content layout applied.

Every slide master has at least one layout. These are the same layouts that appear when you click the New Slide button arrow or the Layout button in the Slides group on the HOME tab. If you modify a layout in Slide Master view, the changes affect the slides that have that layout applied.

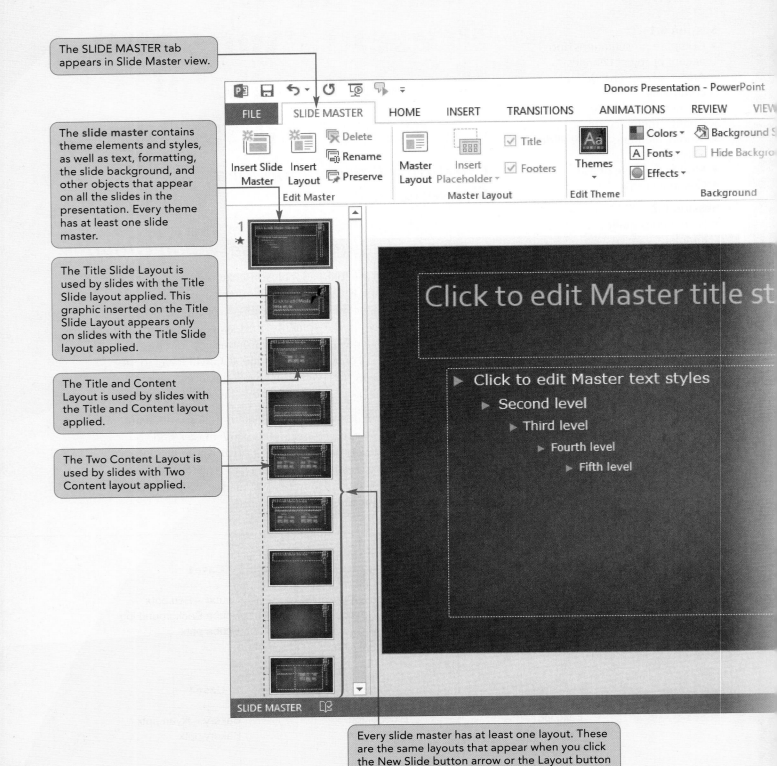

Photo courtesy of S. Scott Zimmerman

Slide Master View

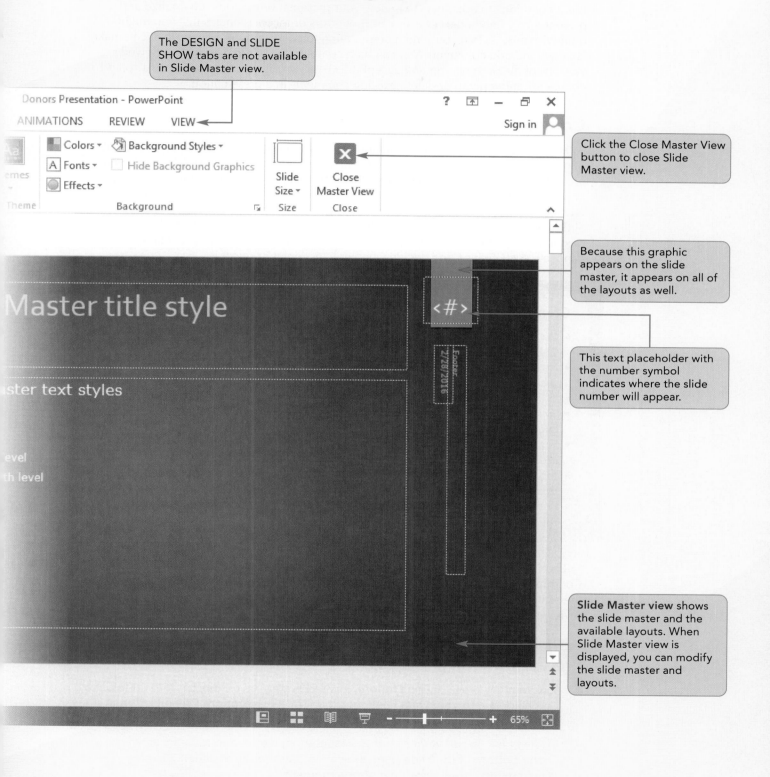

The DESIGN and SLIDE SHOW tabs are not available in Slide Master view.

Click the Close Master View button to close Slide Master view.

Because this graphic appears on the slide master, it appears on all of the layouts as well.

This text placeholder with the number symbol indicates where the slide number will appear.

Slide Master view shows the slide master and the available layouts. When Slide Master view is displayed, you can modify the slide master and layouts.

Sharing and Collaborating with Others

It is a good idea to ask others to review your presentations before you finalize and present them. Another set of eyes can spot errors or inconsistencies that you might otherwise miss. When you send a presentation to colleagues for review, they can make changes and add comments. You can then compare the original and the reviewed versions of the presentation and accept the changes or ignore them. You can also add comments and reply to or delete existing comments in a presentation.

Comparing Presentations

After a colleague reviews a presentation, you can compare it to your original presentation using the Compare button in the Compare group on the REVIEW tab. While you are comparing two presentations, the Revisions task pane appears listing the changes, and change icons appear next to objects that have been changed; you can click a change icon to see a description of the change made. Change icons that appear in the Slides tab indicate changes made at the presentation level. Change icons that appear next to an object in the Slide pane are changes that affect that object on that slide. You can view each change and decide whether to accept it or reject it.

REFERENCE

Comparing Presentations

- On the REVIEW tab, in the Compare group, click the Compare button to open the Choose File to Merge with Current Presentation dialog box.
- Navigate to the location containing the presentation with which you want to compare, click it, and then click the Merge button.
- In the box describing the first change, click the check box to select it to see the change.
- To keep the change, keep the check box selected; to reject the change, click the check box to deselect it.
- In the Compare group, click the Next button to display the next change in the presentation.
- After reviewing all the changes in the presentation, in the Compare group, click the End Review button.
- In the dialog box that opens asking if you are sure you want to end the review, click the Yes button.

Leon created his presentation, and then sent it to Mary Walsh, the Donation Coordinator at ICG, and asked her to review it. Mary made a few changes, and then the sent it back to Leon. Leon asks you to compare his original presentation with the reviewed presentation.

To compare two presentations:

▸ **1.** Open the presentation **Donors**, located in the PowerPoint6 ▸ Tutorial folder included with your Data Files, and then save it as **Donors Presentation** in the location where you are storing your files.

   Trouble? When you open the presentation, a message appears at the bottom of the Slide pane indicating that the presentation includes comments. It will disappear after a moment.

▸ **2.** On the ribbon, click the **REVIEW** tab, and then in the Compare group, click the **Compare** button. The Choose File to Merge with Current Presentation dialog box opens.

3. Navigate to the PowerPoint6 ▸ Tutorial folder and, if necessary, click **Donors - Mary**, and then click the **Merge** button. The Revisions pane opens with the DETAILS tab selected. A description of the first difference between the two presentations appears in a box next to a change icon in the Slides tab. See Figure 6-1.

Figure 6-1 | **Slide 1 after using the Compare command**

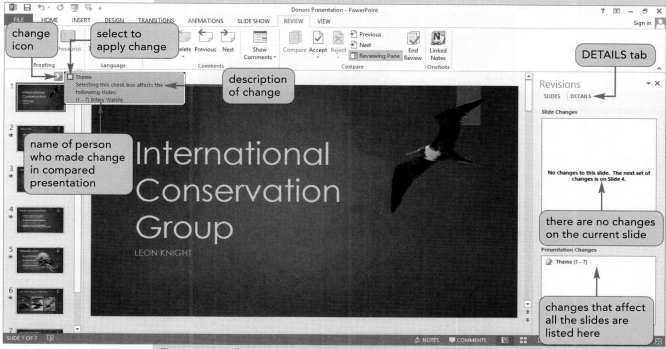

Photos courtesy of S. Scott Zimmerman

Trouble? If the Comments pane opens, close it.

Trouble? If the box containing the description of the Theme change does not appear, click the change icon 📝 at the top of the Slides tab.

In the Slide Changes section, the message that no changes were made to this slide appears. However, in the Presentation Changes section, Theme (1 - 7) appears, indicating that the person who reviewed the presentation made a change that affected the theme. This corresponds to the change icon and description at the top of the Slides tab.

4. In the Slides tab, in the change box, click the check box next to Theme to select it. The change is applied to the presentation and the theme is changed. Leon does not want to make this change.

5. In the change box, click the check box again to deselect it. The theme change is removed from the presentation.

TIP

You can also click the Reject button in the Compare group on the REVIEW tab to reject a selected change.

6. In the Compare group, click the **Next** button. Slide 5 ("Galapagos Islands") appears in the Slide pane with a change box that indicates the slide title was changed. This change is listed in the Slide Changes section of the Revisions pane because the change affects this slide only. See Figure 6-2.

Figure 6-2   **Slide 6 with a change noted**

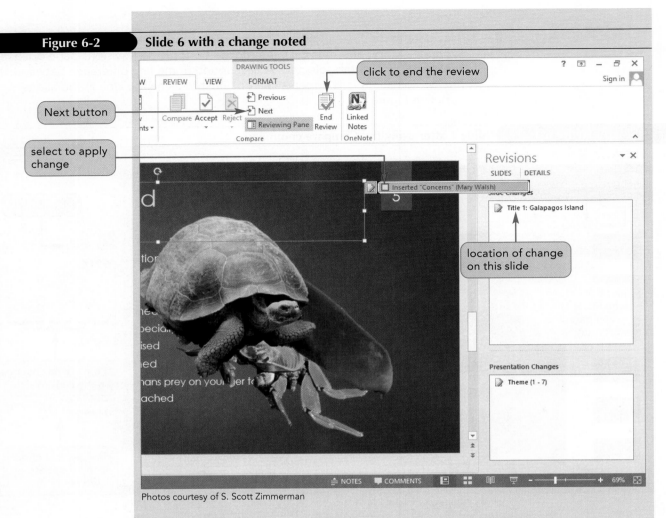

Photos courtesy of S. Scott Zimmerman

7. In the change box, click the check box next to "Inserted." The word "Concerns" is added to the slide title. Leon likes this change so you will keep the check box selected.

8. In the Compare group, click the **Next** button. A dialog box opens telling you that was the last change in the presentation, and asking if you want to continue reviewing from the beginning. Because Slide 1 was displayed in the Slide pane when you used the Compare command, you don't need to continue from the beginning.

9. Click the **Cancel** button. You are finished reviewing the merged changes. In order to accept all the changes you selected, reject the changes you did not select, and remove the change icons, you need to end the review.

10. In the Compare group, click the **End Review** button. A dialog box opens asking if you are sure you want to end the review and warning that any unapplied changes will be discarded.

11. Click the **Yes** button. The dialog box and the Revisions pane close, and the change icons disappear.

Working with Comments

When a colleague reviews a presentation, he or she can add comments to ask a question or make a suggestion. You can also add comments to direct others' attention to something on a slide or reply to a comment that someone else has placed on a slide. When you insert a comment in a presentation, it is labeled with the name of the person listed in the User name box on the General tab in the PowerPoint Options dialog box. You can change this to your own name.

To change the user name in the PowerPoint Options dialog box:

▶ **1.** On the ribbon, click the **FILE** tab, and then in the navigation bar, click **Options**. The PowerPoint Options dialog box opens with General selected in the navigation bar in the dialog box. See Figure 6-3.

Figure 6-3   **General tab in the PowerPoint Options dialog box**

General selected

user name (name on your screen will differ)

user initials

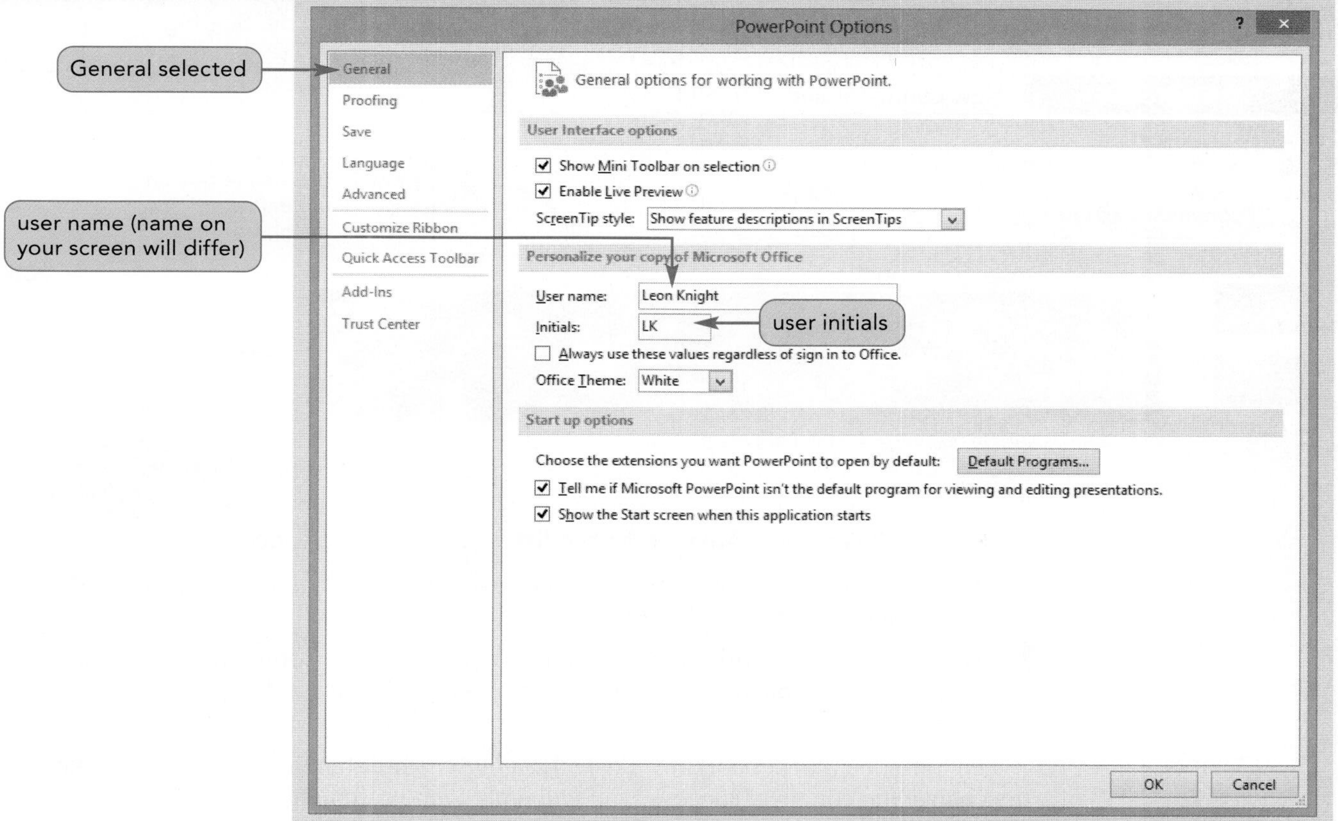

▶ **2.** Note the name currently in the User name box and the initials in the Initials box. If the name and initials in these boxes are not yours, make a note of them as you will need to restore these later.

▶ **3.** If necessary, click in the **User name** box, delete the current name, and then type your name.

Trouble? If you are in a lab and are prevented from changing PowerPoint options, note the name you see in the User name box on the General tab in the PowerPoint Options dialog box because this is the name that will label the comments you add to the presentation.

4. If necessary, click in the **Initials** box, delete the current initials, and then type your initials.

5. Click the **OK** button to close the dialog box.

Now that your name is listed as the user name in the PowerPoint Options dialog box, you can insert a comment that will be labeled with your name.

To insert a comment in Slide 3 in the Donors Presentation file:

1. Display **Slide 3** ("Areas of Concern") in the Slide pane.

2. On the REVIEW tab, in the Comments group, click the **New Comment** button. The Comments task pane appears with a box labeled with the name in the User name box on the General tab in the PowerPoint Options dialog box. (If you performed the previous set of steps, then this should be your name.) A comment balloon appears in the top left corner of the slide. See Figure 6-4.

Figure 6-4   **New comment added to Slide 3**

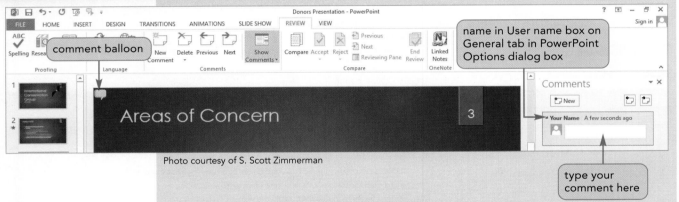

Photo courtesy of S. Scott Zimmerman

3. Type **Please add Amazon to the list.** (including the period).

4. In the Slide pane, drag the comment balloon to position it above the word "Antarctica" in the bulleted list.

5. Display **Slide 2** ("About ICG") in the Slide pane. The Comments pane changes to indicate that there are comments on other slides.

Leon inserted a comment on Slide 4 ("Recent Accomplishments"). Instead of making the change the comment suggests, you will reply to the comment.

To reply to a comment:

TIP

You can also click a comment balloon to open the Comments pane.

1. On the REVIEW tab, in the Comments group, click the **Next** button twice. Slide 4 ("Recent Accomplishments") appears in the Slide pane, displaying a comment that Leon had inserted. A Reply box appears below the comment in the Comments task pane.

2. Click in the **Reply** box, and then type **I agree.** (including the period).

3. Click in a blank area of the Comments task pane. The reply is labeled with your name (or the name in the User name box in the PowerPoint Options dialog box). In the Slide pane, a second comment balloon appears on top of the first balloon.

▶ **4.** Drag the comment balloons to the right so that they do not overlap the text, if necessary.

You will use the Next button in the Comments group to see if there are any additional comments in the presentation. You can decide what to do based upon a comment, and then you can delete the comment when you are finished, if appropriate.

To review and delete comments in the presentation:

▶ **1.** In the Comments task pane, click the **Next** button. Your reply to Leon's comment is selected.

▶ **2.** In the Comments task pane, click the **Next** button. Slide 8 ("How You Can Help") appears in the Slide pane and the comment that Mary added when she reviewed the presentation appears in the Comments task pane.

▶ **3.** Read the comment in the Comments task pane. Mary suggested adding quotation marks around the word "Adopt." Leon agrees with that suggestion.

▶ **4.** In the bulleted list, click to the left of the word "Adopt,", type **"**, click after the word "Adopt," and then type **"**. Now that you've made the change, you can delete Mary's comment.

▶ **5.** In the Comments task pane, point to Mary Walsh's comment. A border appears around the comment and a Delete button X appears.

▶ **6.** Click the **Delete** button X. The comment is deleted.

▶ **7.** On the REVIEW tab, in the Comments group, click the **Next** button. A dialog box opens asking if you want to continue from the beginning of the presentation.

▶ **8.** Click the **Continue** button. Slide 3 ("Areas of Concern") appears in the Slide pane and the comment you inserted is in the Comments task pane. You have seen all of the comments in the presentation.

▶ **9.** In the Comments task pane, click the **Close** button X.

TIP

To hide comments, on the REVIEW tab, in the Comments group, click the Show Comments button arrow, and then click Show Markup to deselect it.

You have finished addressing the comments in the presentation. Next, if you changed the values in the User name and Initials boxes in the PowerPoint Options dialog box, you need to reset them to their original values.

To change the user name in the PowerPoint Options dialog box back to its original value:

▶ **1.** On the ribbon, click the **FILE** tab, and then in the navigation bar, click **Options**. The PowerPoint Options dialog box opens with General selected in the navigation bar.

▶ **2.** If necessary, click in the **User name** box, delete the current name, and then type the name that was originally in this box.

▶ **3.** If necessary, click in the **Initials** box, delete the current initials, and then type the initials originally in this box.

▶ **4.** Click the **OK** button to close the dialog box.

▶ **5.** Save the changes to the presentation.

Modifying Themes

The built-in themes and variants provide many choices for customizing the design of a presentation. However, if you don't like the specific colors or fonts that come with a theme, you can easily change them.

Changing Theme Fonts

Recall that theme fonts are two coordinating fonts or font styles, one for the titles (or headings) and one for text in content placeholders and other text elements on a slide. To change the theme fonts, you click the Fonts button in the Themes group on the Design tab, and then select the coordinating set of fonts from another theme. You can also create a set of custom theme fonts using the Customize Fonts command.

Leon applied the Ion theme with the first variant to the presentation that he created. He would like you to change the theme fonts so that they match fonts used in other ICG company publications.

To change the theme fonts:

1. On the ribbon, click the **DESIGN** tab.

2. In the Variants group, click the **More** button, and then point to **Fonts**. The gallery of theme fonts opens. See Figure 6-5.

Figure 6-5 **Fonts menu listing gallery of theme fonts**

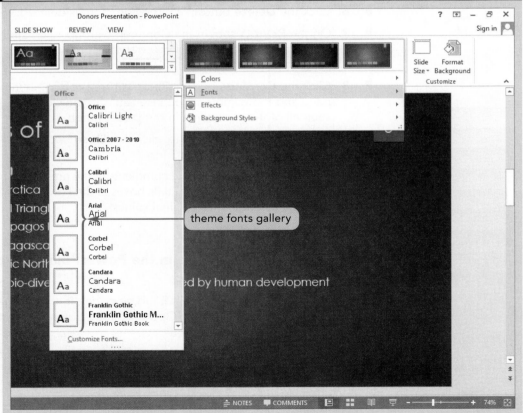

3. Scroll to the bottom of the list, and then click **Consolas-Verdana**. The font of the slide titles change to Consolas and the font of the lists change to Verdana.

4. In the Variants group, click the **More** button, point to **Fonts**, and then click **Customize Fonts**. The Create New Theme Fonts dialog box opens. See Figure 6-6.

Figure 6-6 **Create New Theme Fonts dialog box**

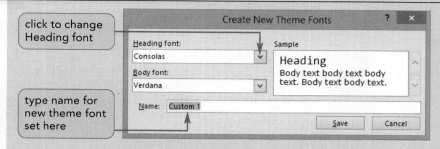

5. Click the **Heading font** arrow, scroll down the alphabetical list, and then click **Corbel**.

6. Click in the **Name** box, delete the text in the box, and then type **ICG Fonts**.

7. Click the **Save** button. Now the custom set of fonts will appear at the top of the Fonts gallery.

When you save a set of custom theme fonts, the set is saved to the computer, and it can be applied to any presentation opened on the computer. If you've applied the custom theme font set to a presentation, that set of custom theme fonts will still be applied to that presentation even if you delete the custom set from the computer's hard drive.

You'll delete the custom theme font set you created from the computer you are using.

To delete the custom theme fonts from the computer:

1. In the Variants group, click the **More** button, and then point to **Fonts**. The custom theme font set you created appears at the top of the menu. See Figure 6-7.

Figure 6-7   **Custom theme font set in the theme fonts gallery**

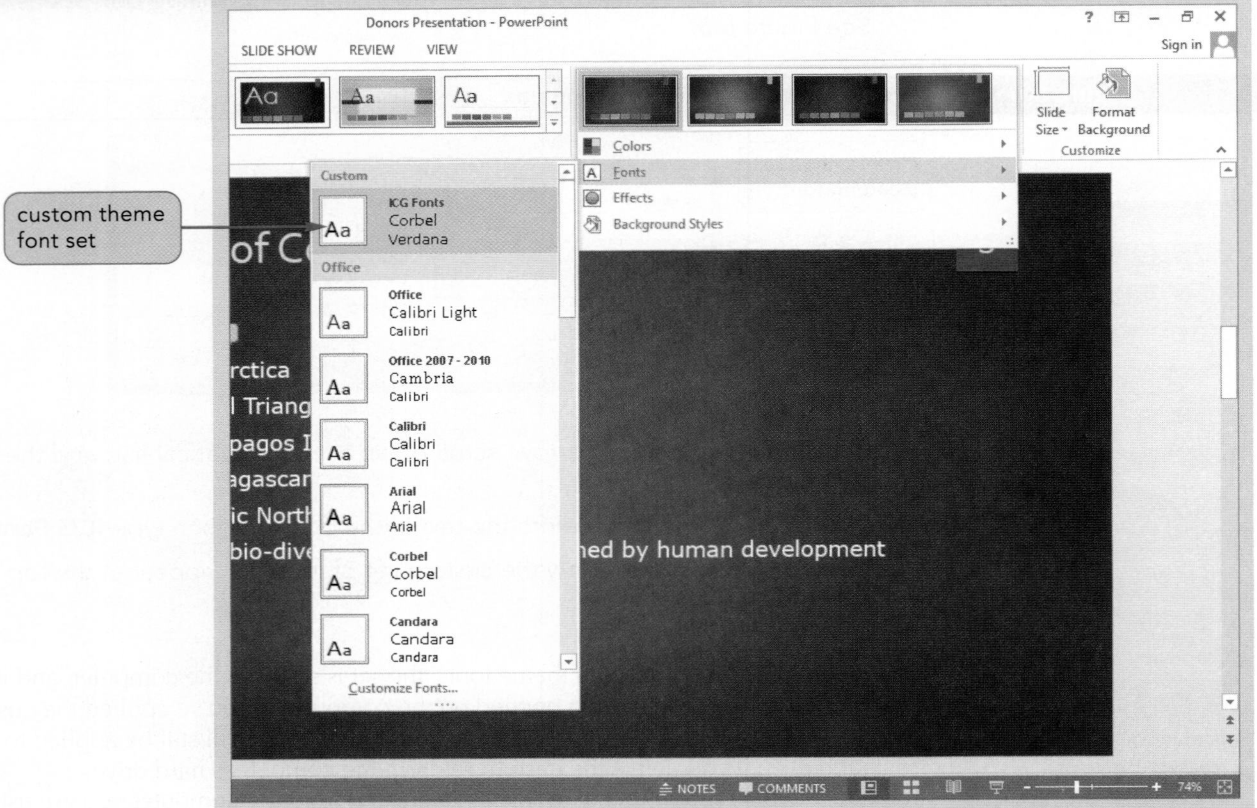

custom theme font set

2. Right-click **ICG Fonts** in the menu, and then on the shortcut menu, click **Delete**. A dialog box opens asking if you want to delete these theme fonts.

3. Click the **Yes** button. The custom theme font set is deleted from the computer. It is still part of the current presentation's theme. You can verify this by looking at the font list on the HOME tab.

4. Click the **HOME** tab, and then click in the **title** text box. In the Font box in the Font group, the font is still Corbel (Headings).

Changing Theme Colors

Each PowerPoint theme has a palette of 12 theme colors associated with it. You can choose another palette of theme colors.

Leon wants you to apply a color palette that uses more green colors.

To change the theme colors in the presentation:

1. Click the **DESIGN** tab.

2. In the Variants group, click the **More** button, and then point to **Colors**. The gallery of theme colors opens. See Figure 6-8.

Figure 6-8 Colors menu listing gallery of color palettes

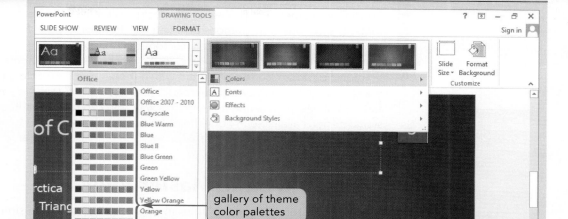

3. Click **Green**. The Green palette is applied to the presentation, changing the slide background color and the color of the rectangle in the upper-right of each slide.

4. Save the changes to the presentation.

As you know, you can click Customize Colors on the Colors submenu to create a custom color palette. You should be wary of doing this without some knowledge of how colors work together. Usually, dark font colors work well on a light background, and light font colors are readable on a dark background. However, not all colors are complementary and some combinations can be visually jarring or illegible. For example, avoid red text on a blue background or blue text on a green background (and vice versa) unless the shades of those colors are in strong contrast. These combinations might look fine up close on your computer monitor, but they are almost totally illegible to an audience watching your presentation on a screen in a darkened room. Also avoid using red/green combinations, which color-blind people find illegible.

Problem Solving: Should You Create Your Own Theme?

PowerPoint comes with professionally designed themes, theme colors, and theme fonts. The various combinations give you hundreds of designs from which to choose. If you decide you need to create a custom theme, you can start "from scratch" and assign every theme color and create your own combination of fonts. But unless you are a graphic designer, consider starting with a theme or theme colors that most closely match the colors you want to use, and then selectively customize some of the colors, fonts, or styles. By creating a theme this way, you can take advantage of the professional designs available in PowerPoint to create your own custom look.

Working in Slide Master View

Slide masters ensure that all the slides in the presentation have a similar appearance and contain the same elements. All presentations contain at least one slide master and one layout. Most themes include multiple layouts. To work with slide masters, you need to switch to Slide Master view. Refer to the Session 6.1 Visual Overview for more information about slide masters.

Leon wants you to make several changes to the look of the slides in the presentation. Because he wants the changes to be applied to all of the slides in the presentation, you will modify the slide master. First, you need to switch to Slide Master view and examine the slide master and its layouts.

To switch to Slide Master view:

▶ 1. On the ribbon, click the **VIEW** tab, and then in the Master Views group, click the **Slide Master** button. The view changes to Slide Master view and a new tab, the SLIDE MASTER tab, appears on the ribbon to the left of the HOME tab. In place of the slide thumbnails in the Slides tab, the layout thumbnails appear.

▶ 2. In the Slides tab, point to the selected layout thumbnail. The ScreenTip identifies this layout as the Title and Content Layout, and indicates that it is used by Slides 2-5 and 7. In addition to placeholders for the title and content, there are placeholders for the slide number, date, and footer, and a graphic—a green rectangle below the slide number placeholder.

▶ 3. In the Slides tab, drag the scroll box to the top of the scroll bar, and then point to the top thumbnail, which is larger than the other thumbnails. This is the slide master, and it is named for the theme applied to the presentation—in this case, it is the Ion Slide Master, as indicated by the ScreenTip because the Ion theme is applied to the presentation. The ScreenTip also indicates that it is used by slides 1-7, which are all the slides in the presentation.

▶ 4. In the Slides tab, point to the second thumbnail to verify that it is the Title Slide Layout used by Slide 1.

TIP

To apply a theme to only one slide or selected slides, right-click it on the DESIGN tab, and then click Apply to Selected Slides.

You can apply more than one theme to a presentation. Usually, this is not a good idea; presentations should have a cohesive look. However, if you want each section of a presentation to have a different look—for example, if your presentation is about different music styles and several slides are about each style—you might want to use a different theme for each section. When there are multiple themes applied to a presentation, each theme has a slide master and its associated layouts.

Modifying the Slide Master

You can modify a slide master in many ways. For example, you can change the size and style of text in the placeholders, add or delete graphics, change the slide background, and change the style of lists. Changes you make to the slide master affect all of the slides in the presentation. For example, if you modify the font, font size, or font style on the slide master, or if you add an image or an animation to the slide master, it will appear on all the slides in the presentation. Changes you make to a layout in Slide Master view appear only on slides with that layout applied.

Leon wants the slide titles to be bold, and he wants the presentation title to be in all uppercase letters. The size of first-level bulleted items in the Ion theme is 20 points. Leon would like you to modify the size of the items in the lists so that the size of the text in first-level items is 28 points. He also wants you to remove the green rectangle behind the slide number placeholder. You will make these changes to the slide master.

To modify the slide master:

1. In the Slides tab, click the **Ion Slide Master** thumbnail at the top of the tab, and then, in the Slide pane, click the border of the title text placeholder.

2. On the ribbon, click the **HOME** tab, and then in the Font group, click the **Bold** button B. The text in the title text placeholder on the slide master becomes bold. Because you changed the slide master, this change affects all of the layouts.

   Trouble? If nothing happened when you clicked the Bold button, the title text placeholder is active, but not selected. Click directly on the border of the title text placeholder, and then repeat Step 2.

3. In the Slide pane, click the border of the content placeholder, and then in the Font group, click the **Increase Font Size** button A˄ twice. The text in the first-level item in the list is now 28 points.

4. In the Slide pane, click the green rectangle behind the slide number placeholder, and then press the **Delete** key. The green rectangle graphic is removed from the slide master. You can see in the Slides tab that it was removed from all of the layouts as well.

Modifying Individual Layouts

Changes you make to the slide master are applied to all of the layouts associated with the slide master, and consequently to all the slides in the presentation. You can also modify individual layouts. When you do this, only the individual layout, and therefore only slides that have that layout applied, are affected.

Leon wants the presentation title to be all uppercase. To have this happen even if someone types the title normally, you will format the title text placeholder on the Title Slide layout to be all uppercase letters. Leon also thinks the slides with Title and Content layout applied would look better if the list items in the content placeholder were left-aligned with the title text, so he wants you to modify the content placeholder on the Title and Content layout. You will modify the layouts now.

To modify individual layouts:

1. In the Slides tab, click the **Title Slide Layout** thumbnail, and then in the Slide pane, click the title text placeholder border.

2. On the HOME tab, in the Font group, click the **Dialog Box Launcher**. The Font dialog box opens with the Font tab selected. See Figure 6-9.

| Figure 6-9 | Font dialog box |

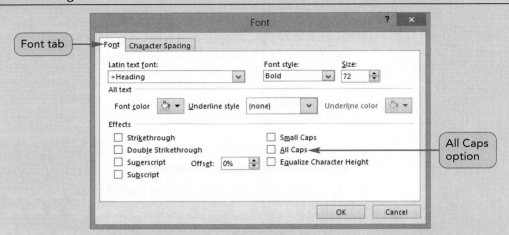

3. Click the **All Caps** check box, and then click the **OK** button. The text in the title text placeholder on the Title Slide layout is all uppercase. Now you will modify the Title and Content layout.

TIP

You can also modify Handout and Notes masters. Click the appropriate button in the Master Views group on the VIEW tab.

4. In the Slides tab, click the **Title and Content** layout.

5. In the Slide pane, click the content placeholder border.

6. Drag the left, middle sizing handle to the left until the content placeholder is as wide as the title text placeholder.

Modifying the Style of Lists

You can modify the style of lists in many ways. For example, you can change the bullet symbol, size, and color or change the font used for numbers in a numbered list. Good presentation design dictates list styles should be consistent across all slides in a presentation. Therefore, when modifying the style of lists in a presentation, you should make these formatting changes to the slide master, ensuring that the changes appear on all slide layouts.

REFERENCE

Modifying the Bullet Symbol

- Select the content text box.
- On the HOME tab, in the Paragraph group, click the Bullets button arrow, and then click Bullets and Numbering to open the Bulleted tab in the Bullets and Numbering dialog box.
- Click the Customize button to open the Symbol dialog box.
- Click the Font arrow, and then click the font you want to use.
- Click a symbol, and then click the OK button.
- Adjust the value in the Size box, if desired.
- Click the Color button, and then click a different color, if desired.
- Click the OK button.

Leon would like you to change the bullet symbol used in the Donors Presentation from a triangle to a semi-circle. You'll make this change on the slide master.

To modify the bullet style on the slide master:

1. In the Slides tab, click the **Ion Slide Master** thumbnail.

2. In the Slide pane, click the border of the content placeholder. Now the change you make to the bullet symbol will affect all bullet levels.

Trouble? If a shape appears to be selected, click a different part of the placeholder border.

3. On the HOME tab, in the Paragraph group, click the **Bullets button arrow**. The Bullets gallery appears. See Figure 6-10. You can select one of the styles in the gallery or open a dialog box where you can customize your bullets.

Figure 6-10 | Bullets gallery

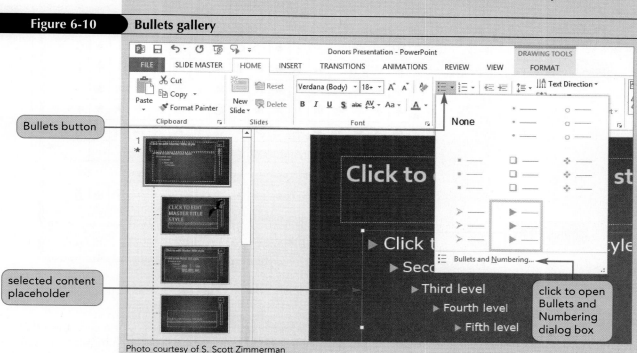

Bullets button

selected content placeholder

click to open Bullets and Numbering dialog box

Photo courtesy of S. Scott Zimmerman

4. Click **Bullets and Numbering**. The Bullets and Numbering dialog box opens with the Bulleted tab selected. See Figure 6-11.

Figure 6-11 | Bulleted tab in the Bullets and Numbering dialog box

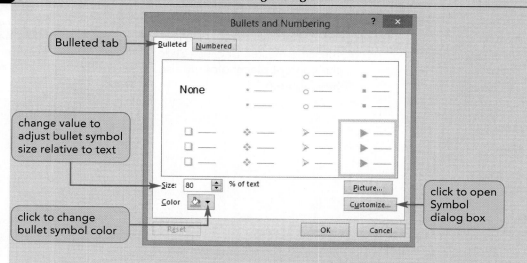

Bulleted tab

change value to adjust bullet symbol size relative to text

click to change bullet symbol color

click to open Symbol dialog box

▶ **5.** Click the **Customize** button. The Symbol dialog box opens.

▶ **6.** Click the **Font** arrow, scroll to the bottom of the list, and then click **Wingdings 2**.

▶ **7.** Scroll to the bottom of the list, and then click the semi-circle symbol as shown in Figure 6-12. All symbols have a name, and this symbol is Wingdings 2: 187.

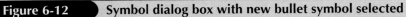
Figure 6-12   **Symbol dialog box with new bullet symbol selected**

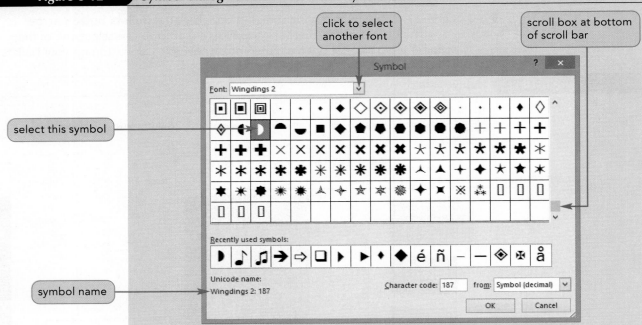

click to select another font

scroll box at bottom of scroll bar

select this symbol

symbol name

TIP

To modify the style of numbers in a numbered list, use the options on the Numbered tab in the Bullets and Numbering dialog box.

▶ **8.** Click the **OK** button. The Symbol dialog box closes and the Bullets and Numbering dialog box is active again.

▶ **9.** Click in the **Size** box, change the value to **100%**, and then click the **OK** button. The bullet symbols in the content placeholder change to the symbol you selected. Now you will examine the changes you made to the slide master in Normal view.

▶ **10.** On the ribbon, click the **SLIDE MASTER** tab, and then in the Close group, click the **Close Master View** button. The Presentation appears in Normal view with Slide 3 ("Areas of Concern") displayed in the Slide pane. The title is bold, the green rectangle behind the slide number is no longer on the slide, and in the content placeholder, the bullet symbols are the semi-circle symbols you chose. These changes correspond to the changes you made to the slide master. Because Slide 3 has the Title and Content layout applied, the content placeholder is also left-aligned with the title text placeholder. See Figure 6-13.

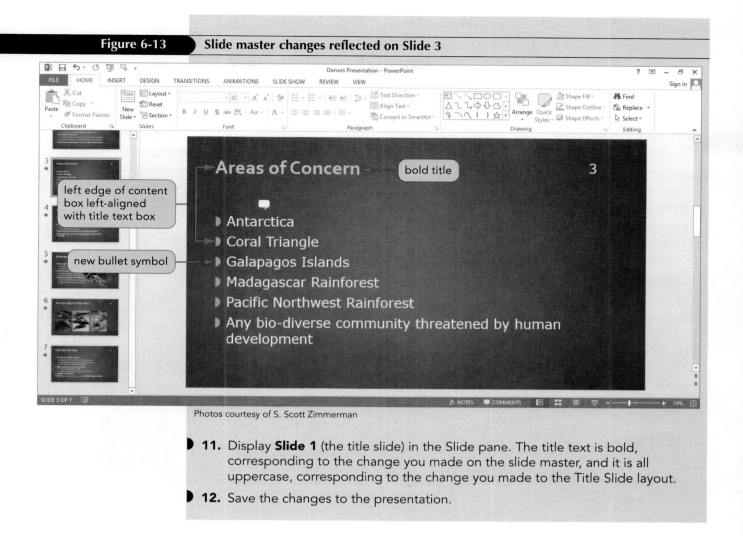

Figure 6-13 Slide master changes reflected on Slide 3

Photos courtesy of S. Scott Zimmerman

▶ **11.** Display **Slide 1** (the title slide) in the Slide pane. The title text is bold, corresponding to the change you made on the slide master, and it is all uppercase, corresponding to the change you made to the Title Slide layout.

▶ **12.** Save the changes to the presentation.

Creating a Custom Layout

If the theme you are using does not contain a layout that suits your needs, you can create a new layout. You do this in Slide Master view. After you create a new layout, it will be listed on the New Slide and Layout menus in the Slides group on the HOME tab.

In the Donors Presentation, Slides 1 through 4 and Slide 7 are slides that present general information about the company and its mission. Slides 5 and 6 are specifically about the new project on the Galapagos Islands. Leon wants to add a section header slide that is filled with a photo before these two slides. He wants you to create a new layout for the presentation so that he can do this. He can then reuse this custom layout to be the section header for slides he will insert later on other location-specific projects.

To create a custom layout:

▶ **1.** Switch to Slide Master view, and then in the Slides tab, click the **Title and Content Layout** thumbnail.

2. On the SLIDE MASTER tab, in the Edit Master group, click the **Insert Layout** button. A new layout is inserted below the Title and Content Layout. The new layout contains placeholders for the slide title and the slide number, date, and footer. See Figure 6-14. You can quickly remove these placeholders by deselecting the appropriate check boxes in the Master Layout group.

Figure 6-14   **New layout added in Slide Master view**

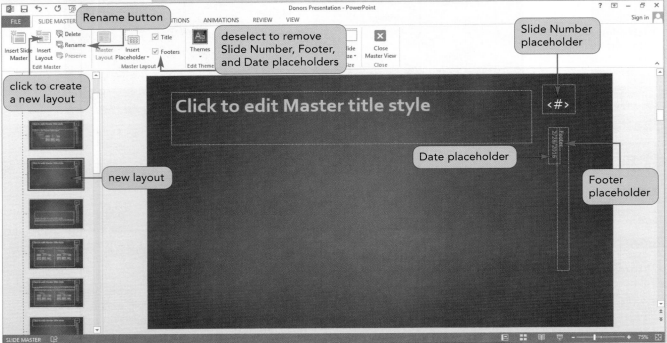

Photo courtesy of S. Scott Zimmerman

3. In the Master Layout group, click the **Footers** check box to deselect it. The Slide Number, Date, and Footer placeholders are removed from the layout. Now you need to add a picture placeholder.

4. In the Master Layout group, click the **Insert Placeholder button arrow**. A gallery of placeholders opens. See Figure 6-15.

Figure 6-15	Placeholder gallery

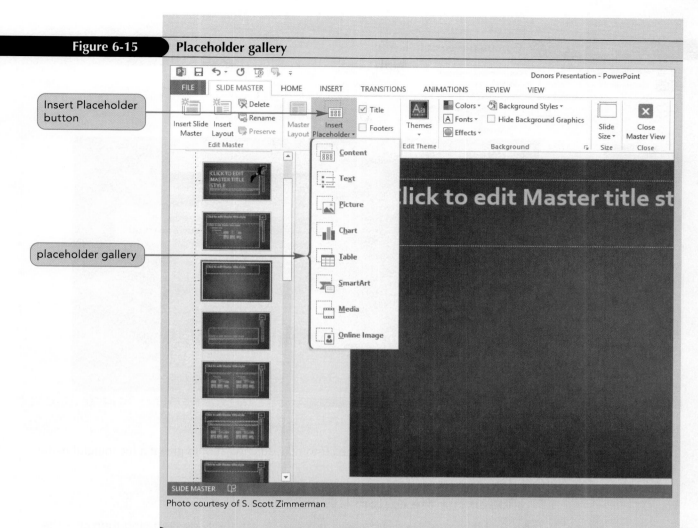

Photo courtesy of S. Scott Zimmerman

5. Click **Picture**. The pointer changes to ╋.

6. Drag to draw a placeholder on the slide that is the same height and width as the slide. On the DRAWING TOOLS FORMAT tab, in the Size group, the measurement in the Shape Height box should be 7.5" and the measurement in the Shape Width box should be 13.33". The picture placeholder is in the layer on top of the title text placeholder.

7. With the picture placeholder selected, on the DRAWING TOOLS FORMAT tab, in the Arrange group, click the **Send Backward** button. Now you can modify the title text placeholder.

8. Drag the title text placeholder so that its left and top borders are aligned with the left and top edges of the slide, and then drag the right, middle sizing handle to the right so that the title text placeholder is as wide as the slide. See Figure 6-16.

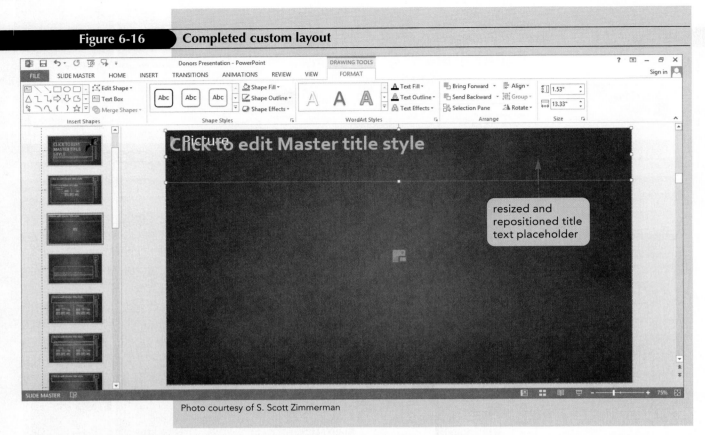

Figure 6-16 Completed custom layout

Photo courtesy of S. Scott Zimmerman

Now that you have created the custom layout, you should give it a meaningful name.

To rename the custom layout:

1. Make sure the custom layout is selected in the Slides tab, and then click the **SLIDE MASTER** tab.

2. In the Edit Master group, click the **Rename** button. The Rename Layout dialog box opens.

3. In the Layout name box, delete the text, and then type **Picture Section Header**.

4. Click the **Rename** button. You're finished working with the Slide Master.

5. On the SLIDE MASTER tab, in the Close group, click the **Close Master View** button.

Next, you will use the custom Picture Section Header layout to create a new slide in the presentation. The slide will be a new Slide 5 so that it appears before the two slides that discuss the Galapagos Islands.

To apply the custom layout:

1. Display **Slide 4** ("Recent Accomplishments") in the Slide pane.

2. On the HOME tab, in the Slides group, click the **New Slide button arrow**. The layout you created, Picture Section Header, appears in the top row of the layout gallery. See Figure 6-17.

Figure 6-17 New Slide gallery listing custom layout

custom layout

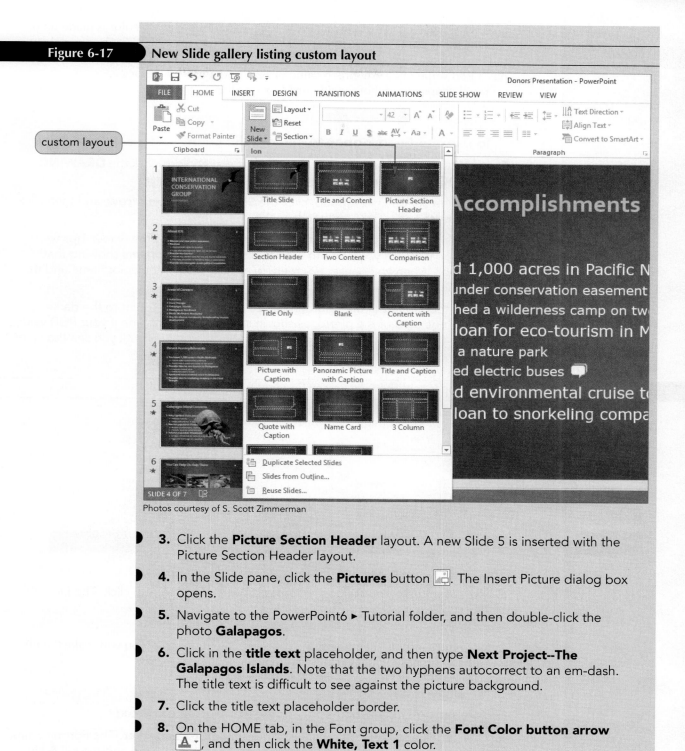

Photos courtesy of S. Scott Zimmerman

▶ **3.** Click the **Picture Section Header** layout. A new Slide 5 is inserted with the Picture Section Header layout.

▶ **4.** In the Slide pane, click the **Pictures** button. The Insert Picture dialog box opens.

▶ **5.** Navigate to the PowerPoint6 ▶ Tutorial folder, and then double-click the photo **Galapagos**.

▶ **6.** Click in the **title text** placeholder, and then type **Next Project--The Galapagos Islands**. Note that the two hyphens autocorrect to an em-dash. The title text is difficult to see against the picture background.

▶ **7.** Click the title text placeholder border.

▶ **8.** On the HOME tab, in the Font group, click the **Font Color button arrow**, and then click the **White, Text 1** color.

The title text placeholder is still hard to see on the picture; in fact, on the left side of the slide, it is harder to see because the photo contains white areas under the text at the point. To fix this, you will fill the shape with a color from the photo.

To fill a shape with a color used on a slide, you click Eyedropper on the Shape Fill menu, and then click an area of the slide. The shape is then filled with the exact color that you clicked. When you point to a color using the Eyedropper tool, a ScreenTip appears listing a general name for the color, such as Red, Gold, or Black, and the color's RGB values. RGB stands for Red, Green, and Blue. Every color is made up of some combination of these three colors on a scale of 0 through 255. For example, pure red has a Red value of 255 and Green and Blue values of 0, but one shade of orange has a Red value of 229, a Green value of 128, and a Blue value of 27.

You'll change the fill of the title text box on Slide 5.

To use the Eyedropper to select a fill color:

1. With the insertion point in the title text placeholder, click the **DRAWING TOOLS FORMAT** tab.

2. In the Shape Styles group, click the **Shape Fill button arrow**, and then click **Eyedropper**. The pointer changes to 🖋.

3. Point to various colors in the photo, pausing to allow the ScreenTips to appear. When you point to a color, a small square appears showing that color. When you pause, a ScreenTip appears listing the color name and the RGB values.

4. At the top left of the photo, near the insertion point, point to the darker orange area of the photo, as shown in Figure 6-18. It's fine if your RGB values do not match the figure exactly, but move the pointer until you see the color name "Gold" instead of "Orange" or "Light Yellow."

Figure 6-18 **Eyedropper tool showing ScreenTip identifying color on slide**

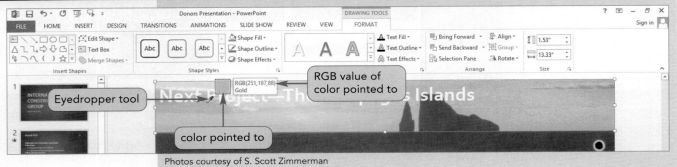

Photos courtesy of S. Scott Zimmerman

5. When the pointer is positioned as shown in Figure 6-18, click. The fill of the title text box changes to the color you clicked.

Now the sunset in the photo is no longer visible. To fix this, you will make the fill semi-transparent so you can still see the picture behind it.

To change the fill transparency of the title text box:

1. In the Shape Styles group, click the **Dialog Box Launcher**. The Format Shape task pane opens with the SHAPE OPTIONS tab selected and the Fill & Line button selected.

   Trouble? If the Fill & Line button is not selected, click it.

2. Click **FILL** to expand the FILL commands. See Figure 6-19.

Figure 6-19   Format Shape pane after selecting a color fill

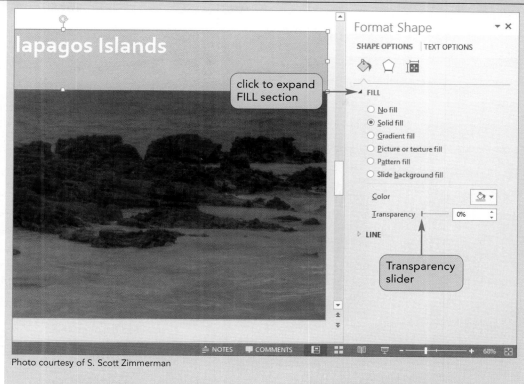

Photo courtesy of S. Scott Zimmerman

Trouble? If the FILL commands are already expanded, skip Step 2.

3. Drag the **Transparency** slider to the right until the value in the Transparency box is **50%**.

Now you can see the photo behind the title text, but the text is again difficult to read. If you use a gradient to fill the placeholder shape and vary the transparency of the gradient stops from 100%—not transparent at all—to 0%—completely transparent, you will be able to see the photo and read the text. You will use the same gold color that you selected with the Eyedropper tool, but the color at the top of the text box will be completely opaque—not transparent at all—and the color at the bottom of the text box will be completely transparent.

To change the fill to a gradient of transparencies:

1. In the Format Shape task pane, click the **Gradient fill** option button. The title text box is filled with a gradient of shades of green. The first stop on the Gradient Stops slider is selected. You want to change the color of this gradient stop to the gold color from the photo.

2. Click the **Color** button. Below the Standard Colors row, a Recent Colors row appears. The gold color you selected in the previous set of steps appears in the Recent Colors row. See Figure 6-20.

Figure 6-20   Color palette showing recently selected color

Photo courtesy of S. Scott Zimmerman

Trouble? If there is more than one color below the Recent Colors label, the most recently selected color—the gold color you selected in the previous set of steps—is the first color in the row.

3. In the Recent Colors section, click the **Gold** color. Now you need to change the rightmost gradient stop to the same gold color.

4. Click the rightmost gradient stop, click the **Color** button, and then in the Recent Colors section, click the **Gold** color. You don't need the middle two gradient stops.

5. Click one of the middle two gradient stops, and then to the right of the stops, click the **Remove gradient stop** button.

6. Remove the middle gradient stop. Now there are only two gradient stops on the slider. You need to change the transparency of the rightmost stop.

7. Scroll to the bottom of the Format Shape pane to display the Transparency options. The leftmost gradient stop is selected, and the Transparency setting is 0%. See Figure 6-21.

Figure 6-21 **Transparency option for gradient stops in Format Shape pane**

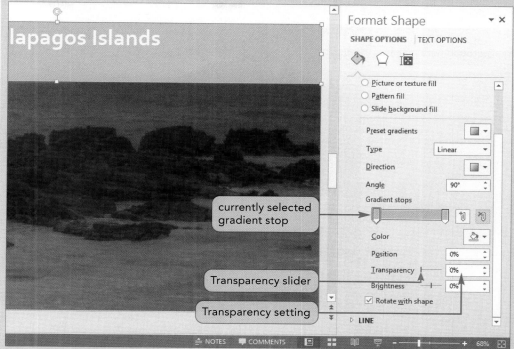

Photo courtesy of S. Scott Zimmerman

8. Click the rightmost gradient stop, and then drag the **Transparency** slider all the way to the right so that the value in the Transparency box is **100%**. The text is still a little hard to read against the mountains, so you will extend the part of the fill that is opaque a little way down.

9. Drag the leftmost gradient stop to the right until the value in the Position box is **20%**. See Figure 6-22.

| Figure 6-22 | Final gradient for the title text box |

Photo courtesy of S. Scott Zimmerman

▶ **10.** Close the Format Shape task pane, and then save the changes to the presentation.

Creating a Photo Album

PowerPoint includes a built-in Photo Album command, which allows you to create a photo album with one, two, or four pictures per slide, and optionally, with titles and captions. The advantage of this feature is that you can insert a large number of photographs all at once into the presentation, without needing to insert each picture individually. To create this type of photo album, you click the INSERT tab, and then, in the Images group, click the Photo Album button to open the Photo Album dialog box. To add a photo, click the File/Disk button, select the photo or photos you want to add from the Insert New Pictures dialog box, and then click the Insert button. To modify a photo, click the check box next to it in the Pictures in album list, and then click one of the Rotate buttons to rotate the picture 90 degrees, and click one of the Brightness or Contrast buttons to make the image brighter or darker or to increase or decrease the contrast. To add text boxes below each photo for captions, click the Captions below ALL pictures check box.

To change the layout of the slides, click the Picture layout arrow, and then click a layout. Note that when you do this, you are not actually changing the layout of the slides. All of the options on the Picture layout menu that do not include a title place the slides on the Blank layout from the Office theme; all of the options that include a title place the slides on the Title Only layout from the Office theme.

In this session, you compared presentations and worked with comments. You also modified the theme by changing the theme fonts and color palette, and you modified the slide master by changing the formatting on the slide master and on individual layouts, by changing the bullet style, and by creating a custom layout. In the next session, you will save the presentation as a template, create a custom show, modify file properties, encrypt the presentation, and mark it as final.

REVIEW

Session 6.1 Quick Check

1. How do you accept a change when comparing two presentations?
2. What name appears above a comment in the Comments pane?
3. How do you create a new theme font set?
4. What is a slide master?
5. How do you change the bullet symbol to a symbol not listed in the Bullets gallery?
6. Describe how to create a new layout.
7. Describe how to add a placeholder to a layout.

Session 6.2 Visual Overview:

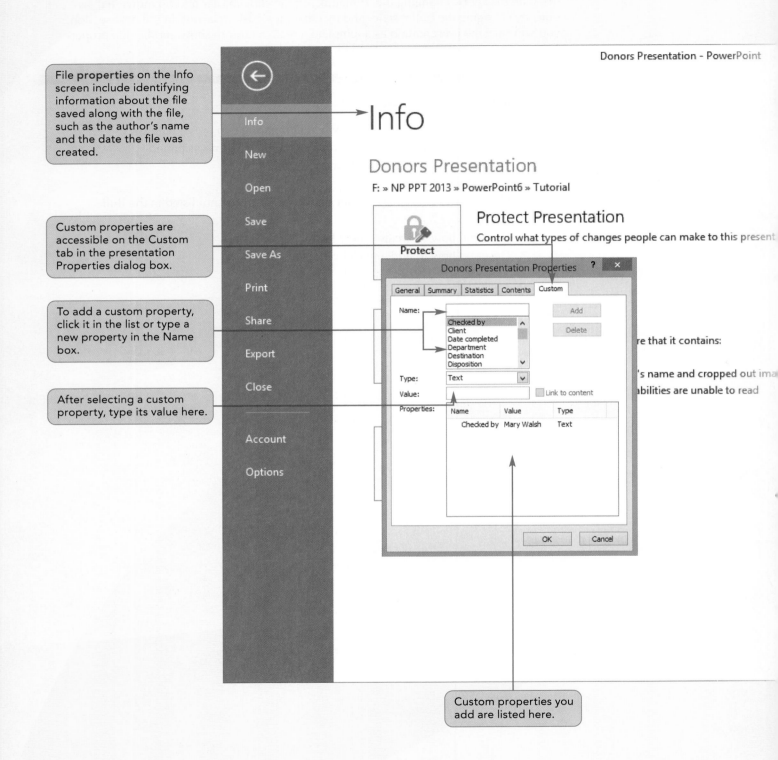

File properties on the Info screen include identifying information about the file saved along with the file, such as the author's name and the date the file was created.

Custom properties are accessible on the Custom tab in the presentation Properties dialog box.

To add a custom property, click it in the list or type a new property in the Name box.

After selecting a custom property, type its value here.

Custom properties you add are listed here.

File Properties

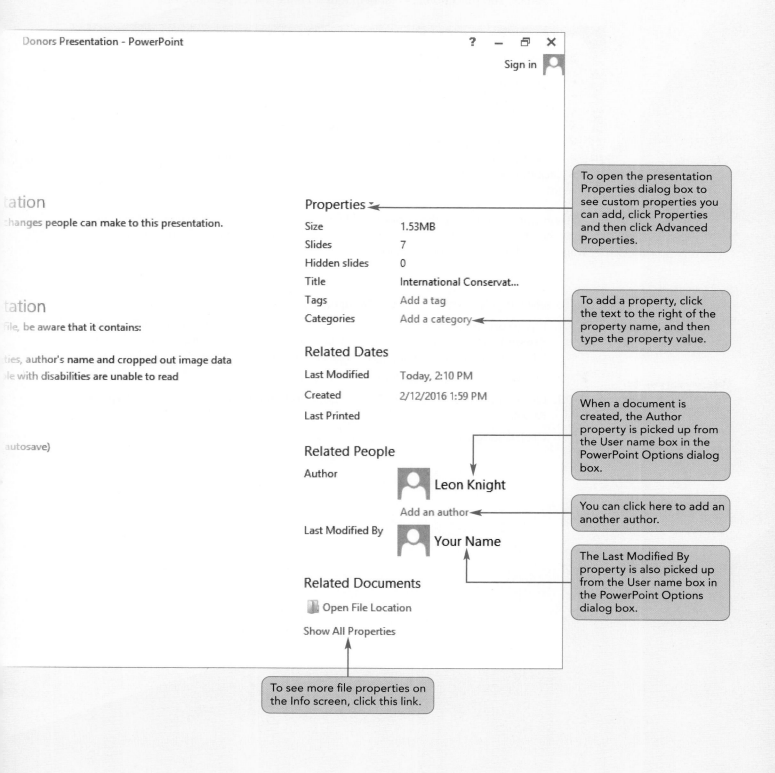

Donors Presentation - PowerPoint

? — ⊡ ✕

Sign in

...tation

...changes people can make to this presentation.

...tation

...file, be aware that it contains:

...ties, author's name and cropped out image data

...le with disabilities are unable to read

...autosave)

Properties

Size	1.53MB
Slides	7
Hidden slides	0
Title	International Conservat...
Tags	Add a tag
Categories	Add a category

Related Dates

Last Modified	Today, 2:10 PM
Created	2/12/2016 1:59 PM
Last Printed	

Related People

Author   Leon Knight

Add an author

Last Modified By   Your Name

Related Documents

Open File Location

Show All Properties

To open the presentation Properties dialog box to see custom properties you can add, click Properties and then click Advanced Properties.

To add a property, click the text to the right of the property name, and then type the property value.

When a document is created, the Author property is picked up from the User name box in the PowerPoint Options dialog box.

You can click here to add an another author.

The Last Modified By property is also picked up from the User name box in the PowerPoint Options dialog box.

To see more file properties on the Info screen, click this link.

Saving a Presentation as a Template

Recall that a template is a PowerPoint file that has a theme applied and also contains text, graphics, and placeholders that help a user create a final presentation.

REFERENCE

Saving a Presentation as a Template

- On the ribbon, click the FILE tab, and then in the navigation bar, click Export.
- Click Change File Type.
- Click Template.
- Click the Save As button to open the Save As dialog box.
- In the File name box, type the filename.
- Navigate to the location where you want to save the template.
- Click the Save button.

Leon wants you to save the customized Donors Presentation as a PowerPoint template. Later, he plans to add a logo and some additional slides that contain information he wants to include in every presentation.

To save a presentation as a template:

1. If you took a break after the previous session, open the presentation **Donors Presentation** you worked on in the last session, and then display Slide 5 ("Next Project—The Galapagos Islands") in the Slide pane.

2. On the Quick Access toolbar, click the Save button 🖫.

3. On the ribbon, click the **FILE** tab, and then in the navigation bar, click **Export** to display the Export screen in Backstage view.

4. Click **Change File Type**. See Figure 6-23.

> Make sure you save the changes to the presentation before continuing.

| Figure 6-23 | Export screen in Backstage view |

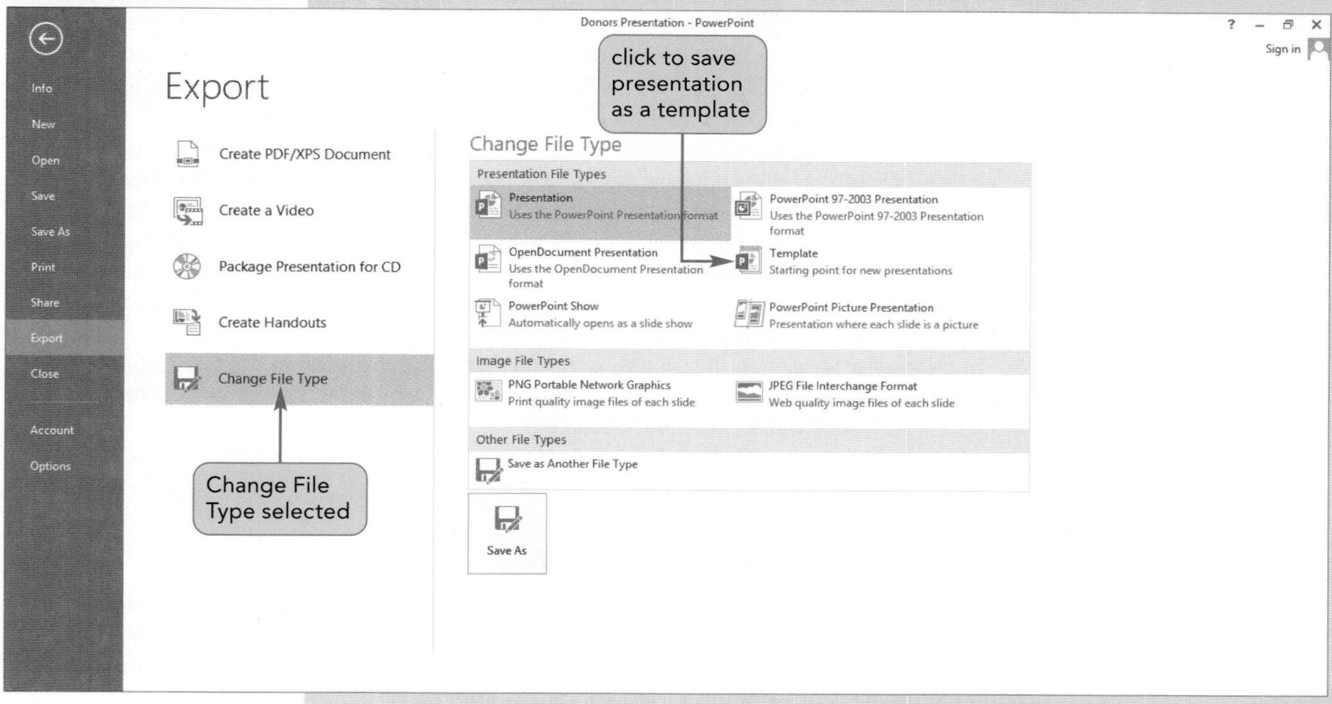

TIP

To change save options, such as whether to always embed fonts when saving, display the Save screen in the PowerPoint Options dialog box, and then select or deselect appropriate check boxes.

5. In the Presentation File Types section, click **Template**, and then click the **Save As** button. The Save As dialog box opens with PowerPoint Template in the Save as type box.

6. In the File name box, type **ICG Template**.

7. Navigate to the location where you are storing your files, and then click the **Save** button. Slides 2 through 8 contain content that is specific to presentations for potential donors and specific to the Galapagos Islands project. Leon wants you to save only the title slide, and he will add additional template content later.

8. In the Slides tab, select Slides 2 through 8.

9. Press the **Delete** key. The slides are deleted.

10. On Slide 1, replace the name in the subtitle with your name, save the changes to the template, and then close the template.

Creating a New Presentation Based on a Custom Template

If you open a presentation template using the Open command in Backstage view, the template itself will open. If you want to create a new presentation based on a custom template, you can double-click it in a File Explorer window or store it in a location that is accessible from the New screen in Backstage view.

To locate the folder that contains the templates that appear on the New screen, click the FILE tab, and then in the navigation bar, click Options to open the PowerPoint Options dialog box. In the navigation bar in the dialog box, click Save. In the Save presentations section, the path in the Default personal templates location is the location where templates that appear on the New screen need to be stored. You can change this location to any folder on your computer or network. A shared network folder is often used to make templates available throughout an organization.

To access templates in this folder, click the FILE tab, and then in the navigation bar, click New to display the New screen. Just above the templates on the New screen, click CUSTOM or PERSONAL, and then click Custom Office Templates.

Creating a Custom Show

A **custom show** is a presentation in which selected slides are included in a version of the presentation or the order of slides is changed without actually deleting or moving slides within the PowerPoint file. Custom slide shows are helpful if you need to quickly create a presentation for a specific audience or if you know you will be presenting to an audience that needs to see only some of the slides in a presentation or needs to see the slides in a different order. They are also useful if you will be using the same slide in multiple custom shows and you need to make a change to the slide; you only need to change it once and the updated slide will appear in all the custom shows in which it is included.

Creating a Custom Show

- On the SLIDE SHOW tab, in the Start Slide Show group, click the Custom Slide Show button, and then click Custom Shows to open the Custom Shows dialog box.
- Click the New button to open the Define Custom Show dialog box.
- In the Slide show name box, delete the text, and then type the name of the custom show.
- In the Slides in presentation box, click the check boxes next to the slides you want to add to the custom show, and then click the Add button.
- To reorder slides in the custom show, select a slide in the Slides in custom show box, and then click the Up or Down arrow.
- Click the OK button.
- Click the Close button.

Leon plans to present to other groups, such as a group of potential volunteers, about the plans for the Galapagos Islands. Therefore, he wants you to create a custom show in the Donors Presentation using the three slides that present information about the Galapagos Islands.

To create a custom show in the Donors Presentation:

1. Open the **Donors Presentation**, and then on the ribbon, click the **SLIDE SHOW** tab.

2. In the Start Slide Show group, click the **Custom Slide Show** button, and then click **Custom Shows**. The Custom Shows dialog box opens.

3. Click the **New** button. The Define Custom Show dialog box opens. See Figure 6-24.

Figure 6-24	Define Custom Show dialog box

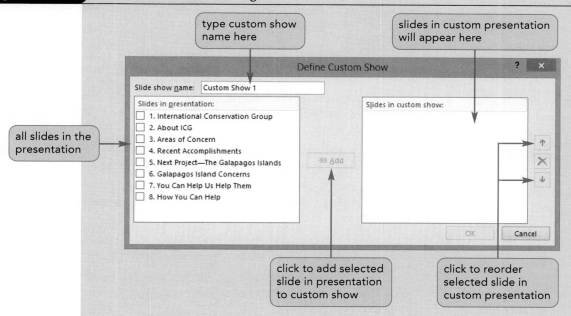

4. In the Slide show name box, delete the text, and then type **Galapagos Presentation**. Next, you'll select the slides that you want to use in the custom show.

5. In the Slides in presentation box on the left, click the check boxes next to **5. Next Project—The Galapagos Islands, 6. Galapagos Islands Concerns,** and **7. You Can Help Us Help Them**.

6. Click the **Add** button. The selected slides on the left are added to the Slides in custom show box on the right.

7. Click the **OK** button. The custom show you created is added to the list in the Custom Shows dialog box.

8. Click the **Close** button in the dialog box.

To run the custom show, you can click the Show button in the Custom Shows dialog box, or you can run it from Normal, Slide Show, or Presenter view.

To run a custom show:

1. On the SLIDE SHOW tab, in the Start Slide Show group, click the **Custom Slide Show** button. The menu now includes the custom show you created. See Figure 6-25.

Figure 6-25 **Custom Slide Show menu listing a custom show**

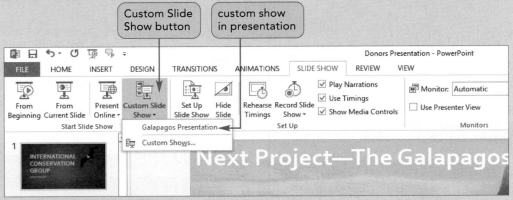

Photo courtesy of S. Scott Zimmerman

2. Click **Galapagos Presentation**. The first slide in the custom show in Slide Show view, Slide 5 ("Next Project—The Galapagos Islands"), appears in Slide Show view.

3. Advance the slide show. Slide 6 ("Galapagos Islands Concerns") appears, showing the first bulleted item and a photo of a crab.

4. Advance the slide show three more times to display each bulleted item and corresponding photo on Slide 6, and then remove the photos and display the complete bulleted list.

5. Advance the slide show again. Slide 7 ("You Can Help Us Help Them") appears, and then three photos animate, one after the other.

6. After the third photo appears, advance the slide show to display the black slide that indicates the end of a slide show, and then advance it once more to return to Normal view.

7. Save the changes to the presentation.

Working with File Properties

You can use file properties to organize presentations or to search for files that have specific properties. Refer to the Session 6.2 Visual Overview for more information on file properties. To view or modify properties, you need to display the Info screen in Backstage view.

Leon wants you to modify the Author property by adding yourself as an author and to add the Status property to indicate that this presentation is not yet final.

To modify file properties:

1. On the ribbon, click the **FILE** tab. The Info screen in Backstage view appears. The document properties are listed on the right side of the screen. See Figure 6-26.

Figure 6-26   Properties on Info screen in Backstage view

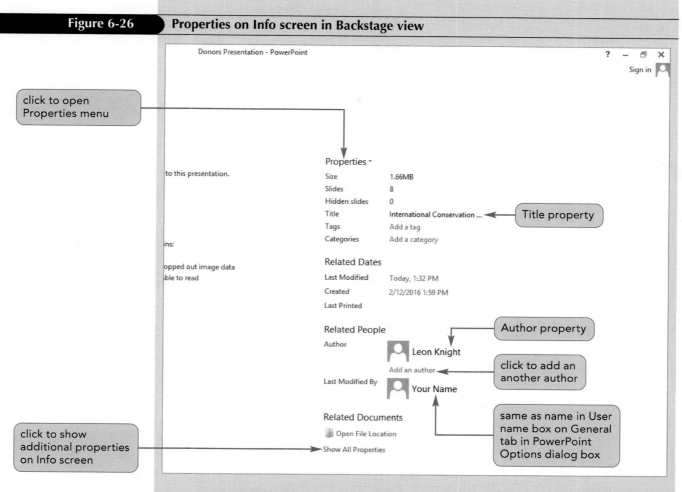

Because Leon created the original document, his name is listed as the Author. The name in the Last Modified By box is also picked up from the User name box in the PowerPoint Options dialog box. Because you have saved the file after making changes, your name (or the name in the User name box on your computer) appears here. You'll add yourself as an author.

2. In the Related People section, click **Add an author**, type your name in the box that appears, and then click a blank area of the screen.

   Trouble? If you pressed the Enter key after typing your name and a dialog box opens, click a blank area of the screen.

3. At the bottom of the Properties list, click the **Show All Properties** link. The Properties list expands to include all of the document properties.

4. Next to Status, click **Add text**, and then type **Draft**.

Leon also wants you to add the Checked by property so that you can list the names of people who have reviewed the presentation. The Checked by property is not listed on the Info screen. To add this property, you need to open the Properties dialog box for the presentation, and then add the property on the Custom tab.

To add a custom file property:

▶ **1.** At the top of the list of document properties, click the **Properties** button, and then click **Advanced Properties**. The Donor Presentation Properties dialog box opens with the General tab selected.

▶ **2.** Click the **Summary** tab. The Author box shows your name next to Leon's name.

▶ **3.** Click the **Custom** tab. This tab lists additional properties you can add. See Figure 6-27.

Figure 6-27   Custom tab in Donors Presentation Properties dialog box

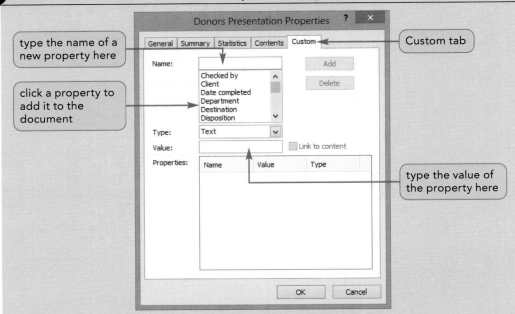

type the name of a new property here

click a property to add it to the document

Custom tab

type the value of the property here

TIP

To create a new property, type its name in the Name box, type a value in the Value box, and then click the Add button.

▶ **4.** In the Name list, click **Checked by**. "Checked by" appears in the Name box above the list.

▶ **5.** Click in the **Value** box, type **Mary Walsh**, and then click the **Add** button. "Checked by" and the value you gave it appear in the Properties list below the Value box.

▶ **6.** Click the **OK** button.

▶ **7.** In the navigation bar, click **Save** to save the changes to the presentation.

Customizing PowerPoint

In PowerPoint, you can customize the ribbon and the Quick Access Toolbar to suit your working style or your needs for creating a particular presentation. To customize the Quick Access Toolbar, you can add or remove buttons and change its location in the window. You customize the ribbon by creating a new group on an existing tab or creating a new tab with new groups, and then adding buttons to the new groups. To customize these elements, click the FILE tab, and then click Options to open the PowerPoint Options dialog box. To customize the Quick Access Toolbar, click Quick Access Toolbar in the navigation bar; to customize the ribbon, click Customize Ribbon in the navigation bar. In both cases, the right side of the dialog box changes to show two lists. On the left is an alphabetical list of commands. On the right, the current buttons on the Quick Access Toolbar or the current tabs and groups on the ribbon are listed. The list of commands on the left are Popular Commands; to see all the commands in PowerPoint, click the Choose commands from arrow, and then click All Commands. To add a command to the Quick Access Toolbar or to the selected group on the ribbon, click the command in the list on the left, and then click the Add button. To customize the ribbon, you must create a new group first. Select the tab on which you want to create the new group (or click the New Tab button to create a new tab), and then click the New Group button.

To move the Quick Access Toolbar so it appears below the ribbon, click the Customize Quick Access Toolbar button to the right of the Quick Access Toolbar, and then click Show Below the Ribbon.

Checking for Accessibility Issues

You already know how to add alt text to objects so that people who use screen readers will understand what is on each slide. You also know how to open the Selection pane and verify the order in which objects on a slide will be identified. You can use the Check Accessibility command to help you identify possible problems on slides that might prevent a presentation from being completely accessible. The Accessibility Checker classifies potential problems into three categories—errors, warnings, and tips. An error is content that is difficult-to-impossible for people with disabilities to access. Content that is flagged with a warning is content that sometimes makes it difficult for people with disabilities to access. And content flagged with a tip shouldn't be impossible for people with disabilities to access, but could possibly be organized in a way that would make it easier to access.

You will use the Accessibility Checker to see if you need to add alt text or change the order of objects on the slides.

To use the Accessibility Checker:

▶ 1. Click the **FILE** tab. The Info screen appears in Backstage view.

▶ 2. Click the **Check for Issues** button, and then click **Check Accessibility**. Backstage view closes and the Accessibility Checker task pane opens. See Figure 6-28.

Figure 6-28   Accessibility Checker task pane listing potential issues

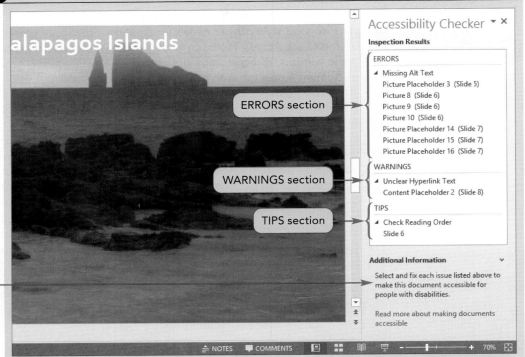

Photo courtesy of S. Scott Zimmerman

You know how to add alt text to objects, so you will let Leon know that the seven pictures listed in the task pane need alt text and find out how he wants to describe them. If you add alt text to an object, it will no longer be listed in the ERRORS section in the Accessibility Checker task pane. The single item in the TIPS section indicates that there might be a problem with the order in which items on Slide 6 are identified.

3. In the TIPS section, click **Slide 6**. Slide 6 appears in the Slide pane. You need to check the order of the objects on the slide.

4. Click the **HOME** tab.

5. In the Editing group, click the **Select** button, and then click **Selection Pane**. The Selection Pane opens. Remember that the objects on the slide will be identified in the reverse order that they are listed in the Selection Pane—in other words, from the bottom layer to the top layer. Picture 8 is the photo of the crab, which appears when the first bulleted item about crabs appears; Picture 9 is the photo of the sea lion, and this appears when the second bulleted item appears; and Picture 10, the tortoise, appears when the third bulleted item appears. If you add alt text to the three photos, this slide should be clear.

6. Close the Selection Pane. The single item in the WARNING section indicates that there is unclear hyperlink text on Slide 8.

> **7.** In the WARNINGS section, click **Content Placeholder 2 (Slide 8)**. Slide 8 appears in the Slide pane, and the Additional Information section in the task pane changes to describe the problem with unclear hyperlink text. You cannot add alt text to text, only to objects. To resolve an unclear hyperlink, you can open the Edit Hyperlink dialog box and change the text to display from the URL to a description of the web page or document to which you are linking; or you can add text to the slide that describes the link.

> **8.** In the Accessibility Checker task pane, click the **Close** button ⊠.

You will let Leon know of the accessibility issues so that he can decide how he wants to address them.

Encrypting a Presentation

To **encrypt** a file is to modify it to make the information unreadable to unauthorized people. When you encrypt a PowerPoint file, you assign a password to the file. The only way to open the file is by entering the password. When you create passwords, keep in mind that they are case sensitive; this means that "PASSWORD" is different than "password." Also, you must remember your password. This might seem obvious; but if you forget the password you assign to a file, you won't be able to open it.

REFERENCE

Encrypting a Presentation

- On the ribbon, click the FILE tab to open the Info screen in Backstage view.
- Click the Protect Presentation button, and then click Encrypt with Password.
- In the Encrypt Document dialog box, type a password in the Password box, and then click the OK button to open the Confirm Password dialog box.
- Retype the password in the Reenter password box.
- Click the OK button.

Leon wants you to encrypt the Donors Presentation file so that it can be opened only by people with whom he has shared the password.

To encrypt the presentation with a password:

> **1.** On the ribbon, click the **FILE** tab to open the Info screen in Backstage view.

> **2.** Click the **Protect Presentation** button. A menu opens listing options for protecting the presentation. See Figure 6-29.

Figure 6-29   **Protect Presentation menu on Info screen**

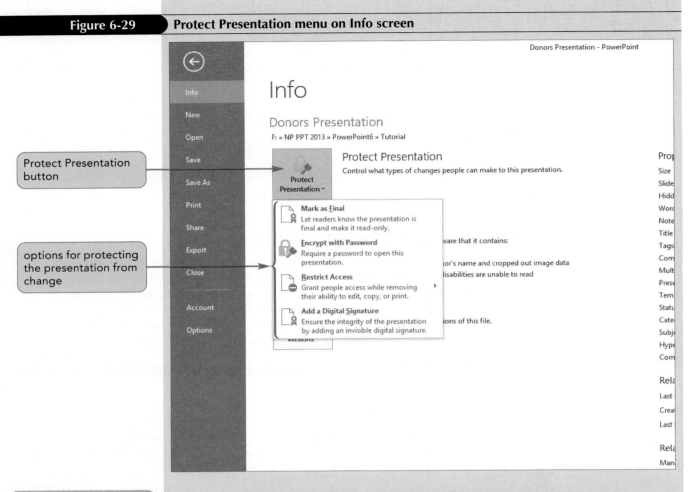

Protect Presentation button

options for protecting the presentation from change

3. Click **Encrypt with Password**. The Encrypt Document dialog box opens. Here you'll type a password.

4. Type **Donors**. The characters you type appear as black dots to prevent anyone from reading the password over your shoulder.

5. Click the **OK** button. The dialog box changes to the Confirm Password dialog box.

6. Type **Donors** again to verify the password, and then click the **OK** button. The Permissions section heading and the Protect Presentation button are orange to indicate that a protection has been set, and the message in the Permissions section explains that a password is required to open the presentation. See Figure 6-30.

Figure 6-30	Info screen after encrypting file

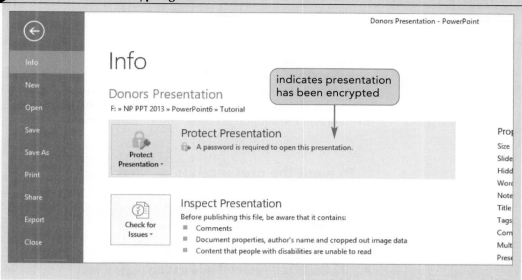

Now, when you save the file, it will be in an encrypted format, so that it can't be opened except by someone who knows the password. (Normally, you would use a stronger password than "Donors," but for the purpose here, you'll keep it simple and easy to remember.)

Decision Making: Creating Strong Passwords You Can Easily Remember

In a world where sharing digital information electronically is an everyday occurrence, a password used to encrypt a presentation is just one more password to remember. When deciding on a password, you should consider a strong password that consists of at least eight characters using a combination of uppercase and lowercase letters, numbers, and symbols. However, this type of password can be difficult to remember, especially if you have to remember multiple passwords. Some people use the same password for everything. This is not a good idea because if someone ever discovered your password, they would have access to all of the data or information protected by that password. Instead, you should come up with a plan for creating passwords. For example, you could choose a short word that you can easily remember for one part of the password. The second part of the password could be the name of the file, web site, or account, but instead of typing it directly, type it backwards, or use the characters in the row above or below the characters that would spell out the name. Or you could split the name of the site and put your short word in the middle of the name. Other possibilities are to combine your standard short word and the site or account name, but replace certain letters with symbols—for example, replace every letter "E" with "#" or memorize a short phrase from a poem or story and use it with some of the substitutions described above. Establishing a process for creating a password means that you will be able to create strong passwords for all of your accounts that you can easily remember.

PROSKILLS

Marking the Presentation as Final

TIP

Another way to allow people to see your presentation without being able to change it is to save the presentation as a PDF or as a picture presentation using commands on the Export screen in Backstage view.

You can make a presentation **read-only**, which means that others can read but cannot modify the presentation. To make a presentation read-only, you use the Mark as Final command, which disables all typing and editing commands. After you mark a presentation as final, you can turn off this status, and then edit the presentation, but this will remove the Marked as Final status.

Leon wants to place the presentation on the company's network so that other people in the company can see it. However, he doesn't want anyone to make any changes at this point. He asks you to mark the Donors Presentation as final. First, you'll change the name in the subtitle text box to your own name.

To mark the presentation as final:

1. At the top of the navigation pane, click the **Back** button to return to Normal view, display **Slide 1** (the title slide) in the Slide pane, and then replace "Leon Knight" with your name.

2. On the ribbon, click the **FILE** tab to return to the Info screen in Backstage view.

3. Click the **Protect Presentation** button, and then click **Mark as Final**. A dialog box opens stating that the presentation will be marked as final and then saved.

4. Click the **OK** button. The dialog box and Backstage view close, and another dialog box opens telling you that the document has been marked as final.

   Trouble? If the dialog box stating that the document has been marked as final does not appear, a previous user clicked the Don't show this message again check box in that dialog box. Skip Step 5.

5. Click the **OK** button. A yellow MARKED AS FINAL bar appears in place of the ribbon, the Marked as Final icon appears in the status bar, and "Read-Only" appears in the title bar. See Figure 6-31.

Figure 6-31   **Presentation marked as final**

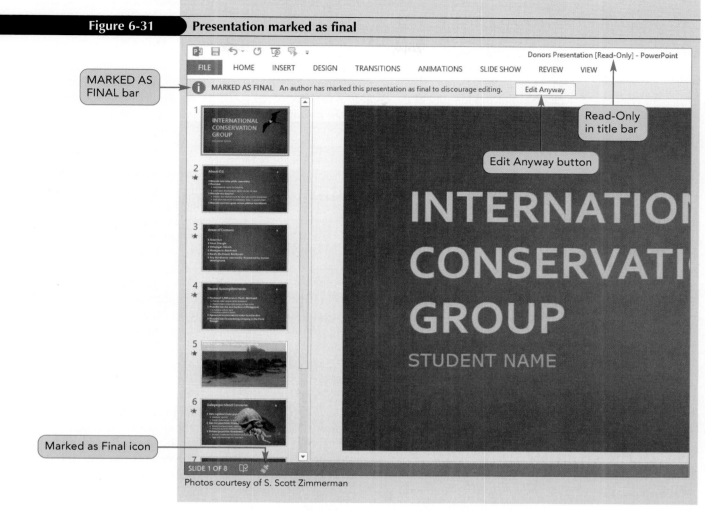

MARKED AS FINAL bar

MARKED AS FINAL   An author has marked this presentation as final to discourage editing.   Edit Anyway

Read-Only in title bar

Donors Presentation [Read-Only] - PowerPoint

Edit Anyway button

INTERNATIONAL CONSERVATION GROUP

STUDENT NAME

Marked as Final icon

SLIDE 1 OF 8

Photos courtesy of S. Scott Zimmerman

Now if you want to modify the presentation, you must remove the editing restriction by clicking the Edit Anyway button in the yellow MARKED AS FINAL bar.

INSIGHT

Adding a Digital Signature and Restricting Access

A **digital signature** is an electronic attachment, which is not visible in the file, that verifies the authenticity of the author or the version of the file by comparing the digital signature to a digital certificate. A **digital certificate** is a code attached to a file that verifies the identity of the creator of the file. When you digitally sign a document, the file is automatically marked as final to protect it from changes. If anyone removes the Marked as Final status so that you can make changes to the document, the signature is marked as invalid because it is no longer the same document the signatory signed. You can obtain a digital certificate from a certification authority.

To add a digital signature to a file, click the Protect Presentation button on the Info screen in Backstage view, and then click Add a Digital Signature. If the Get a Digital ID dialog box opens indicating that you don't have a digital ID and asking if you would like to get one from a Microsoft Partner, that means no digital certificate is stored on the computer you are using. If you click the Yes button, your browser starts and a web page opens listing certificate authorities from whom you can purchase a digital certificate.

If you or your company has access to a Rights Management Server or you are using Office 365 with RMS Online, you can restrict access to a presentation so that others can read it, but not make any changes to it or copy or print it. To do this, click the Protect Presentation button, and then use the Restrict Access command.

Presenting Online

You can run a slide show over the Internet so that anyone with a browser and the URL (the address for a web page on the Internet) for the presentation can watch it. When you present online, you send the presentation to a special Microsoft server that is made available for this purpose. (If you have access to a SharePoint server, you can send the presentation to that server instead.) A unique web address is created, and you can send this web address to anyone you choose. Then, while you run your presentation on your computer in Slide Show view, your remote audience members can view it on their computers in a web browser at the same time. Note that viewers will not be able to hear you unless you also set up a conference call.

In order to present online, you need a Microsoft account (or access to a SharePoint server) and you need to be connected to the Internet. If you don't have a Microsoft account, you can get one by clicking the Sign in link in the upper-right corner of the PowerPoint window or by going to www.live.com. Once you have a Microsoft account, you can connect to the Microsoft server from within your PowerPoint presentation to create the unique web address for your presentation and start presenting online.

To present a slide show online, click the SLIDE SHOW tab, and then in the Start Slide Show group, click the Present Online button to open the Present Online dialog box, as shown in Figure 6-32.

Figure 6-32   **Present Online dialog box**

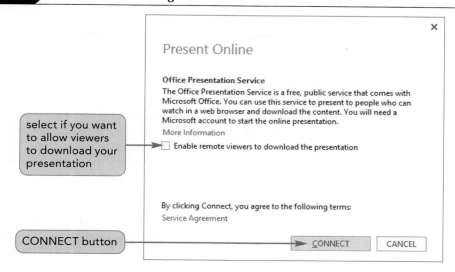

Click the CONNECT button. If you are signed into your Microsoft account in Office or with your Windows 8 account name, the dialog box changes to display the link to your presentation on the Microsoft server and a new tab—the PRESENT ONLINE tab—appears on the ribbon, as shown in Figure 6-33. If you are not signed in to your Microsoft account, you will need to sign in before the link is created.

Figure 6-33   **Present Online dialog box after web address is created**

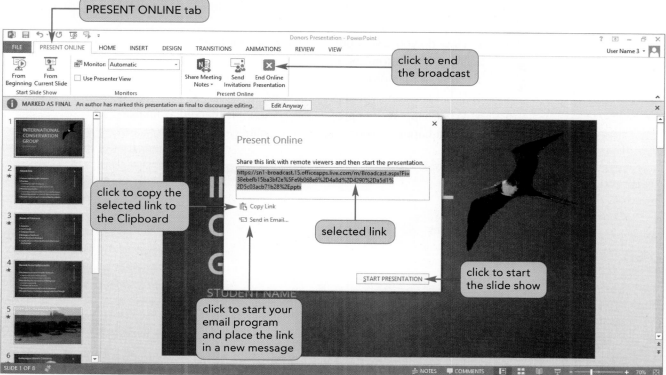

Photos courtesy of S. Scott Zimmerman

To invite people to watch your presentation, you need to send them the link. You can copy the link and send it to people via email, Facebook, or whatever your preferred method of communicating over the Internet is, or you can click Send in Email to open your email program and automatically include the link in the message. If you need to retrieve this link again after you close this dialog box, you can click the Send Invitations button in the Present Online group on the PRESENT ONLINE tab.

To start the online slide show, click the START PRESENTATION button in the Present Online dialog box or click one of the buttons in the Start Slide Show group on the PRESENT ONLINE tab. The presentation appears in Slide Show view on your computer (although you can switch to Presenter view if you prefer). Anyone watching the presentation online will see the first slide in their browser window. You can advance through the slide show as you normally would, and viewers will see the slides on their screens. Note that no matter what transition you see in Slide Show or Presenter view on your computer, viewers watching online will see the Fade transition. Also, not all animations will animate correctly, so if you plan to present online, you should preview the presentation in your own browser first and make sure the animations are acceptable.

To end the online slide show and disconnect from the Microsoft server, click the End Online Presentation button in the Present Online group on the PRESENT ONLINE tab. In the dialog box that opens warning you that everyone watching the online presentation will be disconnected, click the End Online Presentation button.

Note that if you needed to sign into your Microsoft account in order to present online, you are now signed into that account in Office. To sign out, click your user name in the upper-right corner of the PowerPoint window, and then click Account settings to open the Account screen in Backstage view. Below your user name, click Sign out.

REVIEW

Session 6.2 Quick Check

1. How do you save a presentation as a template?

2. What is a custom show?

3. What is a file property?

4. What is an encrypted presentation?

5. What happens to a presentation when it is marked as final?

6. What happens when you present online?

ASSESS

SAM Projects

Put your skills into practice with SAM Projects! SAM Projects for this tutorial can be found online. If you have a SAM account, go to www.cengage.com/sam2013 to download the most recent Project Instructions and Start Files.

PRACTICE

Review Assignments

Data Files needed for the Review Assignments: Interns – Mary.pptx, Interns.pptx, Seals.jpg, Thickness.jpg

The International Conservation Group runs a popular internship program. Leon frequently gives presentations at colleges and career fairs to describe the program to recent graduates. Complete the following steps:

1. Open the file **Interns**, located in the PowerPoint6 ▸ Review folder included with your Data Files. On Slide 1, replace the name in the subtitle with your name, and then save the file as **ICG Interns** in the location where you are saving your files.

2. Compare the ICG Interns presentation with the file **Interns–Mary**, located in the PowerPoint6 ▸ Review folder. Accept the two changes on Slide 5 ("Description of Field Jobs in Antarctica"). Do not accept any other changes, and then end the review.

3. Change the theme fonts to Tw Cen MT-Rockwell, and then customize the theme font set so that Body text uses the Calibri font. Save the custom theme font set as **ICG Fonts 2**.

4. Delete the custom theme font set from the computer.

5. Change the theme color palette to the Blue palette.

6. Modify the Ion Slide Master by using the Font dialog box to format the text in the title text box as Small Caps.

7. Continue modifying the Ion Slide Master by changing the bullet style in the content placeholder to a filled, narrow diamond named Wingdings 2: 183, located in the Wingdings 2 font set. (*Hint*: Drag the scroll box all the way to the bottom; the symbols in this font are organized by name in ascending numerical order.) Make sure its size is 100% of the size of the text.

8. Create a new layout after the Title and Content Layout.

9. Below the title text placeholder, add a Text placeholder that is the same width as the title text placeholder and that is 1.9" high. Reposition it, if necessary, so that the top edge of the Text placeholder touches the bottom edge of the title text placeholder.

10. Below the Text placeholder, add two Picture placeholders that are 3.25" high and 5.2" wide. Position them so that the left edge of the Picture placeholder on the left is aligned with the left edge of the Text placeholder and the right edge of the Picture placeholder on the right is aligned with the right-edge of the Slide Number placeholder, and so they are approximately vertically centered in the space between the Text placeholder and the bottom of the slide.

11. Rename the layout **Text & 2 Picture**.

12. On Slide 5 ("Description of Field Jobs in Antarctica"), change the layout to the custom layout Text & 2 Picture. In the Picture placeholder on the left, insert the photo **Seals**, located in the PowerPoint6 ▸ Review folder. In the Picture placeholder on the right, insert the photo **Thickness**, located in the same folder.

13. On Slide 4 ("Next Internship Opportunity—Antarctica"), fill the title text placeholder with a dark Blue-Gray color that has an RGB value approximately 93, 131, 186 from the very top of the photo. Change the fill to a gradient that uses two gradient stops that both use the color you selected from the photo. Change the transparency of the rightmost gradient stop, positioned at

the 100% mark, to 100%. If necessary, change the transparency of the leftmost gradient stop to 0%, and then reposition the leftmost gradient stop at the 25% position.

14. Save the changes to the presentation, and then save the presentation as a template named **Interns Template** in the location where you are saving your files. Close the template and reopen the **ICG Interns** presentation.

15. Change the name in the User name box on the General tab in the PowerPoint Options dialog box to your name, if necessary, and then insert the following as a comment on Slide 1 (the title slide): **Make sure you mention the number of hours they are expected to work each week**.

16. On Slide 2 ("About the Internship Program"), type the following as a reply to the comment on the slide: **Yes, I think that would be helpful**.

17. Delete Mary's comment on Slide 6 ("How to Sign Up").

18. Create a custom show named **Antarctica** that contains Slide 4 ("Next Internship Opportunity—Antarctica") and Slide 5 ("Description of Field Jobs in Antarctica").

19. Add **Revised** as the Status property. Add the custom property Editor with your name as the value of that property.

20. Check the presentation for accessibility issues. On the slide that is flagged as having unclear hyperlink text, add the speaker note: **Please add text describing the hyperlink**.

21. Encrypt the presentation with the password **Interns**, and then mark the presentation as final.

22. If necessary, change the text in the User name and Initials boxes on the General tab in the PowerPoint Options dialog box back to their original values.

Case Problem 1

APPLY

Data Files needed for this Case Problem: Scuba Background.jpg, Scuba – Ben.pptx, Scuba.pptx

Savoy Scuba Center   Daniel Savoy owns a full-service scuba diving center in Key Largo, Florida. He sells and rents scuba equipment, conducts PADI-certified diver courses, and runs diving expeditions that leave from three locations on the Keys. He asks you to help him prepare a presentation that describes the tours and the services he offers. Complete the following steps:

1. Open the presentation **Scuba**, located in the PowerPoint6 ► Case1 folder included with your Data Files, replace the name in the subtitle with your name, and then save the file as **Scuba Center** in the location where you are saving your files.

2. Compare the presentation to the presentation **Scuba – Ben**. Accept the change on Slide 2 ("Our Tours"). Do not accept any other changes.

3. Change the theme font set to Franklin Gothic.

4. Add the photo **Scuba Background**, located in the PowerPoint6 ► Case1 folder to the Savoy Scuba Slide Master. Resize the photo so it fills the slide, and then send it behind all the other objects on the slide.

5. On the Savoy Scuba Slide Master, change the color of the text in the title text and content placeholders to white. Then change the bullet symbol for all the levels in the content placeholder to a filled, right-pointing triangle named Wingdings 3: 125, located in the Wingdings 3 font set. Change the size of the bullet symbol to 80% of the size of the text.

6. In Slide Master view, on the Title Slide Layout, resize the title text and subtitle text placeholders so they are as wide as the slide, and then remove the footers.

7. On the Title and Content Layout, change the fill of the title text placeholder to the same color used in the content placeholder. Add a white, 2¼-point border around both placeholders, and then remove the footers.

8. In Normal view, on Slide 1 (the title slide), fill the title text box with the Dark Teal color of the ocean water to the left of the title text. Then change the fill to a gradient fill that uses four gradient stops. All four stops should be the same Dark Teal color that you just selected. Set the transparency of both the first stop at the 0% position and the last stop at the 100% position to

100%. If necessary, set the transparency of the two middle stops to 0%, adjust the position of the second stop so it is at 40%, and then adjust the position of the third stop so it is at 60%.

9. Save the changes to the presentation, and then save the presentation as a template named **Scuba Template** in the location where you are saving your files. Close the template.

10. Reopen the **Scuba Center** presentation. If necessary, change the text in the User name and Initials boxes on the General tab in the PowerPoint Options dialog to your name, and then on Slide 2, add the following as a reply to Ben's comment on the slide: **Dan will mention it during the presentation**. Reposition the comment balloons so they do not obscure any text. If necessary, change the text in the User name and Initials boxes on the General tab in the PowerPoint Options dialog box back to their original values.

11. Create a custom show named **Tours** that includes Slides 2, 3, and 4.

12. Add **New Customers** as the Categories property.

13. Check the accessibility of the presentation. On the first slide on which you need to check the reading order, add the speaker note: **Check the reading order on all of the slides with photos**.

14. Encrypt the presentation with the password **Scuba**, and then mark the presentation as final.

Case Problem 2

APPLY

Data Files needed for this Case Problem: Lake.jpg, People1.jpg, People2.jpg, People3.jpg, Service–Blake.pptx, Service.pptx

City of Mesquite, Nevada   Mahendra Kulkami is the city engineer of Mesquite, Nevada. His responsibilities include management of all projects for roadways, sidewalks, parks, running trails, and recreation facilities owned by the Mesquite municipality. Recently, Mahendra oversaw a project in which volunteers were invited to help clean up the shores of Mesquite Lake. He needs to give a presentation on the service project to the Mesquite City Council as part of his regular monthly report. He asks you to help him create the presentation. Complete the following steps:

1. Open the presentation **Service**, located in the PowerPoint6 ▸ Case2 folder included with your Data Files, replace the name in the subtitle with your name, and then save the file as **Service Project** in the location where you are saving your files.

2. Compare the presentation to Service – Blake, located in the PowerPoint6 ▸ Case2 folder. Accept all the changes on Slide 2 ("Overview of Problem").

3. Change the theme font set to Constantia-Franklin Gothic Book.

4. In the Depth Slide Master, change the font style of the title text placeholder to Small Caps.

5. In the Depth Slide Master, change the style of the bullets in the bulleted list to a solid, right-pointing arrow named Wingdings: 232, located in the Wingdings font. Change the bullet symbol size to 80% of the size of the text, and change the color to the Tan, Accent 2, color, if necessary.

6. Insert a new layout after the Title and Content Layout. Name it **Picture Bottom**.

7. In Slide Master view, on the Picture Bottom Layout, add two Text placeholders that are 2" high and 5.5" wide. Position them about one-eighth of an inch below the title text placeholder. Align the left edge of one of the Text placeholders with the left edge of the title text placeholder, and align the right edge of the other Text placeholder with the right edge of the title text placeholder.

8. On the Picture Bottom Layout, add a Picture placeholder the same width as the title text placeholder and 2.5" high, and place it below the Text placeholders you added.

9. Create another custom layout below the Picture Bottom Layout. Name this layout **2 Content 3 Picture**.

10. On the 2 Content 3 Picture Layout, add two Text placeholders that are 2" high and 5.5" wide. Position them about one-eighth of an inch below the title text placeholder. Align the left edge of one of the Text placeholders with the left edge of the title text placeholder, and align the right edge of the other Text placeholder with the right edge of the title text placeholder.

11. On the 2 Content 3 Picture Layout, add three Picture placeholders, each 2.3" high and 3.5" wide. Position them about one-eighth of an inch below the Text placeholders and distribute them evenly in a row, aligning the left edge of the leftmost Picture placeholder with the left edge of the title text placeholder, and aligning the right edge of the rightmost Picture placeholder with the right edge of the title text placeholder.

12. Change the layout of Slide 3 ("Service Day") to 2 Content 3 Picture. Use the Cut and Paste commands to move the "Distributed educational flyers" first-level bulleted item and its sub-items to the text placeholder on the right. In the three picture placeholders, insert the photos **People1**, **People2**, and **People3**, all located in the PowerPoint6 ▸ Case2 folder.

13. Apply the Simple Frame, White picture style to the three photos.

14. Change the layout of Slide 5 ("Next Steps") to Picture Bottom. Use the Cut and Paste commands to move the last two first-level bulleted items and their subitems to the text placeholder on the right. Insert the picture **Lake**, located in the PowerPoint6 ▸ Case2 folder, in the picture placeholder, and then apply the Simple Frame, White picture style to the photo.

15. If necessary, change the text in the User name and Initials boxes on the General tab in the PowerPoint Options dialog box to your name, and then reply to the comment on Slide 2 with **Yes, it is**. If necessary, change the text in the User name and Initials boxes on the General tab in the PowerPoint Options dialog box back to their original values.

16. Delete the comment on Slide 3 ("Service Day").

17. Add **Volunteers** as a Tags property and **Final** as the Status property. Add the custom property Department with the value **DPW**.

18. Encrypt the presentation with the password **Service**, and then mark the presentation as final.

Case Problem 3

RESEARCH

Data Files needed for this Case Problem: Exterior.jpg, Opera.pptx

The Sydney Opera House   The Board of Directors of the Sydney Opera House have decided to increase their fundraising efforts. Marianne Snow-Kimball is an intern at the Opera House. The board asks her to create a basic presentation that each member can use as a basis to create a customized presentation to give to potential donors. Complete the following steps:

1. Open the presentation **Opera**, located in the PowerPoint6 ▸ Case3 folder included with your Data Files, replace the name in the subtitle with your name, and then save the file as **Opera House** in the location where you are saving your files.

2. Examine the slide titles and the content currently on the slides.

3. There are several comments on the slides. Read each comment, and then research the requested information. Add the requested information on the slides.

4. Delete the comments on Slides 2 through 5 in the presentation.

5. On Slide 2 ("History"), insert the picture **Exterior**, located in the PowerPoint6 ▸ Case3 folder. Resize it to fill the slide.

6. On Slide 2, add the Grow/Shrink emphasis animation to the photo. Open the Effect Options dialog box for that animation, and then change the Size to 50% so that the image appears to shrink.

7. On Slide 2, add the Lines motion path animation to the picture you inserted on the slide, and then change the effect to Right.

8. Reorder the animations so that the emphasis animation for the Picture occurs first, then the Lines motion path, then the title text box animation, and then the items in the bulleted list.

9. Modify the start timing for the animations on Slide 2 as follows:
   - Emphasis animation applied to the picture animates On Click
   - Lines motion path applied to the picture, the animation applied to the title text box, and the animation applied to the first bulleted item in the list animate After Previous

- Entrance animations applied to the rest of the first-level items animate On Click
- Entrance animations applied to the second-level items animate With Previous

10. Change the color palette to the Grayscale palette.
11. Change the theme font set to Garamond.
12. On the Music Score Slide Master, in the content placeholder, change the bullet symbol used for first-level items to a double eighth note symbol (♫), named Beamed Eighth Notes, set at 100% of the size of the text, and then change the bullet symbol used for the second-level items to a single eighth note symbol (♪), named Eighth Note, set at 80% of the size of the text. These symbols are both in the Book Antiqua font—scroll to the bottom of the list to find them.
13. On the Music Score Slide Master, change the font size of the title text placeholder to 44 points. Change the size of the text in the first-level items to 28 points, and then change the size of the text in the second-level items to 24 points.
14. Create a Custom Show named **SOH Background** consisting of Slides 2 through 5.
15. Add the custom property "Department" with the value **Board of Directors**.
16. Encrypt the presentation with the password **SOH**, and then mark the presentation as final.

Case Problem 4

CREATE

Data Files needed for this Case Problem: Bakery – Ryan.pptx, Bakery.pptx

Ella's Baked Goods   Ella Stanton began selling homemade desserts and breads at craft shows and county fairs 10 years ago, and she sold out of her supply at every venue. She signed a contract with a local grocery store chain to provide her baked goods to them on a regular basis. She asks you to help her create a presentation that she can give to the bank to request a business loan with a line of credit. Complete the following steps:

1. Open the presentation **Bakery**, located in the PowerPoint6 ▸ Case4 folder included with your Data Files, replace the name in the subtitle with your name, and then save the file as **Baked Goods** in the location where you are saving your files.
2. Compare the presentation with the presentation **Bakery – Ryan**, located in the PowerPoint6 ▸ Case4 folder. Accept the change that adds a new Slide 6 ("Expenses"), and reset the new slide, if necessary. Do not accept any other changes.
3. Read the comments in the presentation, and then delete the comments on Slide 1 (the title slide), Slide 3 ("Current Situation"), and Slide 6 ("Expenses").
4. Refer to Figure 6-34 and modify the presentation to match the slides shown in the figure.
5. Create a custom show named **Financial Info** that consists of Slide 4 ("Snapshot of Financials") and Slide 5 ("2016 Current and Projected Total Sales").
6. If necessary, change the name in the User name and Initials boxes on the General tab in the PowerPoint Options dialog box to your name and initials, and then add a comment on Slide 7 ("Commitment to You") with the text **If you provide photos for this slide, modify the custom layout by replacing the Online Image placeholders with Picture placeholders**. Change the values in the User name and Initials boxes on the General tab in the PowerPoint Options dialog box back to their original values, if necessary.
7. Add the Status property with the value **Draft** to the presentation.
8. Encrypt the presentation with the password **Bakery**.
9. Save the changes to the presentation.

Figure 6-34 **Slides 2-7 in the Baked Goods presentation**

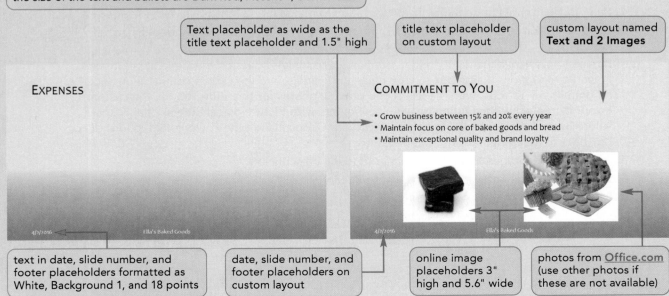

layout changed to Two Content; photo from
Office.com (use another one if this is not available)

first gradient stop in background is Gold,
Background 2, Lighter 80%, positioned at 60%

OVERVIEW

• Started as a hobby 10 years ago
• Four years ago started baking full-time
• Examples of Fairs Attended
  • New England Home Show (Boston)
  • Worcester Spring Home Show
  • Busy Girls Night Out (Swansea)
  • South Shore International Family Festival (Hingham)
  • Newburyport SpringFest

4/2/2016   Ella's Baked Goods

CURRENT SITUATION

• Pending agreement to provide goods to Carter's Markets
• Plan to add third employee
• More capacity needed on current equipment
• Packaging needs to be upgraded
• Production space needs to be upgraded

4/2/2016   Ella's Baked Goods

theme fonts changed to Candara;
theme color palette changed to Red

second gradient stop is Gold, Background
2, Darker 25%, positioned at 100%

layout changed to Two Content; photo from
Office.com (use another one if this is not available)

title text on all slides
formatted as Small caps

SNAPSHOT OF FINANCIALS

• Have cash on hand for 45 days
• Personal credit cards have balance of $1,800
• Personal expenses all up-to-date

4/2/2016   Ella's Baked Goods

2016 CURRENT AND PROJECTED TOTAL SALES

$50,000
$40,000
$30,000
$20,000
$10,000

March (Sales YTD)   June   September (assumes upgrades completed by end of June)   December

4/2/2016   Ella's Baked Goods

bullet style on all slides changed so that the symbols are 120% of
the size of the text and bullets are Dark Red, Accent 1, Darker 25%

Text placeholder as wide as the
title text placeholder and 1.5" high

title text placeholder
on custom layout

custom layout named
Text and 2 Images

EXPENSES

4/2/2016   Ella's Baked Goods

COMMITMENT TO YOU

• Grow business between 15% and 20% every year
• Maintain focus on core of baked goods and bread
• Maintain exceptional quality and brand loyalty

4/2/2016   Ella's Baked Goods

text in date, slide number, and
footer placeholders formatted as
White, Background 1, and 18 points

date, slide number, and
footer placeholders on
custom layout

online image
placeholders 3"
high and 5.6" wide

photos from Office.com
(use other photos if
these are not available)

Aa Verbal Communication

When You Are the Expert

When you give a presentation, you are the expert. Consequently, you need to be sure that you have adequately researched your topic and prepared your presentation so that your audience trusts you as a credible speaker. If you have solid knowledge behind your words, you will feel comfortable explaining the topic to someone who doesn't share that knowledge.

The more you understand a topic, the more relaxed you'll be speaking about it. Audiences will know when you are trying to talk around a topic you don't really understand. You must be able to correctly pronounce and explain terminology, provide additional information or quantitative data to support your main points, and logically guide your listeners through your presentation from beginning to end. You should be able to confidently explain the reasoning behind your arguments and provide support for your claims. You should also be ready to answer all types of questions from the audience and be prepared to counter possible objections that members of your audience might raise. Remember that if your audience consists of non-experts in the field, they will probably have a harder time interpreting any data you give, so you might need to provide additional explanation or images to help them understand the topic. By anticipating questions your audience might ask, you can plan to address those questions and concerns in your presentation. Being well-prepared as the topic expert will help you establish credibility with an audience, and they will trust that your information is correct and accurate.

Finally, try to anticipate what your audience needs to take away from your presentation, and then review it to make sure you are giving this to them. Understanding the needs and expectations of your audience and considering how your audience will use the information that you present will help you adapt your presentation to that audience. This will ensure that your presentation is useful, interesting, and relevant.

Once you've done the background research on your topic and feel comfortable that you can explain it to someone who doesn't have your knowledge, it's time to outline what you plan to say. Consider your main points first. What logical flow must your points have so the audience will follow the presentation to the conclusion? What information and level of detail do you need to convey to the audience? Do you need to do any additional research to be prepared to answer questions or fill gaps in your presentation?

Consider the kinds of illustrations, graphics, and audio or video materials you'll need to support or add further interest to what you plan to say. An image or video clip can go a long way toward making a point and will help you cut back on the amount of text you need to include.

Create a Formal Presentation

PROSKILLS

If you're like many students, you have participated in an internship, a mentored research project, a senior project (sometimes called a capstone project), an honors thesis, or a similar type of experience. Many of these types of experiences require a formal presentation. For example, some colleges and universities hold conferences on undergraduate research at which students present their research or creative works. Most honors students have to give a presentation on and defend their thesis in front of a faculty committee. In this exercise, you'll use PowerPoint to create a presentation that will contain information of your choice, using the PowerPoint skills and features presented in Tutorials 5 and 6.

Note: Please be sure not to include any personal information of a sensitive nature in the documents you create to be submitted to your instructor for this exercise. Later on, you can update the documents with such information for your own personal use.

1. Visit members of your department or talk to your mentor to see various presentations by other students or faculty so that you know the standards and customs of presentation in your discipline.
2. Consider using Word to create an outline of your presentation.

3. Start a new PowerPoint presentation using the theme and variant of your choice.

4. Customize the background, theme, and slide master, and create new layouts, as needed, to suit your content.

5. On Slide 1, give an informative title to your presentation. For example, if you did a research project in art history, you should use a specific, detailed title such as "The Influence of the Friendship and Rivalry between Picasso and Matisse on the Development of 21st Century Modern Art." Include not only your name, but your department and your mentor's name in the subtitle.

6. Create at least six slides in addition to the title slide with information about your project. If you created an outline in Word, import it. Include at least one slide each for the introduction, methodologies, results, discussion, and summary, if applicable to your project.

7. Include at least four graphics—images, charts, SmartArt, or tables. This might include pictures of your experimental setup, graphs of trends, a picture of your research group, or tables that include data gathered or computer-generated statistics. Consider creating the charts or tables in Word or Excel, and embedding or linking them in the presentation. You might also consider slides that consist solely of photographs or other graphics to convey your message. Add a video if it will make part of your presentation clearer.

8. Add sound clips if appropriate.

9. Apply an attractive style and animations to your graphical objects.

10. Apply slide transitions to all the slides in the presentation.

11. Rehearse your presentation, and then record narration for any slides that are not self-explanatory. Add speaker notes as needed to help you remember specific points.

12. Save the presentation with an appropriate name.

13. Export the presentation to Word to create handouts.

14. Encrypt the original presentation with a password, and mark it as final.

15. Give the presentation to your class or at some other venue, as the opportunity presents itself.

OBJECTIVES

- Insert slides from another presentation
- Change the theme fonts
- Modify the slide master
- Modify the background style
- Change slide layouts
- Resize, crop, and reposition photos
- Apply a style to pictures
- Modify the border of pictures
- Insert an online picture
- Fill the slide background with a picture and change its transparency
- Move an object through layers
- Animate objects and modify animation effects
- Add additional animations to objects
- Reorder animations
- Change the start timing of animations
- Apply a transition
- Check the spelling in a presentation
- Add a comment to a slide

Creating a Presentation About a Town Plan for Open Space

Case | *Hamilton Town Council*

Max Carter recently spoke at a town council meeting in Hamilton, Massachusetts about his concern that the town is being developed too rapidly. He wants to present a plan for maintaining open space in town. He created an outline in Word, and wants you to finish the presentation. Complete the following steps:

1. Create a new, blank presentation, and then insert Slides 2 through 7 from the presentation file **Ideas**, located in the AddCases folder included with your Data Files.
2. Type **Plan for Open Space** as the presentation title on Slide 1, and then add your name as the subtitle. Save the file as **Open Space Plan** in the location where you are saving your files.
3. Change the theme fonts to the Franklin Gothic theme font set. Reset the slides, if necessary.
4. In the slide master, change the formatting of the title text placeholder on all of the slides to bold and Small Caps.
5. Change the background style on all of the slides to the Style 9 background style.
6. On Slide 5, crop the photo from the top by about 1½" to just above the highest cloud, and then resize the cropped photo so it is 3" high, if necessary.
7. On Slides 3, 4, and 5, move the photos so that they are top-aligned with the bulleted list. On Slides 4 and 5, align the right edges of the photos and the title text boxes.
8. On Slides 3, 4, and 5, apply the Compound Frame, Black picture style to the photos.

STARTING DATA FILES

AddCases

Ideas.pptx
Rural.png

9. On Slide 6 ("Identify Possible Financial Resources"), insert a photo from Office.com that shows money. Resize it to fill the space, and then apply the Compound Frame, Black style.
10. On Slide 7 ("Good Stewardship Brings Rewards"), fill the background with the photo **Rural**, located in the AddCases folder. Change its transparency to 50%.
11. On Slide 2 ("Overview"), move the title text placeholder to the top layer. Use the Selection pane to help you identify the items on the slide.
12. On Slide 2, add the following animations. (Again, use the Selection pane as needed.)
    - Animate the content placeholder with the entrance animation Wipe and the From Left effect option.
    - Animate the photos named Picture 3 and Picture 4 so that they each appear using the entrance animation Fade, and then add to the photos named Picture 3 and Picture 4 the emphasis animation Grow/Shrink, the motion path animation Lines with the Right effect option, and the exit animation Disappear.
    - Animate the photo named Picture 5 with all of the same animations that you applied to Pictures 3 and 4 except do not apply the exit animation Disappear.
13. On Slide 2, modify the Grow/Shrink animation applied to each photo so the Size setting in the Grow/Shrink Effect Options dialog box is Smaller (or 50%).
14. On Slide 2, change the start timing of the entrance, emphasis, and motion path animations to After Previous, and change the start timing of the 3 first-level bulleted items to After Previous. Make sure the start timing of the 2 second-level bulleted items is set to With Previous. (*Hint*: Move the content placeholder to the top layer so that you can see the bulleted list. Move it back to the bottom layer when you are finished.)
15. On Slide 2, reorder the animations to match Figure 1-1. (*Hint*: Remember you can click the double down arrow in the Animation pane to expand the list of animations applied to the content placeholder.)

Figure 1-1   **Animation Pane for Slide 2**

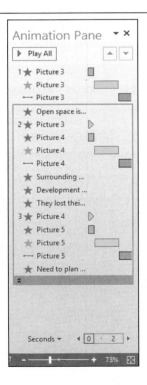

16. Apply the Cube transition to all of the slides.
17. Check the spelling in the presentation and correct errors as needed.
18. Change the name in the User name box in the PowerPoint Options dialog box to your name, if necessary. Add **Create hiking trails?** as a comment on Slide 3 ("Goals").
19. Save the changes to the presentation.

Geddes Trinkets

POWERPOINT

OBJECTIVES

- Change the theme fonts and theme colors
- Modify the slide master
- Change the alignment of text
- Create a new layout
- Duplicate a slide
- Resize and reposition text boxes
- Align objects on slides
- Apply animations and modify the effect options
- Change the start timing of animations
- Change slide layouts
- Insert pictures in content placeholders
- Compress pictures
- Apply transitions
- Cut and paste text
- View a presentation in Slide Show view
- Embed Excel worksheet data
- Link an Excel chart and change the chart type
- Add a speaker note

Case | *Geddes Trinkets*

Erika Geddes owns Geddes Trinkets in Warwick, Rhode Island, a wholesale vendor that distributes wood carvings, ceramic and porcelain figurines, and other handmade items, crafts, and artwork. She is trying to increase her sales volume by convincing established retailers to carry her product line. She wants you to help her create a presentation that will showcase the types of items she sells and explain her pricing and shipping. Complete the following steps:

1. Open the file **Showcase**, located in the AddCases folder included with your Data Files, and then save it as **Catalog Showcase** in the location where you are saving your files.
2. Change the theme fonts to the Candara theme font set, and then change the theme color palette to Median.
3. In Slide Master view, in the Title and Content layout, delete the two graphics at the top of the slide, and then change the alignment of the text in the title text placeholder so that it is left-aligned.
4. Create a new layout by doing the following:
   - Duplicate the Title and Content layout, and then rename the duplicated layout **2 Content and Text**.
   - On the duplicated layout, resize the content placeholder so it is 3.5" high and 5.75" wide.
   - Duplicate the resized content placeholder.

STARTING DATA FILES

AddCases

Chess1.jpg	GermanFigure2.jpg
Chess2.jpg	Intuit1.jpg
CzechDoll1.jpg	Intuit2.jpg
CzechDoll2.jpg	PeruDoll1.jpg
EcuaPots1.jpg	PeruDoll2.jpg
EcuaPots2.jpg	Showcase.pptx
Financial Data.xlsx	Totem1.jpg
GermanFigure1.jpg	Totem2.jpg

- Align the duplicated content placeholder so that its right edge is right-aligned with the right edge of the title text placeholder. Align the original content placeholder so that its left edge is left-aligned with the left edge of the title text placeholder. Align the top of the content placeholders so their top edges are on top of the bottom edge of the title text placeholder.
- Add a Text placeholder below the two content placeholders that is 12" wide and 1" high. Position it so that it is about one-eighth of an inch below the content placeholders. Change the alignment of the text in the Text placeholder to Center, and then remove the bullet symbols by deselecting the Bullets button in the Font group on the HOME tab.
- On the custom 2 Content and Text layout, apply the entrance animation Wipe to the Text placeholder, and then change its effect option to From Left. Change the start timing to After Previous.
- On the custom 2 Content and Text layout, add the entrance animation Shape to the content placeholder on the right; change its Direction effect option to Out, and then change its Shape effect option to Box. Change the start timing to After Previous.

5. Change the layout of Slides 3 through 9 to the custom 2 Content and Text layout. On each slide, insert the pictures located in the AddCases folder that correspond to the title. For example, on Slide 3, with the title "Hand-carved chess set from Africa," insert the picture Chess1 in the content placeholder on the left, and then insert the picture Chess2 in the content placeholder on the right.
6. Compress all the photos in the presentation to 96 ppi.
7. Apply the Wipe transition to Slides 2 and 3 and Slides 10 through 13. Apply the Conveyor transition to Slides 4 through 9.
8. View Slides 3 through 9 in Slide Show view. The Conveyor transition makes it look like the title and the other objects on the slide leave the slide, but the background doesn't move.
9. On Slides 3 through 9, use the Cut and Paste commands to move the title text to the Text placeholder at the bottom of the slide. Make sure there is nothing in the title text placeholders on these slides (that is, so that the placeholder text "Click to add title" appears).
10. In Slide Master view, modify the 2 Content and Text custom layout by deselecting the Title check box in the Master Layout group, and then add a Text Box shape using the Shapes command on the INSERT tab in place of the title text placeholder. Type **Examples of Products** in the text box. Resize the text box, if necessary, so that it is 12" wide and 1" high, and then position it so that its bottom edge aligns with the top edges of the content placeholders. Format the text in the text box so it is Candara (Headings), 36 points, and Olive Green, Accent 3, Darker 25%. Reset Slides 3 through 9, and then view them in Slide Show view again. Now it looks like the title remains on the screen with the background graphic while only the objects change.
11. Open the Excel workbook **Financial Data**, located in the AddCases folder, and then save it as Financial Data Updated in the location where you are saving your files.
12. On Slide 10 ("Wholesale Price List"), embed cells A4 through D16 from the Prices worksheet in the **Financial Data** Excel workbook, located in the AddCases folder. Resize the embedded table so it is 5" high and 8.7" wide, and then center it on the slide. Format the numbers in the Price column in the Accounting Number format with no decimal places.
13. On Slide 11 ("Sales History"), link the chart on the Sales worksheet in the **Financial Data** Excel workbook using the destination theme. Resize the linked chart so that it is 5" high and 9.5" wide, and then center it on the slide.
14. Edit the data on which the linked chart is based so that the sales in 2015 are 20.2 million, and then change the chart type of the linked chart to a Line chart. Save the changes to the Financial Data Updated worksheet.
15. On Slide 11, add **Sales of our products have increased steadily over the past ten years.** as a speaker note.
16. Save the changes to the presentation.

GLOSSARY/INDEX

SPECIAL CHARACTERS

\~(backslash), FM 11
. (dot), FM 16

A

accessibility, presentations, PPT 177–181, PPT 339–341

action button, PPT 207–210
    adding, PPT 207–208
    copying, PPT 208–209
    testing, PPT 209

Action Settings dialog box, PPT 208

active cell The cell in a spreadsheet in which you are entering data., PPT 149–150

Add Animation button, PPT 99

Add or Remove Columns button, PPT 111

adjustment handle A handle that appears on a selected object that you can drag to change the object's proportions without changing the size of the shape., PPT 70
    modifying shapes, PPT 169–170

Advance to the next slide button, PPT 32, PPT 33, PPT 55

alignment
    shapes, PPT 170–171
    text in table cells, PPT 93

alternative text (alt text) Text added to an object that describes the object., PPT 177–178

anecdote, gaining audience attention, PRES 16

animation An effect applied to an object that makes the object appear, disappear, or move., PPT 99, PPT 190–199
    Animation pane, PPT 196–198
    applying, PPT 103–107
    lists, PPT 109–111
    modifying advanced animation effect options, PPT 260–268
    multiple, adding to an object, PPT 192–196
    SmartArt diagrams, PPT 144–145
    start of animation, PPT 107–109
    transitions, PPT 100–102
    triggers, PPT 191, PPT 198–199
    types, PPT 102–103
    video, PPT 115–116

Animation Painter, PPT 99, PPT 106

Animation pane, PPT 196–198

animation sequence number A number that appears next to an object on a slide in the slide pane that indicates the order in which the item will animate during the slide show. The animation sequence numbers only appear on the slide when

the ANIMATIONS tab is selected on the ribbon., PPT 99

Animations gallery, PPT 104

ANIMATIONS tab, PPT 103–111
    Add Animation button, PPT 99
    Effect Options button, PPT 99
    Preview button, PPT 99

annotating slides during a slide show, PPT 288–290

appearance, evaluating, PRES 42–43

Apply To All button, PPT 98

archive A special type of folder containing compressed files., FM 26

arrow button, FM 2, FM 3, FM 11

artistic effects, photos, PPT 166–168

Artistic Effects menu, PPT 167

aspect ratio The ratio of an object's height to its width., PPT 45

audience
    analyzing needs and expectations, PRES 9–10
    anticipating questions from, PRES 35–36
    comments about, gaining audience attention, PRES 17
    connecting to, PRES 39
    eye contact, PRES 39–40
    gaining attention, PRES 15–16
    international, PRES 9–10
    participation, preparing for, PRES 36–37

audio
    playing music across slides, PPT 147
    slides, PPT 145–147

AutoCorrect A PowerPoint feature that automatically corrects many commonly mistyped and misspelled words after you press the spacebar or the Enter key., PPT 10–11

AutoFit A feature that automatically adjusts the size of the font and line spacing in a text box to fit the content., PPT 15

B

background
    hiding graphics, PPT 203
    removing from photos, PPT 164–166
    slides, changing, PPT 200–203
    transparency, PPT 202–203

backslash (, file path, FM 11

Backstage view The view that appears when you click the File tab on the ribbon, and contains the commands that allow you to manage your presentation files and PowerPoint options., PPT 5

backup A duplicate copy of a file., FM 25

Black or unblack slide show button, PPT 55

body language awareness, PRES 39–40

body of presentation, PRES 18–23
    conclusion, PRES 23
    evaluating information, PRES 19
    gathering information, PRES 18
    organizing information, PRES 19–22

border, tables, PPT 90–91

bulleted list A list of items with some type of bullet symbol in front of each item or paragraph., PPT 14–15
    animating, PPT 109–110
    modifying bullet symbol, PPT 316–317

Bullets and Numbering dialog box, PPT 317

business jargon, avoiding, PRES 42

C

category One series of data represented in a chart or graph., PPT 139

category as strategy for focusing presentation, PRES 14

CD, packaging presentations for, PPT 229–230

cell (spreadsheet) The intersection of a row and a column in a spreadsheet., PPT 138
    active, PPT 149–150

cell (table) The area where a row and column intersect in a table., PPT 84, PPT 138
    alignment of text, PPT 93
    changing fill, PPT 90
    filling with pictures, PPT 91–92
    formatting, PPT 273–277

Change New Theme Fonts dialog box, PPT 311

Change your view button, FM 2

Charms bar, FM 4

chart A visual that uses lines, arrows, and boxes or other shapes to show parts, steps, or processes., PPT 138–139, PPT 147–153
    creating, PPT 147–150
    Excel, linking, PPT 282–285
    formatting, PPT 151–153
    formatting chart elements, PPT 285–288
    selecting type, PPT 153

Choose a SmartArt Graphic dialog box, PPT 25–26

chronological organization A presentation organization in which you organize information in a step-by-step fashion or according to a time sequence., PRES 20–21, PRES 22 chronology as strategy for focusing presentation, PRES 14

classification as strategy for focusing presentation, PRES 14

Clipboard A temporary storage area for files and information that you have copied or moved from one place and plan to use somewhere else., FM 21, PPT 22

    moving files, FM 22–23

closing a presentation, PPT 30–31

collaborative presentation, PRES 11

color

    fonts, selecting, PPT 159

    themes, changing, PPT 312–313

    themes, customizing, PPT 211–215

Colors dialog box, PPT 213

column, table

    changing size, PPT 88

    deleting, PPT 87

    inserting, PPT 86–87

    new, inserting, PPT 91

comment, PPT 307–309

compatibility of PowerPoint versions, PPT 230–233

component as strategy for focusing presentation, PRES 14

Compress Media dialog box, PPT 120

Compress Pictures button, PPT 43–44

compressed file, FM 26–28

    compressing, FM 26, FM 27

    extracting, FM 26, FM 27–28

compressed folder A folder that stores files in a format that requires less disk space., FM 2

compressing

    files and folders, FM 26, FM 27

    media, PPT 119–120

    photos, modifying options, PPT 42–44

Computer icon, FM 3

conclusion of presentation, PRES 23

content placeholder A placeholder designed to hold several types of slide content including text, a table, a chart, SmartArt, a picture, or a video., PPT 12

contextual tab A ribbon tab that appears only in context-that is, when a particular type of object is selected or active-and contains commands for working with that object., PPT 7

contrast, photos, PPT 162–163

Convert to SmartArt Graphic button, PPT 24

copy (file) To place a file in a new location that you specify without removing it from its current location., FM 20

    files and folders in File Explorer, FM 20–21, FM 24–25

Copy button, PPT 22

Copy command, FM 21

copy of content, preparing, PRES 44

Copy to button, FM 21

copying Leaving the original selected text or object on the slide and placing a copy of it on the Clipboard., PPT 22

    action buttons, PPT 208–209

    animations, PPT 106

    slides, PPT 28

copyright, PPT 76

Corrections menu, PPT 163

Create New Theme Colors dialog box, PPT 212–213

cropping Removing the parts of a photo you don't want to include., PPT 40

    photos, PPT 40–42

    removing cropped areas from photos, PPT 43

current problem/issue, gaining audience attention/issue, PRES 17

custom gradient, PPT 174

custom layout, creating, PPT 319–329

custom shape, PPT 168–173

    aligning objects, PPT 170–171

    merging shapes, PPT 171–173

    modifying shapes using adjustment handle, PPT 169–170

custom show A version of a presentation in which selected slides from the original presentation are stored in the original presentation file., PPT 334–336

Customize Quick Access Toolbar button, PPT 2

customizing

    PowerPoint, PPT 339

    theme colors, PPT 211–215

Cut button, PPT 22

Cut command, FM 21

cutting Remove the selected text or objects from one location so that you can place it somewhere else., PPT 22

cycle diagram, PPT 24

D

data series The set of values represented in a chart., PPT 139

deductive organization A presentation organization in which you present your conclusions or solutions first, and then explain the information that led you to your conclusions., PRES 19–20, PRES 22

Define Custom Show dialog box, PPT 335

definition, gaining audience attention, PRES 16

delay after animation, PPT 108–109

deleting. *See also* removing

    columns in tables, PPT 87

    custom theme colors, PPT 214–215

    files and folders, FM 25

    rows in tables, PPT 87

    slides, PPT 29–30

delivering a presentation, PRES 32–47

    body language awareness, PRES 39–40

    choosing method, PRES 34

    connecting to audience, PRES 39

    evaluating your appearance, PRES 42–43

    evaluating your performance, PRES 46–47

    eye contact, PRES 40

    grammar and pronunciation, PRES 40–41

    online, PPT 346–348

    preparing for, PRES 34

    preparing for audience interaction, PRES 35–37

    referring to visuals, PRES 42

    rehearsing, PRES 37–38

    setting up, PRES 43–46

    speaking voice, PRES 40

demographics Characteristics that describe your audience., PRES 9

demonstrative presentation Presentation that shows an audience how something works, educates them on how to perform a task, or help them to understand a process or procedure., PRES 6–7

demote To move an item lower in the outline, for example, to change a slide title into a bulleted item on the previous slide or change a first-level bullet into a second-level bullet., PPT 252

DESIGN tab

    Themes gallery, PPT 36–37, PPT 74

    Themes group, PPT 72

desktop, Windows 8 and Windows 7 compared, FM 4

destination file, PPT 271

destination program, PPT 271

Details pane The pane in Windows Explorer that displays the characteristics of the folder or selected object., FM 2

diagram A drawing that visually depicts information or ideas and shows how they are connected., PPT 24

    SmartArt. *See* SmartArt

Dialog Box Launcher, PPT 24

digital certificate A code attached to a file that verifies the identity of the creator of the file., PPT 346

digital signature An electronic attachment not visible in the file that verifies the authenticity of the author or the version of the file by comparing the digital signature to a digital certificate., PPT 346

disk A computer device for storing data., FM 5

displaying. *See also* viewing

    blank slides, PPT 55

Document Inspector, PPT 227–228

dot (.), filenames, FM 16

dragging a file, FM 21–22

DRAWING TOOLS FORMAT tab, PPT 7, PPT 70
    Flip commands, PPT 83

drive A computer device that can retrieve and sometimes record data on a disk., FM 6

E

Edit Hyperlink dialog box, PPT 204

editing
    photos, PPT 162–163
    presentations, PPT 10–11

Effect Options button, PPT 98, PPT 99

Effect Options dialog box, PPT 264, PPT 268

element as strategy for focusing presentation, PRES 14

embedding, PPT 270
    Excel worksheets, PPT 277–282
    pasting and linking compared, PPT 285

emphasis animation, PPT 103

encrypt To modify a file to make the information unreadable to unauthorized people., PPT 341–343

entrance animation, PPT 102, PPT 105

evaluating your performance, PRES 46–47

Excel. *See* Microsoft Excel

exit animation, PPT 103

exiting PowerPoint, PPT 60

exporting presentations to Word, creating handouts by, PPT 290–292

extension The three of four characters that follow the dot in a filename and identify the file's type., FM 16

extract To create an uncompressed copy of a compressed file in a folder you specify., FM 26, FM 27–28

eye contact, PRES 39–40

F

familiar phrase, gaining audience attention, PRES 16

file A collection of data that has a name and is stored on a computer., FM 5
    backup copy, FM 25
    compressed, FM 2, FM 26–28
    compressing, FM 26, FM 27
    copying, FM 20–21, FM 24–25
    deleting, FM 25
    destination, PPT 271
    determining where to store, FM 8
    linking, PPT 211
    moving, FM 20–24
    multiple, selecting, FM 24
    opening, FM 15–16

organizing files, FM 6–8
    properties, PPT 330–331, PPT 336–338
    saving, FM 16–18
    source, PPT 270

File Explorer A Windows 8 tool that displays the contents of your computer and uses icons to represent drives, folders, and files., FM 3, FM 8–14
    changing views, FM 12–13
    compressed files, FM 26–28
    copying files and folders, FM 20–21, FM 24–25
    creating folders, FM 19–20
    deleting files and folders, FM 25
    expanding ribbon, FM 13–14
    moving files and folders, FM 20–24
    navigating to data files, FM 10–12
    opening, FM 10
    opening files, FM 15–16
    panes, FM 8
    renaming files, FM 26
    saving files, FM 16–18

file icon An icon that indicates a file's type., FM 3

file path A notation that indicates a file's location., FM 2, FM 3, FM 10–12

file system An operating system's hierarchy of folders and files, which ensures system stability and enables Windows to find files quickly., FM 6, FM 7

filename The name of a file; provides important information about the file, including its contents and purpose., FM 3, FM 16–17

fill The formatting of the area inside of a shape., PPT 70
    changing to texture, PPT 173–174

Fill command, PPT 79

filler, avoiding, PRES 41

first-level item A main item in a list., PPT 14

Fit slide to current window button, PPT 3

Flip command, PPT 83

folder A container for files and subfolders., FM 5
    backup copy, FM 25
    compressing, FM 26, FM 27
    copying, FM 20–21, FM 24–25
    creating, FM 19–20
    deleting, FM 25
    moving, FM 20–24
    multiple, selecting, FM 24
    organizing folders, FM 6–8

font A set of characters with the same design., PPT 7
    adjusting size, PPT 37–38
    colors, selecting, PPT 159
    tables, changing size, PPT 88
    themes, PPT 35–36
    themes, changing, PPT 310–312

Font Color button menu, PPT 20

Font dialog box, PPT 316

Font group, PPT 19–21

footer Information that appears at the bottom of slides, notes pages, or handouts of a presentation., PPT 121–124

Format Painter, PPT 21

Format Picture task pane, PPT 177

Format Shape task pane, PPT 177

formatting
    cells in tables, PPT 273–277
    chart elements, PPT 285–288
    charts, PPT 151–153
    pictures, PPT 81–82
    shapes, PPT 79–81, PPT 173–177
    tables, PPT 88–93
    text, PPT 19–22

Full Page Slides button, PPT 58

G

GB. *See* gigabyte

geography as strategy for focusing presentation, PRES 14

gesture, FM 4–5

gigabyte (GB) 1 billion bytes of data., FM 6

gradient, custom, in shape, PPT 174

grammar, PRES 40–41

graph A visual that shows the relationship between variables along two axes or reference lines: the independent variable on the horizontal axis and the dependent variable on the vertical axis., PPT 147

graphic A picture, shape, design, graph or chart, diagram, or video., PRES 26
    background, hiding, PPT 203
    as visual, PRES 26–29

group A collection of related buttons for related commands organized on a ribbon tab., PPT 2

H

handout Printed document you give to your audience before, during, or after your presentation. Handouts can be a printed version of your presentation, but they can also be brochures, an instruction manual, booklets, or anything you think will help the audience remember your key points., PRES 38
    creating by exporting a presentation to Word, PPT 290–292
    printing, PPT 58–59

hard disk A storage device permanently housed inside the computer case., FM 6

header Information that appears at the top of notes pages or handouts of a presentation., PPT 122–124

Header and Footer dialog box, PPT 121–122

Help button, PPT 3

hiding background graphics, PPT 203

hierarchy diagram, PPT 24

HOME tab
    Add or Remove Columns button, PPT 111
    Convert to SmartArt Graphic button, PPT 24
    Copy button, PPT 22
    Cut button, PPT 22
    Font group, PPT 19–21

hyperlink, PPT 204–211
    adding action buttons, PPT 207–210
    to another file, PPT 211
    creating, PPT 205–207

Hyperlink to Slide dialog box, PPT 208–209

I

icon, Windows 8 and Windows 7 compared, FM 4

importing Word outlines, PPT 244–247

impromptu presentation, PRES 34

inductive organization A presentation organization in which you begin with the individual facts and save your conclusions until the end of your presentation., PRES 20, PRES 22

informative presentation Presentation designed to inform or educate., PRES 6, PRES 7

Insert Chart dialog box, PPT 148

Insert Hyperlink dialog box, PPT 205

Insert Pictures dialog box, PPT 202

INSERT tab
    Online Pictures button, PPT 74
    Picture button, PPT 39
    Shapes button, PPT 77
    Video button, PPT 111, PPT 112

inserting slides from another presentation, PPT 249–252

insertion point An object on the screen that indicates where text will appear when you start typing, usually appears as a blinking line., PPT 7

intellectual property, PPT 76

international audience, PRES 9–10

introduction, PRES 15–18
    gaining audience's attention, PRES 15–16
    providing overview, PRES 18

J

jargon, business, avoiding, PRES 42

K

key point, identifying, PRES 15

keyboard, Windows 8 and Windows 7 compared, FM 4

keyword Word or phrase that you can enter in as search box that describes an image that you want to search for., PPT 74

kiosk browsing, PPT 225–226

L

language, proofing, PPT 94–97

Large icons view button, FM 3

layer, PPT 257–260

layout The arrangement of placeholders on the slide; in SmartArt, the arrangement of the shapes in the diagram., PPT 11, PPT 24
    custom, creating, PPT 319–329
    SmartArt diagrams, changing, PPT 142–143

library In File Explorer, a container for folders and files that organize files by category-documents, music, pictures, and videos, no matter where these files are stored, such as your hard disk, removable drives, and network., FM 2, FM 3
    linking, PPT 271
    breaking links, PPT 287–288
    Excel charts, PPT 282–285
    options, PPT 283
    pasting and embedding compared, PPT 285
    list, PPT 14–19
    animating, PPT 108–111
    bulleted, PPT 14–15
    converting to SmartArt diagrams, PPT 24–27
    levels, PPT 14
    modifying style, PPT 316–319
    numbered, PPT 16–17
    unnumbered, PPT 17–19

list diagram, PPT 24

Live Preview A feature which previews the change on the slide so you can instantly *see* what the text will look like if you apply that format., PPT 19

M

matrix diagram, PPT 24

merging shapes, PPT 171–173

Microsoft Excel
    embedding Excel worksheets, PPT 277–282
    linking Excel charts, PPT 282–285

Microsoft PowerPoint 2013 A presentation graphics program that you can use to create and display visual and audio aids on slides to help clarify the points you want to make in your presentation or to create a presentation that people view on their own without you being present., PPT 1
    customizing, PPT 339
    exiting, PPT 60
    saving presentations as earlier version, PPT 230–233
    starting, PPT 5–6

Microsoft PowerPoint Compatibility Checker dialog box, PPT 231

Microsoft Word
    creating handouts by exporting a presentation to, PPT 290–292
    importing outlines to create presentations, PPT 244–247
    inserting Word tables, PPT 272–273

Mini toolbar A toolbar that appears when you first select text, and contains commonly used buttons for formatting text., PPT 19, PPT 21

More button A button that appears on all galleries that contain additional items or commands that don't fit in the group on the ribbon., PPT 36

More slide show options button, PPT 32, PPT 33

motion path, PPT 103

mouse interaction, FM 4–5

move (file) To remove a file from its current location and place it in a new location., FM 20
    File Explorer, FM 20–24

Move to button, FM 21, FM 23–24

moving
    photos, PPT 45–47
    slides, PPT 28–29
    text boxes, PPT 48

N

narration, recording, PPT 221–224

navigating to data files in File Explorer, FM 10–12

navigation bar The bar on the left side of Backstage view that contains commands for working with the file and program options., PPT 9

navigation pane The left pane of the File Explorer window that provides access to resources and locations on your computer., FM 2, FM 3, FM 9

nervousness, overcoming, PRES 38

Normal view A view in PowerPoint that displays slides one at a time in the Slide pane, allowing you to *see* how the text and graphics look on each slide, and displays thumbnails of all the slides in the presentation in the Slides tab on the left., PPT 6

note. *See* speaker note

Notes Page view A view in which the image of the slide appears at the top of the page, and the notes for that slide appear underneath the slide image., PPT 49

Notes pane A pane you can display below the Slide pane in Normal view in which in image of the slide appears in the top half of the presentation window and the notes for that slide appear in the bottom half., PPT 49

numbered list A list similar to a bulleted list except that numbers appear in front of each item instead of bullet symbols., PPT 16–17

O

occasion, comment about, gaining audience attention, PRES 17

Office Clipboard A special a Clipboard available only to Microsoft Office applications. Once you activate the Office Clipboard, you can store up to 24 items on it and then select the item or items you want to paste., PPT 24

online delivery, PPT 346–348

online picture, inserting, PPT 74–76

Online Pictures button, PPT 74

Open command, FM 15

opening
    File Explorer, FM 10
    files, FM 15–16
    presentations, PPT 34

optimizing media, PPT 120

Options dialog box, PPT 229

order
    animations, PPT 106–107
    objects on Selection pane, PPT 180
    of reading objects on screen reader,
    PPT 179–180

orientation
    slide shows with two orientations, PPT 257
    slides, changing, PPT 248

outline
    printing presentation as, PPT 58, PPT 59–60
    Word, importing to create presentation,
    PPT 244–247

Outline view The PowerPoint view that
displays the outline of the presentation in the
Outline tab to the left of the Slide pane.,
PPT 252–254

P

Package for CD dialog box, PPT 229

pane, Windows Explorer, FM 8

Paragraph dialog box, PPT 319

password
    encrypting presentations, PPT 341–343
    strong, PPT 343

Paste Options menu, PPT 22–23

pasting Inserting copied or cut text or objects
stored on the Clipboard anywhere in the
presentation or in any file in any Windows
program., PPT 22
    embedding and linking compared, PPT 285

persuasive presentation Presentation designed to
persuade or sell., PRES 6, PRES 7

photo, PPT 38–44
    artistic effects, PPT 166–168
    compression options, modifying, PPT 42–44
    cropping, PPT 40–42
    editing, PPT 162–163
    keeping uncompressed, PPT 44
    removing background, PPT 164–166
    removing cropped areas, PPT 43
    stored on computer or network, inserting,
    PPT 39–40

photo album, creating, PPT 328

picture
    adding to slide background, PPT 100–101
    formatting, PPT 81–82
    online, inserting, PPT 74–76
    resizing and moving, PPT 45–47

Picture Border button, PPT 71

Picture button, PPT 39

picture diagram, PPT 24

Picture Effects button, PPT 71

Picture Styles gallery, PPT 71

PICTURE TOOLS FORMAT tab, PPT 71, PPT 81
    Compress Pictures button, PPT 43–44
    Reset Picture button, PPT 82
    Size group, PPT 45

placeholder A region of a slide reserved for
inserting text or graphics., PPT 2

planning a presentation, PPT 4, PRES 2–11

playback, video, PPT 112–115
    modifying, PPT 114–115

PLAYBACK tab, PPT 115

Play/Pause animation, PPT 191

point A unit of measurement for indicating the size
of text., PPT 14

point of view as strategy for focusing presentation,
PRES 14

pointer, PPT 32

portion as strategy for focusing presentation,
PRES 14

poster frame The frame that appears on the slide
when the video is not playing., PPT 117–118

PowerPoint. *See* Microsoft PowerPoint 2013

PowerPoint Options dialog box, PPT 307

PowerPoint Viewer, PPT 230

Present Online dialog box, PPT 347

presentation A talk (lecture) or prepared file in
which the person speaking or the person who
prepared the file-the presenter-wants to
communicate with an audience to explain new
concepts or ideas, sell a product or service,
entertain, train the audience in a new skill or
technique, or any of a wide variety of other topics.,
PPT 4, PRES 4
    accessibility, PPT 177–181, PPT 339–341
    audience. *See* audience
    body, PRES 18–23
    checking compatibility, PPT 230–231
    choosing when to enhance, PPT 111
    closing, PPT 30–31
    collaborative, PRES 11
    comparing presentations, PPT 304–306
    conclusion, PRES 23
    creating handouts by exporting to Word,
    PPT 290–292

delivering. *See* delivering a presentation
determining form, PRES 5–6
displaying blank slides, PPT 55
dividing into sections, PPT 254–257
editing, PPT 10–11
encrypting, PPT 341–343
focusing, PRES 15
identifying desired outcomes, PRES 7–8
identifying key points, PRES 15
importing Word outlines to create,
PPT 244–247
impromptu, PRES 34
introduction, PRES 15–18
marking as final, PPT 344–345
moving slides in, PPT 28–29
new, creating based on custom template,
PPT 334
opening, PPT 34
packaging for CDs, PPT 229–230
planning, PPT 4, PRES 2–11
printing, PPT 56–60
purposes. *See* purpose of presentation
saving. *See* saving presentations
self-running. *See* self-running presentation
slides. *See* slide

presentation media Visual and audio aids that can
be used to support key points and engage the
audience's attention., PPT 4, PRES 4

presenter The person delivering a presentation.,
PRES 4

Presenter view A view in PowerPoint that allows
you to view your slides with speaker notes on one
monitor, while the audience sees only the slides in
ordinary Slide Show view on another monitor or
screen., PPT 33, PPT 54–55

presenting online, PPT 346–348

Preview button, PPT 99

previewing an animation, PPT 108

printing a presentation, PPT 56–60

problem-solution organization A presentation
organization of presenting a problem, outlining
various solutions to the problem, and then
explaining the solution you recommend.,
PRES 21–22

process diagram, PPT 24

program
    destination, PPT 271
    source, PPT 270

promote To move an item higher in the outline, for
example, to change a second-level bullet into a
first-level bullet or change a first-level bulleted item
into a slide title., PPT 252

pronunciation, PRES 40–41

proofing language, PPT 94–97

property, files, PPT 330–331, PPT 336–338

purpose of presentation
    determining, PRES 6–7
    stating, PRES 17

pyramid diagram, PPT 24

Q

quantitative data, gaining audience attention, PRES 16

question
    from audience, anticipating, PRES 35–36
    gaining audience attention, PRES 16

Quick Access toolbar A row of buttons on a program's title bar that give you one-click access to frequently used commands., FM 3

Quick Access Toolbar Toolbar that contains buttons for frequently used commands., PPT 2

quotation, gaining audience attention, PRES 16

R

Reading view, PPT 55–56

read-only A file status that allows the file to be viewed but not modified., PPT 344

recording narration, PPT 221–224

Recycle Bin, FM 25

Redo button, PPT 22

redoing actions, PPT 22

region as strategy for focusing presentation, PRES 14

rehearsing, PRES 37–38
    slide timings, PPT 220–221

relationship diagram, PPT 24

Remove Background tool, PPT 79

removing. See also deleting
    background from photos, PPT 164–166

Rename command, FM 26

renaming objects on Selection pane, PPT 180–181

Reset Picture button, PPT 71, PPT 82

resizing
    photos, PPT 46–47
    text boxes, PPT 48–49

Return to the previous slide button, PPT 32, PPT 33

reusing slides from another presentation, PPT 249–252

REVIEW tab, Spelling button, PPT 51

ribbon The main set of commands, located at the top of the PowerPoint window, organized into tabs and groups that you click to execute commands you need to work with PowerPoint., FM 3, PPT 2
    expanding, FM 13–14

Ribbon Display Options button, PPT 3

room, familiarizing yourself with, PRES 45

root directory The location at the top of the file system hierarchy where Windows stores folders and important files that it needs when you turn on the computer., FM 6, FM 7

Rotate button, PPT 71

Rotate button menu, PPT 83

rotate handle A handle that appears on a selected object that you can drag to rotate the object., PPT 70, PPT 71

row, table
    deleting, PPT 87
    increasing height, PPT 92
    inserting, PPT 86–87

S

saturation, photos, PPT 163–164

Save As dialog box, FM 17, FM 18, PPT 9–10, PPT 232

saving
    files, FM 16–18
    presentations. See saving presentations

saving presentations, PPT 9–10, PPT 11
    as earlier version of PowerPoint, PPT 230–233
    with new name, PPT 34–35
    as template, PPT 332–333
    as themes, PPT 74

screen reader, order objects are read by, PPT 179–180

ScreenTip Appears when you rest the mouse pointer on a button, and identifies the name of the button; sometimes it also displays a key combination you can press instead of clicking the button and information about how to use the button., PPT 9

scrolling, Windows 8 and Windows 7 compared, FM 4

Search box, FM 2

second-level item An item beneath and indented from a first-level item; sometimes called a subitem., PPT 14

section, presentations, PPT 254–257

See all slides button, PPT 32, PPT 33

segment as strategy for focusing presentation, PRES 14

selecting multiple files or folders, FM 24

Selection pane
    renaming objects, PPT 180–181
    reordering objects, PPT 180

self-running presentations, PPT 218–225
    recording narration, PPT 221–224
    rehearsing slide timings, PPT 220–221
    setting slide timings, PPT 218–219

sequential organization A presentation organization in which you organize information in a step-by-step fashion or according to a time sequence., PRES 20–21, PRES 22

Set Up Show dialog box, PPT 226

setting up for presentation, PRES 43–46

shape, PPT 168–175
    changing fill to texture, PPT 173–174
    custom. See custom shape
    custom gradient fill, PPT 174–175
    formatting, PPT 79–81
    inserting, PPT 77–79

Shape Effects button, PPT 70

Shape Fill button, PPT 70

Shape Height box, PPT 70, PPT 71

Shape Outline button, PPT 70

Shape Styles gallery, PPT 70

Shape Width box, PPT 71

Shapes button, PPT 77

sharing and collaborating
    comments, PPT 307–309
    comparing presentations, PPT 304–306

sharpening a photo, PPT 164

Sign in link Link that appears in the upper-right corner of the PowerPoint window that lets you sign into your Office account., PPT 3

size, slides, changing, PPT 248

sizing handles The small squares that appear in the corners and in the middle of the sides of a border of a selected object., PPT 45

SkyDrive A Microsoft service that provides online storage space for your files., FM 17

slide A page in a presentation., PPT 2
    adding, PPT 11–13
    amount of text to include, PPT 15
    annotating during a slide show, PPT 288–290
    audio, PPT 145–147
    background, changing, PPT 200–203
    blank, displaying, PPT 55
    changing size and orientation, PPT 248
    charts. See chart
    deleting, PPT 29–30
    duplicating, PPT 28
    embedding Excel worksheets, PPT 277–282
    full page, printing presentation as, PPT 58
    inserting from another presentation, PPT 249–252
    inserting photos stored on computer or network, PPT 39–40
    layers, PPT 257–260
    linking Excel charts, PPT 282–285
    moving in presentations, PPT 28–29
    resetting, PPT 247–248
    text boxes, PPT 153–156, PPT 176–177

timing. *See* slide timing
title, PPT 7–8
video. *See* video

slide library A collection of slides saved as individual files on a SharePoint server., PPT 252

slide master, PPT 302

Slide Master view, PPT 303, PPT 314–319
modifying individual layouts, PPT 315–316
modifying style of lists, PPT 316–319
modifying the slide master, PPT 315
switching to, PPT 314

Slide pane Displays the current slide as it will appear during your slide show., PPT 3

slide show
annotating slides during, PPT 288–290
custom, PPT 334–336
running, PPT 52–56

Slide Show view A way to view the presentation such that each slide fills the screen, one after another., PPT 32, PPT 53–54

Slide Sorter view A view in which all the slides in the presentation are displayed as thumbnails in the window; the Slides tab does not appear., PPT 27

slide timing, PPT 216–221
kiosk browsing, PPT 225–226
overriding, PPT 225
rehearsing, PPT 220–221
setting, PPT 218–219

Slides tab A column of numbered slide thumbnails providing a visual representation of several slides at once on the left side of the PowerPoint window., PPT 2

smart guide Dashed red line that appears as you drag a selected object, indicating the center and the top and bottom borders of the object. Smart guides can help you position objects so they are aligned and spaced evenly., PPT 45

SmartArt A feature that allows you to easily create a diagram on a slide., PPT 24, PPT 140–145
animating diagrams, PPT 144–145
converting lists to SmartArt diagrams, PPT 24–27
creating diagrams, PPT 140–142
diagram types, PPT 24
modifying diagrams, PPT 142–144

sort To list files and folders in a particular order, such as alphabetically by name or type or chronologically by their modification date., FM 14

Sound Box arrow, PPT 98

source file, PPT 270

source program, PPT 270

spatial organization A presentation organization that provides a logical and effective order for describing the physical layout of an item or system., PRES 21

speaker note Information you add about slide content to help you remember to bring up specific points during the presentation; also called notes., PPT 49
printing, PPT 58, PPT 59

speaking voice, PRES 39–40

special character, inserting, PPT 94–95

spell checking, PPT 51–52

Spelling button, PPT 51

spreadsheet A grid of cells that contain numbers and text. In Microsoft Excel, a spreadsheet is called a worksheet., PPT 138

staff, assessing, PRES 44–45

Start menu, Windows 8 and Windows 7 compared, FM 4

starting PowerPoint, PPT 5–6

statistics, gaining audience attention, PRES 16

status bar An area at the bottom of the PowerPoint window that provides information about the file and contains commands for viewing the presentation in different ways and for zooming in on the view., PPT 2

storage
files, determining location, FM 8
Windows 8 and Windows 7 compared, FM 4

strong password, PPT 343

style A combination of several formats that you can add to an object., PPT 70
SmartArt diagrams, PPT 144
tables, PPT 89
WordArt, applying to text, PPT 156–159

subfolder A folder contained within another folder., FM 6, FM 7
viewing in File Explorer, FM 9

subitem An item beneath and indented from a first-level item; also called a second-level item., PPT 14

supply need, identifying, PRES 45–46

symbol, inserting, PPT 94–95

Symbol dialog box, PPT 94, PPT 95, PPT 318

T

tab The part of the ribbon that includes commands related to specific activities or tasks., PPT 2

table Information arranged in horizontal rows and vertical columns., PPT 84–93
borders, PPT 90–91
cells. *See* cell
columns. *See* column, table
data entry, PPT 85–86
deleting rows, PPT 87
formatting, PPT 88–93
formatting cells, PPT 273–277
inserting, PPT 84–85

inserting rows, PPT 87–87
repositioning, PPT 93
styles, PPT 89
Word, inserting, PPT 272–273

task pane A pane that opens to the right or left of the Slide pane and contains commands and options related to the task you are doing., PPT 51

technology, assessing, PRES 44–45

template A special type of presentation file that has a theme applied and contains text, graphics, and placeholders to help direct you in creating content for a presentation., PPT 38
saving presentations as, PPT 332–333
themes compared, PPT 38

text
alternative (alt), PPT 177–178
amount to include on slide, PPT 15
formatting, PPT 19–22
table cells, alignment, PPT 93
as visuals, PRES 25–26, PRES 29
WordArt styles, PPT 156–159

text box An object that contains text., PPT 7, PPT 153–156, PPT 176
resizing and moving, PPT 48–49

text placeholder A placeholder designed to contain text, and usually display text that describes the purpose of the placeholder and instructs you to click so that you can start typing in the placeholder., PPT 7

texture, fills, PPT 173–174

theme A coordinated set of colors, fonts, backgrounds, and effects., PPT 35
changing, PPT 35–37
changing colors, PPT 312–313
changing fonts, PPT 310–312
creating, PPT 314
customizing theme colors, PPT 211–215
saving presentations as, PPT 74
templates compared, PPT 38
used in another presentation, applying, PPT 72–74

theme family A theme and its variants with different coordinating colors and sometimes slightly different backgrounds., PPT 35

Themes gallery, PPT 74

Themes group, PPT 72

thumbnail Miniature images of all the slides in the presentation that appear in the Slides tab on the left side of the PowerPoint window when in Normal view., FM 2, FM 3, PPT 6

tile, FM 4

time as strategy for focusing presentation, PRES 14

title slide The first slide in a presentation and generally contains the title of the presentation plus any other identifying information you want to include, such as a company's slogan, the presenter's name, or a company name., PPT 7–8

tone, photos, PPT 163–164

toolbar A set of buttons for completing current tasks., FM 2

touch interaction, FM 4–5

Touch Mode A mode you can switch to if you are using PowerPoint on a device with a touch screen in which the ribbon increases in height so that there is more space around each, making it easier to use your finger to tap the specific button you need. Also, in the main part of the PowerPoint window, the instructions telling you to "Click" are replaced with instructions to "Tap.", PPT 6–7

training presentation Presentation that shows an audience how something works, educate them on how to perform a task, or help them to understand a process or procedure., PRES 6–7

transition The manner in which a new slide appears on the screen in place of the previous slide during a slide show., PPT 98, PPT 100–102

Transition gallery, PPT 98, PPT 101

TRANSITIONS tab, PPT 98, PPT 100–101, PPT 218–219

transparency, background pictures, PPT 202–203

trigger An object, such as a text box or a graphic, on a slide that you click to start an animation., PPT 191, PPT 198–199

Trim Video button, PPT 118–119

trimming a video, PPT 118–119

U

Undo button, PPT 22

undoing actions, PPT 22

unnumbered list A list that does not have bullets or numbers preceding each item. Unnumbered lists are useful in slides when you want to present information on multiple lines without actually itemizing the information., PPT 17–19

USB drive A removable disk you can plug into your computer and use to store files., FM 6

V

video, PPT 111–119
    adding to slides, PPT 111–114
    animation effects, PPT 115–116
    compressing, PPT 119–120
    modifying playback options, PPT 114–115
    poster frames, PPT 117–118
    stored on computer or network, adding to slides, PPT 112
    trimming, PPT 118–119

Video button, PPT 111, PPT 112

VIDEO TOOLS PLAYBACK tab, PPT 112, PPT 113–114
    Trim Video button, PPT 118–119

view, changing in File Explorer, FM 12–13

view button, PPT 3

View tab A tab on the File Explorer window's ribbon that contains options for specifying the view of the window., FM 3

viewing. *See also* displaying
    animations, PPT 106
    files in File Explorer, FM 9

viewpoint as strategy for focusing presentation, PRES 14

visual, PRES 24–29
    graphics as, PRES 26–29
    referring to during presentation, PRES 42
    text as, PRES 25–26, PRES 29

voice, PRES 39–40

W

webinar A presentation in which the audience signs in to a shared view of the presenter's computer screen and calls in to a conference call to hear the presenter over the telephone line., PRES 6

Windows 8, Windows 7 compared, FM 4–5

Windows Explorer A Windows 7 tool that displays the contents of your computer and uses icons to represent drives, folders, and files., FM 2

Word. *See* Microsoft Word

WordArt A term used to describe formatted, decorative text in a text box., PPT 156–159

WordArt gallery, PPT 157

worksheet, Excel, embedding, PPT 277–282

Z

Zoom In button, PPT 3

Zoom into the slide button, PPT 32, PPT 33

Zoom Out button, PPT 3

TASK REFERENCE

TASK	PAGE #	RECOMMENDED METHOD
Accessibility Checker, use	PPT 341	Click FILE tab, click Check for Issues, click Check Accessibility
Action button, add	PPT 207	*See* Reference box: Adding an Action Button
Alt text, add	PPT 177	Right-click object, click Format Object, in Format Shape task pane on SHAPE OPTIONS tab click Size & Properties button, click ALT TEXT, click in Description box, type text
Animation Painter, use	PPT 106	Click animated object, click ANIMATIONS tab, in Advanced Animation group, click Animation Painter, click object to animate
Animation pane, open	PPT 196	Click ANIMATIONS tab, in Advanced Animation group click Animation Pane
Animation trigger, set	PPT 198	Click animated object, click ANIMATIONS tab, in Advanced Animation group click Trigger, point to On Click of, click object to be trigger
Animation, adjust After animation status	PPT 265	In the Slide or Animation pane, select the animation, on ANIMATIONS tab, in Animation group, click Dialog Box Launcher, on Effect tab, click After animation arrow, click option, click OK
Animation, apply	PPT 103	*See* Reference box: Applying Animations
Animation, apply a second animation	PPT 193	Click ANIMATIONS tab, in Advanced Animation group click Add Animation, click animation
Animation, change order	PPT 106	Click ANIMATIONS tab, click animation sequence icon, in Timing group click Move Earlier or Move Later
Animation, modify smooth start and end settings	PPT 265	In the Slide or Animation pane, select the animation, on ANIMATIONS tab, in Animation group, click Dialog Box Launcher, on Effect tab, adjust Smooth start and Smooth end settings, click OK
Audio Clip, insert	PPT 146	*See* Reference box: Inserting an Audio Clip into a Presentation
AutoCorrect, change	PPT 10	Click ⟐ ▾, click command on menu
Bullet symbol, modify	PPT 318	*See* Reference box: Modifying the Bullet Symbol
Bulleted or numbered item, demote	PPT 14, 16	Click bullet or number, click ⇤
Bulleted or numbered item, promote	PPT 15, 16	Click bullet or number, click ⇥
Chart element, add or remove	PPT 151	To right of chart, click Chart Elements button, click element check box or point to element, click arrow, click element
Chart style, change	PPT 151	Click CHART TOOLS DESIGN tab, in Chart Styles group, click More button, click style
Chart type, change	PPT 288	On CHART TOOLS DESIGN tab, in Type group, click Change Chart Type, click chart type
Chart, axis font size, change	PPT 289	Click value in axis, on HOME tab, click Font Size arrow, click size
Chart, create	PPT 148	*See* Reference box: Creating a Chart
Chart, edit data	PPT 151	Click CHART TOOLS DESIGN tab, in Data group, click Edit Data
Chart, vertical axis, change	PPT 288	Right-click vertical axis, click Format Axis, change values in Maximum and Minimum boxes
Comment, add	PPT 310	On REVIEW tab, in Comments group, click New Comment

TASK	PAGE #	RECOMMENDED METHOD
Comment, delete	PPT 311	Click comment balloon, point to comment in Comments pane, click Delete button
Comment, reply to	PPT 310	Click comment balloon, click in Reply box in Comments pane
Compressed folder, extract all files and folders from	FM 27	Click the compressed folder, click the Compressed Folder Tools Extract tab, click the Extract all button
Compressed folder, open	FM 27	Double-click the compressed folder
Custom show, create	PPT 336	See Reference box: Creating a Custom Show
Custom show, run	PPT 337	On SLIDE SHOW tab, in Start Slide Show group, click Custom Slide Show button, click show
Date, display on slides	PPT 121	Click INSERT tab, in Text group, click Header & Footer, click Date and time check box, click Apply to All
Documents library, open	FM 10	In File Explorer, click ▶ next to Libraries, click ▶ next to Documents
Excel chart, link to a slide	PPT 285	See Reference box: Linking an Excel Chart to a Slide
Excel chart data, linked, modify	PPT 287	On CHART TOOLS DESIGN tab, in Data group, click Edit Data, change data in worksheet, on Quick Access Toolbar, click Save
Excel worksheet, embed on slide	PPT 280	See Reference box: Embedding an Excel Worksheet in a Slide
Excel worksheet, embedded, modify	PPT 282	Select worksheet, double-click worksheet, use commands on ribbon to modify worksheet, click blank area of the slide
Eyedropper, use	PPT 326	Click drawn object, on DRAWING TOOLS FORMAT tab, in Shape Styles group, click Shape Fill button arrow, click Eyedropper, click area on slide
File Explorer, open	FM 10	Click 📁 on the taskbar
File Explorer, return to a previous location	FM 14	Click ⬅
File list, sort	FM 14	Click the column heading button
File, copy	FM 24	Right-click the file, click Copy, right-click destination, click Paste
File, delete	FM 25	Right-click the file, click Delete
File, move	FM 21	Drag the file to the folder
File, open from File Explorer	FM 15	Right-click the file, point to Open with, click an application
File, rename	FM 26	Right-click the file, click Rename, type the new filename, press Enter
File, save with new name in WordPad	FM 18	Click the File tab, click Save as, enter the filename, click Save
Files and folders, compress	FM 27	Select the files to compress, click the Share tab, click the Zip button in the Send group
Files, select multiple	FM 24	Press and hold the Ctrl key and click the files
Files, view in Large Icons view	FM 13	Click the View tab, click 🖼 in the Layout group
Folder, create	FM 19	Click the New folder button in the New group on the Home tab
Footer, add to slides	PPT 121	Click INSERT tab, in Text group, click Header & Footer, click Footer check box, click Footer box, type footer, click Apply to All
Footer, don't show on title slide	PPT 122	Click INSERT tab, in Text group, click Header & Footer, click Don't show in title slide check box, click Apply to All
Format Painter, use	PPT 21	Select formatted text or object, click HOME tab, in Clipboard group click Format Painter, select object to format
Format Shape task pane, open	PPT 155	Right-click shape, click Format Shape

TASK	PAGE #	RECOMMENDED METHOD
Gradient fill, position, change	PPT 329	In Format Shape pane, click gradient stop, drag slider to new position
Gradient fill, transparency, change	PPT 327	In Format Shape pane, click gradient stop, drag Transparency slider
Handouts, export to Word	PPT 292	Click FILE tab, click Export, click Create Handouts, click Create Handouts, click option, click OK
Header and footer, add to notes and handouts	PPT 122	Click INSERT tab, in Text group, click Header & Footer, click Notes and Handouts, select check boxes for items to display, type information, click Apply to All
Hyperlink, create	PPT 205	Select object or text, click INSERT tab, in Links group, click Hyperlink, click option in Link to list, click link destination, click OK
Kiosk browsing, set up	PPT 226	Click SLIDE SHOW tab, in Set Up group, click Set Up Slide Show, click Browsed at a kiosk (full screen) option button, click OK
Layout, change	PPT 13	Click HOME tab, in Slides group click Layout button, click layout
Layout, create	PPT 321	In Slide Master view, on the SLIDE MASTER tab, in the Edit Master group, click Insert Layout
Layout, rename	PPT 324	In Slide Master view, on the SLIDE MASTER tab, in the Edit Master group, click Rename, type name, click Rename
Link, break	PPT 290	Click FILE tab, click Edit Links to Files, click link, click Break Link, click Close
Media, compress	PPT 119	Click FILE tab, on Info screen, click Compress Media, click quality option, click Close
Media, optimize	PPT 226	Click FILE tab, on Info screen click Optimize Compatibility, click Close
Motion path animation, adjust	PPT 193	Click motion path, drag red or green circles at ends of the path
My Documents folder, open	FM 10	In File Explorer, click ▷ next to Libraries, click ▷ next to Documents, click My Documents
Narration, record	PPT 222	*See* Reference box: Recording Narration
Numbered list, create	PPT 16	Select list, click HOME tab, in Paragraph group click 📑
Object order on slide, identify	PPT 179	Click HOME tab, in Editing group, click Select, click Selection Pane
Object, delete	PPT 48	Click object, press Delete
Object, duplicate	PPT 165	Click HOME tab, in Clipboard group, click Copy button arrow, click Duplicate
Object, flip	PPT 83	Click object, click DRAWING TOOLS FORMAT tab, in Arrange group click Rotate, click Flip option
Object, move	PPT 45	Click object, drag to new position with 🔀
Object, rename in Selection Pane	PPT 180	Click HOME tab, in Editing group, click Select, click Selection Pane, in Selection Pane click object name twice, edit name
Object, rotate	PPT 83	Click object, drag rotate handle
Objects, align	PPT 170	Select objects, click HOME tab, in Drawing group, click Arrange, point to Align, click alignment command
Objects, move among layers	PPT 261	Select object in Slide or Selection pane, on HOME tab, in Drawing group, click Arrange, click desired option
Online pictures, insert	PPT 75	In content placeholder click 🖼, type keywords in Office.com Clip Art search box, click 🔍, click image, click Insert

TASK	PAGE #	RECOMMENDED METHOD
Outline view, switch to	PPT 254	On VIEW tab, in Presentation Views group, click Outline View
Photo artistic effects, apply	PPT 166	Click PICTURE TOOLS FORMAT tab, click Artistic Effects, click style
Photo background, remove	PPT 164	See Reference box: Removing the Background of a Photograph
Photo brightness and contrast, change	PPT 162	Click PICTURE TOOLS FORMAT tab, in Adjust group, click Corrections, click option under Brightness/Contrast
Photo compression options, change	PPT 43	See Reference box: Modifying Photo Compression Settings and Removing Cropped Areas
Photo, color saturation and tone, change	PPT 163	Click PICTURE TOOLS FORMAT tab, in Adjust group, click Color, click option under either Color Saturation or Color Tone
Photo, sharpen or soften	PPT 163	Click PICTURE TOOLS FORMAT tab, in Adjust group, click Corrections, click option under Sharpen/Soften
Picture, apply effect	PPT 82	Click photo, click PICTURE TOOLS FORMAT tab, in Picture Styles group, click Picture Effects, point to effect type, click effect
Picture, apply style	PPT 82	Click photo, click PICTURE TOOLS FORMAT tab, in Picture Styles group click style
Picture, crop	PPT 40	Click picture, click PICTURE TOOLS FORMAT tab, in Size group, click Crop, drag Crop handles, click Crop
Picture, insert from your computer	PPT 39	In content placeholder click 🖼, navigate to picture file location, click picture file, click Insert
Picture, resize	PPT 46	Click object, drag a corner sizing handle
Placeholder, insert	PPT 322	In Slide Master view, on the SLIDE MASTER tab, in the Master Layout group, click Insert Placeholder arrow, click placeholder type, drag in Slide pane
PowerPoint, exit	PPT 60	Click ✖
Presentation, check for compatibility to earlier versions	PPT 231	Click FILE tab, click Check for Issues, click Check Compatibility
Presentation, check for hidden information	PPT 226	Click FILE tab, on Info screen, click Check for Issues, click Inspect Document, click Inspect, click Remove All next to data you want to remove, click Close
Presentation, close	PPT 30	Click FILE tab, click Close
Presentation, encrypt	PPT 343	See Reference box: Encrypting a Presentation
Presentation, mark as final	PPT 346	Click FILE tab, click Protect Presentation, click Mark as Final, click OK, click OK
Presentation, open	PPT 34	Click FILE tab, click Open, click Computer, click Browse, navigate to location of file, click file, click Open
Presentation, package for CD	PPT 229	Click FILE tab, click Export, click Package Presentation for CD, click Package for CD, click OK or click Copy to Folder, browse to folder location, click OK, click Close
Presentation, print	PPT 57	Click FILE tab, click Print, select options, click Print
Presentation, save as an earlier version	PPT 231	Click FILE tab, click Export, click Change File Type, click PowerPoint 97-2003 Presentation, click Save As, click Save
Presentation, save changes	PPT 11	On Quick Access Toolbar, click 💾
Presentation, save for the first time	PPT 9	On Quick Access Toolbar, click 💾, on Save As screen click Computer, type filename, navigate to location, click Save

TASK	PAGE #	RECOMMENDED METHOD
Presentation, save with a new name	PPT 34	Click FILE tab, click Save As, on Save As screen click Computer, type filename, navigate to location, click Save
Presentations, compare	PPT 306	*See Reference box: Comparing Presentations*
Property, custom, add	PPT 340	Click FILE tab, click Properties, click Advanced Properties, click Custom tab, click property, click in Value box, type property value, click Add, click OK
Property, modify	PPT 338	Click FILE tab, click property box, type property
Proofing language, change for selected word	PPT 95	Select text, on status bar click ENGLISH (UNITED STATES), click language, click OK
Ribbon, expand in File Explorer	FM 13	Click 🔽
Section, collapse/expand	PPT 257	In Slides tab, next to section name, click arrow
Section, create	PPT 257	In Slides tab, click first thumbnail in section, on HOME tab, in Slides group, click Section, click Add Section
Section, rename	PPT 257	In Slides tab, click section name, on HOME tab, in Slides group, click Section, click Rename Section, type name, click Rename
Shape effect, apply	PPT 175	Click DRAWING TOOLS FORMAT tab, in Shape Styles group click Shape Effects, point to a style category, click style
Shape outline, change	PPT 175	Click DRAWING TOOLS FORMAT tab, in Shape Styles group click Shape Outline button arrow, click color
Shape, adjust	PPT 169	Select shape, drag yellow adjustment handle
Shape, apply style	PPT 80	Click shape, click DRAWING TOOLS FORMAT tab, in Shape Styles group, click style
Shape, change fill color	PPT 79	Click shape, click DRAWING TOOLS FORMAT tab, in Shape Styles group click Shape Fill button arrow, click color
Shape, change outline weight	PPT 81	Click shape, click DRAWING TOOLS FORMAT tab, in Shape Styles group click Shape Outline button arrow, point to Weight, click weight
Shape, fill with gradient	PPT 174	*See Reference box: Creating a Custom Gradient in a Shape*
Shape, fill with texture	PPT 173	Click DRAWING TOOLS FORMAT tab, in Shape Styles group click Shape Fill button arrow, point to Texture, click texture
Shape, insert	PPT 77	Click INSERT tab, in Illustrations group click Shapes, click shape, drag on slide
Shapes, merge	PPT 172	*See Reference box: Merging Shapes*
Slide background, change	PPT 200	*See Reference box: Adding a Picture to the Slide Background*
Slide background, change transparency of photo	PPT 202	In Format Background task pane, drag Transparency slider
Slide background, set picture as tiles	PPT 202	In Format Background task pane, select Tile picture as texture check box
Slide Master view, switch to	PPT 316	On VIEW tab, in Master Views group, click Slide Master
Slide number, display on slides	PPT 121	Click INSERT tab, in Text group, click Header & Footer, click Slide number check box, click Apply to All
Slide show, prevent viewer from advancing	PPT 225	Click TRANSITIONS tab, in Timing group deselect On Mouse Click check box
Slide show, run from current slide	PPT 53	On the status bar, click 🖳
Slide show, run from Slide 1	PPT 53	On the Quick Access Toolbar, click 🖵

TASK	PAGE #	RECOMMENDED METHOD
Slide show, run in Presenter view	PPT 54	In Slide Show view, click (•••), click Show Presenter View
Slide show, run in Reading view	PPT 56	On status bar, click ▦
Slide timings, rehearse	PPT 220	Click SLIDE SHOW tab, in Set Up group, click Rehearse Timings, advance slide show, click Yes to save rehearsed timings
Slide timings, set	PPT 218	Select slide thumbnails, click TRANSITIONS tab, in Timing group click After check box, change value in After box to desired timing
Slide, add	PPT 12	Click HOME tab, in Slides group click New Slide button arrow, click layout
Slide, annotate during slide show	PPT 291	In Slide Show view, right-click, point to Pointer Options, click Pen or Highlighter, drag on screen
Slide, delete	PPT 29	Right-click slide thumbnail, click Delete Slide
Slide, duplicate	PPT 28	Click slide thumbnail, click HOME tab, in Slides group click New Slide button arrow, click Duplicate Selected Slides
Slide, move	PPT 28	Drag slide thumbnail to new location
Slides, copy from another presentation	PPT 251	In Slide Sorter view, click thumbnail, on HOME tab, in Clipboard group, click Copy, switch to presentation to copy to, in Slide Sorter view, click location to paste slide, on HOME tab, in Clipboard group, click Paste button arrow, click option for pasting slide
Slides, reset	PPT 249	In Slides tab, click slide thumbnail, on HOME tab, in Slides group, click Reset
Slides, reuse	PPT 251	See Reference box: Reusing Slides from Another Presentation
SmartArt diagram, convert from list	PPT 24	See Reference box: Converting a Bulleted List into a SmartArt Diagram
SmartArt diagram colors, change	PPT 144	Click SMARTART TOOLS DESIGN tab, in SmartArt Styles group, click Change Colors, click color style
SmartArt diagram layout, change	PPT 142	Click SMARTART TOOLS DESIGN tab, in Layouts group, click More button, click layout
SmartArt diagram style, change	PPT 144	Click SMARTART TOOLS DESIGN tab, in SmartArt Styles group, click More button, click style
SmartArt diagram, create	PPT 140	See Reference box: Creating a SmartArt Diagram
Speaker notes, add	PPT 49	On status bar click NOTES, click in Notes pane, type note
Spelling, check entire presentation	PPT 51	Click REVIEW tab, in Proofing group click Spelling
Spelling, correct flagged word	PPT 51	Right-click flagged word, click correct spelling
Start PowerPoint	PPT 5	On Windows Start screen, click the PowerPoint 2013 tile
Symbols, insert	PPT 94	Click INSERT tab, in Symbols group click Symbol, click symbol, click Insert, click Close
Table, add or delete rows and columns	PPT 86	Click in row or column, click TABLE TOOLS LAYOUT tab, in Rows & Columns group, click option
Table, change alignment in cells	PPT 93	Click cell, click TABLE TOOLS LAYOUT tab, in Alignment group, click option
Table, change border width	PPT 278	On TABLE TOOLS DESIGN tab, in Draw Borders group, click Pen Weight button, click weight option, drag on table border

TASK	PAGE #	RECOMMENDED METHOD
Table, change borders	PPT 90	Click table, click TABLE TOOLS DESIGN tab, in Draw Borders group select options, in Table Styles group click Borders button arrow, click border
Table, change cell fill color	PPT 90	Click table, click TABLE TOOLS DESIGN tab, in Table Styles group click Shading button arrow, click color
Table, change column width	PPT 88	Point to column border, double-click or drag
Table, change row height	PPT 92	Point to row border, double-click or drag
Table, change style	PPT 89	Click table, click TABLE TOOLS DESIGN tab, in Table styles group, click style
Table, fill cell with pictures	PPT 91	Click cell, click TABLE TOOLS DESIGN tab, in Table Styles group click Shading button arrow, click Picture, navigate to location, click picture file, click Insert
Table, insert on slide	PPT 85	Click INSERT tab, in Tables group, click Table, click grid
Table cell, rotate text	PPT 276	Select cell, on TABLE TOOLS LAYOUT tab, in Alignment group, click Text Direction, click rotate option
Table cells, merge	PPT 275	Select cells to merge, on TABLE TOOLS LAYOUT tab, in Merge group, click Merge Cells
Template, save presentation as	PPT 334	See Reference box: Saving a Presentation as a Template
Text box margins, change	PPT 156	Right-click text box, click Format Shape, click TEXT OPTIONS, click Textbox button, click TEXT BOX, change values in margin boxes
Text box wrapping option, change	PPT 155	Right-click text box, click Format Shape, click TEXT OPTIONS, click Textbox button, click TEXT BOX, select or deselect Wrap text in shape check box
Text box, insert	PPT 154	Click INSERT tab, in Text group, click Text Box, drag pointer on slide, type text
Text, change format of	PPT 19	Select text, click HOME tab, in Font group click appropriate button to apply formatting
Text, move or copy	PPT 22	Select text, click HOME tab, in Clipboard group click Cut or Copy, click at new location, in Clipboard group click Paste
Theme and theme variant, change	PPT 36	Click DESIGN tab, in Themes group click theme
Theme colors, change	PPT 314	On DESIGN tab, in Variants group, click More button, point to Colors, click palette
Theme colors, custom, delete	PPT 216	Click DESIGN tab, click More button, point to Colors, right-click custom palette, click Delete
Theme colors, customize	PPT 211	See Reference box: Customizing Theme Colors
Theme, apply from another presentation	PPT 72	Click DESIGN tab, in Themes group click More button, click Browse for Themes, navigate to location, click presentation, click Apply
Theme fonts, change	PPT 312	On DESIGN tab, in Variants group, click More button, point to Fonts, click font set
Theme fonts, custom, delete	PPT 313	On DESIGN tab, in Variants group, click More button, point to Fonts, right-click custom font set, click Delete, click Yes
Theme fonts, customize	PPT 312	On DESIGN tab, in Variants group, click More button, point to Fonts, click Customize Fonts, click Heading font or Body font arrow, click font, click Save

TASK	PAGE #	RECOMMENDED METHOD
Touch Mode, switch to	PPT 6	On Quick Access Toolbar, click ▼, click Touch/Mouse mode if not selected, click 👆, click Touch
Transition, change	PPT 100	*See* Reference box: Adding Transitions
Unnumbered list, create	PPT 17	Select list or placeholder, click HOME tab, in Paragraph group click ⊟ or ⊟ to deselect it
User name, change	PPT 309	Click FILE tab, click Options, change user name in User name box, click OK
Video, add to slide	PPT 112	*See* Reference box: Adding Videos Stored on Your Computer or Network
Video, set a poster frame	PPT 117	On play bar, click time to display frame, click VIDEO TOOLS FORMAT tab, in Adjust group click Poster Frame, click Current Frame
Video, trim	PPT 118	Click video, click VIDEO TOOLS PLAYBACK tab, in Editing group, click Trim Video, drag sliders, click OK
View, change in File Explorer	FM 12	*See* Reference box: Changing the View in File Explorer
WordArt shape, change	PPT 158	Click DRAWING TOOLS FORMAT tab, in WordArt Styles group, click Text Effects, point to Transform, click style
WordArt styles, apply	PPT 157	Click INSERT tab, in Text group, click WordArt, click style, type text
Word outline, import	PPT 247	On HOME tab, in Slides group, click New Slide button arrow, click Slides from Outline, navigate to outline location, click outline file, click Insert
Word table, copy from Word document	PPT 274	In Word document, point to table, click Table Select Handle, on HOME tab, in Clipboard group, click Copy, switch to PowerPoint presentation, on HOME tab, in Clipboard group, click Paste button arrow, click option